Closest to the Fire

A WRITER'S GUIDE TO LAW AND LAWYERS

Karen A. Wyle

Published in the United States of America

Oblique Angles Press

ISBN 9780990564140
Printed in the United States of America
Oblique Angles Press

Cover design by Elizabeth DiPalma Design+
Author photo by Kip May
Book Layout ©2013 BookDesignTemplates.com

Contents

*Dedicated to my
wonderful
writing companions*

CHAPTER 1

Why the Title, and Why This Book?

You may be wondering about the title of this book. It comes from an anecdote told about Ulysses S. Grant. General Grant, so the story goes, came to an inn on a stormy winter's night. Rarely elegant in appearance, Grant looked particularly disheveled and weather-beaten on this occasion. A number of lawyers were in town for a court session, and had clustered around the fireplace. One looked up as Grant approached and commented that the stranger looked as if he had "traveled through hell itself to get here."

General Grant allowed as how he had done just that.

"And how did you find things down there?"

"Just like here," replied Grant, "lawyers all closest to the fire."

I borrow this punch line not only to acknowledge the popular view of lawyers as scoundrels, but for another meaning the phrase can bear. Where there's a passionate dispute, whether between friends or strangers, lawyers are likely to be in the thick of it.

Now for the book itself.

First: this book is a resource, to be consulted as needed, or browsed as desired, rather than read straight through in marathon sessions. So don't be intimidated by its length! I wanted to cover as much as I could, but you could make perfectly good use of it without ever getting to most of its content.

So what am I trying to accomplish?

I'd like to decrease the number of howlers in novels and short stories that feature lawyers or legal proceedings. I'd like to reduce the chance that a lawyer, opening your book, will end up laying (or throwing) it down in exasperation and disgust. You'll sometimes consider it necessary to stray from strict accuracy for dramatic purposes, but it always pays to know what rules you're bending or breaking. It'll help you cover your tracks better.

I'd really, really like it if in future, none of your readers torture their own lawyers by declaring, in indignant or piteous or bewildered tones, "But I read about this and I thought I could . . . I thought the judge would . . . I thought the other guy had to . . . ." At least, if your readers are confronting their lawyers in such a way, I'd like them to be more or less correct.

But this book isn't just about avoiding mistakes. It's about discovering possibilities. There are many, many interesting tales lurking in the law, and I'm hoping you'll find some in these pages.

You may already know what legal concepts or proceedings you'll be featuring in your work, or you may be looking for inspiration. Either way, you can use the Table of Contents or the Index to find sections of interest. If you're at all interested in legal settings or plots, go ahead and read more than just the sections you currently need: you'll find plenty to spark your imagination.

I hope that appropriately used, this guide will give at least a few writers the confidence to tackle this potentially fascinating subject matter. And if the legal details of some plot point seem too complicated to cope with, you can probably avoid the situations in which they get complicated, once you know what they are.

In a few places, I'll also throw in some warnings about ways that you, the author, could find yourself in legal difficulties. As noted below, these warnings aren't legal advice! — just signposts identifying possible quagmires.

Next, in true lawyer fashion, I have some caveats.

I am an appellate attorney. I don't do trial work. I listen to recordings of trial proceedings and read trial transcripts, as well as appellate decisions that analyze what went on at trial and the rules that were or were not followed there. This gives me a fair-to-middling knowledge of what really goes on in courtrooms, but a good deal less than what a trial attorney knows. For example, it's possible that some evidentiary rules I discuss will often be ignored in practice, at least in some courts.

I am licensed to practice only in Indiana and some federal jurisdictions, though I'm an inactive member of the California bar as well. I'll try to confine my comments to principles and procedures that are likely to apply nationwide, and to indicate when different states' rules may vary. As for other countries, their legal systems may be very different from what I'll be describing, in many respects. Those differences could make for some fascinating stories. Please write some, and I'll read them with interest!

Legal rules not only differ from state to state: they evolve. I'll occasionally mention some way in which the rules have changed in the past few decades. If your story is set in any time before the present, you should make sure that the rules around which your story turns were the same in that era. (If your story takes place in the future, you have a good deal more latitude.)

To the extent this book gives advice, it's advice about describing legal proceedings, not about taking part in them. This book is not your lawyer, and neither am I (unless one of my clients is reading it, in which case — howdy!) If you need legal advice, please hire a lawyer to provide it.

Will law students find this book helpful? Only if they're cautious about assuming (a) that any particular assertion is correct, either in general or in their state, and/or (b) that their professors would believe it to be correct. Maybe some law student reader(s) will find errors I can fix in the next edition.

Parts of this guide are arranged in more or less the chronological order of a prosecution or a lawsuit, but as I've already indicated, you don't need to read it in order. For that reason, I've sometimes repeated information in two or more sections, though I generally cross-reference between more and less detailed treatments.

One way to prepare for writing convincing legal fiction is to read the work of lawyers, particularly litigators, who write the stuff. Some of you may be leery of this, for fear of accidentally copying these author's styles or plots; but if you don't have that concern, I particularly recommend the novels of Scott Turow. This bestselling author taught writing at Stanford University before going to Harvard Law School. He has been writing and practicing law ever since, with a great deal of high-profile trial work to his credit. John Grisham is another best-selling author of legal fiction with many years of law practice to draw upon.

From time to time, I'll use double asterisks ** to set off what strikes me as an interesting story idea. Some of these will be ideas for the bare bones of an entire story, while others will just be possible bits and pieces. I may write up one or more of these ideas eventually, but that shouldn't stop you from doing the same. As I'll be discussing in 14.M.1., an idea isn't protected by copyright: the law protects only the particular expression of an idea.

Since this is essentially the "miscellaneous notes" section, here's one on pronouns.

We live in a chaotic era where pronouns are concerned. Many readers will no longer tolerate the use of "he" as a pronoun for unspecified individuals. Also, many of the statements in this book apply to multiple parties, or to business entities. I suspect we're moving toward a time when "they" will be an acceptable universal pronoun for formal usage, and I'll be using it in this book.

One final note: the words "lawyer" and "attorney" are interchangeable, except that the latter sounds more formal (and possibly more pretentious). I'll use whichever feels right at the moment.

Enough introduction. Here we go!

Attorneys: Substance and Style

When I talk to lawyers about their pet peeves in legal fiction, one point they often raise is how exciting law practice looks in novels and (especially) in movies and television shows. There are lively moments in most law practices, but much of it is pretty tame, not to say dull.

Of course you don't want your story to be boring, but you could find other ways to acknowledge that reality. In fact, you could highlight the tedium of your lawyer's life — just before you throw it into turmoil.

A. Where They Come From

What sort of people become lawyers?

Some become lawyers, and trial lawyers in particular, because they like to argue. Many captains of high school or college debate teams have gone on to practice law.

Certain cultural backgrounds may predispose people to go into law as a profession. For example, my own background, Judaism, treats the close study of religious texts, and endless discussions of how they should be applied to different facts, as an important religious observance. Religious Jews even spend years studying the disagreements that Jews centuries ago had about these texts. It's not much of a leap from there to reading statutes and case reports, then arguing about how to apply them to a client's case. See why there are so many Jewish lawyers?

A friend of mine who very frequently serves as an expert witness (see 22.H.11) notes that there also seem to be a disproportionate number of Irish attorneys. He has often encountered law firms with names along the lines of Goldberg, O'Hara, Eisenberg, and Murphy.

Some budding lawyers are idealists, burning to put evildoers in prison or to defend the innocent from unjust accusations. Either of these ambitions is all too likely to lead to disillusionment and burnout. Defense attorneys soon learn to assume that almost all their clients are guilty. Prosecutors spend too much time dealing with petty criminals, and even the same petty criminals, time after time. They may well come to feel that their efforts have pitifully little effect on public safety.

Some people go to law school with dreams of dramatic cross-examinations and eloquent perorations to the jury. They soon find that popular culture's portrayal of law practice is poor preparation for the reality. If they're lucky, they'll find their way into a type of practice that lets them try cases more or less frequently. A good trial lawyer has much in common with a good actor, but will spend far less time rehearsing and performing, compared to the hours consumed by the drudgery of trial preparation. Still, a really good trial lawyer may have as strong a personal presence, as much charisma, as any star of stage or screen.

Some lawyers are the children and grandchildren of lawyers, following in the familial footsteps. They at least may have a fairly good idea of what they're in for, as well as a clear career path once they pass the bar.

Then there's the hefty percentage of every law school class that ends up there for reasons other than inherent interest in the law. They may be gifted students who lack confidence that they can handle the transition to the working world, and therefore seek refuge in another three years of study. They may have a passion for theater, or Egyptology, or art history, which they consider it hopelessly impractical to pursue. Law school is the pragmatic compromise, the supposed ticket to financial security.

But things have changed, and more and more law students graduate deeply in debt and with poor job prospects. Some are even using their training to sue law schools for the difference between what they were led to expect and the reality that confronts them. **Such a lawsuit could attract attention from potential employers — which could lead to a job offer invalidating the premise of the complaint.**

Given the amount of confrontation that goes with the territory (or at least, with the practice of law as many attorneys experience it), it's no surprise that substance abuse among attorneys and even judges is common. In fact, it's common enough that state bar associations often have some organization dedicated to assisting attorneys who've sought help with alcohol or drugs, or who've been reported to be impaired on the job. **If you're writing about a lawyer whose hard-drinking days are behind them, you could give the reader a look at them as they join other lawyers at a bar after work. It's not uncommon for such a group to include a couple of lawyers nursing Diet Cokes, and not because they love the taste.**

---

1. A (Possibly Obsolete) Note About Law Schools

I've only attended one law school, and that was long, long ago. I know some things have changed. But at least back then, one was more likely to get a solid preparation for actually practicing law in a less expensive, less "prestigious" law school than in one of the top "elite" schools. The latter prepared their students to be law professors and/or U.S. Supreme Court Justices, rather than divorce lawyers, personal injury lawyers, drafters of wills, prosecuting attorneys, or even high-priced tax or patent or entertainment lawyers. And in-house counsel? We students never heard about them.

Many law school graduates find that their six-week bar exam prep courses (see 2.B.) teach them more about the actual work of the profession than they learned in three years of law school.

Graduates from the most respected law schools are more likely to end up in the larger urban law firms, and getting paid accordingly. They'll also have a better shot at getting the most valued judicial "clerkships," working as assistants for U.S. Circuit Court judges or U.S. Supreme Court justices, positions which can then lead to lucrative law firm jobs, professorships, and/or future judicial appointments.

One very beneficial change at "top" law schools in the last several decades: these schools, like most law schools these days, now have a variety of clinical programs. These programs let students, especially those in the later years, actually get into the trenches under the supervision of a practicing attorney.

B. Becoming a Lawyer

What does it take to turn a lay person into a lawyer?

Well, it used to be easier, or at least a less bureaucratic process, than it is in most states nowadays. Take Abraham Lincoln, for example. Before he became president, he was a very successful trial lawyer. Did he have to go to law school first? Perish the thought! He "read law," studying up on what he'd need to know to practice the profession. He also had to get some Illinois court to certify that he had "good moral character."

Law schools started to pop up in the 1870s. Before that time, most lawyers served apprenticeships and then moved into actual law practice.

Times have certainly changed. As of now, only California, Vermont, Virginia, and Washington (the state, not D.C.) allow the would-be lawyer to avoid law school. Maine, New York, and Wyoming accept some combination of law school attendance, without an actual law degree (Juris Doctor, or J.D.), and apprenticeship.

A discouragingly small percentage of those who try this route actually pass the bar exam (discussed below), but it could be worth a try for the poor, frugal, or impatient aspirant to attorney status. It'll also be harder to recruit clients without that familiar diploma hanging on the wall. However, the sort of self-starter who could pass the bar without going to law school might be particularly well suited to overcoming that difficulty as well.

In many other countries, future lawyers pass from law school to a mandatory apprenticeship before being unleashed on the public. This approach has a good deal to be said in its favor.

Your eager but impoverished protagonist could live in one of the states that allows alternatives to the three-year law school experience, discovering the possibility after despairing of finding a way to afford a legal education. **Alternatively, if you're the dark and cynical type, you could follow someone's descent into crime, meant to fund law school tuition, and have them learn too late that they could have avoided that path.**

Most future lawyers do go to law school. What's that like?

Law schools are almost universally three year programs, though this could change in the future. There was a saying at my law school: "In the first year, they scare you to death; in the second year, they work you to death; and in the third year, they bore you to death." There is, or at least was in my law student days, some truth in that.

First year classes were meant to train the students to "think like a lawyer," applying the framework of the law to increasingly complex fact situations. That comes more naturally for some than for others. The first year curriculum is heavy on basics like contracts, torts, real property, civil procedure, criminal law, and criminal procedure. The student may take more electives in the second year, but each of those electives are still likely to cover a good deal of ground (e.g. Corporations, Income Tax). By the third year, the student, who has most often been in some sort of schooling for fifteen uninterrupted years, is often desperate to get out into the "real world."

Assuming the student manages to graduate, the next serious obstacle looms: the bar exam. The length, details, and difficulty of the bar exam vary (like so much else, as you'll see) from state to state. California has the most challenging bar exam, as measured by the rate at which people pass it. When I took that exam, it lasted three days, an ordeal that left me stumbling around disoriented for hours after I walked out of the third session.

New York also has discouragingly low bar passage rates, although these figures are somewhat misleading: New York allows graduates from overseas law schools to take the bar, and their English language skills are not always up to the task. Even so, your lawyer eager to practice in a big city might fare better in Illinois, which came in 32nd in difficulty in 2013. For what it's worth, the highest passage rate at that time belonged to South Dakota. **A law student approaching graduation and making plans could decide where to seek employment based on where they believed it would be easier to squeak through the exam.**

Every state except the frequent maverick Louisiana includes in its bar exam a section called the Multistate Bar Exam, or MBE. The MBE lasts six hours, usually divided into three-hour morning and afternoon sessions, and includes 200 multiple-choice questions. It covers (in alphabetical order, not test order) civil procedure, contracts (including the U.C.C (see 14.B.1)), criminal law and procedure, evidence, real property, and torts. There's no built-in penalty for wrong answers, which makes various types of guessing strategies worthwhile.

Most states also include state-specific sections covering the law of that state, which may or may not be much different from the law elsewhere. Louisiana, where the law is quite different, does include such a section.

Most states (but not Louisiana) also include either or both of two Multistate Performance Tests (MPT). These 90-minute tests are supposed to assess basic lawyering skills. The test-taker will have to review a case description and/or typical case file materials, and then produce such documents as a memo for a more senior lawyer's review, a brief to be submitted to a court, a contract, or a will.

A little more than half the states (again, not including Louisiana) use the Multistate Essay Exam (MEE). This test includes up to nine essay questions, covering a wide range of legal subjects. These will range from very broad categories like contracts or evidence to somewhat narrower topics like business associations or secured transactions. The questions are drafted so as to require 30 minutes each to answer, but states may give more or less time.

Thirteen states, quite possibly with more to come, administer the Uniform Bar Exam (UBE). This test is supposed to make it easier for lawyers who relocate (see 2.I.) to be admitted to the bar of their new state.

In my opinion, the ordeal of taking and passing the bar has been somewhat neglected in law-centered fiction. An article about the New York bar exam mentions such piquant details as people showing up at 5 a.m. for the 9 a.m. start time, a young woman carrying rosary beads for which someone had obtained a papal blessing, and a young man wearing suntan lotion (not sunscreen?) for the calming associations its odor brought him. The article also mentions the need to leave extra time for the trip to the exam site, **which suggests all sorts of last-minute snafus with which you could torture your protagonist and your readers if so inclined.** **You could also explore different physical settings for the exam, from New York's current huge Javitz Center exhibition spaces (rooms more than five acres across) to some small and stifling classroom. There's room for either agoraphobia or claustrophobia to play a part.** **Or your art could imitate at least one real-life episode by having your test-taker go into labor in mid-exam.** And then, in test sites that assign seats by number and grade exams the same way, **there's the possibility of sitting in the wrong seat and having one's test scores treated as someone else's.**

It may take several months for the law graduate to find out if they have passed the bar exam. Many law firms will hire new associates on the assumption that they'll pass. If that assumption proves overly optimistic, some will keep associates on staff in some capacity while they study some more and try again. **An overconfident young graduate might find out too late that their firm isn't so generous.**

It's not uncommon for would-be lawyers to retake the bar exam one or more times, often with eventual success. At least one persevering fellow passed on the 48th try. **One could, however, easily imagine someone ruining their life with repeated attempts and an escalating obsession with passing the exam.**

Some states, such as Texas, limit the number of attempts to a handful before they won't even look at the results.

It's very common for law school graduates, despite all the time and money they've already spent on legal education, to take special bar exam prep courses. These typically last something like six to eight weeks, although there are marathon courses that last longer. Costs generally exceed one thousand dollars, and may soar to over four thousand. The various prep course vendors tout the higher passage rates of those who take their courses, but I haven't vetted any of those claims.

What if someone can't or won't go through the time-consuming, financially draining process of becoming a licensed attorney? What if such a person just hangs up a misleading shingle and starts taking clients?

Whether or not the pseudo-lawyer actually does a competent job, this constitutes the unauthorized practice of law, and the state organizations in charge of regulating lawyers are quite active in squelching it. Whether due to bar association lobbying efforts or because so many state legislators are licensed lawyers, unauthorized practice of law is typically a crime, most often a misdemeanor (see 29.A.2.). If a formerly licensed lawyer starts practicing law during a period of suspension or after being disbarred (see 4.A.), that could constitute a felony (29.A.3.)

C. Leonardo da Vinci: Not

You remember Leonardo da Vinci, the original "Renaissance man." Sculptor, painter, anatomist, architect, engineer, inventor: he could do just about anything, and do it well.

Very few lawyers aspire to, let alone achieve, such breadth of expertise. Some attorneys in smaller towns, especially those who practice solo or in small firms, will handle a variety of types of cases; but it's more common for lawyers to specialize at least to some degree, though professional rules may prevent them from calling themselves "specialists" unless they've passed certification tests. Family law attorneys don't handle auto accident claims. Lawyers who defend criminal defendants may sometimes handle immigration cases, but are less likely to get involved in litigation about wills and trusts. Other common areas of practice include personal injury and insurance defense. Some subject areas, such as patents and taxes, will be handled almost exclusively by attorneys expert in those fields.

Even within criminal defense, lawyers who typically handle small-time drug cases and burglaries aren't likely to suddenly show up defending someone on a murder charge. In fact, there may be rules specifically requiring a set level of experience before one may undertake such a defense. (See 29.J. for common requirements for attorneys in death penalty cases.)

The "family law" area of practice includes divorce, custody, adoption, and possibly some intrafamily tussles about property. There's a high rate of burnout in this area, especially where custody is concerned: these cases are so intense and heart-wrenching that in some locales, it's hard to find an attorney who will handle a disputed custody case.

One key distinction: not every lawyer is a trial lawyer (aka litigator). Trial lawyers don't even constitute a majority of the lawyers out there. Even in a firm that does primarily or only litigation (trials), some attorneys do only trial preparation and hand off their work to the folks who love the courtroom. It often works out something like the British system, where solicitors prepare cases and barristers try them. And then there are the many lawyers who negotiate contracts, write wills and related documents, draft patent applications, arrange advantageous tax deductions, etc., etc., who never set foot in a courtroom . . . unless they get sued.

A lawyer who doesn't normally handle litigation would be at a serious disadvantage the first time they tried it, no matter how intelligent or how capable within their usual area of practice. **One could have some fun chronicling such an attempt.**

Appellate (appeal) practice isn't as confined to specialists or the equivalent as are some areas of law, and many trial lawyers handle appeals as well; but in my sincere, if not necessarily objective, view (I practice appellate law), there are good reasons for those appealing trial court judgments to seek out a lawyer familiar with the appellate process. Not only do different procedural rules and judicial philosophies apply in trials and appeals, but lawyers handling trials and appeals need somewhat different strengths. Many trial lawyers view research and writing as a somewhat distasteful necessity; many appellate lawyers thrive on it. The techniques effective in presentations to juries will not necessarily be appropriate in an oral argument to an appellate panel, and vice versa. (See Ch. 32, especially 32.J., for how appeals work.)

Then there are the more rarified heights of U.S. Supreme Court practice. There was a time when the principal experts in arguing before that Court were those in the Solicitor General's office, which handles virtually all Supreme Court cases for the federal government. Now, there are many attorneys who appear frequently before the Court representing one private party after another.

Lawyers will sometimes try to help out a good friend or family member by taking a case outside their usual practice area. This is usually the result of fairly intense pressure, as the lawyer is likely to have serious doubts about the wisdom of such representation. **The repercussions could ripple throughout the extended family circle.**

Most if not all states require attorneys to take part in "continuing legal education," abbreviated as CLE or M (for mandatory) CLE, courses in any number of legal subjects. The requirement is meant to keep attorneys up to date on the law. I'm not aware of any requirement that these courses have anything to do with the attorney's area(s) of practice, and some of us frequently take courses because they are offered at a convenient time or place, even though they have little to do with our daily professional lives. **One could write about an attorney tempted to take on a new type of case after encountering the subject in CLE.**

D. Defending the Guilty

As mentioned already, there's one key fact you must understand about criminal defense work: most of a defense lawyer's clients are guilty. If a law student somehow doesn't learn as much before undertaking to represent criminal defendants, they will end up disillusioned in a hurry. And stories where an experienced defense attorney crumples in anguish and doubt because the defendant may be guilty are more or less ridiculous.

That isn't to say that innocent people never get charged with crimes. But that happens a good deal less often than the cops catching someone who's guilty of at least some of the charges that end up being brought. As explained in 9.A., the plea bargaining dance frequently includes prosecutors tacking on a few dubious charges to intimidate the defendant and create some bargaining room.

Why would anyone knowingly make a habit, and a business, of defending the guilty? There are several reasons, any of which could matter more or less to a particular lawyer:

- Even with all the plea bargaining, criminal defense work is likely to involve a fair number of trials. If trials are what get a lawyer's blood pumping, they may choose criminal defense.
- There's an unending supply of clients. Most of them don't have "deep pockets," but a sizable percentage will have some resources they can tap if the lawyer doesn't charge too much. And in a county with overburdened public defenders (see 2.F. and M.), the courts may regularly appoint private attorneys to represent criminal defendants, for a modest fee that's still considerably better than nothing.

- There is, in fact, a place for idealism in criminal defense, but it's about defending basic principles rather than defending lots of innocent individuals. If we value the idea that the government must prove a person guilty beyond a reasonable doubt (see 20.C.) before depriving that person of life, liberty, or property, someone needs to hold the state to that high standard in every single case. The accused must receive a zealous defense, not because they necessarily deserve it, but because we as a society — as well as the occasional completely innocent person charged with a crime — do deserve it.

Such legal idealism can be severely tested when a defendant is generally believed guilty of a particularly horrific crime. Robert Redford's movie *The Conspirator* chronicles one such situation, although I can't attest to its historical accuracy. After President Lincoln's assassination, Mary Surratt, who owned the boardinghouse where the conspirators often met, was one of those arrested, in what may have been an attempt to lure her son John out of hiding. A young Northern Civil War veteran, Frederick Aiken, was appointed to defend Mary, and (according to the film) was much vilified for performing that duty, eventually losing his girlfriend as a result. (The movie, which I haven't seen, may also use the "lawyer appalled that client may be guilty" trope I criticized above, but at least it doesn't attribute such sentiments to an experienced criminal defense attorney.)

A similar and more recent occurrence involved alleged terrorists detained at Guantánomo Bay in the years following the 9-11 attacks. Many attorneys from well-known law firms volunteered to represent the detainees pro bono (without charge). A senior Pentagon official publicly expressed his dismay and suggested that the law firms' corporate clients should boycott these firms. His comments generated an immediate and powerful backlash from prominent lawyers and legal professional associations, as well as some politicians — but whether any corporate CEOs followed this advice is unclear.

E. Pit Bulls and Puppies: Variations in Style

Many clients want an aggressive, take-no-prisoners attorney, particularly in litigation. There are some of those out there, but for quite a while, law school trial practice courses have discouraged that style as counterproductive. The client is usually better off with one of the many lawyers who speak softly and carry a sense of proportion and good people skills.

Hiring a very aggressive attorney has its hazards. When such an attorney cross-examines witnesses, a jury may view the witness as an underdog under attack and ally themselves with the witness emotionally. Coming on too strong in court can also lead to a reprimand from the judge, which undercuts the lawyer's credibility. Besides, a great deal of law practice involves negotiation. Better to choose an attorney who reads people shrewdly and manipulates them deftly.

F. What Newbies Do

Is your protagonist fresh out of law school? Here's what actually happens when newly minted lawyers enter the work force.

Most lawyers in law firms are either partners (co-owners) or associates (employees with some degree of hope of becoming partners eventually). Some law firms also employ staff attorneys, who do work similar to that of associates but aren't on the partnership track, or have a loose arrangement with "of counsel" attorneys, who may or may not get a retainer from the firm and often have a separate law practice as well (unless they're semi-retired).

In large and many mid-size law firms, associates in their first two or three years of practice rarely see the light of day, let alone the inside of a courtroom. They work very long hours to meet their ever-increasing quota of "billable hours," because not everything they do counts as billable.

By the way, there's not necessarily a consensus on the difference between billable and non-billable hours. One possible metric: if someone other than an attorney could easily and properly perform the task (e.g. making copies), any time the lawyer spends on that task is non-billable (though larger firms may itemize time spent by nonlegal staff). And any personal break of more than a few minutes shouldn't be billable . . . which doesn't mean attorneys always keep track of and deduct those breaks.

New associates in large firms may spend months or even years in "document review" for a single huge case. Document review is even duller than it sounds. These unfortunate associates spend their time going through huge amounts of paper, microfilm, and/or digital files, looking for information that can answer "interrogatories" (written questions sent by the opposing party's attorney) or for documents that come within a "request for production" or "subpoena duces tecum" (written requests for documents or occasionally other items, again sent by opposing counsel). And when the opposition answers *their* requests for documents, then these same associates must wade through the avalanche of material provided, looking for those few documents that are worth using in a deposition or at trial. (See 10.A. for more on this process.)

If you want your protagonist to have a professional identity crisis early in their career, stick them in document review. **You could also have your young attorney crack under the strain and start doodling on or annotating the documents. Extra points if you can figure out some plausible way these alterations wouldn't be noticed until trial, though that's highly unlikely.**

New associates are also likely to spend a great deal of time doing legal research and summarizing their research in legal memoranda. As they gain seniority, they may draft more important documents, such as trial briefs (arguing the law to the trial judge) and appellate briefs (the principal vehicle for asserting trial court error to appellate courts). They may also act as "second chair" at a trial, lugging files to and from court, taking notes, and handing exhibits to the attorney actually trying the case.

Some new attorneys actually do try cases. The best quick path to trial experience is to work for the prosecutor's office or for the office of the public defender (see 2.M.). While (as discussed in 9.A.) most criminal prosecutions end in a plea bargain, there are so many criminal cases in most counties that both prosecutors and defense attorneys generally try cases years before junior associates in private practice.

A small, small-town practice will also offer more trial work than the law firm life. And then there's good old nepotism: a young lawyer in Daddy's (or, increasingly, Mommy's) law firm might get to try cases before their peers.

Less likely, but still feasible ways for your protagonist to get thrown into trial work ahead of schedule could include**an urgent request from a friend who (possibly for reasons of local and/or judicial politics) doesn't trust other available attorneys;** or **the sudden incapacity of the more senior lawyer who was supposed to try the case, where the young attorney is intimately familiar with the details and it's for some reason impossible to delay the trial. (Delays of trials, called "continuances," are extremely common, with multiple continuances possible in a single case, so you'll need to have a reason that no continuance will be granted this time.)**

Of course, your new lawyer might try hanging up a shingle as a solo practitioner. However, unless the community is isolated or impoverished enough to be short of lawyers, it'll be hard for the newbie to drum up any business. It might help if they have lifelong contacts with the community; but on the other hand, having everyone know the new lawyer as the Henry boy or the Jameson girl, who should really still be wearing short pants or puffy skirts, could be a hindrance when it comes to the locals entrusting them with their funds or their freedom.

In most law firms, even if the firm handles work in several areas of the law, an associate will be assigned to only one at a time. Some firms rotate young associates through different departments, while others hire new attorneys to work in a specific area and stay there. Someone in a very small firm may handle any business that walks through the door, from contract disputes to divorces to negligence to criminal law, but so general a practice is the exception even for small firms and solo practitioners. It's often better business to develop a reputation for expertise in one or two areas.

To whom can an attorney turn for help with paperwork, legwork, or other tasks?

Law firm support staff typically include secretaries, receptionists, office managers, and the often-indispensable paralegals. Paralegals may do much of the grunt work otherwise assigned to new associates, from witness interviews to document review to preliminary legal research. If, however, they're called upon to write legal documents, they never sign anything they write; and it would be quite risky for a lawyer to send out a paralegal's work product without reviewing it first.

Larger law firms handling family law (divorce or custody) work, insurance defense, and/or criminal law may have a private investigator on retainer or even on staff. A smaller firm in these areas of practice would hire an independent investigator as needed.

Junior associates will almost certainly share a secretary with one or more other attorneys. This can be quite frustrating if, as is often the case, the secretary also works for a senior associate or a partner. Even though the senior attorney may be the one expecting the newbie to turn out work in a hurry, the newbie's work is last on the secretary's priority list. This will be a more important obstacle if your story is set before personal computers became standard equipment for professionals. If every document a lawyer turns out has to be typed (from handwritten or audiotape drafts) by a secretary, and then revised by the same secretary, that secretary holds the lawyer's fate in her (in that era, almost certainly "her") hands. **The evolution of a new lawyer's relationship with an experienced and possibly prickly secretary could be an important secondary theme in your story.**

G. Up or Out: the Partnership Track

Law firms are generally owned by the more senior lawyers as partners. (Technically, whether the firm is a simple partnership, an LLC (limited liability company), or something else may vary.) Most of the lawyers in a mid-size or large firm aren't partners and have no ownership interest in (and no individual liability for obligations of) the firm. They're employees. Traditionally, these employees are called associates. Again traditionally, they're hired in bulk, winnowed out over some period (say five to seven years), and then sent on their way if they don't "make partner." Junior associates are cannon fodder. More senior associates, if they're smart, pay a lot of attention to whether the partners are likely to vote them an invitation to the partnership, and have an exit strategy in place in case the indications aren't favorable. "Lateral" movement from one law firm to another, at a comparable or more senior level, is quite common for associates who have made it past the first two or three years.

For other possibilities, see the discussion of "staff attorneys" and "of counsel" arrangements, above (2.F.).

H. In-House Counsel

Some lawyers, usually lawyers with at least a few years of law firm experience, work for good-sized businesses as in-house counsel. In-house counsel have very different outlooks and responsibilities from lawyers in law firms or with their own law practices. Lawyers who haven't dealt with in-house attorneys much will not necessarily be prepared for these differences.

Lawyers are a law firm's reason for existence, and are therefore on the upper rungs of the firm food chain (though a valued legal secretary or paralegal may in practice outrank a junior associate, or a staff attorney who isn't on the partnership track). In-house counsel sometimes get considerably less respect from the corporate hierarchy, though as noted below, they may command much more respect outside it. Corporate officers sometimes view in-house counsel as necessary nuisances who habitually try to obstruct the corporation's way of doing business. If such officers ask for a legal opinion, and the opinion isn't what they wanted to hear, in-house counsel may be instructed to check with outside counsel, even if outside counsel has less experience than the in-house attorney.

The in-house counsel's position vis-à-vis outsiders, including any outside law firm the company hires, is likely to be considerably more exalted, especially for a company's general counsel. The general counsel will often have a large staff, as well as the ability to choose which law firm will receive the company's lucrative business when hiring outside counsel becomes necessary. If, at any point, outside counsel and the in-house general counsel disagree on such matters as the wording of a settlement, general counsel is likely to prevail.

Being an in-house counsel can also be even more lucrative than being a partner in a successful law firm, though this will depend on the particular compensation package and on how well any corporate stock included in that package performs in any given year. Many corporations recruit top associates from major law firms for such positions. Along with the other benefits, in-house counsel positions tend to have saner and more predictable hours than senior associates, or even partners, in law firms can expect.

In-house lawyers often have to be generalists, familiar with any legal area that could come up and in which they may need to supervise outside counsel.

Any lawyer moving from a firm or a solo practice to an in-house legal department will have habits to un-learn. A lawyer charging by the hour (or more likely, by the tenth of an hour) has little incentive toward brevity or efficiency. In-house counsel, on the other hand, are expected to take up as little of the employees' and officers' time as possible. Also, the lawyer can't go into a discourse on the various possibilities and the likelihood of various outcomes. They will have to go with the answer most likely to be accurate, and to appear decisive. And that answer may well be given in a quick phone call rather than a detailed memo.

In-house counsel will have to learn the office hierarchy, generally far more involved than a law firm's, so as to know who's entitled to take up their time with a question.

A lawyer who hasn't had much direct client contact and moves to an in-house position will have to get used to communicating with lay folk — and with figuring out what important information those folks don't know enough to volunteer, so the lawyer can ask the right questions.

In some jurisdictions, though these may now be in the minority, attorney-client privilege (discussed in 4.D.) doesn't always apply to communications between a corporate officer or employee and in-house counsel. This could be yet another reason that in-house attorneys often respond to questions with a phone call rather than a memo.

If your story involves a large company, **you could feature some interesting conflict between the in-house attorney responsible for hiring and overseeing outside counsel and the outside attorney(s).**

1. Another Option: Working on Retainer

A company (or, conceivably, some wealthy and/or particularly litigious individual) that wants to have an attorney at their beck and call, but doesn't want to employ in-house counsel (2.H., just above), could instead arrange to keep an attorney "on retainer." This use of "retainer" should not be confused with a one-time payment an attorney receives at the beginning of a case, or with "retainer agreements" setting the terms of a single attorney-client representation. Instead, this means paying an attorney to be on call, to take the client's cases as they arise. The payment will probably vary with both the attorney's reputation and the likelihood and frequency of work for this client.

The existence of such a relationship might not prevent the court from granting an attorney's motion to withdraw (see 4.I. and 25.M.).

I. The Out-of-Towners: Pro Hac Vice and Reciprocity

An attorney from the city can show up in a small town courtroom, and the only problem may be the judge's or jury's feelings about snooty city folks. But what if a party tries to bring in a lawyer from out of state?

There's usually a way for lawyers to file a temporary, just-this-once appearance without being a member of the state bar. (The rules governing such temporary appearances are more likely to be found in the court rules about admission to the bar than in the trial rules.) This is most often called appearing "pro hac vice."

Typical requirements for appearing pro hac vice include having a member of the state bar as a sponsor of some kind. The sponsor may need to act as co-counsel in the case, at least on paper. In practice, even if it isn't required, the sponsor or some local lawyer will usually handle routine appearances and filings. The out-of-town attorney may also have to pay some sort of fee. Finally, there's a limit on how often a lawyer may make such an appearance: one may not use repeated pro hac vice applications as a way to practice in two adjoining states without belonging to both states' bars.

It's possible that some state or local rules may require the applicant to show that no one locally available could handle this kind of case. (The Indiana Supreme Court had to step in recently and explain that a particular local rule did not, in fact, include this obstacle.)

What if the lawyer has come to stay? Will they have to take the new state's bar exam, just like the newbies?

That depends. There's no standard approach. Per a chart prepared by the American Bar Association (ABA), half the states have some amount of "reciprocity," allowing lawyers from elsewhere to practice law without jumping through all the hoops required of brand-new attorneys. (For more on those hurdles, see 2.B.) Some states require anywhere from one to seven years of prior law practice. Some also require that the relocating attorney take at least some of the exams new attorneys must take. These might include the multistate portion of the bar exam, and/or a similar multistate exam covering professional responsibility (aka legal ethics). A possibly increasing number of states will allow those who have passed the Uniform Bar Exam, or UBE, to use those prior exam scores for admission.

A few states have reciprocity deals only with a small number of other states, or impose additional obstacles to lawyers not on such a list.

J. Legalese

Like any trade, law uses its own language. Much of it (but by no means all) is loosely descended from Latin, and you'll hear the term "law Latin" used to describe words that started out as Latin and have acquired distinct meanings in the law biz. There are also specialized meanings of common English words.

There's another, more derogatory term often used for the way lawyers talk and (especially) write: legalese. This is often used for phrases, sentences, or longer passages, as well as for individual words.

Here's a small sampling of this specialized legal vocabulary. Please do *not* feel that you should plow through all these definitions, in order, before reading further! You can skip ahead immediately or at any point, returning to this section if and when you feel the need. You can also consult the Table of Contents or the Index to see if there's a more detailed discussion of a word or phrase.

If there's a word in the definition that you don't understand, check whether that word is defined earlier or later in the list. NOTE: if you're recording an audio book or doing public readings, check the pronunciation of these and other such terms.

- Accessory: one who helps someone else prepare for a crime or get away with it. Accessories aren't actually present when the crime goes down. An accessory can't be convicted if the criminal they supposedly helped isn't charged with the crime or gets acquitted.

- Accomplice: one who assists in committing a crime and is actually on the scene when it occurs. An accomplice can be charged and convicted even if the mastermind isn't.
- Additur: a judge's increasing the amount of damages awarded by a jury (allowed in some courts in limited circumstances).
- Admonition: an instruction from judge to jury, telling the jury to ignore something that just happened in court (whether it's testimony or some incident).
- Affidavit: a written statement made under oath or (the nonreligious equivalent) made with an explicit acknowledgment that there are penalties for perjury.
- Aggravating: usually used with "circumstances," meaning some fact pattern that makes a crime or a criminal worse; the opposite of "mitigating."
- Allege/allegation (used in other contexts, but especially often in legal lingo): claim, assert/assertion, as in a complaint or indictment.
- Answer: a defendant's initial response to a complaint.
- Appellant: the party initiating an appeal.
- Appellate: the adjective for "appeal."
- Appellee: the party dragged into an appeal by the appellant.
- Arraignment: the proceeding at which a criminal defendant is officially informed of the charges against them (sometimes combined with a bail hearing).
- Bail: money a criminal defendant has to "post" (give to the court, to be held by the court or some company the court picks) before being released from jail, as a guarantee to ensure that the defendant will show up for trial.
- Bailment: *not* related to bail (except linguistically), bailment is a temporary agreed transfer of control or possession of property from the "bailor" to the "bailee."
- Bequest: personal property (including money) given to someone via a will. (If it's real property, the word is "devise," but bequest is sometimes used to cover both. In fact, I do that myself, in section 14.K.)

- Capital: an adjective meaning that a crime may be punishable by death.
- Cause of action: a valid reason to sue someone. One could also speak of a criminal cause of action, but the phrase is usually used in a civil context. (You're going to see this phrase a *lot* as you read on.)
- Civil: nothing to do with "civility" or politeness, this is the category of law that isn't criminal.
- Common law: a legal system in which courts shape the law via accumulating decisions (aka "precedents"), usually relying on what courts have said in the past but occasionally extending or revising the legal doctrines that have been passed down. The term is also used for the body of law that thus accumulates.
- Complaint: the court filing that starts a civil case in motion (though sometimes used in the criminal context as well).
- Consideration: as with "civil," this has nothing to do with the ordinary meaning of being thoughtful. In legalese, consideration is something received or given up as part of a contract.
- Consortium: sex, but not only sex, and sex only in the context of marriage (so far). The loss of consortium is the loss of the love, emotional support, companionship, and (again) sex, or some of the above, as a result of injury to or death of the spouse. Alternatively: the comparable — nonsexual — loss to a parent when a child dies.
- Conspiracy: an agreement between multiple persons to plan and carry out a crime or tort. A member of the conspiracy may be found guilty of the crime, or liable for the tort, even if they were involved only in the planning phase.
- Constructive: usually paired with the alternative of "actual," this means that some action or inaction is deemed similar to something it isn't. For example, a "constructive eviction" (see 14.D.9.) is a landlord's failure to maintain premises in a livable condition, so that the tenant really can't stay there, whereas an actual eviction is the landlord's intentionally and explicitly kicking the tenant out. Other examples include "constructive fraud" (see 14.F.6.) and "constructive trusts" (see 14.K.10.).

- Contempt: willful (intentional) disobedience of a court's order (civil contempt), or the failure to behave with the necessary decorum and respect in regard to court proceedings (criminal contempt).
- Corpus delicti: this has nothing to do with corpses — unless the trial involves homicide. This phrase can mean the evidence that directly shows a crime has been committed, or the object affected by the crime (the body, if it's murder; the burned building, if it's arson). It often comes up as a contrast to an uncorroborated confession.
- Corroborate: to back up some factual claim with additional evidence. (For example, bruises or other physical evidence of an assault may corroborate the alleged victim's testimony that they were attacked.)
- Counterclaim: a pleading filed by the defendant (see below) in a civil case, equivalent to a complaint filed by a plaintiff, but aimed at the plaintiff who started this particular rodeo.
- Court: not just the place where it all happens, but the trial judge running the show. "The court" exercises "its" discretion, etc.
- Damages (always plural): money the court orders a defendant to pay the plaintiff in a civil case.
- Decedent: someone who died, especially in the probate (wills and trusts) context.
- De facto: in fact, regardless of technical legal categories.
- Defendant: in a criminal case, the one charged with a crime; in a civil case, the party getting sued. A civil defendant can file a "counterclaim" and thus become a plaintiff (see below) and a defendant at the same time. The party filing a counterclaim may also be called a "counterclaimant." (If there are more than two parties, and one defendant sues another, the one suing files a "cross-complaint" and is a "cross-complainant.")
- Deliberate: when the last syllable rhymes with "late," this is a verb and means the jury going off to discuss the case and make its decision. Less often, when the second syllable is emphasized and the last one sounds like "it," this means . . . well, that's hard to say. In the phrase "all deliberate speed," for example, it meant something like "as fast as can be managed without chaos resulting."

- Deposition: a session in which someone gives testimony in an office or meeting room, under oath or affirmation, as part of discovery.
- Devise: a verb or noun, meaning to give real property via a will or the real property so given. (For personal property, see "bequest.")
- Dictum (plural, dicta): language in a court's (especially an appellate court's) written decision, tangential enough that future cases addressing the same issue need not treat it as binding.
- Diminished capacity: some mental condition that makes it impossible to understand certain facts or to form a certain intent.
- Discovery: the pretrial process in which lawyers get information (mostly facts, but also what issues are likely to come up) from the opposition and/or third parties. Forms of discovery include "depositions" (sworn pretrial testimony, often taken in a lawyer's office); "interrogatories" (written questions sent to the opposition); "requests for production," seeking documents or other items fitting some description(s); and "requests for admissions" (what it sounds like).
- Discretion: in the legal context, this really means power — a trial court's power to make a decision based on its assessment of the evidence, the demeanor of the parties, and the feeling in the judicial gut, or a prosecutor's power to decide what charges to bring. When a trial court has substantial discretion to make some ruling, that ruling will be tough to get overturned on appeal. One context in which judges have lots of discretion: family law cases.
- Dismissal (verb form: dismiss): a trial court's order ending a case before a verdict (and most often before any trial). A court dismisses a case that the plaintiff can't win, even if the plaintiff, or the prosecution in a criminal case, proves every fact they claim to be true. A dismissal may also be punishment for party misconduct.
- Dissolution: most often means divorce ("dissolution of marriage"), but can mean unraveling a partnership.
- Document: this word is no longer confined to stuff on paper, but now includes any kind of printout, recording, device, or stored file on which people can put information. So a "request for documents" can have even wider scope than it did a few decades ago.
- Domicile: a home.

- Element: an element of a crime, a tort, etc., is one of the general facts needed to prove that it occurred. An element will be something like "premeditation," while the specific facts that satisfy that element will be along the lines of "Jack T. Ripper bought the knife and the knife sharpening kit, then followed the victim. . . ."
- Exculpatory: evidence that tends to show a defendant's innocence of criminal charges.
- Exigent circumstances: an emergency situation that doesn't leave time for formalities such as getting a warrant.
- Expunge: wipe out, make as if it never happened (though it doesn't necessarily operate quite that thoroughly).
- Fee simple: straight-up ownership of real estate, with no conditions, exceptions, or limitations.
- Fiduciary: used with "duty" or "relationship." A fiduciary has the duty to act solely in the interest of the other party or parties, as opposed to their own.
- Foundation: a metaphor derived from the building trades, this refers to satisfying some sort of prerequisite(s) for introducing a piece of evidence; usually has to do with where the evidence came from and/or how it was stored or transmitted, or with a witness' expertise.
- Habeas corpus: has even less to do with corpses than "corpus delicti" (above). This involves bringing a person into court, specifically a procedure, usually in federal court, where someone is trying to get released from imprisonment or other confinement.
- In camera: doesn't involve photography. This means some sort of hearing, discussion, or interview in a judge's chambers or another place where the public isn't allowed. The place could be the courtroom if the judge kicks out all those who aren't allowed to be present.
- Indictment: the document some jurisdictions use to state what charges are being brought against a criminal defendant, after a grand jury decides to bring those charges.
- Indigent: too broke to pay the various fees charged in a judicial proceeding, and/or to pay for an attorney in a criminal (or a very few

types of civil) proceeding, and/or to pay for a transcript to be used on appeal.

- Infant: not a babe in arms, but under the age of majority (typically 18 these days). (Note: I'm not going to get into the history, but if you're writing historical fiction or even setting your story a few decades back, and if this age threshold matters, research the details.)

- Information: in jurisdictions that don't use grand juries and indictments, the document saying what crimes a defendant is charged with.

- Injunction: a court order that something happen or stop happening. This could be a final judgment, or a court could issue a "preliminary injunction" that would last until the case wraps up (at which point there'd be a final injunction unless the court changed its mind about things).

- Interrogatories: written questions sent by one party to a lawsuit to one or more other parties.

- Invitee: someone explicitly or implicitly invited onto property, especially to serve the property owner's or tenant's interests in some way.

- Jurisdiction: this can either mean the geographical or organizational region in which a legal case is happening (for example, a county, a state, a federal district, or a federal appellate circuit); or the types of cases a particular court is authorized to hear ("subject matter jurisdiction"); or the court's authority to issue rulings that directly affect a particular person or organization ("personal jurisdiction").

- Laches: the failure to pursue some claim within a reasonable time.

- Licensee: someone allowed to come onto property, but who isn't there to confer any benefit upon the property owner or tenant.

- Lien: a creditor's claim to hang onto real or personal property in the creditor's possession until a debt is paid. The most common liens secure debts for work someone's done on or to property (remodeling, auto repair, etc.). Many liens are spelled out by statute, but common law liens can cover a variety of debts. Colleges, for example, have a common law lien on students' transcripts and may refuse to provide those transcripts until outstanding tuition bills get paid. Attorneys are often deemed to have a lien on a client's file, letting them refuse to turn it over to a former client unless and until the client pays the attorney for services rendered.

- Locus delicti: related to "corpus delicti," this means the place where the crime was committed. (For some reason — maybe because it lacks the spine-tingling if confusing suggestion of "corpses" — one doesn't hear this one as much.)

- Malice: it's easier to say what malice isn't than what it is. The legal uses of this word don't match the everyday meaning, and the two most common legal uses don't match each other very closely. In definitions of first degree murder, the term is usually redundant, echoing other elements like deliberate intent or premeditation. In the free speech context, if someone is speaking or writing about a "public figure" (14.F.3.), "malice" means deliberately saying something false or being reckless about whether a statement was true. See also 14.F.10. re "malicious prosecution."

- Mens rea: roughly speaking, this means "state of mind." Mens rea refers to what a criminal defendant knew, or thought, was happening.

- Mitigate/mitigation: where a plaintiff acts to minimize or reduce the damage the plaintiff suffers as a result of someone's tortious conduct or breach of contract. Example: if a tenant skips town halfway through a lease and stops making payments, a landlord can mitigate damages by finding a substitute tenant. In some situations, if the injured party doesn't make a reasonable effort to mitigate damages, they won't be able to collect the full amount of the damage actually suffered.

- Mitigating (as in mitigating circumstances): some fact pattern that makes a crime or a criminal not quite as worthy of condemnation; opposite of "aggravating."

- Motion: a request that a court do something that it wasn't already doing or planning to do.

- Nolo contendere: some jurisdictions allow this plea (also called "no contest") in criminal cases. It's not pleading guilty, as it doesn't admit that one has committed the crime. The defendant is saying, "I give up on fighting this charge, for my own reasons which I don't have to explain."

- Non compos mentis: not of "sound mind," mentally incompetent (for the task under scrutiny, such as signing a will or pleading guilty).
- Ordinance: like a statute, but passed by some local government's equivalent of a legislature.
- Parole: a period following a convicted criminal's time in jail or prison, during which the person lives under various restrictions.
- Perjury: a false statement, significant in the circumstances, that's made with the knowledge that it's false, either under oath or after affirming that one was about to tell the truth.
- Perpetrator: in the criminal context (as used by police and sometimes prosecutors): whoever did or is alleged to have done some criminal act. Short version: "perp."
- Petition: sometimes the same as a motion, sometimes the same as a complaint.
- Plaintiff: in a civil case, the one who starts the litigation ("files suit").
- Pleading: certain key papers filed early in a lawsuit (used mostly in the civil rather than the criminal context).
- Precedent: a previous written ruling by some court. It usually refers to a ruling by a court at least as high up in the judicial food chain as the court that's hearing a case. If the precedent comes from a higher court, the lower court is obligated to rule the same way on legal issues that were decisive in the earlier case. If the precedent comes from a court on the same level of the hierarchy, a court will still think long and hard before taking a different legal path, even if allowed to do so. See "stare decisis."
- Premeditated: planned ahead of time.
- Prima facie: at first glance. Even if the defendant never says a word, there will be some points a plaintiff must prove to win a case. That minimum showing is called a prima facie case.
- Prison: not simply a synonym for "jail," but (usually) a lockup for those who've been sentenced to a year or more of incarceration.
- Privilege: either an exemption (based on a relationship such as attorney-client, doctor-patient, priest-penitent, or spouse-spouse)

from the obligation to disclose information, or immunity from liability from making potentially defamatory statements..

- Privity: the full phrase is usually "in privity with," which means that two people or entities have enough connections between them that it makes sense to treat a contract with, or a suit against, one as involving the other.

- Probate: an area of the law (often handled by one particular judge in a system with multiple judges) that always includes wills and other inheritance issues; is likely to include commitment to mental hospitals and at least some guardianships; and may include some issues that look more like family law (e.g. adoptions). The same word is used for the process a will goes through in the probate court before anyone gets their hands on the property parceled out in the will. (Because of their role in handling inheritance issues, probate courts are sometimes called "orphan courts.")

- Probation: like parole, but instead of rather than following jail or prison time.

- Pro bono: providing legal services for free or at reduced cost.

- Pro se: an individual representing themselves in a legal proceeding.

- Property: means personal property, from cats to cutlery, from junk to jewelry, as well as real property.

- Protective order: similar to a restraining order (see below), often issued by a court against a stalker or an abusive ex, or to prevent disclosure of confidential material.

- Quantum meruit: a remedy used in place of contract remedies in some cases where no contract exists, based on the actual value of services performed.

- Quasi-criminal: a proceeding that isn't technically a prosecution for a crime, but has similar consequences.

- Real property (as opposed to personal property, not imaginary property): land or more-or-less permanent structures on land; real estate.

- Receiver: a person or entity appointed to manage property and keep whoever was previously managing it from dissipating it.

- Recuse (noun form: recusal): for a judge to take themselves off a case because of some personal involvement with the parties or the subject matter.
- Remittitur: a judge's reduction of the damages awarded by a jury.
- Restraining order: not about physically restraining someone, but rather, an order preventing someone from doing something. "Temporary restraining orders" are short-term and are largely meant to keep some situation under control until a court hearing can take place. While different jurisdictions use different terminology, a restraining order is probably issued in a civil rather than a criminal case.
- Riparian: having to do with the right to use or redirect water, particularly in the eastern and midwestern states.
- Scienter: a state of mind required to hold someone legally accountable for some action. It's like "mens rea," but broader, as it doesn't require a criminal context.
- Sentence: the penalty imposed by a judge in a criminal case. (Don't use this to describe a judgment in a civil case, such as tort or breach of contract.)
- Sine die: postponed indefinitely.
- Specific performance: when a court orders someone to fulfill the terms of a contract, rather than to pay money damages for failing to do so.
- Stare decisis: the rule that courts should follow the same legal rules as the courts before them (at least, courts in the same jurisdiction) unless there's a very good reason to change course.
- Statute: a law passed by a legislature, either state or federal.
- Stipulation: an agreement between opposing sides that some fact is established, so that no one has to submit evidence about it.
- Strict liability: a relatively rare type of tort (see below) for which one doesn't have to prove any bad intent or any negligence. Strict liability is imposed in connection with inherently dangerous activities.
- Sua sponte: when the court takes some action on its own initiative, without having been asked to do so.

- Subpoena: an order, under a trial court's authority but generally (at least initially) within an attorney's control, that someone appear to testify at a deposition or in court.
- Subpoena duces tecum: like a subpoena, except that the target must produce documents or other evidence.
- Summary judgment: either a later version of, or the opposite of a dismissal (though it only happens in civil cases), this gives a party a victory without the case having to go to trial. The court decides that despite everything one party can prove, the law dictates that the other party should win.
- Tenants by the entireties: married folk who own property together.
- Testator: someone (male, or the general term) who died and left a will.
- Testatrix: nothing kinky — a female testator.
- Tort: easiest to define by what it isn't. A tort is a civil (as opposed to criminal) cause of action that has nothing to do with contracts, with family law, or with wills and such. Torts come in intentional and negligent flavors, as well as "strict liability." For example, when someone sues for fraud, slander, or invasion of privacy, those are tort actions. When a customer slips on ice in the parking lot and sues the store owner, or sues the other driver in an auto accident for driving carelessly, those are tort actions as well.
- Tortfeasor: the person or entity committing a tort.
- Trier of fact: whoever hears evidence and decides which evidence to believe. If there's a jury, the jury is the trier of fact — but many cases, called "bench trials," are "tried to the court" with no jury involved. In bench trials, the judge is the trier of fact.
- Ultra vires: outside a particular court's jurisdiction.
- Verified/verification (used for written submissions to a court): A document that includes a signed clause, or the clause itself, stating that under penalties of perjury, everything in the statement is true and accurate (typical legalese redundancy) to the best of the signatory's knowledge (that is, as far as the one signing knows).
- Waive/waiver: losing or giving up the right to make an argument, claim some legal protection, or enforce some aspect of an agree-

ment. Waiver can (and in some circumstances must be) intentional, or it can be accidental.

- Willful: on purpose, intentionally, with knowledge. Often part of the phrase "willful and malicious," which means pretty much the same thing. (Outside the U.S., the usual spelling is "wilful.")
- Writ: a court's command that some other official body do something (a "writ of mandate") or stop doing something or refrain from doing something (a "writ of prohibition").

There are also a number of semantic habits lawyers pick up from older lawyers, case reports, contracts, etc. Lawyers tend to use words and phrases like "in reference to," "notwithstanding," "inasmuch as," "hereinafter," and "in accordance with," to name just a few. The contrast between legal writing and less cluttered English calls to mind Mark Twain's evisceration of James Fenimore Cooper's writing style:

"Without any aid from the science of cookery, he was immediately employed, in common with his fellows, in gorging himself with this digestible sustenance." This was a mere statistic; just a mere cold, colorless statistic; yet you see Cooper has made a chromo out of it. To use another figure, he has clothed a humble statistic in flowing, voluminous and costly raiment, whereas both good taste and economy suggest that he ought to have saved these splendors for a king, and dressed the humble statistic in a simple breechclout. Cooper spent twenty-four words here on a thing not really worth more than eight. We will reduce the statistic to its proper proportions and state it in this way: "He and the others ate the meat raw."

And let's not forget that almost any word may be defined, in a contract or statute, as meaning something besides the obvious or accepted. Watch for language like "for the purposes of this section . . . ."

Oh, and there's the structural approach one sees in statutes, which are mostly written by lawyers, either lawyer-legislators or lawyers who work for the legislature and draft the statutes some legislator asks for. Everything's divided into sections and subsections and sub-subsections, all numbered or lettered, and full of cross-references to other sections. You'll be used to it pretty soon — because I've used the same approach in this book. (Hey, I'm a member of the species. . . .)

There's a growing movement to, as a lawyer might say, eschew the incomprehensible intricacies of legal documents (especially in jury instructions — see Section 27.B.). **A young and idealistic attorney could try to push this cause, and might unexpectedly end up discovering that words whose meaning has been established by many decades of usage and court decision are actually *less* ambiguous, for courtroom usage, than "plain English" replacements.**

K. Pro Se, or Courting Disaster

Representing oneself, rather than having a lawyer represent one, is called appearing or acting pro se.

It's a perfectly good idea for a lay person to represent themselves in court — if they should have gone to law school in the first place, have a great deal of time to prepare, and are inhumanly objective about the matter at hand. Otherwise, it's probably a terrible mistake.

Representing yourself in court without adequate legal training is like waltzing through a minefield without a map. In the dark. The odds are enormous that you'll go up in smoke. More prosaically: a non-lawyer acting pro se is likely to miss the chance to introduce crucial arguments and evidence, because they won't know how and when to fulfill procedural requirements.

Given these difficulties, and the possibility of tricking a non-lawyer into making some damaging argument or admission, you might think an attorney would rub their hands in glee when faced with a pro se litigant; but the numerous delays while the judge tries to cope with the pro se party's ignorance can be so maddening that most lawyers dread such cases.

For judges, there's no "up" side. The trial or other hearing is likely to drag on much longer, with a just result much harder to achieve. If the pro se party failed to provide motions or other required documents to the opposing attorney beforehand, it may be necessary to schedule an additional hearing, adding to the court's already overburdened calendar. Moreover, the judge has a very tricky line to walk: how much assistance may they provide before becoming, essentially, an advocate for the unrepresented party? Examples of help that might or might not be excessive (because different appellate courts may disagree) include:

- Relaxing rules of evidence, such as the necessity to lay a proper foundation before admitting documents.
- Overlooking missed filing deadlines.
- Excluding objectionable evidence even though the pro se party doesn't know enough to object.
- Summarizing some key aspect of the applicable law at the start of the hearing, and/or prompting the pro se party as to what is or isn't relevant.

If the judge does decline to enforce some procedural requirement, they had better be even-handed about it, allowing the same latitude to the attorney on the other side.

Pro se litigants may not realize that most civil cases settle without a trial. They may therefore be more resistant to settlement negotiations. They also tend to have inflated notions of what their claims are worth, which makes settlement that much more difficult.

Another legal custom pro se litigants may not understand is the common practice of "taking the matter under advisement," where the judge doesn't decide the contested matter on the spot. Pro se parties have been known to remain for hours in an emptying courtroom, waiting for a ruling that could be days, weeks, or even months away. If a judge is able to rule from the bench and to provide at least a brief explanation of why they so ruled, the pro se party is a little more likely to feel that they had something like a fair hearing.

In criminal cases, because going pro se is such a bad idea, and because defendants have a constitutional right to legal representation (see 2.M.), the judge is supposed to make sure that any defendants stating the intention to represent themselves know how badly it may backfire before allowing the fiasco to unfold. In the civil context, however, urging a pro se party to get a lawyer has occasionally been held improper.

Even lawyers, when they find themselves in the position of litigants, are well advised to hire another lawyer. It's almost impossible to keep your emotions and partisan viewpoint from clouding your legal judgment in this situation. There's an old, wise saying among lawyers: "He who represents himself has a fool for a client."

On the other hand, it's rarely much fun for a lawyer to represent another lawyer. They won't sit back and let their lawyer run things. They're full of tactical suggestions and demands. **One could have some fun with how an experienced, older, crusty attorney deals with being in the position of client for a change, and how their lawyer tries to maintain control of the case.**

---

1. Jailhouse Lawyers

There's one set of pro se parties for whom acting pro se may have fewer disadvantages. I'm talking about "jailhouse lawyers": convicted criminals serving long stretches in prison who pass the time filing lawsuits and petitions on their own behalf, and sometimes assisting fellow prisoners as well. These could include, e.g., belated attacks on a conviction or sentence, claims of mistreatment by prison officials, or claims that a prisoner was improperly denied "good time" credit (early release based on the lack of disciplinary proceedings while incarcerated) or education credit (early release based on, for example, completing a high school equivalency course). Every once in a while, these prisoners have a small or even a large victory to celebrate.

The U.S. Supreme Court held in 1977 that prisoners' fundamental constitutional right to have access to the legal system requires prisons to provide either adequate law libraries or adequate assistance from those trained in the law. However, in 1996, the Court clarified or (more realistically) limited this rule. To gain any relief for insufficient access to the courts, the prisoner must show both inadequate access and some actual injury suffered because of that inadequacy. This "actual injury" requirement includes having to show that the legal action the prisoner was unable to bring was worth asserting, as opposed to "frivolous." These limitations could lead to a Catch-22 loop: **a prisoner might be unable to prove inadequate access to the courts because of their inadequate legal resources.**

The Court also held that the right of access only covered lawsuits challenging either criminal sentences or some condition of a prisoner's confinement. That doesn't, however, preclude a prisoner from learning the ropes on such challenges and using that knowledge for other types of claims. State law may also grant broader access, even for civil lawsuits.

Where the federal court system is concerned, Congress has also erected barriers. The 1995 Prison Litigation Reform Act required prisoners to exhaust all administrative remedies before filing a lawsuit under the federal civil rights statute known as "section 1983" (see 34.M.).

A successful jailhouse lawyer could make an interesting protagonist. Complications could include what has happened at least once: a bar association investigating such a "lawyer," one who habitually assisted other prisoners, for the unauthorized practice of law. Attempts to nail prisoners for unauthorized practice of law usually fail unless the prisoners so served had adequate alternatives, resources giving them meaningful access to the courts.

L. What Good are Lawyers

Many readers may have heard the following quotation, usually attributed to Shakespeare. Shakespeare did in fact write it, but placed it in the mouth of a disreputable fellow named Dick (really):

"First thing we do, let's kill all the lawyers." (*Henry the Sixth, Part II*, IV, ii)

Dick is speaking to, and a follower of, the would-be demagogue Cade, who is plotting to overthrow the government and install himself as king. To put it mildly, neither Dick nor Cade is offered as a reliable commentator on social reform. They disapprove of lawyers because lawyers induce men to make promises for which they may one day be held accountable.

Nonetheless, this is a pretty popular quotation, given that even English majors seldom get around to reading this particular play. What do so many people have against lawyers, anyway?

---

1. Liar, Lawyer

One common meme is the lawyer as liar, brilliantly demonstrated in the Jim Carrey vehicle *Liar, Liar*. This notion may well spring from the undeniable fact that lawyers try to get a jury (or a judge sitting as trier of fact) to believe narratives that may not be true — or at least, to doubt the opposition's narrative, whether or not that narrative is true. Lawyers view this as a necessary evil, or rather, as an essential aspect of the adversary system (whose justification for existence I'll get to shortly). But for many observers, putting the client's interests above the quest for truth is tantamount to lying.

For what it's worth, my experience leads me to believe that outright lying — straightforward assertions by lawyers to judges, juries, or other lawyers of statements they know to be utterly inaccurate — is quite uncommon. Of course, it's a lawyer making this assertion. . . . Ethics aside, a lawyer who deliberately lies to the court could be disbarred from the practice of law if the court finds out, or at least suspended for some long chunk of time. The same is true, though harder to prove, if the lawyer knowingly allows the client to lie on the stand (see 4.F. and 13.I.). There's also the not so minor point that attempting to deceive a court is likely to be disastrously counterproductive, not just in that case but in all future cases before the same judge, or before any judge to whom the deceived judge is likely to vent. (For a lawyer's duty of candor toward the judge in particular, see 4.F.)

As for statements carefully crafted to be ambiguous, or true at some levels but not others, or subtly misleading: well, those may not be exactly rare.

2. On the General Importance of the Law

Aristotle apparently said: "At his best, man is the noblest of all animals; separated from law and justice he is the worst." This is a bit on the conclusory side. For a better explication, I include what I consider the best defense ever offered for elaborate structures of laws, courtrooms, etc., from Robert Bolt's superb play *A Man for All Seasons*. This play purports to tell the story of Sir Thomas More, adviser to King Henry VIII, who eventually ran afoul of Henry's redefinition of the state religion. (The play omits some arguably less laudable aspects of More's life and career — that is, if one is squeamish about such practices as torturing and burning heretics — but that's beside the point.)

At one point in this play, More and his family have reason to believe that a young man, Master Richard Rich, may be spying on More. Rich begs More to employ him, but More has no intention of offering employment to a man he doesn't trust, even in the hope of keeping him out of mischief. Rich leaves, and More's wife Alice, their daughter Margaret, and Margaret's hot-headed love interest Roper all urge More to use his power as Chancellor to arrest the man. More protests that there's no law against being a bad man, and that even the Devil should not be arrested unless he's broken the law.

ROPER So now you'd give the Devil benefit of law!

MORE Yes. What would you do? Cut a great road through the law to get after the Devil?

ROPER I'd cut down every law in England to do that!

MORE (Roused and excited) Oh? (Advances on ROPER) And when the last law was down, and the Devil turned round on you — where would you hide, Roper, the laws all being flat? (He leaves him) This country's planted thick with laws from coast to coast — man's laws, not God's — and if you cut them down — and you're just the man to do it — d'you really think you could stand upright in the winds that would blow then? (Quietly) Yes, I'd give the Devil benefit of law, for my own safety's sake.

The legal system may function based on arcane and convoluted procedures, often applying incomprehensible or artificial distinctions, taking too long and costing too much; but I submit that anarchy, the "law" of strength winning over weakness, with passion or obsession defeating rationality, would be worse.

3. In Defense of Hired Guns, aka

the Adversary Process

Our judicial system doesn't treat truth as unimportant. It just operates on the assumption that the best of various unimpressive options for finding the truth is to have opposing parties try their hardest to persuade the judge or jury of their version of the facts, while poking as many holes as possible in the adversary's version.

What might those other options be?

In criminal cases, many countries use what's called the "inquisitorial" system. These tend to be the same countries that in the non-criminal context use a "civil law" system, which relies on detailed statutes, as opposed to the elaborate, centuries-old structure of judge-made rules called the "common law." In the inquisitorial system, pretrial proceedings are divided into two phases: the investigative phase, where evidence is gathered, and the examining phase, where evidence is scrutinized to decide if a trial should take place. Then, at trial, the judge asks most of the questions. Juries are rarely used, and there are fewer constraints about what sort of evidence may be admitted, given the presumed ability of judges to assess the reliability of witness and to remain unprejudiced by the irrelevant. There are often separate courts for dealing with different kinds of cases, so that the judges have more specialized expertise.

The various phases of an inquisitorial proceeding share a crucial characteristic: it's government employees doing the gathering and scrutinizing and questioning. There's no representative of the defendant directly involved.

We as a society have made and adhered to the value judgment that (in one common formulation) it's better to let ten guilty people go free than to convict and punish one innocent person. (One may always hope that the actual numbers are less lopsided.) For that principle to come close to operating, there needs to be someone with a personal stake in enforcing it: someone familiar with the tools of the system, using them to protect the accused from the governmental juggernaut. Criminal defense attorneys, take a bow.

Theoretically, we could have completely different judicial systems for handling criminal law and for everything else, and try an inquisitorial approach for the latter. There would be no more "cutthroat" divorce attorneys, no more "ambulance-chasing" lawyers handling auto accident claims. We would, instead, be placing significantly more power in the hands of judges. I for one would not envy the judges involved in a family law inquisitorial process. Our current system frequently demands that judges exercise the wisdom of Solomon. How much more would an inquisitorial approach demand?

This hybrid approach would require different educational and training programs for the different kinds of judges, and for attorneys who would practice in these two very different environments. If judges continued to be government employees, the vast expansion of judges necessary would be a major burden on the public purse.

But it could be quite interesting to portray such a mixed system.

M. Right to Counsel

In all criminal prosecutions, the accused shall enjoy the right . . . to have the assistance of counsel for his defense.

So says the Sixth Amendment to the U.S. Constitution. Unstated but essential: if the accused can't pay an attorney, the government must supply one at its own expense — whenever the right exists in the first place.

The interpretation of the Fourteenth Amendment to extend this right into state courts took place in stages: 1932 for capital (death penalty) cases, 1963 for non-capital felonies, 1967 for juvenile delinquency cases, and 1972 for misdemeanors where a convicted defendant could be deprived of liberty (jailed).

What about "infractions" such as traffic tickets? Nope. You're on your own in fighting those.

The Sixth Amendment right to counsel kicks in once someone is formally charged with a crime; but under a chain of U.S. Supreme Court precedents starting with the famous *Miranda* case (discussed further at 34.D.), the right to counsel is also one of the bundle of Fifth Amendment rights you have when you're in police custody and being interrogated. Since 1964 or 1966, depending on how one reads the cases, a suspect who's been arrested but not charged still has a right to an attorney's presence during questioning, and must be told as much. That doesn't necessarily stop police from following the required recitation with hints that only guilty people need lawyers, and that the suspect's troubles will be better solved by just answering a few more questions. . . .

Back to the Sixth Amendment. Once the defendant's been charged, they are entitled to a lawyer's presence and assistance not just during trial, but at various important stages before and afterward. These include the following (listed in the order they occur, with the year the U.S. Supreme Court declared these rights):

- arraignments (since 1961 in capital cases; since 1972, if not earlier, more generally);
- preliminary hearings (1970);
- plea negotiations (2012);
- sentencing after conviction (gradually adopted in a process beginning in 1948 and concluded by 1977);
- appeals "as of right," meaning any type of appeal one may file without the appellate court's permission (1963);
- hearings on whether probation should be revoked and the convicted criminal imprisoned (1967). Many courts extend this right to parole revocation hearings as well.

There's also a right to counsel on appeal and, in very particular circumstances, in some post-conviction relief proceedings (see 32.C.), but it isn't based on the Sixth Amendment. Starting in 1963, the U.S. Supreme Court has held that the Due Process and/or Equal Protection clauses of the Fourteenth Amendment (see 34.G. and 34.H.) require that indigent (broke) defendants, as well as the well-heeled, have lawyers on appeal.

All this protection still leaves some gaps. For example, once the defendant has been charged, they are entitled to counsel at any police lineup, as well as the more suggestive "show-up," where the witness is shown the defendant and asked, essentially, "Is that the perp?" But most lineups and show-ups occur *before* anyone's been charged — and there's no right to counsel at those.

Once a defendant has asked for an attorney, all interrogation is supposed to cease immediately. However, as in the case where a defendant "takes the Fifth" (see 34.D.), the police are allowed to try again after two weeks, if the defendant hasn't been in custody during that time.

What if someone is in jail awaiting trial on one charge, and the police show up to question them on a different one? The U.S. Supreme Court looked at this situation in 2001, and decided (by a 5-4 vote) that the prisoner is out of luck where right to counsel is concerned. They haven't been arrested on the second charge, so even though they're locked up, they aren't "in custody" in a way that triggers the Fifth Amendment-derived right to counsel. And they haven't been charged with the second crime, so there's no Sixth Amendment protection.

In some jurisdictions, the government will provide legal representation in post-conviction relief hearings, even where the Supreme Court doesn't say they must. Similarly, some provide counsel in cases that aren't strictly criminal but could involve loss of liberty, like involuntary commitment to a psychiatric facility (see 13.V.); or in prison disciplinary proceedings; or where fundamental rights are involved, e.g., where the state seeks to permanently terminate the relationship between parent and child (see 14.H.13).

There have even been rulings here and there suggesting that defendants in a much broader array of civil cases should be entitled to government-provided legal counsel. How this could possibly be accomplished has been left unresolved.

Some lawyers work full-time for the state or county, representing the indigent (those who can't afford to hire an attorney). These are "public defenders," often referred to as PD's. Their case load is typically insane. They may meet a client for the first time moments before an arraignment begins. They couldn't possibly give all these desperate souls the sort of careful attention that a lawyer is supposed to owe a client. It's a mess.

Overworked public defenders are likely to pressure defendants to accept plea bargains, whether the defendants insist on their innocence or not. What's more, defendants whose public defenders don't have nearly enough time to spend on each case may not receive the minimum acceptable standard of legal representation, constitutionally speaking. (See 32.C.1.)

Sometimes the court will appoint a lawyer in private practice to represent a defendant on the public dime. The lawyer will probably get paid much less than their usual fee.

1. Waiving or Forfeiting the Right to Counsel

A defendant may "waive" (give up) their right to counsel, choosing to appear pro se (2.K.). It's also possible to forfeit the right to counsel, e.g. by being flagrantly abusive to one's court-appointed lawyer or by stalling too long in hiring a lawyer. Threatening to kill one's lawyer would probably suffice. Some courts would treat a physical attack on the lawyer as forfeiting the right to legal services, but not every court does so, given that the defendant may be tied up or chained during court proceedings. However, this alternative has its own problems, as such restraints would send the jury a very prejudicial message about the defendant's character.

Some jurisdictions recognize a hybrid between waiver and forfeiture, "waiver by conduct," involving less flagrant but repeated conduct toward several successive appointed or hired attorneys.

Before deciding that a defendant has waived the right to counsel, the trial court should tell the defendant that they are giving up a constitutional right and explain the hazards of proceeding pro se. Appellate courts probably won't uphold a trial court's finding of waiver by conduct unless the trial court explicitly warned the defendant that their conduct would, if continued, lead to that conclusion. Forfeiture is different, at least in some jurisdictions: if the defendant's misbehavior is so extreme that a court will find forfeiture, such a warning may not be a prerequisite. In general, though, courts presume that a defendant has *not* waived or forfeited their right to counsel, explicitly or otherwise. A warning would make a trial court's finding of forfeiture easier for the appellate court to swallow.

N. Lawyer Dissatisfaction and its Consequences

Law practice is typically a pressure cooker. Most lawyers work long hours, some appallingly long. Associates in law firms must pile up the billable hours for a firm that may never reward them with a partnership. Solo practitioners and partners in law firms have the constant pressure of finding enough work to pay the bills. Trial lawyers are constantly bombarded with questions and demands from their clients, and unless they're fortunate enough to offload all the boring work on paralegals or junior associates, they spend far more time in the drudgery of trial preparation than in the excitement of a trial. Then there's the constant exposure to human unhappiness, arising both from the causes of legal disputes and from the process itself. (A partial exception: those few lawyers who practice what one lawyer I met calls "happy law," such as setting up small businesses or handling adoptions. But obstacles in either path can still lead to stressed and therefore stressful clients.) Small wonder that job satisfaction among attorneys tends to be low.

The consequences of this pressure and dissatisfaction often include depression, substance abuse, or both. As mentioned in 2.A., many bar associations have organizations, with volunteers supplementing paid staff, that assist lawyers struggling with such problems. They provide this assistance not only as a service to their members, but because either depression or substance abuse may lead an attorney to neglect their work and leave clients in the lurch. **There's tremendous dramatic potential in an attorney's descent into one or more of these conditions, coupled with the efforts of a fellow attorney, often a survivor of same, who attempts to help the sufferer put their life and practice back together. **

O. The Times They Have A-Changed:

Legal Malpractice Suits

Once upon a time, a client whose lawyer screwed up had little recourse.

Professional malpractice means professional performance so slipshod as to fall below the reasonable standard of care in the profession in that particular locale. To show that, one needs an expert in the profession to testify about what the reasonable standard of care is locally, and to explain how the professional in question didn't meet that standard. The problem: lawyers wouldn't testify against lawyers in that way.

That hasn't been true for a while now. **One could write an interesting story about one of the first lawyers to break from that understanding, and what drove him (probably, since most attorneys were male then) to do it.**

If the plaintiff has their expert in hand, and can prove not only that the attorney messed up but that the plaintiff would have been likely to prevail in more competent hands, they can compel the attorney, or their insurance company, to pay damages equal to what that hypothetical competent attorney would probably have won.

The criminal-law counterpart of legal malpractice, asserted in many, many post-conviction petitions (32.C.), is "ineffective assistance of counsel" (32.C.1.).

CHAPTER 3

Fees

A. You Want a Piece of Me?: Contingency Fees

In tort cases (see 14.F. and G.), lawyers are allowed to take a cut of the plaintiff's eventual award or settlement instead of charging by the hour or setting a flat rate. The lawyer may also advance the various up-front costs of the litigation, recovering them upon victory. This is obviously a gamble for the lawyer: no recovery, no fee (and possibly no expense reimbursement, depending on the particular arrangement or the plaintiff's financial situation). Tort lawyers make this gamble in a high volume of cases, hoping it'll pay off in enough of them to provide a reasonable income. Some lawyers will make the same arrangement in a breach of contract case. This sort of fee is called a contingency fee, and it may run as high as 40% or more of the plaintiff's recovery. Sometimes the percentage goes up if the case doesn't get settled and goes to trial.

Some settlements, however, specify that the attorneys will be paid based on time spent rather than a contingency, so tort attorneys are likely to keep track of their time just in case. There are also attorneys who offer clients a mixed fee structure, with lower than usual hourly rates coupled with a lower than usual contingency fee upon success.

Many plaintiffs who've suffered an injury or loss due to someone else's negligence would have no way to afford litigation without contingency fees. Class actions (6.D.) typically involve contingency fees. There's ongoing heated disagreement about whether the availability of contingency fee arrangements is an essential part of keeping corporations in check, or whether it has led to a plague of frivolous lawsuits acting as a drag on the economy.

B. Hourly and Flat Rates

Lawyers who aren't working for a contingency fee have traditionally charged by the hour and billed clients for their time at regular intervals. Quite often, they keep track of their time in increments of one-tenth of an hour.

Lawyers preparing for trial put in an ungodly amount of time. They interview witnesses; review documents; draft interrogatories and requests for production (10.A.); review the results; research many different legal issues; draft follow-up requests; draft innumerable motions; respond to the other side's motions; attend the hearings on those motions; interview witnesses again, to prepare them for trial; organize their research and write trial briefs for the judge; prepare to question witnesses; write and practice opening and closing statements . . . and that's all before the hours, days, or weeks of trial even start.

Multiply all those attorney hours by a hefty hourly fee, and you'll see why any litigation involving hourly fees is something like being caught near an erupting volcano. You may survive, but you'll be lucky to make it with the clothes on your back intact.

How can clients know that their attorneys really worked the hours claimed? The short and oversimplified answer is: they can't. They can request detailed invoices, which at least make it more laborious for the lawyer or law firm to pad the bill. They can also read those invoices carefully. Many years ago, when I worked for a California law firm, a client called to complain that he'd been billed for seven hours of a certain attorney's time on a day when the attorney was out sick. The attorney's tongue-in-cheek response: "I may have been lying in bed, but I was thinking about your case the whole time!" (The bill was corrected.) As with the question of telling outright fibs, I doubt blatant bill-padding is common, but it's possible I'm naive.

It's not unheard of for attorney and client to end up in court, after the principal case is over, fighting over whether a bill is excessive. This sort of dispute can become a battle of the (legal) experts, with lawyer-witnesses for each side giving their views on how many hours, by what level of attorneys, the case reasonably required.

Even if the bill is accurate, hourly billing comes with an unfortunate incentive to spend more time on the case rather than less. A lawyer needn't be consciously succumbing to that incentive for this to be an issue. It's easy to keep researching, or editing and re-editing a brief, past the point where the investment of time and client money really makes sense. Some savvier clients have started requiring their attorneys to submit an itemized litigation budget before the lawsuit is even filed.

Flat fees used to be used primarily for small, more routine legal work (e.g., drafting a simple will, contesting a drunk driving charge). These days, flat fees are increasingly used for a broader range of legal assignments. A flat fee lets clients know exactly how much they're shelling out in the hope of a favorable result. The attorney may still need to keep track of their time, at least at first (see 3.D.) — but once it's clear that the attorney has put in enough time to have earned the flat fee, they can heave a sigh of relief, stop counting minutes, and polish that brief to their heart's content. (Alternatively, the attorney can drag wearily down each new tangent the case throws up, cursing the day they agreed to accept a flat fee.)

C. Your Right Arm and Then Some:

the Cost of Litigation

There are some lawyers who don't earn a whole lot of money: public defenders (see 2.M.), prosecutors, lawyers whose practice is confined to a tiny dot on the map. But even in relatively small towns, most lawyers who bill by the hour earn more than $100 per hour. The larger the city, the larger the law firm, and/or the more senior the lawyer, the higher the rate goes, all the way up to a stratospheric $700 an hour (and that's a 2011 figure) for some New York law firm partners. It shouldn't be hard to get some idea of the typical hourly rate for lawyers in your chosen setting.

Couple that with the amount of legal time involved, which I've already mentioned, and you can see that litigation is a lot more likely to be lucrative for the lawyers than for anyone else involved.

I won't get into the question of whether attorney fees are unjustifiably high, but one must keep in mind that much of that money never gets to the lawyers, even the partners. Those fees pay for every kind of overhead, including office space, support staff, supplies, et cetera. Of course, there may be a circular element to some of these expenses: e.g., in order to impress wealthy clients and get them to pay high fees, the firm needs spacious and fancy offices, which cost a fortune, which require the firm to charge large fees.

D. Refund? REfund?

What if an attorney charges a flat fee, or a minimum amount as a starting retainer in an hourly rate arrangement, and then gets fired? Or what if the case wraps up unexpectedly early and easily? Does the client get a partial refund?

Different jurisdictions may have different rules about attempts to charge nonrefundable fees. The label can be important: an attorney may be able to designate part of the fee as paying for the attorney's availability, or as the fee for the initial stages of the work, without running afoul of professional rules against "nonrefundable" fees. Or the lawyer may have to keep track of their time until it's clear that the hours spent are more than enough to justify the fee. The fundamental issue is likely to be whether the lawyers who run the state disciplinary system think that the arrangement is "reasonable."

Lawyers usually write their own fee agreements. There's a general legal principle (discussed in 14.C.7.) that whichever party writes an agreement will be on the losing end of any dispute about ambiguous language in that agreement. So the lawyer will need to be very careful, and very clear, in describing what portions of the fee are meant to pay for what.

E. Who Pays

Who pays the lawyer?

If you're accused of a crime, and the court thinks you can afford a lawyer, then you have to hire one and pay them (or else represent yourself, almost always a horrendously bad idea — see 2.K.). If you convince the court that you're "indigent" (can't afford to pay an attorney), then the court will appoint one. Most of the time, it'll be a terribly overworked public defender (see 2.M.) who will try to push you through the system as efficiently as possible. Once in a while, a lawyer who usually has paying clients will be roped into defending an indigent client, for much less per hour than they usually charge.

In civil cases, the general rule in this country, appropriately called "the American rule," is that each party pays their own attorney. Here and there, now and then, people try to get this changed and have the loser pay the winner's attorney fees. This would make it easier for people to seek justice through the courts, in cases where contingency fees aren't feasible. However, it would also make it even easier to bully people with the threat of litigation.

The benefits of the American rule can be contracted away. Many contracts include language that lets a party suing to enforce the contract collect attorney fees if that party wins.

In many jurisdictions, the judge in charge of a divorce can decide that one party should pay all or part of the other party's attorney fees. Since the judge is already looking at the parties' present and future financial resources and deciding who should end up with what, this makes a certain amount of sense.

Some statutes encourage private enforcement of their provisions by letting people who sue under those statutes collect attorney fees along with other money damages. Those attorney fee awards, while usually required to be "reasonable," are still based on hourly rates (see 3.B., above) far higher than what most people earn per hour. Statutes like this are often called "fee-shifting" statutes.

Fee-shifting statutes give corporate in-house counsel heartburn. Corporations are very often the defendants in such lawsuits, and no matter the result, they're stuck paying their own legal expenses, whether those include the salaries of in-house counsel, the fees of outside counsel, or both. Meanwhile, plaintiffs with hopes of having their attorney fees reimbursed, or who have arranged with their lawyers to postpone payment of some or all fees until the end of the case, may be profligate with their attorneys' time. Both plaintiffs and their attorneys may be particularly stubborn about settlement demands in cases where a victorious plaintiff will get their attorney fees paid. Even where the defendant is very likely to win, and/or the statute limits the plaintiff's actual damages, the plaintiff may demand a settlement higher than the statutory damage ceiling.

F. Pro Bono - Attorneys Working for Free

It may be hard to believe, but attorneys sometimes work for free. In fact, in many states they're required to do so, for some number of hours per year. Attorneys call this working "pro bono," short for "pro bono publico," or "for the good of the people" in Latin. (As I've already mentioned, the law has a certain fondness for Latin or quasi-Latinate phrases.) Charging substantially less than one's usual rates also counts as pro bono work.

There are entire organizations, often funded in whole or in part by state or federal government, whose purpose is to provide pro bono legal services. Many get their money via grants from the Legal Services Corporation, a "private" nonprofit corporation established by federal statute and funded by tax dollars.

G. The Client's Property Held Hostage:

Attorney Liens

Clients don't always pay their bills. And clients with unpaid bills can get awfully hard to find. What pressure may a lawyer exert in this situation?

In many jurisdictions, the lawyer may hang onto client property until the bills get paid, asserting what's called an attorney's lien. How much pressure this actually puts on the client will vary greatly from one client and case to another.

There are two types of attorney's liens:

- Charging liens, which fasten onto a judgment the client received through the lawyer's efforts in a particular case.
- Retaining liens, which are broader and cover any client property in the lawyer's possession. A common example is the case file, which includes various documents that come either from the client or from one or more courts and would otherwise go to the client, if the client wants them, when the case is over.

If you care to write about an unscrupulous attorney who makes a habit of trying to collect excess fees to which they are not entitled, that attorney could use either type or both types of attorney's lien to put the screws to clients. On the other hand, **your young and struggling attorney could be forced to use this weapon against an unsavory client, who could then resort to violent means to retrieve case files or to coerce the attorney into turning over funds in a trust account.**

CHAPTER 4

The Rules for Attorneys

A. Complaints Against Attorneys

There are rules that lawyers have to follow beyond the rules (e.g., rules of evidence and procedure) that trial judges administer and enforce. These rules are usually called rules of "professional conduct" or "professional responsibility" (and may also be referred to as "ethical" codes), and they're enforced by each state's bar, which in practice means a disciplinary commission working under the authority of the state supreme court. Violating those rules can get a lawyer suspended from the practice of law, or even disbarred (comparable to a priest being defrocked, though not always as permanent). The disciplinary commission also handles complaints that a lawyer has slacked off or neglected the client's interests in some way. This can range from failing to return phone calls (a very common occupational disease) to far more egregious behavior, such as pretending to have filed a lawsuit while actually letting the time run out in which the lawsuit can be filed (see Ch. 11), or settling a case without telling the client and pocketing the settlement.

Who reports a lawyer to the disciplinary commission? It may be a current or former client, opposing counsel, or a judge. Each state has procedures for filing complaints against lawyers. There's an initial inquiry, during which the commission often dismisses the complaint as not worth pursuing. If the commission thinks the complaint could have some merit, it'll notify the target and conduct an investigation. Lawyers who are found to have violated the rules, but who cooperate fully with the commission, have the opportunity to negotiate for a less severe punishment. Lawyers who ignore or defy the commission are more likely to get slammed. If the lawyer's misbehavior has its roots in substance abuse or a mental health issue, as is often the case, the agreement may include getting treatment.

What was that about disbarment not always being permanent? Well, a lawyer can petition to be reinstated, and while it's a long shot, it could happen. It's also possible for a lawyer to practice in more than one state and to be disbarred in only one. **So your protagonist could discover that the smooth-talking fellow in the expensive suit who pocketed their life savings was disbarred one state over for bilking other clients.**

B. Competence

Before a lawyer takes a case, they have the duty to be confident they can handle it competently. One is not supposed to learn a new area of practice at the client's expense (literally or figuratively). Some self-education during a case is to be expected, but the attorney had better know from experience that the amount to be learned is within their capacity. Absent special rules, however, such as the state may have for death penalty cases (see 29.J.), it's up to the lawyer (and the client — caveat emptor!) to assess the lawyer's ability to do the job.

A lawyer with a shaky background in some legal area can bring in more experienced co-counsel, protecting the client while giving the attorney the chance to expand their expertise.

Of course, competence is not merely a matter of experience. Age, illness, or substance abuse can undermine the lawyer's ability to handle a case. **Age, in particular, could provide a complex and poignant problem in self-evaluation for your lawyer protagonist.**

C. Conflicts of Interest

Let's go back to that "hired gun" image. How would you feel if you found out the gunslinger you hired was also working for — or sleeping with — the fellow you hired them to shoot? Would you want to find some barrels to hide behind?

In order to avoid this sort of problem, there are significant limitations on whom a lawyer may represent. The applicable label: "conflicts of interest." The details of the rules may vary from state to state, depending on how precisely the state has adopted the American Bar Association's Model Rules of Professional Conduct, but here are a few basics. If you're going to have a story revolve around conflict of interest, you'll need to study up beyond what I can include here.

Conflicts of interest (which can arise in many contexts, not only in the practice of law) are sometimes divided into "actual" and "potential" conflicts. Basically, there's a "potential" conflict when a reasonable person can see that an "actual" conflict could be on its way. If there really isn't a conflict, but people confused about or ignorant of the facts could think there is, then there's an "apparent" conflict. For example: if someone who owns a business is asked to write an online encyclopedia article about that business, there's a potential conflict of interest before they actually undertake to write it, and an actual conflict once they get started. If they don't own the business, but people think they do, that'd be only an apparent conflict.

The most extreme conflict of interest is simultaneously representing two sides to the same lawsuit. You might think this would never happen; but it's not uncommon for a couple getting divorced, and hoping to keep everything amicable, to ask a single lawyer to handle the matter for both. (I'll get to how lawyers are supposed to handle such requests in a moment.) And busy law firms with many clients have to set up procedures to make sure that none of the lawyers end up representing opposing parties without realizing it. This is a particularly vexing problem for law firms with offices in multiple cities.

What if a lawyer represented Capulet five years ago, and now Montague wants to hire that same lawyer in a case that might affect Capulet's interests? That's probably a no-no, because when the lawyer was representing Capulet, they had the opportunity to learn some of Capulet's secrets, and there's a danger that the lawyer might use some of those secrets against Capulet in the current case.

There may even be a conflict when the current case doesn't directly involve the former client, if the new case could have a negative impact on the former client's interests.

There's a situation not all authorities treat as a conflict of interest: "positional" conflict. What if a lawyer or law firm has been arguing a legal position in one case, and someone else, possibly a larger, richer, more important individual or company, wants to hire the lawyer or the firm to assert exactly the opposite position? What if the cases are in the same court? The answer may depend on whether the lawyer or firm could somehow take both positions and assert the inconsistent arguments without endangering the success of either case. That's a bit more likely if the cases are in different jurisdictions. Where it isn't feasible to handle both cases, the lawyer or firm may be tempted to weasel out of the first case. **If you like subjecting your characters to personal and professional ethical dilemmas, there's material here.**

Problems can arise when lawyers move from one law firm to another, bringing their client histories with them. Even if the new lawyer isn't going to work on a current case, their past representation of a current client's adversary puts the firm in a bind. Must the law firm choose between hiring the lawyer and firing the client? To avoid such painful alternatives, the rules often include some procedure for isolating a lawyer who once represented a current client's adversary, keeping them away from everything connected to the current client's case.

If an attorney is "of counsel" to a law firm, handling some cases for the firm while also maintaining a separate practice, both the attorney and the firm had better be quite vigilant about checking for conflicts of interest.

Sometimes the conflict isn't between the interests of two clients, but between the client's and the attorney's interests. For example, if the attorney owns stock in a company that'll take a serious hit if the client wins, one can reasonably doubt whether the attorney's representation would be as zealous as necessary. Such a conflict will usually involve financial interests, but not always. If the case involves a nuisance action (see 14.D.8.)

against a hog farm with a smelly manure lagoon, and the defendant's attorney lives downwind, the attorney might find it hard to give the case their best efforts, even if property values were somehow not an issue.

Some conflicts of interest can be dealt with by a written waiver from all the clients involved. If a lawyer represents both spouses in a divorce, for example, both of them will have to sign such a waiver. The waiver would specify exactly what the conflict is, and state that the client is fully aware of it and realizes that the conflict could theoretically affect how the attorney represents the client, but consents anyhow.

If a client, or opposing counsel, becomes aware of an attorney's conflict of interest, they can file a motion to have the attorney disqualified.

D. Confidentiality, Attorney-Client Privilege, and Attorney Work Product

There are two related ways in which a lawyer's communications or documents may be confidential: attorney-client privilege and attorney work product.

Attorney-client privilege, unsurprisingly, covers communications between attorney and client, whether verbal or in writing (including email and other supposedly private messages). It applies even before the lawyer is actually hired, during any preliminary consultation — even an informal one that the attorney didn't know was coming. As long as the client intended to ask (or start the process of asking) for legal advice, and reasonably believed that the lawyer had their "lawyer" hat on at the time, the discussion is privileged.

The public policy underlying this privilege is that the legal system works best if clients feel free to be open and honest with their attorneys. While the attorney-client privilege isn't enough to guarantee such honesty, it certainly helps. **One could record the successive layers of deceit and eventual confession in an ongoing attorney-client relationship.**

Clients or potential clients frequently want someone who isn't a party (a spouse, a boyfriend or girlfriend, a parent, a best friend) to attend a meeting with a lawyer, particularly when they're still deciding whether to hire that lawyer. That can be a problem, because technically, anything that's said in front of a nonparty isn't a confidential attorney-client communication. If an adversary somehow finds out about this discussion, they could require the nonparty to disclose what was said, unless some other privilege (e.g. spousal privilege, 22.I.3.) applies.

Lawyers don't want other lawyers looking over their shoulders: hence, the protection for attorney work product. (Technically, this isn't a "privilege.") As long as the attorney doesn't show their notes, drafts, recordings, etc. to anyone except the client(s) and the attorney's support staff, the opposition can't gain access to this material or force the attorney to disclose it.

What if the protected material is disclosed to a third party by accident? Jurisdictions differ as to whether accidental ("inadvertent") disclosure destroys the privileged status. Some say "always," some say "never," and some say "it depends."

One could have a race-against-the-clock attempt to retrieve attorney work product — perhaps a document full of juicy electronic comments — accidentally sent to some third party before the recipient learns of the disclosure and/or sees the material.

What if two parties with separate attorneys, but with some common interest in a case, want their attorneys to work together? In that case, the "common interest privilege" allows the attorneys to share confidential information with each other. Typically the parties would enter into an agreement (e.g. a "joint defense agreement") spelling out the common interest, the present or anticipated proceeding(s) involved, and any other related matters. For example, the agreement might or might not restrict the parties' ability to sue each other in the future in connection with the matter in which both are involved — but even if they retained that ability, they could not use the information exchanged in the current case in any future lawsuit.

Attorney-client *confidentiality* goes beyond just privileged communications. Anything that an attorney learns as a result of representing a particular client is confidential, with the exceptions discussed momentarily.

1. Blowing the Whistle

There are limits on an attorney's obligation to keep the client's secrets. If the client states an intention to kill or gravely injure someone, and the lawyer thinks the threat is more than hot air, the lawyer is permitted to call the police and/or warn the intended victim. The same is true, at least in some states, if the client is about to use the lawyer's services as part of a scheme to commit a crime or perpetrate a fraud that will almost certainly cause damage to someone's property or financial interests. But the lawyer had better be (as the courts often put it) "reasonably certain."

"Permitted to" call the police or give a warning? Do I mean attorneys don't *have* to blow the whistle to prevent a crime, even murder? Well, in most jurisdictions, they don't — at least, that's the rule as far as attorney conduct codes go.

What if the murder/assault/crime/fraud has already occurred? Where financial damage is involved, if there's a chance to mitigate the damage by disclosing confidential client info, some states allow the attorney to do so. But mitigation of emotional harm doesn't count. For example, in many or most jurisdictions, if the attorney knows that a missing person has been murdered and could reveal the location of the body, it's a violation of "professional ethics" to tell the family or the authorities.

California has typically gone to what might be called extremes in protecting client confidences. Until 2004, even a client's plan to commit a future murder had to be kept on the QT.

2. The Fee Exception

There's one situation unrelated to public safety in which an attorney may disclose information the client revealed in confidence or the attorney learned from representing the client.

That's when the attorney goes to court to try to collect all or part of their fee from the client.

Don't tell me you're surprised.

In general, attorneys are supposed to make sure the client knows all about the fee arrangement from the get-go; but there's no obligation to reveal the fact that if attorney and client end up tussling over money, the attorney is allowed to reveal relevant but otherwise confidential client information. **A client might conceivably be very, very peeved at this apparent betrayal.**

E. "Talk to My Attorney"

An attorney may not talk about the case to the opposing party if the opposing party has an attorney of their own.

Is it really that simple?

Is anything in the law that simple? . . . but this rule has fewer exceptions and complexities than most.

If the opposing party's attorney hears about what happened, and for some reason decides that it's OK, then it's OK.

If the opposing party is a corporation or other such entity, then the rule might not apply to a conversation with some lowly grunt with no decision-making power. Some corporate in-house counsel would still raise a stink about such contact.

If the opposing party is a governmental entity, then as long as the attorney makes sure the government lawyer on the case knows what's happening, the attorney can keep trying to persuade government personnel to solve the client's problem.

But if you're a litigant in a case in which your attorney has made an appearance, and the opposing attorney contacts you directly rather than through your attorney, the opposing attorney is way, way out of line.

There's a related rule, the rule against "ex parte" communications. See 10.B.

F. Candor

I've already mentioned the movie *Liar, Liar*. If an attorney actually did what Jim Carrey's character does, routinely presenting the judge with testimony they know to be false, they'd be risking their license to practice law, not to mention a prison term for the crime of "suborning perjury" (13.I.).

Attorneys have a duty of "candor" toward the court and the jury. This duty goes well beyond the obvious starting point of "don't lie to the judge." Mr. Massey in the movie *Intolerable Cruelty* almost certainly crosses the line when he crafts a grossly distorted version of the events his client has already disclosed to him.

If the attorney's client is testifying and lies under oath, the attorney can't just keep asking questions as if all is well. When a client lies on the stand, an attorney will typically ask for a recess, drag the client out of reach, and insist that they correct the false testimony in as undamaging a manner as possible. If the client refuses, the attorney is in quite a quandary, and different states' case law and rules of professional conduct (4.A.) take different approaches to addressing it.

Some courts allow the attorney to blow the whistle and inform the judge about a client's perjury. Others require the lawyer to move to withdraw from the case (see 25.M.). Even if the rules allow the attorney to remain coy as to the reason, the judge will usually know what's going on. Still other courts only allow that option, at least in a criminal case, if the client's interests won't be seriously harmed by the attorney's withdrawal (a pretty tough test to pass). For example, if moving to withdraw would require a continuance (a postponement of proceedings), and the client is in jail, withdrawal could be prohibited. An attorney who can't withdraw may have no choice but to put the lying client on the stand and let the client tell their tale in "narrative" fashion, without the usual question-and-answer format.

Some courts distinguish between strongly suspecting the client is going to lie, or otherwise to present false evidence, and actually knowing it. Where that distinction makes a difference, the lawyer must present the evidence like any other evidence unless they know it's false. Where to draw that line can be quite tricky. This doctrine also tends to encourage lawyers to avoid asking questions and investigating once they become suspicious — a limitation which could adversely affect their effectiveness.

What if a witness other than the client tells a whopper the lawyer wasn't expecting? **This could be a particularly nasty trick for you, the author, to play on an inexperienced trial lawyer.** Again, some states' rules would allow the lawyer to inform the judge (if a recess and a strict talking-to didn't bring the witness around). Where that isn't allowed, the lawyer may have the option of abruptly bringing the questioning to an end and making no further mention of the false testimony for the rest of the trial.

The duty of candor is not limited to presenting evidence. An attorney must not make misleading legal arguments; and if new law would render a previously made argument incorrect, the attorney (in some or all states) must affirmatively come forward with a correction. This is also sound tactics: if the attorney discloses the damaging new case, they can also argue why the case isn't really as damaging or as applicable as it might seem. If it's opposing counsel or the judge's clerk who finds the new authority, the judge will be far less inclined to listen to any such arguments.

There are those who claim that many attorneys not only fail to report when useful cases have been overturned on appeal, but go so far as to *invent* recent useful cases, at least when dealing with judges they know or guess aren't likely to check citations for validity. This may be most likely in court, when attorneys are arguing some motion, rather than in filed papers, which might be handed to a clerk (if that court has clerks) to confirm. **A risky but tempting tactic opposing counsel could use, when faced with such dishonesty, is to invent an even more recent case going the other way and closer to the facts.**

One current hot topic in legal ethics circles: does an associate in a law firm have an ethical obligation to inform the judge if a partner in the firm misrepresents case law?

G. Isn't it Romantic (Not Usually)

In novels, movies, and especially television, attorneys seem to engage in a good deal of sexual frolicking with others involved in their cases or in the court system.

I won't say that attorneys never sleep with their clients/other attorneys in the same firm/opposing counsel/the investigator/the judge. Young attorneys in large firms, with no time for a social life, may from time to time find solace or amusement in each other. Adversaries may find that respect earned in the courtroom gives rise to other emotions. But I think it's safe to assert that most attorneys' sex lives have nothing to do with their work

— except that they may be so overworked and distracted as to frustrate the heck out of their significant others.

In any event, sleeping with a client is a violation of an attorney's code of ethics in most or all jurisdictions.

H. Hawking the Product: Advertising

Whether on TV, billboards, bus stop benches, or the sides of the buses themselves, one can hardly escape attorney advertising these days. But for many generations, the idea would have been unthinkable. Attorneys were supposed to be of a genteel class that wouldn't dream of entering the commercial fray in such a manner.

Even now, there are quite a few restraints, varying from one state to another, on what an attorney is allowed to assert in an advertisement. These rules are usually intended to prevent the advertisement from misleading the potential customer. Rules meant to preserve the decorum of the profession, on the other hand, have loosened up or been dropped altogether.

Promising particular results, including results similar to what others have achieved in the past, or using statistics in a way likely to raise unrealistic expectations would violate current rules. Testimonials about how a particular plaintiff made out like a bandit would have to be most carefully worded to avoid this prohibition. Dramatizations (e.g., two slimy fellows in suits chuckling about how they're going to screw over some injured party, and then exclaiming in dismay at the announcement that the plaintiff has hired a particular law firm) must be clearly labeled as such and may stray over other lines.

One unfortunate attorney received an email from a friendly judge praising the attorney to the skies and recommending that the attorney share the contents of the email with whomever he liked. The attorney forwarded the email to various other attorneys, clients, and prospective clients. He ended up with a public reprimand for supposedly implying that he could influence a government official. The judge resigned.

A lawyer's self-assessment of expertise could be misleading, so states often have minimum requirements of some kind, e.g. a certification based on testing or years of experience, before an attorney may advertise that they "specialize" in any of several fields (again, which fields may vary by jurisdiction). It may or may not be possible to evade such requirements with alternate word choices.

When the bleachers at the stadium collapse, may tort lawyers beat a path to the victims' hospital rooms, offering their assistance? Such in-person solicitation is often prohibited, along with other real-time communications like phone calls and text messages. Even written offers of legal services may be forbidden until some time period after the triggering event; and they must be labeled as advertising matter (as opposed to, say, expressions of sympathy and public-spirited education about how the victim of misfortune could improve their situation).

There are also rules regulating how attorneys may send each other business ("referrals" from one attorney to another). Kickbacks from the lawyer getting the business to the lawyer who sent the client their way are likely to be prohibited unless they're made to a company that exists to make such referrals.

I. Client Trouble: Accepting the Wrong Client

Unless they're in-house counsel (2.H.), public defenders (2.M.), or working on retainer for a major client, lawyers generally aren't required to take on any particular client. With experience, lawyers learn to sniff out clients who are likely to make their lives miserable. Red flags include:

- A client on their third or more lawyer. The more lawyers the client has had, especially if client and lawyer parted ways with some acrimony, the more likely it is that there's another side to the client's litany of incompetent or insufficiently zealous representation.
- A client asking the lawyer to jump into some case in which the client was previously pro se (2.K.). Such a client may not have completely accepted the necessity of paying and listening to a lawyer, and may well have already mucked up the case beyond salvation.
- A client who doesn't listen. Clients who can't or won't pay attention to what the attorney says will be incredibly frustrating to work for, and are likely to injure their cases by ignoring or disobeying the

lawyer's instructions. One very good reason to offer a free initial consultation, whether in person or by phone, is to discover such people before contracting to represent them.

- A subset of such clients: those who, despite the lawyer's explanations, refuse to believe that the legal system operates as it does, instead persisting in expecting the lawyer to use improper tactics or achieve impossible results.
- Another subset: lawyers now stuck in the position of clients (see 2.K. again) and particularly bad at making that transition.
- A client with a conspicuously bad temper. Such a client is likely to turn on the lawyer sooner or later, and/or to misbehave counterproductively (or disastrously) in court.

Of course, your legal newbie could learn any or all of these lessons the hard way.

If a lawyer isn't careful and ends up with the Client from Hell, it may or may not be possible to withdraw from the case, depending on the details.

Of course, the client might make it easier on the lawyer by firing them. Even if the lawyer is a public defender or a court-appointed attorney, the judge will probably allow the attorney to withdraw if attorney and client both desire the split.

Otherwise, whether an attorney needs court permission to withdraw, and whether the court will grant such permission, depends on how serious the problem is between attorney and client and on how much inconvenience and/or expense withdrawal would cause for the court or the parties. If a party has already asked for and received multiple continuances (see 25.E.) and that party's search for new counsel will further delay things, the court may well deny the motion to withdraw. Similarly, if the trial has already begun, and especially if it's well under way, the attorney would have to make a fairly compelling case for why continued representation is essentially impossible or would require the lawyer to violate ethical rules and/or the law.

See 25.M. for more details on how withdrawal and motions to withdraw usually work, including how federal and state courts may differ.

CHAPTER 5

Judges

The most powerful figure in any litigation, with the greatest ability to do justice or to obstruct it, is the trial court judge. And what a challenging job it is! Judges often have too many cases on their dockets to give each case the time they may believe it deserves. They're forced to make crucial decisions, all of which affect people's lives and many of which could transform those lives in crucial and/or devastating ways, based on whatever information the judge receives in a few hours or days. That information may come from attorneys whose competence is questionable — or, even worse, from unrepresented parties (aka "pro se" litigants (see section 2.K.)) who know nothing about how to present evidence or argument in a way the judge is allowed to accept.

So who can "take the bench" (become a judge), and how are they likely to get there, and what could dislodge them once they're in place?

A. The Path(s) to the Bench

Trial court judges may be appointed or elected. The same goes for appellate judges, for that matter, but in my limited experience, they're more likely to go through some more or less elaborate appointment process. Appellate judges, once appointed, may be periodically up for "retention" votes where the electorate votes to keep 'em or throw 'em out.

There are good arguments for either approach to choosing judges. Unfortunately, one common form of the electoral process requires judges to run for office (either with or without a party affiliation), but doesn't let them do the things that candidates need to do to run effectively. For example, in Indiana, a judicial candidate can't personally ask for or receive donations. Someone else, e.g. a treasurer or campaign manager, has to do that. What's worse, a judicial candidate challenging an incumbent judge must tread very carefully in discussing the incumbent's record on the bench.

The U.S. Supreme Court recently ducked a chance to discuss this issue directly. They granted cert (see 32.F.) in a case involving a judicial candidate who was disciplined for mailing and posting online an appeal for contributions. The issue: does a rule prohibiting such an appeal violate the First Amendment (34.A.1.)? Discussions of this issue have often embraced the related issue of whether a judicial challenger has the right to criticize the incumbent. However, the Court didn't reach that question, and held that the "vital state interest" in preserving judges' reputations as independent and even-handed justified prohibiting requests for campaign funding.

Federal judges at all levels are nominated by the President, who often consults with the senators in whose state a federal district court judge will serve, or for appellate judges, some or all of the senators whose states are included in the jurisdiction of that particular Circuit Court of Appeals. Then the nomination goes from just chats with senators to a formal Senate approval process. The Senate Judiciary Committee investigates the nominee, holds hearings, and then reports to the full Senate, recommending that the Senate approve ("confirm") or reject the judge's appointment or else making no recommendation. Assuming the obstacles aren't so great as to discourage either the President or the applicant, the nomination then goes to a vote by the full Senate.

Do all judges start out as lawyers? That's certainly the way to bet, and it's most often a requirement. There are some possibly predictable exceptions, like judges with very limited tasks, and some more interesting ones, like most federal trial and appellate judges — though in practice, it'd be extremely unlikely that a non-lawyer would get the job. But the official who actually hears evidence in many cases may not actually be a judge, but rather, a "magistrate," "referee," or "commissioner." This is especially common in family law proceedings, but magistrates may also preside over civil cases involving smaller sums, and sometimes misdemeanor criminal cases. Whether or not the parties must consent will vary with the type of case and the jurisdiction involved.

Sometimes magistrates and the like issue binding rulings, or rulings that'll be binding unless a party asks for a judge to have a say. Sometimes they make recommendations to a trial court judge, who may well rubber-stamp those recommendations without much scrutiny. And these officials might not be attorneys, even in jurisdictions where the judge has to be.

B. Challenging the Judge

What if the judge assigned to your case turns out to be your ex-mother in law? Or persistent rumor has it that the judge tends to give short shrift to testimony from the racial or ethnic group to which you belong? Or what if a particular judge is known to despise all large corporations, or to treat out-of-town attorneys badly — and you're out-of-town counsel (see 2.I.) for Megacorps?

Depending upon how early a party takes action, there may be a pretty easy way to get out of this bind. The applicable rules may give each of the parties one get-out-of-judge-free card. Early in a trial, or in a new eviden-tiary hearing ordered by an appellate court, a party may be able to file a motion for change of judge without giving any reasons. (Such a rule is sometimes found under a heading about "change of venue" (see 25.C.).)

If a party has waited too long, or if for any other reason this rule doesn't apply, then the party has the far trickier task of asking for a new judge, and/or asking the judge to recuse themselves (remove themselves from the case), based on bias or prejudice. If the judge is favorably dis-posed toward the other guy, it's "bias"; if the judge is unfavorably disposed toward the party seeking recusal, it's "prejudice."

The rules of conduct for judges may require them to avoid even an "appearance of impropriety," which sometimes means they should recuse themselves even if (somehow!) they don't agree that they would be less than impartial. However, judges vary greatly in how willing they are to step aside, and in how personally they take the suggestion that they should do so. And appellate courts are generally quite unwilling to second-guess the judge's decision — though if the problem is blatant enough, they will.

Here's a different, though probably apocryphal, approach to the possible appearance of impropriety, specifically of a conflict of interest. A judge, the story goes, began a case with the following disclosure and statement of intent: "Before I start, I should admit that the plaintiffs have donated to me the sum of $20,000. I should also admit that the defendants have donated to me the sum of $25,000. In order to have no conflict of interest, I am going to remand to the defendants $5,000, and try the case on its merits."

C. Who Watches the Watchers:

Judging the Judge

What happens if a judge misuses their authority? If a judge takes the bench while stinkin' drunk, or hollers at attorneys, or calls the parties names, or declares ten minutes into the trial that they've "heard enough," or dallies with attorneys and bases rulings on that intimate connection . . . do the injured parties have any recourse?

Fortunately, yes. At least sometimes.

Generally, one can't sue judges for how they conduct themselves on cases under their authority. This rule is called "judicial immunity," and it's supposed to protect judicial independence. Given that the rules comes from centuries of case law (i.e., decisions made by judges and followed by other judges), that might not be the only reason it exists.

Judges are, however, answerable to disciplinary commissions, which may be administered by state supreme courts or may be independent agencies. (The situation in federal courts is similar with one key difference: see below.) Parties or attorneys who've suffered from, or at least witnessed, judicial misbehavior may file complaints with the appropriate commission. There are rules of professional conduct for judges, as there are for attorneys.

It generally isn't possible to file such a complaint anonymously, for fairly sensible reasons: it'd be unfair to the accused, and highly impractical for the commission to investigate the complaint.

Typically, the commission will examine the complaint and decide (based on its contents, and perhaps on familiarity with either the judge or the complainant) whether to round-file it or to proceed. If it proceeds, the next step is to inform the judge and ask for a response. Once this happens, the judge would be well advised to hire an attorney who handles these matters. (Feel free to appreciate, **and/or to write about,** the karmic appropriateness of a judge in the position of a client.)

Most complaints against judges don't result in any disciplinary action. In those cases, it's determined that the complaint can't be substantiated, or that the person complaining doesn't understand the rules governing judicial conduct or is primarily upset about an unfavorable ruling. But in those situations where the commission decides the judge has acted improperly, the judge's attorney and the disciplinary commission may work out some sort of agreed sanction (punishment). Otherwise, the court in charge will make factual findings and determine what if any punishment is appropriate. This could range from a reprimand, to reassignment of some of the judge's caseload, to requiring the judge to go into counseling, to suspending the judge for some period of time, to expelling the judge from their job for good.

What's different for federal courts? Well, there's the U.S. Constitution to consider. Under Article III, §1, all federal judges "shall hold their Offices during good Behavior." To kick someone out of a constitutionally established job, one must employ a special procedure: impeachment. If the judge's alleged offense is serious enough to warrant it, the Judiciary Committee of the U.S. House of Representatives conducts an inquiry, and may then ask the full House to vote on impeaching the judge. As with other federal officials (anyone remember President Clinton?), a vote to impeach is a vote to have a trial, not a vote on the merits of the case. The U.S. Senate would hold the trial, and it takes a two-thirds vote of the Senate to remove a federal judge from office.

In the history of this country since the Constitution was ratified, there have been, per one source I consulted, a total of fifteen impeachments of federal judges, of which eight led to convictions and removal from office, though one judge resigned before the proceedings concluded. So the odds of getting rid of a federal judge are pretty low.

1. Judicial Prejudice

Judges being only human, they tend to react according to their cultural programming. One example, according to a recent study of immigration panel decisions: male judges tend to favor female litigants over males, coming down even more harshly on men who displayed more vulnerability than American culture considers "masculine."

Where a judging panel included both men and women, this advantage for women went away, to be replaced by an advantage for men.

Black defendants tend to get longer prison sentences, and are less likely to receive probation instead, than white defendants. According to a January 2005 survey of the research, Latinos were harder hit than blacks when it came to probation versus incarceration in federal court, while the reverse held true as far as length of sentence was concerned, and both groups were far more likely to be incarcerated than given probation in state courts. Black-on-white violence led to particularly harsh sentences. An October 2014 presentation by the ACLU recounted similar results.

D. Supreme Court Justices,

a Law Unto Themselves

Neither trial court judges nor intermediate appellate judges get many chances to shape the law of their jurisdictions. Once in a while, such a judge will end up with a "case of first impression": a case presenting a legal issue that's never been settled by any case in that jurisdiction's appellate or supreme court. The rest of the time, state trial court judges must apply the law as it's been interpreted by the intermediate appeals court. Intermediate appellate courts in some states are pretty much required to follow any earlier decisions by previous appellate judges. In other states, they may disagree or "decline to follow" such cases, but had better have sound reasoning for doing so. All judges in intermediate state appellate courts are bound by the prior decisions of the state supreme court. Federal trial courts must follow the decisions of the U.S. Circuit Courts of Appeals, which must follow the decisions of the U.S. Supreme Court. All state courts at all levels must follow the decisions of the U.S. Supreme Court if those decisions interpret either federal statutes, federal regulations, or the U.S. Constitution.

Which puts U.S. Supreme Court Justices as the tippy-top of the legal pyramid. The only judicial opinions with which they need concern themselves are those of their brother and sister Justices.

CHAPTER 6

Who, What, and Where

I f you as an author have any concern for accuracy, you need to be careful about whether the person bringing suit in your story would have the right to do so, and whether they've come to the right court. These are questions of "standing" and "jurisdiction." There's also the question of whether a claim one could normally bring in state court, based on state law, is "preempted" by some federal statute or regulation.

A. Jurisdiction

Jurisdiction is what determines which court or courts are authorized to hear a case. Ask any lawyer what subjects they found most annoying and impenetrable in law school, and jurisdiction is likely to come up.

There are two basic categories of jurisdiction: "subject matter jurisdiction" and "personal jurisdiction." Subject matter jurisdiction concerns what kind(s) of cases a particular court may hear. It's considered so important that the affected party can't "waive" the issue (ignore it or consent to what happens). At any stage, including an appeal, a party can raise the question of subject matter jurisdiction, or the court can do so — and should, if it realizes there's a problem. **This could be an ironic and (depending on the point of view) miraculous or devastating conclusion to long-running litigation.** At a class I took recently, one speaker told the tale of a federal case dismissed for lack of subject matter jurisdiction something like eight years after it began, and after the plaintiff obtained a large judgment, when a federal judge or the judge's staff figured out that because of the rules for determining the citizenship of limited liability companies, aka LLCs, diversity jurisdiction (see 6.A.1.) didn't exist.

"Courts of general jurisdiction" have subject matter jurisdiction over a broad variety of cases, while more specialized courts like probate courts (see 14.K.2.) only hear a narrow slice of cases. Where a county has a specialized court like a probate court, the courts of general jurisdiction usually can't hear the cases the probate-or-whatever court exists to hear.

Personal jurisdiction is about whether someone can be sued in a court in a particular place (usually a state or some federal district). There needs to be some "minimum contact" between a person or entity and a particular state before one can require that person or entity to defend against a lawsuit in that state. What exactly constitutes a sufficient contact is — like most aspects of jurisdiction — complicated. But if someone has set up a physical place of business in a particular state, or has bombarded its residents with advertising, or wandered about making deals there, they can probably be sued there. Even one contract to deliver a product to someone in the state is probably enough. But selling widgets to distributors that then sell them in a particular state probably won't suffice.

The absence of personal jurisdiction can be waived if the party doesn't assert it at some (usually an early) stage.

The Internet, of course, poses a challenge to centuries-old concepts like personal jurisdiction. So far, it appears that the only way a passive (as opposed to interactive) website can lead to personal jurisdiction is if it's alleged to be defamatory (see 14.F.3.) and is somehow aimed at the residents of that state. Websites that allow a back-and-forth with the user could be enough, depending on how much interaction we're talking about. Commercial websites that let residents of a state buy products will subject the website owner to personal jurisdiction there.

Owning real property in a state lets one be sued there, if the lawsuit has to do with the property, but it isn't enough to establish personal jurisdiction for unrelated suits.

Sometimes there's more than one state or more than one county in which a lawsuit could be brought. That's when the focus shifts from "jurisdiction" to "venue." (Some states' rules treat the assignment of a case to a particular judge as a matter of "venue" as well.) To learn about motions for a change of venue (either type), see 25.C.

1. State versus Federal Jurisdiction

Every state (plus the District of Columbia, aka Washington D.C.) has its own court system. There is also a nationwide network of federal courts. Some cases can only be heard in state court; some can only be heard in federal court; and some can be heard in either. This is a question of subject matter jurisdiction (see above).

With some exceptions, criminal cases are tried in state court. Murder, robbery, arson, kidnapping, burglary: these are generally matters for state courts to address, based on state statutes. If, however, the defendant asserts some right under the U.S. Constitution in connection with their defense, then the issue may work its way up to the state supreme court and then to the U.S. Supreme Court (see 32.F.).

I said "with some exceptions." What exceptions? The more the reach of federal government has grown, the longer the list of federal crimes. The same conduct might violate both a state and a federal statute. Many federal crimes, but not all, are listed in Title 18 of the U.S. Code. I'll highlight a few general categories.

Naturally enough, the federal courts have jurisdiction over crimes directly affecting the federal government: for example, attacking a federal official, evading federal income tax, espionage, or counterfeiting currency (since all currency in this country is issued by the federal government). This principle has been stretched considerably. Bank robbery is a federal offense (though the federal authorities may defer to local authorities and let it be tried in state court) because banks and other similar institutions are insured by the Federal Deposit Insurance Corporation (FDIC). Theft of major artworks from museums is a federal offense (18 U.S.C. §668) if the museum's activities "affect interstate or foreign commerce," a test that is usually applied very loosely indeed (see 34.L.).

The same broad definition of what fits within the federal government's power over interstate commerce has allowed for federal statutes restricting the use, possession, or sale of certain drugs, or the ownership or transfer of certain firearms.

Where a crime takes place in more than one state — for example, kidnapping someone and transporting the victim across state lines — that can be a federal crime, dealt with in the federal courts. Crimes taking place on federal territory, including Indian reservations, also fall under federal jurisdiction.

To sum up: even though the vast majority of criminal prosecutions fall under state jurisdiction, it shouldn't be that hard to write your crime into federal court if that's what you want.

When it comes to civil (noncriminal) law, there are two ways cases can belong in federal court. That sounds simple, but in practice, it can get quite complicated.

"Federal question jurisdiction" covers cases where the plaintiff (the one bringing suit) alleges that the defendant (the one being sued) has violated the U.S. Constitution, a valid treaty, or a federal statute. (I'm using the singular of "plaintiff" and "defendant" for convenience: there could be several of either.) There used to be a monetary threshold (a minimum amount of money at stake) for this sort of jurisdiction, but Congress eliminated it in 1976 (for suits against the U.S.) and 1980 (for all other federal question cases).

The second possibility is "diversity jurisdiction," governed by 28 U.S.C. §1332. To avoid possible state court prejudice against out-of-state parties, the federal courts have jurisdiction over disputes involving more than "the sum or value" of $75,000 (at the time I'm writing), if the opposing parties are citizens of different states or some of them live abroad.

What about corporations? For the purposes of diversity jurisdiction, a corporation is considered a citizen of the state where it's incorporated, plus the state or country where it has its principal place of business. A 2010 U.S. Supreme Court decision defined "principal place of business" as the corporation's "nerve center," "the place where the corporation's high level officers direct, control, and coordinate the corporation's activities." This will most often be the corporation's headquarters.

Litigation can start out in state court and be "removed" to federal court if the federal court has diversity jurisdiction. There are often advantages to being either in state or in federal court. For example, many lawyers consider state court juries as likely to be more generous with tort verdicts than those in federal court. On the other hand, federal procedure may be more streamlined, leading to a shorter trial.

As a result, plaintiffs may "forum shop" by including or excluding defendants based partly on where those defendants live or do business. A defendant can only seek removal to federal court if no defendant is deemed a citizen of the same state as the plaintiff. The federal appellate courts don't currently all agree on whether every named defendant must join in the request. There are more complexities in this game than I can cover here. Judges try to discourage forum shopping, but there's no way to eliminate it entirely.

If a contract specifies that any dispute will be tried in the courts of some particular jurisdiction (see 18.A.), any other court where someone tries to bring the dispute will usually enforce that agreement by dismissing the case. Where the contracting parties are multinational corporations, the specified jurisdiction could be somewhere outside the United States.

2. In Rem Jurisdiction

Most jurisdiction is "in personam" jurisdiction. The foregoing discussion of personal jurisdiction assumes in personam jurisdiction. However, there's also another kind: "in rem" jurisdiction, jurisdiction based on the location of property and concerned with who should get or retain title to that property. Examples of in rem jurisdiction include actions to partition property held by tenants in common (see 14.D.2.), actions to quiet title (14.D.5.), foreclosure actions (14.D.6.), and civil forfeiture actions (34.G.2.).

B. Not Here: Forum Non Conveniens

If there's no jurisdictional rule preventing a case from proceeding in a particular state or county, but the location will be a significant hardship for one or more parties or for many of the witnesses, a party may ask the court to defer to a court in a location that makes more sense, under the doctrine of forum non conveniens. The request will generally come from a defendant, as the plaintiff presumably likes the original location. Trial courts have a good deal of discretion in ruling on such motions. They may also raise the issue on their own, even if none of the parties has done so.

You could have a wealthy plaintiff pick a venue that the defendant and/or several key witnesses couldn't visit without hardship, and give your defendant a sloppy lawyer or none, so that it's only at the last minute that the defendant realizes they have options. Maybe that realization comes after the deadline for seeking a change of venue, so that the newly hired lawyer has to try for some usually unavailable relief.

Of course, the proposed alternative court must be one that could actually accept the case without any problems with personal jurisdiction.

Usually such a motion will involve another court within the United States. If a defendant wants to move a trial overseas, the trial court will consider whether that country's courts will apply U.S. law and whether it's likely to treat the U.S. party or parties fairly.

C. Skin in the Game: Standing

To file a lawsuit, one has to have skin in the game, otherwise known as "standing." A potential plaintiff has standing if they've been injured and damaged in some way by the conduct of whomever they want to sue, or (in some lawsuits against governmental entities) if the government is expected to cause them problems by applying some law or regulation.

If someone is just one of a great many citizens who may be affected by some governmental action, then they don't have standing after all. That sort of impact is supposed to be addressed politically, not judicially. But if a statute was written to protect a particular group of people, the members of that group do have standing.

A related concept is the threshold requirement of a "case or controversy." This means that one can't go to court too soon or too late. Too soon, and the court is being asked to render an "advisory" opinion, concerning matters that haven't yet arisen, even though they're likely to arise eventually. Too late, and the case is "moot": the court's decision can't have the effect it's supposed to have. A case can only be moot when something other than money is at stake. If a prisoner is asking, not that their conviction be overturned, but that they be released on bail before trial, the case is moot if things drag on until after they're tried. If a teenaged girl seeks an abortion in a state where she must obtain either parental consent (which she doesn't have) or a judge's order, the case is moot if she has a miscarriage before the hearing. (It'd also be moot if she gave birth, but that's less likely, since *some* common sense usually enters into scheduling a parental consent hearing.)

On rare occasions, when a case involves some important public policy question and has been thoroughly briefed and argued, the court will go ahead and decide the case even after it becomes moot as to the actual parties. **It could make for an interesting narrative twist if many people have thrown their hearts and wallets into a case that suddenly becomes moot, and are forced to argue that the court should decide the case nonetheless.**

D. All Together Now: Class Actions

You've probably read about class actions from time to time. Maybe you've received some sort of mailing full of fine print, telling you that you're part of a lawsuit you never heard of, and giving instructions about how to opt out of a proposed settlement.

When there are many people who could sue the same defendant for the same reason, based on generally similar facts, some of them may be able to form a "class" and sue that defendant. If, as is generally the case, the underlying claim is a tort claim (see 14.F. and G.), then the class' attorneys, if successful, will get paid by taking a chunk of the eventual award or settlement (see 3.A.). If each individual class member's potential award isn't that great, but there are many class members, attorneys will be more interested in pursuing the case than if they could only get a share of one award. If someone is taking on a large corporation, they'll usually need a large and expensive legal team, and a class action can be the way to get one.

If a class action is brought under some statute that lets the court award successful plaintiffs their attorney fees (see 3.E.), then the attorney fee award will not reduce the class members' recovery.

Class actions may be filed in state or in federal court. 28 U.S.C. §1332(d) covers federal court jurisdiction over class actions. A federal court class action will be dismissed out of hand unless it involves more than five million dollars (as of this writing) *and* there's diversity jurisdiction (see 6.A.1.). It will also be dismissed if too many of the parties are citizens of the state where the lawsuit was originally filed. There's a gray area where it's up to the federal court whether to keep the case or send it back to state court. See the statute for details on these points and a host of others.

Here are a few examples of the types of claims that could end up being combined with other similar claims for a class action:

- International Widget routinely pays women less than men (or vice-versa) in comparable positions.
- Dynamite sticks sold by Acme Explosives are designed or manufactured in such a way that they explode before the fuse has burnt all the way down, causing serious injuries.
- GlamourLife house paint gives off fumes that can cause a nasty skin rash.

See Federal Rule of Civil Procedure (FRCP) 23 for more details of what the federal judicial system requires for a case to proceed as a class action. State court rules are likely to be similar in most respects.

The class will start out with "named" plaintiffs, plaintiffs who say they are representatives of the proposed class. For a class action to proceed, the trial court must agree that the case is a proper one for a class action and "certify" the class. The defendant in a class action will often argue that the case isn't really an appropriate one for class action treatment, and/or that some of the named plaintiffs don't really belong in the class even if the class action proceeds. **Your young, hungry attorney-protagonist could decide to represent a plaintiff who failed at getting a class action certified, or was booted out of the class, in an appeal of the ruling and/or in a separate lawsuit.**

E. Supremacy, aka Federal Preemption

The balancing act between federal and state laws was part of the initial set of compromises in the U.S. Constitution. Here's the relevant language, from Article VI, paragraph 2 (commonly called the Supremacy Clause):

> This Constitution, and the Laws of the United States which shall be made in Pursuance thereof; and all Treaties made, or which shall be made, under the Authority of the United States, shall be the supreme Law of the Land; and the Judges in every State shall be bound thereby, any Thing in the Constitution or Laws of any State to the Contrary notwithstanding.

Note that only those laws "which shall be made in pursuance [of]" the Constitution take precedence over state and local legislation. (For simplicity's sake, I'm going to use "state" to mean "state or local" for the rest of this discussion.) If a law or regulation is unconstitutional, then theoretically it shouldn't preempt anything. **Getting the courts to apply that label is another story . . . one you may enjoy writing if you like your law mixed with politics.**

The caveat for treaties is narrower: if a treaty is "made, under the Authority of the United States," it preempts non-federal law. If the U.S. President enters into some agreement with the leaders of another country, but the U.S. Senate doesn't approve the agreement by a two-thirds majority as is required for treaties, the supposed treaty would arguably not be "made under the authority of the United States" and would not be the "supreme law of the land."

Naturally, a federal law about cooking meth doesn't preempt a state law about licensing cosmetologists. There has to be some direct or indirect conflict with state law. The U.S. Supreme Court has provided some guidance on when there's a conflict and therefore preemption of state law.

First, there's "express," i.e. explicit, preemption, where Congress, or some agency with the power to make binding federal regulations, says in so many words that the law or reg is intended to override state laws on the subject.

Then there's "field" preemption, where the feds are making so many rules on some subject that there's just no room for the state to do the same without stepping on federal toes. If applying the state law would have only an incidental, marginal effect on the federal scheme, there will be no preemption.

Finally, there's the unilluminating label "conflict" preemption: where there's no way to comply with both the state and the federal law.

One question may be whether in regulating some area, the federal government intended to have the laws uniform nationwide, or instead was willing for states to provide more protection for whoever or whatever is being protected. Settling this question could require delving into "legislative history" (committee reports, floor debates, and the like, in which those involved in passing the law explain why they're doing it).

A couple of examples of preemption:

- The FDA (Food and Drug Administration) requires certain nutritional labels on packaged food products. May the state still require more information than the FDA does? May the state still require restaurants to put such information on their menus? (At least one court has answered the second question "probably" — the wishy-washy nature of the answer due to the stage the case was at, with the plaintiff seeking a preliminary injunction (see 7.A.4.).)

- Someone injured in an auto accident might claim that a crucial system in the car was designed in an unsafe manner. But there are Federal Motor Vehicle Safety Standards that in most cases preempt state attempts to say how cars should be designed.

Here's a situation where federal law was held *not* to preempt state law. Plaintiffs claimed that a bank was structuring its overdraft fees and online account statements in a way designed to mislead depositors as to how much money they had at any particular time, and also to impose overdraft fees even though there was actually money in the account at the moment the fee was imposed. The state court held that federal rules allowing overdraft fees didn't cover this territory enough to preempt state claims of breach of contract and of violating a duty of good faith and fair dealing.

With the wild proliferation of federal laws and regulations in recent decades, this issue may come up more and more often, unless some major political shift starts rolling back some of those federal enactments, or at least halts their growth.

CHAPTER 7

Some Basics of Civil and Criminal Procedure

Τ his seems as good a place as any to mention some basics of civil and criminal procedure.

A. Civil Procedure

In law school, I considered Civil Procedure as a compilation of all the dullest bits of innumerable other courses . . . so I won't go on about it at great length. Just assume that everything I say below could come accompanied by a host of "if"s, "and"s, and "but"s.

1. The Complaint and Summons

A civil case usually begins with the filing of a "complaint" and the payment of any necessary filing fee. If the plaintiff, the person or entity filing the complaint, can't afford the fee, they may ask the court to find that they're too poor and allow them to file "in forma pauperis" or some such status, without paying this and various subsequent fees.

It's also likely that the plaintiff's attorney, or a plaintiff who's acting pro se (see 2.K.), will be required to file a form called an "appearance." The appearance contains such info as contact information, the type of case being commenced, the names of all the parties, and perhaps whether the plaintiff or plaintiff's attorney will or won't accept certain kinds of delivery of papers (e.g. by fax and/or email).

More and more courts, including many if not all federal courts, now require that complaints be filed with the court electronically, though they may exempt pro se litigants (again, see 2.K.) from this requirement.

But filing the complaint isn't enough: one has to get it to the defendant or defendants (whoever one is suing), and it must usually be accompanied by another document called a "summons." The contents of the summons are similar to the contents of an appearance, with the important addition of the amount of time the defendant has to respond or the date when a response is due, plus a warning that the defendant could lose the whole case if no response is made (see 27.A.).

The complaint and summons are then "served on" the defendant(s). Unlike what happens with "service" of various documents filed later on, it's usually some government functionary who serves the complaint and summons, after receiving copies from the plaintiff/plaintiff's attorney. These documents can be served by mail, by personal delivery, or by leaving them at an individual's known place of residence. If all these methods are impractical, the complaint and summons can be served by "publication" in some appropriate journal.

You'll notice that delivering the summons to the defendant in person isn't the only option. That means that "ducking" service, avoiding process servers by ingenious or desperate measures, isn't really worth the effort. The court will just let the plaintiff move on to one of the other methods.

Organizations are usually required to designate an agent for service of process (as it's called). Corporations, for example, must often specify an agent for service at the time the corporation is registered with state officials.

It's not uncommon for a defendant to claim later that the summons was never served at all. If, however, the defendant knows about the litigation and files an appearance, the court is likely to have jurisdiction over that defendant in any case.

Just how much detail does the plaintiff need to include in the complaint? In the 19th century and before, the process of constructing one's complaint was highly technical and complicated, and often took several tries to get to an acceptable version. Nowadays, though, there are two basic approaches to this question: "notice" pleading or "fact" pleading.

Notice pleading requires only enough verbiage to give the defendant(s) a general idea of what claim the plaintiff(s) will be asserting. For example, with the exception of a few types of cases, including fraud (14.F.6.), the Federal Rules of Civil Procedure require federal plaintiffs to include "a short and plain statement of the claim showing that the pleader is entitled to relief." (But see below about what's happened in the federal system in the last few years.) Some states use notice pleading in most cases, but require fact pleading for fraud and/or some other claims.

In jurisdictions that require fact pleading, the plaintiff must include enough factual detail to indicate that if the plaintiff proves those facts, the plaintiff will be entitled to relief. It may or may not be necessary to name the cause of action (type of claim) that the alleged facts would successfully establish.

There's currently some confusion on the federal level because, while the wording of the rule remains unchanged, 2007 and 2009 U.S. Supreme Court opinions moved a great deal in the direction of requiring fact pleading rather than notice pleading. These opinions' emphasis was on the need to include more than formulaic recitations of the elements of some cause of action, but they went on to require the inclusion of facts that could establish that cause of action.

If a plaintiff isn't sure which of two legal theories it'll be feasible to rely on, the plaintiff may be able to employ "alternative pleading," where different "counts" (sections) of the complaint make different and possibly even contradictory factual allegations.

In any case, complaints usually have numbered paragraphs. Those numbers become important once it's time for the defendant to respond.

2. The Defendant's Turn: Answers and Counterclaims

So much for the plaintiff. What options and requirements apply to defendants?

Let's start with a form of response that's no longer much in use: the "demurrer." Back when the pleading requirements for complaints were

more onerous, demurrers were often used to point out the technical defi-
ciencies of the complaint. To the extent demurrers still exist, they're now
more likely to be called "motions to dismiss for failure to state a claim on
which relief can be granted" (or similar language).

The defendant usually files an "answer" to the complaint. The answer
may include a "general denial" of the complaint, or it may go through the
numbered paragraphs of the complaint and, as to each such paragraph,
either "admit" the paragraph's allegations, "deny" those allegations, or state
that the defendant lacks a sufficient factual basis either to affirm or to deny. The last of these options is functionally equivalent to a denial. Failure
to deny allegations in one of these ways constitutes an admission of their
truth.

Answers are also used to assert most "affirmative defenses." An affirmative defense is a reason, other than the plaintiff's factual allegations
being false or unprovable, why the plaintiff should lose. (One also sees
affirmative defenses in criminal law, serving a similar function.) While the
plaintiff generally has the burden of proving the facts that would establish
the claim, the defendant usually has the burden of proving an affirmative
defense.

Here are some possible affirmative defenses:
- accord and satisfaction (e.g. the debt was already paid);
- the debt in question has been discharged in bankruptcy (see 14.R.);
- duress;
- estoppel (Ch. 17);
- no valid contract exists because of a failure of consideration (see
  14.C.2.);
- fraud (14.F.6.);
- laches (17.A.);
- res judicata (Ch. 28);
- Statute of Frauds (14.C.3.);
- statute of limitations (Ch. 11);
- lack of jurisdiction (6.A.);
- improper venue (25.C.);
- insufficient service of process (7.A.1., just above);
- the same action is already pending in another court of the same
  state.

But this is by no means an all-inclusive list.

As already mentioned, affirmative defenses also exist in the criminal context, but they're generally raised first at trial rather than earlier. See 13.E.2., 13.E.3., 13.R., and 13.T. for some examples.

A few of the affirmative defenses typically raised in civil cases may be asserted by a motion to dismiss rather than being included in the answer. Which ones (once again) vary from place to place, but they may include lack of jurisdiction, improper venue, insufficient service of process, and failure to join (that is, to name in the lawsuit) some necessary party. Also, as I mentioned just above, the defendant could use a motion to dismiss to make the argument that the complaint fails to state a claim on which relief can be granted.

The defendant needn't remain exclusively on the defensive. Defendants can file counterclaims, which are essentially complaints aimed back at the plaintiff. The plaintiff would then have to file an answer and/or a motion to dismiss the counterclaim. The counterclaim would still be active even if the court dismisses the original complaint. This is one reason why suing someone primarily to make their life miserable can backfire. **Your story could include some obnoxious character smugly contemplating the defendant's distress at being sued . . . and the karmic wheel turning and presenting a longer and more serious counterclaim.**

If there are multiple defendants, one defendant may make a claim against another defendant. That's called a cross-claim or cross-complaint. If there are multiple plaintiffs and they have a falling-out, one plaintiff could file a cross-claim against another.

Counterclaims can name new parties, dragging them into the lawsuit. For example, the defendant's counterclaim could claim that some third party conspired with the plaintiff (see 14.F.9.). **This could be an example of "punching back twice as hard." **If a good-sized company is trying to use litigation to drive some little guy out of business, the defendant's counterclaim could target the plaintiff's most important customer and claim a conspiracy between the two.** But the defendant had better have some basis for this claim, or the new party could end up being able to sue for malicious prosecution or abuse of process (14.F.10.).

3. Filing and Service of Later Documents

Documents that follow the filing of a complaint, such as answers, counterclaims, motions, discovery requests (see 10.A.), trial briefs, etc., are served by the parties' attorneys (or by unrepresented parties) directly. Traditionally, service was by mail (sometimes required to be certified or registered mail) or by personal delivery, though local rules or customs might allow such variants as leaving the papers in an attorney's courthouse mailbox. These days, service may be made by fax or email in some places, though (as mentioned above) those innovations may require the recipient's prior consent. Any or all of these methods, or some newfangled online system, may be required or allowed for filing papers with the court as well. It's common for the rules to require service to take place no later than the time a document is filed with the court.

Again, in many or all federal courts, electronic filing and service of documents may be required for all attorneys, with no option for refusing to accept electronic service.

For purposes of service or filing by mail, the time a party deposits the papers in the mail is usually the time that counts.

4. Temporary Relief: TROs, Preliminary Injunctions, and Suchlike

Sometimes the plaintiff (or a counterclaimant) claims to need immediate relief before the case is actually tried. The most urgent version of such relief is a temporary restraining order (TRO). Sometimes the party seeking a TRO doesn't even want to tell the other party about it, because of what that other party is likely to do if they know (hide property, threaten or attack someone, grab the child and flee the state, etc.). Then the party seeking a TRO would file an "ex parte" application for it, which might be granted with the proviso that there will be a hearing with all parties present within a few days afterward. (For more on ex parte communications with a court, see 10.B.)

A preliminary injunction may be requested after a TRO is in place, or initially. If granted, it will usually last until the case is finished. A preliminary injunction will be granted only if the court decides that the plaintiff is likely to win and get the same relief in a permanent way at the end of the case. The court will also have to be convinced that waiting until the end of the case to grant this relief would lead to some "irreparable" — irreversible — harm. Also, as with any injunction, the court will need to decide that just ordering someone to pay someone else money isn't going to be good enough to set things right. (See 30.A.)

A variant on all this: temporary custody or visitation orders in family law cases. They're often intended to preserve the status quo. These sometimes pose constitutional questions, as when a party asking for a temporary visitation order isn't a parent. As discussed in 14.H.10., any parent who's fit to raise their child is assumed to know whether contact with a particular non-parent is a good idea, and overcoming that assumption may require more of a hearing than usually happens before a temporary order gets issued.

There's another, rarely used form of temporary relief: appointment of a receiver. Where it appears that property involved in a case is likely to be frittered away, or to disappear in some other way, before the final decision as to what should happen to it, the judge may appoint a receiver to take over management of that property. This occasionally occurs in a divorce where one or both spouses own a business. The court might also appoint a receiver where a plaintiff is trying to get a trustee (14.K.10.) replaced or a corporation dissolved; or where a creditor makes a convincing argument that the debtor's primary asset won't last until the end of the case without intervention; or where there's a dispute over ownership of real property and no one is taking care of the property in the meantime.

B. Criminal Procedure

I'll be dealing with various aspects of criminal procedure later on. Here are the basics, with cross-references to some more detailed discussions.

Caveat: when legal authorities use the term "criminal procedure," they're sometimes referring to matters beyond procedure as such, including a criminal defendant's constitutional rights. What I'm setting out here is more limited, similar to what I've already summarized for civil cases.

A criminal prosecution begins with either a grand jury hearing (see 19.A.), whose goal (for the prosecution) is an indictment, or with the alternative filing of a document called either a "criminal complaint" or an "information." Not all states actually use grand juries, let alone use them for all prosecutions, so the filing of an information is quite common.

After a criminal complaint or information is filed, it's up to the defendant whether or not to request a preliminary hearing, at which a judge would decide whether the evidence favoring the prosecution is strong enough for a trial to take place. (Again, see 19.A.)

If there's a grand jury hearing and an indictment, the defendant will probably be arrested after the indictment is filed. In any event, unless they've already arrested an alleged perpetrator at or near the scene of a crime, the police will go to a judge or magistrate and obtain an arrest warrant. To do so, they'll need to submit a writing under penalty of perjury, called an affidavit, or give testimony under oath, setting forth the probable cause for the arrest. A criminal complaint or information may serve this purpose: if it doesn't contain the necessary oath or affirmation, the officer submitting it could supply that in person. (See 34.B. and 34.B.2.)

Once the police have their arrest warrant, they can arrest the person named in that warrant anywhere they can find them. Sometimes the attorney for the accused will negotiate a time and place for the accused to surrender to the police.

Once a person has been arrested, they'll be "arraigned," brought into court to hear the charges against them and plead guilty or not guilty. Either before or at the arraignment, they'll find out how much money they'd have to post as bail in order to be released pending trial, if bail is available for that crime. (See Ch. 12 re the basics of arrest, 12.A. and 34.C. re bail.)

Most prosecutions end with a plea bargain rather than a trial. (See 9.A.)

Anyone accused of a misdemeanor or a felony has a right to a trial by jury. However, most criminal trials end up being "bench trials," with the judge ("the court") acting as the "trier of fact," i.e. deciding what evidence is true and false. (See 19.B.)

The prosecution must prove a defendant's guilt beyond a reasonable doubt. (See 20.C.; for some related complexities, see 20.D. On the question of whether jurors must unanimously agree on guilt or on related questions, see 19.C.)

If the court believes the prosecution hasn't actually proved the defendant's guilt beyond a reasonable doubt, the court can under some circumstances order the defendant acquitted (found not guilty), or set aside a jury's guilty verdict. (See 27.D.)

For how criminal sentencing works if the defendant is convicted, see Chapter 29, especially 29.B.

CHAPTER 8

Are We There Yet?, Part One:
The Pace of Legal Proceedings

A. Intro: "Abandon All Hope "

Lawsuits are hell. Or would be, if Hell were expensive.
Like Hell, they last forever.
Like Hell, they often end up making you regret whatever you did to get there.

I've sometimes thought that every courthouse door should bear the same inscription that greeted those entering Hell in Dante's *Inferno*: "Abandon all hope, ye who enter here."

That's obviously an unfair and jaundiced view. As I said earlier, the judicial system, with all its faults, is a better way to resolve disputes than, say, mortal combat. Sometimes, justice is done, and done without overwhelming unintended consequences for the parties.

But if you're going to write about litigation, you should keep in mind the enormous financial, logistical, and emotional burdens involved.

B. How Long, Oh Lord ...

The U.S. Constitution's Sixth Amendment guarantees criminal defendants a speedy trial. Different jurisdictions set different limits on the maximum elapsed time between some triggering event and the time the trial takes place. However, a defendant in any court is entitled to argue that under federal law, their trial has been unconstitutionally delayed.

Federal law on this subject is not cut-and-dried: various circumstances besides the amount of time that has passed will be weighed in determining whether the charges must be dropped. If at least a year has passed since the triggering event, the defendant starts out ahead: the trial court is supposed to presume that the defendant's right to a speedy trial has been violated, and the prosecution will be playing defense. Factors to be weighed include the reason(s) for the delay and any prejudice the defendant has suffered because of the delay.

What sort of prejudice? Well, if the defendant couldn't make bail or is for some other reason locked up awaiting trial, that's an obvious injury. If the charges have been widely publicized, the defendant's reputation and/or livelihood may be in ruins.

The triggering event could be arrest, or the presentation of formal charges in an indictment or some other charging instrument. The alert reader may spot a loophole here: the government can take its sweet time investigating the crime and preparing to bring charges. However, the statute of limitations (see Ch. 11) will in most cases put some limit on how much time can pass, typically some number of years, after the commission of a crime before someone is charged.

The speedy-trial guarantee only applies to delays that are not, directly or indirectly, of the defendant's making. If the defense, for any logistical or tactical reason (and the former could include the attorney's schedule), seeks any delays, those delays don't count for speedy-trial purposes.

One could create some suspense by giving a prosecutor a case with a potentially fatal weakness, one that further investigation might or might not resolve, and a clock getting dangerously close to the limit.

In general, the federal constitutional guarantee of a speedy trial doesn't apply to "delinquency" cases against juveniles (see 13.W.). State time limits for those proceedings vary. If a prosecutor asks the court to try a juvenile as an adult, due to the heinous nature of the crime, speedy trial rights might kick in when the judge grants that request. **A crafty defense attorney might decline to oppose such a request if they figured that the prosecution will almost certainly miss an impending speedy-trial deadline. But if the lawyer figures wrong, this could be a very damaging decision for the client.**

Civil trials are a very different story. With no constitutional limitations, things can drag on for months and years — and only the starting date matters for statute of limitations purposes.

Given the need, just discussed, to keep criminal prosecutions on track, civil trials are sometimes bumped by a higher-priority criminal case on the court's calendar.

The party with the deeper pockets (i.e., more financial resources) might pile on more and more "discovery" requests (see 10.A.). On the other hand, a large corporation has so many records that combing through them to see what material falls within a discovery request can become very time-consuming and expensive.

The party with the most to gain if witnesses disappear, die, or find their memories fading might file repeated requests for "continuances" (postponements) of preliminary hearings and evidentiary hearings (see 25.E.).

A particularly bitter case, and/or one involving particularly stubborn or vindictive litigants, can drag on for many years, going up on appeal several times over one issue or another. One sees some family disputes, such as will contests, in this sad category. And that's not even counting all the post-divorce custody/parenting time disputes that simmer and bubble over from the day after the divorce until the youngest child reaches legal adulthood.

Charles Dickens presents the ultimate fictional example of an endless, and endlessly expensive, trial in his novel *Bleak House*. **SPOILER ALERT:**

A probate dispute drags on for generations, blighting the lives of the litigants and costing some of them their sanity. In the end, just as a new will is brought to light that would finally resolve the case in a young man's favor, the attorneys inform the court that the entire enormous estate over which they've been fighting has been consumed in "costs" (including attorney fees). The shock to the young man's already weakened constitution proves fatal. The Chancery Court system shown in this novel differs substantially from any current American court setup, but some veterans of litigation may still find that the tale rings true.

CHAPTER 9

Alternatives:
Plea Bargains, Settlement, and ADR

I 'll be discussing trials at length later on. However, most cases, whether civil or criminal, never get that far.

A. Plea Bargains

Most criminal cases never go to trial. If they did, the already overburdened judicial system would grind to a halt. The lubricant: plea bargains.

In a plea bargain, a prosecutor offers to let the defendant plead guilty to a lesser charge than the one they are initially facing, or to one of several charges, and/or to receive a lighter sentence than they could get if convicted of the charged crime. This is possible because prosecutors have discretion (a much-used legal term meaning "it's up to someone or some administrative body") about whether to press a particular charge. Because this is such a crucial stage in most prosecutions, the defendant is entitled to a lawyer during plea negotiations, whether or not they can afford one. (See 2.M.)

Pleading to one of several charges or to a lesser charge may not require judicial approval, but plea bargains involving the sentence require the judge to go along. A judge can torpedo the negotiations by refusing to do so. Then, either the negotiations start over, or the case goes to trial. A judge may well refuse to accept a plea agreement if the defendant continues to assert their innocence.

The judge may consider the agreed sentence too light, especially if the case has started to receive a lot of publicity. The reverse doesn't seem to happen much, but it could: **what if the judge has some reason to doubt the guilt of a defendant who has (as the saying sometimes goes) "copped a plea"?**

Recently, it's become more common (per statutes in some states) for the alleged victim to have input as well. **The victim's objection to a plea bargain has obvious dramatic potential.** For a highly dramatic, though futile, portrayal of such objections, see Jodie Foster's performance in the movie *The Accused*.

Because it's assumed that the prosecutor and the defense attorney will at least discuss a plea bargain, the prosecutor may throw in tangential charges which could then be bargained away.

Plea bargains may depend on the defendant testifying against co-defendants. Minor players in a criminal enterprise may be arrested and charged in order to obtain their "cooperation" via a plea bargain.

Unless the plea agreement explicitly allows the defendant to appeal some issue (for example, a claimed violation of a constitutional right, or whether the prosecutor interpreted the statute correctly), accepting the bargain means giving up the right to appeal. If the agreement does allow an appeal, it's a "conditional" agreement, and will be enforced unless the appeal succeeds. Most appeals don't. (See 32.J. for why.)

Obviously ripe for dramatic treatment: the dilemma of a falsely accused prisoner who for whatever combination of reasons (e.g., poor or no legal representation, or highly misleading circumstantial evidence) feels compelled to plead guilty and agree to years of imprisonment.

What if either the prosecution or the defendant wants to get out of a plea agreement?

Well, first, has the deal already been accepted by the other side? Plea agreements, like other agreements, are contracts. If an offer is withdrawn before it's accepted: no contract. (See 14.C.1.)

If, as is common, the deal includes a requirement that the defendant testify against someone else, and the defendant backs out of doing so, the deal is off. Unless there's some such failure to fulfill the terms of the bargain, it's tough for the prosecution to withdraw from a plea bargain. Bureaucratic confusion, leading to acceptance of a plea agreement that a higher-up would have vetoed, probably won't do the trick. Even if the prosecution blows it big time — for example, by failing to notify the victim of the impending deal where (as in Indiana) the state constitution requires that the victim be consulted — that might not be enough to torpedo the deal if the prosecution misled the trial court about whether the requirements had been followed.

The sooner the defendant tries to withdraw after agreeing to the deal, the better their chances. If the defendant wants out and prosecution witnesses have become unavailable in the meantime, it's particularly unlikely that the court will grant the request.

If the defendant didn't have a lawyer when they agreed to the deal and subsequently gets one, that significantly increases the odds that the judge will grant relief. And if the defendant had a lousy lawyer (say, one who didn't investigate the facts or the law), and pled guilty *because* of the lawyer's bad advice, then if and when the defendant wises up, they may be able to get the deal thrown out.

A judge is usually obligated to let the defendant back out if:
- the defendant wasn't in an appropriate mental state to make the deal (drunk, drugged, mentally disabled);
- the defendant's lawyer didn't mention such details as that the deal would allow the defendant to be deported with no additional proceedings;
- the lawyer accepted the deal without *asking* the defendant;
- the judge got too heavily involved in the negotiations that led to the deal (though one may need a change of judge, or an appeal, to prevail on this argument);
- the defendant was coerced, in some way other than vividly presenting the alternatives, into making the agreement;
- new and compelling evidence of innocence emerges.

1. Maybe I Didn't Do It, But Punish Me Anyway:

No Contest Pleas

Sometimes a plea bargain involves pleading "nolo contendere," or "no contest." Where available, this means accepting all the immediate consequences of pleading guilty, including a fine and/or court-ordered restitution and/or probation and/or jail/prison time (see multiple sections of Ch. 29) — but without admitting the facts that add up to guilt. Such a plea might (but doesn't always) prevent the self-proclaimed victim or someone else from treating those facts as already proved in a later proceeding, such as a civil suit based on the same events. (See the discussion of offensive collateral estoppel in Ch. 28.) **This type of plea could provide a more nuanced approach to the story line I suggested in 9.A, above.**

Some jurisdictions either won't accept no contest pleas or won't accept them in certain kinds of cases, such as those involving sexual misconduct.

A judge might not accept a no contest pleas, even where otherwise allowed, if the defendant simultaneously declares their innocence. Some judges might also balk if the defendant has proclaimed innocence in public statements and/or through traditional or social media. **One could have an inexperienced judge thrown into confusion by a defendant who goes this route.**

2. Distinction and a Bit of a Difference:

Alford Pleas

The Alford plea, named after the party in a 1970 U.S. Supreme Court case, is very much like a no contest plea, but there are subtle differences.

An Alford plea doesn't go so far as to admit guilt, but it essentially admits that the prosecution has enough evidence to prove guilt of the pled charge, and/or a greater charge, beyond a reasonable doubt. That makes it more likely that a plaintiff in a subsequent civil suit will be able to rely on the plea as proving the facts underlying the criminal charge (again, see Ch. 28).

In states that accept Alford pleas, as opposed to no contest pleas (9.A.1.), in cases of sexual misconduct, the convicted defendant could find themselves in a serious quandary. Sentences for sexual crimes may include, as a condition of probation or parole (29.F.), an order that the defendant complete a counseling program. Such programs typically require those attending to admit guilt. Otherwise, they're "resisting" therapy, and could be kicked out of the counseling program. That in turn could be treated as a probation or parole violation, which could send the defiant defendant back to prison.

B. Settlement

A settlement is the civil version of a plea bargain. (Or conversely, a plea bargain is a settlement reached between a criminal defendant and The People or The State, as represented by the prosecutor's office.) At any stage prior to the judge's issuing a final order, the parties can agree to some sort of compromise.

To put it mildly, settlements are encouraged. Judges are far too busy to preside over any case that doesn't *have* to be tried.

Even if the case has already been tried, a settlement can save the judge or jury some work. It can, however, be terribly frustrating for jurors who've spent hours or days concentrating, discussing, and arguing to be told it was all for nothing. **Imagine a drama with the intensity of *Twelve Angry Men*, but involving some emotionally charged civil trial, ending in the announcement of a settlement before a verdict is reached — perhaps a settlement quite different from where the jury was heading.**

It's common for the judge to set a date for a settlement conference, either early on or after most discovery (10.A.) has been completed. Some judges or magistrates actually preside over such conferences. **Depending on the personality of the judge and the intensity of their desire to settle the case, this could make for a dramatic or a comedic scene.**

In major civil litigation with large sums at stake, either or both sides sometimes stage mock trials, often administered by jury consultants (see 19.D.1.). The mock trial may help the lawyers decide on an acceptable ballpark or range for the settlement amount.

Even without taking judicial pressure into account, both plaintiff and defendant often have strong incentives to settle. The plaintiff gets a guaranteed amount, instead of risking spending all that time and money and ending up with nothing. It's also likely to be much easier to collect the agreed-upon amount than to enforce a money judgment (see Ch. 33). The defendant, on the other hand, gets a known damage award without rolling the dice on what a judge or jury might do. For all these reasons, the cases that actually go to trial are likely to be close calls on the law and/or the facts. Of course, they may just feature particularly stubborn or antagonistic parties who can't stomach anything short of a pitched battle and the chance of total victory.

If a settlement is reached, it is incorporated in a court order, and becomes as binding as any other order. Indeed, it could be more binding: some settlements prevent parties from raising various issues on appeal.

C. Special Paths to Settlement: ADR

Alternative dispute resolution, or ADR, provides several structured paths to settling a civil dispute before trial. The two most common types of ADR are arbitration and mediation.

1. Arbitration

Arbitration means putting the outcome of a dispute in the hands of someone who's neither judge nor juror. Many contracts, including the contracts consumers sign with various big companies, include a provision that instead of going to court, the parties will submit any dispute to arbitration, thereby waiving the right to a regular trial. (Instead, or in addition, such contracts may say that any lawsuit has to happen in the courts of, and/or under the laws of, some particular state. See Ch. 18.)

In "binding" arbitration, the arbitrator has the last word even more than a judge would, because there's typically no appeal from the arbitrator's decision. "Nonbinding" arbitration is a trial run, used as a way to give the parties an idea of who has the stronger case. It may be possible for the parties to turn a nonbinding arbitration decision into a binding one, by agreeing to it or by waiting more than some specified amount of time to go to court.

Arbitrations are usually less formal than trials, and the rules that govern what kind of evidence can be submitted tend to be more lax than the rules at a trial. The process may also be less expensive.

Who will the arbitrator be? As with so much else, that depends on where the lawsuit is happening. In some jurisdictions, arbitrators have to be either lawyers or judges. Retired judges often make good money as arbitrators. Sometimes, arbitrators will be experts in the particular field involved in the dispute. Most contracts with arbitration clauses designate that an arbitrator should come from the American Arbitration Association (AAA) or from JAMS (which used to be an acronym for Judicial Arbitration and Mediation Service). Both AAA and JAMS have good reputations for neutrality. However, **if you want to feature a contract written by some less scrupulous company, the arbitration clause might require that the arbitrator come from an organization with whom the company is a little too cozy.**

Often, under the terms of the contract or local court rules, both parties will have a chance to rule out, or "strike," one or more choices of arbitrator, with the arbitrator left standing getting the assignment. Sometimes there's a panel of arbitrators rather than a single arbitrator. In such cases, there are usually three arbitrators, one selected by each side and the third selected by the first two.

Given this setup, arbitrators will have trouble staying in business if they acquire a reputation for being pro-plaintiff, pro-defendant, or otherwise biased. Many litigators worry that to avoid such a perception, arbitrators may make a point of "splitting the difference" between the parties and/or alternating which side they favor. **This could be a plot point in a story where one party has a very strong case, one that would almost certainly prevail in a court trial.**

2. Mediation

A mediator doesn't make decisions. Instead, a mediator makes it unnecessary for anyone to make a decision about who's right or wrong.

Unofficial mediation may start with Aunt Jane or Granny or a preacher, hauling the disputants into the study and saying, "Y'all talk this over right now!" This intimidating relative or other acquaintance then interrupts when anyone starts yelling or repeating themselves, and drags the discussion back to the issues, and browbeats the participants into reaching a compromise. Or it may be some less confrontational friend going back and forth, in person or by email or suchlike, helping the two sides inch toward a reasonable middle ground.

There is, however, a professional alternative.

Professional mediators are trained to help the parties to a dispute move from repeating the positions they've staked out, and airing their emotions, to focusing on what it is the parties actually need to get or to prevent. The goal is an agreement that both sides can live with. Just as with the more informal alternative, the mediator may bring the parties together in one room, or shuttle back and forth between the two. However, in the latter case, the parties are likely to be in rooms near each other to make the process more efficient.

Mediation can take place before anyone has sued anybody, but it's more common after a lawsuit has been filed. In some places, the lawsuit can't proceed until the parties have at least tried mediation; in others, it's purely voluntary, or will be voluntary unless a particular trial judge insists on it.

Mediation, if successful, is generally a good deal cheaper than trying a case. The mediator's bill may be split equally between the parties, or not, depending on the circumstances and what the judge thinks of those circumstances.

Besides ending hostilities sooner and costing less, mediation has two big advantages over full-scale litigation:

(1) It may actually be the end of the dispute. Because the mediator's focus is on what feasible measures the parties can accept, they're less likely to revisit the matter and file motions for modification, petitions for contempt, etc.

(2) The parties and mediator can get creative. While there will be some limits, a mediated agreement can often include provisions that a court wouldn't otherwise have the authority to impose. For example, one or both parties might make some concession or provide some benefit on an

issue that isn't involved in the lawsuit itself. Arbitration isn't usually this flexible where remedies are concerned.

Mediation is not an all-or-nothing proposition. The parties can agree on some points while litigating the rest. However many points get settled in mediation, if a lawsuit has already been filed, then a judge will need to incorporate the agreement into a court order before it's binding. There may, however, be limits on whether and how a party can back out of the agreement before the judge acts.

Mediation may sound like a process incompatible with the presence and usual mindset of attorneys. Indeed, in family law cases (such as divorces), it's fairly common for mediation to take place without attorneys present, though the attorneys will still review any agreement before it's submitted to a court. In other civil cases, the lawyers typically take part, often presenting summaries of their clients' positions and of the evidence favoring those positions, and otherwise playing an active role in the discussions.

What's said in mediation is likely to be confidential — within certain limits. A proposed compromise typically can't be used as evidence of the strength or weakness of a party's position. However, what a party says during mediation can be used to prove such things as a witness's bias, or that a party has unduly delayed the proceedings or obstructed a criminal investigation.

Mediation is a relatively new aspect of U.S. civil litigation, but it has great potential for fictional treatment. Emotional scenes, emotional breakthroughs, long-hidden grudges, long-hidden traumas . . . the possibilities are legion.

Mediation is available as an option in some criminal cases, most often fairly minor misdemeanors, especially where the parties have some preexisting relationship. The process is often called victim-offender mediation. It's been happening since the 1970s, but it's still a good deal less common than civil or family court mediation.

Prosecutors don't usually take part; defense lawyers sometimes do (but see below). Sometimes this mediation takes place after the case has been concluded, to help the parties move forward rather than to decide the outcome of the case.

Most of the criminal cases mediated involve vandalism, minor assault, theft, or burglary. Since the result could be a lesser penalty, defendants may feel some pressure to participate. That raises constitutional concerns if the program requires, as some do, that the defendant admit guilt in order to take part. Another such concern: since mediation isn't part of the usual criminal process, the defendant has no guaranteed right to have counsel present. And in states where mediation confidentiality is more limited, defendants could find their words or actions during mediation coming back to haunt them during a later criminal proceeding.

3. The Clients Rebel

There's one other way to settle a civil case, uncommon but potentially satisfying to your readers. As discussed in 4.E., attorneys are not allowed to contact the opposing client, but there's nothing to stop clients from getting in touch with each other. A litigant could decide that months or years of distracting and expensive litigation just aren't good business, and may contact the opposing party directly to negotiate a settlement. If both parties are corporations, this would probably involve a meeting between the CEOs (chief executive officers). Then, a reasonable compromise reached, the two CEOs can fire their attorneys. Where these negotiations have gone smoothly, they may even go off together into the proverbial sunset, becoming partners in some future business venture.

D. Mistrials and the Alternative

A mistrial is a judicial misfire. Instead of the neat progression from initiation of the case to pretrial procedures to trial to verdict, things somehow go awry.

The best-known type of mistrial is a "hung jury," a jury that can't agree on a verdict. (You can see the British version of this situation near the beginning of Dorothy Sayers' detective novel *Strong Poison*.) In places where the traditional requirement of a unanimous jury is still observed, a single juror can "hang" the jury. In jurisdictions that have moved to some type of majority vote, anything less than the required number of votes for a particular verdict yields a hung jury as well. If a jury reports to the judge that it's deadlocked (unable to reach agreement), the judge will frequently order the jurors to keep trying anyway. There's a jury instruction many judges give to a potentially hung jury, urging the minority jurors to seriously consider what the majority are saying, and reminding all the jurors that another jury wouldn't be any better equipped than they are to decide the case. But sooner or later, if nobody budges, the judge will have to declare a mistrial.

In a criminal case, it'll then be up to the prosecution to decide whether the odds of doing better the next time around are good enough, or the case is important enough, that it's worth going to trial again. The prosecutor could offer a better plea bargain than was offered before, in an attempt to avoid the choice between another whole trial and letting the defendant off entirely. These tactical decisions will be affected by how close to unanimity (or to the required number of votes) the jury got. A judge could, however, preempt those decisions by dismissing the charges.

In a civil case, if the plaintiff decides it's worth the expense and other burdens of going through a second trial, there will be one.

A mistrial may also result from someone violating the rules so egregiously that the judge decides a fair trial has become too unlikely. (Unless the judge is unusually humble about their ability to disregard prejudicial evidence or attorney misconduct, this will only happen in a jury trial.) Maybe one or more jurors slept through crucial testimony. Maybe one of the attorneys ignores the judge's pretrial ruling that the jury must not hear certain evidence, and mentions that evidence in opening or closing argument or while examining a witness. None of these situations will absolutely, inevitably result in a mistrial — but they easily could.

What if it's the judge's conduct that undermines the trial's fairness? Maybe the judge commented in front of the jury that no one in their right mind would believe the defendant's story, or that defense counsel was a liar, or that defense attorneys are all liars. The proper defense response to such comments is to move for a mistrial, whether or not the judge is likely to regain their professional objectivity enough to grant it. Denial of the motion under such circumstances will very likely be reversed on appeal (see Ch. 32).

The alternative to a mistrial, when someone has said the wrong thing in front of the jury, is an admonition to the jurors to ignore what they've heard. The judge and the attorneys pretend to believe that the jurors will actually be able to comply with this instruction. In fact, few attorneys believe that it's possible to, as the saying goes, "un-ring the bell" by telling the jurors to act as if they never heard it ring.

In the case of an allegedly sleeping juror, one may see a comparable charade: the judge asking the juror whether they actually heard all the evidence, and the juror (suppressing a yawn) solemnly averring that yes, indeed, they heard every word.

How different can the new trial be from the old one?

Well, the judge — whether it's the same judge or a different one — doesn't have to decide the same way on questions like whether some piece of evidence should be admitted or kept out. **An attorney who argued for and managed to get a mistrial could be taken aback when the opposition wins some evidentiary battle that it lost the last time around.**

CHAPTER 10

Surprise: No Surprises

A. Discovery

Courtroom surprises are great fun in books and movies, but the modern American justice system aims to avoid them.

As part of the process called "discovery," parties must usually disclose to each other the witnesses they intend to call. Potential witnesses and other third parties can be "deposed," required to testify outside the courtroom (typically in a lawyer's office) under oath. In addition, each side can ask the other detailed written questions (interrogatories). Interrogatories can ask about the positions the opposition will be taking on any number of factual issues, or can seek clues as to where additional evidence might be found. Parties can also be asked to admit disputed facts, via the appropriately named Request for Admissions. Failure to respond to and deny Requests for Admissions within the time period provided is likely to mean that the party who should have done so is treated as having made whatever damaging admissions are contained in the document. **One could have some fun with this, particularly in a comic or satirical piece where exaggeration or ribaldry is feasible.**

Parties can also require each other to disclose documents and other physical evidence (using a "Request for Production"), although there are grounds for resisting some such requests. They can even ask people or organizations who aren't part of the lawsuit to turn over relevant documents or items, using a paper called a "subpoena duces tecum." These demands may be excessive, used to intimidate the opposition or to inflict large amounts of attorney fees, and discovery disputes often address the scope of the demand.

As mentioned in 8.B., discovery requests can be a major burden on individuals or (especially) companies that have a great many records to look through. The rules governing discovery predate computers, email, and text messages: while the rules do contemplate requiring parties to sift large quantities of paper, parties must now try to figure out just which electronic records and communications come within a discovery request, and how to supply them without disclosing private or confidential information. The burden that discovery imposes on corporate resources will often induce the corporation to settle a case it might otherwise fight.

When a party knows that some requested document will help the opposition, one common tactic is to hide the needle by piling a haystack on top of it. A party may turn over thousands of irrelevant documents, including multiple copies of the same one (e.g., ten recipient's versions of the same email). Parties may also delay producing evidence helpful to the opposition's expert witness until after the expert has filed a report, in the hope that neither the expert nor the trial attorney will realize the report needs to be amended.

When a party will be calling an expert witness at trial (see 22.H.11.), some jurisdictions will allow discovery of early drafts of the expert's report. The federal courts used to take this view, but changed their rules in late 2010.

The movie *My Cousin Vinny* does a wonderful job of accepting the mundane nature of the discovery process while still surprising the audience. The inexperienced lawyer-protagonist learns about the discovery process fairly early in the movie, and we see him (briefly) talking to witnesses and asking them questions. However, we don't find out the point of those questions until his utterly masterful cross-examinations of the witnesses. (NOTE: see 22.H.5., about cross-examination, for the possible drawbacks of how Vinny conducts one of these crosses.)

My Cousin Vinny also demonstrates how one can, in limited circumstances, bring in last-minute evidence (a document or, as in the movie, a witness). To do this, one must persuade the judge that one couldn't have known about the evidence earlier; or else, that the evidence is necessary to respond to the other side's unexpected evidence, which one couldn't reasonably have predicted. Caveat: at least one attorney I know believes that Vinny's objection to such a witness should have been sustained.

And in case anyone's seen the movie *Primal Fear:* one may not avoid disclosing witnesses ahead of time on the ground that "the Sixth Amendment says I can."

How is technology changing the discovery process? I've already mentioned the proliferation of electronic files, but there's also something of a solution to that. It's called "technology assisted review," or TAR, or for some reason, "predictive coding." TAR uses computers to replace the paralegal(s) or attorney(s) sifting through multiple documents. At least one federal opinion has language assuming that TAR will be more accurate than error-prone humans performing the same task. However, TAR can potentially give rise to new disputes based on the particular software and how it was programmed. **And then there's the possibility of hacking.**

One caveat to all this: some attorneys are incompetent or lazy, and as a result don't do much (if any) discovery. If you want your lawyer-protagonist to pull off an otherwise unlikely evidentiary surprise, give the lawyer such an opponent.

B. Ex Parte Communications

If a party to litigation (criminal or civil), or that party's attorney, talks to or otherwise contacts the judge without the other party or the other party's attorney present, that's an "ex parte" communication.

Except in certain emergencies spelled out in state or local court rules, it's not supposed to happen. How often it happens, or more specifically, how often it's tolerated, seems to vary a good deal from one county to another. Parties representing themselves ("pro se" litigants) sometimes run afoul of this prohibition by writing a letter to the judge without sending a copy to the other side.

When is an ex parte communication actually allowed? Answer: when some irreparable harm is threatened, and (a) the attorney hasn't been able to reach opposing counsel in the limited time the situation allows, or (b) telling opposing counsel what's going on will make the harm a lot more likely. Under such circumstances, a judge may issue a temporary restraining order (abbreviated as TRO) crafted to prevent the harm until the court

can hear both parties argue about what should happen next.

CHAPTER 11

Waiting Too Long: Statutes of Limitations and Repose

F or most crimes (more on that in a minute) and for all civil litigation, there's a limit on how long one can wait before initiating court action. This limit, which varies from one crime or cause of action to another, is called a statute of limitations. The general idea is that after some years have passed, memories have deteriorated, documents have disappeared, and an adequate examination of the facts is less likely. But for serious crimes, those considerations become less important. And in civil cases, some are likely to involve less transitory evidence than others.

Let's start with how long the state has to charge someone with a crime.

With murder, it's easy: there's no statute of limitations. **The murder could have taken place before most of the people in town lived there or were even born, but if the evidence turns up, the prosecution can proceed.**

Once we get past murder, there's more variation among the states. Many, but not all, states have no statute of limitations for kidnapping, arson, sexual offenses involving minors, and/or forgery. Colorado, apparently not content to leave treason prosecutions to the federal government, not only provides for prosecuting it but places no limitation on when. In Arizona and California, make off with public money and you'd better keep running: no statute of limitations. So check your locale if you're going to make the statute of limitations an issue in a case other than murder. You may need to find out in what "class" of felony or misdemeanor your crime falls: many states have specific statutes of limitations for each such class.

If a potential defendant is on the run and has left the state, or is otherwise living in hiding, the statute is generally "tolled," meaning the clock is paused during the time the defendant couldn't be arrested. The idea may be that if someone's living a normally visible life and isn't getting into any further trouble, they may eventually be considered a reformed character — a notion less likely to apply to someone who's actively evading justice. **Your story could include a fugitive who thought they waited just long enough before turning up, only to realize the rule didn't work that way.**

Sometimes the statute is tolled until evidence first surfaces that a crime has occurred. This may be true in child molesting cases, and in cases involving malfeasance in public office (and there may be some interesting metaphors lurking there . . .). There's often a specific extension of the statute based on the age of the victim, and sometimes the extension is measured by x number of years added once a minor victim reaches some particular age.

The number of years during which the state can file charges for any particular offense varies from state to state, but for more serious felonies, it's likely to be from five (more often six) to 10 (rarely, 15) years. The low end of the felony scale: most often three years, but sometimes two. The typical term for misdemeanors is one to two years, but a few states go up to three or even six.

Wyoming, now, is one tough state: as of this writing, it has no statute of limitations on any crime, period.

The U.S. Supreme Court has held that if a criminal statute of limitations is ambiguous, or if it's unclear which statute applies, the matter must be resolved in favor of the accused. On the other hand, some states look favorably on both civil and criminal statutes of limitations, and interpret any exceptions narrowly. Given the competing public policy interests, one can't count on a state tipping one way or the other without checking.

If a prosecutor can sell the court on a particular offense being "continuing" for some length of time, then the statute of limitations won't kick in until the conclusion of that ongoing course of conduct. One of the more clear-cut examples is possession of contraband (or of anything the particu-lar person isn't legally allowed to have): the clock doesn't start ticking until the alleged possessor gets rid of it. Failure to register for the draft, hiding assets from a bankruptcy court, or conspiring to commit a crime would also involve ongoing conduct. So does kidnapping, but unless we're talk-ing about holding a victim for months or years, the added time available for prosecution isn't likely to be crucial.

When it comes to civil cases, contract cases tend to have longer stat-utes of limitations: often six years, sometimes as much as ten. Some states have the same limitation for oral as for written contracts, while others have shorter ones for oral contracts, often about half as long as for written contracts. This difference corresponds to the likelihood that the evidence necessary to establish an oral contract (testimony, based on memory) will fade or be harder to obtain as time passes.

Similarly, disputes involving real property tend to have longer statutes of limitations, similar to those for written contracts, presumably because at least some of the evidence isn't going anywhere. That's not always the case: some states have a statute of limitations for written contracts that's twice as long as the one for real property disputes.

Statutes of limitations for claims of physical injury are generally a good deal shorter than those for written contracts, and often shorter than those for oral contracts and/or real property disputes. Statutes of limitations for damage to personal property fall all over the place, sometimes being iden-tical to those for real property disputes, sometimes coming closer to those for physical injury.

A statute of limitations may be tolled during a period when the would-be plaintiff is unaware that the cause of action exists. This could, for ex-ample, happen if medical malpractice only manifests itself in symptoms after the statutory period has run. The statute of limitations may also be tolled when the potential defendant deliberately conceals key facts. This is an example of "equitable estoppel" (discussed in Ch. 17).

Sometimes there are two different statutes of limitations that could ar-guably apply to the same case. For example, there could be a special statute of limitations for cases with a certain remedy, and it could be inconsistent with the statute covering some cause of action that allows for that remedy.

When that happens, you'll need to see how the particular state (or the federal government) resolves the contradiction.

One could sometimes get some degree of relief under the common law from mistakes like filing a lawsuit in the wrong court, if the statute of limitations ran before the mistake could be corrected. The remedy, where it existed, involved filing a paper sometimes called a Journey's Account (as in, journeying to the correct court). Some states have replaced this common law doctrine with statutes called Journey's Account Statutes. If for some reason you want to delve into such details, you'll need to check whether the state in question follows that common law doctrine or has a statutory equivalent (or neither).

There's a different set of statutes that can cut off the right to sue when the statute of limitations wouldn't: statutes of repose.

Statutes of repose crop up most often in product liability and in the probate context. One may also find them in connection with construction projects. Statutes of repose cut off all claims some number of years after a specified event — an event *other than* the injury (financial or personal) over which someone wants to bring suit. For example, a statute of repose might bar any will contest brought more than X number of years after an estate was opened. Or lawsuits related to a construction project might be cut off Y years after the project is "substantially completed."

For the most part, the various equitable factors that "toll" a statute of limitations, like a plaintiff's inability to discover their injury or the plaintiff's status as a minor, don't affect application of a statute of repose. Such a statute involves a calculation, on the part of lawmakers, that the disadvantages of open-ended litigation outweigh the possible injustice to claimants whose injuries occur, or who discover their injuries, too late.

Statutes of limitations are probably better known and understood by the public at large than statutes of repose. **A fledgling attorney might get in trouble by assuming that the same equitable rules apply to both.**

CHAPTER 12

Arrest Basics

When may the police arrest someone? And what happens when someone gets arrested? And what's "booking," as in "Book 'im, Danno"? (That was a phrase commonly used in the TV series *Hawaii 5-0*, originally shown from 1968 through 1980. I understand it's used in the current reboot version as well.)

As mentioned later (34.B.2.), the police may arrest someone if (a) they see the crime take place; (b) they have an arrest warrant; or (c) they have "probable cause" to believe that the person they're arresting has committed a crime, or was just about to. In this context, "probable cause" means there were "facts and circumstances" (there's the usual legal tendency to say everything twice) that made the officer's belief reasonable.

Here's the usual procedure, with a hypothetical Jane Doe as the subject.

Once Jane is arrested, she's "booked." This takes place at a police station. The police ask Jane for basic info like her name, address, and birth date. If she lies about any of those, her lie won't hold up very long if she's carrying a driver's license, credit card, or other such material that has the correct details: the police will usually search her clothes, and maybe her body as well. Even if she was arrested for something minor, the police may make her strip naked, and she may have to help them peer into various private areas and openings that could be used to smuggle small objects.

Jane also gets her picture taken, typically facing front and to both sides. That's the "mug shot." The police take her fingerprints as well. Unless they're using some newfangled gizmo, this involves an officer pressing each of her fingers, one at a time, onto an ink pad and then rolling the fingertip from one side to the other on a piece of cardboard. Even if the fingerprints are taken in this low-tech way, they'll be scanned and entered into an FBI database that's available to law enforcement all over the country. In some places, Jane may have to provide a DNA sample as well, typically via a cheek swab.

Then Jane is put in a holding cell for a bit or moved to the jail, where she'll be for a while.

What about her phone call? Surprise: that's not always permitted. If it is, Jane won't get to make it until after booking. There may be limits on whom she is allowed to call, and/or on the apparent purpose of the call (trying to arrange for bail or getting hold of a lawyer would be acceptable). How will the staff know whom Jane is calling and why? It's likely (and signs in the jail may warn new arrivals) that someone will be listening to and/or recording the call. So this is not a time for Jane to blurt out anything she doesn't want to hear later in the courtroom. Jail phone systems are supposed to have attorney phone numbers programmed in, so attorney-client phone calls won't be listened to or recorded. Assuming such systems are both reliable and consistently used, there's the question of how often they're updated. **You could explore this issue by having your criminal defense attorney fresh out of school or new to the state.**

While Jane is cooling her heels, the police will probably check whether there's an arrest warrant out there with her name on it, on some other charge than the one that got her arrested this time. If there is, she can usually kiss the idea of bail goodbye. Otherwise, she'll get a bail hearing (also called a "bond" hearing) . . . eventually. For very common offenses like DUI (driving under the influence), at least if it's the first time she's been charged with it, there may be a standard bail amount that Jane can pay without going to court first. If that option isn't available, she'll have to wait until she's "arraigned" — brought to court to hear the charges against her and to tell the judge whether she'll plead guilty or not guilty — and then ask for a lower or no bail.

Where there's no preset bail, it may take several days before the bond hearing takes place, especially if Jane is arrested on a Friday. There may be a statute limiting how long they can make her sit in the poky before the hearing.

A. Bail

As noted earlier, bail is money a criminal defendant (or those close to them) can pay as a guarantee that the defendant will show up for trial. If bail is set and paid, the defendant is released "on bond" pending trial. If the defendant doesn't show up to be tried, the money is forfeit.

Bail bondsmen make bail into a business. They typically charge 10% of the total amount of the bail. Pay that percentage, and the bondsman comes up with the rest — but the payment is nonrefundable. This shifts the risk of the defendant's flight from the defendant's family and friends to the bondsman, who will try to manage that risk in a manner similar to an insurance company. The setup arguably undercuts the primary reason for bail, namely the defendant's disinclination to impoverish their loved ones. Bail ends up being used to decide which defendants will have a chance to stay free before trial and which will await trial in the local lockup (aka jail). But the courts hang onto the legal fiction that the amount of bail is calibrated to assure the defendant's presence at trial.

Poor defendants with poor families may find even the 10% bail bond fee impossible to pay; or the family may have wrenching choices to make, such as whether to leave a loved one in jail or else go hungry, forego needed medication, or risk homelessness. A defendant not out on bail stays in jail.

The more serious the charge and the fewer ties the defendant has to the community, the higher the bail. If the defendant ever failed to show up for a court hearing in the past, especially after bail was posted — in which case it's called "skipping bail" — that's the kiss of death.

Some jurisdictions have special bail rules for particularly serious crimes such as murder. For example, they might allow bail to be denied "where the proof is evident, or the presumption strong" (the Indiana Constitution's language). And in some cases, including (but not necessarily limited to) capital crimes, there is no bail.

CHAPTER 13

What's It All About:
Substantive Principles (Criminal)

Many novels involve criminal trials. It's the obviously dramatic way to write courtroom drama. So naturally, I'll provide some pointers about criminal law — but I can't come close to covering all the myriad ways that the State can criminalize behavior. There's also quite a bit of variation in how different states define even the classic crimes. Take this as a preliminary, basic orientation.

A. An Introductory Note about Criminal Intent

First, let me mention a point on which it's easy to get confused: criminal "intent."

As I write this, the U.S. Supreme Court has just reminded us lawyers that criminal statutes are assumed to require the state to prove "criminal intent," even if they don't say so. However, that's not the same thing as the sort of "intent" required by crimes such as first degree murder (13.E.) and various types of "attempt" (13.P.). And it certainly doesn't mean intent to break the law: as discussed in 13.S., "ignorance of the law is no excuse" (usually).

Instead, all it means is that most of the time, the prosecution must prove that the defendant was aware of the facts that make their conduct fall within the definition of the particular crime. For example, to be guilty of burglary (13.G.), the defendant doesn't have to know that opening an unlocked door satisfies the "breaking" requirement, but they do have to realize that they're opening a door. Another example: to commit theft (13.H.), the defendant must know that the property belongs to someone else.

B. Having it Both Ways:

Prosecutorial Inconsistency

Let's say the police arrest two disreputable characters in a darkened alley, moments after shots rang out. There's a hastily wiped pistol on the ground next to the corpse. Both guys claim the other did the shooting, and while they may have been acting together in some way (see conspiracy (13.Q.) and felony murder (13.E.1.)), the evidence against either is awfully thin. Any reasonable jury would figure that one of these two fellows is guilty of murder — but if the two are tried in a single trial, the defense can use the possibility of one defendant's guilt to negate the other's guilt beyond a reasonable doubt (20.C.).

What can the prosecution do?

The prosecution can move for (request) separate trials. And in some jurisdictions, the prosecution may (so far) be able to get away with feeding one version of events to the judge or jury in one trial, and an inconsistent version in the other. In 2005, the U.S. Supreme Court hinted that this trick might violate the defendants' due process rights (34.G.), but it's never actually resolved the question.

Given that many readers may find this tactic intrinsically dishonest, its use in your story could get the readers' blood pumping.

C. Categories

As discussed further in the section on criminal penalties (at 29.A.), crimes are divided into felonies and misdemeanors. Violating a city ordinance is usually an "infraction," which doesn't always count as a criminal offense.

Practically speaking, felonies and misdemeanors are distinguished by the penalties attached to them. A felony is usually any crime for which one may be sentenced to more than one year in prison; a misdemeanor sentence is anything less, and generally served in the county jail rather than state prison (unless we're talking about federal offenses).

The distinction has other effects. See the discussions of "felony murder" (13.E.1.) and of citizen's arrests (13.U.).

There's another way to categorize crimes: "malum in se" versus "malum prohibitum." The former are crimes that violate most people's morality, like murder, rape, and theft. The latter — a category that has mushroomed (an understatement unless one is visualizing a nuclear mushroom cloud) — covers more recently invented crimes that are on the books to serve some indirect social purposes. (Several commentators have noted that just about every American has unwittingly committed one or more felonies, especially felonies found in federal statutes.) See 13.E.1., below, for a situation where these categories could make a difference, namely in deciding whether someone's guilty of involuntary manslaughter.

D. The Model Penal Code

The criminal codes of the various states would vary even more than they do if not for the Model Penal Code (MPC), completed in 1962. Compiled by the American Law Institute, it was considerably better organized than many states' prior criminal statutes. Most states adopted at least some, and often many, of its provisions. The MPC offered not only definitions of specific offenses, but an overall approach that started with such definitions, then moved on to possible justifications that would negate criminal liability, and finally to excuses that might reduce or even eliminate any punishment.

Not all details of the MPC have proved equally persuasive. The doctrine of felony murder (see 13.E.1.) has survived despite the MPC's abandonment of it. On the other hand, despite the MPC's treatment of the question, relatively few states have been so severe as to treat an attempt to commit a crime (13.P.) as harshly as the actual completion of it.

A general caveat: by the time you read this, the MPC or portions of it may have been revised, and various states may have adopted or rejected those revisions.

E. Murder Most (and Less) Foul

Naturally, murder is the go-to crime for fiction. The details of what constitutes murder, and if it does, what exact variety of murder, vary a good deal from state to state. If your story is set in a real location, check its statutes.

Most people, when they say "murder," are referring to what's most often called first degree murder: an unlawful, unjustified, premeditated killing "with malice aforethought." The latter term doesn't have much to do with "malice" in the lay sense. In fact, it's not all that clear what it does mean, as many definitions of the phrase repeat (at least to some extent) other parts of the definition of first degree murder, like intent or premeditation. Other definitions treat "with malice" as meaning "without legal excuse."

Some states classify certain approaches to committing murder, like poisoning or lying in wait, as "first degree" — though poisoning and lying in wait would seem to meet the tests of intention and premeditation in any event.

Where there's still a death penalty (29.J.), it's usually limited to first degree murder.

Second degree murder is generally murder committed on the spur of the moment, without "premeditation" or "deliberation," and without adequate excuse.

If there's an excuse that most people can identify with but don't consider an actual justification, then you might be in "voluntary manslaughter" territory. The line between second degree murder and voluntary manslaughter is sometimes difficult to draw. One commonly used example of voluntary manslaughter is killing "in the heat of passion": for example, when a husband shoots his wife and/or her lover after catching them in the act. **If a grieving parent killed a Westboro Church protester who showed up at their soldier son's funeral with a "God says it served them right" sign, that could come under the same rubric.** Another such excuse would be a verbal threat by someone who'd attacked the defendant in the past. In any case, the provocation must come just before the homicidal response, and the defendant must actually be affected enough to lose control of their emotions.

If our old friend Jane Doe fully intended to beat someone to a pulp, but didn't plan to kill them, she could be guilty of second degree murder if they die. If Jane does something extremely reckless without giving a hoot whether people get killed, and people do end up dead, that could be second degree murder as well. If she's extremely reckless and should have known people would get killed, but it's not so clear that she wouldn't have cared, some jurisdictions would call her conduct voluntary manslaughter, while others would call it involuntary manslaughter or criminal negligence. When a drunk driver kills someone, that's usually some version of manslaughter. Some states have a separate category of "vehicular manslaughter."

Who has to prove what (or, in legalese, who carries what burden of proof) to distinguish between murder and manslaughter, or between degrees of either, varies from place to place. (See 20.D. re burden-shifting.)

1. Murder Without Killing: Felony Murder

If a defendant is something of a bad guy, and really unlucky — what in Yiddish we'd call a schlemiel — they can be guilty of murder without killing anybody. That's right: if somebody dies as a result of something that the defendant or their partner in crime does while committing a felony, they may have committed "felony murder." And the penalty for felony murder can be just like the penalty for any other kind.

States differ as to what sorts of felonies can lead to a felony murder charge if someone dies, but violent felonies are most likely to qualify. A few states include a wider range of felonies: there have been felony murder convictions upheld for helping a minor obtain alcohol or assisting in illegal drug possession.

Traditionally, felony murder could carry the death penalty if the felony fell (so to speak) within certain categories, typically arson, rape, or robbery. However, since 1982 (when the U.S. Supreme Court decided *Enmund v. Florida*), a felony murder conviction can't lead to a death sentence for a defendant who participated in the felony with no intent to kill.

The death doesn't necessarily have to result directly from any act of the defendant. For example, in some states, if a police officer fires at the fleeing culprits and the bullet hits an innocent bystander or one of the defendant's accomplices, that still counts. The idea is that the defendant set off the chain of events that led to the shooting and the resulting death.

Under the "merger" doctrine, if the felony is an assault, and all the elements of "assault" are also elements of murder, the prosecution can't convict someone of felony murder based on an assault that results in someone's death. In such circumstances, the State must prove all the elements of murder, not just those that add up to "assault." (More generally, the merger doctrine prevents convictions for two crimes when all the elements of one are also included in the other.)

If someone dies as a result of the defendant committing a misdemeanor, that might amount to involuntary manslaughter. Some states limit this rule to misdemeanors that are *malum in se* (wrong in themselves, like assault) as opposed to *malum prohibitum* (wrong because of the legal context, like fixing someone's plumbing without a plumbing license). (See also 13.C. re this distinction.) Some states also treat a death resulting from a "non-dangerous" felony as involuntary manslaughter rather than felony murder.

2. Self Defense and Defense of Others

State laws differ quite a lot, once again, concerning when people are allowed to use lethal force to defend themselves. (There's been a fair amount of inaccurate publicity on this issue in recent years, often discussing so-called "Stand Your Ground" laws in cases where such laws are irrelevant.)

One key factor is where the defendant was located when someone threatened their safety. Under the "Castle Doctrine," if someone is in their own home, they are allowed to use whatever level of force is reasonably necessary to protect themselves. At least, they can do so if the attacker isn't a police officer. If an overzealous officer of the law, not in uniform, breaks into someone's home waving a gun, and the various incoherent things they're yelling don't include "Police!" . . . what happens if the homeowner assumes the intruder is one of the local drug dealers and shoots first? This is currently a hot-button political issue in many states.

If someone is out on the street and is threatened with violence, whether they have to run for their life (if there's somewhere to run) depends on where they are. Traditionally, folks in this situation have a "duty to retreat" if possible. However, at the time I'm writing this, just under half the states in the U.S. have "Stand Your Ground" laws that dispense with this requirement, or else never had a duty to retreat in the first place.

How much force is one allowed to use? That depends on what one reasonably fears will happen if one doesn't do whatever one is contemplating doing in self-defense. The dividing line is between deadly force and everything less — even though one may not know, in the stress and confusion of the moment, which one is using.

If a person reasonably fears that they are about to be seriously injured or killed, they may use deadly force without violating the law (assuming they don't have an opportunity and a duty to retreat instead). Of course, whether such a fear was "reasonable" may depend on hotly disputed facts. **You could have your protagonist defend their life against an attacker, only to find themselves vilified as a racist thug or wannabee cop while the attacker is posthumously treated as a martyr.** (Whether this story idea mirrors actual events in recent American history is a thicket I won't venture into.)

What's "serious" injury, or, per some formulations, "great" or "grievous" bodily harm/injury, may vary from state to state. If your defendant was trying to prevent a rape or kidnapping, their defense will be different if the state's statute explicitly allows use of deadly force in that situation. If not, they will need to fall back on the likely consequences of a kidnapping (i.e. death) or the likelihood that a rapist would seriously injure or kill the victim. Some states' case law settles the latter question by defining rape as serious/great/grievous bodily harm.

What if the accused started the fight in the first place? If the fight was over and the person they attacked decides to come back for more, it won't matter that the accused started it the first time. Similarly, if the accused started it, but wasn't using deadly force, and the intended victim ups the ante and uses deadly force, the original aggressor may then use deadly force as well without being guilty of homicide.

What if the accused was defending someone else? The key is whether the person they were defending could legally have used the same amount of force to defend themselves.

What if the accused believed someone needed defending, but was mistaken? What if the apparent violence was actually street theater, or a (really dumb) psychology experiment? In a few states, the accused would be out of luck; but in most, if that belief was reasonable, they have a valid defense.

A few states allow defense of others only if one has a special relationship with them, such as with a child or a spouse.

The wrinkles added by different states can be piquant. For example, Alabama allows deadly force to repel forcible entry into a licensed federal nuclear power facility.

Self-defense and defense of others are (appropriately enough) affirmative defenses. This means that the defendant has the initial task of raising the issue and presenting some evidence to support it. Once that happens, some states leave the burden of proof on the defendant, requiring the defendant to show that more likely than not (by a "preponderance of the evidence"), their action was justified. In others, once the defendant has raised the issue and supported it in some way, the prosecution has to prove beyond a reasonable doubt that the facts *didn't* justify the use of lethal force.

3. The Insanity Defense

This defense (which could theoretically be used for various crimes, not just murder) gets a fair amount of attention, and triggers quite a bit of indignation; but it isn't used all that often, and succeeds even less frequently. That's because the most common formulations are very hard to prove — and in most states, the defendant does bear the burden of proof, though only by a preponderance of the evidence, the "more likely than not" standard (see 20.A.).

The traditional formulation, known as the *McNaughton* rule, goes like this: due to mental disease or defect, the defendant did not understand the nature or quality of their act, or did not understand that it was wrong. "I thought the preacher's head was a giant poisonous insect! That's why I whacked it with a frying pan!" That's a failure to understand the nature or quality of one's act. "I thought I was in the National Post-Apocalyptic Army and we had to shoot anyone who couldn't contribute a long day's labor!" One could define that various ways, but it's probably a lack of understanding that it was wrong to shoot the nice old man in Apartment 37B. The federal courts use something very close to the *McNaughton* standard.

A more recent variant of this test, adopted by about half the states, asks whether the defendant had "substantial capacity either to appreciate the criminality of their conduct or to conform their conduct to the requirements of the law." The latter part of this test is pretty vague, and brings to mind the name, at least, of one of the less common alternative tests, the so-called "irresistible impulse" test, also known as the *Durham* rule. (Those of you who've read or seen *Anatomy of a Murder* will probably remember "irresistible impulse." And by the way, finding one ancient case that rules the defendant's way, as in that story, wouldn't help if there were more recent cases from the same court going against them.)

In fact, the rather forgiving *Durham* rule went well beyond the notion of "irresistible impulse," providing a defense if the unlawful act was the "product of mental disease or mental defect." Defense attorneys found this rule very useful indeed — so much so that courts and legislatures eventually abandoned it in most jurisdictions.

A related defense, again not confined to murder prosecutions, is "diminished capacity." The idea is that because of mental limitations the defendant was born with or that resulted from illness or injury, the defendant couldn't form the mental state required for murder or some other crime. This defense doesn't usually aim so high as to get the defendant entirely off the hook, but rather seeks conviction of some lesser offense for which proof of (for example) premeditation or intent isn't required.

The factual issue of whether the defendant met the applicable test may lead (as so many issues do) to a battle of the experts. Interesting questions may also arise as to what sort of behavior indicates sanity. For example, in one recent Indiana case, the trial court (in a bench trial) rejected the defendant's insanity defense, based in part on the fact that the defendant had requested an attorney and that the request "suggest[ed] some comprehension of her legal jeopardy." The Indiana Court of Appeals held that this use of the defendant's exercise of her right to counsel violated her right to due process (34.G.) and constituted fundamental error (see 22.M.1.). **Your story could involve similar facts, and be set in some jurisdiction that hasn't considered the issue.**

F. Rape

The definitions and proof requirements for rape have changed quite a bit, and for the better, in recent years.

For example, it used to be legally impossible for a husband to rape his wife. He was entitled to marital sex, any time, any way, end of story. Also, actual physical force — not the threat of force, not any other sort of coercion or intimidation or chemical sneakiness — used to be an essential element of the crime, with a few exceptions discussed below. The victim had to have put up a pretty fierce fight, or she was presumed to have consented. The prosecution had to prove "penetration" (although a forcible sex act that didn't include that detail could be punishable as "sodomy" or "sexual assault"). And rape, by definition, only happened to women.

Rape was also treated differently from other crimes on a procedural level. The state couldn't rely on the victim's testimony, but needed some other evidence such as bruises, torn clothes, medical testimony, etc. (See also 22.F. re other situations when "corroborating" evidence is required.) Sometimes, the victim had to take her complaint to the authorities within some set period of time (the Model Penal Code, in 1961, specified three months) — often a much shorter period of time than was required by the statute of limitations (see Ch. 11) for other violent assaults. Even where that wasn't the case, the victim's failure to go to the police could be used against her. And for many years, judges instructed juries that rape charges were "easy" to make and difficult to prove, and told them to scrutinize the victim's testimony more closely than they would other sorts of testimony.

All these elements started changing in the early 1970s, as part of the wider societal shift concerning male/female relationships and roles.

By now, all fifty states can charge a husband with raping his wife, although not all of them treat marital rape and nonmarital rape as equivalent. During a transition period in the 1990s, many states had three defined classes of rape victims: those not married to the rapist, those married but no longer living with him, and those married to and living with him. It often took violence or injury to make rape of a live-in spouse criminal, and the penalty might be less severe. Some states retain some of these distinctions to this day.

Instead of requiring the use of actual force, the prosecution may now rely on other sorts of coercion such as threats. The use of greater amounts of force or of force causing physical injury may constitute a more serious degree of rape.

A victim is no longer required to risk life and limb fighting off the attacker. And of course, we now acknowledge that men can be raped . . . although the vast majority of such assaults take place in prisons and are never charged. (Some states have different statutes for rape of men, but the penalties are equivalent.)

The special procedural approaches to rape have also been abandoned in most states. Where the "prompt complaint" doctrine survives at all, it's mainly for spousal rape alone.

Vocabulary note: current state statutes usually don't include the word "rape." It's all "sexual assault" in various degrees.

Even when proof of actual force was generally required, there were exceptions for unconscious or mentally incompetent victims; for those below the age of consent (see the discussion of "statutory rape," coming up in 13.F.1.); or for those whose consent was obtained under false pretenses. The false pretense that may come first to mind, a false promise of marriage, isn't included: that constituted the separate crime of "seduction." But impersonating a spouse (or, probably, a significant other) constitutes rape by deception. So does disguising the initial stages of rape as a medical examination.

In and/or after the 1990s, as societal attitudes about rape charges changed, the federal courts and a number of states made a significant change in their evidence rules. As discussed in 22.J., a prosecutor or plaintiff usually may not use a defendant's prior "bad acts" to show that they are the sort of person who would commit the alleged crime or tort; but these jurisdictions now allow the prosecution to introduce evidence of sexual assaults the defendant previously committed, in order to show the defendant's "propensity" to commit the presently charged sex offense. The rules vary as to how far back in time the prosecution may reach for such prior offenses.

One area of considerable ferment is the burden of proof concerning consent. You should check the laws of the state where your story takes place, for the period when it takes place. Lack of consent is still an element of the crime of rape, to be proved by the prosecution, but a verbal objection may theoretically be enough to satisfy the state's burden. If the defense claims the alleged victim consented, how much proof on this point (if any) does it take to shift the burden back to the prosecution? Courts disagree, and some have gone back and forth on the issue. (For more on shifting burdens of proof, see 20.D.) Proving lack of consent beyond a reasonable doubt can be very difficult in cases of "acquaintance rape"; but (goes the counter-argument) proof of guilt in criminal prosecution must remain difficult, no matter the crime in question, in order to protect the rights of the accused.

Because lack of consent is an essential aspect of rape, it is inevitable that many defendants who can't plausibly deny the sexual encounter itself will instead claim that the alleged victim consented to have sex. And if allowed to, such a defendant might introduce any evidence that makes it appear more likely that the alleged victim *would* consent, including anything they can dredge up about the alleged victim's sexual history. A victim brave enough to cope with telling a roomful of strangers at least some of the details of a sexual assault, and then being interrogated by the defendant's attorney, possibly with reporters at hand, might find the likelihood of being portrayed as a slut one ordeal too many.

A caveat: a law professor who studied this issue around 1980 told me that despite poring over trial transcripts for months, he found no 20th century instances where trial lawyers actually used this tactic, despite its common appearance in novels and movies. If indeed such an attack on the woman's reputation had become rare, even before the laws I'm about to discuss, such forbearance probably resulted from tactical assessments by defense counsel that attacking so sympathetic a witness would alienate the jury. However, even if the victim has become relatively safe from such attacks in the courtroom, publicity outside that forum can be ruthless if and when the court allows the victim's identity to be disclosed. Some media outlets self-impose limits on such publicity, but in our freewheeling Internet era, those limits have become less significant.

In the mid-1970s, states began to adopt what are known as "rape shield laws," which now exist in every state (and in D.C.). These laws limit the use of evidence of the alleged victim's past sexual conduct. Most commonly barred: general "reputation" evidence, e.g., that the man or woman is generally believed to be promiscuous, or specific evidence of how many previous sexual partners they have had. The defense may still offer evidence of a sexual relationship with the defendant, either before or after the alleged rape. There are other exceptions, varying by state; and there is the overall limitation that concern for the victim' feelings does not trump the defendant's constitutional right to a fair trial. Judges get the unenviable task of trying to weigh how much harm proffered evidence would do to the victim against how crucial that evidence is to a fair trial. **This task could make for some gut-wrenching and/or thought-provoking stories.**

One line of questioning not barred by rape shield statutes, at least those of which I am aware: whether the alleged victim has a financial motive for the accusation For example, the defense may ask whether the alleged victim consulted a tort lawyer before going to the police. And any imprudent comments to friends about cashing in by targeting a celebrity would certainly come in as impeachment evidence if discovered.

The viewpoint that accusation equals guilt or that all men are potential rape time-bombs can victimize people as well. Some college campuses have lately adopted policies that treat the failure to get "affirmative consent" to any degree of sexual contact as sexual assault — at least for school disciplinary purposes, which may include expulsion and damning entries on school records, with catastrophic results for the alleged offender's career and reputation. The most extreme interpretations of these policies might include someone walking up and kissing a girlfriend or boyfriend without getting explicit permission. How could that get anyone in trouble? **Well, what if the couple break up a month later, and the ex is feeling vindictive?** There's also serious potential for selective prosecution, where various factors unrelated to the underlying conduct determine whose life gets ruined. To make matters worse, the student disciplinary proceedings typically lack any semblance of due process (see 34.G.): the accused student may not be able to confront the accuser, let alone have an attorney present or benefit from any presumption of innocence.

There's also the minor difficulty that actual sexual feelings may be less politically correct, so that repeated interruptions of ongoing intimacy to ask "May I?" end up derailing the encounter.

1. Statutory Rape

Just as there's a minimum age for entering into an enforceable contract, there's a minimum age (which, yet again, varies considerably from state to state) for consenting to sexual activity. Having sex with someone who's legally unable to consent, but with no claim that the partner didn't intend to consent, is often called "statutory rape," although the state's criminal statutes are more likely to refer to some numerical "degree" of rape.

The age at which one is permitted to have sex without potentially getting one's partner arrested is typically called the "age of consent." Just how serious a crime it is to reach below that minimum depends not only on where it takes place, but on the age of the older partner and the age difference between the two. Sometimes, the term "age of consent' is used for the age after which statutory rape ceased to be a possibility, regardless of the age of the older partner. That age varies, from state to state, between 16 and 18, with 16 considerably more common. Where the older partner is within a few years of the younger partner's age, some states attribute the power of consent to children as young as 12 or 13. **A family that moves to such a state from a state where consent is legally impossible until the age of 16, 17 or 18 could be in for some serious culture shock. And a family moving in the opposite direction could end up with a teenager in terrible legal trouble.**

2. Child Molesting

In my professional lifetime, the legal landscape has gone through several transformations where sexual abuse of children is concerned. Some decades ago, prosecutors and the general public assumed this crime was extremely rare. When people began to realize that such abuse was not so rare after all, the pendulum swung to believing any claim that was based at least in part on the child's report, on the assumption that children would never lie about or invent such an experience. More recently still has come some recognition that improper methods of questioning, or deliberate attempts to shape the statements of children (e.g. in nasty divorce litigation), may sometimes lead to inaccurate statements by children or even, most cruelly, the distortion of children's memories. (For more on how eyewitnesses, children or adults, may come to believe "memories" that never occurred, see 22.H.10.)

Most of us, when we hear about "child molesting," envision a prepubescent child victim. However, if a teenager barely under the state's age of consent (see above) sleeps with their significant other, the latter may not only be prosecuted for child molesting, but may be burdened with lifelong inclusion in a sexual offender registry. **A parent who disapproves of a child's romantic partner can cripple that partner's life prospects.**

G. Robbery versus Burglary

Robbery and burglary are not synonyms.

Burglary is something people do to property. Robbery is something people do to other people to end up with their property.

To be less cute and more specific, burglary means going onto real property and/or into a building without permission, and either taking personal property or intending to.

Statutes defining burglary tend to speak in terms of "breaking and entering." "Breaking," however, doesn't mean what it would in other contexts. The lightest of pushes with a pinky finger, causing a door that's not quite closed to open wide enough for someone to walk through, counts as "breaking." So does opening an unlocked door, forcing someone else to open the door (locked or unlocked), or pushing someone out of the doorway. Intending to commit a crime once inside usually makes this a felony.

As for "entering": yeah, that actually means going inside.

Robbery requires the threat or use of force to deprive someone of property they own or control. It can be property they currently possess (such as a wallet), or property they can get to (such as the contents of a safe). "Force," even if used rather than threatened, doesn't have to mean someone gets hurt, just as "breaking" doesn't have to mean destruction.

The boundary between robbery and burglary can get blurry. If the burglar injures someone in the course of the burglary, that may be "felony burglary" rather than robbery.

H. Theft

While we're talking about taking personal property, let's get "theft" out of the way.

In criminal statutes, the term "theft" can be quite broad, sometimes including such offenses as embezzling money from one's employer or swindling investors with lies about the project in which they're investing. What tends to come to mind when we hear "theft" — taking personal property from someone with the intention of keeping it — is often called "larceny." Larceny is by its nature nonviolent. It may be divided into "petty" and "grand" larceny, or into various degrees of larceny, based on the value of what's stolen. Broader theft statutes, or specific theft statutes such as auto theft, may be divided similarly (hence the term "grand theft auto").

Prosecutors prefer broad theft statutes to sets of more specific ones, because the defense might be able to prove that what happened doesn't fit the pickier definitions in the latter. When stuck with more specific statutes, the prosecution may be able to use a kitchen-sink approach and charge the defendant with a few related crimes.

1. Embezzlement

Embezzlement requires a victim that had reason to trust the thief.

More specifically: embezzlement is the theft of money or other property by someone who had a position of responsibility regarding those assets. People embezzle from clients and from employers.

The required elements: (a) there's a fiduciary relationship between the victim and the defendant (the sort of relationship that justifies the former relying on the latter, discussed further in 14.P.); (b) the defendant acquired that property through that relationship; (c) the defendant actually took ownership of the property or transferred it to someone else who wasn't entitled to it; and (d) the defendant did all this intentionally, not through carelessness.

"Accounting embezzlement" is the use of accounting tricks to hide the fact that one has removed or hidden funds for one's own use.

I. The Truth, and Not the Truth: Perjury

You may have heard the comment that it isn't the crime that gets you, but the cover-up. With perjury, the crime and the cover-up are the same.

Perjury includes lying under oath — that is, intentionally making a false statement after having taken an oath to tell the truth — in a judicial or administrative proceeding, or intentionally making a false statement in that setting after having affirmed that one will tell the truth under penalty of perjury. (Yes, that sounds circular.) There's one more element: the false statement has to be "material" to (of some substantial importance in) the proceeding in which the party took the oath or made the affirmation.

It's also a crime, "subornation of perjury," to induce someone else to perjure themselves. If an attorney knowingly presents perjured testimony in court, even if it wasn't the attorney's idea, the attorney could be found guilty of this crime.

Differentiating facts from inferences or opinions, or mistaken beliefs from deliberate falsehoods, may add some complexity to this apparently simple picture.

Whether testifying with reckless disregard of the truth counts as perjury may not always be clear. The key could be whether the one testifying believed their testimony to be false.

For another way a false statement can get someone in very big trouble, see the federal statute at 18 U.S.C. §1001, discussed next.

J. The Wide Net of 18 U.S.C. §1001

Perjury, as just explained, has a fairly limited context. The federal crime of "false statement," as it's commonly known, has a far greater reach — and several of the mighty have fallen as a result.

18 U.S.C. §1001 is up there with RICO (see 15.C.) as a way for the federal government to ruin people for conduct no one would expect to have that consequence. (It can also be used to pressure such people into cooperating with some investigation into a more logical target.) Here's the key statutory language:

> Except as otherwise provided in this section, whoever, in any matter within the jurisdiction of the executive, legislative, or judicial branch of the Government of the United States, knowingly and willfully—
> (1) falsifies, conceals, or covers up by any trick, scheme, or device a material fact;
> (2) makes any materially false, fictitious, or fraudulent statement or representation; or
> (3) makes or uses any false writing or document knowing the same to contain any materially false, fictitious, or fraudulent statement or entry;
> shall be fined under this title, imprisoned not more than 5 years or, if the offense involves international or domestic terrorism (as defined in section 2331), imprisoned not more than 8 years, or both. If the matter relates to an offense under chapter 109A, 109B, 110, or 117, or section 1591, then the term of imprisonment imposed under this section shall be not more than 8 years.

The rest of §1001 provides exceptions for what parties to litigation, or their lawyers, say in or to the court, and also for some statements to or in Congress that don't pertain to either investigations or payments. So the federal government can't throw members of the House or Senate in prison for lying in their speeches and press conferences.

That bit about a "materially" false, fictitious, or fraudulent statement? The materiality test is satisfied if the statement is "capable of influencing" the decision of the federal entity to which the defendant made the statement.

Here are some things the prosecutor *doesn't* have to prove to nail someone under §1001:

- That the defendant lied under oath or after affirming their statement to be true under penalties of perjury.
- That the defendant lied directly to a government official. If the subject of the statement is somehow under federal government jurisdiction, and the statement makes its way to some federal official, that's enough. (Example: lying on a timesheet that somehow gets submitted to the feds.)
- That the defendant knew the federal government would end up receiving the false statement.
- That the false statement had anything to do with a separate crime, let alone that the defendant committed any separate crime.
- That the statement actually had any effect on anyone whatsoever.

For more information, ask Martha Stewart, home interiors guru, who went to the federal penitentiary for the way she described a stock transaction that was publicized as, but legally wasn't, illegal insider trading (see 15.B.).

Or go chat with movie director John McTiernan. McTiernan got a phone call during dinner one day from someone who, without identifying themselves or their business, asked questions about a divorce attorney McTiernan had once hired, and about how often McTiernan had hired a certain investigator linked to that attorney. McTiernan figured the caller was a reporter, gave a casual, off-the-cuff answer, and got off the phone as soon as he could. In fact, McTiernan had hired the investigator not once, as he told the anonymous caller, but twice. The caller was actually with the FBI, and McTiernan was charged with a criminal violation of §1001. After a complicated court battle, during which another similar count and a perjury charge were added, McTiernan went to federal prison, paid a hefty fine, and was prevented from practicing his profession for years before and after his prison time.

If you want to write about a Kafkaesque tale of the out-of-control exercise of federal power, 18 U.S.C. §1001 will come in very handy. (For another situation prone to abuse of government power at multiple levels, but technically on the civil front, see "civil forfeiture" (34.G.2.).)

There's no foolproof way to avoid a §1001 prosecution, even if you never say anything false to anyone in your life, since you could still be accused of doing so. However, a good start is to decline to speak to any federal agent without an attorney present.

K. Blackmail

Blackmail is an interesting legal critter because, unlike perjury and perjury's civil cousin defamation (see 14.F.3.), it's every bit as illegal if the defendant was telling the truth — or rather, threatening to tell it.

Blackmail is threatening to reveal damaging information about someone unless the target pays some demanded sum of money (or provides something else of value). The word for this sordid form of extortion has an almost quaint origin: Scottish chieftains charged a sort of protection fee for protecting a farmer's livestock and crops from raids — including raids by the chieftains or their henchmen. (Why that was called blackmail I don't know.) Now, however, the blackmailer is more likely to be refraining from an action otherwise considered good citizenship, namely blowing the whistle on criminal conduct. The federal blackmail statute reaches no further, and in fact, applies only if the compromising information involves a violation of federal law. In common law and in most (if not all) states, however, the information can be anything that would harm someone's business or reputation. The threat may involve disclosure to some particular individual or audience, or wider publication. These days, one could expect social media to be involved.

A related offense: "extortion," which may include similar threats to those in blackmail as well as threats of physical harm to be inflicted on the target or the target's loved ones. Where extortion includes threats of exposure rather than violence, it would cover verbal threats where blackmail would be announced in writing.

Blackmail is usually a felony. One can only speculate about why lawmakers have traditionally been so sensitive to the possibility that secret, damaging information may be revealed.

Murder mysteries have often involved victims of blackmail who finally turn on the blackmailer. The police and/or private detectives who uncover this motive often express sympathy with the victim-turned-perpetrator.

L. Intimidation and Threat

Scaring someone, or specifically making them afraid you'll hurt them, may or may not constitute the crime of "intimidation," depending on why you're doing it.

"Intimidation" in the criminal context often means trying to frighten someone into doing or not doing something that's part of some judicial or police process. If, for example, the perpetrator's goal is to keep someone from talking to the police, or testifying, or testifying truthfully, that's criminal intimidation. The prosecution will have to prove that the words or actions amounted to a threat, and probably that the object of that threat was aware of it. But if the object of the threat was too stout-hearted to be actually concerned, that's not a defense.

Some states have broader definitions of this crime, omitting the requirement that the action the defendant is trying to cause, or to prevent, be connected to the legal system in some way. Recently, some states have also criminalized "ethnic intimidation": causing property damage or making physical contact with the victim, or plausibly threatening to do so, because of the victim's race, national origin, gender, religion, etc. There are also differences from one jurisdiction to another as to whether it's enough that the target felt threatened, even if the speaker didn't have that intention.

Related statutes sometimes criminalize threats of violence (and usually have "threat" in the title).

A charge of criminal intimidation or threat, especially if threatening intent isn't an element, can raise questions of whether the defendant's First Amendment right to freedom of speech (see 34.A.1.) is being infringed. As I write, the U.S. Supreme Court just ducked the chance to decide whether a rapper's lyrics posted on Facebook, and other Facebook posts, about violence against quite a few specified people could be punished under a federal threat statute without violating the rapper's freedom of speech.

M. Trespass - Criminal Version

Is it a crime, or just a tort (14.D.7.), to ignore a "no trespassing" sign? That depends.

Once upon a time in merry old England, "trespass" was primarily treated as a crime. Then it evolved into a tort, to be addressed via a lawsuit rather than criminal charges, unless combined with some sort of violence or disturbance. Nowadays the pendulum has swung part way back: some states make it a crime to enter onto someone's property "unlawfully" — which sounds tautological, but essentially turns civil trespass into a crime as well. Other states require an "unlawful purpose" before trespass becomes criminal. In that case, the phrase means an intent to commit some other crime (either any old crime or one of a list).

Sometimes criminal liability depends on a warning, whether verbal or via a sign or such, that people should stay away unless invited.

N. Resisting Arrest

One of what you could call "piggyback crimes," the charge of resisting arrest (either a misdemeanor or a felony, depending on the details) could stick even if the charges behind the original arrest end up dropped.

First of all, who's doing the arresting? If it's a citizen's arrest (13.U), "resisting arrest" doesn't apply, though some other sort of assault charge might. The person doing the arresting has to be a law enforcement officer by at least some elastic definition. A park ranger might count. In some states, a private security guard who's also an off-duty police officer would count also.

Mouthing off briefly at the arresting officer, whether the officer is arresting the loudmouth or someone else, wouldn't amount to resisting arrest. Violently interfering with the arrest, however, would. A prolonged, loud, threatening series of comments might. Violent resistance will most likely be charged as a felony rather than a misdemeanor.

What if the initial arrest is unlawful? Some states will allow the use of reasonable force to resist an unlawful arrest. Others, more concerned about the safety of the police and/or of the person getting arrested, don't have that exception.

What if the arrest is proper, but the way it's done isn't? Let's say, for example, that the police are beating a prisoner who didn't attack them first. The victim of that beating is probably allowed to use just enough force to protect themselves — at least, if there's a helpful video from a by-stander or police body camera, showing what really happened. . . .

O. Disorderly Conduct and Sometimes-Separate Related Offenses

"Disorderly conduct" is a pretty broad umbrella. It may include public intoxication; fighting; hollering loudly and/or obscenely in public; or pret-ty much any other public conduct that annoys the police. It may or may not include such possibly separate offenses as "disturbing the peace," "inde-cent exposure," loitering, prostitution, or obstructing traffic. Depending on the state and the circumstances, disorderly conduct may be a misde-meanor or (much less often) a felony.

Some states extend the idea of disorderly conduct to telephone or online behavior, using it to reach various kinds of harassment.

When disorderly conduct involves speech, especially speech directed at police or other government agents, the charge raises constitutional issues: was the defendant exercising a First Amendment right (or similar state constitutional right) to freedom of speech? See 34.A.1. for more on how these lines are drawn.

Aside from the free speech issue, catch-all crimes of this sort may be enforced in an arbitrary manner, or may be used to target individuals or groups against whom a police officer has some particular animus.

P. Close but No Cigar: Attempt as a Crime

What if someone fully intends to commit a particular crime, but doesn't pull it off? In many cases, they can be charged with a crime anyway: "attempt."

It's common for some crimes to have their own specific "attempt" version, especially attempted murder.

Unlike some other indirect ways of imposing criminal liability (like felony murder, discussed in 13.E.1.), criminal attempt requires the specific intent to commit a particular crime. Recklessly risking the harm a particular crime would inflict is not enough. Similarly, it's logically or psychologically impossible to attempt to commit criminal negligence or criminal recklessness.

But one doesn't need a declaration along the lines of "I meant to kill the son of a bitch!" Intent may be inferred from circumstances, such as (for example) the use of a deadly weapon in a manner likely to cause death or great bodily injury. Whether the inference is compelling enough to constitute proof beyond a reasonable doubt could be a point in contention.

Attempt's other key element, though its exact definition may differ: getting pretty close to success.

Generally, the state must prove either an act that reveals the guilty intent, or an act that goes beyond preparation and sets the crime in motion. The latter can be tricky, as not everyone will agree on when preparation crosses the line into something more.

Acts that might be found sufficient include (among others): lying in wait, stalking, following, etc.; enticing the victim to a location; casing the joint; unlawful entry; and possession or manufacture of items appropriately used in the crime and not reasonably explained by some innocent purpose, especially when found near the planned location of the crime.

What if the person who intended to commit the crime changes their mind before actually doing so? This possibility is called "abandonment," and in some, though by no means all, jurisdictions, it's a defense to the crime of attempt. In those jurisdictions, the outcome might turn on whether the trier of fact (the judge in a bench trial, or the jury) believes that the defendant had really reversed course, was just pausing to build up nerve, or was hovering in indecision. Per the Model Penal Code (see 13.D.), the defendant must abandon the effort to commit the crime, or better yet, prevent it from being committed, "under circumstances manifesting a complete and voluntary renunciation of his or her criminal purpose." Realizing that one's likely to get caught and prudently waiting for a better opportunity doesn't qualify as sufficiently "complete" or "voluntary." "Beat it — the cops!" is not abandonment of attempt. Deciding it's safer to pick another victim won't cut it either.

What if, for some reason unknown to the would-be criminal, the crime would have been impossible to perform? This often arises in the case of a police sting operation, as where an undercover police officer shows up with fake drugs. Not surprisingly, given how useful the police find such maneuvers, a defendant's mistake about such facts is rarely if ever a defense to a prosecution for attempt. But if the defendant actually knew the drugs were fake, or knew about whatever other circumstances made the crime impossible, then they would lack the necessary specific intent to commit the underlying offense. **It could be fun to start by getting the reader to assume that an actual crime almost occurred, then show that the facts weren't as they seemed (say, a police officer had been disguised as the intended victim), and finally, reveal that the accused knew about the setup all along and was yanking the official chain.**

Q. Conspiracy and Related Crimes

Moving further away from commission of a specific crime, we have the broad separate offense of conspiracy.

"Conspiracy" is a wide net, cast to catch those who can't be shown to have actually committed a particular crime. (A defendant might be charged with both attempt to commit a crime and conspiracy to commit it, if there's evidence to support the former.) If two or more people agree to cooperate in some illegal endeavor, and (at least in most jurisdictions) if any conspirator committed at least one "overt act" intended to further that endeavor, the state can charge another conspirator with "conspiracy" even if the crime never happened, or if the defendant can't be proved guilty of all the elements of the basic crime.

Ignorance of the law (in this and other contexts) is no excuse. (See 13.S.) If the defendant agreed to help do something they thought was legal, and (where necessary) took some small step toward making it happen, they are out of luck.

The agreement needn't be in writing, or even spoken out loud. It can be "tacit," understood without being made explicit, and can be proved by circumstantial evidence. In other words, if the alleged conspirators *acted* as if they were pursuing an illegal goal, the trier of fact can find that they agreed to pursue that goal.

Many jurisdictions will not allow the use of a co-conspirator's guilty plea as evidence of the defendant's agreement to commit the crime, or as evidence of guilt generally. However relevant evidence of that plea might be, they view it as against public policy, on the grounds that it blurs the line between proving the defendant's guilt and proving someone else's. But it's perfectly okay for the prosecution to call this co-conspirator and have them testify about the conspiracy, the agreement, etc. In fact, the co-conspirator's plea bargain may require them to do so.

Theoretically, "knowledge" or "approval" of the conspiracy isn't enough, but when the trier of fact may infer agreement from behavior, that's not a very powerful distinction. **One could tell the story of some low-level employee targeted by an overzealous prosecutor, or used as a lever to try to get some more important target — maybe someone who cares about that employee — to accept a plea bargain.**

Someone can become part of the conspiracy after a crime was committed by helping to conceal it.

It takes at least two to tango, conspiracy-wise, but if all the conspirators except one die before being charged, the prosecutor can still nail the survivor. Similarly, at least in some states, the defendant is still on the hook if their co-conspirator is somehow immune from prosecution, e.g., manages to successfully assert an insanity defense.

A corporation (see 14.U.1.) can commit conspiracy, but not internally. In other words, if employees within a corporation conspire to break the law, they aren't making the corporation criminally liable for conspiracy (even assuming it's proved that they acted as agents for the corporation) unless they bring an outsider into it. That's probably just the logic of corporate law at work: a corporation is a single entity, so it can't conspire with itself.

If the other conspirators change the goal of the conspiracy without cluing the defendant in, the defendant isn't guilty of conspiring to commit that new crime. But the defendant may have to prove the change, and their ignorance of it — at least by a preponderance of the evidence (see 20.A.).

One can withdraw from a conspiracy; but if one's co-conspirators committed any crimes before that point, one can still be found guilty of those. And one will have to prove that one withdrew.

What are the penalties? That varies. In some jurisdictions, the penalty for conspiracy to commit a particular crime is the same as for actually committing it.

Some states have a lesser version of the same idea, called "aiding and abetting" or acting as an "accessory," for those who were less involved in the criminal endeavor. (In at least some jurisdictions, this is different from being an "accomplice," which may require having been present.)

By the way, the idea of conspiracy also exists in tort law (14.F.9.). It doesn't provide a separate cause of action, but lets a plaintiff sue a conspirator along with the primary "tortfeasor."

R. Necessity and Duress

Here's what "necessity" and "duress" mean (in the criminal context), and the (sometimes minimal) difference between them. Both of these affirmative defenses have obvious dramatic possibilities.

Necessity means that one had to commit a criminal act to prevent some worse alternative. For example, one had to kick in a neighbor's door in order to save them from a fire.

Of course, that's too easy an example. Few prosecutors would charge that hero in the first place. Here's a situation that's gone to trial at least once (and might have different results in different courts, though I'd think the defendant's chances are pretty good): Husband and Wife are out for a drive. They're in an accident, and one of them (say Wife) is injured. Husband rushes her to the hospital without waiting for police to arrive and investigate. He's charged with a hit-and-run, and asserts necessity — the need to get Wife immediate medical attention — as a defense. Key facts in such a case would include how serious her injuries appeared to be (in light of whatever Husband knew about Wife's underlying medical condition), and how quickly it could be presumed that the police would appear.

The technical elements of the necessity defense focus on what the defendant believed and whether that belief was reasonable. That is, the defendant must have "reasonably believed":

- that the threat existed;
- that the threatened harm was worse than the harm done by the criminal act;
- that the threatened harm was imminent (so no time to brainstorm other solutions, seek help, etc.); and
- that there was no less harmful (and/or less criminal) way to avert the threatened harm.

Also, one can't use necessity as a defense if one's own behavior caused the threat. In the previous example, if Husband got into the accident because he was drunk, he can't use necessity as a defense against the hit-and-run statute, even if Wife did need to get to the hospital immediately.

And there's the awkward fact that by arguing necessity, the defendant is admitting that they committed the alleged violation in the first place.

Given that we're talking about letting someone off the hook for violating the law, the necessity defense isn't allowed too wide a scope. Averting economic harm, no matter how serious, is not (in most jurisdictions) a sufficient "necessity." So poor old Jean Valjean's theft of a loaf of bread to feed his sister's family in *Les Miserables* probably wouldn't be excused as "necessary."

What if the greater harm is about to happen to the future defendant? This issue has come up when prisoners escape prison and assert that their escape was necessary to prevent their being raped or otherwise injured. The results in these cases are split. At best, the necessity defense is allowed only if the prisoner turned themselves in as soon as they were safe (for the moment). Given the tendency for courts to assume, or pretend, that officialdom always does its job properly and would have intervened to protect the inmate, it will often be difficult or impossible to prove that the prisoner had "no less harmful alternative."

We're now close to the border between "necessity" and "duress." Let's say that instead of beating or stabbing a fellow prisoner for the fun of it, Crazy Jack threatens to stab your hapless protagonist unless the latter starts a fire to distract the guards while Jack escapes. That's the beginning of a duress defense. With duress, the defendant committed a criminal act because someone threatened them (or someone else) with physical harm.

Duress differs from necessity in one key respect: belief in the danger, even reasonable belief, isn't enough. The threat must actually have been made. This may be a distinction without a difference if the defendant is the only witness to the threat itself.

As with necessity, the threat must have been immediate, and there can't have been a way to escape, or help the other threatened person escape, without committing the criminal act. At least, the defendant must have reasonably believed that they lacked other options.

The common law required a threat of death or serious bodily harm. In the milder modern era, this requirement has been relaxed somewhat.

There's a limit to what society forgives someone for doing under duress. No matter what some sick psycho demands, one can't use duress as a defense against intentional homicide or an attempt at same. However, duress may well knock the crime down from murder to some degree of manslaughter.

S. Ignorance Won't Help

With so many criminal statutes and other regulations out there, it's often said that most of us have probably violated a few without knowing it, and that no one could possibly keep up with them all. But in general, that's no defense. As the much-cited maxim goes: "Ignorance of the law is no excuse" — at least, unless a police officer wasn't quite up on the law that determines whether a search was legal or not (see "good faith exception," at 34.E.1.).

There are criminal offenses where one necessary element of the crime is some sort of knowledge — but that's pretty much the only time that it matters whether the defendant knew they were breaking the law, for purposes of guilt or innocence. When it comes to a prosecutor deciding whether to bring charges, or (following a conviction) what sentence they decide to seek, the perpetrator's level of knowledge is more likely to be of interest.

A real-life example that got a fair amount of attention: a young mother of two who thought her Pennsylvania concealed carry license allowed her to carry her pistol (obtained for self-protection) in New Jersey was thrown in jail, and only escaped a years-long prison sentence because of popular outcry. The outcry was particularly intense because the same prosecutor gave lenient treatment to a spouse-abusing sports figure. You should be able to conjure up fictional examples of this principle in action.

T. Entrapment

A successful entrapment defense means that the police worked really hard to try to get someone to commit the crime.

Entrapment involves some fairly fuzzy lines. It's not enough for the cops to provide the opportunity. It's not enough if they cajole, persuade, or even lie. The amount and intensity of persuasion or coercion makes the difference.

States take either an "objective" or a "subjective approach" — though "objective" essentially amounts to the jurors' subjective view, rather than the jurors' reading of the defendant's subjective view. Per the "objective" test recommended by the Model Penal Code, if the police conduct would induce Joe Law-Abiding Citizen to commit the crime, there's entrapment. With the "subjective" test, the jurors assess the defendant's "predisposition" to commit the crime: if they were predisposed to commit it, then the police inducements were just gravy, and the defendant is guilty. The defendant's rap sheet, gang affiliation, etc. then become relevant, even though that evidence would normally be excluded as clouding the issue of the defendant's guilt re this particular crime. No surprise: the subjective test leads to fewer acquittals. And most states use it.

Let's say a disguised police officer — a big, muscular fellow with tattoos — tells a teenage boy living in a gang-ridden neighborhood that if he doesn't go pick up a shipment of drugs, the members of one of the local gangs will set him on fire. Under the objective test, a jury is likely to find entrapment. But if the teenager has been arrested for previous activity associated with drug trafficking, the subjective test will likely allow this police tactic to succeed.

The same pair of results would apply if, instead of threatening the accused, the officer spent weeks befriending him, promising to find his family a safer place to live and to protect the youngster's mother when she walks home from her job late at night — if only the youngster will run this one little illegal errand.

In states using the objective test, the burden of proving entrapment is on the defendant, though only by a preponderance of the evidence (see 20.A.). In states using the subjective test, the defendant has to prove that the police induced them to commit the crime, but then the government, to win a conviction, has to rebut that showing or prove that the defendant was predisposed to commit the crime, in either case beyond a reasonable doubt.

U. Citizen's Arrest

Yes, there is such a thing as a "citizen's arrest." And it's not just for citizens.

Once again, the details vary by state; but if a regular person, not any variety of police officer, sees someone commit a crime, that private person is allowed to detain the culprit until the police show up. They may even use force — in some states and under some circumstances, deadly force — to keep the criminal from running away.

What if someone has what they consider good reason to believe the crime was committed, but didn't see it? Generally, that'll be good enough if the crime is a felony, as opposed to a misdemeanor.

That's assuming the would-be hero wasn't mistaken. If the crime didn't occur or the person grabbed didn't commit it, the person who undertook the "arrest" could be liable for various crimes or torts (e.g. assault, battery, false imprisonment, slander), depending on the details of what occurred.

Your protagonist could have a vertiginous journey from fear of confrontation to triumphing over fear to public adulation to public disgrace.

V. Involuntary Commitment

A person doesn't have to be convicted of a crime to be locked up. And the basis for confining such a person needn't be proved beyond a reasonable doubt.

Like the criminal justice system, the involuntary commitment process seeks to protect the public. However, it also exists to protect people from themselves. The touchstone: is the subject a danger to others or to themselves?

It used to take no more than a preponderance of the evidence (see 20.A.) to get someone involuntarily committed. In 1979, however, the U.S. Supreme Court ruled that the Constitution required application of the somewhat tougher "clear and convincing evidence" standard. But what, exactly, has to be shown by this amount of evidence? What is the definition of "danger"? This will vary from place to place, and very likely from one year or decade to the next.

Involuntary commitment is a species of preventive detention, and thus an exception to the usual rule that people can't be detained because of what they might do in the future.

The commitment process starts with a "hold," a brief period of confinement, typically 72 hours. This may be referred to as "emergency detention" and/or "observational institutionalization." (The former may include temporary treatment.) State law will determine what kind of folks are authorized to initiate such a hold, but they're likely to include police officers, some mental health professionals, and possibly members of some sort of "mobile crisis team." Any authorized person may contact the police (unless they are the police) and ask that someone be detained and transported to a psychiatric facility.

Within the time specified for the hold, the commitment can be extended if the designated number of qualified people (usually psychiatrists or other mental health professionals, which may include social workers) examine the person and tell the court that longer confinement is necessary to protect the person or the public. A diagnosis of mental illness may also be required.

Most states also provide for the alternative of mandatory outpatient treatment. This is less restrictive in physical terms; but in terms of treatment the patient would like to reject, it may be more coercive, since patients in a psychiatric facility, at least in some states, have the right to refuse treatment.

How hard is it to prove one's sanity? More than one intrepid researcher has feigned mental illness in order to investigate conditions in psychiatric facilities — and not all found it easy to regain their freedom. For example, there's the story of reporter Elizabeth Jane Cochrane, pen name Nellie Bly, who went undercover in a mental institution in 1887 (admittedly a different era where the law of involuntary commitment was concerned). She put on an act while staying at a boarding house, and dropped it upon reaching the Blackwell's Island asylum — only to find the diagnosis of mental illness confirmed no matter how she acted. After ten days in appalling conditions, her newspaper sent an attorney to get her sprung. In the early 1970s, psychologist David Rosenhan recruited eight people to briefly fake auditory hallucinations and try to get admitted to a variety of psychiatric hospitals. All were admitted easily; all resumed normal behavior immediately upon admission; and all were forced to admit psychosis and start taking anti-psychotic medication in order to be released, after hospital stays from seven to 52 days, with an average of 19 days. (**Any of these "pseudopatients" could be the basis of an engrossing story.**) In yet another undercover investigation in the late 1990s, reporter Kevin Heldman claimed suicidal behavior, was admitted after a ten-minute intake interview, then stopped exhibiting symptoms and asked to be released at the end of 72 hours. No dice, he was told. He spent about a week longer in the hospital, of which he spent around six minutes talking to a psychiatrist.

Must treatment be *available* to the involuntarily committed? In 1997, the U.S. Supreme Court ruled that such availability isn't constitutionally required. The same 5-4 decision allowed indefinite involuntary commitment of violent sexual offenders, and didn't even require conviction of a violent sexual offense as a prerequisite.

Combine this ruling with state laws that can make teenagers who sleep together into sexual offenders (e.g., if one or both are below the age of consent), and it wouldn't take too blatant an abuse of authority for a law enforcement official or medical professional, who also happened to be the outraged father of some teenaged girl, to get her swain locked up for what could turn into life.

W. Delinquency - Like and Unlike Crime

There's great dramatic potential in the intersection (or perhaps the more appropriate metaphor would be collision) between the adolescent years and the criminal justice system. During the most tempestuous and volatile years of a young person's life, the carelessness or lousy decision of a moment may have life-changing consequences — though those consequences will probably be less severe than for an adult lawbreaker.

On the other hand, juvenile "delinquency" doesn't always mean conduct that would get an adult into trouble with the law.

One might assume that all minors (usually meaning those under 18 years of age) are under the jurisdiction of the juvenile justice system, but in some states the cap is 16, with anyone older treated as an adult. A trial court can also decide that a youngster charged with a serious crime should be tried as an adult. Most states set a minimum age below which a child can't be handed over to the regular criminal justice system; but not all do so, and the minimums that do exist vary, some going as low as 10 years old. A few states automatically try "emancipated" minors (14.H.11.) as adults. Some states have guidelines for particular crimes, with the minimum age for trial as an adult varying by crime. During the 1990s, many states made it easier for juveniles to be "waived into" adult court.

What's the difference? There are several, some where being in the juvenile justice system is advantageous to the juvenile and others not.

First, the favorable differences.

- There's a greater emphasis on rehabilitation and less interest in punishment where juveniles are concerned.

- A child or teenager found "delinquent," the juvenile equivalent of guilty, can be sentenced to confinement in a juvenile corrections facility or even in an adult jail or prison — but in most states, that confinement can last no longer than the juvenile's 21st birthday. There's a certain inconsistency here, with the threshold to adulthood different for confinement than for the earlier stages of the process. "Until 21" may be a relic from a time when more adult rights and privileges (e.g. voting) kicked in at 21, and/or it may be the shortest acceptable time to keep some delinquents off the streets. In states that don't have this limitation, the 21-year-old inmate could be transferred to an adult prison after reaching that age, in what's called a "blended" sentence.

- The court has and often uses various less severe options (not all unique to delinquency), including probation; community service; counseling; fines; restitution (compensation paid directly to the victim); electronic monitoring; or some combination. The juvenile may even get off with no more than a verbal warning from the police, without going to court at all. In that event, the police may or may not hold the juvenile until a parent or guardian can show up. If they don't, the parent or guardian might not even find out what happened.

- Disposition may be "informal," with an appearance before either a probation officer or a judge, rather than formal, with charges and all that follows them. The case may also be "diverted" (a procedure also available in some adult courts, and called "deferred adjudication" or "pretrial diversion" (see 29.A.2.)): the juvenile follows some required procedure such as counseling or community service, and if they do this successfully, the delinquency case never proceeds.

- Even when the juvenile is charged (which involves a "petition" for a finding of delinquency), they are more often than not allowed to remain at home pending the fact-finding hearing.

- Juveniles' records may be sealed against public view, either automatically or upon the juvenile's request. (In the latter case, a fee may be required, and there may be some set time period before the records will be sealed.) In addition, the juvenile's delinquency record may be "expunged," largely deleted from public records (see 32.G.), once the juvenile turns 18.

- A few states, including Indiana, have taken action to address the possibility that kids arrested for delinquency have been abused or neglected. Did the juvenile learn violent behavior at home? Did they steal food because they're the only one feeding themselves and their siblings? Indiana recently passed a law requiring that when a juvenile is arrested and detained, at least in a juvenile detention facility, that those in charge of processing new admissions investigate whether the juvenile has in fact been abused or neglected. If they decide that the juvenile is a Child in Need of Services (see 14.H.13.), the juvenile will be treated as "dual status" (subject to both delinquency and CHINS procedures), and may end up being treated in less confining or coercive ways. A multi-state organization called Models for Change is promoting such legislation.

On the other hand, juveniles' constitutional rights in delinquency proceedings are fewer than those of criminal defendants.

- There's no trial by jury. The juvenile might not initially realize this. **A young man could have nightmares of a jury where every member is his mother — or his girlfriend's father.** **On the other hand, the trial judge might actually *be* his girlfriend's father. A battle might then ensue over whether the judge should recuse himself (see 5.B.).**

- There's no right to a public hearing (the flip side of the protection involved in sealing records).

- In the relatively few cases where the court doesn't let the juvenile stay home pending the hearing, there's no right to bail.

- When a minor is put on probation, it's likely to be for a longer period than an adult would get. And the conditions may be more numerous, as well as particularly galling, e.g., behaving respectfully towards the juvenile's parents. There may also be "post-disposition" hearings at regular intervals, where the court checks up on how the juvenile is doing.

The movement toward private prisons in this country is controversial and hotly debated, but private correctional facilities for juveniles are far more common. At least some studies have concluded that the privately run facilities do at least as good a job as the public. (A writer could easily imagine and describe appalling conditions in either sort of facility, though the details might differ.)

Whether public or private, a residential facility for delinquent offenders may be anything from a camp comparable to a summer camp, to a home-like environment, to something much like adult prison.

Some ways a kid can end up in court aren't even crimes. "Status offenses" like truancy, underage drinking, "habitual disobedience," and running away from home are illegal only because it's a juvenile who's committing them. Status offenses may or may not be called "delinquency," but they can have serious consequences. While a status offender shouldn't end up in a "correctional facility" (see the discussion of JJDPA below), they could be placed in a special "school." A record of status offenses may also play a role in how seriously a court or other official takes some subsequent offense.

The federal Juvenile Justice and Delinquency Prevention Act (JJDPA) attempts to govern state handling of juvenile offenders via the usual federal tactic of withholding funding to states that don't go along. (Historical note: the JJDPA was first passed in 1974. More than forty years later, we still don't have all states complying with all its provisions.)

The JJDPA prohibits holding status offenders (with a few exceptions) in "secure detention" or "secure correctional" facilities. It also (as of 1980) limits the amount of time that juveniles found delinquent may be held in adult jails or prisons to a few hours. Per the original act and ever since, if juveniles *are* in a facility with adult prisoners, they are not supposed to have any contact with those prisoners, meaning they can't be in cells with or next to the adults or share common spaces with adults. (Please note: by the time you read this, the details may have changed. For example, there's some pressure from law enforcement agencies to weaken the no-contact-with-adults provision so that it would allow occasional sporadic contact.)

All well and good — unless the juvenile has been kicked out of the juvenile justice system and tried as an adult. Some of these protections still theoretically apply, but not all.

If a juvenile is tried, convicted, and sentenced as an adult, presumably for a serious crime, that juvenile is likely to end up in prison with adults. Many juveniles will be smaller and weaker than almost all the adult inmates, easy prey for all the kinds of violence that inmates manage to inflict on each other. When not being victimized, the youngster will be learning how to live in a world of criminals, as well as how to commit various new crimes. What sort of bleak and stunted future will the young prisoner have when they are finally released?

Some states do try to separate juveniles convicted in adult court from adult prisoners. But in a terrible example of the law of unintended consequences, one all-too-common way of separating juveniles from adult inmates is to separate juveniles from human contact altogether — to place them in solitary confinement, with all its psychologically destructive effects (see 29.G.).

You could alternate between a youngster in solitary, chronicling their struggle to stay psychologically whole, and the family that at first has no idea what's happening (or may even have precipitated it by their response to the child's earlier mistreatment by other inmates); then begins to suspect; then struggles to find out for sure; and then, finally, hires a lawyer to get the child moved to a facility where they can be confined in a safer and less destructive way.

The U.S. Supreme Court has, at least, held that juveniles may not, even in adult court, be sentenced to life in prison without possibility of parole for crimes other than homicide. Nor may the state enact a sentencing scheme which *requires* a trial court to sentence juveniles convicted of homicide to life in prison without possibility of parole.

X. Criminal Contempt

Criminal contempt doesn't have to occur in a criminal case. Whatever the underlying litigation, acting up in court, or challenging or undermining the court or the judicial process in some other way, can result in a criminal contempt charge. (Warning: this is yet another area where definitions tend to vary. I'm using what I consider the clearest and most common.)

Direct criminal contempt involves actions during a proceeding, committed in the judge's presence. Examples of indirect criminal contempt include ignoring an order to show up and threatening the judge or a witness (if the threat is made somewhere other than open court).

Indirect criminal contempt is generally treated like any other criminal charge. Direct criminal contempt: not so much. The judge's power to punish direct "contemptuous" conduct is surprising, and controversial in some legal circles, because in some jurisdictions, it's a criminal penalty imposed with relatively few procedural protections. Just how few varies. Some states will provide the subject (the "contemnor" in legalese) with a lawyer if they don't already have one; others won't. Some let the offended judge decide the penalty; others don't. Some allow the contemnor to appeal immediately; others don't, although if I were advising someone in that situation, I might recommend trying a writ of habeas corpus (32.E.).

The judge may be able to find the contemnor in contempt on the spot and impose punishment just as quickly. That punishment may be a fine or jail time. A day or two in the slammer is typical, but in rare cases it can be as much as six months. The judge does have to put the order and its basis on the record.

CHAPTER 14

What's It All About:
Substantive Principles (Civil)

A. Introduction: Civil Law

E ven though so many courtroom dramas focus on criminal prosecution and defense, there's a great deal of drama to be found in the
enormous umbrella category known as "civil" law. There can be a
major David versus Goliath power differential, as in "little guy takes on big
corporation" (perhaps the most common scenario in fiction outside of the
criminal context); or there can be the equally compelling situation of former friends, neighbors, or relatives dragging each other through the
courts, airing each other's secrets, risking what should be permanent and
nurturing relationships.

Back to David and Goliath for a moment. If the law gives David
enough advantages over Goliath, David could end up the stronger party in
a legal dispute. Many corporate officers, general counsel, etc. would argue
that the legal system is currently skewed in David's favor. That's an argument I'll stay out of. However, there's some basis for concern about juror
attitudes. Most potential jurors have been exposed to a good deal of fiction
and rhetoric that paints people who work for or run corporations as
greedier and less ethical than the rest of humanity.

B. Models and Uniforms

Much of the similarity between one state's law and another comes from their similar origins. We inherited a good deal of our legal system from pre-Revolutionary British law. State courts also pay attention to what other state courts are doing, so as the law evolves in one state, others may decide they like the new direction.

However, there's another mechanism for serving those goals, especially in areas where predictability and uniformity have practical advantages, such as the law surrounding commercial transactions. Some group of legal experts can come up with a Model Code or Uniform Code, and put it out there for state legislatures to enact and/or for state courts to track. We've already discussed the Model Penal Code (13.D.), but there are many more specific model codes in the civil context.

There are a great many Uniform Codes or Acts and a few Model Codes or Acts. One that might reasonably feature in a story of some kind is the Uniform Child Custody Jurisdiction and Enforcement Act (UCCJEA), whose goal is to reduce tussles between different states in child custody cases. (See 34.K. for a few details.)

1. The Uniform Commercial Code

Perhaps the most frequently adopted uniform code is the Uniform Commercial Code (U.C.C.), which covers, among other topics, sales of goods; negotiable instruments (checks and so forth); and secured transactions (where a seller or lender hangs onto some sort of rights to the item the deal covers).

Every state in the U.S. has adopted at least part of the U.C.C., usually most or all of it (and, again usually, including Article 2, which deals with the sale and purchase of goods). Louisiana, with its fondness for its French origins, differs from other states on many legal points, and has declined to adopt that portion of the U.C.C. dealing with the sale of goods.

C. Promises, Promises: Contract Law

The first thing to remember is: one may not (successfully) sue someone just for breaking a promise. There has to be more.

Contract law isn't all based on the original common law any more. As mentioned just above (14.B.1.), almost all the states have adopted the Uniform Commercial Code's provisions governing sales of goods, although a few states have tinkered with the details. If the legal aspects of buying and selling "goods" (oversimplified definition: physical property that can be moved from one place to the other, or will become movable in the future) are important to your story, check for your location's version of the U.C.C. It includes technical details I won't attempt to cover here.

Most of the time, if someone is suing about a promise, there needs to be a contract. The basic ingredients of a contract are an offer, acceptance of the offer, and something called "consideration."

By the way, I'll be talking about "both" parties, but there can certainly be more than two. If one of three or more parties breaches the contract, it may or may not be obvious who should sue whom. If you want to include such a story line, I'll leave it to you to hunt down more details.

1. Offer and Acceptance

The terms of the offer and of the acceptance need to match. If I offer X + Y, and you respond with, "OK, Y + Z," that's not an acceptance. It's a counteroffer; and once you make a counteroffer, you can't hold the other party to the original offer. But if you respond by asking whether Y includes Z, that doesn't keep you from accepting the offer, whatever the answer to your question. **There's potential comedy, or a setup for bringing a character to the boiling point, in an extended back-and-forth between some reasonable person and an indecisive and/or detail-obsessed Other, the latter making countless counter-offers and then wanting to revert to some already rejected offer.**

Offers don't last forever. They may come with explicit expiration times, or the time to respond may be what's reasonable under the circumstances. Under the U.C.C., if a buyer or seller of goods promises to leave an offer open, it must stay open for as long as was promised or for three months, whichever is shorter.

If the offer has expired, or is withdrawn, before the other party tries to accept it, that attempt doesn't make a binding contract. This means that exactly when the "acceptance" happened can be crucial. Most of the time, mailing an acceptance means the contract exists as soon as someone drops that acceptance in the mail (but *not* when that person hands it to a friend to mail).

An "option contract" is a contract that give one party the right to buy or sell some item later at a certain price. It's potentially two contracts in one: the first is an agreement to keep a second offer available for some specified time period. That first contract has to have consideration (discussed below in 14.C.2.). Once that first-stage contract is in place, the party making the offer to buy or sell something must keep that offer open throughout the option period, and a counteroffer from the other party wouldn't affect that obligation.

Things can't be left too vague. A contract has to have a certain degree of specificity. "We'll figure out later how many widgets I'll deliver and what you'll pay me" — an "agreement to agree" — isn't a binding contract: it gives no rights to either side. What specifics are required will depend on the type of contract. For example, for a valid contract to sell goods, the offer must generally specify what is being sold, the delivery date, and the price. Under the U.C.C.'s provisions re the sale of goods, if the time of payment isn't mentioned, payment is assumed to be due at the time of delivery. Many invoices have language about when payment is due, such as 30 days from the date of the invoice; but an invoice the buyer doesn't sign or otherwise treat as a contract isn't part of the contract.

Whether a seller could, in a lawsuit, actually rely on the U.C.C.'s payment-on-delivery rule (assuming the state has adopted it) instead of the seller's invoice terms might get complicated: the buyer might be able to claim a waiver based on the seller's previous acceptance of payments made per the invoice. This is just one example of how the way the parties actually deal with each other can change what's enforceable in the original contract.

Most people think of contracts as promises going both ways (what's technically called a "bilateral" contract), but a contract may be based on only one promise. A "unilateral" contract starts with a promise to respond in a certain way to a particular action. Restaurant challenges like "eat the whole giant steak in 30 minutes and it's free" are unilateral contracts. The restaurant makes the offer; the customer accepts by eating the steak within the specified time.

---

2. Consideration:

What You Get or Give or Give Up

Consideration can't be something that's already happened. Let's say I find your lost wallet, which contains a lottery ticket. In gratitude, you promise to share any proceeds with me. You then win a prize. We don't have a contract, because your promise came after the value (the returned wallet) that you received from me.

"Consideration" doesn't have to mean a benefit to both parties. One or both can give something up instead. This is "detriment" as consideration.

There's an old folk tale I read as a child that illustrates this point. It may have been one of those told about legendary prankster Till Eulenspiegel. Till, if it was he, offers an annoying gentleman a deal: if the latter will bend over a barrel and take three whacks with a belt, Till will pay him some enticing sum. The man endures two resounding whacks, groaning that it will be worth it to get the money — but Till then announces that the deal had placed no time limit on when Till would administer the third whack, and he's in no hurry. . . . As a contract, this has a few problems, but consideration isn't one of them. There was sufficient consideration in this deal, even though Till was not to receive any benefit (other than schadenfreude, i.e. delight in the suffering of another), because the other contracting party was to suffer the detriment of being thwacked.

What other problems? Well, the two parties understood the deal very differently. The man assumed that he would receive three whacks in a row, within a very limited period of time. Till intended to delay the third whack indefinitely. The two parties didn't have a "meeting of the minds."

Also, a contract to let someone hit you would probably be deemed unenforceable as against public policy. (See 14.C.8.)

Some written contracts are coy about what the actual consideration is. Instead of including it, they'll mention some trivial amount, like one dollar; or they might say something like "for one dollar and other good and valuable consideration." Or the consideration could really be that small, as might be the case in a model release (where someone consents to have their photograph used in all sorts of unpredictable ways). In any of these situations, you have what's called "nominal" consideration.

Under the common law, nominal consideration was usually enough to make a binding contract, assuming everything else was in order. Nowadays that's less certain, although it may be more likely to be sufficient in an "option contract" (see 14.C.1. above).

Contract requirements such as consideration can get tricky where one agreement grows out of another. For example, the intermediate appellate court for Indiana has held that under some circumstances, an agreement to guarantee the performance of one party to a contract needs no consideration beyond the consideration that makes that primary contract valid. (However, as noted in 14.C.3. below, the agreement had better be in writing.) **This could be an area where "a little learning is a dangerous thing." A potential guarantor, seeking to put an end to a cousin's or in-law's repeated requests, could assume that the promise to guarantee a payment or other performance wasn't binding because the guarantor wasn't getting any benefit from that promise beyond an amorphous reduction in family friction.**

3. The Statute of Frauds

Does a contract have to be in writing? Can it be a "handshake deal" instead, with no paper involved? Often, it can; but there are limits. Those limits generally go by the name of a centuries-old English statute, the "Statute of Frauds." Different states have varying versions of this statute, but usually, the following kinds of contracts can't be enforced without some written note or memo containing the key terms:

- Contracts that can't be performed within one year of when they're made.
- Contracts to transfer some interest in real property.
- Prenuptial and postnuptial contracts.
- Contracts "in consideration of marriage," where one party promises to marry the other in exchange for some other consideration, like a transfer of property.
- Contracts for the sale of goods worth more than some set amount (currently $500 in the U.C.C. (14.B.1.) as adopted by most states, but may be higher in a few states, and may have been lower in a few states in the past).
- Contracts in which one party guarantees some obligation of the other party or promises to pay the other party's debts.

Some states also include certain life insurance contracts, contracts for someone to include property in a will, or contracts that give a realtor a commission upon the sale of real estate.

Sometimes, if the contract has been partially performed already, that partial performance may be raised as a defense to the claim that a contract is unenforceable because of the Statute of Frauds. But whether part performance rescues the entire contract, or just lets someone recover compensation for the part actually performed, varies from one state to another. Under the U.C.C. in its pure form, it makes a difference if goods are specially manufactured for the seller and can't be sold elsewhere, and if the manufacturing process began before the buyer repudiated the contract (that is, said they weren't going to abide by the contract).

4. Capacity to Contract

Can anybody and everybody enter into a binding contract? No. The issue of whether someone may enter into a contract is called "capacity." If some permanent or temporary quality prevents someone from making a valid contract, that's called "incapacity."

One common type of incapacity is age. A minor doesn't have the capacity to contract. At least, any supposed contract wouldn't be binding on the minor, unless the minor's parent or guardian agreed also. However, the contract is "voidable" rather than "void ab initio," meaning that if the minor wants to hold the other party to the contract, they may do so. **Someone attempting to cheat a minor by entering into a contract with the expectation that it's meaningless would be in for a nasty surprise.**

Age is a legal incapacity. There can also be fact-based incapacity, when the potential contracting party is not mentally capable of understanding what the contract entails. This incapacity may be permanent, or temporary (caused by illness or intoxication, for example).

Capacity has special implications if one party to the contract is a corporation: not every employee or board member or officer is authorized to act on the corporation's behalf. However, even if the corporate bylaws say otherwise, vice presidents may be treated as having "apparent authority" to sign contracts. Any employee whose title includes the word "representative," such as a sales representative, may also be viewed as having apparent authority. More generally, "apparent authority" means that something a company has done, whether it's giving someone a particular title or providing them with the trappings of authority (e.g. corporate stationery), has led reasonable observers to believe that the person is an agent of the company and has authority to enter into contracts. If this impression of authority is the corporation's or other company's doing, a contract such a person signs will probably bind the company. But if the other contracting party knows, or should know from some action of the company, that this person wasn't authorized to enter into contracts after all, there's no binding contract.

5. No Contract But:

Promissory Estoppel and Quantum Meruit

If there's no contract, is there no hope? Well, there are circumstances that let someone sue someone for breaking a promise, even without a contract.

Promissory estoppel is an "equitable" remedy. (For more on equity and equitable remedies, see 19.B. and 30.A.) If a person reasonably relied on the promise, and incurred some cost or other detriment because of that reliance, they can recover some amount of damages via promissory estoppel.

For example: I tell you I'll let you live in my guest house on the beach, rent free. We're old friends, and I owe you a favor, so it's reasonable for you to believe me. You give up your small, airless apartment with a view of nothing, and you rent a U-Haul. You and your U-Haul show up, and I've changed my mind. You can sue for what's called promissory estoppel.

There could be some interesting gray areas about what reliance is "reasonable" if the parties had some sort of romantic history. . . .

If someone can recover damages for promissory estoppel, what can they get? That's a matter of dispute. Most likely, they can get the costs they incurred because they relied on the promise: in my example, the U-Haul rental, the cost of traveling to the guest house, and maybe the degree to which temporary housing exceeds the rent they were paying on the apartment. Courts in some jurisdictions will instead award the value of what the person was promised, namely the amount that it should cost to rent the guest cottage for some reasonable length of time. (As to the damages one gets for breach of an actual contract, see 30.B.1.)

Another way to obtain quasi-contractual legal relief without a contract is through "quantum meruit," law Latin for "as much as is deserved." This is another equitable remedy, meant to prevent unjust enrichment. As in many equity cases, a great deal will depend on what the state legislature and/or a particular court thinks is fair or unfair, just or unjust, given the facts at hand.

In situations where someone provided services under circumstances where they had a reasonable expectation of getting paid, the court may take evidence of what such services would generally cost in the relevant marketplace and award that amount. Quantum meruit may also be invoked to pay someone who provided professional (e.g. medical or firefighting) services in an emergency — but not if that particular professional or agency is known to provide such services at no charge. In either case, the person required to pay will have benefited from ("used" and "enjoyed") the work performed.

Quantum meruit is sometimes divided into two categories: contract implied by the facts, and contract "implied" by law, which really means that public policy dictates the plaintiff should get paid. The former category would cover the "reasonable expectation of getting paid" scenario. The latter would cover some situations where emergency services are provided. Not every state will make this sometimes tricky distinction. In an "implied by law" quantum meruit case, recovery may not include the profit the plaintiff would have been able to include in an actual contract. Also, it may not be possible to successfully sue a government under an "implied in law" quantum meruit theory: that isn't really a contract cause of action, and sovereign immunity (Ch. 16) might preclude it.

Quantum meruit could also apply if someone unwittingly entered into a contract with the wrong party. For example, if someone (perhaps, in this scenario, a tenant or a house guest) claimed to be the agent for a homeowner and hired a contractor to install a swimming pool, then the contractor might be able to recover the usual cost of that service from the homeowner even though no binding contract exists. The outcome could depend on whether the homeowner was in a position to know the work was going on. If the homeowner was out of the country throughout the time the pool was being installed, and played no role in the deception, equity might not dictate that this innocent owner be held responsible. In that case, the contractor might have to go after the supposed agent based on some tort cause of action, possibly fraud (14.F.6).

Sometimes even a party who has breached a contract may recover in quantum meruit for the value of the products or services that party provided before the breach. Any such recovery, however, would be offset against the damages the breach caused to the other party (see 30.B.1.).

6. Modifying a Contract

What if one or both parties want to change the terms of a contract? That's very much like making a contract in the first place, and similar rules will apply — with some exceptions.

The original contract may (and very often does) spell out how any changes, or "modifications," must be made. Frequently the modifications must be made with all the formalities used in the formation of the original contract.

A change in the contract, like the contract itself, usually requires consideration. Exception: under the Uniform Commercial Code, when "merchants," people whose business is buying and selling, modify a contract, there doesn't need to be new consideration for the change. Merchants make so many modifications that it'd be too cumbersome to keep track of who gained or lost what by each little adjustment.

So if you have a publishing contract, and your agent or editor tells you that there's suddenly a new contract provision, that's only true if you agree to the new language. However, if the original contract puts the burden of objecting on you, and if you fail to take whatever action would keep the new language from being incorporated in your contract, then you're stuck. All the more reason to read that original contract *very* carefully.

7. It Doesn't Mean THAT!: Construing the Contract

What if at some point, the parties to the contract disagree on what the contract means?

There are several principles the courts apply in interpreting contracts. First of all, there's the distinction between "ambiguous" and "unambiguous" contracts. A contract is "unambiguous" if the meaning seems clear when some stranger reads it. In that case, the courts generally won't listen to an argument that the words really mean something else because of a discussion that wasn't written into the contract. But if the words of the contract are ambiguous, one may use "extrinsic evidence" to clarify them. Extrinsic evidence is evidence of discussions, events, trade practices, etc.

There's language in many written contracts saying that every bit of the agreement has been written down and included. In that case, the court won't look at extrinsic evidence about what anyone said, or even what anyone wrote in a separate document, if that evidence would add to or conflict with the contractual language.

Another rule, one that actually tends to benefit the little guy (!), is that if contractual language is ambiguous, that language will be construed against the party who drafted it. It makes sense: that's the party who had the chance to make things clear, and didn't. So when, for example, a bank hands a borrower some long document full of fine print, if there's anything in it that hasn't already been clarified by decades of disagreements, then in case of a dispute about the meaning of a clause, that clause should be interpreted in the borrower's favor. (However, there may be exceptions, or places that apply the rule less broadly. See, for example, 14.G.3. re how liability waivers may be interpreted.)

If different states would interpret the terms of the contract differently, then the inclusion of a "choice of law" clause (Ch. 18), saying which state's law will govern in the event of a dispute, can be key. The contract may also specify in what state's, or even what country's, courts any dispute will be tried (see 18.A.). And whether a party to the contract can go to court at all could depend on whether there's a clause requiring any disputes to be submitted to arbitration (see 9.C.1.).

8. Oh No You Don't: Limits on Enforceable Contracts

There are limits to what a contract may cover and what it may include.

Some subjects are off limits as "against public policy." You can't, for example, contract to sell your children. Couples planning to adopt a not-yet-born baby can agree to pay the mother's expenses, but any payment the mother gets for the act of giving up the child is prohibited. (See 14.H.14.) **One can imagine creative ways to get around this limitation, with unusually defined or just plain imaginary expenses.**

Other restrictions concern employment contracts: for example, an employer can't make an employee agree never to join a union. Now that we have several federal and some state laws requiring landlords, employers, etc. to make various accommodations to people with disabilities (see 34.H.), a landlord-tenant agreement can't include a flat ban on medically necessary animals like seeing eye dogs, although the tenant could have some hoops to (metaphorically speaking) jump through. **Given the animals that are sometimes claimed to be medically necessary these days, like psychological "support" animals, your story could explore the boundaries of this rule.**

Even though divorce settlements often include agreements on child custody (14.H.8.), some states (e.g. California) have public policy restrictions on the content of such agreements, and most or all states require a judge's approval for such agreements.

Some types of contracts are allowed, but with limitations. For example, non-compete clauses in employment contracts or in contracts to purchase a business may purport to limit what sort of jobs someone can take, or what professional practices they can start up after they leave their current position. These clauses get close scrutiny, and it's not uncommon for a court to find that a particular example is too broad to be enforced. The basic rule is that people can't indefinitely contract away their ability to make a living in their chosen field, and any restrictions along these lines are disfavored. (See 14.L.4.)

If one party is actually incompetent to understand contracts, or presumed (e.g. because of age) to be so, the contract will be either void or voidable (see 14.C.4.). That's why parents or guardians are called upon to sign contracts (including waivers of liability) for their kids. But what if one party doesn't realize the other is under 18 years of age? While there may be a tort remedy, such as fraud, the contract itself won't be enforceable if the minor or the minor's parent/guardian wants to get out of it.

Contracts made under duress are against public policy. Blackmail is one dramatic example of such duress. There's also economic duress. For example, let's say you contract with a moving company to take all your worldly goods across country. When the truck reaches Iowa, the company insists on raising the price, threatening to dump everything in a cornfield unless you pay up. That's duress, in the contract context, and you won't owe the extra money even if you signed a contract modification. (But it may cost you some legal fees to assert that defense.)

"Undue influence" may arise most often in the probate context (say, where a sick and elderly person makes a last-minute new will leaving everything to the caretaker (see 14.K.4.)), but it can also be a basis for attacking a contract. To claim undue influence in this context, one must show that one party to the contract had some particular weakness that could be exploited (e.g. intellectual limitations, a tendency to drunkenness, a pathologically trusting nature), and that another party had a special relationship with the first that made it easier to exploit that weakness.

If one party enters into a contract based on the other party's lies about or concealment of something that could reasonably have changed the first party's mind, that fraud or concealment may make the contract unenforceable. The rules can get complicated, and are more likely to vary from state to state, where concealment/nondisclosure is the issue.

Even if no one intentionally lied or hid the facts, if the parties were both mistaken about some important fact, or were talking past each other and didn't have the same understanding about what the contract was about, the contract may be unenforceable based on "mistake." If both parties were confused, it's "mutual mistake"; otherwise, "unilateral mistake." (See 30.C. for an example of mistake, probably unilateral mistake, and an appropriate remedy.)

A contract may be unenforceable because, for reasons not under a party's control or not within that party's contractually assumed risk, it becomes impossible (or a great deal more difficult and/or expensive) to perform. A contract between a theater and a magician for a series of performances would become impossible if the magician were *actually* to disappear. . . . However, if the contract included some provision for the magician's death or incapacity, it would remain enforceable. A contract to sell a mansion would be impossible to perform if a massive earthquake struck the location and the mansion slid into a crevasse — unless the contract dealt with who would owe what in the event of interference by natural disaster.

A contract for something basically innocuous, like a loan or the sale of goods, can be so incredibly one-sided as to be "unconscionable." Unconscionable provisions are often found in "contracts of adhesion": contracts full of legal boilerplate, presented on a take-it-or-leave-it basis by big businesses to everyday consumers. Contracts of adhesion are not themselves unconscionable or against public policy, but their contents may be unconscionable. The likely disparity in bargaining power between the parties is a contributing factor. Hiding disadvantageous terms in boilerplate makes them more likely to be unconscionable. Examples: hidden fees that greatly increase the price; disclaimers of warranties (that is, language eliminating various remedies state or federal law would otherwise provide for shoddy products or services — see 14.C.9., below); language applying the terms of the current contract to a significantly different previous contract between the parties.

9. The Catch-All Covenant and Implied Warranties

There's something called an "implied covenant of good faith and fair dealing" (not always used with "implied" attached). States vary quite a bit as to which contracts include it. Where this implied covenant does exist, it's a sort of catch-all, meant to foil a party's attempt to slither between the explicit terms of the contract, or to rely on technicalities to deprive the other(s) of what they reasonably expected to get out of the arrangement. You'll need to check how far your state is willing to go in this direction.

Indiana, for example, recognizes this implied contract term (at the moment, anyway) in employment and insurance contracts only. On the other hand, a few states (e.g. Nevada) even allow tort, as opposed to contract, lawsuits based on this idea if the parties have a fiduciary relationship (see 14.P.).

Contracts for the sale of consumer products generally come with an "implied warranty of merchantability." This implied warranty comes from the U.C.C. (see 14.B.1.). It adds to such contracts a set of promises, implied by operation of law. These promises include that the goods are of "fair average quality" for goods described as in the contract, and that they are fit for the ordinary purposes for which people use such goods. "Fit" means that they can be used, safely and without any significant alteration, for such ordinary purposes, whether those purposes are consumption (food products), construction (nails, ladders, boards, etc.), application to the skin (cosmetics), or whatever.

Other parts of the implied warranty of merchantability are tied to the particular contract. The goods must, for example, be "adequately" contained, packaged, and labeled if the contract requires that they be in containers, packaged, or labeled. The goods may also have to meet any applicable industry standards.

This set of implied warranties, like implied warranties in general (though states can make exceptions), may be waived by acceptance of an "as is" contract, or by sufficiently conspicuous language in a contract saying that no implied warranties apply. Also, if the buyer has inspected the goods as thoroughly as the buyer wished to inspect them, or has been given and rejected the opportunity for such an inspection, the buyer can't make any claim based on the implied warranty if that inspection would have revealed the defect.

Some, but not as many, states have also adopted the U.C.C.'s "implied warranty of fitness for a particular purpose." This applies when the seller has reason to know for what purpose the buyer is buying the goods, and that the buyer is relying on the seller to provide goods that will serve that purpose. If this warranty exists under the state's laws, then the goods had better be suitable for the intended purpose, or the buyer has a claim for breach of contract.

10. Third Party Beneficiaries

In some circumstances, a contract may be enforced by a third party. If the point of the contract, some part of the consideration, was to benefit that third party, the "third party beneficiary" has an enforceable legal claim on the promised performance. The benefit must have been part of the intent behind the contract, and the beneficiary must be identified, either by name or as a member of a defined class. Life insurance contracts are a common example.

11. Bailment

One particular subspecies of contract is the arrangement between a "bailor" and "bailee" (noun: bailment). Any time you surrender some item of property temporarily, with the reasonable expectation of getting it back later, you've got a bailment going on. Examples include checking your coat at the opera, the arrangement made when you park your car in a parking garage, and renting a storage unit. The one leaving personal property with the other is the bailor; the one accepting temporary custody of the property is the bailee.

Legal authorities differ on the extent to which bailments are contracts, or are like other contracts. Bailments are usually classified as for the benefit of the bailor, the benefit of the bailee, or the mutual benefit of both. A restaurant that provides free parking is setting up a bailment for the benefit of you as bailor, while a library loaning you a book counts as a bailment for the benefit of you as bailee. On the other hand, some authorities state that a bailment must include not only delivery of and acceptance of the property, but consideration, as in other types of contracts. Even the "benefit" categories are fuzzier than they look. If the restaurant provides "free" parking to its customers, it also benefits, by getting the patronage of those who will only go to restaurants that make parking convenient. Even the library is being allowed to serve its designated purpose: if no one came to borrow books, it's likely the library would lose its funding after not too long.

Those categories do count, however, when it comes to the duty the bailee has to the bailor. If the bailment is mainly for the bailor's benefit (like the coat check or free parking), the bailee is only required to avoid gross negligence or bad faith. If the bailment is more or less equally for mutual benefit, then we're in standard negligence territory, with the bailor required to exercise reasonable care in looking after the property. If the bailment is for the bailee's benefit, like the library lending you a book, you owe a duty of "extraordinary" care, something close to strict liability: lose or damage the book, and you may have to replace it even if the damage largely resulted from some unpredictable event.

One can imagine disagreement over which category of bailment was involved and hence which standard of care applied. If a movie star borrows a diamond bracelet to wear on the red carpet, and the entire glittering assemblage is taken captive by a band of robbers, is the actress responsible for the unforeseeable loss? Did the substantial publicity the jewelry designer expected to gain from the loan render the bailment one for mutual benefit?

D. Property, or What is Real

What is real? No, strike that. (That's something lawyers say when they're speaking in court, on the record, and change their minds about what they should be saying.) What is real property?

"Real property" is land plus "fixtures," which means stuff built on the land that isn't going anywhere in a hurry. All other property is "personal property." The boundary between the two may not always be clear. A house is real property, but what about a mobile home? or one of those houses that someone puts on a *very* big truck and hauls to another location? Different jurisdictions may answer these questions differently, either in general or in particular factual situations.

There's more than one type of ownership of real property. If you own it, completely, every which way, then you own it "in fee simple" or (in some places) "fee simple absolute." However, there are many types of partial ownership.

1. Ways of Partly Owning Real Property

Here are a few forms of partial ownership of real property, which I'll illustrate with a fellow named Joe Doakes as the owner.

- Fee tail: the real property goes to Joe and his direct ("lineal") descendants. If you've read much 17th or 18th century British literature, you may have read about estates being "entailed." That's the same thing. A "fee tail male" meant the property was entailed to male descendants only; the less common "fee tail female" meant only female descendants could benefit.
- Conditional fee simple: Joe owns the property unless some specified event occurs. This condition would appear in the written legal instrument that conveys the property to the owner. For example, Joe's wife's rich uncle might give Joe and his bride a deed to a country cottage as a wedding present, but the deed includes the condition that if the two of them get divorced, the property comes back to the uncle, who may then decide whether it should go to the ex-wife or to some still-married family couple. **Such a condition might easily be forgotten over the years, and then rediscovered and used to create all sorts of difficulties.**
- Life estate: Joe has full use of the property and any income it produces until he dies. After his death, the property goes to some other person or entity, not of Joe's choosing.
- Leasehold: if Joe leases or rents property, he theoretically owns a piece of it, namely the right to keep leasing it per the terms of his lease agreement.

    What's the difference between renting and leasing? The terms are often used interchangeably, but to the extent they're different, rentals usually cover shorter periods and are likely to be automatically renewed unless someone takes action to terminate them. Leases cover a longer, set period, and may or may not have automatic renewal provisions. Often, if a tenant stays on after a lease, it's converted to a month-to-month rental. (See 14.D.9., below.)

- Remainder: Joe owns a remainder interest in the property if he stands to end up with the property after the owner of a life estate dies, or if the owner of a conditional fee simple interest runs afoul of the condition. **The emotional situation could get complicated if Joe has some emotional connection to the owner of the life estate or of the conditional fee simple.**
- Lien: Joe does work on someone else's real property, so he may have a claim on that part of its value that corresponds to the amount owed for the work. By the way, the same goes for some kinds of personal property, like motor vehicles: your auto mechanic may have a lien on your car or truck until they get paid. (See also 3.G. re attorney liens on client property.)
- Easement: if Joe has the right to cross his neighbor's field to get to his own, he has an easement. This concept has so many twists and turns and details that I discuss it in more depth in section 14.D.1.a., below.

It used to be that a deed or a will giving real property to Joe Doakes on-ly gave Joe a life estate. To give him a fee simple absolute, the grant had to specify "Joe Doakes and his heirs." Nowadays, Joe's heirs are assumed to benefit as well, and the grant is only limited to a life estate if it says so ex-plicitly (e.g., "to Joe Doakes for his life").

a. Easements

If a utility company can meddle with a strip of your property in order to keep supplying gas or electricity or phone service, that company has an easement. Like the right to cross a neighbor's field, this is an "affirmative" easement: it lets the holder of the easement take some action. There are also "negative" easements, which let the holder prevent others from acting. For example, if you have the legal right, based on some previous transac-tion or inheritance, to prevent your neighbor from building a structure that blocks your view, you have a negative easement. Another example: if the previous owner of your house was worried that construction next door might undermine the stability of their own property, they might have paid the next-door neighbor for a negative easement preventing the neighbor from expanding a basement in the direction of their property. As explained below, that's probably the kind of easement that would benefit you as the purchaser of the property, and would also bind subsequent purchasers of the neighbor's property.

More terminology: the one who benefits from an easement is called the "dominant tenant" (really). Any property that's worth more, or easier to use, because of the easement is the "dominant estate." The party and property on the other end of the deal are called the submissive — no, sorry, the servient tenant and estate.

Even more terminology, related to the preceding: "appurtenant easements" versus "easements in gross." Appurtenant easements are the ones that benefit a piece of land rather than just an individual. If the land is transferred, it'll be assumed that an appurtenant easement is transferred along with the land unless the transfer document (the deed or will) says otherwise. An easement in gross is for the benefit of a particular person, whether or not that person continues to own any particular piece of land. There's still a servient estate, but no dominant estate to match.

Example: Old T. Imer owns land that includes a pond. There's a path to the pond from the nearest public road, running through Imer's land. If all the local families have an easement to use that path in order to swim in the pond, the locals have appurtenant easements, and any new locals will get to go swimming as well. (This sort of appurtenant easement, for the benefit of many people based on where they live, is also called a "public easement.") If no one gets to use the pond except Imer, but Sweet B. Jane's mother is buried next to the pond and she's allowed to use the path to pay her respects, she has an easement in gross. Easements giving someone to right to hunt and fish on property are usually treated as easements in gross.

What if the ground cover is hardy enough that from season to season, you can't tell exactly where the path used to be? Then there'd be a "floating easement," letting the locals get across in some reasonable way that doesn't cause any more trouble than the original route.

Some states may require that an appurtenant easement be necessary for the enjoyment of the dominant estate: for example, where the only driveway to a house originates on or crosses someone else's property.

You can't sell an easement in gross, the kind that's just for your use, unless the owner of the servient estate (the property you're skipping across, or whatever) agrees, or unless the easement is for a commercial purpose. But if the owner of the servient estate sells their property, you get to keep right on skipping: the easement in gross survives that transfer. That's true for appurtenant easements as well: in the pond example, the locals get to keep using the path to the pond even if Old T. Imer sells to Young S. Quirt.

Public easements, like the one to cross Imer's land to the pond, are an example of tenancy in common (see 14.D.2., just below).

This troop of locals following their tradition probably acquired their claim by what's called adverse possession (see 14.D.10.).

---

2. Ways of Sharing Ownership of Real Property

More than one person can own a piece of real property (or any lesser right in that property). There are three basic types of ownership of any real property interest. Some of these may also show up in ownership of personal property.

- Tenancy in common: two or more people or entities own the property together, and either one may transfer their interest to anyone else. If any of the tenants in common get tired of the arrangement, they can go to court and get the court to partition (divide) the property. It's presumed that all the tenants have the same right to possess the property, but this can be changed by the terms of the property grant.

- Joint tenancy: when two or more people (actual humans, not corporations and such) own property in this manner, the death of one passes their interest to the other(s). Each has a "right of survivorship" in the property. Any of the joint tenants may sell or give away that right — but that action turns the joint ownership into a tenancy in common, and no one has a right of survivorship any longer.

  At common law, one had to prove four "unities" to show that property was held in joint tenancy: time, title, interest, and possession. In other words, the joint tenants had to have acquired their interests at the same time and through the same instrument (say, a deed or a will); they all had to have the same amount of ownership; and they all had to be entitled to full possession of the property. Many states still follow these rules, at least where land is involved. If these four "unities" exist, the property will probably be treated as a joint tenancy, even if nothing specifically labels it as such.

- Tenancy by the entirety (or entireties): basically a joint tenancy for a married couple. This is an option a married couple can decline, although state law may presume that when spouses acquire property together, they acquire it this way. Given the nature of this tenancy, neither party may sell or give their interest to anyone else without the other's consent. If the couple divorces or the marriage is annulled, the court handling the dissolution or the annulment will decide what happens to the property.

When someone talks about a "deed" to property, without any qualifier, they're probably talking about what's sometimes called a "grant deed." (Just to confuse us, some people will describe a quitclaim deed (see below) as a grant deed.) A grant deed describes what interest is being transferred, and guarantees (a) that it hasn't been sold to anyone else, and (b) that the buyer has been told about any encumbrances (mortgages, liens, easements, etc.) on the property. Both the grantor, the one transferring the property, and the grantee, the one receiving it, sign the deed in the presence of a notary public or similar official. A "warranty deed," often used in mortgages, adds the seller's commitment to defend the purchaser's title against anyone showing up later and claiming rights to the property.

If you give someone an instrument saying, "Whatever interest I own in this property, if I own any, is now yours," without guaranteeing or describing any particular ownership interest, that's a "quitclaim deed." These are often used in divorces, or conversely, for giving a new spouse title to property. It's quicker than checking out all the possible claims to the property, so it's used when speed is useful, and also when the less cooperation someone needs from a former owner (e.g. an about-to-be-former spouse), the better.

A "beneficiary deed" is a future transfer of property to one or more beneficiaries, and takes effect only when the grantor dies. This isn't anything to count on, as the grantor may take it back later, or sell the property to someone else.

If property is sold for nonpayment of real estate taxes, the purchaser usually gets a "tax deed."

A deed can be used to record a "life estate" in property. As already noted (14.D.1., above), this is the right to use the property during the grantee's lifetime. The grantee can't bequeath it (see 14.K.5.) or transfer any rights that would outlast the grantee.

A "deed of trust" is used in some states as part of the process of mortgaging property. The borrower transfers title to a third party, a trustee, who holds it until the mortgage is paid off and then transfers it back. If the borrower defaults on the underlying loan, the trustee may sell the property and pay the lender from the proceeds, returning any amount left over to the borrower. (See also 14.D.6.)

3. Restrictions on the Use of Real Property

Just because someone owns real property doesn't mean the owner may do whatever they want to it or on it. Local zoning ordinances can limit what kind or size of outbuildings may be added, or prevent the owner from subdividing the property (carving it into smaller lots with houses on them). Other ordinances may set up numerous procedural hurdles for major subdivision projects. And then there are "restrictive covenants."

Restrictive covenants may be found lurking in the deed, and bind each successive purchaser of the property. They may be enforced by the other property owners whose deeds include the same covenant.

The usual intent behind restrictive covenants is to maintain property values throughout a neighborhood. The covenant may be negative (e.g., a prohibition against parking cars on the front lawn, or a limitation on how many unrelated people may share a house) or affirmative (a mandate to keep the grass cut or the house painted). **Someone casting off the bonds of conventional employment to run their own business detailing guitars or making driftwood sculptures might run afoul of a restrictive covenant they'd never noticed, one blocking business activities in a residential neighborhood.**

Not so long ago, it was common for blacks or Jews to be kept out of particular neighborhoods by restrictive covenants preventing homeowners from selling to them. In fact, such language is still in some deeds, even though it's no longer enforceable because of civil rights laws. **There are dramatic stories waiting to be told about homeowners attempting to integrate their neighborhoods, and the legal and social opposition they faced.** **But restrictive covenants can be more petty, such as prohibiting holiday decorations outside certain dates — and the battles that result from challenges to such restrictions may be every bit as fierce.**

The courts aren't fond of restrictive covenants in general (i.e., such covenants are "disfavored"), since they limit what people may do with their own property.

If the neighbors have put up with earlier violations of the same covenant, the property owner who finally gets sued can defend against the suit by claiming "acquiescence." Whether that defense succeeds will depend on factors like how often the neighbors let similar matters slide and how similar they were, as well as how close together the defiant owner's house is to the house of whoever's suing.

4. Recording an Interest in Real Property

Rights in property often depend on the right being properly recorded in a county's records office. When two people or entities both have claims to property, the one who records the claim first is likely to prevail, although it can get a good deal more complicated.

There are actually two different land recording setups in the U.S. The one I've started describing, and will go back to describing in a minute, is the most common. However, in certain locales in eleven states, there's an optional alternative known as "land registration" (aka the Torrens title system). With land registration, a court determines that someone has title to land, and then a certificate of title is registered. Essentially, the fighting about who owns what land takes place early on. Now back to how it usually works.

The function of a recording office (typically called something straightforward like County Recorder's Office or Recorder of Deeds) is to give notice of a claim to ownership. Someone thinking of purchasing real property, or lending money against it, can check the files for deeds and other ownership documents to see whether someone else has an earlier claim. The history of the property's ownership, as traceable at the recorder's office, is called the "chain of title." If our old friend Joe Doakes fails to make his ownership part of the chain of title by recording his deed-or-whatever, and someone else shells out money for that property, that purchaser may be able to jump ahead of Joe in terms of first claim on the property. Whether that happens will depend on what variant of the recording system the state uses (see below).

Statutes about recording claims to real property can be "race" statutes, "notice" statutes, or "race/notice" statutes.

With a race statute, whoever records their instrument first has the superior claim. This has enough drawbacks that there aren't many of these statutes still around.

With a notice statute, what counts is whether a subsequent claimant actually knew or had reason to know about an earlier claim. If whoever had the earlier claim recorded it before the second purchase, then that later purchaser could have known by checking the chain of title. The legalese for "shoulda known better" is "constructive notice," and that's enough for the second purchaser to lose. But if neither claim was recorded when the second purchase was made, the second purchaser wins even if the earlier claimant gets to the records office first.

With a race/notice statute, in order to prevail the later purchaser has to have purchased in good faith, with neither actual nor constructive notice of the earlier claim, *and* needs to record first.

If Joe didn't pay for his interest, but received it as a gift or an inheritance, then he can't trump an earlier claim on the property even if that earlier claim wasn't recorded. Similarly, buying stock in a corporation doesn't work like buying an interest in real property the corporation owns: an unrecorded earlier claim can still win out.

Depending on state statute, some types of claims on real estate, like a contractor's lien, don't have to be recorded right away to be effective. Real estate taxes, if unpaid, may let the taxing governmental unit take the property, but the government doesn't have to record a tax lien: we're all supposed to know what can happen when we don't pay real estate taxes.

In bankruptcy (see 14.R.), a debtor's unrecorded transfer of an interest in real property may be treated as void.

Most often, the instrument someone is recording must be witnessed before a notary public (aka "notarized"), but in some places any old witness' signature is enough.

All kinds of deeds, as well as leases (at least long-term ones), mortgages, easements, and court orders affecting ownership of property, may be recorded.

---

5. Actions to Quiet Title

If two people (or other entities) are squabbling over who owns some piece of real property, one of them can bring an action to "quiet title," asking a trial judge to declare that they are the true owner and thus clearing the title of other claims.

An action for quiet title is essentially an action for a "declaratory judgment," but one that comes up enough to have its own name. (Any time a plaintiff asks the court to decide who's right without also doing something else like awarding damages or requiring or prohibiting some conduct, that's an action for a declaratory judgment. See 30.A.)

---

6. Foreclosure

Outside the realm of criminal law and child custody, there are few situations more dramatic than someone losing their home, especially if the property has been in the family for generations, or if, conversely, home ownership has been out of reach for the homeowner's family and has finally been achieved. Any number of financial reverses, including job loss and medical crises, can make it difficult or impossible to keep up with mortgage payments. And well-intentioned government programs meant to encourage home ownership sometimes had the unintended consequence of planting people in homes they couldn't afford to keep paying for.

Most people who "own" real estate don't own it outright, free and clear. Rather, they own it subject to one or more mortgages. Mortgages are security interests in real estate, which means that as part of some loan arrangement, a bank or other entity (or, rarely, an individual) is given what you could call conditional ownership of part of the real estate. If the borrower, aka the "mortgagor," stops paying the mortgage on the agreed terms (amount and schedule), the holder of the mortgage, the "mortgagee," may start the process known as foreclosure. If that process grinds through to its conclusion, the real estate is sold at auction, and the mortgagee gets the money owed on the property; those holding more junior (later in time or in legal priority) security interests in the property, including liens (see 14.D.1.), get the next shares; and the mortgagor gets any money that's left.

If, as is true too often these days, the real estate is "under water" — meaning the property's value has decreased to less than the amount outstanding on the loan — then the mortgagor gets nothing. Sometimes, the mortgagee could still sue the mortgagor for the sum the sale proceeds didn't cover. This is called seeking a "deficiency judgment," and whether it's possible depends on state law and on the terms of the mortgage. A mortgage that doesn't allow the mortgagee to seek a deficiency judgment is called a "non-recourse" mortgage. Quite a few states require mortgages on residential real estate to be non-recourse.

How long the process of foreclosure takes, and to what extent the courts get involved, depends on whether we're talking about "judicial" or "nonjudicial" foreclosure. Some states allow the streamlined nonjudicial foreclosure if the mortgage included a "power of sale" clause authorizing it, or if the parties to the arrangement used a "deed of trust" instead of a mortgage in the first place. A deed of trust designates some trustee as the legal owner of the property, while the buyer gets "equitable" ownership. The deed of trust must be recorded, like other documents showing ownership of real property (14.D.4.). If the buyer pays off the loan, well and good: the trustee is then required to convey legal title to the purchaser, in another recorded document. But if the buyer defaults on the purchase loan, the trustee may foreclose on the property without troubling any court about it. Once the trustee sells the property, the successful bidder gets a document conveying both legal and equitable title, which is recorded in its turn. The proceeds would be handled as in a foreclosure based on a mortgage.

188 • SUBSTANTIVE PRINCIPLES (CIVIL)

Just how much faster is a nonjudicial foreclosure than a judicial foreclosure? That depends on state law. In some states, it's very short indeed, as little as two weeks. In others it's over 100 days.

A judicial foreclosure is a lawsuit, but unless the defendant is in better shape than most to defend against it, it goes relatively quickly. However, it's always worth the debtor's while to examine the paperwork as thoroughly as possible. In recent years, for example, some mortgagors discovered that their mortgages had been bundled and resold to investors, and that somewhere along the line, someone had failed to dot some essential "i"s. That discovery brought quite a few foreclosures to a screeching halt. **You could chronicle this almost-miraculous deliverance from the POV of the debtor rescued from homelessness, though you'll have to research the details.**

In states with particularly clogged courts, such as New York, a judicial foreclosure may typically take years.

One way to halt a foreclosure is to declare Chapter 7 or Chapter 13 bankruptcy (14.R.), though whether that ultimately prevents the loss of the property will depend on the type of bankruptcy, whether the property is the debtor's primary residence, the other debts involved, and a host of other factors.

The mortgage or deed of trust will usually specify how long the creditor must wait for a loan payment before starting the foreclosure process. But the creditor must beware of waiting *too* long: the foreclosure process must begin within the time set by the applicable statute of limitations (see Ch. 11).

Some lenders are willing to negotiate with at least some borrowers to avoid a foreclosure. They might be willing to try a lower payment for some period of time while the borrower tries to regain their economic footing. The federal Department of Housing and Urban Development (HUD) offers free counseling services to try to make this happen. Some state agencies may do the same.

Even after foreclosure has begun, a debtor can get the property back by paying the outstanding debt plus certain costs the lender has incurred. This is called "redemption." In quite a few states, the debtor can even redeem the property within some set time after it's been sold at auction. This is more likely to be possible in a judicial than a nonjudicial foreclosure. The availability of redemption, and how long it stays available, may also depend on how much of the original debt remains unpaid. Sometimes, as in Iowa (per a 2010 source), the creditor can avoid the possibility of redemption by agreeing to a "foreclosure without right of redemption," which lets the borrower delay the sale; or the creditor can cut the one-year post-sale redemption period in half by agreeing not to seek a deficiency judgment.

You could tell the story of a naive borrower who started out not understanding the risk of foreclosure. When they fell behind in their payments, the mortgagee could mislead them into thinking it could obtain a deficiency judgment that would ruin their family, pressuring them to allow the foreclosure without a fight. After the homestead, or the farm, went under the auction hammer and was purchased by a particularly despised enemy, they could find out about the right of redemption. Then you could give them a windfall of some kind and a happy ending, or send them into even more perilous circumstances in search of the money for the payoff. . . .

7. No Trespassing

While "trespass" can be used in various more or less archaic ways (not even including prayers for divine forgiveness), I'll stick to the usage that means coming onto land without permission. This may be a crime (probably a misdemeanor (29.A.2.)) or an intentional tort (14.F.2.a.).

The landowner isn't the only one who can sue for trespass. Anyone with a right to occupy the real property, such as a tenant or someone living with a tenant, may do the same.

Trespass isn't limited to walking/running/driving onto land. Setting an object in motion such that it ends up on the land — for example, launching pumpkins with a catapult to celebrate the harvest season — is also trespass if the owner or resident hasn't expressly or implicitly given permission. (Showing up at the launch site and cheering loudly when a pumpkin splatters on your property would be implicit permission.)

Even someone authorized to come onto the land, like a mail carrier, can commit trespass if they go beyond the authorized errand. If the mail carrier is also a Peeping Tom and looks through the windows on their route, that's trespass.

The trespasser doesn't have to know that they are on forbidden turf; they only have to know that they are doing whatever brought them onto that property. Sleepwalking presumably wouldn't suffice, but absentminded strolling probably would.

With an exception noted below, the landowner can sue for trespass even if the trespasser didn't cause any damage, but given the "American rule" that each party generally pays their own attorney fees (3.E.), this would be an expensive luxury unless one sued in small claims court (22.A.).

Where the trespasser does cause damage, however, the standard is something close to strict liability (14.G.4.). Unlike negligence damages, the trespasser may be on the hook for damages no reasonable person would have foreseen. And in some states, if the trespass meets the definition of "criminal trespass," the plaintiff can collect multiple, such as treble, damages (see 30.B.3.).

Trespass can occur below ground, by tunneling or otherwise disturbing the earth. However, here's the exception I promised you: this sort of trespass does require some sort of damage or interference with the owner-or-tenant's ability to use and enjoy the property.

What if the alleged trespasser also has a right to the property? This question usually arises in the landlord/tenant context, when the landlord shows up and insists on entry over the tenant's protests. This is common enough that many states have some separate legal framework ensuring that the landlord's action won't be analyzed according to the rules usually governing trespass. (See 14.D.9.) Those separate rules will probably apply even if the person in possession is no longer entitled to be there under landlord-tenant law.

What if a passerby sees some dangerous event unfolding, and would have to enter on someone else's property to provide assistance? Fortunately, there's an exception for what would otherwise be trespass when someone acts to protect people from injury or property from damage. (However, if the would-be good Samaritan ends up causing more damage than they prevented, things could get sticky.) If someone in this position is charged with criminal trespass, this could be an occasion to use the "necessity" defense (13.R.).

If what's trespassing is an object or structure rather than a person, that may constitute a "continuing" trespass. The damages might be the cost of removing the object or structure, and repairing any damage done by either the object or structure or its removal. If that's impractical, damages might be based on how much a structure's presence diminishes the value of the property.

What if the trespasser gets hurt in mid-trespass?

Landowners and tenants don't have the same duty to keep the property safe for trespassers as they do for "invitees"; but if they know that people habitually tromp through, they have the duty either to keep the trespassers out or to exercise reasonable care to make the property safe for those who show up. (For more about invitees, and about duties of reasonable care, see 14.G.) If there's an "attractive nuisance," some feature likely to lure children, onto the property, then there's a duty to take reasonable precautions to prevent that harm. ("Attractive nuisances" should be distinguished from the "nuisances" discussed in 14.D.8., just below.) For example, a swimming pool otherwise accessible to a moderately determined child should have a fence around it sufficient to keep most children out.

What's considered an attractive nuisance may vary from state to state. Ponds, unlike constructed swimming pools, are generally not so considered, and the same usually goes for a man-made pool made to look like a natural feature of the land. One of the earliest setups found to be an attractive nuisance was a railroad turntable, which children treated as a type of playground equipment, and which the court found "irresistible." Construction sites have gone in and out of the "attractive nuisance" category: at one time they were protected by statute in many states, but they're now more likely to be assessed on a case-by-case basis. Discarded refrigerators count as attractive nuisances — and many have proved deadly, though modern rules require they be (theoretically) capable of being opened from the inside, and local ordinances usually require the doors to be removed before disposal.

Holes in the ground or near the ground, such as tunnels, wells, or holding tanks, are sometimes considered attractive nuisances, especially if there's some construction or debris nearby that makes it easier for a child to get into them.

Results have varied as to whether parked cars can be attractive nuisances. Most often, they aren't so treated, perhaps because there are so very many of them everywhere, and a contrary ruling would seriously undercut the notion that one needn't spend a great deal of time, attention, or expense on preventing harm to trespassers. Similarly, neither a farmer's livestock nor the fence needed to keep animals from straying is likely to be deemed an attractive nuisance. On the other hand, farm machinery left overly accessible just might.

What about actual play equipment? If it's accessible to children younger than those for whom it's designed, it may well fit the bill.

The rules discussed above concern unintended harm to trespassers. Premeditated harm, as in setting traps for trespassers, is a different story. Any trap that constitutes deadly force is a definite no-no. If the trap would inflict less damage, there may still be a statute or ordinance prohibiting it. If not, the landowner had better be very sure how much damage it can do — and even more careful to prevent guests or invitees from stumbling across it.

8. The Common Enemy and Other Nuisances

The people we're closest to are sometimes the ones we fight with most fiercely. And I'm not (this time) talking about family: I mean those in geographical proximity. That is, neighbors.

There are several legal battlegrounds on which neighbors face each other. I mentioned one, enforcement of restrictive covenants, a bit earlier. Another involves the concept of "nuisance," and in particular, "private nuisance."

A nuisance, legally speaking, is something a property owner does that bothers those nearby without the property owner actually coming onto anyone else's property or physically removing anything from that property. A "public nuisance" is one with a broad enough reach that the government gets involved to protect the general public. The effects of a "private nuisance" are felt closer to the source.

What sort of effects? The nuisance can be almost anything that affects the senses (or goes beyond them to actual bodily functioning): loud noises, nasty smells, bright lights at night, clouds of smoke, gaseous clouds . . . .

To be actionable (bad enough that the neighbor can sue), the nuisance has to be substantial, and it has to be ongoing. (While some authorities say "continuous," I'm fairly confident that recurring noises/smells/etc., with no end in site to the recurrence, will suffice.)

The usual remedy for a nuisance: injunctive relief (see 30.A.). If the plaintiff wins, the defendant is ordered to stop doing whatever's preventing the plaintiff from enjoying life on their property

Context matters. Noise that would count as a nuisance in a quiet semi-rural neighborhood may not be a nuisance in the middle of a downtown city block. Smells that a court would deem a nuisance near a restaurant may be viewed as just part of the landscape in farm country. If you decide to build your mansion downwind of a hog farm, you probably — although people keep trying — don't get to shut down the farm because of the stench. This is called the "moving to the nuisance" rule.

One fairly important indicator of context: zoning. If the property is zoned for what the landowner is doing on it, and they aren't doing it in an unusually obnoxious fashion, they probably won't be enjoined from continuing to do it.

One frequently fought battle between neighbors involves water. Mr. Dry puts in a new driveway or otherwise alters the topography of his property, and now Mr. Wet has a lake in his front yard.

Mr. Wet may well be out of luck, at least as far as legal action against Dry is concerned. Water that comes and goes as a result of weather, rather than following a fixed course like a creek, is called "surface water." Surface water is usually treated as a "common enemy" (a somewhat bleak way of looking at nature). A property owner is entitled to deal with it in whatever way is convenient for that owner; and, similarly, if the owner wants to make some otherwise permissible changes in their property, they don't have to revise their plans because those changes might increase the runoff next door. Whether they'll start a generations-long feud by ignoring those effects is another story.

If, due to a feud already established, Mr. Dry deliberately *collects* rainwater and arranges for it to flood Mr. Wet's yard, that's another story, one with "private nuisance" and possibly "intentional infliction of emotional distress" (14.F.8.) in the title.

For other kinds of water issues, see 14.E.

---

9. Landlord-Tenant Law

Take real property law and contracts, stir, season with equitable remedies, and you might have landlord-tenant law.

The landlord's first obligation is to actually deliver possession of the premises to the tenant. If a previous tenant doesn't leave on schedule, it's the landlord's job to get rid of them, via procedures discussed below.

The premises must be delivered in a condition that poses no notable threats to health or safety. Another way of saying this: by making a dwelling available for lease or rental, the landlord gives the place an "implied warranty of habitability." (See 14.C.9. for more on implied warranties.) If that doesn't happen, or if the premises — through no fault of the tenant — come to need some sort of repairs to keep them in that condition, the landlord must take action, or the tenant will be able to move out and stop paying rent on the basis that the tenant has been "constructively evicted."

Once the tenant has moved in, must the landlord respect the tenant's privacy? In most states, statutes or judge-made case law say "yes," at least to some extent. In those states, absent an unexpected emergency, a landlord may not just show up and march in without giving advance notice (sometimes specified by statute, sometimes just "reasonable"), and may only enter for certain purposes. Those purposes typically include inspections, maintenance, repair, or showing the place to prospective future lessees. The lease may also spell out the landlord's right to enter for various purposes and/or the amount of notice needed before doing so.

In general, residential tenants have greater legal protection than commercial tenants, because the latter are dealing with the landlord on a more equal footing and can presumably negotiate lease terms to their liking. Corporate tenants, however, had better make sure that the lease names the corporation rather than any individual as tenant, to keep the individual from being on the hook for the lease. Also, commercial leases may have terms limiting the kind of business the tenant is allowed to conduct. The purpose of such terms could be to protect the landowner from anything from strict liability for hazardous uses (see 14.G.4.), or to avoid violating some other lease that protects the other lessee from local competition. Commercial leases may also have staggered start dates for various obligations, from paying rent to insuring the premises to opening for business. And commercial leases may deal with who is allowed to make what kind of alterations to the building, where a residential lease would seriously limit what the tenant could do (e.g. no nail holes in the walls).

Once upon a time, a tenant was on the hook for the rent even if the landlord didn't keep their part of the bargain, and would have to sue the landlord separately for any relief. These days, the duty to pay rent is generally treated as dependent on the landlord fulfilling their own obligations.

If the tenant leaves before the lease term is up and stops paying rent, and the tenant didn't have a good enough reason (such as constructive eviction) to leave, the tenant will still owe the balance of the agreed lease payments. However, the landlord may have to do their best to mitigate (lessen, alleviate) damages by searching diligently for another tenant.

How can a landlord get rid of a deadbeat or otherwise troublesome tenant?

It used to be acceptable for the landlord to use "self-help," whether that meant tossing possessions into the street or turning off necessary utilities or changing the locks or actually dragging the tenant off the premises. That's generally prohibited by statute nowadays; and if the landlord ignores the statute, the landlord could end up paying the tenant's attorney fees as well as damages. As a result, it can take quite a while to actually evict someone. The landlord must give notice and then go to court. (The necessary court action may have some quaint name like "unlawful detainer.") The statute may give the tenant some set period to fix the problem (start paying rent, stop selling drugs, stop making meth . . .). The eviction process is likely to take more than a month and could drag on for several months.

What constitutes a renewal of the lease? That depends on the language in the lease, and/or on the parties' behavior.

Staying on after the lease ends and continuing to pay rent is called a "holdover." If the lease doesn't specify that renewal must be by express written notice, a holdover would convert the lease into a month-to-month arrangement (unless the lease spells out some other consequence). That's assuming the lease was originally for a longer period.

10. Adverse Possession

Property can change hands in various ways: sale, gift, inheritance. To recap the previous discussion (14.D.2.): ownership of real property is generally shown in a document called a "deed." The deed usually specifies exactly what rights in what property are being transferred, but a "quitclaim deed" says only that whatever rights one party has in the property are being transferred to someone else.

There is, however, another way for real property to change hands, a way brimming with storytelling possibilities.

"Adverse possession" is the rather dry name for a situation rife with dramatic potential: if someone takes over and uses land that doesn't belong to them, blatantly enough and for long enough, they can make it their own.

The technical, legalese term for the person who starts out as a trespasser and ends up the landowner is the "disseisor," but that label has largely fallen out of use, with the more prosaic "adverse possessor" taking its place.

Generally, for adverse possession to take place, the use of the land must be "actual," "open and notorious," "exclusive," "hostile," and "continuous." (The language of real property law tends to have that full-bodied, antique flavor.)

What these mean:

- "Actual": The details may vary from state to state, but in general, the adverse possessor must be making some physical use of the land. Paying real estate taxes on the land, while possibly necessary, wouldn't be sufficient.

- "Open and notorious": One can't just sneak onto the land in the dead of night and clear away all signs of one's use before the morning. People have to be able to see what the adverse possessor is up to.

- "Exclusive": Whatever individual or group is claiming to have acquired the property has to be the only individual or group that's been using the property. The owner one is trying to dispossess definitely can't be using it at the same time.

- "Hostile" (also known, less colorfully, as the "adverse" in "adverse possession"): the rights claimed and acted upon by the claimant must be inconsistent with the original owner's rights. If the owner has given permission for the use, the claimant flunks this test.

- "Continuous": someone can't just show up once in a while and then claim adverse possession. The adverse possessor needs to be there, making use of the land, on a regular basis. Depending on the type of property and its location, "regular" may mean just about every day (for a house in a residential neighborhood) or less often (say, for a house in an area where all the houses are vacation rentals).

In some jurisdictions, if someone's in the process of setting up adverse possession and then voluntarily transfers their interest to someone else, the time the first and second person spend possessing the property may be "tacked" together to reach the amount of time required by statute. The transfer would have to be in writing, and might have to be drafted as if the first person already had title to the land.

What does it take to interrupt "continuous" possession? Well, if the legal owner sues to establish once and for all that it's their goldarn property, and if they pursue the case all the way to a judgment, that'll do it. But if they sue and then drop the suit, that won't.

How long does all this take? The required period varies from state to state, but it's usually at least 10 years.

Why should the law turn squatters into property owners in this way? Well, in a way, adverse possession is a special variant of that old standby, the statute of limitations (see Ch. 11). You don't want some mustachioed villain to be able to ride in waving an old and long-ignored piece of paper, saying that the house Miss Mary has lived in all her life, and taken care of, and expected to die in, was technically never hers. Where would Miss Mary go?

If it's the local public as a whole that adversely possesses an easement, that may be called a public easement (14.D.1.a.) or an "implied dedication." In some states, the amount of time required for adverse possession of a public easement is quite short, as short as one year. In response, property owners may install a gate across some publicly used path and close it for one day a year. Even a public property owner may take such action in order to keep the rest of the public at bay. For example, the University of California at Berkeley is reported to close all streets on campus one day a year in order to retain exclusive control of those streets. That way, the university can construct a building where there used to be a street without claims that it's interfering with a public easement.

E. Water Rights in the East and West

When the United States extended itself to the west, some new rules evolved to deal with the different conditions. For instance, it's a lot drier out there. The western states have a quite different approach to water rights and usage than the moister Midwest and East Coast.

The English approach adopted by the earlier, eastern-er states is called the "riparian water rights doctrine." Under this approach, anyone who owns land near a body of water has the right to make a reasonable use of that water. All such landowners, aka "riparian owners," have equal rights to use the water, with no priority setup and no possibility of losing that right while the riparian ownership continues to exist. There's no equivalent of adverse possession (see 14.D.10.) for riparian rights.

In the western U.S., there's a different setup, called the "appropriation" or "prior appropriation" doctrine. The difference in climate, what with water refusing to fall from the sky in ample and predictable quantities, is only one part of the explanation. The other lies in the history of the region. The first major water uses involved mining and irrigation, neither necessarily located near bodies of water. And much of those activities took place on land still owned by governmental units.

How does the prior appropriation doctrine work? Well, first of all, the state or the general public is deemed the owner of the water. By a process that may include the grants of actual permits, the state parcels out the right to use water based on the purpose for which it'll be used, with "beneficial" uses usually required. The more the public benefits from the water usage, the more water the user has the right to use. Beneficial uses include the early uses already mentioned, mining and irrigation, as well as the provision of drinking water for both humans and farm animals. In the last few years, "beneficial" uses have come to include environmental dust control, as well as the arguably more frivolous, if economically advantageous, production of fake snow.

These rights are treated as property, and may be transferred like other property. But if the user stops using, they may lose those rights.

There's also a role for first-in-line priority. Early on, "first come, first served" was sometimes the only rule. Then it was incorporated into the prior appropriation doctrine as a decisive factor in times when water is scarce. Under those conditions, the users ahead in line, called "senior appropriators," get to satisfy their entire needs before the latecomers, the "junior appropriators," get so much as a drop.

Many years after the prior appropriation doctrine came to govern bodies of water, similar rules came into effect in many states for "groundwater" from other sources such as springs and underground waterways. Even states with riparian systems for surface water may use some form of appropriation system or registration system for groundwater. Which states do what with groundwater gets more complicated than I plan to get into here.

States that use the prior appropriation doctrine for all surface water include (perhaps surprisingly) Alaska, as well as Arizona, Colorado, Hawaii (another surprise), Idaho, Montana, Nevada, New Mexico, South Dakota, Utah, and Wyoming. California, Kansas, Nebraska, North Dakota, Oklahoma, Oregon, South Dakota, Texas, and Washington use it for at least the land closest to bodies of water.

F. Torts: Introduction and Intentional Torts

So what's a tort?

I often define torts by subtraction. A tort is a civil cause of action that isn't about a contract, isn't (at least not primarily) about ownership of real property, doesn't involve the interpretation of a will or trust, and doesn't concern divorce, custody, or other family law issues.

There's another, somewhat counterintuitive aspect to the definition of a tort. Even if you can make a plausible case for describing someone's conduct as tortious, if your damages are limited to what's called "economic loss," your options may be limited as well.

A substantial majority of states in the U.S. follow the economic loss rule. States started to adopt or to reject this rule in the mid-1960s, so if you're reaching further back, you can probably ignore it. The federal courts have followed the economic loss rule in admiralty cases since 1986, but different federal circuits disagree about whether to follow it in other cases.

Among the states that follow this rule, the details vary from state to state, but the basics will be something like the following. Where the lawsuit arises from a defect in a product or a service, and nothing other than that product, or whatever the service covered, is damaged or lost or destroyed, you generally have to pursue contract remedies. Unless some exception applies, only if some *other* property is damaged, etc., or someone is injured may you go after the different and often broader tort remedies (see 30.B.2. and 3.).

What if the defective product is used in another product and makes the second product defective as well? Some courts will draw fine lines here, treating the claim as falling in contract or tort depending on whether the second product is physically "damaged" (tort), or just too flawed to be marketable (contract). Another similarly finicky distinction: if the defective product simply falls apart, that's economic loss, but if its defects cause it to bash itself into some other object, you're back in tort country. It quite likely won't matter that the plaintiff had no stake in the other object, and thus isn't economically harmed by that other object's post-collision condition.

At least one state, Maryland, will (last time I checked) allow a tort recovery for "economic" loss if the product or service was so defective that it *could* have caused death or severe physical injury, even though it didn't actually do so.

As for the usual exceptions to the economic loss rule, they include, among others, legal malpractice (2.O.), breach of duty by a fiduciary (14.P.), and some other situations comparable to the latter. Some states also treat suits against particular kinds of contractors, such as those involved in residential construction or design professionals, as exempt. **What combination of policy arguments and political connections led to each such exception might be worth discovering.**

Rather than simply limiting a plaintiff to contract damages, the application of this rule may prevent the plaintiff from recovering any. This could occur where the contract explicitly limits warranties (guarantees, either stated or implied by law, about the usability or quality of the product or service) or limits the available remedies in some way. And if the parties didn't have a contract in the first place, the would-be plaintiff may be out of luck unless they can make a case for a quantum meruit recovery or for promissory estoppel (14.C.5.).

There are two broad classifications of torts: intentional torts, and negligence. Most tort claims involve negligence — so let's start with intentional torts, and get them out of the way.

Intentional torts, as you'd expect, are torts based on something the actor (or "tortfeasor," if you want to get fancy and Latinate) did on purpose, or in some cases did without giving a damn what happened. Some of these torts are the civil equivalents of various types of crimes.

1. Battery

When a person hits someone, or otherwise touches them in a harmful or offensive way, without permission, that's "battery" in the civil context, though it may (at least in some jurisdictions) be "assault" when it's treated as a crime. There is some controversy as to whether lack of permission/consent is an element of the tort, or whether, on the other hand, consent is an affirmative defense. The vagueness and subjectivity of the term "offensive" may be responsible for this confusion.

"Assault," in the civil context, would be the attempt or threat to commit battery.

2. Conversion and Related Torts and Proceedings

Treating someone else's personal property as if it were one's own — using it without permission, selling it, taking it and refusing to return it, or messing with it in some other way — constitutes the tort of "conversion."

Damages for conversion usually equal the fair market value of the property prior to the conversion. The aggrieved party may, but doesn't have to, accept the property back as part of the process. If the owner of the property just wants the property back, and the person who took it isn't obliging, then traditionally the owner would sue not for conversion but for "detinue," or else bring an action in "replevin." "Detinue" applies when someone was originally entitled to hold onto property, as in a bailment (14.C.11.) and then refused to return it. "Replevin" would be used by someone who's entitled to possess property they don't actually own, through some contractual arrangement with the actual owner, if some unauthorized third party has gotten hold of it.

These days, there are likely to be statutory substitutes for both detinue and replevin, with more boring labels. Typically a plaintiff would claim the right to possess the property and file a bond. The sheriff then seizes the property and returns it to the plaintiff until the court settles the question of who's entitled to hang onto it. Perhaps to discourage malicious or mischievous use of these proceedings, the amount of the bond is usually required to be one and a half or two times the value of the property. The defendant may have the option of filing a "counter replevin" bond that would let them hang onto the property while the court makes up its mind. As with appeal bonds (see 32.I.), and unlike bail bonds (12.A.), these bonds are likely to cost as much, in cash or in some other security, as the amount in question.

a. Trespass to Chattels

Trespass can involve land, aka real property (see 14.D.7.), or "chattels," aka personal property.

"Trespass to chattels" (nice archaic ring to that phrase) is essentially a type of conversion. If Jack interferes, on purpose, with Jill's possession of personal property, and Jill was entitled to possess it, and Jack wasn't, then Jack has trespassed.

3. Defamation (Slander and Libel)

First, the difference between slander and libel: slander is spoken, while libel is written.

What about Facebook posts? If they're written, it's libel. If someone posts a link to an audio or video file, whatever is said out loud in that file could be slanderous. What if someone posts a video that includes text? I'm guessing that text, if defamatory, would be libel rather than slander. An altered photo or video that shows a man getting unduly friendly with a goat would probably be treated as libel. These distinctions may be drawn differently in different jurisdictions.

What difference does it make whether it's slander or libel? That depends on where you are. In some jurisdictions, it's a lot easier to collect damages for libel than for slander. This distinction probably predates our confusing online era, and made sense when a written falsehood was more likely to endure and spread than a spoken one. Some jurisdictions have kept up with the times and treat libel and slander similarly.

One recent lawsuit emerging from our Internet culture: as I write, someone is suing YouTube, the popular video site, for libel. YouTube allegedly removed a video due to what YouTube viewed as an attempt to inflate the number of "clicks" recorded, posting a takedown notice that the video's content had violated YouTube's terms of service. The plaintiff alleges that this notice could lead folks to conclude that the poster did something more nefarious, such as copyright infringement.

What a plaintiff must prove to establish slander or libel depends on the plaintiff. As a matter of First Amendment law (34.A.1), if someone is a "public figure," then before they sue for defamation, they had better be able to prove that the speaker either (a) knew the statement was false or (b) acted with "reckless disregard" of whether it was true or false. The legal tag for this extra element is "actual malice"; but "malice" in the everyday sense, an emotional motivation, is not the point. Knowledge is. (For some discussion of these distinctions, you could check out the movie *Absence of Malice*, starring Paul Newman and Sally Fields.)

As for who's a "public figure":

- Celebrities: check.
- Politicians: check.
- People involved, voluntarily, in some event of substantial public interest, especially if they're deliberately using the media in some way: well, that's less cut-and-dried, but they probably count as public figures. The courts may refer to such people as "limited public figures."

Someone can be a public figure in some contexts and not in others. If you're a character actor whose face is vaguely familiar to millions, your right to sue for defamation may be limited if the statement concerns your career, but if it's about your sexual proclivities, you're not exactly fair game.

It can also matter who the defendant is. Given the First Amendment's guarantee of freedom of the press, there are somewhat different rules for suing newspapers and other media, even when no public figure is involved. The plaintiff may have to prove that the media defendant was negligent; and unless the plaintiff proves the same "actual malice" as in cases involving public figures, the defendant can't be made to pay punitive damages (see 30.B.3.).

One key distinction to be made, though it can be quite complicated to make it, is between "fact" and "opinion." An opinion, even a vehemently negative one, is only defamatory if, in context, it implies the existence of defamatory *facts* that the listener or reader doesn't already know. This kind of statement is sometimes called a "mixed" statement of opinion.

Take this example: "That butcher of a surgeon botched things so badly, I'll never walk without a limp again!" According to some analyses, that's a statement of opinion, and the surgeon can't sue over it, because the under-lying facts — that the surgeon operated on the unhappy patient — are known to the listener. Whether the surgeon is responsible for the patient's limp, this argument runs, is a statement of opinion that doesn't imply the existence of undisclosed facts. (I for one can imagine a contrary argument about implied underlying facts.) On the other hand, here's an easier case of implied facts: "Your fiancée will kill you before the honeymoon's over" suggests some fairly detailed knowledge of previous murders or current plans.

What if the nasty, horrible thing someone says is true? Well, in the U.S., that's an absolute defense. We get to tell unpleasant truths about each other, at least as far as defamation is concerned. Using the truth to interfere with contractual relations (see 14.F.4., just below), or to cause emotional distress on purpose (14.F.8.), may be another matter.

Of course, having a defense may mean having to assert and/or prove that defense, as opposed to being safe if the plaintiff can't prove the oppo-site. (Quick distinction: sometimes, a party has the burden of "going for-ward" with certain evidence, and then the other side has the burden of disproving it; other times, the party that raises a defense has to prove it as well. See 20.D.) Does the plaintiff in a defamation case have to prove that the statement is false? If so, why do courts talk in terms of truth as a "de-fense"? If this is important for your story, you'll need to study up on the law of the particular state.

What if the speaker told a falsehood by mistake, and there's no public figure or matter of great public interest involved, but the speaker had a good reason for making the statement? They may be in luck if the circum-stances mean the statement was "privileged." For example, one can't be sued for slander based on testimony given in court. Courtrooms are handy that way: the judge may say anything they like without fear of slander lia-bility. Similarly, legislators may hurl outrageous accusations at each other without slander liability. Spouses may say whatever horrible thing they like about each other without being sued for it. These are "absolute" privi-leges.

Then there are the more limited "qualified" privileges. When a poten-tial employer asks a past employer about an employee's performance, the past employer may have a qualified privilege to answer those questions (although these days, most aren't willing to risk being entangled in litigation in the first place, and give only minimal information). Citizens testifying before legislative committees, statements warning others of a dangerous situation or condition, and statements made in official government reports are among those protected (somewhat) by qualified privilege. A plaintiff trying to overcome a qualified privilege would need to show that the defendant abused the privilege. This means either that the defendant's statement, in content or context, somehow went beyond the scope of the purpose for which the privilege was recognized in the first place, either in its content or in how widely it was publicized; or that it was motivated primarily by ill will.

Qualified privileges may also apply in a few other tort cases, including suits for intentional infliction of emotional distress (14.F.8.) and malicious prosecution (14.F.10.).

What it takes to collect damages for defamation depends on just what the defendant said. Slander or libel "per se" (as opposed to "per quod") is so likely to be damaging that the plaintiff doesn't have to actually prove damage. Examples of "per se" defamation would include statements about the plaintiff's professional competence (i.e., lack of); claims that the plaintiff had a "loathsome disease"; or accusations of serious criminal conduct. Saying a woman was "morally impure" used to count as defamation per se, but I wouldn't want to bet on that still being the rule in all jurisdictions. **If that rule hasn't been explicitly abandoned by statute or case law where your story is set, it could make for an interesting legal controversy.**

If, instead of saying that a surgeon was blind as a bat and all thumbs (defamation per se), the defendant said the surgeon had dented their car and then refused to pay for body work, that'd be defamation per quod. It's got nothing to do with the surgeon's professional competence, and it doesn't accuse the surgeon of serious criminal conduct. If the surgeon wants to sue, they will have to show that the accusation caused them some actual harm.

4. Interference with Business or Contractual Relations

Interference with a contract and interference with business relations are closely related. Which label applies depends on whether someone's trying to prevent a business relationship from forming, or to bust up one that already exists.

The precise elements may vary from one jurisdiction to another, but a typical statement of the elements for interference with contractual relations would be something like:

(a) a valid contract existed between some third party and the plaintiff;

(b) The defendant knew about this contract;

(c) The defendant intentionally acted to interfere with the contract;

(d) The plaintiff suffered some financial or other harm as a result of the defendant's actions.

The defendant might have persuaded, bribed, or threatened the third party to breach the contract, or might have somehow prevented either party from performing the contract.

Move the action earlier, to before the formation of the contract, and you have interference with business relations. Spreading vicious rumors about a plaintiff, so as to drive people away from the plaintiff's business, would be one approach (and would double as defamation, discussed in 14.F.3. above). Specifically dissuading a third party who was contemplating doing business with the plaintiff would be another.

If the defendant had a legally recognized justification or excuse for saying or doing whatever interfered with the contract or the relationship, then there's no tort liability. In fact, the absence of such a justification or excuse is sometimes an element of the tort, which means the plaintiff is in the difficult position of proving a negative. (The rule may be phrased in terms of having to prove the defendant's "improper purpose.") That would probably involve evidence from which the trier of fact could infer that the plaintiff was motivated either by greed (if the plaintiff could redirect the benefits of the arrangement) or by spite. Not all states follow this approach: some make justification or excuse an affirmative defense. Future clarifications in the Restatement of Torts, a uniform statute (see 14.B.) much consulted by state legislatures and courts, could settle this question.

One could have a lot of fun thinking up creative and/or outrageous ways for feuding ex-friends or ex-spouses to discourage people from shopping at the other's store or using the other's services.

Damages for these torts could include the money the plaintiff would have made out of the contract the defendant sabotaged or prevented. In some cases, punitive damages (see 30.B.3.) may be awarded as well. For a more complete and satisfying revenge, the plaintiff may also be able to get an injunction (see 30.A.) to prevent the defendant from benefiting from the interference — say, from taking a job or performing work of which the plaintiff was deprived.

---

5. Unfair Competition

"Unfair competition" is a category of intentional torts that can overlap various other areas of the law.

State common law or statutes on unfair competition may deal with some practices nowadays covered by federal antitrust statutes (15.A.) or federal trademark law (14.M.2.)

Unfair competition also includes disclosure of a previous employer's confidential information. Sometimes, especially if it involves a customer list, this same conduct could also be a violation of a non-compete agreement (see 14.C.8 and 14.L.4.); or it could constitute the theft of a trade secret (14.M.4.).

Other forms of unfair competition include:

- "Trade libel": the intentional "publication" (i.e. communication) of false factual information about a product or service, resulting in pecuniary (financial) loss to the plaintiff. The defendant has to have known the information was false or been recklessly indifferent to its truth or falsity.
- False advertising, including bait-and-switch advertising.
- Using someone's well-known name or likeness to help sell a product or service without their permission (also sometimes treated as an invasion of the person's "right of publicity," discussed in 14.F.7.).

- "Predatory hiring": hiring away a competitor's key people with inducements that aren't usually available in that industry, like big signing bonuses or salaries well above marketplace normal.

The federal government has taken over some aspects of unfair competition law and given them to the Federal Trade Commission (see 15.A.) to enforce.

6. Fraud

This tort is also called "deceit," which has a nicely personal and archaic ring to it. Basically, a person lies, intending someone to take (or refrain from taking) action based on that lie, and the poor dupe does just that.

As is common with "intentional" torts, it's just as bad if the person acts "recklessly," saying something that's likely to deceive without caring whether it does.

The basic elements of fraud: the defendant (1) made a false statement that (2) they knew to be false, (3) under circumstances where the plaintiff could reasonably believe the defendant knew the facts; and (4) the plaintiff relied on the statement and (5) thereby suffered harm. Some states add the separate idea that the statement was "material," i.e. relevant and important to the plaintiff, but one could say that's already covered in the requirement that the plaintiff's reliance harmed the plaintiff in some way. Some states will also include as an element the defendant's intention that the plaintiff rely on the statement.

What about a promise someone doesn't intend to keep? If the other elements (knowledge that one is lying, plausible setup, success in leading the victim to swallow the lie, and where applicable, intent that the other person rely on the lie) are present, then that's likely to be enough. One possible example: an employer luring someone to take a job with phony promises about salary, responsibilities, etc. With that sort of fraud, as opposed to some more blatant swindle, it could be tricky to prove the defendant's intent to deceive if the defendant covered their tracks well.

"Constructive fraud" isn't really fraud at all, because the defendant doesn't have to know they were lying. As with other uses of the adjective "constructive," the term "constructive fraud" is used when other circumstances make it appropriate, according to the accumulated wisdom of the common law, to treat one thing as if it were another. Constructive fraud substitutes a fiduciary relationship (see 14.P.) for the missing element of deceit. Constructive fraud, then, requires the fiduciary relationship plus a false representation about something that matters to the plaintiff; an intent that the plaintiff rely on that false statement; a plaintiff who actually did rely on it; and harm to the plaintiff. Basically, fiduciaries are required to be especially careful about what they say to those who rely on their judgment, and if they aren't, they can be sued for constructive fraud.

7. Invasion of Privacy

Those of us who are not public figures have some right to privacy. Even for a public figure, there are limits to the degree to which people are allowed to intrude on their life and (a separate issue) publicize its details.

One only has invasion of privacy where there's a reasonable expectation of privacy in the first place. If someone leaves embarrassing information lying about (or, these days, puts it out on social media), then repeating it wouldn't be invading the privacy the person already disdained. Listening outside someone's window and then telling the world what was said, on the other hand, would.

If people gossip about what they overheard, isn't that free speech (34.A.1.)? And if it's true, it isn't defamation, right? Well, freedom of speech, and its practically conjoined twin, freedom of the press, have their limits. Repeating what most people would consider personal and private information, offensive to have spread around, falls outside First Amendment protection unless the context makes it newsworthy. (Jane Nobody's teenage abortion: not newsworthy. Polly Politician's career as a prostitute before she began a crusade for tougher prostitution laws: newsworthy.) And while a true statement isn't defamation, invasion of privacy has different rules.

One area where state laws often differ, and are still evolving, is the extent to which one is permitted to record either one's own conversations with others, or the conversations and interactions of other people with each other, without the other person's or other people's consent. Common examples of such activities include recording phone conversations to see what a possibly-errant spouse is up to and using "nanny cams" to check up on those in charge of one's children. One is more likely to be liable for invasion of privacy if one isn't a party to the conversation or present on the scene — but even if one is recording one's own plus someone else's activity, one might be held to have invaded the other person's privacy. Whether it's worth that legal risk, where it exists, will depend on the importance of what one could discover.

"False light" invasion of privacy comes closer to, but is still different from, defamation. Say a newspaper publishes what would be an innocuous photograph near an unrelated and shocking headline, and the layout could lead people to think the headline refers to the person in the photograph. That could make the newspaper liable for a "false light" tort, if the judge or jury thinks the layout was done recklessly.

If someone uses a person's name or picture in an advertisement without permission, they've "appropriated" the name or the "likeness." That can be a tort within this general category, especially if the one doing the appropriating has made money by doing so, or is likely to. Some states treat this as an invasion of privacy, while others use the related concept of a "right of publicity," discussed further below.

Photographers who take photos of those who aren't celebrities, politicians, et cetera are well advised to have the subjects sign model releases. These releases, if written carefully enough, allow the photographer or any agent of the photographer to publish the image. Without a solid model release, doing so might be an actionable invasion of privacy and/or a violation of the right of publicity — although if the use is "editorial," it could be neither. Editorial usage of a photo would be certain uses in a newspaper or magazine story, such as a story about the location where the photo was taken. The less prominent the person's image is in the photo, the less likely such a usage will cause problems. (Model releases are typically very broad, and while they may include language about "in exchange for fair consideration," there's often little or no actual consideration involved. The more pervasive, lucrative, and/or embarrassing the use of the photograph, the more likely that this sort of release would be found insufficient as a contract. See 14.C.2.)

Where it exists, the right of publicity is the right to exploit one's own "name, image, and likeness" (or other such language) for commercial purposes. "Image" probably means a still photograph or video, where "likeness" would be something painted or drawn. In some jurisdictions, recognizable voices, signatures, and/or characteristic mannerisms or gestures might be protected from unauthorized broadcast or imitation.

Celebrities may be most likely to claim violations of the right of publicity, though the majority of jurisdictions that recognize it at all treat everyone as possessing it. Thus, while the paparazzi might not, as discussed above, be violating a celebrity's privacy by capturing and selling the celebrity's photo, they may be violating this related right.

Violations of the right of publicity may also constitute unfair competition (see 14.F.5.). Some celebrities even hold trademarks (14.M.2.) covering one or more aspects of their identities.

Some states treat the right of publicity as intellectual property that can be inherited or bequeathed (see 14.K.5.). These include Tennessee and California, so the estates of The King, aka Elvis, and of Marilyn Monroe still control and benefit from commercial uses of those deceased stars.

8. Intentional Infliction of Emotional Distress

Intentional infliction of emotional distress is a relative newcomer, given that most torts have a legal history measured in centuries.

If someone threatens to show up on your next birthday and kidnap you, or calls you every Saturday at noon to tell you how worthless you are and how glad they are to have divorced you, what can you sue them for? Eventually there had to be an answer, and here it is.

The elements of the tort:

- The conduct must either be intentional or reckless (meaning that the tormentor didn't care whether they were tormenting the victim or not).
- The conduct must be "extreme" and/or "outrageous." Whether the harassing ex in my example above would meet that test is not entirely clear. But if the calls come at midnight instead of noon, that should do it. This test is more likely to be met when there's a pattern of conduct (as with the ex); when the defendant was in a posi-

tion of power over the plaintiff or had a fiduciary duty (see 14.P.) toward the plaintiff; or (at least in some states) when racial or ethnic epithets were used. Given changing societal norms, we can expect epithets concerning sexuality or gender identity to be added to the list, where they haven't been already.

- The plaintiff must actually suffer severe emotional distress, and it must have been caused by the defendant's conduct. Proving these two points could have its complexities. If the plaintiff was in company when the events occurred, or called for assistance shortly thereafter, then whoever else was present could testify to the plaintiff's reaction. (That testimony could include what the plaintiff said, even though that would be an out-of-court statement: it could be offered as evidence of the speaker's state of mind, and it might also constitute an "excited utterance." See 22.K.) Otherwise, you'd have only the plaintiff's word for how upset or frightened they had been, and why.

Cross-examination on these points could easily lead to the infliction of more distress. Could the plaintiff subsequently sue opposing counsel, if the cross arguably went beyond the permissible zeal of an attorney examining an opposing party? I wouldn't bet on it: there are privileges that apply to what goes on in a court proceeding. Frustration with that rule could drive the plaintiff to seek payback of a less formal sort . . . .

In general, acting within one's rights isn't intentional infliction of emotional distress, even if it's likely to be very upsetting to someone. For example, landlords get to evict tenants if they follow proper procedures (see 14.D.9.), even if the tenants have nowhere to go. But if the landlord makes a point of gloating, describing all the terrible things that'll happen to the tenant once they're living on the street, that's probably enough (if the homeless former tenant can find a lawyer to handle the lawsuit). See also the discussion of "qualified privilege" as a defense to defamation (14.F.3.).

One use sometimes made of this tort: to force bill collectors to back off (though the federal government and some states also have laws limiting bill collection behavior).

Naturally, people have tried to push the boundaries of this tort and sue for *negligent* infliction of emotional distress. The drawbacks of such a tort are obvious: we could all end up suing each other for hurt feelings. Courts have therefore drawn the line and held it, except for one special circumstance. If a party's negligence (for example, in the operation of a vehicle) causes serious physical injury or death, and a member of the victim's immediate family witnesses that event, the family member may be able to sue. (So far, injuries to or deaths of pets don't cut it, **but your near-future story could break some new ground there.**) The plaintiff formerly had to prove that they had suffered some physical impact, however incidental or slight, and some jurisdictions still have this requirement, but others have abandoned it.

9. Conspiracy in Tort

The notion of conspiracy, more familiar in criminal law (13.Q.), also crops up in torts. It's not often a separate cause of action, but it can net the plaintiff additional defendants to add.

One key distinction between the criminal and civil versions involves intent. While ignorance of the law is generally no excuse in criminal prosecutions (13.S.), conspiracy to commit a tort requires awareness that the goal of the conspiracy is to commit a tortious and potentially harmful act.

As with criminal conspiracy, this civil version requires agreement on the plan, as well as an "overt act" aimed at achieving it by one or more of the conspirators.

10. Malicious Prosecution and Abuse of Process

Let's say Harry Hatfield decides to use the judicial system to make Maggie McCoy's life miserable. Whether he sues her, persuades someone else to sue her, or talks a prosecutor into charging her with a crime, Ms. McCoy has a tort tailor-made for taking revenge if she emerges triumphant. It's called malicious prosecution.

Malicious prosecution requires the plaintiff to prove (a) that the now-defendant (the S.O.B.) was responsible for the plaintiff's legal troubles; (b) that the ruling or verdict was in the plaintiff's favor; (c) that the defendant lacked any reasonable grounds, or (per some formulations) lacked "probable cause," to believe the lawsuit or prosecution was justified; and (d) that the defendant acted with "malice."

For more on "probable cause" in other contexts, see "probable cause" for conducting a search or making an arrest (Ch. 12 and 34.B.), and the "probable cause" a judge may find at a preliminary hearing (19.A.). As for what puts the "malice" in a "malicious prosecution": while actual hostility or ill will would qualify, it isn't essential. The plaintiff could satisfy this requirement by showing that the defendant intended to use the legal system to gain some advantage or satisfaction at the plaintiff's expense. That is, the advantage or satisfaction must have been something more than what any successful plaintiff in a civil case, or any victim of a crime for which the perpetrator was convicted, would experience.

Caveat: at least in some jurisdictions, the person whose actions give rise to a criminal prosecution isn't liable for malicious prosecution if the prosecutor independently investigated and decided it was worth bringing charges. See also the defense of "qualified privilege" (discussed re defamation in 14.F.3.).

Unlike malicious prosecution, abuse of process doesn't require that some earlier case end in favor of the party who wants to invoke it. Abuse of process can involve initiating a lawsuit, or it can refer to some process within a lawsuit, such as discovery (see 10.A.). Otherwise, it's quite similar to malicious prosecution: the plaintiff will need to prove that the defendant wasn't justified in taking the action in question and had some improper purpose for doing so.

Both these torts are hard to prove: how do you prove someone's purpose? **Of course, some malicious people like to brag about how they've put the screws to people they hate, and if the plaintiff finds those who heard such boasts and persuades them to testify, the bully who tried to use the court system as a weapon may get their just desserts.** On the other hand, **someone with a righteous case who got out-spent and out-lawyered, and lost a case as a result, could then discover that the victor wasn't content with one victory and was suing for malicious prosecution in the hope of completing the ruination of the pipsqueak who dared to seek justice. Or you could start with the latter situation, only to have the bully's big mouth thwart them at the last.**

G. Negligence and Related Tort Concepts

Negligence is biiiig business for lawyers. Every slip-and-fall case against a supermarket: negligence. Every auto accident case: negligence again.

Negligence, in a nutshell, is unreasonable carelessness that causes someone foreseeable harm.

Well, that's skipping a step. Person (or Company) A can't be liable for negligence toward Person B unless A owed B some "duty of care."

This concept springs from the relationship or lack of relationship between the parties. A store has a duty of care toward its customers, a school toward its students, a guardian toward their ward, a trustee toward beneficiaries. Drivers have a duty of reasonable care toward others using the roadways. A duty can also arise from a statute, such as federal statutes or regulations laying out safety precautions employers must take in the workplace. At least some states hold that natural gas companies have a duty of reasonable care as to how they distribute gas, because it's a "dangerous instrumentality." This duty includes the more specific duty to warn customers, and anyone else they could reasonably expect to encounter the gas they distribute, about its various hazards. (Compare this with the more extreme approach of "strict liability," discussed in subsection 14.G.4. below.)

"Duty" is a concept that tends to expand or contract or sprout exceptions in order to avoid unjust results. For example, one has a duty of care toward people who come onto one's property (in the "real property," house-and-yard-or-building-and-parking-lot sense) at one's express or implicit invitation. These folks are called "invitees," and they include customers of a business. If the person is allowed onto the property, but is there to serve their own purposes rather than those of the property owner, they are a "licensee." Invitees may be entitled to a higher degree of care for their safety than licensees, although the rules covering the two have converged in at least some jurisdictions. But if the person injured was trespassing, that duty may disappear (see 14.D.7.).

The duty of reasonable care toward invitees is sometimes called "premises liability." It can include the duty to protect invitees from each other.

Let's say a bar keeps serving someone after they are clearly drunk. Then that person attacks another customer. If the injured customer sues, the bar could be liable for negligently continuing to serve the drunken patron. Whether the bartender should have foreseen the violence may depend on the factual details. **Would the attack be less foreseeable if the attacker was wearing a priest's collar?**

A contract can create a duty where none existed before. For example, if a contractor agrees to follow safety regulations, and failure to do so leads to someone's injury, the contractor may be held to have had a duty to that person. That still leaves open the question of whether the failure to follow the regs could have been expected, by a reasonable person, to cause the injury.

A statute can create a duty, for negligence purposes, if it was meant to protect (a) a class of people to which the plaintiff belongs from (b) the sort of harm that actually occurred, and (c) the harm came from the hazard the statute was dealing with.

Generally speaking, no one has a duty to come to the aid of another. But once people do get involved and try to help others, they have a duty to be careful about it. Does that discourage people from trying to help others? Indeed it does. That's why some states have "good Samaritan" statutes that limit the liability of would-be rescuers, at least to some extent.

Back to that definition of negligence as unreasonable carelessness that causes someone foreseeable harm. The technical term for the "causes someone foreseeable harm" part is "proximate cause." (Don't confuse this with "probable cause," discussed in 34.B.) The most famous case illustrating this concept is *Palsgraf vs. Long Island Railroad*, a 1928 New York case that could be summarized as "Rube Goldberg goes to court."

In *Palsgraf*, a gentleman was trying to catch a train. Two helpful railroad employees, one on the train and one on the platform, shoved and hoisted and generally tried to help him get on the train. In the course of this maneuver, the man dropped a small package he was carrying. The package, unbeknownst to the railroad employees, contained fireworks, which hit the track and went kablooey. The shock of the explosion caused a set of scales on the other end of the train platform, many feet away, to topple onto Mrs. Palsgraf, injuring her. She sued the railroad for the actions of its employees (another topic, addressed in 14.Q.). She won, in the trial court and on appeal, until another appeal brought the case to New York's highest appellate court. (This is a good time to note that not all state courts fitting that description are called the whichever-state "Supreme Court." A "Supreme Court" may actually be an intermediate appellate tribunal. That's true in New York, although there are four "appellate divisions" of that intermediate "supreme" court. The highest court in New York is called the "Court of Appeal," a label more commonly for intermediate appellate courts. See how easy it is to get tripped up on the details?)

Back to Mrs. Palsgraf. The majority of the New York Court of Appeal held that the railroad had no duty of care toward Mrs. Palsgraf in relation to the fireworks, and thus no liability for her injuries, because the employees did not know about the fireworks and could not have been expected to foresee the bizarre sequence of events that ended up affecting her. In contrast, if the man trying to board the train had been injured in that attempt, his injury would have been foreseeable.

The ruling in *Palsgraf* was not, in fact, couched in terms of "proximate cause," but it is commonly cited as an example of that principle.

One could have fun inventing other similarly unlikely and complicated ways for some poor soul to be injured, as either the focus of a story about a personal injury lawyer or as background information describing that lawyer's range of cases.

What if some unrelated event, occurring after the defendant's action, contributes to the plaintiff's injury? That's called an "intervening" cause. The key question is whether that subsequent event was sufficiently foreseeable that society should still blame the injury on the defendant's conduct.

What if the negligent party didn't realize that someone who could foreseeably be injured was unexpectedly vulnerable? The negligent driver should have foreseen that someone might be crossing the road; but they couldn't have foreseen that the person in the crosswalk had brittle bone disease. Well, too bad for the driver. This rule is sometimes called the "eggshell skull rule," or for the full-sentence version, "You take your victim as you find them."

Another effect a statute can have, besides creating a duty, is to get the plaintiff past having to show that the defendant failed to act with reasonable care. If the plaintiff shows that the defendant violated a statute passed to protect the public, that's called "negligence per se," and all that's left is to show that the negligence proximately caused the injury.

Situations where more than one person or entity contributed to harm the plaintiff, or where the plaintiff contributed to their own injuries, raise the issue of "contributory negligence" and/or "comparative negligence." "Contributory negligence" is the older term, and in most contexts has been superseded by "comparative negligence." You'll need to check your jurisdiction and your time period to see which would apply.

The idea behind "contributory negligence" was that if the plaintiff's own carelessness contributed to the injury, they didn't deserve a judgment in their favor. That's pretty harsh, and it's on the way to being obsolete, except for (surprise, surprise) where the defendant is a governmental entity. In most states, a plaintiff has to be at least as negligent as the defendant (or all the defendants taken together) before recovery is barred. A few states use a "pure" comparative approach, in which a plaintiff who's found to be 90% negligent can still collect 10% of their damages from the 10% negligent defendant. Any of these approaches require the trier of fact to calculate just how much the various parties were at fault. **You could chronicle a jury's attempts to evaluate a messy situation, rife with human error, and to come up with numbers that somehow represent each party's contribution to the disaster.**

There's a related concept, "assumption of risk," according to which a plaintiff can't collect for injury that they knew might happen and voluntarily risked. This doctrine has fallen somewhat out of favor as "contributory negligence" has yielded to "comparative negligence," which can take such factors into account with arguably better precision.

What about careless kids? Are they held to the same standard of "reasonable" care? Well, that'd hardly be reasonable, would it? A child can be negligent, all other factors being present, if they are more careless than one could expect of a child of similar age, intelligence, and experience. In some states, however, children under some particular age are presumed to be incapable of negligence — or rather, presumed to be at an age when no one can expect anything better of them.

1. Medical Malpractice

Like legal malpractice, medical malpractice used to be very difficult to bring into court, and for similar reasons. (See 2.O.)

The movie *Not As a Stranger*, from 1955, includes an exchange between a brilliant and highly respected doctor and a medical student. The latter says something about how he needn't know everything being taught in some class because only seventy percent of the material would be on the exam. The doctor goes into a rant of sorts about how doctors are the only people who can get away with killing people — so the student had better learn it all, not just seventy percent.

Those were the days (for doctors, if not for patients or their loved ones).

It's not that the idea of suing a doctor for what's now called "medical malpractice" is anything new. The idea goes all the way back to the law of ancient Rome and, in theory, has continued to be around ever since. In practice, however (no pun intended), such lawsuits were rare in the U.S. until the 1960s. The key factor may have been the development of cracks in the metaphorical dam where expert testimony was concerned. Once doctors began to move away from the notion that one Just Didn't testify against a fellow doctor, these lawsuits became much more feasible.

Proving medical malpractice requires proving what the doctor actually did, that the doctor's actions or inactions caused the patient's injury, and how the doctor's conduct differed from the "reasonable standard of care" for doctors in that location and with that specialty. Damages can include resulting medical costs, lost income, lost future earning potential, "pain and suffering," and/or loss of consortium (see 30.B.2.). The judge or jury may have the challenging task of figuring out just what an arm, a leg, an eye, a kidney, et cetera is worth.

Now that doctors get sued for malpractice, they have to pay hefty sums for malpractice insurance. That financial burden has made it harder to find doctors in certain particularly risky specialties, such as obstetrics. Unless a woman prefers to use a midwife anyhow, this could be pretty alarming to discover when already pregnant.

To cope with this problem (or, for the more jaundiced, to tilt the balance away from injured patients back toward prestigious and wealthy doctors), many states place limits on the size of medical malpractice awards, and/or require that medical malpractice claims go first to a special review board staffed with medical professionals. This is supposed to reduce the likelihood of experts-for-hire bamboozling jurors with baseless claims about the effects of this or that medical procedure. Where there's such a board in place, the patient may be required to file a claim with that board within a pretty short period of time.

2. Wrongful Death

Here's a relatively new category of lawsuit which doesn't fit neatly into the negligence-versus-intentional-tort divide.

"Wrongful death" lawsuits as such didn't exist at common law, but states (by court decision or statute) started allowing them in the last century or so. By now, every U.S. state has a statute on the subject.

In some states, only the personal representative of a dead person's estate (14.K.6.) may bring a wrongful death action. Where that's the rule, any damages recovered may become part of the estate, to be handled like any other portion of the estate that wasn't dealt with specifically, or they may go directly to the survivors. Other states let the survivors sue directly. Survivors (also known as "real parties in interest" when it's a personal representative who sues) are those who suffer some sort of legally recognized harm because of the death. They include spouses, children, parents, and in some states "life partners" and/or anyone financially or logistically dependent on the deceased. In at least a few states, someone who thought they were legally married to the deceased can sue where some other "significant other" can't. **Whether the would-be plaintiff or beneficiary of a lawsuit really had such a belief could be an issue.**

Some states will also let siblings or grandparents sue and/or recover damages. That's especially likely in the case of grandparents who were raising a child whose death is at issue. One gut-wrenching distinction between different states: some will and some won't let parents-to-be sue for wrongful death when a fetus is killed.

Some government employees and agencies in some states (or within the federal system) may be immune from wrongful death liability. (See Ch. 16.) When the law doesn't provide that protection, it's not uncommon for the agencies involved in building or maintaining a roadway to be sued for wrongful death after a fatal auto accident. Such accidents also tend to lead to wrongful death actions against automakers, and/or any company involved in the design or manufacturing process for the automobile whose claimed defects contributed to the death. An employer who allowed dangerous conditions to exist at the workplace may also end up a defendant.

When someone's death was in some way caused by either that person or someone else getting drunk, the bar or bartender, or even the hospitable friend, that served the final drink or three can be sued for wrongful death.

The most commonly available damages in a wrongful death suit are "pecuniary" damages: damages to compensate for some financial loss resulting from the person's death. The easiest such losses to determine would be medical and funeral costs. Beyond those, the size of the damage award may depend on predictions about how much the deceased would have earned for the rest of their life. **That's a debate which could dredge up aspects of the person's health, past history, etc., that the family would rather have kept quiet.** Experts may be called by one or both sides on such subjects as how much the deceased's household services were worth in financial terms.

More controversial, especially in the time period when these lawsuits were first allowed: damages for emotional injury. Where allowed, these could include emotional anguish (or the more traditional term "pain and suffering" more often used for physical anguish); loss of protection; loss of affection and nurturing; and loss of "consortium" (see 30.B.2.) for spouses. There are also damages that fall somewhere in the middle, such as loss of a parent's guidance as young people begin to make their way in the larger world.

Most states don't allow the award of punitive damages (see 30.B.3.) in wrongful death suits.

3. Waivers of Liability

You've probably seen them dozens of times, and so have your potential readers. Whether you're renting skis, or your child is taking gymnastics, or your other child is going on a field trip, you're going to be asked to sign a form full of fine-print legalese. The gist of it: no matter what happens, and no matter what basis those events might provide for a lawsuit, you're waiving (giving up) the right to sue.

So do the waivers work? If something horrendous happens, has that signature really prevented you from making the bastards pay?

Not always.

First, let's recall the principles of interpreting contracts. Yes, this form is a contract, or it couldn't bind anyone in the first place. In exchange for handing you the skis or taking Junior to watch cows get milked, whoever tells you to sign the form is asking you to give up some of your legal rights. Now who wrote that form? You certainly didn't. It's the other party to the contract who drafted, or copied, or paid someone to draft that language. That means that if there's anything unclear in that fine print, you should get the benefit of the doubt as to its meaning.

For example, sometimes, even though a parent is signing a form so a child can take part in some activity, the language goes something like this:

"I recognize that this activity may result in serious and even fatal injury, and I release [whichever organization] for any liability, whether or not due to negligence or intentional action by any agent or employee, for any injury, loss or damage I may suffer. . . ."

Who's going to be standing behind that cow, anyhow? It's not the parent that might get kicked. Yet the parent, in this example, isn't explicitly being asked to give up their child's rights, or to waive a claim for injuries to the child. That language may well be interpreted as letting the parent sue on the child's behalf if Bessie gets rough.

Different jurisdictions may read identical language more or less broadly. For example, the Florida Supreme Court recently (in 2015) resolved a conflict between Florida's lower appellate courts and held that a liability waiver at a resort village, applicable to "any and all claims and causes of action of every kind arising from any and all physical or emotional injuries and/or damages which may happen to me/us," insulated the park from negligence liability even though it did not explicitly say as much. The injured party did not, however, raise the claim that a release of negligence liability was unconscionable (see 14.C.8.), an argument some courts might accept. More might do so if the release purported to cover even "gross negligence" or "recklessness."

In its ruling, the Florida Supreme Court asserted that most other states would examine the details of the situation and would at least consider including a negligence claim in the release's scope, even without an explicit reference to negligence. As a justification of sorts, the Court noted that even if the release did refer to negligence, many consumers wouldn't understand it anyway.

4. Strict Liability

Some activities are considered so inherently dangerous that if people engage in them and someone gets hurt, the injured party may recover damages, period. The plaintiff doesn't have to prove the defendant negligent in the usual sense (let alone that the defendant meant any harm). In these situations, the courts impose what's called "strict liability" on the person or company whose actions or omissions caused the harm.

What sort of activities would these be? Here are a few:

- Anything much to do with blowing things up: actual demolition, storing explosives, or transporting explosives. The same goes for handling highly flammable materials. However, this may not apply if the explosive or flammable materials are stored in a remote location where they would normally do no damage, unless they're stored in an unusual and questionable way.

- Keeping wild animals in captivity, except for zookeepers and others required by their job to do so.

- Keeping a dog or other pet that's already proved itself to be vicious. The requirement of such proof is often called the "one free bite" rule. However, some jurisdictions have eliminated it and now impose strict liability for even a first injury caused by a domestic animal.

The notion of strict liability got its start in England in 1868. If your historical fiction is set in the U.S. at or before that time, it shouldn't include strict liability.

Perhaps the most common application of strict liability is the defective manufacture of products. This application of the concept got started in California in 1963.

You might think that a defect in designing a product, or in warning people about how to use it, would be treated the same way as defective manufacture, but in general, you'd be wrong. Maybe design is recognized as inherently more difficult, more creative, harder to predict and control, than manufacturing. As for warnings, what's an adequate warning is partly a matter of predicting how people will interpret it, which can be pretty tricky. There are books and websites that collect what seem like ridiculous warnings that someone's lawyer thought were necessary. Often these warnings are the result of some past litigation.

How to manufacture an existing product, on the other hand, seems pretty cut-and-dried. So if the plaintiff proves that something about the way the product was manufactured caused a defect that in turn caused damage or injury, they probably doesn't have to prove anything else for a finding of strict liability.

H. All in the Family

The most heart-wrenching, draining, bitterly fought civil actions may be family law disputes. That should come as no surprise. Divorce, in particular, combines the loss of a mate with the possible loss of children, home and property. Take people's most deeply rooted drives and needs, mess with several of them all at once — and you have an explosive situation.

1. Marital Time Travel, aka Annulment

Marital time travel!

All right, that's a rather fanciful way of describing annulment. But annulment can have its share of fiction.

While divorce ends an existing marriage, annulment proclaims that whatever the parties thought and no matter how long they lived as husband and wife, they were never legally married to begin with.

A marriage can be annulled if:
- One or both spouses were below the age of consent and didn't have their parents' or guardians' consent.

- One spouse was coerced into marriage or for some reason (temporary or permanent mental incapacity) lacked the capacity to consent.
- One or both spouses were induced to marry based on fraudulent representations, and thus didn't effectively consent.
- The spouses were too closely related to legally marry in the state where the marriage took place.
- One spouse was already married and had not been divorced or widowed. **Here's a twist you could explore: what if one spouse was already married, but fights the annulment action by trying to get the earlier marriage annulled? Since annulment undoes the marriage as if it had never happened . . . .**
- The marriage has never been consummated (the spouses have never had sex with each other).

And in some states, with the potential for a nasty dispute indeed:

- One spouse is impotent (not just on one or two occasions, but as a permanent and probably incurable condition) or persistently refuses to have sex with the other.

What happens to the couple's property if the annulment comes after years of living together? It's not treated the way marital property (see 14.H.2., below) is treated in a divorce. Instead, the court will come as close as it can to restoring the property picture that existed before the marriage. If there are children, someone will end up paying child support, and some sort of spousal support (well, formerly-thought-to-be-spousal support) may be ordered for a while. Given how fiendishly difficult it could be to get this right, the trial court will probably have even more of a free rein in handling the mess than it would in a divorce.

If there are children of the now-voided marriage, they won't be legally treated as illegitimate.

---

2. Marital Property

Even before any disruption of the marriage, there are ways that marital property is different. The main one: tenancy by the entirety (sometimes called tenancy by the entireties), a form of joint ownership of real or personal property that's only available to married couples (see 14.D.2.), and which may have special benefits (including, sometimes, extra protection in bankruptcy (14.R.)). But the context for most discussions of what's "marital property" is impending divorce.

California is a "community property" state. So are quite a few other Western and Southwestern states. (The rest are sometimes called "equitable dissolution" states.) In community property states, any property acquired during marriage, with certain exceptions, is presumed to belong jointly to both spouses. In a divorce, it'll be divided equally unless some good reason is established for a different result. This will be accomplished either by parceling pieces out evenly or by otherwise ensuring that both spouses end up with equal value. "Otherwise" might mean that one spouse has to pay cash to the other, either all at once or at monthly intervals. Such payments are called "equalization" payments or judgments.

The exceptions about what counts as community property typically include property acquired by will or inheritance; property swapped for other property owned before the marriage; property one spouse acquires after a formal legal separation; property the spouses agree won't count as marital property (an agreement that could be part of a prenuptial agreement (see 14.H.3.)); and judgments one spouse obtains against the other spouse.

Even with the exceptions, the notion of "community property" may sound far-reaching. However, there are other states, including ho-hum, stolid, midwestern Indiana, where all the property that either spouse *brings into* the marriage is *also* treated as marital property. The wife's family business, the husband's army pension, the wife's grandpa's collection of spittoons, etc., all go into the "marital pot," also called the marital estate.

However the marital estate is defined, many states other than community property states also presume, as a starting point, that the entire marital estate should be divided equally. However, even if there is such a presumption, the trial court may have the discretion (authority, legal power) to decide otherwise, though it may have to consider certain factors and/or to explain its reasoning in some detail.

Pensions and other accrued retirement plans (see 14.S.) can trigger some of the most intense battles and strongest emotions. The idea of the now-despised spouse siphoning off some large portion of what the worker earned from years of toil can push folks over the edge.

Not only the spouses' assets but their debts are dealt with as part of the marital property division.

In a community property state, debts incurred before the marriage will usually remain the obligation of the party who incurred them, while debts from the marriage are likely to be treated as marital debt. However, if a spouse used some separate source of credit, such as a credit card in their name only, for some expenditure that didn't benefit the marriage, it might not be lumped in with other marital assets and debts.

In some other states, debts a party incurs before the marriage, like assets brought into the marriage, will be part of the marital estate, but who ends up required to pay them may depend on many factors. Important caveat: whatever the divorce court orders as to liability for a debt won't be binding on the creditor. Whatever remedies the creditor has under the contract from which the debt arose will still remain. However, if the creditor goes after one ex-spouse for a debt the other was supposed to assume under the divorce decree, the party who paid the debt can go back to court to seek reimbursement from the one who was supposed to pay it.

3. Prenuptial and Postnuptial Agreements

Prenuptial agreements (a term often shortened to "prenups," with the occasional variant "premarital agreements") are agreements made between prospective spouses, and are meant to nail down a distribution of property in the event of a divorce. The assumption giving rise to a prenup is that if they do get divorced, the couple will prefer their agreed-upon arrangement to the application of the state's usual rules for dividing marital property. It's rather like writing a will for a marriage: the couple is indicating where they want their property to go if the marriage dies. The alternative, no prenup, is the post-marital equivalent of relying on intestacy laws (14.K.1.).

However, while just about everyone accepts the fact that they'll eventually die, the death of a marriage is thankfully far less certain. So some people avoid prenups as suggesting an insufficient faith in or commitment to their future spouse, or even for superstitious reasons.

Courts used to be pretty hostile to prenuptial contracts, but that hostility has faded. Still, if the parties didn't have separate lawyers look the contract over, the court will give it a good hard look on its own, especially if one party was substantially richer and/or more sophisticated than the other.

Prenups are particularly likely to be used in situations like these:

- The couple have children from prior marriages or other liaisons, and want to be sure the property they had before this next marriage will go to those children.
- One or both spouses are coming into the marriage with substantial debts, which one or both of them feel should not end up the responsibility or partial responsibility of the other.
- One of the spouses is much wealthier than the other, and needs reassurance that their intended isn't a gold-digger.

Even without this sort of special reason, a prenup is sometimes thought to reduce the likelihood of a drawn-out battle over property in the event of a divorce. In some cases, it may not work out that way: the two can, after all, battle over the validity of the prenup, and *then* over the property if the prenup is thrown out. But many times, the existence of the prenup will make the idea of a court contest (even) less appealing, because it's less likely to be fruitful.

What if the parties didn't do a prenup, but later wish they had? Perhaps one spouse has separate property and is considering selling it to help buy marital property. Or one of them has a chance to join a partnership, but the partners want to make sure the spouse has no claim on the partnership assets in the event of divorce. Or maybe one of them just inherited a bundle, and is feeling bitter about the possibility that half of it might go to the other if things go sour.

What's left is a somewhat more problematic animal called a postnuptial (or postmarital, or reconciliation) agreement. It can cover the same ground as a prenup. However, courts are less receptive to postnuptial agreements, and scrutinize them more carefully. There are several reasons:

- This reasoning is fortunately obsolete in this country, but a married couple was once viewed as a single legal person, which therefore couldn't contract with itself.
- The spouses are contracting away rights that (in some sense) they already have. Courts will be on the lookout for any sign that a more

dominant spouse pressured the other into the postnuptial agreement while actively contemplating or planning a divorce.

- Some view the availability of postnuptial agreements as encouraging divorce. The notion is that without this way of easing the path to divorce, the couple would just suck it up and stick it out. How the marriage would be affected if the couple instead gave up the advantageous property purchase, or one of them lost out on the chance at a partnership, is apparently not worth considering.

By the way, there's a bit of business involving a prenup in the movie *Intolerable Cruelty* that makes zero sense. "The Massey prenup," drafted by crack divorce attorney Miles Massey, has never been broken. At a certain point in the movie, one lawyer makes a point of trying to get a look at the Massey prenup, and another lawyer objects vehemently. This is absurd: the prenup would be an exhibit in multiple divorce cases, and thus a matter of public record. While it's possible that details of particular prenups would be confidential and therefore "sealed" (see 22.D.), the legal terms of the contract wouldn't be.

4. Divorce: From Fault to No-Fault and Other Wrinkles

Through the 1960s, married couples in the U.S. could only obtain a divorce based on "fault," usually meaning misconduct of one (and only one) of the spouses. The grounds for divorce included adultery; abandonment for some specified period of time; deliberate infliction of physical or emotional pain (often called "cruelty"); and commission of a felony that landed a spouse in prison. Sometimes, the hardly intentional or culpable ground of "impotence" or other inability to have sexual intercourse also sufficed. (See 14.H.1. for the alternative of annulling a marriage under such circumstances.) The more "fault"-like version of this ground was "constructive abandonment," in which one spouse stopped assenting to sexual relations with the other. A sufficiently long separation of residences provided another relatively neutral ground for divorce in at least some states.

Defenses to an action for divorce included the "them too" defense, known as recrimination. Success with this defense resulted in a Pyrrhic victory: the mutually misbehaving couple remained married.

If the blameless spouse decided to forgive and forget, that decision constituted "condonation" and provided another defense to divorce. In some states, this defense would require specific proof of forgiveness, such as the injured spouse's resumption of sexual relations.

In the many cases where both spouses wanted out of the marriage, but neither of the spouses had committed acts necessary for a divorce, it became common for the spouses and their attorneys to put on a fictional performance in court, with most often the wife testifying that the husband had been physically abusive or unfaithful. Sometimes, the couple would arrange for the wife to come home and find the husband with a supposed lover hired for the occasion, but the wife's testimony would still contain some falsehoods as to the context of this "discovery." If the court decided to notice the staged nature of the event, that would constitute "collusion," a defense to divorce, and the couple would have the choice of either staying married or of trying a more convincing performance later on. Or they could bite the proverbial bullet and arrange for one of them actually to commit an action that would justify the divorce. This agreement would constitute "connivance," though once again a court might well decline to act on any suspicions it might have. **Either approach could make for colorful fiction, with anything from a farcical to a tragic tone depending on your preference.**

Since another name for false testimony is "perjury," a crime (see 13.I.), this situation was quite unsatisfactory from a public policy point of view, what with couples often having to choose between perjury and continued marital misery.

In January 1970, the governor of California signed the country's first "no-fault divorce" statute into law. This statute introduced the ground of "irreconcilable differences," and made no-fault divorce available to couples who both desired a divorce as well as spouses who were alone in wishing to end the marriage.

The trend toward no-fault divorce took off from there, with nine states adopting the innovation by 1977, and all but South Dakota and New York offering some form of no-fault divorce by 1983, though some states retained the more traditional form of divorce as an option. New York, the last holdout, accepted no-fault divorce in 2010.

What conditions must still be satisfied for a divorce? For example, must at least one of the parties move out of the marital residence? One sometimes reads about couples who have split up but still share a residence either for economic reasons or to maintain a stable environment for their children. According to a recent California Supreme Court decision, California spouses had better plan for a period of living apart if they want the state to consider them legally separated and grant them a divorce. **You could write about a couple who had planned to divorce while still sharing a residence, possibly a couple who had only reluctantly decided to formalize their relationship in the first place, who consider changing their minds about the divorce when the necessity for a relocation is thrust upon them.**

5. Child Support

The question of child support, paid after, and sometimes during, a divorce by the noncustodial parent (see 14.H.8. below) to the custodial parent, is almost always complicated and can be horrendously so. There will usually be some starting point as to what percentage of the noncustodial parent's income must go toward child support, and what expenses it's supposed to cover. The custodial parent's income will also be a factor. Even when the court doesn't diverge from the standard allotments, it must determine what the parents' income is, and deal with changes in that income or unpredictable income streams. Hostile ex-spouses will be ordered to keep each other up to date on every change in their personal or professional lives that could affect the numbers. When they don't, it's back to court they go.

The more often the children stay overnight with the noncustodial parent, the more deductions get made from what would otherwise be that parent's child support obligation.

One interesting wrinkle: at least in some states, a court can decide that a parent who doesn't earn much money could be earning more, and that they've got no good reason not to earn more. A court could even accuse the parent of deliberately keeping their income low to avoid paying more child support (though this always struck me as a somewhat unlikely cut-off-nose-to-spite-face maneuver). In these situations, a court may be able to "impute" to the parent an income higher than what they're actually earning, and base their child support obligation on that imputed income. **A parent who's using their new freedom to leave a well-paid but suffocating job and pursue their artistic dreams could find themselves having to defend that decision in court.**

6. Spousal Support

Spousal support used to be called alimony in most states, and it used to be commonplace. The prevailing assumption was that only husbands worked outside the home and brought in most of the marital income. Once hubby moved out, wifey was presumably incapable of supporting herself without assistance.

The transition in this country from "fault" to "no fault" divorce (discussed further in 14.H.4., above) had a substantial impact on alimony awards. In the era when all states required wrongdoing by one spouse as a prerequisite for divorce, the amount of alimony might increase according to whether and how much the husband was at fault. Starting in 1969 with California, most states switched to a "no fault" model without that prerequisite.

The latter stages of that change coincided with the entry of more and more middle-class married women into the workplace, in a gradually increasing variety of positions and pay scales.

The result was a de-emphasis on alimony as a replacement for a departing husband's income. Instead, alimony or spousal support, also called spousal maintenance, flowed toward whichever spouse would stand more in need of it after the divorce; and increasingly, such support became temporary, lasting only long enough for a spouse who had done little and/or low-paying work outside the home to prepare for longterm self-support. This sort of award is often called "rehabilitative" maintenance. Rehabilitative maintenance awards last only a few years.

A spouse may still receive longterm support if they have some physical or mental disability that will prevent them from becoming self-supporting in the foreseeable future.

A spousal maintenance award may end before it otherwise would if the recipient remarries, though this is not necessarily automatic.

The amount of any spousal maintenance award will be highly fact-sensitive. Unlike child support, which is often determined according to minutely detailed mathematical formulae based on parental income and custodial arrangements, the trial court tends to have few guidelines to work with.

What about the spouse who works hard to put the other through many years of professional education, only to be served with divorce papers once the lucrative job offers come in? Some states award what they call "reimbursement alimony" in this situation.

---

7. Guardians ad Litem

In any case involving the well-being of a child (such as custody, visitation, adoption, guardianship, or termination of parental rights, all discussed below), the trial court may appoint a neutral third party called a guardian ad litem (GAL for short) to help the judge out. A GAL may be a lawyer or therapist, but isn't always. The GAL's job is to act as a sort of assistant fact-finder, interviewing parties and other people who know the parties, investigating the situation so that the judge is not limited to relying on the evidence the parents or other contestants bring to court. Depending on the circumstances and the local rules and customs, a GAL's involvement with the child and the family may be fairly limited or may stretch on for years.

See also 14.I. re the use of guardians ad litem in adult guardianship proceedings.

---

8. Custody

There are two kinds of custody: "legal custody" and "physical custody." Physical custody is what most people think of when they hear the word "custody." It means where the children will live. Legal custody is about making decisions like where the children will go to school, what their religious training will be, and what doctors they will see when they're ill. It's simplest when the same parent has both kinds of custody.

Once upon a time, the "tender years" doctrine led judges to assume that young children should live with their mothers. (Farther back than that, in merry old England, it was assumed that both wives and children pretty much belonged to the husband/father, and if the wife ran off or the husband kicked her out, the kids stayed with Daddy.) In recent decades, at least theoretically, the parents start off with an equal claim to custody.

When one parent gets legal custody or physical custody or both, that parent has "sole" legal and/or physical custody. However, this doesn't mean that the other parent won't get visitation or (the more contemporary term) "parenting time" with the children. (See 14.H.9., below.)

Even if one parent is making the major decisions about the children's lives, the other parent is not supposed to be shut out. Usually, a parent with sole legal custody must still keep the other parent informed about things like school grades and activities, medical problems, and travel plans.

If the judge thinks the parents can work together well for the children's sake, the judge may award "joint" custody. Joint legal custody means the parents make important decisions about the children together. Joint physical custody means the children live half the time with one parent and half the time with the other. As you might expect, joint custody of either type is the exception rather than the rule — though some politically active fathers, who believe that mothers still have the advantage where custody is concerned, are pushing for a presumption in favor of joint custody.

Whatever the court orders, either parent can go back to court later, arguing that the order didn't work the way the judge intended, or that circumstances have changed and the custody or parenting time arrangements should change as well. Translation: there may be truces, but the war very often continues until the youngest child is a legal adult.

9. Visitation aka Parenting Time

Unless there is some special reason why it shouldn't happen, the "non-custodial" parent will still get to spend quite a bit of time taking care of the children. This is called "visitation" or (more recently) "parenting time." Many states have detailed guidelines about what sort of parenting time the noncustodial parent will get, spelling out different schedules for different ages of the children and for various circumstances (e.g. summer vacations, holidays, birthdays). There may also be different rules depending on how far away the parents live from each other. The guidelines may spell out just when one parent should ask the other parent to take care of the children instead of calling a babysitter.

There may be ways that a custodial parent can prevent the other parent from getting visitation, or get the court to impose limitations such as supervised visitation. It's likely that the parent seeking such restrictions will have the burden of showing that normal parental visitation will pose a danger to the child — though if the noncustodial parent originally agreed to such restrictions, the burden may be on that parent if they challenge the restrictions later. Sometimes a noncustodial parent who isn't allowed actual visitation will be allowed some sort of remote virtual contact such as Skype, and/or letters and/or phone calls. A noncustodial parent who does have normal visitation could also be granted such privileges.

If the custodial parent hasn't quite met the threshold for getting the other parent's physical visitation disallowed, the court may still order such precautions as giving the child a cell phone for contacting the custodial parent and forbidding the noncustodial parent from taking the phone away or exercising any control over it.

One unusual condition with particular dramatic potential: the court might forbid the noncustodial parent even to inform the child that they are the child's mother or father. That's a condition that could be challenged on constitutional grounds. (See 20.B., 34.G., and 34.G.1. for more on fundamental parental rights.)

When parents hate each other too much for the child to go from custodial to noncustodial parent, or vice versa, without some scene that might traumatize or even endanger the child, a government agency, or a private organization developed for the purpose, may be used as a site for one parent to drop off the child and the other to pick up.

10. Non-Parent Visitation

Almost every state has a law about which most parents know nothing unless they find themselves in court, forced to defend the decisions they've made about who gets to spend time with and look after their children.

It's usually grandparents who can sue the custodial parent if the parent cuts off contact between the grandparent and the child, or even just refuses to allow the type or amount of visitation that the grandparent wants.

Most often, only a single (widowed, divorced, never-married) parent can be hit with such a lawsuit, but in a few states, even married parents raising their children with no legal complications are vulnerable.

Theoretically, the trial court must start out by assuming that the parent knows what they are doing and knows what's "in the child's best interests" (i.e., what's best for the child). The U.S. Supreme Court established this principle in 2000 and held that the petitioning grandparent-or-whoever must overcome that presumption. However, the Court didn't say how or by what margin of evidence that presumption should be overcome. As a result, some states set the bar much higher than others for the petitioning grandparent. In states that demand less, especially if the trial judge had been on the bench for a while before the year 2000, the parent is often put in the position of having to prove that this particular grandparent really shouldn't have this particular kind of visitation.

These cases can be every bit as intense, bitter, harrowing, and expensive as custody litigation between parents. All sorts of family secrets may be dredged up. The children may feel caught in the middle and somehow responsible. The funds intended for family vacations, or music lessons, or college, or even the mortgage, go to legal fees instead. Certainly, the parent could give up the battle — but **they may be trying desperately to defend their children against a grandparent who drinks to excess, or refuses to acknowledge their declining physical and mental abilities, or blames the surviving parent for the other parent's death, or abused other children in the family. All the while, the judge may spend the trial looking at cute pics of their own grandchildren.**

Things can get even worse for the parent who agreed to a visitation order and then regrets it, or the parent who resisted such an order and lost. At least one state, California, has a statute criminalizing "deprivation of child custody," which includes court-ordered non-parent visitation.

What about former step-parents? Some states might lump them together with other non-parents, but it appears that most recognize a special interest in allowing step-parent visitation, at least in some cases. According to one source, 23 states have statutes allowing for step-parent visitation, while 18 others have some way of allowing judges to award it.

11. Emancipated Minors

It had to happen sooner or later: there's a way for kids to divorce their parents.

Actually, it's been possible for quite a while, although only about half the states in the U.S. have specific written procedures for it. It isn't called divorce, though, but "emancipation." That's apt enough: emancipation means freedom from parental control. It means the parents are no longer entitled to decide where the child will live, which church the child will attend, or what medical treatment the child will receive. On the other hand, as with other forms of emancipation, it means the child must take responsibility for their own maintenance.

Two traditionally adult activities, marriage and military service, bring about emancipation — once one has o'erleaped any age or parental consent restrictions for those activities. If the minor becomes emancipated first and then wishes to marry while below the usual age of consent, they may still need parental approval. And emancipation doesn't get a minor out of going to school.

The minor will probably need to inform their parents about the petition, or else explain to the court why that would be a really, really bad idea.

The minor will need to show the court that they are capable of financial self-support, and generally able to be self-sufficient without getting into any serious difficulties (or without being more likely to do so than folks over 18).

If parents have consistently failed to provide care and support, emancipation is in some cases an appropriate alternative to shunting the minor into the foster care system.

The process can work in the opposite direction: if a child is both self-sufficient and sufficiently difficult to control, the court may recognize reality and declare that since the parents no longer *can* play a parental role, they no longer must do so. A parent may petition for such an order.

12. "Parental Privilege"

Who gets to hit kids without being charged with a crime? Parents, that's who, though within limits. (Well, maybe other kids, too; but right now I'm talking about parents.)

This is one of those areas where similar vague terms, such as "reasonable force," "reasonable corporal punishment," and "discipline," have changed over time — though not necessarily as much as you suppose. In at least some places, for example, a parent may beat a sufficiently troublesome child (or rather, more likely, teenager) with a belt and assert "parental privilege" as a complete defense to any prosecution.

Which doesn't mean it wouldn't lead to a CHINS proceeding (see 14.H.13., coming right up). **The opportunities for a clash of cultures, perhaps involving a family of immigrants or a family that has moved from the country to the city or vice-versa, are legion.**

13. Children "In Need of Services" and Termination of Parental Rights

When parents are unfit (abusive or neglectful), the government, often a county government, can step in and take the children away, putting them in foster care. If the parents don't straighten up, or don't convince the authorities that they've done so, then the government can take the most drastic action available: permanently ending the parent-child relationship.

Termination of parental rights is the last step in a drawn-out process. An earlier stage involves some agency with a name like Department of Child Services (DCS) or Child Protective Services (CPS) filing papers claiming that a child is something like a Child in Need of Services (CHINS). (Check the names and abbreviations used in the state you're writing about.) If the child is found to be a CHINS, the parent(s) may or may not be offered various "services" like training in parenting techniques, drug abuse rehabilitation, supervision, etc. Children are often taken from the parental home and placed in foster care, which may or may not be a cure worse than the disease.

Those who work in DCS-type agencies often feel that they "can't win for losing." Whatever they do, they're accused either of too aggressively breaking up families, or of too carelessly leaving children in homes where they're abused or neglected.

In any event, if whatever DCS has done to improve the home environment doesn't work or hasn't worked well enough, then DCS will file new papers seeking to terminate the parent's parental rights. Whatever they're required to prove to make this happen, the U.S. Supreme Court has decreed that they'll have to prove it by "clear and convincing evidence" (see 20.B.). However, the deck has often, by this time, been stacked against the parent. The earlier proceedings that culminate in a termination hearing involve lower standards of proof, and the parent may not have been represented by counsel in those earlier proceedings. The witnesses for DCS will be well-known to the judge. During much of this process, the children are already in foster care or otherwise living outside the parental home, and any progress they make toward physical and emotional health may be attributed to that removal. **A parent may be struggling to overcome their past, to reform, to pull their life together, only to find that the personnel on whose testimony or reports the judge relies have refused to adjust their picture of the parent.**

DCS may be required to prove that it has a satisfactory plan for the child's future, but this requirement often has little substance. In Indiana, for example, DCS will be deemed to have such a plan if it hopes the child will be adopted at some point, even though there are no adoptive parents in the offing and no particular reason to expect them to appear.

Also, the procedural setup may actually favor DCS. In Indiana, for example, the Court of Appeals has somehow decided that it should be especially deferential to trial court decisions in termination of parental rights cases, even though the fundamental human rights at issue might dictate the opposite approach. Also in Indiana, termination of parental rights cases are the *only* cases in which a parent who's appealing the termination may not, even under extraordinary circumstances, get an extension of any applicable deadline. **If the parent has hired a solo practitioner to appeal the termination order, with no paralegal or secretary backing them up, and the attorney gets hit by a truck while driving frantically to file their brief on the last possible day, then theoretically, the parent is out of luck. There are constitutional considerations that might lead the appellate court to find a way around this rule.**

If a parent is in prison and is likely to remain there for much of the child's childhood, the odds of termination go up substantially. **A parent wrongfully convicted of a serious crime faces not only the loss of freedom, but the loss of their children as well.**

I haven't seen actual statistics on this, but it's my impression that the vast majority of CHINS and termination cases involve parents with drug addictions and/or convictions. If we ever turn from the "drug war" to more pragmatic approaches to the problem of drug abuse, we may see a welcome decline in these heart-wrenching cases.

By the way, when parents are for any reason not able to care for their own children, but the situation may improve with time, a relative or friend may end up as the child's guardian. Sometimes this is an informal arrangement, but a guardian may also be court-appointed. See 14.I.

14. Adoption

Years ago, I attended a conference where one of the speakers addressed branding. Her practice, as I recall, included both adoptions and helping people start new businesses. When asked, she would say that she practiced "happy law."

And adoption has great potential to bring happiness: a renewal of hope, the beginning of love.

But there's plenty of possibility for dramatic tension — and even, unfortunately, for heartbreak. The latter is most likely to arise from one of three situations: (a) the birth mother changes her mind within the period when that's possible; (b) a father surfaces who wasn't properly informed of the pregnancy; or (c) the child has serious medical or psychological problems that weren't disclosed.

Adoption is a matter for states to control, but most states' statutes derive from the 1994 Uniform Adoption Act. (If your story predates it, dig deeper.) For simplicity, I'll summarize that Act's provisions . . . or rather, a few of them, as the Act is well over a hundred pages long. If this partial summary doesn't cover a desired plot point, you'll need to go to the Act and/or the statutes of the state in question.

One initial note: the scenario many people associate with adoption is not, in fact, the typical one. At the time the Act's introductory language was written, less than one-third of all adoptions in the U.S. involved adults adopting unrelated infants. The rest consisted of stepparent or relative adoptions and adoptions of older children (many of whom had spent years in foster care, with the adoptive parents and/or a string of earlier foster parents).

The Act was designed to put an end to several prior practices that existed in one or another state, including:

- Prohibiting adoptions based solely on such factors as race, ethnicity, marital status, or age. Caveat: if the biological parent has requested an adoptive parent with certain characteristics, including race or ethnicity, that request may be honored, and may even get high priority, second only to the prior adoption of a sibling by the same adoptive parent.
- Concealment of relevant medical or genetic information.
- Failure to notify parents or possible parents that adoption proceedings were occurring.

Not every parent is legally authorized to place a child for adoption. To do so, a parent must have "legal custody," whether or not that parent has "physical custody" (see 14.H.8.). **A would-be adoptive couple, or an agency, could discover too late that the parent who gave the child up for adoption did not have legal custody.**

Adoption creates a legal parent-child relationship indistinguishable from the biological relationship — except where it doesn't. Other state laws may in fact distinguish between biological and adoptive children in such areas as child support and inheritance. Usually, though, biological and adoptive children are in fact treated identically where both child support and inheritance are concerned.

An adoption in another U.S. state is generally treated as if it occurred in the state at issue, an application of the "Full Faith and Credit" clause of the U.S. Constitution (see 34.K.). Whether the same is true for an adoption in another country depends on whether any circumstances exist that would violate the Hague Convention on Intercountry Adoptions. At least, that's the case if the adoption took place after the U.S. signed that treaty, effective 2008. Also, many of the following rules don't apply if the child is a Native American. I'll summarize separately the rules that apply to such children.

Adoptions may be set in motion by the parent(s), or by an agency whom either the parent(s) or the government have authorized. Governmental agencies get involved when the parent's rights have been terminated (see 14.H.13.).

If the adult wishing to adopt a child is married, their spouse must join in any petition to adopt, unless the two are legally separated or the spouse has been declared incompetent.

Except under circumstances I'll get to in a moment, the following people must consent to the adoption:

- The biological mother (or adoptive mother, if the child has already been adopted one or more times).
- The mother's husband.
- A man who used to be her husband, if the two were divorced or officially separated less than 300 days before the child's birth. This includes a man who tried to marry the mother or thought he had married her, even if the marriage was for some reason invalid.
- A man who's been found by a court to be the father, or who's signed an acknowledgment of paternity, if he's *also* financially supported the child as best he can and visited or communicated with the child.
- A man who's taken the child into his home and treated the child as his own before the world at large.

The unifying factor in these provisions: sperm ain't enough. Unless the parents are or were married, only a man likely to be the father who has also acted like a father has the right to block an adoption.

If the parent has already relinquished the child to an agency for adoption, the agency is the one doing the consenting instead of that parent.

If the child is 12 years old or older, the child also must consent, unless a court determines otherwise. **One could have a 12-year-old child trying to convince a judge that the prospective parent was some sort of bad guy, despite a clean report from the evaluator.**

Now for those exceptions. Here's when consent isn't required.

- If someone's parental rights have been terminated by a court (again, see 14.H.13.), their consent or lack of same becomes irrelevant.

- If a parent has been judicially declared incompetent, the Act says their consent isn't required. **This strikes me as a potential legal quagmire, as incompetence may not be permanent — unlike losing one's parental rights to an adoptive parent.**

- If there's a proceeding for adoption, or for terminating a parent's rights, and the parent doesn't show up or file an appearance in the case within the required time, the process can go on without them. However, if the parent later convinces a court that they missed the deadline because of "excusable neglect," the adoption may be undone, and the process would have to start over. **If you want a story full of stomach-clenching complications in the adoption process, this could be one.**

- If the child has a guardian, the court can decide that the guardian's refusal to consent to the adoption is not in the child's best interest, and allow the adoption to proceed anyway.

While a grandparent's consent isn't required, grandparents are supposed to be told about the adoption petition ("given notice") if they're grandparents by way of a deceased parent of the child.

A parent may not consent, in the sense of giving irrevocable, binding consent, to the adoption before the child is born. While this rule applies to both parents, it was probably in greater part a recognition that a woman might not accurately predict how she will feel once she has given birth. In an earlier era, it was not uncommon to prevent the woman from seeing, let alone holding, the baby, so as to minimize the likelihood of this emotional transformation.

Where a man isn't already legally acknowledged as the father, there may be paperwork he can sign before the birth that precludes his being treated as the father for adoption purposes — in which case his consent isn't needed. (Terminology note: I'm using "consent" where the Act uses either "consent" or "relinquishment." The difference: "consent" means approving adoption by a particular adoptive parent. "Relinquishment" means that an agency takes charge and finds the adoptive parent.)

If the parent is still a minor, they are supposed to have access to counseling and to a lawyer's advice. What's more, that lawyer shouldn't be the lawyer who is representing the adoptive parent or the agency. If these rules aren't followed, **you could have a situation where a teenager signs a consent form without meaning to give up the child permanently.**

Before giving consent, the parent must be provided with quite a bit of information, including the meaning and consequences of adoption; the availability of legal and personal counseling; the legal consequences of lying about who the father is; what sort of private medical information the adoptive parents will be getting; and under what circumstances, if any, the child will be informed of the parent's identity. (We'll get to the issue of "open" versus "closed" adoptions shortly.)

Once the child is born and the parent consents to adoption (which may not happen immediately after the birth), there's a period within which the parent may still change their mind. Per the Act, that period is relatively short (though still agonizingly long for the adoptive family): within 192 hours (eight days) of the birth. However, this is one area where states still differ substantially: the parent may have fewer than eight days, or as much as 30 days.

If the biological parent goes to court and shows by "clear and convincing evidence" that their consent was obtained by fraud or duress, they can revoke that consent. Fraud might include, e.g., the assurance that "this is just paperwork to make some tax stuff easier, but really, you're still the mother," or "this is the only way you can get little Sally the medical treatment she needs." In this context, duress can range from literal arm-twisting to threats ("sign that baby over or we'll call Immigration"; "sign or we'll tell the cops where you stash your smack").

If at any point the court finds out that there's a man who may be the father and hasn't received notice of the adoption proceeding, the court is supposed to find out if the man can be identified, located, and notified. If his name or location isn't known, but there's a decent chance that a published or publicly posted notice would attract his information, that notice should be published or posted. I would expect more and more courts to require some sort of use of social media in this quest.

However, if the state has a "putative father registry" which men who might have ended up fathers are supposed to check, then any father who hasn't registered might be out of luck.

Adoptive parents aren't allowed to pay a birth mother a fee for giving up her child. (See also 14.C.8. re unconscionable contracts.) But if something can credibly be called an expense of pregnancy or childbirth, the adoptive parents are allowed to pay for it. Examples: medical bills, hospital bills, prenatal medication, living expenses for a little while before and after the birth, and psychological counseling during a similar period. If the adoptive parents are caught overstepping these bounds, that usually won't keep the court from approving the adoption. There may be statutory penalties of some kind. If those penalties are financial, the adoptive parents might view them as just another related expense.

Even where the biological parents actively choose the adoptive parents and place the child with them, the Act and statutes that follow it (unlike the more common practice before the Act's adoption) require a formal evaluation process administered by some governmental body. Stepparent adoptions are exempt from these requirements, unless a court decides an evaluation is a good idea.

The evaluation process provides the possibility of bureaucratic interference due to personal animosity, a bureaucrat's self-importance, turf battles, etc. As one check on such possibilities, a would-be adoptive parent who's had custody of the child for six of the previous 24 months, or for half of the child's life, can sue an agency that refuses to place the child with them. If the plaintiff establishes by a preponderance of the evidence (see 20.A.) that the child has a substantial emotional tie to them, and that the adoption would be in the child's best interest, the court is supposed to order the adoption.

Evaluations must be made or updated no earlier than (per the Act) 18 months before the child is placed for adoption. **Of course, a great deal can happen in an adult's life in that much time.** Similar concerns could arise if the requirement of a pre-placement evaluation is waived**, as can happen "for good cause shown" or (alternatively) when a parent directly places a child with a relative for adoption. Caveat: I don't mean to suggest that there can't be good cause for having the placement come before the official evaluation. For example, where a foster parent wishes to adopt the child, it would be cruelly absurd to require that the child be removed until the evaluation had taken place. Query: did any state require this sequence of events before the Act came along? If so, **there's a sad story to be told.**

Unless a prospective parent has already been through the evaluation process, the Act forbids them from publicly advertising their wish to adopt.

Evaluations involve personal interviews with and home visits to the prospective adoptive parent, as well as interviews with others who know the parent. **If there are buried resentments between the would-be parent and some "friend" or relative, they could erupt during this process.** One way and another, the evaluator is supposed to come up with a report so extensive and detailed as to impress the average private detective. This includes requiring the prospective parent to have their fingerprints taken.

After collecting all this information, the evaluator has to absorb it and decide whether anything they have learned raises "a specific concern" that allowing the adoption would pose a significant risk of physical or psychological harm to the child. This concern could be based on the needs or vulnerabilities of the particular child, or it could be more general, extending to the subject's suitability to adopt any child.

If the evaluator doesn't approve the adoption, the would-be parent has 90 days to ask a court to review the evaluator's decision. At this point, the burden of proof (by a preponderance of the evidence) is on the one seeking to adopt.

When the adoption is in process before the child is actually born, there are procedures for releasing the child to the adoptive parents directly from the hospital. If the first in the series of forms is filed after the child's birth, and the next isn't filed on time, the appropriate department will investigate whether the child ended up with someone other than the approved parent. If that somehow happened, the agency will enlist the necessary forces to have the child removed. **One can imagine what the approved adoptive parent would go through if the baby had disappeared between the first and second form, possibly handed over to a relative or to the biological mother's boyfriend.**

Before the child actually moves in, the adoptive parent is supposed to receive a written report with such info as prenatal care, the child's medical condition at birth, any drugs taken by the mother during pregnancy, and known diseases or hereditary risks of disease. For a child older than infancy, the report should also include social histories of the child and the child's biological parents, including school history, racial/ethnic affiliations, abuse or neglect proceedings involving the child, identities of those with whom the child has lived or visited on a regular basis, and what relationship(s) the child had with those previous caregivers. This report should also note if the child has managed to get in legal difficulties of their own (criminal proceedings or, more likely, the juvenile equivalent, "delinquency" proceedings (see 13.W.)).

If this sort of information only becomes available to the relevant agency after the child has moved in with the adoptive parent, that information is to be included in a supplemental report. **The appearance of such a report could be a significant obstacle. The delayed information could pertain to the child themselves, or to the biological parents. For example, the biological parents could have started showing signs of some degenerative disease after the delivery of the initial report.**

As noted above, many termination of parental rights proceedings (14.H.13.) take place without a particular adoption on the horizon; but any time there are two known biological parents and at least one hasn't consented to the adoption, there will be an associated termination of parental rights action, or the equivalent. The biological parent's consent won't be required, and their rights will be terminated, if the court finds either of the following:

- The biological parent has "abandoned" the child. That means that they have failed, for however long state law or a particular judge thinks is too long, to visit or communicate with the child.
- The biological parent has failed to support the child.

In stepparent adoptions, this decision may be made as part of a consolidated proceeding that ends with approving the adoption.

The details of when a biological parent may veto an adoption — particularly a parent who was somehow prevented from being part of the child's life — will vary from case to case and state to state. In such cases, there is likely to be tension between the parent's fundamental rights and what the court perceives as the child's best interest, where the adoptive family offers an immediate loving environment. However, the court walks a fine line: it may not terminate a parent's rights simply because it views the prospective adoptive family as a "better" choice. (And yes, this will often be a distinction without a difference, and the "best interest" standard has certain inherent tendencies toward inconsistency and subjectivity.)

Unless the court decides, for "good cause" (another squishy standard), to set aside these requirements, it may not grant a petition for adoption unless 90 days (or any state's varying number) have passed since the petition for adoption was filed, and the child has been in the petitioner's custody for those 90 days. (Exception: stepparent adoptions, which have different rules.)

So, those 90 days have finally passed, and the adoption is granted. The parents can finally rejoice and relax, no? Well, not quite. The biological parent, or another adult who sought to adopt the child, may appeal within the state's appeal deadline (see 32.A.) — and while the appeal will be "expedited" (given priority), it will still take months to resolve. There are also other ways to challenge a judgment after the time to appeal has expired, though the grounds for such a challenge are fairly limited (see 32.D.). Per the Act, no such challenge may be brought later than six months, even where a comparable challenge to some other kind of judgment might be brought within a year or even later. (Again, check state statutes to see whether they use the Act's six-month deadline.)

If the father, perhaps a previously unidentified father, is in the military, the Soldiers' and Sailors' Relief Act (see 14.T.) could allow an even later challenge.

Adoptive parents whose attorney was less than fully informed, or didn't communicate all the details and possibilities, might be very unpleasantly surprised by any of these late-coming challenges.

Adoption means not only a new start, but a new (amended) birth certificate, to be substituted for the original certificate in the appropriate registrar's files unless for some reason the court, the adoptive parent, or the (twelve years old or older) child doesn't want one.

Stepparent adoptions are exempt from some of the usual procedures and obstacles for the sensible reason that the custodial parent — who is, as a matter of constitutional law, presumed to have the child's best interests at heart — has already, in a sense, "vetted" the stepparent. In the event the custodial parent dies, this reasoning leads to a surprisingly sensible and compassionate result: the stepparent may still petition to adopt the child, in the same manner as they would have before that tragedy, as long as the child had already lived with the stepparent and the deceased parent for a year.

The Act also tacitly acknowledges the likelihood of nonmarital intimate partnerships by allowing the custodial parent's significant other to pursue an adoption on the same terms as a stepparent, so long as the custodial parent consents. (If your setting is a state with a more conservative legislative bent, check whether this is one part of the Act that the state didn't go along with.)

While in most or all states, adoption by a "stranger" will terminate a non-parent's right to get court-ordered visitation (and might also put an end to visitation under an existing order), a stepparent adoption has no automatic effect on such visitation orders. However, the trial court overseeing the adoption will probably review any existing orders of this kind (at least if asked to do so) to make sure they're still in the child's best interest under the changed circumstances. The court may also authorize continuing visitation between the child and the former parent.

A stepparent adoption also won't interfere with the child's right to inherit property from the biological parent if that parent dies without a will (see 14.K.1.). (This doesn't work in reverse: the biological parent can't inherit from the child, if the child dies first.)

Can same-sex partners adopt a child?

I wouldn't attempt to put forth a scorecard on this rapidly changing question. At least half the states allow the same-sex partner of a biological parent to adopt the child. Some states allow gay married couples to adopt; others (not always the same ones) allow gay individuals to adopt. Some states may now distinguish between gay married and unmarried couples.

It's legally possible to adopt an adult, although different procedures apply. At least, the procedures applicable to adoption of competent adults and of emancipated minors (see 14.H.11.) differ from those used for minors and for incompetent adults. Adults may adopt adults in order to formalize some longstanding informal relationship; or to ensure that there's someone, or the right someone, in position to inherit an estate (though entirely cutting out a spouse or children may not be feasible — see 14.K.3.); or because a noncustodial parent who opposed a stepparent adoption can no longer prevent it once the child turns 18.

Spouses can't adopt spouses. (Ick.)

From the early 1900s until around the early 1980s, "closed adoptions" were the norm in the U.S. Birth parents learned nothing about those who adopted their children, and couldn't dream of receiving updates or playing any part in their children's lives. Adoptive parents knew next to nothing about birth parents. Children had no established means of finding out their origins.

Nowadays, "open adoptions" are the norm, although the degree of contact between birth parent(s) and adoptive parents and the amount the child knows about the birth parent(s) vary greatly. Where contact between birth parent and adoptive family has not been maintained, either party can go to registries which facilitate contact by mutual consent.

Of course, not every birth parent wants to be found out. The biological mother may have hidden the fact of her pregnancy from her family or from the man she met thereafter. If her religion condemns unwed motherhood, the consequences, if her secret is revealed, could range from divorce to excommunication to "honor killing."

If a biological parent has chosen to remain anonymous, the adoptive parent or an adult adoptee can still obtain medical and other background information via records maintained by the court or the adoption agency. **Of course, if what the adoptee wants to know is whether she is related to her fiancé, "nonidentifying" information won't be good enough.** In that case, the adoptee can go to court and explain the compelling reason she needs to know her parentage — and why that reason outweighs the harm that could be done by the disclosure.

It was once common for authorities to remove children from their Native American tribes, on one or another (if any) pretext, in order to place them in more "civilized" family settings. According to some figures, this was happening to 35-40 percent of Native American children. Rather later than you'd think, in 1978, the federal government addressed this practice in the Indian Child Welfare Act. Where the parents could no longer have custody, this statute gave other Native American family members priority, and after them, any member of the child's tribe.

Things can get messy (to understate things) if the child's tribal origin is mixed, or if the mother is not Native American and the father has disclaimed paternal responsibility. It's even worse when a claim is asserted after a child has lived for months or years with a non-tribal family. There are many who feel that the statute's goals of righting historical wrongs and preserving Native American tribal identity should not be attained at the cost of separating children from loving parents.

15. The Missing Marriage License

Finally, here's a situation straight out of today's headlines (well, today's Indiana case reports) that's just begging for a fictional treatment.

Many states require that a couple wanting to get married have a marriage license on hand to show whoever's going to perform the ceremony, and/or that the license be filed with the county clerk after the ceremony. **In one Indiana divorce proceeding, it developed that the day before the wedding, the bride-to-be *burned* the marriage license and (according to her) told her groom she had done so. The appellate court affirmed the trial court's ruling that the two were never legally married, and thus retained the rights and only the rights of two unmarried persons. The not-actually-a-husband argued that at least, his not-a-wife should be equitably estopped (see Ch. 17) from denying her marital status. The Court of Appeals rejected that argument, holding that because there was evidence to support the conclusion that the not-a-husband knew all along, equitable estoppel did not apply.**

I. Guardianship

There are two basic categories of guardianship, either of which can lead to dramatic conflict: guardianship of a child, and guardianship of an adult. When someone seeks guardianship of a child, the struggle is between the would-be guardian and the child's parent or parents. Where the focus is an adult who is allegedly unable to care for themselves, then that adult, as well as any alternate guardian, can oppose the petition.

For children, when parents are struggling with substance abuse or other problems that make their fitness questionable, guardianship with a relative as guardian may be an alternative to placing a child in foster care. It's not uncommon for the arrangement to be by mutual consent of the parent and guardian, at least in the beginning. Later, however, disagreement about the duration of the guardianship and the parent's ability to resume parental duties may land the parties in court.

There's a more limited form of guardianship called "conservatorship," "guardianship of the estate," or "conservatorship of the estate," in which the guardian is put in charge of someone's assets and finances only. Guardianship, or (as it's sometimes known) "conservatorship of the person," has the potential to be considerably more drastic: the guardian may end up responsible for all the "ward's" physical needs, including food, shelter, and health care, as well as for managing the ward's money and property. Depending on the circumstances, the guardian may have the power to decide whether the ward can retain a driver's license, own a firearm, enter into contracts, get married, or even vote.

With such rights at stake, due process requires a fairly high degree of procedural protection for the potential ward. While the details may vary, the subject of the petition is likely to be entitled to notice of and attendance at all proceedings; representation by counsel; examination and cross-examination of witnesses; and a "clear and convincing" or comparable standard of proof. The subject in an adult guardianship proceeding may also demand a jury trial, although this rarely occurs (**which would make for a more interesting story if it did**). At least one state, Kentucky, requires, rather than just allowing, a jury trial before a guardian may be appointed for an incapacitated adult.

It's common in guardianship cases for the court to appoint a guardian ad litem, aka a GAL. A GAL is *not* a guardian in the sense we're talking about, but rather a temporary assistant fact-finder who can interview and investigate the parties in ways the trial judge cannot. (See 14.H.7. for other uses of guardians ad litem.) The court may also appoint a doctor or other professional (e.g. a social worker) to examine the potential ward.

Guardians are typically required to make regular reports to the court, often annually. Some guardianships over adults last as long as the ward does, while others are terminated when the ward regains the capacity to handle their own affairs. Where the ward is a minor, changes in the parents' circumstances, as well as the child's, may provide grounds for terminating the guardianship.

Guardians may be paid for their services, and if so, that payment may come from the ward's assets. If at some later time the guardianship ends or different guardians are appointed, the ward, or the succeeding guardian, might try to reclaim those payments on the basis that the previous guardians mishandled the assets in some way. **A battle could ensue as to whether, for example, the purchase of a larger house in which both the guardian and the ward were to live was for the ward's benefit or the guardian's.**

By the way, the fact that someone has a guardian does not, by itself, mean that the person is incompetent to testify (see 22.H.2.).

J. Children with Money

Here's a recipe for drama, with possibilities for comedy, tragedy, noir, or farce: take the emotional intensity and complexity of parent-child relationships, and throw in the crazy-making effect of large amounts of money.

When children have lots of money due to an inheritance, it sometimes happens that a guardian of the estate (see 14.I.) gets appointed to oversee and protect that wealth. But one of the common ways that kids get rich is by employment in the entertainment industry. And some unfortunate history has led to laws in some states meant specifically to protect such youngsters.

These laws are sometimes called Jackie Coogan Laws, because of the impetus to the enactment of the first one (in California, naturally). Jackie Coogan was a very successful child actor in the early part of the 20th century. He earned about $4,000,000 (something like $67,000,000 in today's dollars) in the course of his career, all paid to his parents. When he reached his majority and tried to get hold of it, it turned out his parents had spent most of it, and it took an expensive lawsuit to recover the rest. The legislative response, in 1938: the Child Actors Bill, which required that a portion of a child performer's earnings be paid directly to a trust account, and that someone other than the parents had to be the trustee. The trust assets were paid to the performer when they reached their majority.

Per the current version of California's statute, all the child's earnings technically belong to the child, and (more to the point) 15% must be paid into a trust account. If the parents don't set up a trust, that percentage goes to the Actors Fund of America (which, despite its name, is available to professionals in all areas of performing arts and entertainment).

A few other states, including New York, home of Broadway, have similar laws. But most don't. And people keep finding loopholes in the laws that exist, leading to legislative tinkering, in an ongoing and somewhat depressing race between legislation and greed. **Your story could deal with some ingenious loophole, or be set in a state that lacks legislative protection for child performers.**

K. Will We, Won't We: Wills and Trusts

The laws governing what people leave behind them when they die, and how, are extremely complex, and I'll just be scratching the surface. But before I dive into those details, let's talk about the dramatic possibilities.

A will is the ultimate "last word." There's no rebuttal, no comeback. Whatever the deceased thought of someone when the will was written, there's no more chance to change their mind.

A will can air long-suppressed resentments, or reveal secret relationships. It can continue a family feud, or rise above it; or, by the way the will disposes of financially, sentimentally, or symbolically valuable property, it can start a new one.

Due to the tradition of reading the will aloud to the beneficiaries, it used to be customary (or at least, literature from centuries back suggests it was customary) for testators to use their wills as a way to pontificate to a captive audience, inflicting on them various lofty sentiments about life, death, and morality — or, alternatively, unloading on the bereaved the hurt feelings and resentments of a lifetime. (The multi-volume 18th century novel *Clarissa* provides one example of the former.) There's no reason you can't have a contemporary testator do the same. But even without such explicit language, a will is often a revelation of the testator's preferences and loves and hates.

Wills very often give particular items of property to some designated person or persons. Items for which there's no specific directions constitute the "remainder," and will be distributed as the will dictates. There may, however, be items that are left by category (e.g., "the jewelry," "the furniture") to some group of beneficiaries, in the touching hope that these beneficiaries can decide amicably who gets what. **Your account of the no-holds-barred brawl that takes place instead could include the decades-old feuds and animosities that make ownership of some brooch or nightstand seem terribly important to the combatants.**

1. If There Isn't Any Will: Intestacy

What someone leaves behind to be parceled out is their "estate." Before getting into how wills work, I'll touch on what happens if someone never gets around to any kind of "estate planning" (setting up the future distribution of their property). If someone doesn't make a will or put their assets in trust or otherwise arrange what will happen after they die, they will die "intestate," and state law will determine who inherits what.

While the details and definitions vary significantly from state to state, here's the usual priority lineup:

First comes the spouse. That's current spouses, not exes. Things get complicated where the spouses are legally separated and/or in mid-divorce, or have lived apart for decades. Check the law of the state your characters are in. **A marriage from decades back, never revealed to the children of a later relationship and never formally dissolved, could lead to a will contest. If the later relationship was, or purported to be, a marriage, there could be other major complications, as that supposed later marriage would have been void.**

In states that have civil unions, domestic partnerships, and suchlike quasi-marital relationships, the rules re spouses apply. (That's one of the reasons to have such legal categories in the first place.)

That doesn't mean the spouse gets everything, at least if the deceased had children. But in most states, the spouse gets what may be the single biggest chunk, because the rest will be divided among "children," "parents," and/or "siblings," plural (assuming there's more than one child, parent, or sib alive at the time). Some states, however, make life simpler by dividing the estate equally between the surviving spouse and each child.

There are also states, or at least one state (Montana), where the current spouse and any children from previous liaisons split the estate, while the descendants of the deceased and the current spouse get nothing — unless the spouse has children from some other relationship, in which case it's apparently presumed that they might siphon off some assets that should be used for the children of the marriage, and the children of the marriage get half of whatever's left over after $150,000.

In states like California, where most property acquired during the marriage is "community property" (see 14.H.2.), the spouse gets all of the community property, and the divvying up starts after that.

And so on. You'll have to check the law of the particular state whose courts are handling the estate (usually the legal residence at the time of death).

Of course, there are children and children. The deceased might have adopted children (whose treatment is usually the same as biological children); or foster children, biological children adopted by others, posthumous children (historically of men, **but these days, potentially of women as well**), and/or children born outside of wedlock. **You could really make your readers' heads spin if the deceased had some of each.**

And what's a "sibling"? Half-siblings may be treated differently from full siblings. Half-sibs often receive half as much as full siblings.

Story possibility: someone who knows the deceased left them out of the will, but who would get a share under intestacy laws, gets hold of and hides the will and/or blackmails the lawyer who drafted it. (You'd have to make sure that this person wouldn't get a share despite the will's provisions. See 14.K.3., below.)

There are some types of property that aren't subject to these intestacy rules, because they aren't handled by wills in the first place. Those include property held in certain kinds of trusts (see 14.K.10.), and insurance policies or retirement accounts that provide for a named beneficiary.

Even if someone does write a will, and succeeds in doing it properly (see 14.K.2., next), then all these rules may still apply if there's any property the will doesn't cover.

2. Ways of Making a Will

There are simpler and more complicated ways of writing a will. The simplest, relatively speaking, is to actually *write* it, by hand. A will that's entirely handwritten by, as well as signed by, the "testator" (the one whose death it's all about), is called a "holographic" will. (Ghostly 3D effects not required.) The rules vary significantly from state to state, but in some, the requirements for proving that the testator actually wrote the will and meant what it said are less rigorous for holographic wills. Even in states that don't cut holographic wills in general much slack, they're more likely to do so for people in certain dangerous professions or situations. This makes sense, because the rationale for being less picky about holographic wills is that they're more likely to be created in emergency situations, when the testator (a) is forced by circumstance to contemplate their demise, and (b) doesn't have access to an array of witnesses, lawyers, etc.

Holographic wills are easier to forge, due to the lack of witnesses, and may also be more likely where the deceased was an unsophisticated sort, which could lead to bequests that have unintended consequences. **Your story could involve both problems, and include a dispute over whether the deceased was unsophisticated *enough* to have made some problematic decision.**

In a few states, there's a somewhat similar, though more restricted, option called a nuncupative will. A nuncupative will isn't even written down: it's stated orally by someone "in imminent peril of death" (phrasing from an Indiana statute) who then dies because of that peril. These wills require at least two disinterested witnesses. (Vocabulary note: that doesn't mean they're bored, just that they have no stake in the outcome.) One of the witnesses must write the details down within some set period of time, and then submit them to the probate court within some other deadline. Once written down, the will may also have to be notarized.

This kind of will doesn't automatically revoke previous wills, and there may be a limit on how much property it can dispose of. **Dramatic possibilities leap to mind, starting with getting the testator into the perilous situation. If the peril is external danger, rather than illness, there could be three friends sharing that danger, taking turns telling the others what they want done with their property. Whose will is actually at issue in probate court could be revealed only at the end of the story.** (I may write this one myself — but go ahead and write it also, if you're so inclined! Of course, you don't need my permission: ideas aren't subject to copyright. See 14.M.1.)

Except for holographic wills, a will isn't valid unless it's been "witnessed." State law prescribes how many witnesses are needed, plus any special requirements for witnesses, but a witness must always be a legal adult, and should not be a beneficiary of the will. This last can be important: if the will gives, or could under any circumstances (e.g. the prior deaths of other beneficiaries) give anything to the witness, then if there aren't enough other surviving witnesses to satisfy the law, the beneficiary-witness might not get what the will would otherwise give them. In some states, for example, someone in this position may only receive what they'd have gotten if the deceased had died without a will (i.e.., whatever the intestacy laws would have provided). (Here's a question I haven't researched: what if the will actually met the requirements for a holographic will, even though it wasn't intended as one, but was improperly witnessed by a beneficiary? **Could be worth exploring….**)

What are witnesses for, and what do they actually have to "witness" (observe)?

Well, they don't have to know what's in the will. **(One could, however, have an unscrupulous witness persuade the testator that such knowledge is in fact necessary.)** However, if there's been a series of wills and/or codicils, it'd be a good idea to show the witness the date or some other information that'd make clear just which version they're witnessing.

A witness isn't just a possibly unpaid notary public, stating that some-one signed a paper. Witnesses do need to be in a position to know several facts:

- That the person who supposedly signed the will really did so. They don't have to see the person sign it, if that person assures them af-terward that yes, they signed it, and yes, that's their signature right there. (The converse, however, isn't true: the person making the will is generally supposed to watch the witnesses sign it.)

- That the testator was "of sound mind": not drunk, not stoned, not senile, and generally capable of understanding what's in the will and what they're doing by signing it. There's substantial overlap with what's necessary for a witness to be "competent" to testify.

  The witnesses need to be of sound mind also, at least when they're doing the witnessing. It'd be a good idea to choose witnesses who are likely to be of sound mind in the future, if called upon to testify.

- That aside from the testator's *capacity* to understand that they were making a will and what its contents were, that the testator *actually did* appear to understand these things. Since a stranger may be less attuned to the testator's facial expressions, body language, and ways of expressing themselves, it may be desirable to choose a friend or relative. That's if the testator can find one who (a) isn't a beneficiary and (b) isn't so upset about being excluded that they're likely to sab-otage the process later. . . . (Maybe an acquaintance would be the best bet.)

It's good to choose witnesses who are likely to outlive the testator, so they can testify in the event of any will contest. **Of course, if the person contesting the will — possibly someone who would have been in better shape under a previous, revoked will, or someone who'd do well under the intestacy rules — were to start killing off witnesses, things could get dicey. (If the murderer doesn't get to all the witnesses before the probate pro-ceeding, but has killed off enough to bring the remaining witnesses below the required number, then those who want the will to stand would need to prove that the dead witnesses (a) are really dead and (b) really did witness the will.)**

The executor of the will (the poor bloke saddled with making sure that all the will's instructions are followed — see 14.K.6.) could be a witness, as long as they aren't also a beneficiary or potential beneficiary. As for whether it's a problem for the executor, or any other witness, to be paid for services in executing or otherwise handling the will: maybe. The further back in time you go, the more likely this sort of arrangement is to disqualify someone as a witness.

Wills are likely to include, or to be accompanied by, an "attestation clause" and/or a "self-proving affidavit." Of the two, the latter currently appears both more common and more useful.

An "attestation clause" may appear just below the testator's signature. With a smaller or larger helping of legalese, it essentially states that the witnesses were present (possibly specifying the date and location); that they saw the testator either sign the will (or, if physically incapable of signing, direct someone else to sign it), or else identify the signature as their own; and that the testator appeared to be acting voluntarily, to be old enough, and to be of sound mind. Probably the main reason these clauses are no longer universally used is that the witnesses may still need to show up in the probate court to say the same things (that is, to "prove" the will).

A "self-proving" clause or affidavit, on the other hand, is usually enough to allow the witnesses to stay home. (A few states are not be so accommodating, and still require witnesses to appear.) The self-proving affidavit covers essentially the same ground as an attestation clause. It may or may not have to be a separate document. In some states, it's all right if the self-proving affidavit was executed later than the will itself.

Unlike wills in general, many states require self-proving affidavits to be notarized. On the other hand, some states are satisfied if the affidavit or clause includes a statement that the witnesses are signing under penalties of perjury. That just means they know that if what they're signing is false, they can be charged with the crime of perjury (13.I.).

3. Stiffing the Family

Can a testator leave their entire estate to strangers, cutting off spouse and children without a penny?

Not exactly.

Most states have statutes that let a widow or widower who's been left out of the will, or even one who's dissatisfied with what the will allotted them, "elect to take against the will". The surviving spouse will then get whatever share of the estate the statute specifies. Before these statutes were passed, the common law made a similar provision for widows ("dower" rights) and widowers ("curtesy").

Many states also provide for a "homestead allowance" and/or a "family allowance," letting the surviving spouse and/or dependent children claim some specified amount(s) for living expenses before the rest of the estate is distributed. There may also be a homestead "exemption," letting the surviving family stay in the family home for some period of time, regardless of what the will says should happen to it.

4. Undue Influence

Whatever type of will you're writing about, one fertile ground for conflict is the possibility of undue influence, especially when a spouse or child receives less than they expected.

The concept is similar here and in the contract context (see 14.C.8.); but it may be more likely to arise in the case of a will, since most people (in modern developed countries, at least) are old when they die, and thus more likely to have some degree of declining mental function and/or dependence on others. If a will, especially a will made late in life, cuts out typical beneficiaries in favor of the deceased's lawyer or caretaker or recently acquired spouse or girl/boyfriend or cult leader, it's quite likely the spouse or children will claim undue influence and contest the will.

To recap what undue influence means: whoever's challenging the will would need to show that the testator had some intellectual or psychological weakness the beneficiary was able to exploit, and had a relationship with the beneficiary that made it easier for the beneficiary to take advantage of that weakness.

5. Special Vocabulary

There's some Latin-derived vocabulary that can make a big difference in who gets what: "per capita" and "per stirpes." These terms may be used in a state statute about intestacy, or may turn up in the language of a will.

"Per capita" comes from the Latin for "by the head." With per capita distribution, all living members of some group (such as grandchildren of the deceased) get an equal share. "Per stirpes," Latin for "by branch," bases the distribution on more factors. If the deceased had two children, one of whom had one child and the other of whom had ten, the grandchild with no siblings would get half of the "grandchild" share and the ten siblings would equally split the other half.

Is that all? No. Let's say that under the intestacy statute or the will, the children of the deceased are to split the estate. If that's a per capita distribution, then if one of the children dies, the others get it all and share equally. If it's a per stirpes distribution and the deceased child had children of their own, then those children split the share that would have gone to their parent.

And an oft-ignored technicality: an "inheritance" is what someone gets under intestacy laws. A "bequest" or "devise" (the latter word used for real property) passes via a will. The verbs: "inherit," "bequeath," and "devise."

6. The Executor

Who gets saddled with keeping track of all the details and making sure the money and property get where they're supposed to? If there's a will, it'll usually name someone (or some organization, like a bank) the testator trusted to be the executor. The term "personal representative" may also be used. If someone dies intestate, the probate court will appoint a personal representative. For simplicity, I'll just say "executor" for the rest of this discussion.

Issues of conflict of interest may arise, although most states will let a beneficiary serve as executor — probably because it's a fairly thankless task unless someone makes a paying profession of it, and ruling out beneficiaries would make executors hard to find, at least for smaller estates. In fact, while ideally the executor should be capable of handling the job, executors may be chosen more for their perceived concern for the decedent's wishes than for their expertise in handling all the details involved. (See below re the help they're allowed to hire.)

If following the provisions of the will involves transactions such as selling real property or stock holdings, and the executor has the chance to make a sweet deal with their own company, that'd be an example of a conflict of interest that could make the court step in.

Executors do get paid, though the applicable statute may put a cap on that payment, typically a percentage of the estate's value. The executor may also hire those with expertise they lack, such as lawyers, realtors, and accountants, and pay them with funds from the estate.

If the executor is handling the estate's assets recklessly, or in a way that benefits them at the expense of the beneficiaries, a beneficiary or a creditor of the estate can ask the probate court to remove the executor. There usually has to be a showing of pretty severe misconduct before that request will be granted.

7. Changing One's Mind: Codicils and Revocations

There are two basic ways to change one's mind about the contents of a will. There's a certain morality-tale fitness about the fact that the way that seems easier is in fact more likely to lead to trouble. That deceptively simple approach: the codicil.

A codicil is an amendment to a will. It can make a minor change (the bequest to the local animal shelter now goes to a rescue organization for pureblood Pomeranians), or it can radically change the winners and losers. The problem: it's not always so straightforward figuring out what the codicil is intended to change and what provisions it means to leave untouched.

A codicil has to meet the same technical requirements as a will. Now that word processors and digitally saved documents are the rule, it's usually almost as easy, and less problematic, to write a new will.

But then there's that old will to be dealt with.

Physically destroying a will generally counts as "revoking" it: that is, undoing it, invalidating it. Writing "revoked," "null and void," or some such language on every page would be one method, though burning is more traditional and shredding would be an acceptable modern alternative.

What about copies of the destroyed will? If the destruction of the original is a proved fact, a copy will be useless. If there's no such proof, it's still generally assumed that a missing original was destroyed; though some courts will, these days, accept a copy into probate if whoever presents it makes a credible case that the testator *didn't* destroy the original.

The most reliable way to revoke an old will is to start by making a new one that dots all the necessary technical "i"s. The testator should make sure the new will explicitly revokes *all* prior wills and codicils. Then they should go on an orgy of destruction, thoroughly obliterating every original, paper copy, and digital copy of the old will(s) they can track down. But the testator must make very sure the new will is technically satisfactory before revoking the old will, or they could end up intestate, with the blunt instrument of intestacy law (see 14.K.1., above) governing who gets what. **This could be an ironic conclusion to a story of old and new wills, inconsistent codicils, questionable copies, and so on.** Another, classic ironic conclusion: that of Charles Dickens' *Bleak House* (already mentioned in 8.B.). **SPOILER ALERT:**

> A particular will contest had gone on for decades, even generations. The strain of uncertain expectations even proved fatal to one possible beneficiary. When a new, more recent will finally emerged that would settle the case quite neatly, there was never an opportunity to present it: just before the new will was to be introduced, it was revealed that the entire huge estate had been entirely consumed in "costs" (primarily legal fees).)

8. Take It or Leave It: No Contest Clauses

Wills frequently provide that anyone who contests the will loses whatever bequest the will had bestowed upon them. Such a provision is known as a "no-contest" clause (not to be confused with the "no contest" or "nolo contendere" plea sometimes available in criminal cases (9.A.1.)). Of course, this has no practical effect if a will gives someone nothing at all. That's a good reason for even the hurt or vindictive testator to throw a substantial bone to anyone who'd reasonably expect to be included.

9. The Rule Against Perpetuities

Since the 17th century, in Britain and then over here across the pond, there's been a limit on how far into the future one may reach when disposing of one's property in a will, a trust, an option, or any other way. This limit, which applies to both real and personal property, is usually called "the Rule Against Perpetuities." Where it still exists (see below), it provides that any attempt to dispose of property is void (of no effect) if the designated recipient *might* acquire the property more than 21 years after every identifiable person alive at the time of the disposition has died.

Believe it or not, that's oversimplifying things. For one thing, the usual term isn't "acquired." The rule speaks in terms of when the interest in the property "vests" or "is vested." To oversimplify yet again, an interest in property "vests" when the ownership of the property no longer depends on future events.

If part of a bequest, or whatever, violates the Rule Against Perpetuities, that isn't supposed to invalidate the entire bequest. There's another seemingly simple principle that could be very tricky to apply.

The complexities of the Rule Against Perpetuities can drive a law student to tears and a lawyer to drink. (In recognition of this fact, the Supreme Court of California held in 1961 that it wasn't malpractice for an attorney to draft a will that ran afoul of the rule.) If you're going to work it into a story, you'll have some homework to do.

Apparently, for purposes of this rule, an embryo or fetus is "alive." **One could try to pull this definition into a debate about abortion or the morning-after pill.**

In the movie *Body Heat*, set in Florida, the Rule Against Perpetuities provides a legal error in a will, an error necessary to make a nefarious plot come off. A twist that may interest some film buffs: the movie doesn't give the will's details, but according to UCLA law professor Michael Asimov, the most likely use of the rule in the will would not actually have been an error under the law of Florida at the time the events take place. Apparently the movie was originally set in New Jersey, whose more traditional version of the rule fit the plot better, but was moved to Florida because of a Teamster's strike.

All this may soon be a quaint pile of legal rubble in the dustbin of history. Many states are abolishing or limiting the Rule Against Perpetuities, authorizing the creation and maintenance of "perpetual trusts" or something almost as long-lasting.

10. Avoiding Probate: Trusts and Pay On Death Accounts

A will's progress through "probate," the legal procedure for "proving" (authenticating and administering) a will, is likely to take months or years, even if the will isn't contested. Many people, especially those with substantial assets to leave, try to pass those assets on in ways that avoid the probate courts. One often used vehicle: trusts (specifically, "testamentary trusts"). A person may set up a trust and put some or all of their assets in it, retaining control by making themselves the trustee (or one of the trustees, with appropriate safeguards as to what the others may do). At the time of some future triggering event, such as the deaths of all the trustees, the assets can go to one or more beneficiaries. The person setting up the trust and putting assets in it is the "settlor," the "trustor," or the more modern "trustmaker." And none of this involves the courts (unless something goes wrong). That also means the matter can be kept private, which probate proceedings cannot.

Trusts can also be used to limit the extent to which an intended beneficiary can impoverish themselves, lay waste to the family estate or business, etc. **A beneficiary may be fiercely resentful of having to come cap in hand to a trustee — perhaps a family member with whom they have a relationship of mutual detestation — in order to make significant expenditures of what they regard as their rightful inheritance.** **A trustee's control of family assets can also be used to thwart political ambitions or projects.**

Many charities are set up as trusts, administered by a chain of trustees over the decades and centuries. Pension plans are also typically trusts, with the retired employees as beneficiaries.

The tax consequences of putting property in trust will differ from the consequences of hanging onto it or of disposing of it in other ways. I won't attempt to go into the details.

A trust can be revocable or irrevocable. If one doesn't fear changing one's mind, and wants to ensure the beneficiaries that they'll eventually receive the trust assets, one can make it irrevocable. However, a trust meant as an alternative to a will is likely to be revocable, in case (a) the settlors turn out to need the assets for their own purposes or (b) events shed new light on the extent to which the beneficiaries deserve the settlors' largesse. However, if the goal is to avoid estate tax, only certain kinds of irrevocable trusts will do the trick.

Even where a trust is irrevocable, the passage of time may cause sufficient changes that the original terms no longer serve the trust's purpose, or the purpose itself is viewed as contrary to public policy. In that case, either the trustees or the beneficiaries may file an action seeking court-imposed changes. Examples of trusts that would currently be held to violate public policy include those that condition a benefit on the recipient's permanently refraining from marriage, or marrying only within a particular racial group. For now, however, a condition that the beneficiary marry within a particular religion is still acceptable. But a condition that the beneficiary *practice* a particular religion may not be. A payment that occurs after a beneficiary gets divorced may be all right — unless it's read as meaning to encourage that divorce. **One could have fun setting one's story in the future and playing about with what that future culture would consider contrary to public policy.**

The trust should spell out in detail what powers each of the trustees has. The trustees actually have legal title to the trust property, but are bound to exercise it for the purposes set forth in the trust. It is, however, perfectly all right and very common for the trustees, particularly professionals such as bankers and (yup) lawyers, to be paid some sort of fees, as well as having any expenses reimbursed.

A trust (leaving aside implied or constructive trusts, discussed below) must be established by documents specifying just what property is included. The "corpus" of the trust, the stuff it covers, can be real property, or tangible personal property, or intangible personal property. Intangible property could be, for example, a vested interest in some future payment, or a chose in action (14.N.).

A trust's assets don't have to be explicitly named if it can be clearly ascertained from the trust instrument what was intended. Beneficiaries don't have to exist yet: for example, they could be not-yet-born children of the settlor. For a private trust, meant to benefit particular people, the Rule Against Perpetuities" (see 14.K.9., just above) acts as a limit on how far in the future the trust may reach; but for charitable trusts, which at least theoretically benefit the public at large, that rule doesn't apply.

The probate court's equity jurisdiction, and/or state statutes, will usually give the court some authority to oversee the administration of the trust. For example, the court might limit the trustees' compensation to some percentage of the trust assets.

Some people set up a trust, but also execute what's called a pour-over (hyphen optional) will. A pour-over will leaves anything that isn't already in the trust to the trust. It's a catch-all safety measure in case the testator didn't get around to transferring all assets to the trust. It may also be useful when an asset that would otherwise go into the trust during the trustor's lifetime is harder to manage when owned by a trust. For example, some states and some insurance companies make it difficult to buy or sell a motor vehicle owned by a trust. Some sorts of corporate stock are not easily administered by trusts. Transferring property to a trust may give the assessor an opportunity to reassess the property for tax purposes.

The chief disadvantage of a pour-over will is that of all wills: probate court. Whatever assets are still there for the will to pour to the trust will take some time getting there. The trustee will have to keep being a trustee for longer, instead of getting out from under as soon as the assets already in the trust are distributed to the beneficiaries. However, if there wasn't much property left to be poured over, the estate may qualify for expedited "small estate" procedures. Those procedures generally aren't available for real estate, which would be a factor in favor of transferring real estate to the trust beforehand.

Another way to avoid probate, at least for bank accounts: "pay on death" (POD) accounts, sometimes called "poor man's trusts." These accounts can transfer money to one or more beneficiaries, who simply need to go to the bank with the death certificate of the person who set up the account.

Someone setting up a POD account can instruct the bank, via a beneficiary designation form, that the various beneficiaries should collect different amounts (though how thoroughly and effectively this binds the bank may vary). If all the beneficiaries die before the person who set up the account, then the account's assets become part of the general estate after all.

Where there's a conflict between a POD account and the will, the POD account's terms usually win, unless the will specifically mentions and overrides the POD account.

Some states also allow real property to be handled the same way, with instruments called beneficiary deeds or transfer on death deeds. It's surprisingly straightforward — but where's the authorial fun in that?

Well, actually, there are some potential disadvantages to POD accounts:

- Some states won't let people name organizations, such as charities, as beneficiaries.
- The bank could fail, which will make more difference if the account exceeds whatever federal or other insurance is around at the time.
- One can't name alternate beneficiaries ahead of time (**so there's once again room for a killer or serial killer to wreak havoc**).
- If whatever estate does exist doesn't pay any estate tax due (see 14.O.4.), the account could be frozen.
- If the beneficiaries are minors when the relevant death occurs, courts must get involved after all.
- Some states won't allow any changes to the account, once established, unless the beneficiary or beneficiaries consent.
- If so much of the potential estate goes into this account that it doesn't leave the percentage state law requires be left to someone, such as a spouse, things can get messy. Similarly, one can't use such accounts to avoid paying creditors.
- Last and usually least: the bank may charge service fees.

There's one type of trust that isn't planned and has nothing to do with avoiding probate. Sometimes, a court will decide that property held by one person or organization should have belonged to or been used for the benefit of someone else. In that case, the court can order the property held in an "implied trust" or "constructive trust" for whoever should have owned it or gotten its benefits. This means that the legal owner must manage the property for the benefit of the person who should have owned it. An "implied" trust is one the trustor intended to create, but somehow didn't. A "constructive" trust is created by a statute and/or a court to alleviate some injustice.

Such an arrangement might not last long, as the beneficiary may not trust the "trustee" to perform as trustees should, even if the "trustee" is an innocent recipient of property mishandled by another.

L. Employment

Here's where I'll discuss a few topics having to do with employer-employee relationships.

By the way, there's one such topic, employer liability for employee actions ("respondeat superior"), that I'll save for 14.Q.

---

1. "At Will" Employment

"At will" employment could be called (with apologies to those who dislike word play) "fire at will." It means that the employer doesn't need any special or reasonable cause to fire (aka terminate) the employee. If there's no employment contract saying otherwise, employment is usually presumed to be "at will." (Montana may be alone in limiting at-will employment to an initial probationary period, if it still does.)

If a written contract says employment is "at will" or that employees may be fired "for any cause" or "without good cause," that's more than enough to settle the issue. If there's no contract as such, but only some written employment "policy," that'll usually be further support for the presumption of at-will employment. But if either a contract or a written policy says that employees may only be fired for good cause, or for certain specified causes, that should be enough to rebut that presumption. If the employer, or someone working for the employer and in charge of hiring, makes verbal promises along those same lines, then the employee can at least make a fight of it, especially if they relied on those assurances.

There's a difference between no cause and a cause that's against public policy. Except for very small companies, racial or gender discrimination is one of the prohibited bases for firing someone. Another is retaliation for having reported the employer's violation of a statute or regulation: for example, telling health/safety officials about a restaurant's dirty kitchen, or reporting sexual harassment. Employees also can't be fired for exercising various legal rights or fulfilling legal duties (voting, serving in the military, taking family or medical leave provided by law or regulation).

According to some sources, federal law now treats discrimination based on sexual orientation or transgender status as gender discrimination. Some states do as well.

With any of these prohibited bases for firing someone, the employer may claim that the employee was really fired for some other, permissible reason. Rules vary as to who bears the burden of proof: does the employee have to prove that they were fired for reporting illegal conduct, for example, rather than for poor work quality, or does the fact that the employee blew the whistle mean the employee wins *unless* the employer proves some legitimate basis for firing the employee?

The federal statute prohibiting various kinds of discrimination, Title VII of the Civil Rights Act of 1964, is administered by the Equal Employment Opportunity Commission (EEOC), which sometimes files its own lawsuits on the terminated employee's behalf. The EEOC also acts as a gatekeeper: an employee wanting to file their own lawsuit under federal anti-discrimination laws must usually start by making a claim to the EEOC and getting a "right to sue" letter. One exception: gender discrimination claims under the Equal Pay Act, for which the plaintiff can skip this step, though the details of remedies available under Title VII versus the Equal Pay Act won't always make that the best option.

Going the federal route has pluses and minuses. On the plus side, there are a host of remedies available, including:

- reinstatement, if both the plaintiff and the court think the employer and employee could somehow work together in the future;
- back pay (the wages the employee would have earned if not fired) through the time of trial;

- front pay (future wages), if the employee can show (which could be difficult) that they won't be employed in the future, or (more likely) won't earn as much as before the termination;
- lost benefits (insurance and the like that the employer provided until the termination, and possibly pensions that would have vested (see 14.S.) in the time between termination and trial);
- "pain and suffering" (emotional trauma, stress-related physical symptoms);
- out of pocket costs like job search expenses or medical treatment for those stress-related symptoms;
- attorney fees and other costs of the lawsuit;
- punitive damages (30.B.3.) for the nastiest employers.

Age discrimination lawsuits under federal law, however, offer more limited remedies. Out of pocket costs, pain and suffering, and punitive damages aren't available, though there may be a penalty equal to the back pay award if the employer either knew it was breaking the law or obviously didn't care one way or the other (i.e., was "reckless" about the possibility).

If the plaintiff proceeds under federal anti-discrimination laws, there are limits on the amount the employer can be made to pay for some of these types of damages (specifically, for out of pocket costs, pain and suffering, and punitive damages combined), with the limits based on the size of the company. That maximum amount currently ranges from $50,000, for the smallest companies covered by federal law, to $300,000 for the largest.

State laws treating some basis for termination as against public policy may provide more or less generous relief, with perhaps the broadest range to be found in the area of punitive damages.

In any of these lawsuits, as well as in a suit claiming someone was fired in breach of an employment contract, the plaintiff must try to make things better for themselves — to "mitigate" their damages. Damages for lost wages and benefits, whether past or future, will be reduced by the amount the employee was actually able to earn via substitute employment, or by the amount the trier of fact thinks the employee should have been able to earn with reasonable effort. The plaintiff usually won't get injunctive relief like reinstatement in a state breach of contract case, whether the contract is for employment or otherwise. (See 30.A. and B.)

2. Labor Law

The at-will employment doctrine is one of the few areas where employers, or employers and employees (depending how you look at it), have the autonomy to decide the details of the employer-employee relationship. Federal labor law governs, or could be revised to govern, just about everything else, including wages earned; hours worked (including what constitutes overtime and who gets it); workplace safety; workers' compensation for workplace injuries; pensions and various other benefit programs; and unpaid leave of absence for childbirth, adoption, and serious illness. I won't cover all these regulatory schemes in detail, but I'll attempt to sketch an overall picture.

a. Employers and Unions

In one of many sweeping assertions of power under the U.S. Constitution's Commerce Clause (see 34.L.), Congress adopted the National Labor Relations Act in 1935, and has amended it in major and minor ways over the years. The NLRA's provisions are administered by the National Labor Relations Board (NLRB).

The NLRA concerns "collective bargaining" between employer and employees — in other words, unions. It applies to most private employers, with a complicated set of exceptions having to do with the amount of business a retailer does, the total amount of business done by various other categories of businesses, or the amount of the business' interstate commerce. If your story depends on the NLRA applying or not applying, you'll have to look up the details.

This is important: if your story is not set in the present day, don't assume that current labor laws were in effect! It took decades of battle — in many cases literal battle, with people injured or killed — before union representation became relatively routine in many industries.

The NLRA doesn't apply to state and local governments in their capacity as employers, or to those who employ only agricultural workers, or to interstate airlines and railroads. (Neither does federal workers' compensation law.)

Employees are allowed to vote for a particular union to represent them in bargaining with the employer, or to vote against any union representation. The union selected by a majority of the employees becomes the exclusive representative of all the employees. Once a union is chosen, the employer must negotiate with the union representative about "wages, hours, and other terms and conditions of employment" (including such matters as overtime pay, sick leave, and health benefits).

Once those negotiations are finished, the employer may not make changes in any of the areas negotiated without further negotiations. Nor may the employer go around the union representative and deal directly with the employees.

To get the union selection process started, or to try to change which union is representing the employees (to "decertify" the existing union), at least 30% of the employees need to file a petition with the NLRB Regional Office.

Once there's a negotiated contract, the terms of that contract may remain in effect even after it expires, while negotiations for the next contract continue.

What if an employee thinks unions are counterproductive parasites, or bitterly opposed the particular union that won the election? Must that employee pay union dues? That depends on whether the negotiated contract says so, and on whether a state "right to work" law says that payment of union dues can't be compulsory.

Employees who don't unionize may act as a group, which the law calls "engaging in concerted activity." But however united they are in their demands for some term or condition of employment, they have less powerful weaponry than unionized workers. For example, if they engage in a synchronized work stoppage, a "strike," they may not have the same protections as striking union workers would. If the work stoppage doesn't end with the employer making concessions *and* agreeing not to retaliate, the employer may be able to discipline or fire the employees. However, this rule isn't as cut and dried as many employers think it is (and that's as far as I'm going to wade into the complexities of the issue).

Unions may call a strike when negotiations are not going as they like. Unless the strike is called for an unlawful purpose — for example, a strike demanding that the employer stop hiring workers of some particular ethnicity — the striking workers will have some legal protections, but the details vary with the purpose of the strike. If the union strikes to demand economic concessions, the employer may hire replacements. If those replacements are qualified and actually do the work, and if the employer outlasts the strikers to the point where the union essentially surrenders and wants to end the strike, the strikers might not get their jobs back — at least not until there are new openings for which they're qualified. (At that point, if the strikers haven't found comparable employment elsewhere, and if the union asks that they be reinstated, the employer must comply.) All of which means that a strike for economic benefits is somewhat risky.

On the other hand, if the employer has been committing "unfair labor practices" — various kinds of interference with the right to unionize or the union's right to bargain, or refusal to handle grievances in the agreed-upon fashion — then striking employees can't be fired or permanently replaced. If the employer has to hire people to do the work during such a strike, those people get the boot when the strike is over.

By the way, unions can also be guilty of unfair labor practices, including picketing that physically presents nonstriking workers from getting to work, threatening employees who refuse to join the union, retaliating against employees who try to institute changes in how the union operates, and other similar misbehavior.

There's an exception to most of what I've just said: if the negotiated contract prohibits strikes during some specified period, the only protected strikes are those concerning some types of unfair labor practices. But walking out because working conditions have become unsafe doesn't violate a no-strike provision.

If the union doesn't authorize a strike and some of the employees strike anyway, that's a "wildcat" strike, and if it violates an existing contract, those employees may be fired or otherwise disciplined.

Whatever protections strikers have may disappear if the strikers engage in certain kinds of misconduct, including violence or the threat of violence; "sitdown strikes," where the workers stay on the premises without working and effectively deprive the employer of the use of the premises; or blocking passage in and out of the building.

A union can't strike or picket at a health care institution without giving (currently) 10 days' written notice to the institution and to the Federal

Mediation and Conciliation Service. The FMCS is a federal agency that serves not only hospitals and the like, but all sorts of industries and government agencies, and not only with labor disputes but with other kinds as well. **And I'd guess it could give rise to many an interesting story.**

Sometimes, instead of striking, unions turn to a "slowdown," with employees working more slowly than the job requires. Related tactics are the "sickout," with a large percentage of the workforce calling in sick, or "working to rule," where employees start following technical requirements usually honored in the breach. Working to rule may be a tactic difficult to counter ("Judge! They're following all the regulations!"), though employers sometimes try, with such labels as "malicious compliance." Slowdowns and sickouts are considered unlawful labor tactics and can get the employees fired.

The employer-initiated version of a strike is a lockout, where the employer tells the employees not to come to work until they're ready to accept the employer's terms. In a lockout, as in a strike triggered by unfair labor practices, the employer may only hire temporary replacements for the union workers.

b. Federal Regulations re Wages and Benefits

Per the Fair Labor Standards Act (FLSA), which Congress passed in 1938, it's no longer up to Congress to make and change the rules about minimum wage, overtime, youth employment, and recordkeeping for all these: that's now done by the Employment Standards Administration's Wage and Hour Division, part of the Department of Labor. The states may set their own standards if they favor employees more than the federal standards do.

The FLSA covers nearly all employers, due to a particularly elastic interpretation of "commerce": using the U.S. mail or the telephone to reach someone, or be reached by someone, in another state, or taking or placing orders in another state, subjects a business to the statute. Small farms and a few other businesses with little paid labor are explicitly exempted.

The FLSA defines the normal work week (at least, for purposes other than the "Affordable Care Act") as 40 hours; sets the federal minimum wage; requires that men and women get equal pay for what's deemed equal work; restricts use of child labor; and says who must get overtime for what sort of work. A plaintiff who sues under the FLSA and wins must receive an award of attorney fees as well as damages. This differs from how most statutory "fee-shifting" provisions (see 3.E.) work: usually, it's up to the judge to decide whether to award attorney fees to the victor.

These rules apply to workers not in unions as well as to union members. But they make a major distinction between the workers whose wages, etc. are regulated, "non-exempt" workers, and others, the "exempt" employees.

"Exempt" employees are supposed to be "white collar" types. Young lawyers working long days, late nights, and numerous weekends can only dream of getting overtime pay, for example.

To be "exempt" (makes it sound like a favor, doesn't it?), a worker must earn a "salary" rather than an hourly wage. There are some complex rules about how to define a salary for exemption purposes, which I won't go into. Here's one that's easy: the salary must be above a statutory minimum, or the worker is still covered by the FSLA standards, which means they are entitled to overtime pay and other benefits.

This minimum salary is fairly minimal at the moment: just $23,600 per year, amounting to $455 per week. At 40 hours per week, which of course may be a good deal less than an exempt worker is required to work, that'd come to around $11.38 an hour. However, a possible rule change has recently been announced that would raise the threshold from $23,600 to $50,440. If this change goes into effect, which would happen sometime in 2016, employers might have to provide overtime and related benefits to many more workers, although other exemption rules (see below) might limit the new rule's impact. On the other hand, employers could respond by cutting the hours newly exempt employees work, and/or by reducing salaries in order to make the time-and-a-half of overtime lower as well. Formerly exempt employees might also find that their employers could no longer provide various flex-time arrangements and/or nonstandard benefits.

As for the remaining rules about what sorts of employees are exempt: oversimplifying somewhat, those exempt include management, supervisors, and various professionals. The latter include engineers, accountants, teachers, clergy, architects, doctors, dentists, registered nurses, pharmacists, and scientists. On the other hand, bookkeepers and LPNs (licensed practical nurses) aren't exempt, so they're covered by the rules on wages, overtime, and the rest. Some of these rules may also change under the latest proposal, though that's up in the air, with public comments solicited on what changes should be made. One of the possibilities: employers might need to look at the percentage of an employee's time that was spent on more managerial or professional tasks, as opposed to more clerical or routine ones. That, in turn, could mean employees having to keep track throughout the day of which kind of work they were doing.

c. Unpaid Internships

What about unpaid interns, for whom the only compensation is the training they receive, the experience they gain, and the connections they form? Is that allowed?

In 1967, the Department of Labor put out some guidelines on when an unpaid internship arrangement was allowed. These guidelines listed six factors to be considered, all of which had to apply for unpaid internships to be permissible. These guidelines may not have applied in the for-profit private sector, but in 2010, the Department put out similar guidelines that did.

In June 2013, a federal district court in New York issued rulings that sent a substantial ripple through business and professional communities where unpaid internships are common. The plaintiffs in the case, unpaid interns, had sued to claim compensation under the Fair Labor Standards Act and similar New York labor laws. They did not claim that unpaid interns should always be treated as employees: they proposed a rule that if an employer received an immediate advantage from the intern's work, the FLSA should apply. The district court certified a class (see 6.D.) and issued a partial summary judgment order (see 25.I. and 32.A.) to the effect that the plaintiffs were "employees" under the FLSA. The defendants were allowed to file an interlocutory appeal (again, see 32.A.), and on July 2, 2015, the Second Circuit Court of Appeals reversed that order.

The Second Circuit reaffirmed that labeling someone an unpaid intern did not settle the question of whether they should receive FLSA protection. It declined to follow the Department of Labor's six-part test, but it also rejected the plaintiffs' suggested approach. Instead, it adopted the defendants' suggestion of a "primary beneficiary" test: whether the intern counted as an employee should depend on whether the intern or the employer received the greater benefit from the arrangement. If the employer benefits more, the intern is an employee. The court also adopted a non-exclusive list of seven factors for courts to consider. These factors emphasize the intern's participation in formal education programs, which may make it more difficult for employers to use unpaid interns who aren't also pursuing some relevant studies at a college or trade school.

The court also found that the district court had applied the wrong test for whether to certify a class. Even if that had not happened, the standard the Second Circuit adopted for deciding which interns must be paid is so fact-based that it would be hard for any large collection of interns to be certified as a class in future (again, see 6.D.). Without the incentive of a large, collective award, will attorneys be willing to take on unpaid internship cases? Maybe. Remember, the FLSA requires attorney fee awards when plaintiffs prevail, and the amount isn't linked to or limited by the damages the plaintiff gets.

Actually, I've oversimplified what happened at the Second Circuit. What really happened might be worth some fictional imitation.

In its analysis of the "employee or not an employee" question, here's how the court summarized the defendants' position:

> The defendants urge us to adopt a more nuanced primary beneficiary test. Under this standard, an employment relationship is created when the tangible and intangible benefits provided to the intern are greater than the intern's contribution to the employer's operation.

Read it as many times as you need to. Read it one more time than whoever proofread the opinion. What this actually says is something like this: employers only have to pay interns if the intern is already getting more out of the relationship than the employer is getting.

It's backwards. There's no way that's what the court intended.

For the rest of the opinion, the court never actually restates which way the balance should tip in the "primary beneficiary" test. Instead, it says things like: "[T]he proper question is whether the intern or the employer is the primary beneficiary of the relationship."

I've checked a few news reports and commentaries on this case, and so far, they're all ignoring this error. I expect that by the time this book comes out, someone will have caught the error and fixed it. **But what if that never happened? People see what they expect to see: that's why it's so hard to proofread one's own writing. What if some case crucial to your protagonist's fate or fortunes contained such an unintended switcheroo? What if no subsequent court case at the same (or a higher) level of the judicial hierarchy had clarified the matter? Since common sense actually does play a role in interpreting statutes and cases, at least some lower courts would probably follow the obvious intention. However, some lower courts might conceivably feel obligated to follow the rule as stated until the higher court could set things straight. This could create a window in which your protagonist would have some leverage for a favorable settlement.**

d. Employee or Independent Contractor?

One way many employers try to avoid the many rules governing employer-employee relations is to declare that the people doing the work aren't employees at all. No, they're "independent contractors," and therefore don't need to be paid overtime, given vacations, etc., etc.

The precise analysis a court will use to decide whether someone's an employee or an independent contractor will differ from place to place, but whether or not the FLSA applies, certain factors are usually considered:

- Who supplies any tools or equipment the worker uses to do the job;
- Who determines the worker's schedule, and what happens if the worker doesn't show up for work;
- Who controls other aspects of how the work is performed (the "right of control" test);
- How financially dependent the worker is on the business (the "economic realities" test).

3. Mother's Milk

Unlike the situation generations ago (for those of you too young to remember it), many mothers return to work within a few weeks or months of giving birth. There's a medical consensus that breast milk is the best food for infants for the first six months or longer. How can a mother keep nursing once she's away from home for eight hours or more?

Except for those very few workplaces that provide nurseries, the only way is for the mother to use a breast pump (or to express milk by hand, almost always a slower and more difficult process), and to refrigerate the milk for later use.

Since a 2010 change in the federal Fair Labor Standards Act, federal law requires employers with more than 50 employees to provide some sort of space, not in a bathroom, where mothers can pump breast milk undisturbed and in privacy. More than half the states have their own laws on the subject as well.

But many employers somehow haven't got the word. And while the U.S. Department of Labor's Wage and Hour Division at least theoretically enforces the federal rule, some state statutes are as toothless as the babies whose health they're meant to protect.

4. Non-Compete Agreements

Non-compete clauses, or (for a bit more gravitas) covenants not to compete, restrict someone's right to work in a particular field, in some location or locations, for some period of time. These are usually paragraphs in some more extensive contract. They've traditionally been used to safeguard trade secrets (see 14.M.4.); to prevent key employees from going out on their own and taking customers with them; to protect the employer's investment in expensive training; or to make sure that a deal to buy an existing business doesn't turn into a sucker play. The agreement may include, or be coupled with, an agreement not to hire away the other party's employees, or not to solicit the other's clients, or not to use any confidential information.

Some centuries back, English common law rejected all such agreements as improper restraints of trade. That started to change in the early 17th century, and in modern times these agreements are disfavored rather than prohibited. They still get pretty close inspection from the courts, since they restrict people's rights to practice their profession or otherwise earn a living as they see fit.

It's acceptable for an employer to condition an offer of employment on a non-compete agreement. In this situation, employment is the consideration (see 14.C.2.) the new employee receives. States differ, however, about the situation where an employer presents a current employee with such a provision. Some will treat continued employment (i.e., "we won't fire you if you sign") as proper consideration, while others require something more. The trend may be toward requiring additional consideration.

The geographical scope and duration of the agreement must be reasonable in light of the interest to be protected. For example, in an industry where technical advances become obsolete within months, a non-compete agreement lasting for ten years is likely to be held excessive. Similarly, if someone buys a business whose customer base is entirely in one state, and the seller agrees not to start a similar business anywhere in the U.S., that restriction is likely to be narrowed by the court or thrown out altogether. (Courts take both approaches to overbroad non-compete agreements, depending on state law, the circumstances of the case, and the particular judge's attitude toward competition.)

California is particularly hostile to non-compete agreements, enforcing them only in a few situations involving ownership of a business or of shares in a business. Notwithstanding the attitude of this entertainment-obsessed state, radio and television personalities elsewhere are often required to sign non-compete agreements. One currently open question: if someone successfully sues in some other state to enforce a non-compete agreement that California would reject, do California courts have to recognize that judgment under the Full Faith and Credit Clause (see 34.K.)? **The dramatic potential of stories featuring celebrities could add interest to a story based on such an agreement.**

For some reason, non-compete clauses are becoming more common in low-level jobs, such as sandwich shops, where neither trade secrets nor training investment seem to explain their necessity. **You might want to explore this as an example of corporate overreach and predict one or another outcome.**

M. Intellectual Property

Intellectual property (IP) law may not be as intimidatingly arcane as tax law, but it gets intricate enough, and I'm providing only an introductory overview.

I'll start with copyright — which you as an author had better get to know, to some extent, for your own protection. Again, I am *not* offering legal advice about this subject. But it never hurts to know, if and when you need legal advice, what your lawyer may be talking about. And just as authors sometimes write about authors, you may want to write about authors with copyright problems.

For example, you could put your POV character(s) on either side, or both sides, of one of those suits where Nobody S. Heardofme sues Best Seller, claiming that the latter's latest book was based on a story they showed the famous author at a conference.

1. Copyright

Copyright law derives from the congressional power to "promote the Progress of Science and useful Arts, by securing for limited Times to Authors and Inventors the exclusive Right to their respective Writings and Discoveries." That "limited time" has gotten longer and longer.

Originally, per the Copyright Act of 1790, copyright protection lasted 14 years, renewable for another 14 years if the author (or whatever creator) was still alive. To have that protection, the author had to dot some i's, such as including a copyright notice. By 1831, the term had increased to 28 years plus a renewal for 14, but it was necessary to register one's copyright. In 1909 came another increase, up to 28 plus 28. This statutory scheme was accompanied by state-administered "common law" copyright that governed unregistered works.

The federal 1976 Copyright Act provided the biggest increase yet, one that remains somewhat controversial in its extent: the author's life plus 70 years. (It's actually more complicated than that, with different terms for "works for hire" (see below) and for works that were published before 1978. Check http://www.copyright.gov/circs/circ15a.pdf for details.) And it's no longer necessary to include a copyright notice if the work was first published in or after March 1989. Nor is registration strictly necessary, though as I explain in a minute, it can be awfully handy.

The 1976 Copyright Act also brought all copyright law under federal control — except for what the federal law doesn't cover, namely expression that has never been captured in any tangible form. So a dance or speech that somehow, nobody has recorded on their cell phone could still be subject to the state's common law copyright.

But what does having a federal copyright mean? Here's a basic overview: the author of an artistic work owns the copyright from the moment of the work's creation, assuming it's in fact an original work and the author hasn't contracted away their copyright. The owner of the copyright has exclusive control of the work unless and until they contract away any rights.

Copyright doesn't cover ideas, such as "the idea of hunting a formidable whale at the lead of an eccentric captain" (an example used in one federal case), or, say, a rich handsome fellow with a scary secret falling in love with an inexperienced young woman (as in *Twilight* and *Fifty Shades of Grey*). Rather, it protects the particular expression of an idea. The dividing line between an idea and the expression of an idea can be elusive. One sees such hair-splitting as distinguishing between, on the one hand, "events" and "plots" in a story (not subject to copyright) and on the other hand, "storylines" (subject to copyright). (To which I respond: c'maahhhn.)

If an employee creates work that can be copyrighted for their employer, that's "work for hire," and the employer owns the copyright. (As to who's an employee as opposed to an independent contractor, see 14.L.2.d.) "Work for hire" also includes certain types of work listed in the Copyright Act, but *only* if they're produced per a contract that specifically says the work is to be considered work for hire. That list: contributions to collective works, portions of motion pictures or other audiovisual works, translations, supplements to another author's work (such as forewords, tables, or charts), compilations, instructional texts, testing materials, and atlases.

One can also transfer the copyright in an existing work, either entirely or piecemeal. Some of the sleazier publishing contracts have the effect of giving the publisher all or almost all of the rights that are normally part of the copyright bundle, such as publishing the work in various formats, authorizing adaptations for movies or TV, translating the work, and so on.

The copyright owner has the exclusive right to prepare or authorize preparation of "derivative works," those based on or adapted from preexisting works. If anyone puts out an unauthorized derivative work, or otherwise infringes a copyright, the copyright owner can get a court to enjoin (prohibit) the offending work's publication, distribution, etc., and to order impoundment (seizure) of all copies and any plates, et cetera, used to produce them. As far as I know, the statute hasn't been revised to reflect POD (print on demand) or ebook publishing, but presumably, any impoundment order nowadays would include some appropriate measures to prevent the use of digital files.

Many people mistakenly believe that one has to take some official action in order to have a valid copyright. As indicated in the little historical summary up above, that's no longer true. "Publishing" the work (a legal term whose meaning gets complicated) starts the clock running on the life of the copyright, but it does not create the right itself. Registering a copyright is very useful from a practical viewpoint, as it allows the owner of the copyright the option of collecting the damages listed in the federal statute without proving any actual damage; but unregistered works are still copyrighted works.

If the owner *has* registered the copyright, either before the infringement or within three months afterward, that owner has the choice of asking for the infringer's entire profit from the derivative work, plus any actual damages suffered from the work's publication, or of receiving the preset amounts set forth in the statute. Those preset amounts range from as little as $200.00 (if the court finds that the infringer had no clue that they were infringing) to as much as $150,000.00 (if the copyright owner proves that the infringer knew darn well what they were doing). That's for each work whose copyright was infringed.

Federal court decisions, and particularly those of the Circuit Courts of Appeal and the U.S. Supreme Court, add some wrinkles.

To prove copyright infringement, one has to start by proving that the copyright work was, well, copied. One does that by proving (1) that the alleged infringer had access to the original work, and (2) that there's a "substantial similarity" between the original work and the work alleged to violate its copyright. The defendant can still get out from under by proving that they created the work independently, without any reliance on the copyrighted work. People do sometimes have similar inspirations, and some ideas seem to bubble up out of the zeitgeist in several places at once. If one can convince the suspicious copyright holder, or the trier of fact, that this happened, that'll be the end of the matter.

There are various tests for "substantial similarity." One is "literal similarity," the verbatim copying or paraphrasing of the original work. The other kind of similarity is "nonliteral" similarity, most important if there is "comprehensive nonliteral similarity," where "the fundamental essence or structure of one work is duplicated in another." Some courts default to relying on that mythic figure the "reasonable observer," asking whether that admirable arbiter would find the works, as a whole, substantially similar.

Not every type of word arrangement can be copyrighted. Titles, whether of books, stories, or songs, have no copyright protection. Song lyrics, on the other hand, do.

What about nonverbal works of art?

Music can be copyrighted, and those who hold the rights to it tend to enforce that copyright militantly. Whether or not two pieces of music are similar, and if so, why, has led to some interesting litigation. The 1970 release of "My Sweet Lord," a song by George Harrison (originally one of the Beatles), was held to have infringed on the copyright of the 1963 hit pop song "He's So Fine," composed by Ronnie Mack and recorded by The Chiffons. More recently, the family of deceased singer Marvin Gaye won a verdict against Robin Thicke for infringing the copyright of Gaye's "Got to Give it Up" in Thicke's "Blurred Lines." While one fact hurting Thicke's case was his admission that he'd felt inspired by Gaye at the time he composed "Blurred Lines," the case has brought up and stirred much discussion about whether current U.S. copyright law is out of step with contemporary techniques of musical "sampling" and such. As I write this, the legal battle is still continuing.

Dance choreography is protected, but only once it's been "fixed" in some sort of recording. Similarly, a speech isn't protected until it's been written down or recorded.

Here's a creative area full of potential for character-driven drama: fashion design, with its many idiosyncratic, emotional, and/or flamboyant practitioners. At present, there's no U.S. copyright protection for fashion design as such, because clothes are "useful articles" and one can't copyright same. Only if some design element can be defined independently of a piece of clothing — for example, a pattern of sequins — is it protected by copyright law. There have been repeated efforts in recent years to amend the law for some degree of fashion protection. **Your designer could be pushing legislation and finding it difficult to collaborate with some influential but fashion-oblivious legislator. Or a plot to kidnap, blackmail, intimidate, or kill a rival designer could grow out of frustration with the lack of legal avenues for relief.**

The 1998 statute updating federal copyright law added a single exception to this "useful article" limitation: boat hull designs. **If you're interested in the more technical sort of historical fiction, you might explore how this came about, and all the political machinations that made it happen.** The apparent justification: boat hull designs can take years of hard work, taking into account multiple technical factors, without meeting the high originality requirements for a patent (see 14.M.3.). In fact, a Florida statute protecting boat hull designs was struck down as pre-empted by federal patent law. But as soon as the boat is available, the hull design can be copied in a few hours with a simple mold if some federal law doesn't step in to prevent it. The same rationale may apply to who knows how many other designs that don't have this protection, and **your historical novel could feature designers frustrated by this unequal treatment.**

---

a. Fair Use

The "fair use" of a copyrighted work isn't an infringement, even though access and similarity are undisputed. The relevant factors are:

(1) the purpose and character of the use, including whether such use is of a commercial nature or is for nonprofit educational purposes; (2)

the nature of the copyrighted work; (3) the amount and substantiality of the portion used in relation to the copyrighted work as a whole; and (4) the effect of the use upon the potential market for or value of the copyrighted work.

Factor (3), as applied to song lyrics, means there's no such thing as fair use where they're concerned. Songs, at least the modern variety, are short enough that any portion is too substantial for fair use to apply.

Some common types of "fair use" have solid public policy benefits to recommend them. Satire and parody, so important in our political culture, generally constitute fair use of the underlying material. Serious critical commentary and educational discussions are likely to fall within fair use if they don't go overboard on how much they quote.

There is one aspect of the notion of "fair use" that comes from case law, rather than from the copyright statute: the notion of a "transformative" use. As the U.S. Supreme Court put it in 1994, in the first major case exploring this idea, a "transformative" use "adds something new, with a further purpose or different character, altering the first with new . . . meaning, or message. . . . [T]he goal of copyright, to promote science and the arts, is generally furthered by the creation of transformative works. Such transformative works thus lie at the heart of the fair use doctrine's guarantee of breathing space." That 1994 opinion cited a 1990 Harvard Law Review article by Judge Pierre N. Leval. Leval put the point this way: "[if] the secondary use adds value to the original — if [the original work] is used as raw material, transformed in the creation of new information, new aesthetics, new insights and understandings — this is the very type of activity that the fair use doctrine intends to protect for the enrichment of society."

If you think fan fiction deserves this label, you're not alone. There is at least one group, the Organization for Transformative Works, pushing for the recognition of fan fiction as meeting this definition and thus falling within the "fair use" exception.

b. Public Domain

If a work of art has outlived its copyright, or the copyright owner decides to donate the work for unrestricted public use, or it was created by a federal government official while that official was officially working, then it's "in the public domain" and may be used or distributed by anyone. (A few states' constitutions or statutes put government artwork in the public domain as well.) Fortunately, no one can get hold of it and acquire the exclusive right to sell it to everyone else. It's free to all comers.

A copyright owner who wishes to put work in the public domain must express that choice by some positive act or declaration. A growing number of visual works are being placed in the public domain via the Creative Commons organization. Creative Commons also provides several different limited licenses that copyright holders can publicly associate with their works, allowing the reproduction or distribution of those works for specified purposes.

2. Trademarks

A trademark can be made of words, images, sounds, or some combination, but its purpose is specifically to identify a good or service, or the entity that supplies that good or service. It's the symbol of a brand. Trademarks can protect consumers who trust in the quality of a branded product. They also protect the investment that may make a particular brand worth more in the marketplace than a product equivalent in every aspect except cachet.

Actually, if the mark identifies a service rather than a product, it's a "service mark." And musical phrases are technically known as "sound marks." When we get around to having public odor dispensers, we'll probably have "odor marks" or "smell marks." I'll mostly use "trademark" as shorthand for "all kinds of marks" in this section.

Unlike copyright protection, trademark protection is about who gets there first. No matter how independent someone's path to a particular trademark, they don't get to keep it if they get there second. Once someone has registered the trademark, no one else may use the same brand name or logo or whatever (within limits discussed below), even if the late-comer thought of it in a public place, shouted "Eureka!" at the top of their lungs, and described it on the spot in excited detail.

Finally, copyrights and patents have, and by Constitutional command-ment must have, limited terms — but a trademark, though it expires regu-larly, may be renewed indefinitely.

The law of trademarks, like so much of our legal framework, comes from English common law. And unlike the copyright arena, the common law lingers more substantially for trademarks. Misappropriation of a trademark is one of several torts classified as "unfair competition" (14.F.5.).

Common law protection for trademarks under state law is based on their actual use, and limited to the geographical areas where they're used. This can create problems when people start a business in one state and then want to expand nationwide.

Federal trademark protection, on the other hand, *is* nationwide. So if some little company registers its trademark while operating out of Po-dunk, it can take its time expanding into New York or L.A. If the holder of a registered trademark establishes that it's been infringed, the holder can collect the damages spelled out in the statute. I'll describe these in a mo-ment.

The holder of a trademark can harness the power of the Customs Ser-vice to keep products with infringing marks out of the country. After a mark has been registered for five years, the mark becomes "incontestable," which means it's a lot harder to defeat its enforcement in court. (Yes, there are details. No, I'm not going to go into them.)

Registration also makes innocent mistakes less likely, as it's easier to find a registered trademark in a search.

Oh, and registration lets the holder put that cute little circle with an R in it next to the trademark.

The federal statute, usually called the Lanham Act, was passed in 1946. (Like many federal statutes, and unlike copyright and patent statutes, its only justification (as falling within Congress' constitutionally delimited powers) is the Commerce Clause (34.L.).) The Lanham Act defines a trademark as "any word, name, symbol, or device, or any combination thereof . . . used by a person . . . to identify or distinguish his or her goods, including a unique product, from those manufactured or sold by others. . . ." Despite this "person/his or her" phrasing, business entities can and very often do hold trademarks and other marks.

Here's a bit more about the registration process, including a recent procedural ruling that could provide frustration for your protagonist.

Whoever wants to register a trademark starts by applying to the U.S. Patent and Trademark Office (PTO). An examining attorney with the PTO checks, among other things, whether the mark the applicant wants to register is confusingly similar to one that's already registered. If the examining attorney refuses the registration application for any reason, the applicant has the option of appealing to the PTO's Trademark Trial and Appeal Board.

If the Board agrees with the examining attorney, the applicant has two quite different avenues for further appeal: the U.S. Court of Appeals for the Federal Circuit, or a U.S. District Court. Heading to the Court of Appeals means an appeal much like any other (see 32.J.): the reviewing court will look only at the record of proceedings, and won't hear new evidence. Appeal to the federal district court, and the applicant can bring in new evidence, including expert witnesses; and if the applicant loses there, they can still appeal.

Sounds like a good strategy, doesn't it? But according to the Fourth Circuit Court of Appeals, if an applicant chooses the district court route, then even if they win and the PTO's initial decision is reversed, they'll have to pay the PTO's attorney fees. This holding seems to be based on statutory language which hadn't been enforced before. So unless things change, that trademark had better be valuable indeed if an applicant is going to head to federal district court to try to register it.

To successfully sue someone for infringing a trademark, a plaintiff has to prove all of the following (with an exception discussed below):
- That the plaintiff owns a valid trademark.
- That the defendant used that trademark or a similar mark without the plaintiff's permission.
- That the defendant's activities had a "substantial effect on" interstate commerce. This test is satisfied by, e.g., advertisements distributed

or broadcast in more than one state; moving the marked goods between states; advertising the marked goods on billboards along interstate highways; or (ironically) sending the mark to another state in an effort to register it as the defendant's trademark.

- That the defendant's use of the trademark is likely to cause confusion among consumers. This is a crucial limitation. Would consumers be likely to assume some connection between the trademarked goods (or services or music) and whatever the defendant is peddling? The bar is lower if the defendant's goods (etc.) compete directly with those of the plaintiff. If the plaintiff's trademark covers luxury bath soap and the defendant's similar mark is used to sell charcoal for backyard grills, it may be tougher to convince the judge or jury that consumers are connecting the two.

So what can a plaintiff get by proving federal trademark infringement? The award can include some combination of the following:

- The profits the infringer made from their use of the trademark. The plaintiff only has to show the defendants' gross sales of the infringing product or service. It's up to the defendant to show their expenses in bringing in those sales.
- Any profits the plaintiff can show they lost due to reduced or diverted business.
- The costs of the litigation, such as filing fees.
- In rare cases, the plaintiff's "reasonable" attorney fees.

Perhaps because it may be tough to prove damages, the court can give the plaintiff up to three times the proved damage amount ("treble" damages, discussed in 30.B.3.).

If the plaintiff can show that the defendant "willfully and maliciously" (knowingly) used a counterfeit mark, the court can award three times the defendant's profits or three times the plaintiff's damages, whichever amounts to more; plus reasonable attorney's fees; plus (if the court feels like it) prejudgment interest (30.B.1.a.).

In the mid-1990s, Congress made life easier for holders of "famous" trademarks by passing the Federal Trademark Dilution Act. A trademark or other mark is sufficiently famous if it's "widely recognized" by U.S. consumers — except that the tests are more complex than that makes them sound, and include scope of advertising and of sales as well as actual recognition.

This statute replaces the requirement of showing likely consumer confusion with the lesser burden of showing the likelihood of "dilution by blurring." Factors in deciding whether that's likely include the similarity between the marks; just how "distinctive" and how widely recognized the famous mark is; and whether the defendant has been trying to establish, or has succeeded in establishing, a link between the famous mark and the defendant's own product. A variant of dilution by blurring, "dilution by tarnishment," is any "association arising from the similarity between a mark or trade name and a famous mark that harms the reputation of the famous mark."

You could find a way to have your character disregard this danger and end up facing twelve lawyers from Great Big Corporation across the courtroom.

If the defendant has managed to register their mark, however, then fame isn't enough to get the holder of the famous mark any relief.

Of course, if a trademark is famous, there may be other reasons to play around with it besides the hope of commercial gain. The Dilution Act specifically states that noncommercial uses of the mark don't violate the statute. The concept of "fair use," important in copyright litigation (see 14.M.1.a.), crops up here: the statute's examples of acceptable noncommercial use include such fair uses as comparisons between products, as well as criticism or parody of the mark holder and/or the goods or services it provides.

Can you, as an author, mention a famous mark in your book? Well, your intent in publishing the book is presumably commercial, at least in part: you'd like to sell a few, wouldn't you? So if you mention the product in a nasty way, or in a humorous way that a humorless corporation might consider nasty, you'd better go all the way to parody — and be prepared to establish as much in federal court.

In 1999, after society had well and truly entered the brave new world of the Internet, Congress amended the Lanham Act to address "cyberpiracy" or "cybersquatting." If some enterprising and computer-savvy person figures out what domain name the holder of a trademark is likely to want, and grabs it for themselves in order to extort money from or annoy the holder, they have violated federal law. **One could easily imagine some smartass 12-year-old getting into a world of trouble doing this as a prank.** (The details are in 15 U.S.C. §1125(d). There are lots of them.)

As noted above, a trademark can be a logo, a slogan, or a name. It can even be someone's family name. **Many a downtrodden employee probably dreams of cutting loose, starting a small business, and nailing up a sign with their name on it. Which is fine — unless someone else has already grabbed it.**

I'll give you an example from my own family history.

After being laid off at age fifty, my father, undaunted, decided to start his own engineering company. Not being particularly given to flights of fancy, he decided to call it Wyle Engineering Corporation. All well and good, until he heard from Wyle Labs, a very, very big company that provides (in their words) "specialized engineering, scientific and technical services." They didn't fancy his using the name Wyle on his separate little engineering company.

If he'd held fast and let them sue, would he have won? Maybe. But the fact that both companies did engineering, and that Wyle Labs had unquestionably been using the name longer, would have made things dicey. Dad didn't take the chance. Wyle Labs didn't mind co-existing with Charles Wyle Engineering Corporation, aka CWEC, so that's what Dad's company became.

What if my father had been a baker, starting up Wyle's Particularly Palatable Pastries? He'd have had a better chance, because there'd be much less chance of confusion. People would be less inclined to assume that Wyle Labs had branched out into the pastry business.

There's a similar story whose ending I've always particularly liked. **If no one has written it up, either as nonfiction or in fictionalized form, somebody should.** It's the story of the Lost Name Steak House and Saloon, in Mooresville, Indiana. Some years back, this establishment had a different name (possibly the name of the owner's family, though I don't actually know). Unfortunately, another, presumably better established restaurant had a similar name and decided to throw its weight around. Undaunted, the owners made a virtue of necessity, and changed the name to commemorate their losing battle.

Sometimes the little dog picks the fight with the Great Dane. Amazon Bookstore set up shop in Minneapolis, Minnesota in 1970, focusing on feminist fiction and nonfiction. As Amazon, the web site, took off, Amazon Bookstore started encountering the classic signs of consumer confusion. Customers and suppliers looking for the online retailer were tying up its phones and its sales personnel. So in 1999, they sued Amazon for common law trademark infringement. Amazon's strategy, which proved a public relations fiasco, was to focus on the Minneapolis bookstore's lesbian clientele, contending that the two retailers were in different enough businesses that Amazon the defendant wasn't infringing on Amazon the Lesbian Plaintiff's trademark. The parties settled the lawsuit in November of 1999, with the bricks-and-mortar bookstore assigning its trademark to the online retailer and receiving in return a license to call itself Amazon Bookstore Cooperative.

Even if a big company doesn't really believe some small-potato outfit using a similar trademark will be any threat to its business, the company may feel some pressure to get tough anyway. To keep a trademark, the holder must show that they've zealously protected it. Let a few minor infringements slide, and when a more important one occurs, there's a chance the courts will decide the company doesn't own that trademark any more.

Are there limits to what can become a trademark? Sure. Trademarks need to be "distinctive," as that term is defined in the relevant case law. There are five degrees of distinctiveness, from least to most distinctive: "generic," "descriptive," "suggestive," "arbitrary," and "fanciful." "Suggestive," in this context, doesn't mean racy, more's the pity — rather, it means that the words or image suggest the subject matter, like Coppertone® suntan lotion, or the intentionally misspelled Gleem® toothpaste. An "arbitrary" trademark is one that uses existing words or images that have nothing apparent to do with the goods one is selling, e.g., Camel® cigarettes or Apple® computers. A "fanciful" trademark is something made up from scratch, like Clorox® bleach, Kodak® film, or Xerox®.

Suggestive, arbitrary, and fanciful marks are deemed distinctive enough to make valid trademarks, without the need for any additional proof. If a plaintiff claims that "North Pole Tours," say, is a trademark, they're in generic or descriptive territory, and they'll need to show that they've already managed to establish the words or image in the public mind as signifying their particular product.

One can't use the flag of a state or country as a trademark. One can't use anyone's signature or portrait without that person's written consent. And there's a special rule about using the name, signature, or portrait of a deceased President of the United States during the life of "his widow" without that widow's consent. Whether "widow" will be defined to include "widower," when appropriate, remains to be seen.

What if the PTO or its Trademark Trial and Appeal Board doesn't like a particular trademark?

The Lanham Act allows rejection of a proposed trademark if it "[c]onsists of or comprises immoral, deceptive, or scandalous matter; or matter which may disparage or falsely suggest a connection with persons, living or dead, institutions, beliefs, or national symbols, or bring them into contempt, or disrepute." To the extent the difference between "scandalous" and "disparag[ing]" has been defined, here's a somewhat oversimplified version of those definitions: "scandalous" means that a substantial portion of the general public finds the mark shocking and offensive, while a proposed mark "disparages" a person, entity, or group if the person or entity, or a substantial portion of the group, reasonably views it as insulting.

This provision has been at the center of an ongoing tussle between various Native American activists, the Washington Redskins football team, and most recently the Trademark Trial and Appeal Board. That board has twice found the trademark Redskins to be offensive to and thus "disparaging" of Native Americans. The first decision, in 1999, was reversed for insufficient evidence and on procedural grounds, but the second, in 2014, was affirmed at the U.S. District Court level in July 2015. The Redskins' management argued that these restrictions violated the First Amendment (see 34.A.1.), but the court took the position that trademarks, since they're licensed by the government, are actually government speech which the government may restrict. Further appeals are likely.

However one acquires a trademark, and however one has defended it, there's still a way to lose it. If enough people start using the product's trade name as a common noun — if they talk of blowing their nose on a "kleen-ex" when they mean any and every kind of paper tissue, or "xeroxing" no matter what kind of photocopier they use — then someone who wants to use that no-longer-unique label in their advertising may be able to do so.

One could imagine a carefully planned campaign to make this happen, probably using social media. You'd have to come up with an adequate motivation, since a trademark once lost in this way could probably not be resurrected by anyone else.

One can also lose a trademark by failing to follow the procedures for keeping it. Per the current rules, those involve filing a form with the U.S. Patent and Trademark Office no later than the sixth year after the trademark was first registered, again before the 10th year, and every 10 years after that. The form lists the items the holder is selling that use the trademark, and must come with a photo showing that use. And there's a fee, currently $100.00.

3. Patents

Patent law doesn't sound that complicated at first glance, but in practice, it may be even more insanely complicated than tax law. If you want to have your story turn around patent law, I suggest finding a patent lawyer to grill. With luck, they'll be satisfied with an acknowledgment, rather than your life savings.

I will, however, mention a few points.

There are three basic types of patents:

- "Utility patents," for new and useful material objects (machines, gizmos, widgets, and pieces of such) or processes (usually industrial or technical).
- "Design patents," for original ornamental designs for manufactured items.
- "Plant patents," for brand-new types of plants, whether invented or discovered. The plant must not have been found in an "uncultivated" area. (Is this the Patent Office version of *Star Trek*'s Prime Di-

rective?…) With certain exceptions, the plant must be "asexually reproduced," reproduced in some way not involving seeds. It also can't be a "tuber-propagated" plant . . . except when it can. (These exceptions apparently have something to do with situations where the part that propagates is also the part that people eat. So???) One may only get a plant patent on an entire plant, not some portion of it; but one may get a utility patent on the method used to engineer a plant.

In general terms, a utility patent covers how a useful item works, while a design patent covers how a useful item looks. The U.S. Patent and Trademark Office has this to say about that distinction: "Both design and utility patents may be obtained on an article if invention resides both in its utility and ornamental appearance. While utility and design patents afford legally separate protection, the utility and ornamentality of an article are not easily separable. Articles of manufacture may possess both functional and ornamental characteristics."

Utility and plant patents usually last either 20 years from the date the application was filed or 17 years from the time it was granted, whichever is longer. (That gives some idea of how long the process can take.) However, if the patent application refers in certain ways to an earlier application, the term may be 20 years from the date of that earlier application. And there are other wrinkles for patent applications filed overseas.

During the term of the patent, the patent holder must pay the required "maintenance fees" to keep the patent alive. (There's nothing like these maintenance fees in the copyright area. See 14.M.2. re keeping a trademark alive.)

Design patents last 14 years from the date they're granted.

Patents are like copyrights in that it's not enough to have a general idea. The application will need to describe the process, machine, design, or whatever in detail. This description is called the "disclosure."

Folks who need to remember the essential requirements for patents sometimes use the shorthand N-U-N, which stands for Novel, Useful, Non-obvious. To oversimplify somewhat, one can't patent anything that's been previously described or used, anywhere. (That's the "novel" requirement.) Whatever one is patenting has to be useful, or at least have the potential to be useful, to someone, somehow, somewhere. And whatever the device/process/thingie adds to existing knowledge can't be obvious to every halfway knowledgeable person; and it can't be just an obvious combination of prior knowledge.

Who may apply for a patent?

- The actual inventor. If there are several, they apply jointly. (Just paying for the R&D doesn't make someone a joint inventor.)
- The estate of a deceased inventor.
- The guardian of an "insane" inventor. **If the guardian and the inventor had very different views of how the invention should be used, and it was the guardian's machinations that got the inventor declared insane in the first place. . . .**
- If no actual inventor is interested, or the inventor can't be found, someone with a proprietary (ownership) interest in the invention may apply; but that owner may only apply on behalf of the inventor.

Once one manages to get a patent, what does that do? It lets the patent holder prevent other people from making, using, selling, or trying to sell whatever's been patented. The patent doesn't confer an affirmative right to do those things; but such a grant isn't needed, unless there's some legal obstacle (say, an environmental regulation), and a patent wouldn't remove that obstacle.

If someone infringes a patent, the patent holder can sue in federal court, getting an injunction to make them stop the infringement and/or collecting damages. If the patent holder can prove that the infringer made money that would otherwise have gone to the patent holder, the damages would include that lost profit. To prove that, the holder has to be able to prove (a) a demand for the product; (b) that no non-infringing substitutes are out there; and (c) that the holder could have manufactured and marketed the product themselves. If the plaintiff can't prove such damages, they'll get a reasonable "royalty": what someone would owe, per unit sold, if the patent holder granted the seller a license to make and sell the product.

One may assign (transfer, sell or give away) a whole or part interest in a patent. In that case, the person or company to which the interest is transferred may then make or use or sell whatever-it-is to their heart's content, and they won't have to ask the original patent holder's permission. Assign in haste, repent at leisure.

Patents have no effect internationally. One must apply for a patent in each country where one wants the exclusivity it may afford. And the patent laws elsewhere can be quite different.

By the way, the phrases "patent applied for" and "patent pending" don't provide any protection to, or impose any obligation on, anyone.

Current hot topics in patent law include attempts to patent people's genetic code. **Future hot topics could include patents on people's neural patterns.** Patent issues with serious public health implications would include when medical patents should expire and what sort of reverse engineering of much-needed medicines should be allowed.

4. Trade Secrets

Like the expression covered by a copyright, the invention covered by a patent, or the symbology of a trademark, trade secrets are made up of information. However, the law governing trade secrets themselves is quite different from the federally controlled, tightly scripted processes in place for copyrights, trademarks, and patents.

Hold on: what's a trade secret?

A trade secret is information used in someone's business which the business keeps secret, and which gives the user a business advantage over competitors who don't have that information. A few examples of the sort of information that could be a trade secret: a special alloy or compound used in some product; the design of a product or some component of a product; a special manufacturing technique that either makes the product different or makes it cheaper to produce; a recipe or its ingredients; a customer list or other customer information. States have differed, however, on when customer lists and the like should be treated as trade secrets.

Trade secrets don't have to involve desirable products or services, or info about what makes those products so good or those services so sought-after. They may instead involve blind alleys and fruitless experiments. Let the competition waste their resources exploring such!

The common law protected trade secrets by treating the improper use or disclosure of a trade secret as an intentional tort (14.F.), a type of unfair competition. But determining whether information was actually a trade secret could be quite complicated. The courts balanced six factors: how widely the information was known to those inside the business; what precautions were taken to prevent the information leaking out; how many outsiders actually had got hold of the information; how difficult and/or expensive it had been to develop the information; how difficult and/or expensive it would be for outsiders to come up with the information on their own; and how much of a competitive advantage the information gave its owners.

The Uniform Trade Secrets Act (UTSA) first came out in 1979, and was amended in 1985. (Re: uniform statutes generally, see 14.B.) As of 2013, 47 states, plus Washington, D.C., the U.S. Virgin Islands, and Puerto Rico, had enacted the UTSA, though they haven't all enacted it exactly as written, and their variations also vary from each other's. For example, some adopted the 1979 version and haven't gone back to conform their state statutes to the 1985 amendments. Also, several states have added explicit protection of customer lists.

The UTSA defines trade secrets as (simplifying what I regard as unnecessary legalese) information that has economic value because other folks who might use it don't know it and can't readily find it out without cheating. That paraphrase, however, leaves out one key element in the definition. The UTSA tightened up the definition of a trade secret, at least compared to some common law approaches, by making the owner's efforts to keep the information secret a part of the definition itself. Under the UTSA, it's not a trade secret if no one's taking much trouble to keep the information secret in the first place. And the UTSA requires "reasonable" precautions, not just any old efforts at secrecy.

The UTSA also took a step in the other direction: it doesn't limit trade secrets to secrets that cost a lot of money or effort to discover. However, courts may still consider all six of the common-law factors, even those that emphasize money spent or efforts made.

Courts enforcing the UTSA, like those following the common law of trade secrets, can issue injunctions preventing the competitor from using the trade secret. Victorious plaintiffs often get an injunction against future use along with money damages for past use. Money damages may be based on the plaintiff's lost income or on the defendant's unjust enrichment.

Both measures can be complex to calculate, but unjust enrichment may be somewhat easier to determine.

There's another option available in "exceptional circumstances": a "royalty injunction," letting the competitor keep using the secret as long as it pays a reasonable royalty to the owner of the secret. Royalty injunctions are more likely to be available when the competitor acquired the secret without realizing the secret had been misappropriated. States differ quite a bit about whether a royalty injunction requires a showing that the plaintiff will otherwise suffer irreparable harm, as injunctions generally do (see 30.A.). The UTSA doesn't specifically include that requirement; and since the irreparable harm requirement generally refers to the notion that money damages aren't good enough (see 30.A. again), an "injunction" that requires the payment of money might reasonably be supposed not to need such a showing.

The UTSA also lets the plaintiff collect treble (triple) damages (see 30.B.3.) and attorney fees for "willful and malicious misappropriation" of a trade secret. However, not all courts have been eager to award such damages and fees: some are unwilling to interpret "willful and malicious" as it's frequently interpreted in other contexts, namely meaning "on purpose and knowing you were breaking the law." These courts require that the competitor have some motive that goes beyond just trying to out-compete the plaintiff. And the UTSA also lets the court give attorney fees to a victorious defendant if the court decides the plaintiff pursued the action in bad faith (without any good reason to think the lawsuit could succeed).

There are ways a competitor may legally get hold of and use a trade secret. Unlike the situation for patents, it's okay to discover the secret by reverse engineering the product or process and figuring out how to duplicate it. The competitor may discover the secret by their own independent efforts. **This could lead to an ironic scenario: two competing companies, both devoting precious resources and considerable energy to guarding the same secret from each other.** Given these legitimate alternatives to improperly getting hold of a trade secret, the plaintiff must show that the defendant had access to it.

If the owner of the trade secret lets it leak through inadequate precautions, then it's fair game: under the UTSA, it ceases to be a trade secret at that point, and in general, trade secrets are protected for only as long as the secret is properly kept.

Is anyone surprised that the federal government has gotten involved? The federal Economic Espionage Act of 1996 ("EEA") makes some activities involving trade secrets into federal crimes, and also allows the U.S. Attorney General to go into federal district courts to get an injunction. The EEA reaches theft of trade secrets and various related activities that either:

(a) are pursued with an intent to benefit a foreign government, or with the knowledge that one will be providing such a benefit; or

(b) involve "a trade secret, that is related to a product or service used in or intended for use in interstate or foreign commerce." That's a pretty broad category, especially given how interstate commerce is currently defined (see 34.L.).

The owner of the stolen trade secret can't use the EEA as the basis for a civil suit, although Congress is currently working on changing the EEA to add a civil cause of action.

N. Second-Hand Claims, aka Choses in Action

What would you call it if someone encouraged someone else to start a lawsuit? What if the instigator hoped for a piece of any eventual judgment?

These days, even if you call it by the derogatory term "ambulance-chasing," lawyers are allowed to do it, though there are limits (including rules about how soon after a tragedy a lawyer may attempt to capitalize on it). But it can also be called "maintenance," or (if the lawyer would get a share of the judgment) "champerty"; and it used to be strictly verboten. The proliferation of lawsuits was, at that time, recognized as bad for society in general. **A story involving either the shameless pursuit of a particular case, or the pushy legal advertising that used to be against legal ethics rules (see 4.H.), could be used to support the public policy behind this prohibition.**

A claim on which a lawsuit can be based is called a "chose in action," and it meets some definitions of personal property, definitions that apply in some but not all contexts. (One definition it may not meet: the kind of "property" that gets divvied up in a divorce.) The rules about whether a particular chose in action may be assigned (transferred) under what circumstances, and how the resulting lawsuit would proceed, are complicated and may vary from one jurisdiction to another. For example, according to some sources, a claim for fraud (14.F.6.) can't be assigned before the lawsuit based on that claim has begun. Similarly, one may not be able to assign a claim for legal malpractice (2.O.). The common thread might be that these claims are based on a relationship between the parties that involved trust and/or integrity.

There's also a distinction between "legal assignment" and "equitable assignment" of a chose in action, based on the degree of formality involved. Whether it makes a difference may depend on the nature of the underlying claim. If you want the character to whom the chose in action is assigned to be able to sue in their own name, you'd better have the assignment in a writing that satisfies the requirements of a contract (14.C.).

O. Taxes

Of all the legal subjects best addressed by specialists, tax law may be the most impenetrable (with patent law also in the running for that title). I am no specialist. The details are very, very complex, and if you want your story to depend on them, you'll have a good deal of research to do (or to hire). I'll just sum up some types of taxes and who imposes them, and make a few comments about each.

---

1. Income Tax

First there's income tax. This tax comes in three flavors: federal, state, and (in some places) local. Given that many people who refer to the two certainties of "death and taxes" are thinking of income tax, it may surprise some that federal income tax didn't exist until the Sixteenth Amendment to the Constitution in 1913. Initially, the bite was more of a modest nibble.

World War I changed things for those in the upper brackets, and if you pay taxes in the USA, you know the rest.

Automatic withholding of income tax by employers didn't come in until 1943, during World War II, when presumably collection of maximum taxes seemed quite important. Withholding has the effect of disguising the amount of tax collected, and even leading many people to view the return of excessive tax collected (tax refunds) as some sort of windfall, rather than the repayment of an interest-free loan.

The federal tax code has become unbelievably complicated, to the extent that the staff of the I.R.S. (Internal Revenue Service) help lines frequently give incorrect answers. As mentioned in 17.B., receiving such erroneous advice doesn't protect a taxpayer from the consequences of the error — **a situation ripe for indignant fictional treatment.**

One reason for all the complexity is that for many years now, tax law has been used for social engineering, to encourage or discourage many kinds of behavior. Want more people to own homes, or contribute to charity, or use energy-saving devices, or make their homes less energy-leaky, or use more mass transit, or run small businesses? Give 'em a tax break if they do. (**One could come up with interesting constitutional challenges to, or political campaigns making an issue of, what charities get "recognized."**) Those are a few of the more well-known deductions with a social goal, but there are many, and accountants and tax attorneys help those who can afford the service find and take advantage of as many as possible. Some tax breaks are only available for a limited time; others have been around for decades.

Various proposals are floating around for simplifying the tax code, which would almost certainly involve getting rid of many of these tax breaks. Whether a simplified tax code would stay simple for long is anyone's guess, **but one could have fun with a cynical near-future narrative where it doesn't.**

Scam artists or deluded optimists periodically come up with various claims that no one really has to pay federal income tax. They're wrong, **but one could base a story on such claims, using either a comic or a tragic treatment of your protagonist's fate.**

Most, but not all, states impose their own income tax. Seven states (as of this writing) don't: Alaska, Florida, Nevada, South Dakota, Texas,

Washington, and Wyoming. Two states, New Hampshire and Tennessee, tax only the income from interest and dividends. These states may make it up, to some extent, with higher property, fuel, and/or sales taxes, though most have lower overall tax burdens than states that do impose income tax.

---

a. Income Tax Audits

The idea of having the IRS question the accuracy or truthfulness of your income tax return is scary enough, even if you're unusually confident that you dotted every "i." Tax audits happen rarely, and aren't always catastrophic or even damaging when they do; but there's certainly story potential in the worst possibilities.

More than 99% of all individual income tax returns sail through without any level of audit. If a taxpayer isn't reporting income from a farm, a business, or rental property, the odds of an audit go way down to .4 (that's point-4) percent, or approximately 1 in 250. Of those income tax returns that do get extra attention, something like 70% are handled by exchanges of mail rather than an in-person interview. A little under 10% of audits of any kind result in no changes — and a few (which, given hundreds of millions of taxpayers, means tens of thousands) of audits actually end with the taxpayer getting an unexpected refund. **You could have a taxpayer in crisis, perhaps something reminiscent of poor George Bailey's troubles in *It's a Wonderful Life,* and have the relief come not from generous neighbors but from an audit that goes decidedly in the taxpayer's favor.**

The IRS uses computer algorithms, supplemented with random looksees, to decide which returns are worth a second look.

In a mail review, the taxpayer gets a letter listing what documents should be mailed to verify something in the return. In-person audits may be "field audits," where the IRS agent comes to a home or place of business, or "office audits," where the taxpayer comes to an IRS office with records in hand. **A field audit could be complicated by an outspoken or emotionally unstable employee, or by the need to conceal evidence of some wrongdoing unrelated to income tax.** **An office audit could turn into a farce if the documents were particularly hard to transport, or if the taxpayer didn't pay attention to which sorts of documents the notice said to bring and hauled in every piece of paper in the building.**

The auditor could be double-checking what is there in the return, such as allegedly dubious deductions, or trying to sniff out what isn't there, as in additional income.

If an accountant or CPA or tax preparation service prepared the tax return, the taxpayer can hire them to come along to an in-person audit. In fact, the taxpayer can even hire someone like this to go to the audit instead of the taxpayer, as a "personal representative." The IRS has a form (a "power of attorney" form, used in this and many other situations) that such a representative would have to fill out. The taxpayer could also hire an accountant or a tax lawyer who didn't help with the return initially.

If a taxpayer tries to go it alone and decides mid-audit that they're in over their head, a federal statute called the "Taxpayer Bill of Rights" allows them to call a halt until they can get reinforcements in.

Most in-person audits only take one session of about two to four hours, but one may schedule a follow-up if necessary.

What sort of facts — aside from the types of income I've already mentioned — are more likely to get someone audited?

Well, there's reporting a whole lot of income, with the odds climbing as the amount goes up.

There's a mismatch between what the taxpayer reported and some other document the IRS received, such as a W-2 from the employer or a 1099 form from someone who hired the taxpayer for some independent project. Failure to report a foreign bank account is particularly dicey. And there's a form that casinos file for at least some gambling wins, so if that win doesn't show up in the winner's return, there'll be trouble.

Deductions higher than some IRS-computed average might do it, including unusually generous charitable deductions. (**A white-collar type suddenly having qualms of conscience about their lifestyle and deciding to share the wealth could find that indeed, no good deed goes unpunished.**) Deductions for business travel and entertainment also get a somewhat skeptical eye, as do claims that a motor vehicle is used 100% for business.

Filing a Schedule C, as businesses must do, will make one a more likely target; and if the business involves lots of exchanges of cash, an audit is more likely still. **If you want to drag a young entrepreneur through the wringer, it's not implausible.** There's also the tricky line between a business and a hobby. One may write off expenses for a hobby, but only up to the amount of income it brings in. After a few years of "business" losses, the IRS may decide the taxpayer isn't in business after all. (Possibly-still-current rule of thumb: if someone makes a profit three out of five years, they're in business. If the business is breeding horses, the IRS understands how tough it is, to a point, and only requires a profit for two years in seven.) Gambling is one of those hobbies-or-businesses, but with its own wrinkles: only professional gamblers may deduct food and lodging expenses, even if an amateur gambler makes a profit (i.e., their expenses add up to less than their wins).

Home office deductions tend to be taken by those who don't actually meet the fairly strict requirements, so such deductions get a second look. What requirements? The taxpayer must use the space "exclusively and regularly" for business. If they also play games on the computer in that room, they can try claiming that they'd do the same thing, for as many hours of the day, at a regular office . . . but I wouldn't count on that argument succeeding, **unless it turns out the auditor is also a games fanatic.**

The rules about who may deduct what sort of stock trading losses are tricky enough that such claims get extra scrutiny. Similarly, the rules about taxation of alimony, aka spousal maintenance or spousal support (14.H.6.) are so complicated that the IRS may not unreasonably hope the taxpayer messed up in some way. **An ex-spouse already pushed to the brink by divorce proceedings could tumble or dive right over the edge if audited because of much-resented alimony payments.**

2. Sales Tax

Then there's sales tax.

So far, we don't have a federal sales tax, although there are frequent proposals for either supplementing or replacing the federal income tax with a federal sales tax. Typically, this would include exemptions or income floors to protect low-income residents.

There are also folks who want the U.S. to follow the lead of, among others, the European Union by imposing "value added taxes" (VATs).

VATs can add a whole lot to the cost of a product because they're multi-level, taxing value added to a product at any stage of its production and sale. Don't hold your breath on these showing up in the U.S. any time soon.

At the time I'm writing this, Alaska, Montana, and Oregon have no state sales tax of any kind, although local municipal entities in these states may impose their own. New Hampshire has a tax on restaurant meals, car rentals and lodging, possibly because so many tourists consume these during the state's colorful autumn. Delaware's tax on gross business receipts indirectly raises the costs of goods and services.

3. Property Tax

Property tax may be the most infuriating, at least for some, because it taxes people simply for owning something that they've already (possibly) bought and paid for. And if they don't pay the tax, either through ignorance of its existence or through some other mistake, they can lose that bought-and-paid-for property for good.

The taxing authority (a local government, usually a county) can put a tax lien on the property — and that lien has higher payment priority than the mortgage. If the overdue tax isn't paid or a payment arrangement made, the county can sell the property at a tax sale, pay itself the tax out of the proceeds, and give the former owner what's left over. If some savvy party, possibly with help from whoever's organizing the sale, is the only bidder and gets the property cheaply, the owner will end up with considerably less than the fair market value of the property minus the unpaid tax.

Despite notification requirements, it somehow seems to happen from time to time that people don't even hear about the tax being overdue, or they receive incorrect assurances about the urgency of the situation, until the property has been sold.

However, all is not necessarily lost. The owner has a "right of redemption." Within some period of time (how much being determined by statute), the owner can pay the back taxes, along with various legal costs, and regain ownership of the property. Of course, those legal costs make it difficult to come up with the necessary cash in time, especially if the owner didn't hear about the sale immediately.

If the owner believes the necessary steps (e.g. proper notice) weren't taken or that some fraud was involved, they can sue. One approach would be an action to "quiet title" (see 14.D.5.).

4. Estate Tax

The two supposed certainties of existence, death and taxes, sometimes overlap. Estate tax piggybacks on one of our strongest instincts: to care for our loved ones as best we can, even after we're gone. Property that is passed on via someone's will is subject to federal estate taxes and possibly state estate (or in some states, "inheritance") taxes. Some states apply the same exemptions as the feds do, but in others, the state tax reaches assets that the federal tax doesn't.

Not every bequest or inheritance gets taxed. (I use both terms because "bequest" means a transfer via a will, while "inheritance" covers transfers of property upon the death of someone without a will (14.K.1.).) The federal estate tax doesn't usually reach property left to a spouse or to a federally "recognized" charity. There's also a hefty amount, currently more than five million dollars, that may be bequeathed in a will before any estate tax kicks in, unless that amount has been reduced via the linked gift tax (see 14.O.5., just below).

Of course, if someone has spent their life accumulating a multi-million dollar fortune, five million may not seem so hefty, and the feds may not be the folks he'd want to see benefiting from it. That's why there's a thriving legal industry devoted to finding ways for the wealthy to avoid estate taxes, via certain kinds of trusts and other devices that effectively pass property on without the use of a will. (See 14.K.10.)

As with income tax, estate tax is one of many, many ways that the federal tax structure is used for social engineering: to assist preferred causes, activities, or groups and to discourage others.

Estate taxes can be a hot-button political issue. It offends many people very deeply that even after someone has died, the government will grab for the assets they worked so hard to give to their children. Voters who will never amass anything like the amounts necessary to trigger the tax may still vote to put an end to it.

The law of unintended consequences may assert itself in this area as well. There are folks worried that when there's a major change coming in the details of estate tax, people will actually try to schedule deaths — their own, or more problematically, the deaths of others — so as to reap the maximum benefit of that change. **If you're game for some technical details, this motive could provide the climax of a whodunit.**

5. Gift Tax

Now we come to gift tax. As a special case of the principle that no good deed goes unpunished, we have the IRS decreeing that not too many gifts should go untaxed. Realistically, if there's going to be an estate tax, there must be a gift tax as well, or any wealthy person whose death is not a completely untimely surprise will evade the estate tax with premortem gifts.

If gifts made by one person to another within one year exceed a designated amount (which has risen over the past several years, year by year, and is currently $14,000), these gifts may be taxable. There's also a lifetime exclusion (also called an exemption) linked to the estate tax floor. This means, for example, that if, during your lifetime, you give away two million dollars, the estate tax floor drops by two million dollars, and if your estate exceeds that lesser amount, it becomes subject to estate tax.

Also, gifts given within three years (per the current rules) of death are subject to the estate-tax rules rather than the gift-tax rules. These aren't the only connection between federal estate taxes and gift taxes: if you're wading into those waters, you'll need to find most of the details somewhere else.

Transfers of assets over one million dollars, whether by gift or bequest, may also (in some circumstances) be subject to a "generation-skipping transfer tax." In general terms, it's intended to make sure that even if the wealthy give or bequeath large sums to grandchildren or great-grandchildren, the family still gets hit with gift and/or estate taxes at least once for each (approximate) generation.

State gift taxes are rare and getting rarer. Where they exist, they also tend to be connected to the state's estate/inheritance tax.

Financial note: I've been talking about bequests, gifts, etc. worth a certain amount — but who determines their worth, if they involve something other than cash or the equivalent? The federal standard is "fair market value," which sounds straightforward but can in fact be a time-consuming (aka expensive) figure to determine.

P. Fiduciary Duty

In what sort of relationship can you count on another person to think only of your needs and desires rather than their own, and always to act solely in your interests?

No, youngsters, it isn't marriage (at least not on this planet among this species). But this is what people are entitled to expect from anyone who owes them a "fiduciary" duty. A fiduciary is supposed to have, or act as if they have, complete loyalty to the principal (the person or entity on the other end of this relationship). In a fiduciary relationship, the principal relies upon and trusts someone for assistance or protection. However, this reliance and trust must be reasonable under the circumstances. One can't just saddle someone with this responsibility willy-nilly. The fiduciary must agree to take on such responsibility, or at least agree to assume some position that comes with a legal or ethical duty of loyalty. That agreement might conceivably be insufficient if the fiduciary obviously (*really* obviously) lacked the necessary expertise and mental capacity for the job.

Attorneys have a fiduciary duty toward their clients. Corporate directors have a fiduciary duty to corporate shareholders. Legal guardians have a fiduciary duty toward their wards. Asset managers have a fiduciary duty to those whose assets they manage.

But wait, you may ask: don't some of these people get paid? How is that in the principal's interest? Wouldn't the principal be better off getting all this loyalty and assistance for free?

Well, since there'd be very few available attorneys, asset managers, corporate directors, etc., if payment weren't allowed, all that's required is that the principal know about and agree to the compensation, and that the compensation be "reasonable" (one of the law's favorite adjectives).

Remedies for breach of a fiduciary's duty will depend on the particulars, but are likely to include compelling the errant fiduciary to turn over any profits gleaned from the breach.

Q. Blame the Boss - Respondeat Superior

Who has a "deeper pocket" (more financial resources to pay a judgment), the employee or the employee's boss? Usually the latter. So it's handy for plaintiffs that under some circumstances, they can sue the employer for an employee's tortious conduct. The law-Latin name for this doctrine is "respondeat superior," which means "let the superior answer," and the common law has recognized it for centuries.

The basic idea: the employee, as agent of the employer (the "principal"), is doing the employer's bidding, and therefore the employer should be held responsible for any damage that results. The key issue is usually whether the employee was in fact acting within the scope of their employment at the crucial time. This can be a tricky question, depending on what might seem like minor factual details. For example, whether an employer is responsible for injuries suffered in an auto accident, where the driver at fault got drunk at a company party, may depend on the amount of pressure on employees to attend the party and where the crash took place. There's also a fine line, drawn in different places in different jurisdictions, between a minor personal detour (e.g. a trip to the proverbial water cooler) during the workday and a more significant "frolic." (I'm not sure how many folks have committed torts while at or en route to the water cooler, but I won't rule it out.) Finally, the employer's apparent attitude toward certain conduct, and the extent to which the employer encouraged, tolerated, or discouraged it, may make a difference. **Did the repo company hire felons and retired boxers?** Or ** did it screen such people out and put its new hires through training in defusing potentially violent confrontations?**

R. Bankruptcy

Bankruptcy is almost as complicated as tax or patent law, and if you're intrigued enough by this summary to write about it, what I have to say is just a starting point.

First, it's almost all federal. One of Congress' enumerated powers, per the U.S. Constitution, is to enact "uniform Laws on the subject of Bankruptcies." The current federal law is called, unsurprisingly, the Bankruptcy Code. (See the discussion of Chapter 7 property exemptions, and the discussion of "clawback," for how state law can still enter in.)

There are Federal Rules of Bankruptcy Procedure, supplemented by local rules in various bankruptcy courts. Each federal judicial district — of which every state has at least one, and more populous states have many — has its own bankruptcy court. No other court, state or federal, has jurisdiction over a bankruptcy unless the debtor appeals. (There may be circumstances where the government appeals, but I haven't been able to find any references to them.)

The debtor may appeal the bankruptcy court's decision to a federal district court, and from there, if still determined to keep fighting, to a regular federal appeals court (Circuit Court of Appeals). If the bankruptcy court is in the First, Sixth, Eighth, Ninth, or Tenth Circuits, the debtor has another choice for the first appeals stage, a special appellate panel for bankruptcies (called, again straightforwardly, a Bankruptcy Appellate Panel, and staffed by bankruptcy judges). From there, once again, the appeal could move into the regular federal appeals system.

The goal of bankruptcy is to allow people with crushing burdens of debt to start over, while giving fair treatment to the various creditors who supplied the debtors with goods, services, or money. At least, that's the ideal. Which side in general, or which creditors in particular, are likely to benefit most and least may be expected to shift back and forth with the political winds and resulting changes in bankruptcy law.

The immediate benefit of filing for bankruptcy is that it calls off the hounds. As soon as one files, an automatic stay puts a halt to all efforts by all creditors to collect debt. From that point, it's up to the bankruptcy court to decide who gets what.

Individuals and businesses may file for bankruptcy. The rules are different for sole proprietorships (businesses built around the work of one person, run by that person) than they are for corporations and other businesses: sole proprietorships, like individuals, can (with certain exceptions discussed below) have their debts "discharged" (eliminated) in bankruptcy, but other businesses, including corporations, generally can't. For the latter, bankruptcy will involve "reorganization" of their debts, with repayment schedules the financially tottering business can actually handle, and/or liquidation of assets (sale of those assets for cash).

Much of the actual work in a bankruptcy happens in an administrative office rather than in court, in meetings with an appointed trustee. That's oversimplifying, of course. . . . There's a whole department called the U.S. Trustee. The U.S. Trustee appoints Chapter 7 trustees, who get one-year assignments to panels and are then are randomly assigned to particular Chapter 7 bankruptcies. (We'll get to the chapter numbers and what they mean in a moment.) Most Chapter 11 bankruptcies don't have trustees, but if they do, those trustees are appointed by the U.S. Trustee. Chapter 13 bankruptcies are administered by private trustees, but the U.S. Trustee supervises them. Trustees appointed or supervised by the U.S. Trustee are often called "case trustees."

There are five different types of bankruptcy, usually referred to by the number of the Bankruptcy Code chapter that covers them. So here they are, in numerical order.

Chapter 7 bankruptcy is often called "liquidation," even though there may not be any assets worth liquidating. It's for those individuals and businesses whose situation is too dire for reorganization alone. Creditors get paid according to a fixed priority. The lower a creditor falls on the priority list, the more likely that creditor will end up getting paid only a small percentage of the original debt, or even nothing at all.

The following priority order summary is a broad and oversimplified version of the complex reality.

Secured creditors are first in line. Secured creditors are those who loaned money against the security of real or personal property, with (in other circumstances) the right to take that property and sell it for repayment if necessary. Employee wages count as unsecured debt, but unpaid employees are in the category of "unsecured priority debts," which get paid before all other unsecured debt. All wage claims get paid before any employee benefit plans (see 14.S.).

Last in line, after all other unsecured creditors, come the corporate shareholders. Holders of preferred shares edge out holders of common stock, bringing up the rear. (For the distinction between preferred and common stock, see 14.U.1.)

If the same asset has been used as security for multiple loans, as in a first and second mortgage on real property, then a junior "lien" (claim on property) only counts as secured if the value of the property is more than enough to satisfy the more senior lien(s). If the property is not currently worth that much, the junior lien is said to be "stripped." Once the bankruptcy has concluded, all lienholders will be required to file the necessary paperwork to clear the property of the liens. (See 14.D.4.)

The trustee may sell all assets except the "exempt" ones in order to pay creditors. As for what assets are exempt under Chapter 7, this is one area where state law does come into play. States are allowed to come up with their own lists of exempt property. Some give the debtor a choice between the default federal list and the state list. Exempt property is likely to include at least some of the equity in the debtor's home, as well as a car. Household goods will probably be exempt unless they're particularly valuable. Some states exempt any property held by a married couple via a tenancy by the entirety (see 14.D.2.). In sum, the bankrupt doesn't have to start over with nothing.

If the state's exemption for a house or a car isn't its full value, but is capped at some dollar amount, and the house or car is worth more, the trustee may be able to sell the asset and give the debtor the amount under the cap.

The federal exemption setup and the setup in some states gives the debtor a "wild card" exemption for some amount, to apply to whatever property the debtor chooses. This exemption may be combined with others: for example, to make a car fully exempt so it won't be sold.

If the costs involved with selling an asset make the sale impractical, the debtor gets lucky and keeps the asset.

Chapter 7 bankruptcy is only available below certain income levels. As the least complicated sort of bankruptcy, it's usually over with within a few months.

Chapter 9 bankruptcy is only for "municipalities" (local government entities like towns or cities). There's no legal way for a bankruptcy trustee to liquidate a municipality's assets and distribute them to creditors, so this sort of bankruptcy tends to be a more limited version of what happens under Chapter 11.

Chapter 11 bankruptcy, sometimes called "rehabilitation," is for individuals and (especially) businesses whose affairs aren't so hopeless. (It can also be called "reorganization," but so can Chapter 13, which in some ways it resembles.) The bankrupt tries to work out changes in loan terms — reductions in interest, reduction of the principal (the original amount borrowed), stretched-out repayment schedules — that will let them get back on their feet. If the bankrupt isn't doing too well at handling the reorganization process, a trustee may be appointed; but the trustee doesn't sell anything off, only keeping an eye on the way the individual or business conducts financial operations.

As for discharge of debt under Chapter 11: for business entities that are still operating a business, the reorganization plan (once "confirmed" by the court) acts as a contract between the debtor and the creditors, replacing pre-bankruptcy contracts. It's a little different for individuals, whose debts are discharged later in the process (and if you want the details, go find a bankruptcy attorney to explain them). There's an "out" for an individual who can meet the requirements for a "hardship" discharge. What's required for a hardship discharge is a showing that (a) the unsecured creditors have gotten paid more than they would have if the debtor had gone into Chapter 7 on the date the plan was confirmed, and (b) what's been done is the best the debtor can do.

One interesting question that may arise in a Chapter 11 bankruptcy: are the owner's social media accounts personal, or assets of the business? The bankruptcy court may decide that whatever the owner thinks, the way the account is used makes it a business asset that must be passed along to whoever runs the company during the reorganization. The owner of a gun shop recently spent seven weeks in jail for civil contempt (see 30.D.), resisting an order to turn over the passwords for Facebook and Twitter accounts he insisted were personal. In the judge's view, the owner's frequent posts from gun shows, political posts in favor of gun owner rights, and so on meant that the account was being used primarily to boost the business. The owner still contends otherwise, but eventually yielded up the passwords in order to get out of jail.

Chapter 12 is only for family farmers and fisherfolk with a regular income from that activity, and lets them keep farming or fishing during the bankruptcy proceeding. It's similar to Chapter 13.

Chapter 13, which may be called "reorganization" (see above) or "adjustment of debts," is available only to individuals, but includes individuals operating as sole proprietors of businesses. Like Chapter 7, it has a financial ceiling above which it can't be used, but a ceiling involving the amounts of secured and unsecured debt rather than income. The focus of Chapter 13 bankruptcy is the repayment plan, a road map for at least partially satisfying creditors over time, which the bankruptcy court must approve. Payments are made through the bankruptcy trustee. The debtor stays in possession of various valuable assets that would be liquidated in a Chapter 7 bankruptcy; but in the end, the debtor may only keep those assets if any secured loan against the assets is fully paid. A debtor who can't come up with an adequate plan may have to go into Chapter 7 instead. Chapter 13 bankruptcies typically take from three to five years to complete.

Exemptions play a somewhat different role under Chapter 13: the absence of sufficient nonexempt property can keep the debtor from getting a Chapter 13 bankruptcy at all. In Chapter 13, the debtor pays off creditors on a monthly basis, over time, with disposable income (income not needed for the debtor's living expenses during that time). Some of that disposable income goes to pay secured creditors and other high-priority debts. There's supposed to be some left for unsecured creditors, and those creditors are supposed to end up no worse off than if the bankruptcy were in Chapter 7 and the debtor's nonexempt assets were being sold for the creditors' benefit. So if the debtor's disposable income isn't enough to pay creditors at least as much, over the lifetime of the repayment plan, as they'd get from a sale of the debtor's nonexempt assets, the debtor is left with Chapter 7.

What debts may and may not be discharged in bankruptcy is likely to change over time, as Congress keeps tinkering with the Bankruptcy Code. Some debts can't be discharged no matter what sort of bankruptcy the debtor goes through. These non-dischargeable debts currently include: child support; spousal support; loans not listed in the bankruptcy paperwork; loans incurred after filing bankruptcy; debts obtained by fraud; judgments for damages awarded to compensate for willful and malicious injury to people; and judgments for damages due to death or personal injury inflicted while driving under the influence of alcohol or other drugs.

Tax liens and most other tax debt can't be discharged in Chapter 7 and aren't exactly discharged in Chapter 13, but they're significantly easier to handle under Chapter 13. For example, under Chapter 13, the plan can sometimes put other urgent creditors ahead of the tax repayment. What matters is that the tax debt gets paid by the end of the bankruptcy period. The tax man won't wait nearly that long in Chapter 7 bankruptcies.

Some types of debt may be discharged in Chapter 13, but not in Chapter 7. These currently include judgments for willful and malicious injury to property; debts arising from property settlements (as opposed to support) in divorce proceedings; and debts incurred in order to pay tax debt that is not itself dischargeable.

Caveat: I've been oversimplifying (really!). In Chapter 7, creditors can try to prevent discharge of a debt by filing an objection. Grounds for the court to refuse discharge include (and this is *not* an exhaustive list) fraudulent concealment or transfer of funds in order to hide assets, as well as failure to obey court orders (orders that might involve documents to be provided, or financial management courses to be completed). Some of these grounds can also prevent discharge of debt in a Chapter 12 or 13 bankruptcy, but creditors have no say in those cases.

If the debtor lies to the bankruptcy court and is found out later, the discharge of debt can be revoked upon request of a creditor, the case trustee, or the U.S. trustee. Details of when this may happen, etc., vary with the type of bankruptcy.

Most bankruptcies are voluntary, initiated by the debtor; but in some circumstances, a creditor can throw an individual into Chapter 7 bankruptcy as a way to increase the creditor's chances of getting paid. Per the current rules, the creditor must have an unsecured claim of at least $15,325 (*don't* rely on this figure being accurate whenever you're reading this book!), and the individual must have no more than eleven unsecured creditors in all (same caveat). If the debtor has twelve or more unsecured creditors, it takes at least three creditors acting together to start Chapter 7 proceedings, and their claims must total at least that same amount. The debtor can try to convert the bankruptcy to Chapter 13. The debtor can also contest the bankruptcy on the grounds that the requirements haven't actually been met; and if they are correct, the creditor responsible may end up paying damages, court costs, and attorney fees. Aside from that risk, bankruptcy offers debtors powerful enough protections that the creditor may be better off hoping the debtor stays *out* of bankruptcy.

If a debtor decides to go through bankruptcy and makes that decision in a hurry, that debtor could have some serious problems — and so could people to whom the debtor made payments or gave gifts. That's because the bankruptcy court can look back in time and retroactively reclassify loan payments and other transfers the debtor made.

The bankruptcy court will presume that the debtor has been insolvent (debts exceeding assets) for 90 days before filing the bankruptcy petition. State law can lengthen that period to several years. The court can, and very likely will, go after any payment the debtor made (whether or not it's in cash) to a creditor during that time. This type of transfer is called a "preferential" transfer, and the procedure of undoing it is known by the picturesque and graphic label of "clawback."

If the debtor made a payment or other transfer to what the law calls an "insider" (family, friends, business partners) during the *year* before filing, that's also considered preferential and gets "clawed back" the same way. **Even giving one's sweetheart an engagement ring months before your finances went bust might constitute a preferential transfer.**

Any transfer that's worth something and doesn't involve an exempt expense, and that's made within two years (or some period specified in state law, another state-by-state difference) before the filing, may be clawed back if the trustee shows that it was intended to hide assets or otherwise thwart the bankruptcy process. Such transfers are called fraudulent transfers. Example: you sell your new Mercedes to a cousin for the cost of a broken-down Volkswagen, knowing your cousin owes you a favor and will reverse the transaction when the coast is clear.

Are there any defenses to clawback? Well, if the transfer wasn't one-way — if the debtor received something of equal value at the same time — then clawback may not be appropriate. And there's some sort of possible exception for transfers made "in the ordinary course of business," though I haven't tried to figure out the limits of that defense.

Individuals and businesses can file for bankruptcy more than once; but the number of years they have to wait varies with the type of bankruptcy the debtor went through the first time and the type the debtor now wants to file.

What if the bankruptcy court refuses to OK a bankruptcy plan? Or what if the court approves the plan, and a creditor wants to challenge it? Whether either a debtor or a creditor can appeal the bankruptcy court's decision varies from one federal circuit to another. The matter gets even more complicated because the statutes governing bankruptcy are pretty murky about what sort of decisions are "final" enough to be appealed, and the rules on finality are different than they are in other cases (see 32.A.).

If you're wondering how someone who needs to file bankruptcy can afford to pay a bankruptcy lawyer, never fear: bankruptcy lawyers don't count as "creditors" and thus don't have to accept whatever partial payment (sometimes a pittance) must content the bankrupt's creditors. However, the bankruptcy court will be able to review the lawyer's charges and decide whether they're reasonable, although the mechanism for doing so varies with the type of bankruptcy.

For Chapter 7 and Chapter 13 bankruptcies, the local bankruptcy court may well have rules setting fees which will be assumed to be reasonable. Such fees may be called "presumptively reasonable" or "no-look fees."

The amounts will probably vary according to the cost of living in the area, although some locales allow higher fees than you might expect. For example, per a 2005-2009 study, fees in the Midwest were on the low end, which is hardly surprising, but fees in the Southwest tended to be highest. At that time, fees for a Chapter 7 were likely to be near $1,200 in the lower-cost court districts, and up to $2,500 on the higher end.

Where a fee schedule of this sort does exist, most bankruptcy lawyers charge according to it: it's too much hassle to do otherwise. Just what work is included in a particular no-look fee will vary from court to court.

Given the greater complexity of Chapter 11 reorganizations, one doesn't usually find presumptive fee schedules in those bankruptcies.

S. Green Pastures:

Pensions and Other Retirement Benefits

Whether as a subject of union negotiation, or an issue in a divorce where the spouses' assets are being divided, retirement benefits can arouse strong passions indeed. (Once, in mediation training, I played the role of a mediator while the instructor played that of the husband. He illustrated the typical depth of feeling on this subject by abruptly lunging forward, grabbing my chair, and shaking it, bellowing, "You're *not* going to take my pension!")

A pension is a "defined benefit plan" where, once an employee has worked for some amount of time and earned some particular salary or range of salaries, they are entitled to receive a payout based on those numbers, distributed at some regular interval (often monthly). Health care coverage after retirement doesn't count because the amounts to be paid are unpredictable, but the legal status of such coverage is similar.

Pensions used to be much more common than they are now. These days, "defined contribution" plans, in which both employer and employee contributes some amount with every paycheck, dominate the retirement landscape. Examples of defined contribution plans include Individual Retirement Arrangements (IRAs), 401K plans, profit sharing plans, and employee stock ownership plans. But perhaps twenty percent of those employed by private companies, and a higher percent of government employees, still have pensions to look forward to. Whether they should be counting on those pensions, or other retirement benefits like health care, to last for life is another matter, discussed below.

The key threshold to cross, with a pension or other retirement-related benefit such as post-employment health care, is when the benefit has "vested." A retirement benefit is vested when there is no remaining condition to be fulfilled before the employee is entitled to it. The benefit can vest before the employee may actually start collecting it, as long as the only thing left to happen is the passage of time. (If the universe ends and time is destroyed along with space, the issue will presumably be moot.) If the employee must work for months or years longer before having a right to collect the benefit after they retire, the benefit isn't vested yet.

In many jurisdictions, there used to be a presumption that benefits lasted as long as the retiree lived. As a result, some union or employment contracts were vague on the subject. As I write this, the U.S. Supreme Court has recently ruled (in a case about retiree health benefits) that no such presumption applies, and that the matter must be decided based on the principles for analyzing ambiguous contracts. (The legalese used was whether the benefits had "vested for life.")

With defined contribution plans, employees have an immediate vested right to get their own contributions back, but it may take years before the employee has a vested claim to the amount the employer kicked in.

How many years? To answer that, I'd have to be an expert on ERISA, the federal Employment Retirement Income Security Act. That's a very complicated statute I'm not going to describe or analyze in detail. Somehow, federal constitutional limitations notwithstanding, ERISA covers almost all private (nongovernmental) employers who offer pension plans or other retirement benefits, though churches are exempt. (There are some other exemptions as well. I told you it was complicated.) The plans covered include not only pensions and defined contribution plans but various kinds of plans related to health care, such as insurance, HRAs (health reimbursement accounts), and flexible spending accounts, scholarship programs, training programs, travel insurance, housing assistance, prepaid legal services plans . . . so many that if you're writing about any benefit provided by a private employer, you can't rule out ERISA having something to say about it.

T. Soldiers' and Sailors' Relief Act

There's all sorts of things it's harder to manage when you're away from home serving your country. And the sort of problem that could land you in court definitely fits that bill. The Soldiers' and Sailors' Relief Act is intended to reduce the chance that serving in the military will lead to some legal disaster on the home front.

I'm not going to go into all the ins and outs and "if"s and "but"s, but a member of the U.S. armed forces may be eligible for one or more of the following:

- reduced interest rates on various debts, including mortgage or credit card debt;
- protection from being evicted from a rented dwelling, if the rent is less than $1,200 per month;

and relief that's particularly important for those posted far from home:

- a delay in anything going on in civil court, including foreclosure (see 14.D.6.), bankruptcy, divorce, or a lawsuit, and protection against default judgments.

My sources differ as to whether members of the National Guard, Air National Guard, or Reserves have any rights under this statute when they're not on active duty. Clearly, those on active duty benefit more. Even if there is theoretically some coverage for those not on active duty, the following details make pretty clear that it'd be hard to invoke the statute under those circumstances.

For any debt that predates active military service, the service member can request that the interest be reduced (if it was higher) to 6 percent per year until they leave active duty. The creditor may then try to show that the member's service hasn't really "materially affected" the member's ability to pay the interest they originally agreed to pay.

As for eviction protection: once again, the landlord may try to prove that the service member or someone else in the family could actually pay the rent. If that doesn't fly, a court may give whatever relief it considers "just," with a three-month stay as one of the possible options.

The delay of court proceedings also depends on circumstances (like an extended and distant deployment) justifying it.

U. Corporations: What Makes Them Special

1. Corporate Form and Function

There's another word with which just about every English-speaker is familiar, but which is really a legal term: corporation. For those on the leftward end of the political spectrum, it's often used in some negative context: for them and many others, it usually means some great big company, probably one of a chain of companies, with tentacles reaching throughout the country or farther. All of that can be true; but a company fitting that description doesn't have to be a corporation (though most are), and a corporation can be as small as one person (though I'd guess that most have at least a handful of owners, aka stockholders or shareholders).

The details that follow will be of use if you decide to set your story in a corporate boardroom rather than, or in addition to, a courtroom. There's plenty of dramatic potential in the power plays that take place within a corporate structure and between corporations, or between a corporation and groups of shareholders. And if you wish to use the "evil corporation" trope, these details may help you do so with accuracy.

Basically, a corporation is a type of business, made possible by state statute, in which only designated assets are at risk when the business . . . does business. A contract or, especially, a tort judgment (see 30.B.) can be ruinous for a business that hasn't incorporated. If the defendant is the sole proprietor of a business, a plaintiff wielding such a judgment could potentially seize everything the defendant owns. A plaintiff with a judgment against a normal partnership can reach anything that *any* of the partners owns, even a partner who had nothing to do with the transaction or event leading to the judgment. By satisfying the requirements for setting up and running a corporation, the owners of that corporation can risk only the assets they decide to expose. Of course, those assets have to be sufficient to support the business, or at least to attract any necessary additional investment.

Ownership of a corporation is indicated by "shares" of its "stock." The owners get value for their shares either by getting "dividends" (cash distributions of some of the corporation's profits, typically paid four times a year ("quarterly")) or by reselling their shares (though there may be limitations on when and to whom they may sell).

The owners of the corporation can't directly run it, at least not in their capacity as owners. They have to elect a board of directors, which hires (and can fire) officers to run it. If the corporation is small enough, the owners may be the directors as well. For corporations large enough for their stock (see below) to be sold on the New York Stock Exchange or the alternate NASDAQ exchange, a majority of the directors must be "independent," neither current nor recent officers or employees. The board of directors must also have a separate Audit Committee of similarly independent directors with established financial literacy, while yet another independent committee establishes the officers' salaries and other compensation.

There are regular meetings for the stockholders, at which they can make changes in the bylaws (written rules) that govern the corporation, or replace directors, or decide whether to sell the corporation to an interested buyer. If the shares of a corporation are traded on a stock exchange, then a "hostile takeover," the purchase of control of a corporation without stockholder agreement, is also possible.

Some corporations have two types of stock, "common" and "preferred." The distinction is perhaps counterintuitive: holders of "common" stock may vote on who becomes a director, while holders of "preferred" stock may not. On the other hand, preferred shares come with almost-guaranteed dividends whose value is known in advance. Common shares don't. (I say "almost" because when times are tough, a corporation may be able to suspend dividend payments on preferred stock.) Also, in the event of bankruptcy (see 14.R.), preferred stockholders get paid before common stockholders. Most shares in public companies, shares people can buy on the stock market, are common stock. (See also 15.B.)

If the corporation ends up in court, it's more likely that it will be required to have a lawyer to represent it, rather than some officer or director or shareholder acting the way a pro se individual (2.K.) would. Even in small claims court, corporations may need to hire attorneys if the amount exceeds some pretty small sum.

I am not in a position to confirm or rebut this, but a lawyer I know who recently retired as a corporation's general counsel (see 2.H.) tells me that government regulators often treat corporations as "guilty until proved innocent," viewing them with suspicions based on a few well-publicized instances of corporate misbehavior.

2. "Piercing the Corporate Veil"

Ain't legalese poetical sometimes? This often-used phrase comes into play when someone, or many someones, use the pretense of a corporation to limit their liability without actually following all the rules that come with corporate existence. A plaintiff proving such a failure to follow the rules can get to the owner's assets after all.

3. Limited Liability Partnerships and LLCs

This is a complex hybrid beastie. While the details will vary from state to state, possibly even more than the details of corporate structure, the basic idea is that there is (usually, though not always) at least one general partner with the usual partnership exposure to liability, and then a host of limited partners whose exposure is limited to some fixed investment. The partners can run the business directly without a board of directors. There are no shares to be bought or sold. It's not uncommon for law firms to use this form of partnership, or the somewhat similar LLC.

CHAPTER 15

Federal Law with Both
Civil and Criminal Aspects

I'll be addressing two potentially huge topics in a limited, cursory way: antitrust and RICO. Antitrust, as a concept, predates the federal statutes that must now dominate any discussion of it, although the common law more often talked about "restraint of trade." RICO is a specifically federal and statutory response to the existence of organized crime; but it's frequently used well outside that original context. Both the federal antitrust statutes and RICO have both criminal and civil aspects.

A. Antitrust

So what are these "trusts" that "antitrust" law goes after?

Historically, "trusts" were big corporate holding companies (companies that exist only to own stock in and control other companies), used to create a monopoly or similar market-dominating setup. A business or set of businesses with a monopoly has complete control of the market in some commodity or service and can set prices, availability, and features just as it likes. Where there's a monopoly, there's no competition — and the basic American idea of how an economy should work includes plenty of competition.

330 • FEDERAL CIVIL/CRIMINAL

Federal regulation of trusts began near the end of the 19th century. Before that, there were some state antitrust statutes. Indeed, some still exist, to deal with anticompetitive operations so completely intrastate (within one state) as to avoid even our modern hyper-expansive view of the U.S. Constitution's Commerce Clause (see 34.L.). For the rest, three federal statutes (let's not count statutes that amended those three) govern.

The Sherman Act came first (in 1890). It prohibits unreasonable "restraints of trade" and any monopoly or attempt to monopolize. The language of the Sherman Act was on the vague side, and rigorous enforcement didn't really get started until the establishment of the Federal Trade Commission (FTC) in 1914. Then things slacked off for a while (partly due to President Coolidge's philosophy that "the business of America is business"). But Franklin Delano Roosevelt was elected in 1932 and took office in 1933, the same year the Antitrust Division of the Attorney General's office was established. Enforcement of federal antitrust laws started to pick up and gain steam in the mid '30s. It hasn't particularly slowed down since then.

The FTC may issue "cease and desist" orders under these statutes, but it's the Antitrust Division that does the litigating.

Targets of Sherman Act enforcement include "cartels," groups of producers who band together to control quantities, price, etc. For example, if OPEC (Oil Producing and Exporting Countries) were under U.S. jurisdiction, it would qualify as a cartel. In the 1920s and 1930s, the U.S. light bulb market was controlled by a cartel known as the Phoebus Cartel, which limited how many hours a light bulb could be expected to last (no more than 1000) in order to ensure that consumers and businesses would have to purchase more bulbs.

The Antitrust Division sometimes tries to go after international cartels that (unlike OPEC) are active in the U.S., especially since 1993, and has managed to successfully prosecute members of around 20 such cartels. (See below for more about criminal prosecutions.)

Here comes a bit of geometry: restraints of trade are either "horizontal" or "vertical." A horizontal restraint of trade involves an agreement among direct competitors in some industry, either manufacturers, wholesalers, or retailers of some product or set of products — an agreement not to compete all that hard. A vertical restraint of trade may occur when some entity buys up or controls multiple links in the production and distribution chain, e.g. manufacturers *and* wholesalers *and* retailers for some product.

Horizontal agreements to divvy up the market and/or charge certain prices are per se illegal, meaning no one has to prove that the agreements actually affect the market: that's conclusively presumed. A "concerted refusal to deal," namely a boycott of some business that isn't part of the club, is another horizontal restraint of trade that's illegal per se. "Collusive bidding," agreeing to submit bids different from the bids that would be submitted for a truly competitive purpose, is also per se illegal. Other arrangements, including vertical restraints of trade, are evaluated under the "rule of reason," which looks at all the circumstances to see whether the setup actually hurts competition or whether it might, on balance, actually boost it. (Historical note: between 1911 and 2007, vertical price-fixing was illegal per se.) There's an in-between category for arrangements that haven't been held to be illegal per se, but sure *look* anticompetitive. These arrangements, appropriately enough, get a variant of "rule of reason" analysis called "quick look."

In a good historical illustration of the notion of "unintended consequences," the Sherman Act was at one time used to target labor union activities, on the grounds that unions were labor "cartels." But then the Clayton Act came along.

1914's Clayton Act, in addition to exempting various union and agricultural activities, prohibited mergers and acquisitions that would tend to create a monopoly or have the effect of substantially reducing competition. When you read about the FTC investigating a proposed merger between Verizon and AOL and either approving it or disapproving it, the Clayton Act is the reason why. Companies over a certain size have to file paperwork and submit to scrutiny before proceeding with such deals.

The Clayton Act also added to antitrust law the categories of "tying arrangements" and "exclusive dealing arrangements." In a tying arrangement, a seller agrees not to sell to any buyer who refuses to buy certain other goods — or who *does* buy certain goods from a competitor who's not part of the deal. Tying arrangements fall under rule of reason analysis. So do exclusive dealing arrangements, in which a buyer agrees to buy only from one seller.

The Federal Trade Commission Act largely, but not entirely, overlaps with the Sherman Act. It reaches not only "unfair methods of competition" (see also 14.F.5.) but various "unfair or deceptive acts or practices." Only the FTC sues under this Act. The FTC also enforces quite a few more specific "consumer protection" statutes, including the Equal Credit Opportunity Act, the Truth-in-Lending Act, the Fair Credit Reporting Act, the Cigarette Labeling Act, the statute that's supposed to get us onto a "do not call" registry, and a few others.

As for what's an "unfair" act or practice, that's anything "likely" to cause substantial injury to consumers that (a) the consumers can't reasonably avoid and (b) isn't outweighed by benefits to consumers or to competition. This is obviously not the most precise standard imaginable, and political views (plus potentially other political concerns) are likely to affect the weighing process.

Most antitrust enforcement actions are civil suits by affected individuals or businesses or by the federal government, but blatant and high-volume violations of the Sherman Act can result in criminal charges.

The usual penalty for criminal conviction under the Sherman Act is a hefty fine (up to $1 million for an individual and $100 million for a corporation), and/or up to 10 years in prison (for whichever individuals the prosecution can nail). The corporate fine can go even higher if doubling the amount the corporation gained, or the amount the victims lost, would go over that limit. The Division has a "leniency" policy, also called "amnesty," which gives immunity from prosecution to the first company to come forward and cooperates in an antitrust inquiry. It also provides confidentiality to those who apply for this amnesty. Since around 2000, this amnesty is granted automatically once the program requirements are met.

Awards in civil suits under the Sherman and Clayton Acts usually (with a few exceptions) include treble, as in tripled, damages (see 30.B.3.), as well as attorney's fees and court costs. Plaintiffs in a civil suit under either of these statutes can also try to get an injunction (see 30.A.) against anticompetitive activity that threatens to inflict economic injury.

Things have actually gotten a bit easier for those sued for violating the Sherman Act since the 1970s. As of that time, the plaintiff has to plead enough facts to make the anticompetitive conspiracy not just "conceivable" or "possible," but "plausible."

So what counts as economic injury for antitrust purposes?

Well, if the anticompetitive activity leads to prices higher than they'd otherwise be (which might take expert testimony to prove), the excess counts as injury. This might be asserted by a class action (see 6.D.) if the amounts involved wouldn't be worth asserting by a single plaintiff. A competitor whose business ended up struggling due to anticompetitive practices could assert their lost sales. A would-be business owner who couldn't enter the market because of antitrust violations could claim the loss of potential profits — which could set up quite a battle about whether those profits were indeed likely.

Here's something that *isn't* "economic injury" to a competitor: a big-box store comes to town and offers lower prices than the local merchants (or it buys one of the local stores and digests it, thereby lowering its prices). And the opposite, price-fixing resulting in higher prices, won't lead to "economic injury" to a competitor who can also collect those prices.

Under federal antitrust law, only a person or company that purchases directly from the potential defendant, not indirect purchasers further down the line, will have a claim. (There are exceptions for some situations where the defendant owns or effectively controls the intermediate sales link.) State antitrust laws often extend relief to indirect purchasers as well.

Some kinds of corporate cooperation are perfectly legal. For example, if we didn't let companies share technical standards, there'd be no such thing as "a" USB port. We have all sorts of standardized products: from nuts and bolts (one of the first standardized products) to power cords to computer accessories like monitors and keyboards.

The American National Standards Institute (ANSI) is a nonprofit organization that coordinates the development of voluntary standards in multiple industries. ANSI also works with similar foreign and multinational organizations to ensure that at as many American products as possible will be commercially viable overseas.

Standardization got its start around the beginning of the 20th century. Coincidentally, this is not long after the adoption of the first federal antitrust statute, discussed above. **If you write alternative-history fiction, you might take a look at what sort of world we'd live in and what its technological level would be if the authorities in the U.S. and/or elsewhere had managed to strangle standardization in its proverbial crib.**

The antitrust authorities do keep an eye on just how competitors work together in developing or changing standards. For example, a company whose patented technology is inextricable from some technical standard may throw its weight around and extract anticompetitive concessions from the rest of the industry. Such conduct is called a "patent holdup." Standard-setting organizations try to prevent it by requiring that any crucial technology be licensed on reasonable terms in order to be included in a standard. The Antitrust Division has gotten involved by giving its views on various licensing setups. The FTC sued companies that tried to "game" the system by claiming that technology they had developed was non-proprietary and would remain available to all comers, while simultaneously applying for patents on that technology. Private companies have brought similar suits.

Participants in standardization talks may also be accused of straying off-topic and colluding in other, less tolerated ways. It's okay to talk about what a USB port will be like, but not to set prices or control the supply of USB flash drives.

B. Securities Regulation

"Securities regulation" primarily means regulation of the markets in which people buy and sell common stock, or shares, in publicly owned corporations. (See 14.U. for more on common stock.) If things are working the way they should, how much people are willing to pay for stock in a corporation will depend on the corporation's economic prospects, which in turn will depend on such factors as what goods or services the corporation sells, how well it's managed, whether it's being sued, whether a competitor has just come out with a better and cheaper version of what it's selling, etc. The goal of securities regulation is sometimes said to be ensuring that potential stock purchasers get accurate information about such facts. But sometimes, it's more about leveling the playing field.

Starting in 1933, federal statutes have set up an elaborate structure for regulating the sale and purchase of stock. I'm not going to go into much detail about it: if you're interested enough in the stock market to set a story in it, you probably know more about this regulatory structure than I do. But the Securities and Exchange Commission (SEC) is at its center.

The Securities Act of 1933 prohibited fraudulent sales of securities. Such fraudulent sales would include selling stocks after misleading potential purchasers in any way about the corporation's financial well-being or the value of its products. One example: the so-called "pump and dump" scheme, where someone connected with a corporation releases misleading or outright false information to make a stock seem more valuable than it is. Once the price goes up, those behind the "pumping" sell some or all of their shares at the inflated price. Those who purchase during the time the stock is inflated, and don't sell almost immediately, ends up with stock worth a good deal less than they paid for it. This is most likely to be attempted with stocks that aren't vigorously traded as a rule, and therefore attract less scrutiny.

Another tactic: setting up a corporation with a name similar to an existing and valuable corporation, then selling its stock to investors who don't take sufficient care to notice the difference.

The current regulatory setup includes many safeguards that make it far more difficult to deceive the public about such matters, or about the activities of the corporation's officers and directors. Corporations must publish quarterly financial statements, and annual statements accompanied by the opinion of an outside auditor. Annual proxy statements disclose all officer compensation. All major contracts must be filed as exhibits to an annual required filing. And so on. The advent of the Internet has made all such filings immediately available for scrutiny by the SEC and the public at large.

The drafters of the Securities Act of 1933 didn't think to include any provisions about fraudulent purchases. Naturally not: how can one make a fraudulent purchase? Well, it turns out one can. A company president proved that in 1942: he issued dubious pessimistic statements about corporate earnings and took advantage of the resulting lower stock prices to buy the company's stock more cheaply. Rushing into the breach, the SEC issued a regulation under section 10b of the statute. That regulation may be found at 17 C.F.R. (Code of Federal Regulations) 240.10b-5, and is called 10b-5 or 10b5 for short.

Here it is:

> Employment of Manipulative and Deceptive Practices: It shall be unlawful for any person, directly or indirectly, by the use of any means or instrumentality of interstate commerce, or of the mails or of any facility of any national securities exchange, (a) To employ any device, scheme, or artifice to defraud, (b) To make any untrue statement of a material fact or to omit to state a material fact necessary in order to make the statements made, in the light of the circumstances under which they were made, not misleading, or (c) To engage in any act, practice, or course of business which operates or would operate as a fraud or deceit upon any person in connection with the purchase or sale of any security.

What if someone doesn't lie, but just uses the truth that they learned from their corporate position or their connections to the corporation to make a killing on the stock market? Some countries have no problem with letting the people who know the most about a corporation use that information to their advantage. In the U.S., however, such "insider trading" is sometimes a violation of 10b5. It's covered in 10b5-1, which states that prohibition of "manipulative and deceptive devices" in the statute's section 10(b) includes "the purchase or sale of a security of any issuer, on the basis of material nonpublic information about that security or issuer, in breach of a duty of trust or confidence that is owed directly, indirectly, or derivatively, to the issuer of that security or the shareholders of that issuer, or to any other person who is the source of the material nonpublic information." There's a lot more, and quite complicated, language having to do with how to establish an affirmative defense to the claim of a 10b5-1 violation.

I'm not sure how long the language about "duty" has been in this rule, but whatever the language, the SEC used to apply 10b5-1 with a broader brush. For a long time, the SEC took the position that anyone with insider info, however acquired, had the choice of disclosing it, refraining from trading in the stock of the business in question, or breaking the law. However, a 1980 U.S. Supreme Court decision refused to allow the SEC to go that far. The defendant in that case, *Chiarella v. U.S.*, worked for a printer hired to print corporate takeover bids for a corporation hoping to acquire certain target corporations. The employee figured out the identity of the target corporations and bought their stock, then sold it after the takeover bids were announced. The court held that someone who's not a corporate officer, but who deduced insider information and made stock purchases accordingly, did not violate 10b5. According to *Chiarella*, failure to disclose insider information violates the rule only if the person with the information has some duty to disclose it. A corporate officer or director has such a duty to the corporation's stockholders, but the defendant held no such position. He had no prior dealings with whoever was selling the stock, and was not a fiduciary (see 14.P.) for those sellers. As to whether he owed a duty to the printer's customer, that possibility wasn't raised at trial and thus couldn't be used to nail the fellow.

If, instead of gleaning his information from documents at the printer's, this gentleman had been tipped off by a corporate insider in exchange for some personal benefit, that benefiting insider would have breached their own fiduciary duty and would be liable under 10b5. What about the outsider, or the "tippee?" The U.S. Supreme Court recently refused to review a Second Circuit decision that tippees will be criminally liable only if they knew about both the improper source of the information and a benefit to the insider "tipper," and that this benefit to the tipper must be more than the gratification of helping out a friend or a fellow alumnus, though it could be a benefit to the tipper's reputation or professional standing. Previously, the Ninth Circuit had allowed a conviction of the tippee based on proof that the tipper intended to benefit the tippee, with a friendly or familial relationship between the two providing sufficient basis. Current betting is on the Second Circuit's view, though the Supreme Court's denial of cert (see 32.F.) does not actually decide the question.

Current regulations make it difficult to keep insider trading from public notice, and reduce its likely profitability. Corporations must disclose most stock transactions by officers or directors within two days. If the purchase and sale (or sale and purchase) of corporate stock by an officer or director occurs with the two transactions within six months, the excess of the sale price over the purchase price must, with a few exceptions, be paid over to the corporation.

"Willful" violations of federal securities law may lead to criminal prosecution. What constitutes a willful violation, however, is not entirely clear and consistent. The exact meaning of this language may depend on whether the feds are looking to impose a fine or to throw someone in prison. In the latter case, per a 1997 U.S. Supreme Court decision, the government, at least in a case under Rule 10b5, must prove the defendant's "culpable intent" as well as their "breach of a recognized duty."

It turns out there's some overlap, and some inconsistency, between federal antitrust law and federal securities law. When that happens, according to a series of U.S. Supreme Court decisions starting in 1963, the securities regulations generally trump antitrust, with the person or company in question receiving immunity from antitrust enforcement. **If you enjoy historical research and the fiction that can spring from it, you might explore the legal proceedings and any turf battles preceding this detente.**

State laws venturing into the realm of securities regulation have the picturesque nickname of "Blue Sky" laws. They may, among other possibilities, prohibit fraud in the sale of securities, require brokers and dealers to register, require registration of the securities themselves.

There's a uniform statute (see 14.B.) called the Uniform Securities Act. First proposed in 1930, it was substantially rewritten in 1956, and 37 states ended up adopting all or part of it. Subsequent revisions made little difference until the 2002 version, which led to revisions in the statutes of at least 15 states. Again, I won't attempt a detailed summary. The uniform statute emphasizes such issues as fraud, misleading statements, and undisclosed conflicts of interest. It covers investment advisers as well as those who actually trade in stock. It also includes registration and record-keeping requirements. The administrator of this setup may suspend or revoke a registration in the event of misconduct. The uniform statute also has some interconnections with federal securities law. It provides for civil liability to aggrieved private parties, as well as criminal prosecution for most "willful" violations.

One area where states still tend to disagree: whether to treat annuities (contractual arrangements that provide periodic payouts) as securities subject to regulation. The Uniform Securities Act doesn't regulate "fixed annuities," which provide regular predetermined payouts, but does regulate "variable annuities," in which the amount of the payout depends on the success of the investments made by the annuity fund management.

Unless something has changed recently, New York has held out against adopting any Blue Sky laws, either based on the Uniform Securities Act or otherwise.

C. You Too May be Treated Like a Gangster: RICO

It all started with some very frustrated law enforcement folks. They were having a devil of a time getting juries to convict gangsters. Oh, they finally got Al Capone on taxes, but wasn't there some easier way?

Enter the Racketeer Influenced and Corrupt Organizations Act (RICO), in 1970. RICO was designed to make it easier to convict participants in organized crime by focusing on how organized crime actually functioned, and to nail the kingpins rather than just the small fry actually doing the murder, shakedowns, pimping, drug dealing, etc. It did this in several ways:

- Focusing on "patterns of racketeering." This was supposed to mean multiple violations of the sort of laws organized crime might violate in the regular course of business.
- Including those who initiated the criminal activity, even if they weren't out on the streets committing violent acts and so forth.
- Providing for pretrial restraining orders seizing the assets that would otherwise pay for the finest criminal defense teams.

At some point after RICO was passed, and certainly by the 1980s, the feds figured out that RICO could be a handy tool well outside its original context.

Various portions of RICO deal with investing proceeds from a pattern of racketeering in an "enterprise," or using such proceeds to maintain an interest in the "enterprise," or conducting the affairs of an "enterprise" through a pattern of racketeering. Most courts require the defendant to be someone or something other than the "enterprise," though the minority view has been gaining adherents. Where there's a requirement of two separate participants, that requirement may be satisfied even if there's only a sole proprietorship involved, if there's some formal separation between the individual and the business or if the business has employees. Where a corporation is the target, sometimes the corporation is the "enterprise" and its officers or employees are the participants. Where a civil suit is contemplated, this may raise the tactical problem of whether the lawsuit is financially worthwhile, since many courts won't allow the use of a "respondeat superior" approach (see 14.Q.) to let the plaintiff sue the corporation for its agents' misdeeds.

So what makes up a "pattern of racketeering activity"? A business (again, potentially including an individual in business as a sole proprietorship) may be accused of violating RICO if it uses the U.S. mail or telephone twice in 10 years for a "predicate act." A "predicate act" is any of a list of underlying crimes that might not be so serious, if RICO wasn't available to ratchet them up. Use the mail or the phone at least twice in 10 years for one of these acts, and that's deemed a pattern of racketeering activity.

What are these predicate acts? There are many, and some are awfully easy to commit. Here are a few examples of some "predicate acts" that may not immediately make you think of gangsters and the like:

- Selling (or maybe just distributing) a video of a live musical performance without permission.
- Using income that came from collection of a gambling debt, if the gambling involved violated any federal, state, or local law, in interstate commerce (which includes a whole lot of types of economic activity).
- Using income from "usury," charging more interest than some law allows, to acquire any interest (such as corporate shares) in any entity involved in interstate or foreign commerce.
- Selling goods or services with counterfeit trademarks.

- Obstruction of justice, of an investigation, or of state or local law enforcement.
- Making a false statement in a passport application.
- Interstate transportation of a stolen motor vehicle or other stolen property.
- Criminal infringement of a copyright.
- Violating restrictions on payments to a labor organization.
- Harboring an illegal immigrant.
- Conspiracy to participate in any of these (or the many other listed) acts.

Some of these federal crimes may, for a criminal conviction, require proof of some sort of intent — but under RICO, the only elements the prosecution must prove beyond a reasonable doubt, the usual standard for criminal prosecutions, are the "pattern" elements. The underlying crime, the predicate act, need only be proved by only a preponderance of the evidence! (Yes, I find this shocking.)

Also, as already mentioned, under RICO the feds can seize or freeze *all* the assets of the business involved at the time of indictment, *before* any proof that the predicate act has been committed. Those assets may be the defendant's only chance of hiring a sufficiently able and experienced attorney. The pressure to accept a plea bargain can thus be overwhelming.

The penalties for violating RICO include very long prison terms and forfeiture of assets unrelated to the criminal activity.

As mentioned above, RICO also has a civil side, allowing suits in both state and federal court. A successful plaintiff can collect treble (triple) damages (see 30.B.3.). One new twist currently in the news: some spouses of the wealthy, claiming that their spouses have hidden assets, are trying to pull their divorce actions into federal court and use civil RICO. So far, this hasn't succeeded, but stay tuned.

RICO has been used against many organizations unrelated to organized crime, including Catholic dioceses, Major League baseball, companies that hired illegal aliens, and anti-abortion activists who blocked entrances to abortion clinics.

D. Admiralty

Admiralty law, also called maritime law, covers a good deal of what happens at sea or on other navigable bodies of water, or on ships or boats that travel on such waters. I'll only be dipping a few toes, so to speak, into this extensive and complex area of law.

Article III, §2 of the U.S. Constitution extends the federal judicial power to "all Cases of admiralty and maritime Jurisdiction." The Judiciary Act of 1789 placed these cases under the authority of the federal district courts. (The current version of this jurisdictional grant is found at 28 U.S.C. §1333.)

Admiralty has its own common law, i.e. its own generations' worth of case precedents building on each other. If a case arises that falls into some gap in that law and isn't covered by a federal statute, then the court will look to more general common law for guidance. Congress' authority to legislate in this area is based at least in part on the Commerce Clause (34.L.). For those who distinguish between "admiralty" law and "maritime" law, the former means admiralty common law and the latter, a broader category, also extends to federal statutes on maritime matters.

What waters fall within admiralty jurisdiction? Well, the "high seas," to start with: the oceans where ships from any nation may be found and where no country claims exclusive authority. U.S. admiralty jurisdiction also covers America's "territorial seas," also called "territorial waters," meaning the inland edge of the ocean. The current international consensus is that territorial waters extend 12 miles from shore.

Admiralty jurisdiction extends to "navigable waters" inland as well. Navigable waters are those which can be traveled for purposes of commerce, including the movement of passengers. It isn't necessary that these waters be already so used, only that they could be. If a lake or pond or river is entirely contained within the land of a single state, with no sources or outlets that flow into or out of an ocean or a waterway in another state, then admiralty jurisdiction can't reach it.

The removal of a natural or man-made obstruction may turn a waterway into a navigable one. Conversely, the construction of such an obstacle may remove the waterway from admiralty.

Admiralty jurisdiction extends to cases arising from activity on vessels that could travel navigable waters, even if the vessel wasn't doing any such traveling when the relevant events took place. A vessel, per the federal statute, is an "artificial contrivance . . . capable of being used . . . as a means of transportation on water." Not long ago, a federal district court and the Eleventh Circuit Court of Appeals both decided that a "floating home," a wooden house-like structure with empty space below the main floor into which water could flow, met the definition of a vessel, even though it was never meant to convey anyone or anything from place to place. The U.S. Supreme Court disagreed, holding that a large floating object with no means of steering or propulsion wasn't a vessel after all.

While parties may normally choose which states' law will apply to their contractual dealings (see Ch. 18), one may not contract one's way out of admiralty jurisdiction.

Where the maritime element of a situation is incidental compared to the aspects that concern a local jurisdiction, state courts may take over. And the federal statute giving admiralty jurisdiction to the federal courts contains a "saving to suitors" clause that lets plaintiffs bring suit in state court in most admiralty cases. Once a plaintiff makes that choice, the defendant may not "remove" the case to federal court unless there's some basis other than admiralty, such as diversity jurisdiction (see 6.A.1.), for that transfer. **You could follow the travails of a state court judge, possibly new to the bench or (on the other hand) weary and ready to retire, trying to make sense of admiralty law.**

The substantive law governing the case will still be admiralty law rather than the state law applicable to similar cases. Thus, a suit for damage to cargo would not be decided based on the state's negligence law (14.G.), and a claim that one is entitled to possess cargo would not fall under the state's precedents or statutes governing conversion, detinue, or replevin (14.F.2.) However, the court may provide common law remedies available in state court, even if they wouldn't be available in a federal admiralty action.

Admiralty cases in federal court may only be tried to a jury in cases falling under the Jones Act, which provides a framework for seamen (ship crew members who satisfy certain requirements) to bring negligence actions following personal injury.

If one is bringing an admiralty action "in rem" (see 6.A.2.), that action must stay in federal court.

If a case could come into federal court based on either admiralty or diversity jurisdiction, then the plaintiff must explicitly designate it as admiralty or it will be handled under normal federal court procedures. In that event, trial by jury would be available.

The U.S. does not attempt to apply its admiralty law to ships that legitimately fly the flags of other nations, even if they are moving about in U.S. waterways. But if the ship has so little connection with that other country that it has no business flying its flag, the federal courts will treat it as subject to their jurisdiction and apply U.S. admiralty law.

Naturally, humans on board ships can breach contracts, commit torts, or commit crimes. Thus, courts administering admiralty law can deal with the same breadth of legal issues as other courts normally do. However, in the last several decades, starting in 1972, the U.S. Supreme Court has used its position as administrator of the federal court system to cut back somewhat on admiralty jurisdiction in tort cases. This still-developing limitation requires a "maritime nexus," meaning (a) some connection between the events giving rise to the action and traditional maritime activity, as well as (b) some potential for the events to disrupt maritime commerce. This latter test is not as restrictive as it might seem at first glance. For example, a collision between two pleasure boats or a fire on a docked pleasure boat can satisfy the maritime nexus requirement.

Similarly, there are some limits on the contract cases that will come under admiralty jurisdiction. To fit within admiralty, contracts that involve ships and boats are supposed to have something to do with the maritime activities, the operation or navigation, of the ship. A lawsuit filed because a painter adorned a boat with *Sweet Valley* instead of *Sweet Sally* might not satisfy that test. However, the contract cases that have been held to fall within or outside admiralty jurisdiction do not sort very neatly into coherent categories.

There will, of course, be some causes of action that can only occur on land, as well as others that need the maritime setting. The latter would include violation of rules governing shipping lanes or rights of way in water — as well as the exclusively maritime crime of piracy. **If you plan to write about pirates operating in U.S. coastal waters or on some U.S. river, you'll need to bone up on admiralty law.**

Other criminal cases that would be handled under admiralty jurisdiction include shipboard mutiny or any sort of shipboard assault.

The Federal Rules of Civil Procedure (FRCP) cover admiralty cases unless (e.g., in criminal cases) those rules have nothing to cover the occasion, in which case the court will follow the Supplemental Admiralty Rules. Those rules also trump the FRCP in the event of any conflict.

Shipowners are presumed to have a duty of reasonable care toward their passengers where possible negligence is at issue (see 14.G.).

Admiralty law differs in some respects from its land-based counterpart. For example, there are far fewer applicable statutes of limitations (Ch. 11). Instead, courts sitting in admiralty (another way of saying that the judge is wearing their proverbial admiralty hat) apply "laches," the equitable counterpart (17.A.). Oral contracts, which are often invalid on land (see 14.C.3.), are generally valid at sea. Joint and several liability (see 30.B.4.), a damages rule whose use and parameters vary greatly among states, does apply in admiralty. Special rules, some of them found in the Jones Act already mentioned, also govern the damages recoverable by seamen injured on board ship.

A federal statute called the Limitations Act lets shipowners limit their liability in cases of accident. Oversimplifying quite a bit: if the accident resulted from circumstances outside the owner's "privity or knowledge" (essentially, the owner's knowledge and control), and if the owner takes the required procedural steps in federal court, the owner's total liability for damages will be limited to the value of the ship and its cargo *after* the accident. There Limitations Act includes quite a few exceptions. One concerns liability for personal injuries and deaths, which may, for some categories of vessels, require increasing the available damage fund by a set amount per ship tonnage.

Another area of maritime law concerns the recovery of vessels and cargo sunk or otherwise lost at sea. Occasionally the concept of salvage is applied more broadly when there is a "maritime connection" between the sunken object and traditional maritime activities. For example, at least one court has treated the recovery of a seaplane as salvage. Another allowed a salvage action for cash found on a floating corpse.

There are two categories of salvage, contract salvage and "pure" salvage. The distinction may be obvious, as when the owner of the vessel or cargo hires salvage services; but there are also salvage contracts implied by law, when the circumstances suggest that a rational owner would have entered into a salvage contract had the owner been informed of the circumstances at the time. If the owner or other person in charge of the vessel explicitly rejects the offer of salvage, no contract will be found and no salvage award given.

Pure salvage occurs when someone seizes the opportunity presented by a maritime misfortune. The doctrine arises from the public policy benefits of encouraging recovery of vessels or goods that would otherwise be lost forever. Pure salvage has three elements:

- Reason to believe, at the time, that the vessel or cargo would be destroyed or damaged (or damaged further) if no one acted to salvage it;
- Voluntary action intended to salvage vessel or cargo, not based on any preexisting duty or obligation; and
- At least partial success. There is no award for a valiant but futile effort.

A minor role in the salvage operation, such as standing by to provide some necessary service or conveying messages, can suffice.

How much of the recovered material a "pure salvage" claimant (or "salvor") will receive depends on such factors as the effort and skill used in the recovery, the amount and cost of specialized equipment used, the value of the property, the level of danger the material was in, and the level of danger the salvors faced. Different courts will place these factors in different orders of priority.

Salvors may also collect money damages for damage to their own property during the operation and for expenses they incurred.

A salvage claim may be brought against the owner(s) of the vessel or cargo, or against the recovered material itself via in rem jurisdiction (mentioned above). A pure salvage claim will generally be brought in rem.

If some of those involved in a salvage operation concentrate on saving lives rather than property, they too may share in the salvage award. If only lives are at stake, however, the general maritime duty to preserve life at sea whenever possible precludes any award.

The law of salvage sometimes bumps up against, and is hard to distinguish from, the common law doctrine known as the "law of finds." When any valuable item, be it sunken ship or treasure buried on land, has been given up for lost, the law of finds takes over. Admiralty courts prefer to apply the law of salvage, which leaves some portion of the ship's or cargo's value for the owner, rather than the law of finds, which follows a "finders keepers" approach. Unless the owner or the owner's insurance company has explicitly given up hope of salvage, or the claimant has discovered an obviously ancient shipwreck for which no heirs have come forward, the situation probably falls under salvage. Ships owned by the U.S. or some foreign government are unavailable for "finding," on the theory that governments never give up searching for their sunken ships. There are also federal statutes that make some shipwrecks unavailable under the law of finds, giving title to the wrecks to either the federal or some state government.

CHAPTER 16

Sovereign Immunity:
Suing the State

I t may not surprise you that there are extra obstacles in the way of anyone attempting to sue a government body or official. "Government of
the people, by the people, for the people" is all very well, but letting
the people sue the government? . . . And yet it can be done.

"Sovereign immunity" is the doctrine that someone may only sue the
federal or a state government, or its officials and employees, if that government says they may. At one time, the definition was simpler: sovereign
immunity meant no lawsuit, or at least no tort action (see 14.F. and G.). If
governments wanted to enter into contracts, which is unavoidable in any
developed country short of an absolute dictatorship, they pretty much had
to allow some recourse for the other contracting party in the event of a
breach.

Then governments started loosening things up, or "waiving" their tort
immunity via various statutes. For example, the Federal Tort Claims Act
spells out when and how one may sue the feds over (like it says) a tort
claim.

One crucial factor is the government's consent. If the government enters into a contract, it's implicitly consenting to be sued for breach of that
contract. A statute waiving immunity gives explicit consent to certain lawsuits not based on contract.

It's more likely a government agency may be sued for negligence than for an intentional tort, though there may be ways to go after the government-employed individual who committed the latter.

Under the Federal Tort Claims Act and similar state statutes, tort claims don't go straight to court. The claimant has to start by filing a claim with the agency involved (using some "administrative" procedure). Then, if the agency decides its people didn't do anything wrong, there are ways to take the matter to court. However, the trial court won't start from scratch: it'll give at least some deference to the agency's findings.

The same sorts of questions that arise in suits against private employers (see 14.Q.) come up here as well. Was the government employee acting within the scope of their official duties?

States may draw a line between the exercise of "discretionary" duties, which require judgment and are immune, and "ministerial" duties, where the state employee simply follows procedures and dictates provided by others, and which are not immune. Other states differentiate between "planning" decisions in which a state official must weigh policy and politics (immune) and "operational" actions that do not rise to that level (not immune).

State statutes may place a monetary cap on damages available in actions, or some actions, against the state. In class actions (see 6.D.), if the state offers to settle and some members of the class accept that offer, the agreed payments may exhaust the funds available under the cap and leave the more stubborn plaintiffs unable to recover at all.

The question of whether municipalities (towns, cities, counties) may assert sovereign immunity is a complicated one. If a lawsuit seeks damages or costly injunctive relief, and would therefore have an impact on the state treasury, it may be treated as a suit against the state for sovereign immunity purposes. Where that isn't the case, municipalities may have sovereign immunity in some situations, depending at least in part on whether the state's constitution provides for it. As for what happens in suits against municipalities under the federal statute known as "section 1983," see 34.M.

At least according to some authorities, "sovereign" immunity covers states, while "governmental" immunity covers municipalities when they have such immunity.

Woven into all this is the Eleventh Amendment to the U.S. Constitution. The Eleventh Amendment protects states from lawsuits in federal court brought by other states or foreign governments, or by their citizens. In 1890, the U.S. Supreme Court interpreted this amendment as also prohibiting lawsuits by private citizens against their own states. The state may, however, waive its Eleventh Amendment protections against suit. Also, a long and sometimes contradictory series of U.S. Supreme Court decisions established that when Congress is exercising certain constitutionally authorized powers, it may abrogate (set aside) a state's Eleventh Amendment immunity. The various federal and state statutes effectively removing Eleventh Amendment protection in various areas make for the patchwork of state immunity and vulnerability summarized above.

All this makes for one of the more complicated and confusing areas of the law (as opposed to all those nice straightforward areas . . .). So if your story involves a suit against a government or its agents, plan on doing, or hiring, some research.

CHAPTER 17

Fairness in Action: Equitable Estoppel

Remember "promissory estoppel," the alternative sometimes available to someone who doesn't have a contract to rely on (14.C.5.)? That's just one example of a broader principle: "equitable estoppel."

The underlying principle behind equitable estoppel is sometimes stated as "he who seeks equity, must do equity." (This phrasing predates inclusive pronouns for unknown individuals.) However, this statement is a bit narrow, as equitable estoppel may arise in proceedings where no one has gone to court asking for an equitable remedy. (See 19.B. for what sort of actions are viewed as "in equity.")

The more accurate and broader way to describe equitable estoppel is that it protects parties against certain unfair results that could arise from the application of the usual legal rules. Often, the situation involves various sorts of misleading conduct, whether or not the actor meant to mislead. Caveat: the details of various sources' definitions of equitable estoppel don't always cover the exact same territory.

One common example of equitable estoppel is where there's an ongoing business relationship and one party has consistently waived (been willing to overlook) a requirement in the underlying contract. That party can't suddenly start enforcing the requirement, if the other party relied on the first party continuing to waive the requirement and would be injured by the sudden change of attitude. This could, for example, arise in a lease where the tenant has been violating some term of the lease right along, and the landlord never bothered to mention the violation or object to it until the landlord has some other reason to want the tenant gone.

In promissory estoppel, someone acted reasonably in relying on a promise, and equity therefore provides a remedy (though not a traditional contractual remedy) rather than leaving the person empty-handed for lack of a contract. On the flip side, if someone is induced by misleading or out-right false statements to enter into a contract, the other party may be equi-tably estopped from enforcing that contract.

A related doctrine, "judicial estoppel," may be asserted to prevent someone from switching positions on some factual or legal point that came up in the same or an earlier proceeding. For example, if John sues for custody of Junior and asserts that Junior is his son, he can't later turn around and claim that he has no duty to support Junior — at least, not un-less he can show that he acquired relevant new information in the mean-time. (This doctrine is related to "collateral estoppel" (see Ch. 28), but has more to do with an individual's conduct, rather than how an issue was previously resolved.) In some jurisdictions, judicial estoppel only applies if the person changing positions prevailed with the original position. This rule could be viewed as protecting the judicial system from looking foolish for having upheld a position later contradicted by the victor.

A. Laches

Some authorities include the doctrine of "laches" in equitable estoppel. "Laches" prevents a potential plaintiff from bringing suit after too much time has elapsed. Unlike a statute of limitations or a statute of repose (see Ch. 11), laches doesn't involve a specific time limit for a specific kind of lawsuit. Instead, it's a case-by-case determination that the would-be plain-tiff had more than enough time to act, and the intended defendant would be unfairly disadvantaged by the overly delayed suit.

On the other hand, equitable estoppel can also act to toll a statute of limitations (that is, to prevent it from expiring).

B. Limits of Equitable Estoppel

Even where state actors such as prosecutors act unfairly, equitable estoppel is generally unavailable to defendants in criminal trials, although doctrines like entrapment (see 13.T.) have a similar flavor.

The government also benefits from another limitation.

Let's say your eyes are glazing over as you stare at your income tax return. You call the IRS, wait on hold for some ungodly amount of time, and finally get to ask your question. You inquire as to the meaning of some confusing language, or provide some facts and ask whether you need to report certain income. You're lucky (you think): you get a nice clear answer, telling you what you may and may not do. You rely on that answer as you fill out your return. Then, a few months later, you're audited and assessed interest and a penalty for taxes the IRS now claims you owed all along.

Sounds like a great trigger for equitable estoppel, doesn't it? But the maxim that applies isn't anything about equity; instead, it's our old friend, "Ignorance of the law is no excuse" (13.S.). As a Minnesota federal judge put it in 2012: "[A] mistake of law by a government agent, acting without audit or examination, does not amount to an act or interpretation upon which the taxpayer could justifiably rely. *Those who deal with the government are expected to know the law and may not rely on the conduct of government agents contrary to the law.*" (That's my emphasis, not the judge's, who presumably found this language less ironic than I do.)

CHAPTER 18

Choice of Law

By now you're probably quite tired of my saying how this or that doctrine or rule may vary from state to state. But at least, you may assume, once you know what state your courtroom is in, you know what the law is.

Not so fast!

"Choice of law" rules may, under some circumstances, dictate that the law of another state, such as (for example) the state where the defendant lives, should apply rather than the law of the state where the trial takes place. And guess what? Even these "choice of law" rules may vary from state to state!

It's also common for contracts with big companies, companies which do business in multiple states, to include in the contractual boilerplate a provision that any controversy will be dealt with according to the laws of a designated state.

One might expect the chosen state to have laws favorable to the company whose contract language specifies it, at least in the kind of controversy likely to arise. There are, however, neutral and legitimate reasons for such contract clauses. If a contract involves a corporate takeover or some other transaction potentially affecting a corporation's structure or control, it's better all round to have a judge who's knowledgeable about corporate law. A state like Delaware, where many corporations are incorporated, will have many such judges.

Whatever the pros and cons for the various parties, if your story involves residents of different states suing each other, or residents of one state who get embroiled in a lawsuit in another, you'll once again have homework to do. And if your story involves a large company, you'll need to pick an appropriate state's law to apply.

A. Forum Selection Clauses

Contracts likely to contain choice of law provisions may also state that the case will be tried in the courts of a particular state or city (or, more rarely, another country). Even if there's no such provision, a court unfamiliar with the law of some other state might encourage or require that the case be heard in that state.

As with choice of law clauses, there are legitimate reasons for a contract to pre-select the forum where disputes will be heard:

- When a corporation is one of the parties in a lawsuit, it may have to produce multiple employees and boatloads of documents in court. That's less of a burden if the court is local.
- Some jurisdictions, and especially some counties, are notoriously pro-plaintiff. The judges may even be local plaintiff's attorneys who more or less pass the position of judge back and forth between them. Even where neither of these problems exist, it's easy for a lawyer to urge a small-town jury to stick it to a big-city corporate defendant. Forum selection clauses often designate large cities where juries will be less inclined to side reflexively with a corporation's opponent.

Judges and Juries

The United States didn't come up with the idea of juries, but we use juries far more than any other country I know of, especially in civil (as opposed to criminal) trials. That doesn't mean every case is tried to a jury, however — far from it. Not very many are (again, especially in civil trials).

A. The Other Kind of Jury

The kind of jury that hears evidence at a trial is technically called a "petit jury" (law French for "little jury"). The other kind is, logically, called a "grand jury," as "grand" is French for "large." Less logically, a grand jury may in fact have fewer members than a petit jury: the numbers vary from as many as 23 to as few as two, depending on the state.

Grand juries, when they're actually used, are part of criminal procedure. All states provide for the use of grand juries, but not all states actually use them, and those that do may use them only for serious felonies. They are convened (summoned, called up) to assess evidence offered by a prosecutor and decide whether there is probable cause to believe criminal charges are justified. If the answer is "yes," the result is an "indictment."

The alternative to convening a grand jury is for the prosecutor to file an "information" setting forth the charges, after which the defendant may request a preliminary hearing. The judge then decides, based on the evidence presented at this hearing, whether there is probable cause to hold the defendant for trial. While a preliminary hearing is an adversary proceeding, the judge will interpret the evidence in the light most favorable to the prosecution. Given this systemic advantage for the prosecution, defense counsel may offer little or no evidence or waive the hearing altogether — a tactic that also avoids giving the prosecution a crack at the defense witnesses (those already identified) any sooner than necessary.

The prosecutor (whether in a grand jury proceeding or in a preliminary hearing) is under no obligation to present a balanced view. They are free to give the jury only the evidence most damaging to the potential defendant. For that reason among others, it's often said that a prosecutor could get the typical grand jury "to indict a ham sandwich." (In one of life's little ironies, the original phrase-maker, New York Chief Judge Sol Wachtler, was later indicted for extortion and related charges, to one of which he pleaded guilty.) However, if the prosecutor doesn't really want to bring charges and has yielded to political pressure to do so, they may supply the grand jury with information undercutting their own case, as happened in 2014 when a grand jury had to decide whether to indict police officer Darren Wilson for shooting 18-year-old Michael Brown. **You could put together a riveting fictional treatment of such a situation using multiple points of view: a prosecutor trying to comply with the political diktat to convene a grand jury while still serving their own sense of justice; one or more jurors; the politicians pushing for an indictment; and the victim or their relatives.**

Grand jury proceedings are short on protections for the potential defendant. Normal rules of evidence don't necessarily apply, especially if the jury asks to see some material that would be excluded at a trial. For example, the only federal rules of evidence that apply to grand jury proceedings are those dealing with privilege (see 4.D. and 22.I.).

Generally, the potential defendant may not have their lawyer present in the room, but must ask for permission to leave the room and consult. There is no judge to observe and control how the prosecutor addresses the subject or characterizes evidence. Witnesses don't hear each other's testimony, and there are no reporters: the proceedings are confidential. Transcripts are made, but access to them is tightly controlled. (If someone ends up indicted, their defense counsel can then get access to the transcript of anything they said to the grand jury. Lawyers for other people charged with a crime may be able to get a transcript, but only if they can meet some substantial burden like showing "great prejudice" that would otherwise result.)

Of all those involved in grand jury proceedings, the only people who may later talk about what went on are the witnesses.

There are justifications offered for all this secrecy: that witnesses would otherwise be reluctant to come forward, and that the reputations of the subjects would be tarnished by the revelation that they were targeted. Given how rarely the subjects go unindicted, the latter explanation rings a bit hollow.

It's not uncommon for subjects of grand jury proceedings to later be charged with perjury on the basis of their testimony. Rather than taking that chance, the subject may limit their testimony by invoking the Fifth Amendment's protection against self-incrimination. However, if that fact somehow becomes known despite the requirement of confidentiality, it may in some jurisdictions be used to support an unfavorable inference in related civil proceedings. In other words, as discussed in 34.D., while no judge or jury is allowed to infer guilt of a *crime* based on someone's invocation of the Fifth Amendment, judges and juries in *civil* cases may be allowed to treat that silence as evidence of a tort, say, if the information comes their way.

Grand juries, once sworn, may meet periodically over months or even years, considering multiple cases. Their members are thus even more likely than members of petit juries to be elderly and retired.

Grand juries needn't be unanimous, though the percentage needed to return an indictment varies from state to state. (For that matter, petit juries aren't always required to be unanimous for the defendant to be convicted. See 19.C.)

If the grand jury refuses to indict, the prosecutor may still ask a judge for permission to file charges — but given how rarely this occurs, the judge may be skeptical about the existence of probable cause.

B. Judge or Jury?

There are some kinds of cases that may or may not be tried to a jury, and other kinds of cases where there will *never* be a jury.

In a criminal case where there is a possibility of more than six months' imprisonment, a defendant has a right to trial by jury. In some states, a defendant facing less than six months also has that right. A defendant charged with an infraction, such as a parking ticket, probably can't get a jury trial.

Almost every state provides trial by jury in civil cases as well as criminal — but the U.S. Constitution doesn't require them to do so. Federal constitutional protection for the right to trial by jury comes from the Seventh Amendment, part of the Bill of Rights. As discussed further in Chapter 34, the Fourteenth Amendment, passed after the Civil War, was eventually held to implicitly include or "incorporate" key portions of the Bill of Rights, making them apply to state laws and state courts; but the right to a jury trial in a civil case was not one of those so included. However, most state constitutions include this right as well. Louisiana's does not, but state statutes fill the gap to some extent, although only for cases in which the amount at stake exceeds $50,000.

In civil cases, whether one has a right to a jury trial generally depends on how much money, if any, is at stake, and on the archaic historical distinction between "at law" and "in equity," with only the former tried to a jury. In general, in most states, any sort of family law case (divorce, custody, child support, paternity) will *not* be tried to a jury. In other sorts of civil cases, the distinction may be related to what remedy the plaintiff (the person bringing suit) is seeking. A remedy other than money damages is more likely to mean a suit in equity, tried to a judge. Preview of coming attractions (30.A.): in general, if money can fix it, money is all the plaintiff can get. If money can't fix it, as where unique property is at stake, the plaintiff can get other kinds of relief, such as a judge ordering someone to do or stop doing something (injunctive relief).

The very entertaining movie *Intolerable Cruelty* (already mentioned a couple of times) gets this wrong. Highly successful Beverly Hills divorce attorney Miles Massey, in the course of constructing a false narrative to assist a client, informs her that "the jury" or "the jurors" (I forget which) will eat the story up. California does not appear to be one of the few states that allow a jury to hear divorces under some circumstances. States that do *may* include Georgia and Texas, but if this issue matters in your story, you should check the law of the state in question.

Having the right to a trial by jury doesn't mean it's always a good idea. A criminal defendant doesn't have to take advantage of their right to a jury trial. If a defense depends on some legal principle that the average juror might not "get," the defendant could be better off having a trial judge hear the case without a jury. (A lot depends on the reputation of the particular judge.) For example, defense counsel may want a case tried to a judge instead of a jury if the defense hinges on the existence of reasonable doubt. If a defendant does not plan to testify or to offer their own version of events, but instead intends to rely on the weakness of the prosecution's case, a judge may be a better bet, as jurors (the judge's instructions notwithstanding) tend to expect an innocent person to speak up and assert innocence. A trial to the judge is called a "bench trial." Whoever ends up deciding where the truth lies, be it the jury or a judge, is called the "trier of fact."

The defendant's waiver of trial by jury must be made with full knowledge of the rights they're giving up. If the transcript of the trial proceedings doesn't demonstrate such knowledge, the defendant can later get the resulting guilty verdict set aside. (See 32.B. and 32.J.)

In a civil case where the right to a jury trial applies, a party can waive (give up) that right. However, if another party wants a jury, and follows the right procedures to make that desire known, then a jury will hear the case.

C. A Dozen - or Not

Not all juries have the traditional twelve members. In some states, civil or even criminal jury trials may have six or nine members. A twelve-member jury is still probably the most common in criminal trials, but is not constitutionally required.

Nor must a jury always be unanimous. Unanimity is traditional, and the U.S. Supreme Court at one time considered it required in criminal trials; but in 1972, it changed its collective mind, at least where state courts are concerned. A pair of cases led to the somewhat puzzling result that federal, but not state convictions require a unanimous jury. However, almost all states do require a unanimous jury verdict for a criminal conviction. In civil jury trials, there's more variation: something like a third of states allow a civil litigant to prevail on the basis of a majority verdict.

These two elements, size and unanimity, do overlap. In a 1979 case, the U.S. Supreme Court held that if a jury in a criminal case is as small as six members, they must all agree for the conviction to be constitutional under the Sixth and Fourteenth Amendments.

Unanimity isn't always a simple matter. Must the jury agree unanimously on what happened, or only on the ultimate verdict? If different views of certain facts would change which statutes the defendant was found to have violated, the jury in any jurisdiction requiring unanimity would have to unanimously agree on those key facts. But what if different scenarios could lead to conviction for the same crime? In this situation, in at least some jurisdictions, the jury need not unanimously pick one scenario over another. For example, several federal appellate courts have held that where the defendant was charged with possession of a firearm by a convicted felon (see 34.A.2.), the jury need not unanimously agree on which of two or more possible firearms the defendant possessed. Per this analysis, they must only agree on the "element" of possessing a firearm. The U.S. Supreme Court held in 1991 and 2013 that this distinction between "elements" of a crime and the "means" used to commit the crime, with unanimity required only for the former, was constitutionally acceptable. But where the distinction should be drawn is not always clear.

Such complexities often arise in child molestation cases. The abuse may occur over months or years, and the child's memory of exact dates, locations, and other details may be fuzzy. Must the jurors unanimously agree on which particular event took place?

If the indictment or information (see 19.A.) specifies the date the crime was committed, then the answer will probably be yes, that unanimity is required on this fact. (A prosecutor may be able to avoid this problem by giving a range of dates rather than a specific date.) However, if the judge doesn't adequately explain that requirement in the jury instructions, and the defendant fails to object to those instructions (or objects but offers an incorrect instruction as an alternative), then the jury's failure to agree on the details may not matter. As discussed at 22.M.1., failure to object to some error at trial almost always limits the defendant, in a later appeal, to the argument that the trial court committed "fundamental error." In child molestation cases, the credibility of the alleged victim is generally the crucial issue, and where the jury clearly believed the child was telling the truth, the possibility that different jurors had different episodes of abuse in mind isn't enough to pass the very limited "fundamental error" test.

D. Picking the Jury

Jury service can be disruptive of anyone's life, and the pay is minimal (typically less than thirty dollars a day). Nor are employers usually required to make up the difference. Most (*not* all, so check!) states prohibit an employer from firing a juror because they are absent for jury duty, but that's not much consolation for days or weeks of lost income. So a potential juror may well wish to dodge this duty — but that's not so easily done. Those most likely to be excused, or in some states excused automatically, are members of the armed forces; those whose job involves public safety on a daily basis (such as firefighters and police officers); and pregnant women. An urgent temporary reason, such as the need to care for a very sick family member, may suffice if the judge sympathizes. The longer the trial is expected to last, the better the chance that someone whose professional or personal situation will collapse in ruins if they are absent that long will be excused.

A juror does have to be able to understand English well enough to follow the proceedings, and can't be in such poor physical condition as to make reliable daily attendance, or remaining awake and alert throughout the day, impossible. Nor may a juror be a minor, or a convicted felon whose civil rights have not been restored (see 32.G.).

Those least likely to try to get out of jury service are often retired people with little to fill their days. One is therefore likely to see a disproportionate number of such people on juries.

Lawyers rarely end up on juries. Many jurisdictions used to automatically exempt lawyers from jury duty, and even though that's changed, it's generally easy for them to get themselves excused. The judges don't want lawyers to miss hearings because they're on a jury somewhere. Besides, both judges and lawyers know that a lawyer on a jury could be something of a wild card. **Try it: put a lawyer on your fictional jury, giving the other jurors alternate views of the law, letting them know just what might be going on in the many "sidebars" (muttered conferences between the judge and the attorneys), and so on. If you try this, I'd recommend getting an actual lawyer to advise you.**

Given this possible outcome, one of the lawyers trying the case is likely to use a peremptory challenge, if necessary, to keep a fellow lawyer off the jury. (See 19.D.1., below, re peremptory challenges.)

It does, however, happen that a lawyer ends up on a jury. It's happened to other lawyers I know, and it happened to me. In my case, from what I could gather, the defense wanted me there because voir dire (again, see 19.D.1) revealed my membership in the American Civil Liberties Union, which stoutly defends the rights of criminal defendants; while the prosecutor, it turned out later, wanted an informed inside view of how a jury had viewed his case.

1. Voir Dire and Challenging Jurors

Once anyone who's going to be excused has headed home, how is a jury chosen from the general "jury pool" of potential jurors to serve in a particular trial?

Jurors are chosen by a process called "voir dire," which is French for "to see to say" and originally meant an oath to tell the truth. The voir dire process is designed to flush out any juror who shouldn't be on the jury, and to give the attorneys some chance to shape the jury to their liking.

Either the judge, the attorneys, or both will ask the jurors questions. Often the jurors are asked to fill out questionnaires as well, with information like age, profession, health, and prior involvement with the judicial system. A juror who doesn't answer these questions honestly can end up in serious trouble. In fact, the potential jurors are usually asked to swear that they'll answer truthfully. If they're caught in a lie, they might be charged with perjury.

If an attorney doesn't want a potential juror to end up on the jury, they may "challenge" the juror. There are two types of challenges: "for cause" and "peremptory."

A challenge for cause should be used when that juror can't competently and fairly serve on that particular jury. Maybe the juror is friends with — or an enemy of — the defendant, or one of the attorneys, or an important witness. Maybe the juror hates black people, and the defendant is black. Maybe the juror or a member of the juror's family was the object of a similar civil suit, and thus likely to favor the defendant. Or maybe the juror or family member was the victim of a similar crime, and thus likely to favor the prosecution. Maybe the juror admits that they could never award any damages to someone who was even a little bit responsible for an accident. (Under comparative negligence principles, a plaintiff who's less than 50% at fault may still be able to recover some of their damages. See 14.G.) Maybe the juror is phobic about firearms, and the exhibits will include them.

The attorneys may make as many challenges for cause as they like, although it's up to the judge whether or not to buy the attorney's argument and send the potential juror packing.

In cases where the death penalty may be imposed, the state may challenge jurors for cause if they say that they could never vote for that penalty, or that they could not be impartial in a case where that penalty (so to speak) hangs over the defendant. Critics of this process contend that "death qualified" jurors, as those who pass these tests are called, tend to be more inclined to favor the prosecution at the guilt-versus-innocence phase of the trial. There are limits: the state may not challenge for cause to every juror who has any doubts or scruples concerning the death penalty. Jurors who strongly favor the death penalty can also be weeded out.

An attorney uses peremptory challenges to try to get a jury who will decide the case their way. Each attorney has a limited number of peremptory challenges, or the process would go on forever. For major trials, or when representing well-heeled clients, attorneys may pay pricey jury consultants to tell them what ages, ethnicities, professions, etc. they should try to get on the jury. Whether these consultants are worth their pay, I couldn't say. **One could have fun, in a farce, with a supposed jury consultant who was actually an impostor and made outrageous recommendations about which potential jurors to challenge and which to keep.**

Obviously (I hope), a potential juror's race does not justify a challenge for cause. But what about peremptory challenges that eliminate most or all jurors of a particular race?

The rules here are similar to some states' rules about firing employees. In states with "at will" employment (see 14.L.1.), you may fire an employee for any arbitrary, silly reason, but not for the wrong reason, such as racial discrimination. The same goes for gender. In the jury context, a lawyer may decide to waste their peremptory challenges by doing their best to stack the jury with blondes, or getting rid of anyone who looks like their brother-in-law; but if their peremptory challenges will have the result of eliminating all jurors of a certain race or gender, they'll have to prove that that isn't their goal, and that they have some other, "neutral" explanation for the challenge in question.

One may not strike jurors based on their religious affiliation; but if their particular religious beliefs would actually prevent them from fulfilling their duties as jurors, one may challenge for cause.

2. Blue Ribbon Juries

Sometimes, in complicated civil cases, instead of hoping that ordinary jurors will understand the necessary expert testimony, the court may decide to choose a jury with a head start. A jury, grand or petit (see 19.A.), whose members already have considerable expertise in the subject matter may be called a "special" jury or a "blue ribbon" jury, and its use goes back hundreds of years, though it is not particularly common these days.

The use of a blue ribbon jury in a criminal trial raises concerns about the defendant's right to trial by a jury of their peers. The word "peers" is not part of the Sixth Amendment, but the courts have interpreted that amendment to include it, although what is required is a general cross-section of the population rather than a jury tailored to match the defendant's demographic. The U.S. Supreme Court rejected this argument against blue ribbon juries in 1947, and that decision has not been overruled, but the practice appears to have been abandoned throughout the U.S.

One could write about someone determined to get on a special jury due to some personal interest, hacking and/or otherwise faking their way to selection with phony credentials and then trying to keep up the facade as the trial proceeded.

E. Controlling the Jury

Once the jury has been chosen, the jurors will be asked to take an oath, typically en masse. The oath's contents are usually on the general side. For example, here's one from California: "Do you, and each of you, understand and agree that you will well and truly try the cause now pending before this court, and a true verdict render according only to the evidence presented to you and to the instructions of the court?" Sometimes the oath will include "so help you God" language, in which case a juror could indicate a preference to affirm rather than swear. A juror taken by surprise with such an oath might be embarrassed to speak up; **but they might resent the ambush, and be more likely to misbehave (see below) as a result.**

Unlike the oath to answer questions truthfully during jury selection, this oath usually does not, practically speaking, carry with it any possibility of punishing a juror who violates it. See below for the latitude jurors have in performing their duties.

Jurors are generally told not to read newspaper or other media (including Internet) accounts of the trial, and not to discuss the case with each other or anyone else until it's time for them to deliberate (discuss the evidence and decide on a verdict). Judges and attorneys are resigned to the fact that jurors will do some of this, but they hope to keep it to a minimum. It's particularly tricky these days to try to keep jurors from deliberately looking things up online, or stumbling on information in someone's Facebook post. (Jurors are frequently sent out of the room while the attorneys argue about what evidence should be admitted, so media and online sources may know about witnesses or exhibits that the judge decided the jury shouldn't see.)

In a particularly controversial trial, the jury may be "sequestered": essentially incarcerated, made to spend nights and weekends in a hotel under supervision (and perhaps without computers and cell phones). This practice has become less and less common, particularly as a response to general pretrial publicity. It is now likely to be reserved for cases where someone has attempted to intimidate jurors, or where some highly interesting fact, likely to be particularly well publicized, must be kept from the jury. Disadvantages of sequestering the jury include increasing the chance that jurors will drop out, which in turn can lead to a mistrial if the court runs out of alternates (see 19.F., below). There is also the possibility that jurors desperate to go home may be too willing to compromise on a verdict. Finally, the demands of work and family life make it more likely that a potential juror will have to be excused if sequestration is likely, which increases the difficulty of finding the appropriate cross-section of the population (see 19.D.2.).

Sequestration is even rarer in civil cases than in criminal trials, and when it occurs, it is likely to start later, when deliberations begin.

One alternative to sequestration, though it is also considered somewhat extreme, is to keep the jurors' identities confidential rather than including them in the public record, referring to the jurors only by number. Given the public policy favoring public access to government records, as well as the view that freedom of the press (34.A.1.) includes some degree of access to information about the operation of government, this secrecy is generally intended to last only through the end of the trial, though court personnel sometimes continue it for longer.

It used to be generally prohibited for jurors to take notes during the trial, perhaps on the theory that they would miss some evidence while writing other evidence down, or that their notes might over-emphasize some points. The reality that jurors won't remember anything close to all the evidence without taking notes has led to changes in this rule, at least in some courts. This sort of rule may vary not only from state to state, but from county to county. A judge in Indiana just sentenced a juror to 30 days in jail for contempt of court because he took notes on his cell phone.

Also, in some courts jurors are now allowed to ask questions, most often by giving them in writing to the bailiff, who will submit them to the judge for review and possible use. I heartily approve of this trend. As already mentioned, I managed to make it onto a jury once and experienced firsthand the frustration of having a pertinent question that the attorneys didn't address.

Oh, you want to know what that question was? Well, it was a robbery case, and one of the alleged robbers was still on the lam. The prosecution's main witness was a large young man. The defendant was a scrawny little fellow. The defense theory (if I recall, after all these years) was that the prosecution's witness and the missing robber had actually conspired to rob the place. The prosecution insisted that no, the defendant and the missing robber had intimidated the witness into handing over the money. I don't believe there was any evidence that the robbers were armed. The other jurors and I wanted to know: how big was the missing robber? If he wasn't much bigger than the defendant, we were far from sure that the two of them could have intimidated the witness into much of anything.

Speaking of frustration: let's address the generally thankless task of the alternate juror.

F. Alternate Jurors

In many criminal and some civil cases, one or more alternate jurors are chosen to hear all the evidence — and then, most likely, get no chance to say or do anything about it. Alternate jurors are spare parts, available in case so many jurors get sick or are removed for misconduct that there wouldn't otherwise be enough jurors left to decide the case. Without the alternates, the judge would have to declare a mistrial, which means the whole trial has to be redone from scratch (see 9.D.). In some jurisdictions, the jurors don't know until just before they start to deliberate which ones will be the alternates.

Alternate jurors sit with the rest of the jury throughout the case. If they aren't needed by the time the jury goes off to deliberate, they may be dismissed; or, in some jurisdictions, including the federal courts, the judge has the option of retaining them in case a juror takes ill during the deliberations. If an alternate replaces a juror after deliberations have started, the jury must start deliberating all over again. The judge would need to make sure, if there was any doubt, that the alternate hadn't been exposed to any information that was supposed to be kept from the jury.

Even if the court rules prohibit letting alternate jurors remain with the jury during deliberations, violating that rule probably won't be reversible error (see 32.J.1.) if no one objected at the time, as long as the jurors were instructed not to let the alternate join in the deliberations.

G. Jury Nullification and Other Shenanigans

One open secret about juries is that in criminal trials, jurors don't have to do as they're told. This is a big part of why we have juries at all. They're a failsafe against laws that may be unduly harsh or out of step with current societal values. If the law is unjust, the jury may simply refuse to apply the law. Such a refusal is called "jury nullification." This power can be extrapolated from several U.S. constitutional provisions. In addition, four states, Georgia, Indiana, Maryland, and Oregon, have state constitutional provisions or statutes saying the jury is the judge of, or has the right to determine, both "the law" and "the facts" of the case. (In Indiana, it's Article I, §19 of the state constitution.) Twenty more states have more limited provisions that apply to civil suits for libel, presumably due to the importance those states accord to freedom of speech.

Judges, understandably, would just as soon that jurors didn't know they have this option. The defense generally won't be allowed to argue that the jury should ignore the law. The most the defense may be able to do is get a jury instruction (see 27.B.) citing the "judge of the law and the facts" language if it exists in that state — and then largely contradicting it by saying that the jury should follow the law as the judge has explained it to them. **A clever defense attorney might be able to hint, just enough, at the possibility of jury nullification that even if the trial judge intervenes and tells the jury to ignore what the attorney said, the jurors will have picked up the clue.**

If a jury does break the rules, it's not so easy to do anything about it, especially if the verdict's already in.

During a trial, including while the jury is deliberating, there are various things a judge can do if informed that a juror has misbehaved. If, for example, some other member of the jury reports that a juror has hidden a powerful motive to rule for one party or the other, or has done significant research into some factual or legal issue, the judge may dismiss that juror and interrogate the other jurors to see whether their own ability to deliberate impartially has been affected. The judge could admonish (lecture) the other jurors, reminding them of their duty, or could even surrender and declare a mistrial (see 9.D.). It's anybody's guess what most judges would do if confronted, mid-trial, by the knife-shopping expedition out of which Henry Fonda's character made such hay in *Twelve Angry Men*. **But one could base a story on such events, aiming for anything from farce ("but *Henry Fonda* did it!") to tragic irony (e.g. an acquittal prevented by a mistrial, followed by conviction of the innocent defendant in a second trial).**

The options of judge and parties become much more limited once the verdict is in and the case is over. Rather than open the floodgates to endless accusations and second-guessing about how a verdict was reached, the courts have generally treated past jury deliberations as close to sacrosanct, refusing to hear statements from jurors about what was said or done during deliberations. Another pragmatic calculation supporting this policy: the likelihood of uncovering juror misconduct after the fact is probably less than the likelihood that dissatisfied parties or their allies would try to persuade, bribe, or intimidate former jurors into accusing their fellows (or even themselves) of such misconduct, especially in controversial cases where jurors are sequestered until and only until a verdict is reached.

Federal Rule of Evidence 606(b) implements this principle (for both trial juries and grand juries in federal courts) as follows: "During an inquiry into the validity of a verdict or indictment, a juror may not testify about any statement made or incident that occurred during the jury's deliberations; the effect of anything on that juror's or another juror's vote; or any juror's mental processes concerning the verdict or indictment. The court may not receive a juror's affidavit or evidence of a juror's statement on these matters."

Not all states strike this same balance. Some jurisdictions, applying what is sometimes called the "Iowa rule," allow juror statements if offered to show that a juror lied during the "voir dire" process (see 19.D.1.), though not to show misconduct during actual deliberations.

Juror misconduct or other skulduggery, such as attempts to influence the jury, can be proved by "extraneous" or "non-juror" evidence, such as testimony from court personnel or other witnesses to the event.

CHAPTER 20

Burdens of Proof

Any writer planning to deal with criminal trials should understand the "beyond a reasonable doubt" standard of proof. And anyone writing about other sorts of trials should realize that this standard doesn't apply.

How does the jury know what standard to apply? We'll get to that a little later (27.B.), when we talk about jury instructions.

Lawyers and judges usually speak in terms of "burdens" of proof. Let's start with the easiest burden to carry: proving a case by "a preponderance of the evidence."

A. Fifty Plus One: Preponderance of the Evidence

In most civil trials, whoever has the burden of proof on a particular issue has to prove the point by "a preponderance of the evidence," essentially anything more than 50%. So if, in the view of the "trier of fact," the evidence favoring the plaintiff is just a bit more plentiful or persuasive than the evidence favoring the defendant, and the plaintiff's burden is "preponderance of the evidence," then the plaintiff wins.

This standard is viewed as most appropriate when money or property is at stake; no fundamental rights are involved; and society has no great stake in who ends up winning. Most of the time, when there there's a dispute about money or property, the main concern of society as a whole is

372

that the dispute be settled peacefully, rather than that one or the other party end up victorious.

B. "Clear and Convincing"

(Whatever That Means)

In civil cases where fundamental rights are involved or there's a significant societal stake, you'll usually find that the plaintiff's case must be proved by "clear and convincing evidence," or some similar term. This is a higher threshold than "preponderance of the evidence," though its precise meaning is harder to pin down, and different courts' definitions differ. One thing is clear: this is not as high a hurdle as "beyond a reasonable doubt."

(For more on what constitutes a "fundamental right" in constitutional law, see the discussions of "substantive due process" and equal protection at 34.G. and 34.H.)

"Clear and convincing evidence" is the minimum burden of proof constitutionally permissible in termination of parental rights cases (cases where the government is seeking to permanently sever the connection between parent and child). Some states apply this burden of proof in less extreme parental rights cases, e.g. cases where a grandparent is suing for visitation with a grandchild over the parent's objection. (The grandparent, not the parent, must prove their case by clear and convincing evidence in these jurisdictions.) It may also be used in cases where a guardian seeks to discontinue life-sustaining medical treatment for someone unable to make that decision for themselves.

Clear and convincing evidence is the usual standard of proof for writs of any kind. Thus, while guilt in criminal proceedings must be proved "beyond a reasonable doubt" (see 20.C. below), if an already convicted defendant attempts to have the conviction set aside in a habeas corpus proceeding (see 32.E.), then the clear and convincing evidence standard will apply.

C. Beyond a Reasonable Doubt

In our system, criminal defendants are considered innocent unless and until proved guilty beyond a reasonable doubt. Many other countries' systems do the same, and several international treaties also require the use of that standard.

The novel *Presumed Innocent* has a wonderful passage in which a particularly defense-friendly judge explains things to the jury. I urge you to read the passage in its entirety, but I'll summarize it here. The judge asks a potential juror whether or not the defendant is guilty. The man says he doesn't know — and the judge dismisses him from the jury on the spot. The judge then explains that as the potential jurors sit in court and look at the defendant, they must say to themselves, "There sits an innocent man."

Depending on the crime(s) with which the defendant is charged, the prosecution may have to prove a list of factual generalizations about the crime, called the "elements" of the crime, beyond a reasonable doubt. (See the descriptions of various crimes in Ch. 13 for examples of elements.) The State doesn't have to meet this burden of proof for every detail that's part of the prosecution's story, but must satisfy that burden for at least some facts that match each of the required elements.

This standard does *not* mean "beyond any conceivable doubt." Different judges in different states will define the term slightly differently, but here's one fairly typical example of a jury instruction on reasonable doubt, from Connecticut.

> The meaning of reasonable doubt can be arrived at by emphasizing the word reasonable. It is not a surmise, a guess or mere conjecture. It is not a doubt raised by anyone simply for the sake of raising a doubt. It is such a doubt as, in serious affairs that concern you, you would heed; that is, such a doubt as would cause reasonable men and women to hesitate to act upon it in matters of importance. It is not hesitation springing from any feelings of pity or sympathy for the accused or any other person who might be affected by your decision. It is, in other words, a real doubt, an honest doubt, a doubt that has its foundation in the evidence or lack of evidence. It is doubt that is

honestly entertained and is reasonable in light of the evidence after a fair comparison and careful examination of the entire evidence.

Why do we set such a high bar for the prosecution? Why isn't one of the looser standards good enough?

For one thing, the stakes are highest in a criminal prosecution. The defendant may lose their freedom. That's only possible in a very few circumstances, and for a much shorter maximum time, in civil cases. (See 30.D. for the details.) And in rare criminal cases, which were a good deal less rare when this standard first evolved, the state may take someone's life.

Another point: in most civil cases, the government acts as an intermediary between private parties and/or an enforcer of agreements between private parties. There are more exceptions now than there were when the "beyond a reasonable doubt" standard first appeared (see, e.g., 15.A., 15.C., and 34.G.2.); but by the time those exceptions developed, the basic difference in standards of proof in criminal and civil cases was well established.

Here's another justification, one more potent now than in the early years of our republic. These days, state and local governments have deep reservoirs of taxpayer money to draw upon. That means the prosecution is likely to start with a major tactical advantage. Holding them to a very tough standard acts as some compensation for that advantage.

D. Ping, Pong: Shifting the Burden

Sometimes the burden of proof goes back and forth between the two sides of a case. This usually occurs where one side asserts an affirmative defense of some kind (see 7.A.2.). For example, if a criminal defendant is on trial for murder and asserts that they acted in self-defense, they'll have to start off with *some* evidence, enough to indicate that self-defense is an issue that may be involved. Often this initial showing only has to be enough to meet the "more likely than not" preponderance of the evidence standard. Once that burden is met, the prosecution has to disprove self-defense beyond a reasonable doubt. But if the defendant doesn't make that initial showing, the prosecution doesn't have to disprove self-defense at all, let alone beyond a reasonable doubt. (You can imagine, **or show,** how confused a jury could get if asked to keep track of all this.)

Other affirmative defenses involving the same back-and-forth burden-shifting include insanity (see 13.E.3.), duress (13.R.), necessity (a close relative of duress, also at 13.R.), and entrapment (13.T.).

Burden-shifting also occurs in many types of discrimination claims. Typically the plaintiff must show that the defendant's conduct or policy had a "disparate impact" on members of the protected class (see 34.H.) compared to those not within that class. Once the plaintiff has made that prima facie case, the burden shifts to the defendant to show that the policy or conduct was necessary. If the defendant makes that showing, the burden shifts back to the plaintiff to show that some less discriminatory alternative was available.

CHAPTER 21

Open and Shut: Opening and Closing Statements

B efore we get to the substance of a trial — the meat, as it were (with apologies to my vegetarian and vegan readers) — let's talk about the outer layers of the sandwich: opening and closing statements.

A. Opening Statements

An opening statement doesn't have a great deal of scope for dramatic flourishes. It's meant to be a preview or road map for the trier of fact (judge or jury) of what the actual evidence will show. It's not supposed to include "argument," explanation of how the law and/or facts add up to a particular verdict. Many lawyers push up against the line on this rule, but overdo it and the judge may reprimand the lawyer — always damaging, and not how your lawyer character wants to start a trial. (And by the way, it's permissible, though not common, to object during an opening statement.)

That isn't to say one can't achieve eloquence in an opening statement, but it has to be done by a carefully crafted description of the evidence. The movie *Suspect* provides an example of riding the line between acceptable and unacceptable in a very effective opening statement. In *My Cousin Vinny*, on the other hand, the novice litigator played by Joe Pesci clearly crosses that line. His entire opening statement: "Uh... everything that guy just said is bull****. . . . Thank you." The judge quite properly struck that opening statement as argumentative.

If you want your lawyer to break that rule in a major way, you'll need to set up some reason for an exception. In my novel *Division*, for example, I realized during the editing process that I'd gone and strayed from the proper confines of an opening statement. Rather than shed a tear and hit "delete," I took advantage of the fact that the proceeding (a) takes place in the future (b) before a judge, rather than a jury, and had the judge explain that she would give counsel some latitude:

> "Counsel, a caution to you both. I have a pretty good idea how you came to be representing these litigants. I have no quarrel with public-ity as a quid pro quo — up to a point. I have approved broadcast of these proceedings, but any grandstanding, any rehearsals for movie roles, and that broadcast will end. Understood?"

> It was.

> "That said, this is a somewhat atypical proceeding, and we are al-lowed some procedural latitude. If you wish your opening statements to vary somewhat from the traditional summary of facts to be proved, I will allow it. Particularly if it obviates the necessity for closing statements."

The first opening statement will come from the party who carries the burden of proof: the one who will lose, automatically, if they don't prove whatever the type of case requires. The other party usually has a choice between going next, before any evidence is presented, or saving ("reserv-ing") their opening statement until just before they present their own evi-dence. Pick whichever sequence fits your own dramatic needs.

B. Closing Statements

Next to unlikely cross-examinations, some of the most dramatic mo-ments in fictional law practice may come in closing statements. This isn't

100% unrealistic: closing statements are where an attorney can to some extent cut loose. Whereas (there's a lawyer word for you) an opening statement is not supposed to include any argument, a closing statement should. The closing is where the lawyer can tie together the evidence that's been admitted, explaining what it all means and why the jury (or the judge as trier of fact, if there's no jury) should view the evidence in a particular way.

Whether this dramatic presentation makes much difference is another matter. Some attorneys say that judges, as triers of fact, pay little attention to closing arguments. Even a jury may have already made up its mind before the closing arguments roll around. Reasonably, however, one can expect a closing argument to make more of an impression on a jury than on a judge, because the jurors are less jaded, and because fictional treatments have predisposed them to listen to closing arguments.

There are potentially persuasive arguments the lawyer is not allowed to make in closing. A lawyer may not, for example, argue that they personally believe their client is telling the truth (although it wouldn't surprise me if lawyers ride the edge of this rule fairly often). The forbidden argument we'd probably see most often, if allowed: that the judge or jury in a criminal case should draw unfavorable inferences from the defendant's silence. As explained in 34.D., the prosecution may not suggest that an innocent defendant would protest innocence or explain themselves; and the trial judge should make sure the jury knows that any such inference is prohibited.

CHAPTER 22

Order in the Court: How Trials Work

Trials aren't necessarily about the evidence. They're about persuasion — which is a matter of using, massaging, and/or diverting attention from the evidence. They're about manipulating witnesses, opposing counsel, the judge, and the jury. (Trial judges, at least experienced judges or judges who used to be trial lawyers, are harder to manipulate.) So the better you are at writing clever and manipulative characters, the more engrossing *and* true-to-life your trials will be.

But while you're at it, please try to get the technical details right as well.

A. The Exception: Small Claims Court

Much of what I'm about to say doesn't apply in one type of courtroom: small claims court. Depending on the county setup, this may be a separate courtroom, or just one function of a court that also handles normal civil cases and/or criminal cases.

Small claims courts exist to handle claims that don't involve much money. The maximum amount may be in the range of four, six, or ten thousand dollars. Usually the plaintiff is seeking money damages of some kind, but some small claims courts also have jurisdiction over evictions, and/or the authority to grant equitable relief such as protective orders or injunctions (see 30.A.).

The defining characteristics of small claims court are (relatively speaking) informality and simplicity. Though the details will differ from place to place, the judge and parties may not be bound by the usual rules of evidence, and pretrial discovery (see 10.A.) probably won't be allowed. The judge will usually try to keep the hearing very short and efficient. The usual goal is for parties to be able to present their cases and defenses without an attorney. However, if a corporation is a party, that's allowed only for the smaller claims.

It may or may not be possible to file a counterclaim (see 7.A.2.) in small claims court. If the counterclaim is over the monetary limit, it's less likely, and filing such a counterclaim could require moving the entire case into the more formal court.

Some jurisdictions let a party who loses in small claims court bring the case into the more formal court for a second try. Others require the loser to seek relief from the appellate court, as in any other kind of case.

B. Battle Inside, Buddies Outside

Non-lawyers, especially clients who loathe the opposing party, sometimes assume that their lawyers will harbor similar feelings about opposing counsel. They may be shocked, or feel betrayed, to find that outside the courtroom, the two lawyers appear to be on perfectly friendly terms. (They might be even more dismayed to find out that their lawyer is married to opposing counsel, as in the movie *Adam's Rib*, featuring a married prosecutor-and-defense-attorney couple. Such a highly unusual arrangement could only continue if no one objects. **Conceivably, however, a party could decide that such a relationship would provide an advantage.**)

It's hardly surprising that opposing counsel are often friends outside the courtroom. They practice in the same jurisdiction for years and see each other often. They belong to the same professional associations, and will socialize together at both formally organized association functions and more casual gatherings. They also have a great deal of shared experience and personal temperament in common, more than they're likely to have in common with their clients.

Clients rarely find out about another aspect of such familiarity. Sometimes, and more often in particularly chummy legal communities, opposing counsel are very frank with each other about what they see as the strengths and weaknesses of their client's case, especially when discussing a possible settlement (see 9.B.). To avoid violating ethical rules, such attorneys must make sure their discussions focus on the information exchanged in discovery (10.A.) and the applicable law, without straying into any confidential client information (4.D.). Some attorneys will consider this approach incompatible with "zealous" representation of their clients.

It's also fairly common for one or both attorneys to be friends of the judge. After all, most judges used to be attorneys in the same community, and even after they take the bench, they attend many of the same bar association functions as their former peers. Professional ethics dictate that these friendships have no effect on the judicial proceeding.

It's possible, of course, that such familiarity has bred contempt or hostility rather than friendlier feelings. Antagonism, like friendship, is not supposed to affect how lawyers and judges conduct themselves during litigation. Whether negative feelings are harder to suppress in this context is a matter for psychologists **and storytellers** to ponder.

Sometimes, in counties with elected judges, one attorney is or recently was the judge's campaign manager. That's the point at which some opposing counsel might reluctantly decide to, or be pressured by the client to, file a motion asking the judge to recuse themselves (see 5.B.). Of course, that could be counterproductive if the judge found the suggestion of bias insulting, and not only denied the motion but held a grudge. A motion for recusal might be more likely, and perhaps have fewer disadvantages (as in less to lose), when the attorney and the judge have a history of personal dislike.

Of course, there will be cases that challenge friendships between attorneys or between lawyers and judges: either because the facts are so provocative, or because a lawyer uses tactics that opposing counsel or the judge considers unfair or unethical.

C. Quaint Legal Customs

1. The Stage and the Actors

You've almost certainly seen what courtrooms look like, with the raised pedestal for the judge known as the "bench," and the probably raised seat in which witnesses sit to testify, called the "witness stand" (despite the sitting) or sometimes the witness "box."

And you've seen the judge's black robes, under which they could be wearing whatever strikes their fancy, though some locales may have their rules on the subject. We've discarded the British custom of robes for the lawyers, and wigs for judge and lawyers, but we still cling to the judge's robe.

And you may well have seen the bailiff, the employee in charge of moving people in and out of the courtroom, the one who gives orders like "Please rise" just before the judge enters. The bailiff may also promise that parties who come forward will be heard, and recite some devout formula like, "God save the [United States/State of [Whichever]] and this honorable court!"

The bailiff is often the person who administers the oath to witnesses. The bailiff provides security, which may be a crucial function in cases where emotions run high and/or parties have nothing to lose by relieving their feelings in a violent manner. If the jury is sequestered (housed in a hotel overnight for one or more nights), the bailiff will guard them and keep an eye on them to make sure they stay put. The bailiff may also be stuck with various paper-shuffling duties, stocking courtroom supplies and moving exhibits around.

Oh, about that oath: however secular some people believe our society has become, many courts still ask witnesses to swear on a Bible or some other appropriate holy book unless the witness requests otherwise (see 22.H.4.).

Back to customary clothing. Attorneys for the Office of the U.S. Solicitor General, which represents the federal government before the U.S. Supreme Court, traditionally wear "morning coats" (formal coats with two tails, among other features). Justice Elena Kagan, back when she was the Solicitor General, eschewed this tradition, but it survived her tenure nonetheless. Since young deputies in that office may have little occasion for such attire, not to mention insufficient clothing budgets to pay for it, the office has "loaner" coats available. These may or may not fit the particular deputy. Also, depending on how recently another attorney wore the loaner coat, it may or may not have been cleaned since the prior use. If the deputy who wore it last had a particularly rough session before the Court, they may have left some souvenir of the experience in the form of perspiration.

2. Addressing the Court

Lawyers and parties should address judges as "your Honor." Lawyers appearing for oral argument in an appellate court start by saying, "May it please the Court" — unless they're addressing the U.S. Supreme Court (and perhaps some state supreme courts), in which case they say, "[Mr./Ms.] Chief Justice, and may it please the Court."

3. Thanking the Judge - No Matter What

"Thank you, your Honor."

This common utterance doesn't, as you might think, mean that the judge has just ruled in the lawyer's favor, or even that the judge has promised to keep an open mind. It is just as likely to follow a negative or even a devastating ruling: it's essentially the "thank you, sir, may I have another" of legal practice. It's what a lawyer says after the judge has ruled, whatever the ruling.

It's just good manners, courtroom style.

D. Confidential Filings

In general, case files are public records. That means John Q. Public and M.E. Too may drop by the courthouse, or wherever the records are stored;

jump through whatever hoops the court clerk has established under local or state rules; and look at those records or even have copies made.

So does that mean that if a company sues an employee for breaking a non-compete agreement (14.L.4.) by sharing the company's trade secrets (14.M.4.) with a competitor, the company has now shared those secrets with the world? If a husband and wife are getting divorced and (as is common) are required to submit one or more years' tax returns to the court, can every con artist and identity thief in town have their social security numbers for the asking?

Fortunately not. While the details will (again) vary, there are ways to keep certain filed documents or portions of documents confidential or "sealed."

And oy, can those procedures be a headache.

In Indiana, for example, the administrative rule covering how to exclude material from public access — itself part of a much longer rule about public access in general — is three dense pages long (plus another page of commentary). And many of the sub-paragraphs cross-reference each other, or other rules, or statutes. Just one example of this rule's requirements: sometimes a party has to file two versions of the same document, one redacted (that is, with the confidential material taken out), and the other on green paper. When one has to do this and when one may file only the redacted version is just one of the complexities.

If a party fails to follow the rules about how to get or hang onto that coveted "confidential" label, that party might (depending on how unforgiving the rules are in that jurisdiction) lose the benefits of confidentiality. Hello, duplicate secret sauce in the burger joint across the street.

Sometimes it's necessary for counsel to see confidential information that the client shouldn't. In those situations, the parties will enter into a confidentiality agreement specifying how to handle such material. The court then enters this joint agreement as a protective order, which lets the court enforce the agreement. If either side then violates it, the court can hold that party and/or attorney in contempt (see 13.X.). The protected materials will be labeled with language like "Confidential — Subject to Protective Order," and will be filed under seal (legalese for confidential, as noted above).

E. Stipulations

Sometimes, to save everyone's time and the court's patience, counsel for both parties agree to certain facts. These facts would normally fall into one of two categories:

(a) Facts that are undisputed, and would be a boring nuisance to prove;

(b) Facts that the other side can almost certainly prove, and which might be more damaging when presented in a full-blown evidentiary way.

Of course, the opposition may not want to stipulate to facts in the latter category — but the side that does prefer a stipulation may be able to plausibly assert that they could put up a decent fight to get the evidence excluded (kept out). Or at least they can bluff.

What if a party stipulates to some damaging fact and later on finds evidence that contradicts it? In some states (e.g. Indiana), they're out of luck unless they can show they were led to make the stipulation by something like fraud or undue influence. In others (e.g. Illinois), they may be able to get out from under if they can prove the stipulation is untrue. **If your story is set in one of the more lenient jurisdictions, you can have your lawyer discover the key evidence at the last minute — or is it too late? . . . If your courtroom is in a state that treats even false stipulations as binding, your countdown could be to the moment that another lawyer, maybe someone more senior than your intrepid main character, is about to make the fatal stipulation.**

F. Testimony is Evidence -

But Not Always Enough

I've had many a client insist that there was no "evidence" of some disputed point — only to reveal, in the next breath, that their ex, or neighbor, or whoever their opponent may be, testified to the point at trial. Don't make their mistake. Repeat after me: Testimony Is Evidence. In many situations, a single witness' testimony, even without any additional ("corroborating") evidence, is enough to prove a disputed point.

There are times when the sworn word of a single witness is *not* enough. For example:

- At least in some jurisdictions, testimony from an accomplice is not enough to convict someone of a crime. Some of these jurisdictions have exceptions in cases (such as receiving stolen property or forcing someone into prostitution) where corroborating evidence would be particularly hard to come by.

- In some jurisdictions, including those that follow the Model Penal Code on this point, one may not establish that a witness' testimony was false, for the purpose of proving perjury, if the only evidence of that falsity is the contrary testimony of one other witness.

- In federal patent cases, per the most recent info I've found, the uncorroborated testimony of a (self-proclaimed) inventor that their invention came first, before the patent on file, is not enough to invalidate that patent. But federal appeals courts *would* accept the testimony of a single witness who has nothing to gain by testifying that some third person came up with the invention first. (If you're going to have your story turn on such matters, you're safer setting it in the latter 20th century, in case things have changed since then.)

There's a lovely label, and a matching objection, for truly bizarre testimony: "incredible dubiosity." That can mean the testimony is inherently improbable, or that it's completely uncorroborated *and* appears coerced and/or equivocal (the witness acts doubtful about their own testimony). If such testimony is the only evidence, it won't suffice to sustain a criminal conviction, and might not be good enough for civil liability either. However, courts are very reluctant to apply this label. **Still, you could have fun coming up with testimony that would merit it.**

An area in which corroboration requirements were, for many years, very common is also one in which they are particularly controversial. In most or all states, prosecutions for sexual assault (13.F.) used to require corroborating evidence of some sort: the alleged victim's testimony wasn't enough to sustain a conviction. The Model Penal Code, which dates from 1962, included this requirement. The rationale was that false accusations of rape were particularly likely, motivated by anything from "sexual neurosis," female fantasy, jealousy, spite, or morning-after shame about consensual intercourse. A related phenomenon was the giving of what is known as a "cautionary instruction": in this context, jurors would be told that rape was a charge easily made and difficult to disprove, and that they should therefore scrutinize the testimony of the alleged victim more closely than the testimony of other witnesses.

By 1990, most states had rescinded the corroboration requirement. The sexual assault cautionary instruction has also been disapproved in most states, by statute or case law, but is still allowed (though not required) in a few.

The frustration, humiliation and fear that many rape victims must have suffered due to these requirements has obvious story potential. On the other hand, as discussed in 13.F., there's reason for concern that in administrative proceedings in various universities, the pendulum has swung too far in the opposite direction, treating the accused as guilty until proved innocent. **Your story could take the reader inside the trauma of a falsely accused student.**

G. What Evidence?: Spoliation

Have you ever wondered why parties who discover damaging information don't just destroy it, instead of waiting for the other side to make some request that covers it?

Or maybe your inherent decency has prevented you from thinking along those lines. Rest assured, though, that the idea has occurred to others, some of them prosecutors who find they've dug up evidence favorable to the defendant.

And then there's evidence favorable to the other side that just *happens* to get damaged or destroyed. Routine housekeeping and storage space maintenance, don'tcha know.

"Spoliation" — a word easily confused with "spoilation," which isn't a word but would cover the concept nicely — means the intentional or negligent destruction or significant alteration of relevant evidence.

A few states have recognized spoliation as a separate tort. That's more likely when someone who isn't involved in a lawsuit or potential lawsuit, some person or entity who for some reason had a duty to preserve evidence, destroyed or altered it instead. Who has a duty to preserve evidence?

Anyone who controls that evidence and should know (i.e., "could reasonably foresee") that the evidence might be relevant to an existing or possible court case. Just when that's foreseeable can get complicated, and I'm not going very far into that thicket; but a non-party isn't likely to have a duty to preserve evidence unless there's a statute saying so, or unless that non-party contracted to preserve the evidence, or the non-party had already been served with a subpoena duces tecum requiring them to deliver the evidence somewhere. A cautious attorney could create the necessary foreseeability by telling the non-party in so many words that some document or object may be required as evidence in upcoming litigation.

The question of what's foreseeable enough to create a duty to preserve gets especially tricky in family law cases. If one spouse suspects the other of cheating, does that mean a divorce proceeding is foreseeable, and the suspicious spouse must refrain from deleting emails or texts that would help an opposing counsel find hidden assets? The answer is far from clear.

The scope of what's considered "relevant" evidence for purposes of spoliation is fairly broad, broader than the definition a judge will apply at trial when deciding whether to admit or exclude evidence. Some, but not all, jurisdictions put the burden on the party alleging spoliation to prove that the missing evidence was probably relevant. To avoid a Catch-22 situation, courts generally don't require such a strong showing that only the missing evidence would suffice to make it.

Most of the time, it's a party to the litigation or potential litigation who claims the other party (or one of multiple other parties) committed spoliation. And some of the available remedies are quite karmically appropriate. The most common remedy is for the judge to infer, or instruct a jury to infer, that the missing evidence would have damaged the one who screwed with it (the "adverse inference" remedy). An instruction that the jury should draw this adverse inference will almost certainly do major damage to the spoliator's case. In Scott Turow's novel *Presumed Innocent*, where a glass with fingerprints on it goes missing before any defense expert can examine it, the judge uses a slightly milder variant of this instruction, telling the jurors that they could decide the missing glass was enough to raise a reasonable doubt about the defendant's guilt.

In more egregious cases, where a party's conduct stinks to high heaven and the destroyed evidence was crucial to a fair trial, the party who went to such lengths in order to prevail may be declared the loser, either by dismissal of a plaintiff's complaint (see 25.A.), or by entering a default judgment (27.A.) against a defendant.

Another possible remedy, if the spoliated evidence was examined by an expert witness before it met its fate, is to exclude the testimony of that expert. Similarly, a party may be prevented from presenting testimony about what the evidence would have shown.

Oh, and the party who spoliated evidence may also be fined.

And if the judge thinks the party's lawyer was involved: hoo, boy. Watch the sanctions fly.

The severity of the remedy will probably depend both on the importance of the evidence and the court's view of how culpable the spoliator is. On the latter point, the closer events come to common office procedures (whether re aging piles of paper or re electronic clutter), the less severe the sanction. But if the court thinks the party's "routine" has been tailored to maximize the destruction of material that may end up damaging some day, that's a different story. Where computer files are involved, some courts have used experts to supervise discovery in the first place, so as to reduce the chances of lost evidence, as well as to assess the likelihood that a loss was indeed accidental.

Corporations routinely send out a notice as soon as a lawsuit appears on the horizon, instructing everyone who might conceivably have any relevant files to hang onto them. However, with such notices going out to dozens or hundreds of people, it's easy for accidental spoliation to occur.

You could use spoliation to combine suspense with a very satisfying comeuppance, starting with the innocent party's lawyer suspecting that some favorable evidence had been either destroyed, or altered to make it unfavorable; chronicling the hunt for proof, as time remorselessly runs short; and finishing with the hammer blows of judicial retribution. **Or you could have your story spring from accidental spoliation of evidence that would have favored the party who lost or destroyed it, with the frustrating and ironic result that the jury was allowed to presume the opposite.**

Some jurisdictions have special rules for deciding whether the prosecution in a criminal case has committed spoliation, or at least spoliation that requires reversing any subsequent conviction. The question arises when the police or prosecution controls "exculpatory" evidence, evidence that would help the defense.

In Indiana, for example, the key distinction is between "potentially useful evidence" and "material exculpatory evidence." If the most a defendant could claim is that the material, if tested, might have yielded results useful to the defense, loss of such evidence does not violate the defendant's due process rights (see 34.G.) unless the defendant can show the government agents acted in bad faith, intentionally destroying the evidence to hurt the defendant's chances. If, however, the police or prosecution realized before the loss or destruction of the evidence that it was exculpatory, and if there's no still-available evidence that serves the same exculpatory purpose, then the conviction must be reversed, no matter how the evidence came to be destroyed.

Given how difficult it can be to prove the government's "bad faith," not all states follow this approach. Some use more complex balancing tests involving the degree of bad faith if any, the exculpatory value of the evidence, and the alternative evidence still available.

H. Witnesses

1. Preparing Witnesses

It'd be so much easier for trial lawyers if they could control witnesses like puppets, making sure they didn't contradict what they'd said earlier (to the lawyer or opposing counsel or somebody else), and keeping them from talking too much. . . .

There are a few key precautions trial lawyers can take instead.

- Ask witnesses the planned questions ahead of time, more than once, with the latest run-through near the time of trial. Tell the witness that if the other lawyer asks whether they've been asked the same questions before, it's okay to say "Yes." Don't tell them what to say (at least not unless one can be very subtle about it), or that's "coaching," and the witness may admit on cross-examination that they were coached. Do instruct them to tell the truth — and make sure they know it's just fine to tell opposing counsel about *that*.

- More generally, teach witnesses to answer the question concisely and then *stop talking*. That's especially true when opposing counsel is cross-examining the witness, but it holds even when the lawyer who called the witness is asking the questions. Amplifying, explaining, rambling: these can all give the opposition new nuggets to exploit.
- Subject them to some mock cross-examination and deal with any problems that arise, such as obvious loss of confidence, loss of temper, or descent into inarticulate gibberish. Repeat as necessary — and if the witness can't hack it, see if there's another witness who can cover the same territory.

Bottom line: the attorney must do whatever they can to come to court with a calm and articulate witness.

2. Competence to Testify

A witness may only testify if they are "competent" to testify. Competence has both a general and a specific component. A witness must be capable of recalling facts and speaking the truth about them, and must know the difference between truth and falsehood. The witness must also have direct personal knowledge of the facts of the particular case.

In the federal system and in most or all states, a witness is presumed competent to testify in general, unless they fall within some category deemed incompetent by a statute or case law, or a category where it's up to the judge to decide. Child witnesses, for example, may be presumed competent; or the competence of children in general or children under some specified age may depend on the judge's assessment of whether they know (a) the difference between truth and lies and (b) the importance of telling the truth. Some states will presume a child witness is competent in criminal cases, or in criminal cases where the child is alleged to be the victim.

The common law disqualified as incompetent any witness who had been convicted of a felony. The federal courts no longer follow this rule, but some states do, at least if the conviction took place in that state. **One could explore state pride and prejudice with a scene where attorneys argue about whether a felony conviction from a neighboring state really means so much less than a local one.**

You might assume that someone with a serious mental illness is presumed incompetent to testify. Currently, in most jurisdictions, you'd be wrong. The judge will examine the witness' ability to perceive things and events, and to report those perceptions coherently, and will then decide based on that assessment whether the witness may testify. Obviously, the mental illness may affect the weight that the trier of fact gives the witness' testimony. **The direct and cross-examination of a schizophrenic witness, a manic witness, or a paranoid witness could include riveting details, and the jury's reactions to the witness could create a good deal of tension as to the result of the trial.**

There's some overlap between the law of privileges (22.I.) and the notion of competence to testify. For example, Missouri law states that the following folks are "incompetent to testify": "[a]ny person practicing as a minister of the gospel, priest, rabbi or other person serving in a similar capacity for any organized religion, concerning a communication made to them in their professional capacity as a spiritual advisor, confessor, counselor or comforter."

Can animals ever be competent to testify? **Several science fiction authors have addressed this question, with animals either altered to be more intelligent or discovered to be so — but there's always room for a fresh take on the idea!** Outside that genre, evidence has on occasion been taken from animals, but whether it's classified as "testimony" is another story. For example, in 2008, a French court apparently used a dog's reaction to a suspect ("furious" barking) in a proceeding about whether to launch a full murder investigation in a case that might or might not have been suicide. Some news stories described the dog as a "witness," but one could also characterize the demonstration in other terms. (Something similar was attempted, also in France, in 2014, but fell flat: the dog showed no interest in the suspect.)

3. Children in Chambers

When children do have their say, they don't always do it by testifying as other witnesses do, perched on the witness stand with everybody watching. Where a child's evidence or viewpoint is needed, judges may interview the child "in chambers" or "in camera" (same thing). Such interviews can make for compelling scenes, whether by promoting the plot or illuminating the character of the child or the judge. But you'll have to do some homework: the details of such interviews vary widely from state to state and from judge to judge, and will depend on many factors. You'll have less studying to do if you set your story in one of the many states that don't have statutes on the subject, and then make up a county in that state.

Here are some of the questions that may be answered differently in different courtrooms and/or different types of cases:

- Must the parents consent to the interview?
- May the parents be present during the interview?
- Will the attorneys be present?
- If a guardian ad litem (14.H.7.) has been appointed, may that guardian be present?
- Will the child take an oath to tell the truth?
- Will the interview be recorded (by audiovisual means and/or a court reporter transcribing it)?

State rules may allow in camera interviews in bench trials, but not in jury trials. Or they may allow them for younger children, but not older.

Many courts have held that if the judge relies to any extent on the child's statements in the interview, the interview must be recorded and the record (or transcript) available to any appellate court. If, for example, the judge gave custody to one parent based in part on the child's wishes as expressed in the interview, and the interview was not recorded, the losing parent's due process rights (see 34.G.) would arguably be violated. However, those rights don't go so far as to allow the parents or their attorneys to cross-examine the child in chambers, or to impeach the child's statements with prior inconsistent statements (see 22.H.7.). And in some states, a party's failure to request that the interview be recorded may be treated as a waiver of any right to that recording. **If you set up your story so there's no recording of an in camera interview, you could later have crucially conflicting accounts of what either the child or the judge said or did.** **Or a parent's attorney could read the transcript of the issue and have a hunch that something's missing, only to seek out the audiovisual recording and find that it's missing or has been edited.**

Similarly, in some courts where attorneys are allowed to be present, the party may be held to have waived that right if they agree to a private interview between the child and the judge.

Some courts that don't always allow attorneys to be present will allow the attorneys to submit questions beforehand, and/or will have the transcript read to the attorneys before the child leaves and let them submit follow-up questions.

Some states require the judge to find that testifying in the presence of the parties or the attorneys will harm or upset the child before excluding parties or attorneys from the interview.

And whatever the rules, if any, not all judges bother to follow them — at least in civil cases.

In criminal cases, the defendant's right to confront and cross-examine witnesses (34.F.) precludes a cozy, private interview with the child witness. However, the possible trauma to the child, and the further possibility that a child (especially a child victim) will be intimidated by the defendant's presence, frequently require some compromise procedure. The usual compromise: testimony by closed circuit television, with the prosecution and the defense attorney in the room with the child and able to communicate with the defendant (in the courtroom watching the feed). If there's a jury, they also see the testimony via the television feed.

4. So Help Me God - or Not

Has any movie ever shown a witness who *doesn't* swear to tell the truth, the whole truth, and nothing but the truth, "so help me God"? There's an alternative the movies don't usually feature.

A witness may affirm under the penalties of perjury that they'll tell the truth, the whole truth, et cetera. The federal courts currently use an affirmation with no religious language. In some courts, the possibilities will be thrown together: "Do you solemnly swear or affirm . . . so help you God?" **A sufficiently stiff-necked nonbeliever might object to that phrasing.**

One could also have some fun with a witness that insisted on taking the reference to "the whole truth" literally, and providing it expansively.

The wording of either an oath or affirmation may vary from court to court, and even from witness to witness. Montana, for example, has a statute allowing courts to "vary the mode of swearing or affirming to accord with the witness's beliefs whenever it is satisfied that the witness has a distinct mode of swearing or affirming." The federal rules take a similar approach, requiring only that the oath be "in a form designed to impress that duty on the witness's conscience." California has a simplified version for child witnesses.

---

5. Direct, Cross, Redirect, Recross

When an attorney calls a witness and asks that witness questions, that's called "direct examination."

On direct examination (often just called "direct" for short), the attorney is not supposed to ask "leading questions." Leading questions contain the substance of the answer. Questions that can be answered with a "yes" or "no" fall into this category. There's an exception for preliminary questions to establish the witness' background or expertise. That exception aside, leading questions — including the intimidating, thundering subset of "Isn't it the truth, Mr. X, that . . ." — are reserved for cross-examination ("cross" for short), when an attorney is questioning a witness called by the other side.

Different jurisdictions will have different rules about whether questions asked on cross-examination may address matters that weren't brought up on direct. However, the witness' credibility is always at issue, so the cross-examining attorney can always challenge that credibility. (There are rules about what evidence may be raised, and in what manner, to try to prove the witness a liar or a fool. See 22.H.7. re impeachment of witneses, below.)

There are many unrealistic cross-examinations in fiction. The typical "Perry Mason moment," where a rigorous cross breaks down the guilty party's defenses and yields a shouted or blubbering confession, might have occurred in recorded history, but at best it's exceedingly rare. (For a nicely done example of this unrealistic trope, see the climactic courtroom scene in the movie *A Few Good Men*.) Not only are witnesses unlikely to break down and confess on cue, especially after testifying to the contrary minutes before, but the aggressive behavior that usually triggers the confession in such stories is called "badgering the witness" and will almost certainly draw a successful objection from opposing counsel. Even standing close to the witness, or approaching the witness to hand them an exhibit, is allowed only with the court's express permission (though judges no doubt vary in the distance they'll tolerate in their courtrooms). The usual form of this request: "Permission to approach the witness?" Some attorneys will tack "Your Honor" on the end.

If you want a more realistic example of a once-in-a-lifetime devastating cross, check out the cross of Dr. Kumagai in Scott Turow's novel *Presumed Innocent.* The witness is not a murderer: just an incompetent hack, hoist on his own petard. (That may be oversimplifying what occurs, but to judge for yourself, you'll need to read the book.)

Much as I and many other movie viewers love *My Cousin Vinny's* scenes of cross-examination, one of those crosses, that of the witness with the dirty screen window and obstructed view, could be called sarcastic. Jurors may not react well to sarcasm, especially when directed at a witness: it can inspire protective feelings toward the witness and thus be counterproductive. (The touch of sarcasm at the end of Turow's Dr. Kumagai cross comes after the jury has every reason *not* to feel that way.) A better approach may be Vinny's gentle and very effective cross-examination of the older lady with the thick glasses.

Cross-examination is not a time for arguing one's case. If the attorney tries to insert any appreciable degree of argument in their questioning, the opposing counsel is likely to object. (The usual form of this objection: "Objection: argumentative.") If there's a jury, the trial judge may admonish them to ignore what the lawyer had to say. That's hardly the sort of message a lawyer wants the jury to receive.

Another tactic attorneys are not supposed to use on cross, no matter how often you've seen it in film or television: reminding the witness that they are under oath and subject to perjury laws. This is considered argumentative, and may also violate rules against asking a witness to comment on the law.

One oft-debated topic in the legal community is the extent to which "good faith" should constrict the scope of a cross-examination. This may be a question of evidence law, of professional ethics, or both. The basic question is: may a lawyer insinuate, and try to get the jury to believe, something that isn't true — or at least, something the lawyer has no reason to believe is true? If a witness said they were walking by and saw the accident, and there's no reason to think otherwise, may the lawyer try to plant doubts about the witness' presence? If the attorney knows the witness has perfectly good eyesight, may the lawyer ask questions designed to raise doubts about the witness' vision?

Suffice to say that there are plenty of litigators who think this is a necessary aspect of zealously defending one's client, and others (at least some of whom actually practice courtroom law) who disagree.

A similar question arises when the attorney has dug up something on the Internet and wants to use it in cross-examination. Whether it passes the "good faith" test may depend on the source: a comment board where people habitually froth at the mouth and hurl outrageous accusations? Or the website of some professional organization, helpfully making the standards of that profession available to the general public?

If the online info passes that lawyer's, and that judge's, "you're citing *what?*" test, then the witness could be questioned about it *if* the information makes some significant fact more or less likely. It could be especially important if the information directly or indirectly undermines the witness' credibility. (Direct: info about a perjury conviction or a famous fraud scheme. Indirect: the info contradicts some part of the witness' version of events, though not on a point that's crucial to the substance of the lawsuit.)

None of this means that the online information necessarily gets admitted into evidence. In my "online professional standards" example, it might, once a proper foundation is laid establishing that these really are the standards of that organization, which really publishes them online. Otherwise, probably not: all that goes into evidence is the witness' response to whatever questions the attorney got to ask.

What happens after cross-examination? Very often, the attorney who first called the witness tries to repair any damage by what's called "redirect" examination. Redirect is supposed to cover only what was in some way touched upon in the cross-examination. But no, that isn't the last word either: opposing counsel gets another chance, called recross. This can go on until no one can think of anything else worth asking, or until the judge loses patience.

Sometimes, an attorney may decide that any repair work they could do on redirect is less important than avoiding recross. That's a very reasonable calculation when the witness has more or less fallen apart on cross: opposing counsel may be able to make matters significantly worse if given another crack at the now-fragile witness. If an attorney refrains from redirect or recross, the witness is excused and the trial moves on.

When two or more attorneys are representing one party, it's good courtroom etiquette, and sometimes required, that only one of them gets involved in dealing with a particular witness. You see this rule in action in the movie *Anatomy of a Murder*, where Jimmy Stewart's character protests to the judge about the two prosecuting attorneys taking turns making objections. There's one situation, however, where stepping on co-counsel's toes (metaphorically speaking) may be unavoidable: where co-counsel isn't actually counsel yet, but a legal intern allowed to represent the client under an actual lawyer's supervision. If the intern is wandering off course, it's still better to ask the judge for a moment to confer with the intern; but if things are going too wrong, too fast, it may be necessary for the lawyer to jump in, and most judges will be tolerant about it.

6. Hostile Witness

There's one situation where attorneys get to treat their own witnesses the way they may already treat the other side's witnesses. That's when the attorney calls a witness who has no interest in helping their side, but who has helpful testimony to (grudgingly) offer. Such a witness is aptly named a "hostile witness," and may be asked leading questions (and badgered to the same limited extent as a witness on cross-examination).

Tactical note: I recently heard about a trial lawyer who called an important opposing witness as a hostile witness, quite a while before the witness would otherwise have testified. This gamble worked out well: opposing counsel hadn't gotten around to preparing the witness, who fell apart quite satisfactorily.

For an unusual, hilarious, and enormously satisfying example of examining a hostile witness, see lawyer Vinny Gambini question his furious fiancée in the movie *My Cousin Vinny.*

7. Impeaching the Witness

A witness' credibility is always crucial. How may it be established, and how attacked?

Let's start with the second question.

How may an attorney attempt to prove that a witness' testimony should not be believed? This process is called "impeaching" the witness ("impeachment" as a noun), and there are several possible approaches — but not all of them are always permitted.

When impeaching a witness, one must usually start out by confronting the witness with the supposedly damaging facts (though, cue the old refrain, this may vary from state to state). Then, if the witness refuses to admit those facts, one may sometimes bring in "extrinsic evidence" such as other witnesses or documents to make the point. The lawyer can't skip directly to that other evidence, even though it might have more dramatic impact: they must "lay a foundation" by giving the witness a chance to explain matters in a more face-saving manner. Some places will let the lawyer lead with the extrinsic evidence if it shows a criminal conviction for certain felonies, not just on the heavy end of the spectrum, like murder and rape, but down the ladder to burglary. One may also be able to offer direct proof of criminal convictions for crimes involving dishonesty or false statement (see 13.I. and 13.J.). Caveat: using any of these convictions gets a lot tougher once the conviction or the former felon's release from prison took place more than 10 years ago. At that point, the impeaching attorney may have to convince the judge that the "probative value" of the conviction substantially outweighs the extent to which it'll prejudice the jury against the witness or the defendant.

In jurisdictions that require the lawyer to start by letting the witness explain a prior conviction, **it could be entertaining to show how a witness attempted to explain, for example, a ten-year-old conviction for selling fake luxury goods.**

One way to impeach a witness is to expose the witness' bias (predisposition in favor of a person, group or viewpoint) or prejudice (the opposite, a predisposition against). Bias often arises from a relationship with the party in whose favor the witness is testifying, or identification with a group to which that party belongs. Prejudice may be based on personal experience with a party or a group, but it may be an attitude derived from the witness' upbringing, or based on cultural stereotypes, or the result of the media's presentation of some relevant events. If the witness denies the bias or prejudice, the lawyer may bring in extrinsic evidence if there is any.

If the witness has been careless enough to make some prior statement that conflicts with what they are saying now, aka a "prior inconsistent statement," then under some circumstances (also discussed in 22.K.), one may offer proof of that prior statement to impeach the witness. Some jurisdictions require that the prior statement must have been made under oath, either in a courtroom or a deposition. This is more likely if that jurisdiction allows the prior inconsistent statement to be admitted for its truth, rather than only for impeachment purposes. See below (as well as 22.K.).

An attorney may try to trigger an inconsistent statement by asking the witness a series of minor questions similar to questions asked years before in a deposition (see 10.A.). A particularly sneaky attorney might even tweak the wording of one or more of these questions, to increase the chances of an answer inconsistent with the answer given at that long-forgotten deposition.

If a witness does make a statement inconsistent with a previous sworn statement, the attorney who called that witness can attempt some damage control on redirect by clarifying the prior and current answers, or by emphasizing the unimportance of the details. Of course, they will have to do so without asking leading questions (see 22.H.5.).

As mentioned above, in some jurisdictions, including federal courts, once the opportunity appears to introduce a prior inconsistent statement, the judge or jury gets to consider that statement in deciding the ultimate issues in the case, not just in deciding whether the witness is truthful. When that's possible, a witness called to serve one side can become one of the most important witnesses for the other.

An attorney may attempt to show that the witness has a bad reputation where truthfulness is concerned. This is one situation where one needn't start by letting the witness explain things away. Instead, one may use another witness, after demonstrating that this second witness has adequate knowledge of the first witness' reputation. Or an impeachment witness could have direct personal experience with the first witness, showing the first witness' problems with the truth.

Finally, there's attacking the witness' "competency" (22.H.2.), either in general (the witness could not, unlike Hamlet, tell a hawk from a handsaw), or about the issue at hand (maybe the witness claimed to have been sitting up in bed when they saw the defendant looking in the victim's window, but the witness' bedroom has no view of that window).

A related concept, impeachment by contradiction, lets an attorney do an end run around certain evidentiary obstacles. For example, one normally can't introduce evidence of a conviction if that conviction was later overturned because the police violated the defendant's Fourth Amendment rights. But if the defendant "opens the door" by testifying on direct examination that "I've never even seen a cannabis plant and wouldn't know it if I saw it," the prosecution could ask about, and if necessary prove, the defendant's prior conviction for running the largest cannabis farm in the state, even though that conviction was overturned on appeal. Supposedly, the trier of fact (whether judge or jury) only gets to consider this evidence in assessing the defendant's truthfulness. Whether jurors could achieve such mental self-discipline is another story.

Another example of impeachment by contradiction: one may offer evidence of a defendant's or other witness' otherwise inadmissible "bad acts" (22.J.), if the witness was careless enough to testify that they never did anything of the sort.

By the way, whatever a lawyer or jury may assume about whether religious beliefs make people more likely to tell the truth, you probably can't use the witness' religion as impeachment material. At least, not directly. One may raise the witness' religion if the tenets of that religion make the witness more likely to be biased toward, or prejudiced against, someone about whom they're testifying. (Here's a question I haven't seen addressed: if the witness has chosen to swear rather than affirm, piously declaiming "so help me God" with a hand on the Bible, could a lawyer impeach the witness by showing that they're actually an atheist, or a member of some religion with no "God" in the conventional sense, and therefore wouldn't take that oath seriously?)

Of course, if evidence is relevant to the underlying issues in the case, not just to whether a witness is truthful, one may offer it directly, even if it also tends to prove that the witness is a liar.

a. Bolstering

Getting back to the first question (way back at the start of this section), how may one bolster a witness' credibility? That's actually harder than attacking it. Generally, one may only do so in response to impeachment. The attorney is not allowed to ask questions or introduce evidence to show the witness' reputation for truthfulness unless the opposition has already attacked that reputation. It is not permitted to show that the witness has asserted the same facts under oath in the past (a prior consistent statement), unless the opposition has dredged up a prior inconsistent statement first. If one side brought in Farmer Tom to testify that a witness who testified earlier is known throughout the county as a lyin', cheatin' S.O.B., then and only then may the other side bring in Pastor Tim to testify that on the contrary, everyone knows the earlier witness' word is their bond.

A prosecutor is not allowed to bolster a witness' credibility by implying that the government knows facts it isn't allowed to disclose which support the witness' credibility. Presumably this rule arose because some prosecutors were doing just that.

b. You're In the Army Now: Impeaching Military Officers

As mentioned in the movie *A Few Good Men*, it's a dangerous business to impeach a witness in a military tribunal, at least if that witness is an officer. The Uniform Code of Military Justice, Article 89, makes it an offense for members of the armed forces, and certain other folks connected thereto, to "behave[] with disrespect" toward a "superior commissioned officer." Theoretically, "truth is no defense"; but if the lawyer's possibly disrespectful conduct results in the superior officer being arrested and/or disgraced, it's presumably less likely that the lawyer will get court-martialed in their turn.

8. Cussing

Lawyers, of course, must keep their courtroom language strictly G-rated. But what can they do about witnesses who cuss?

This issue arises in the legal comedy *From the Hip* when a witness describes someone as an "asshole." Judge and lawyers then discuss whether this term may remain on the record, with the lawyer in charge of the witness arguing that this is a term with no adequate synonyms.

If the witness' language appears to be rubbing the judge or jury the wrong way, the lawyer could ask for a moment to confer with the witness, and then use whatever approach is most likely to induce the witness to exercise some restraint.

There is the related issue of when a witness should recount someone else's language without edits. Police officers often find it awkward to quote foul-mouthed defendants, and sometimes need to be reassured that it's necessary to give the fact-finder a complete and accurate picture of what occurred.

9. One (Question) Too Many

One of the important lessons trial lawyers must learn is to avoid, whenever possible, asking a question to which they don't know the answer. This advice is often phrased as "Don't ask one question too many." In trying to emphasize a favorable fact, the attorney may undercut it, or worse. For an attorney to assume they know where a line of questioning is going, when in fact they don't, can lead to disaster — and to very enjoyable fiction.

To make this point effectively, I'm going to resort to several spoilers. Yes, I said **SPOILERS AHEAD**. If you haven't seen the movie *Anatomy of a Murder* (or read the book, which probably has the same moment), skip ahead now. Ditto if you care about a much less important spoiler in *My Cousin Vinny.*

All righty, then. In *Anatomy of a Murder*, Army lieutenant Frederick Manion is accused of murdering Barney Quill, a local innkeeper whom Manion's wife has accused of raping her. There's no doubt that Manion shot Quill. Manion is claiming temporary insanity — but the subtext of the defense strategy is the not-legally-recognized doctrine, "He deserved killin'." Mrs. Manion, a notorious flirt, claims that Manion tore off her panties, but the panties haven't been found. Working for Quill at the inn is the lovely young Mary Pillant. At a key point in the trial, Mary testifies that she found a torn pair of panties, of the correct brand, in the inn's laundry. The hard-charging prosecutor subjects Mary to a withering cross-examination, aimed at suggesting that she was actually Quill's mistress and is testifying falsely out of pique that Quill was larking about with Mrs. Manion. Mary is at first confused and distressed; then, when she understands what the prosecutor is getting at, more acutely distressed. She denies being Quill's mistress, and stammers something like, "Barney Quill was . . . was . . . ." The prosecutor then makes the classic error of asking one question too many: "Barney Quill was *what*, Miss Pillant?" Well, guess what? Quill was Mary Pillant's father, and only compelling evidence would have made her speak ill of him posthumously.

In *My Cousin Vinny*, one of the two defendants has chosen a public defender (see 2.M.) over the inexperienced Vinny. The PD is cross-examining an eyewitness. He extracts the admission that the witness wears glasses and was not wearing those glasses at the time he allegedly saw the defendants, about 50 feet away, running out of the store. Rather than leaving well enough alone, the PD tries to underscore the witness' testimony with a question repeating it, emphasizing the witness' being so far from the boys and not having on his "necessary prescription eyeglasses" — only to have the witness clarify that the glasses in question were *reading* glasses.

A related principle suggests that the attorney not give an unfriendly witness rope with which to hang the attorney's client. For example, in the trial of former football coach Jerry Sandusky on multiple counts of molesting young boys, Sandusky's defense attorney asked one of the victims,

"Didn't you tell us that Jerry treated you like a son?" The devastating, and not really unpredictable, reply: "No, he treated me like a son in front of other people. Outside of that he treated me like his girlfriend."

One anecdote, possibly apocryphal, is often used to illustrate the one-question-too-many principle, and also falls into that related "rope for hanging" category. An attorney is representing a man accused of biting off another man's ear. The defense attorney asks a witness, "Did you actually see my client bite off the man's ear?" The witness admits that they didn't. The fatal additional question: "Then how can you be so sure?" The response: "I saw him spit it out."

You may, by this time, be asking how an attorney can ever be sure they know what the witness will say in answer to a question. Of course, they can't be absolutely sure. One function of leading questions in cross-examination (see 22.H.5.) is to minimize the chance of a damaging, unexpected response. If it appears that the witness is beginning an answer that will include more than "yes" or "no" (plus null words like "sir" or "ma'am"), the attorney could interrupt and ask the court to instruct the witness to answer the question directly.

Another failsafe is having evidence available to impeach any undesirable answer (see 22.H.7.).

10. The Problem with Eyewitness Testimony

For some undoubtedly interesting reasons based in evolutionary psychology and sociology, we tend to believe people who tell us what they've seen and heard. If they declare it under oath, we believe it even more. The trouble is that eyewitness testimony is far less reliable than we're apparently programmed to assume. There's been extensive research over the last several decades suggesting that countless people have been convicted based on the sincere but erroneous testimony of eyewitnesses.

Our memories are not, as we sometimes assume, a sort of recording that's made and then remains unchanged (except for some fading). Rather, we construct our memories, filling in many blanks with anything from our imaginations to unrelated details. For example, I might see Joe Blow on the elevator, then leave the building and see a street robbery. I didn't get a great view of the robber, but I confuse and combine the two memories, so that I remember seeing Joe Blow commit the robbery.

Over time, we also reconstruct our memories; and we believe our reconstructions at least as much as we believe the initial construct.

Sometimes the details that become part of reconstructed memory are introduced by some player on the prosecution team. One much-litigated instance is the overly suggestive lineup. Say the police call a victim or other witness in to try to pick the perp in a lineup, and only one of the people in the lineup matches the witness' previous description (e.g., is black, has a beard, wears glasses, is tall or short or fat or skinny). There's a danger the witness will adjust their memory to match the single person in the lineup who comes closest to what they remembered. It's even worse if the cops confront the witness with a single person or photograph. (When it's a person rather than a photo, this is called a show-up, also discussed in 2.M.)

Questioning can also plant false memories. In one experiment, test subjects who had visited Disneyland as children were shown what looked like advertisements featuring Bugs Bunny at Disneyland. Then they were asked if on those childhood visits, they had shaken hands with an employee dressed as Bugs Bunny. Quite a few of them remembered that experience — even though Bugs Bunny isn't a Disney character and wouldn't (absent some unlikely practical joke) be at Disneyland at all.

This effect can be quite subtle. It's been demonstrated that even the words used in a question, such as "crash" as opposed to "accident," can lead to a witness remembering details that match that word choice, like broken glass that wasn't present in the actual scene.

Memory distortion due to questioning is even more likely in children than in adults. It now appears that most of the cases involving the alleged bizarre Satanic abuse of children in day cares were "proved" with child eyewitness testimony contaminated by overeager investigators.

Questioning under hypnosis may, for some people, be especially likely to plant and cement (to mix metaphors) a false memory. A witness who's been hypnotized may thus be particularly unreliable. Yet a jury could assume the opposite.

Some, but not all, judges will allow expert testimony from memory experts about the possibility of memory contamination. Others find it too inconsistent with the traditional preference for eyewitness testimony, and/or the traditional role of the trier of fact in assessing credibility.

One could set up some colorful and intriguing scenarios of memory contamination, including the POV of a witness who finds it impossible to believe that their memory has been so affected. On the other hand, there have been victims who testified against alleged assailants and saw them convicted, only to come to the horrified realization that their memories were tainted and unreliable. **You could tell the story of such a victim who, years later, was struggling to right the wrong they unwittingly committed.**

11. Expert Testimony

Many cases involve scientific or technical complexities beyond the everyday experience of most jurors or even judges. In these cases, one or both sides call expert witnesses to educate the trier of fact. Often enough, one ends up with a "battle of the experts." **One could show such a battle from the point of view of a bewildered juror: how on earth are they supposed to know whom to believe?**

A list of all the possible areas for expert testimony would be very long indeed. Here's an alphabetical sampling of just a few fields from which expert witnesses may come: accident reconstruction; alteration of audio or video recordings; blood spatter pattern analysis; climatology; computer forensics (aka recovery and/or analysis of computer files); electrostatic properties of materials (sometimes relevant to whether or not arson caused a fire); facial reconstruction (from, e.g., a partial skull); false confessions; feather analysis; fingerprint comparison; handwriting comparison; hypnotism; plant botany; pollen analysis; serology (examination of bodily fluids for DNA markers and the like); soil analysis; and voice spectrography (a method of comparing voices). And here's an exercise you might want to try: come up with situations in which each of these experts would testify. Some, like accident reconstruction and blood spatter, are obvious, but others will take more thought — **and could be used in more unusual stories.**

Expert testimony can be very powerful indeed. A witness can't testify to a legal conclusion, but an expert's opinion on some technical issue can point quite strongly in the direction of one.

Experts aren't "paid for their testimony." But they are paid by the side using them (with the possible exception, discussed below, of indigent criminal defendants), usually on an hourly basis, for the time they spend testifying, and the time they spend preparing to testify, as well as for any travel expenses they may incur. It's not allowed to pay experts via a contingency fee (see 3.A.): that would provide too direct a financial incentive to give testimony helpful to the plaintiff.

There are two related threshold questions concerning expert testimony: who's an expert, and what testimony will be admitted as expert testimony? The focus, logically enough, is usually on the latter. It doesn't do a party much good to have an acknowledged expert in the courtroom if the court won't admit the evidence the party is paying that expert to present.

There are two commonly used tests for deciding what is admissible expert testimony. The older one, still used in a few states, is the *Frye* or "general acceptance" test: the scientific basis for the testimony "must be sufficiently established to have gained general acceptance in the particular field in which it belongs." The more recent *Daubert* standard, initially an interpretation of Federal Rule of Evidence 702 and now incorporated in it, has supplanted the *Frye* test as the majority approach.

F.R.E. 702 currently reads as follows:

RULE 702. TESTIMONY BY EXPERT WITNESSES

A witness who is qualified as an expert by knowledge, skill, experience, training, or education may testify in the form of an opinion or otherwise if:

(a) The expert's scientific, technical, or other specialized knowledge will help the trier of fact to understand the evidence or to determine a fact in issue;

(b) The testimony is based on sufficient facts or data;

(c) The testimony is the product of reliable principles and methods; and

(d) The expert has reliably applied the principles and methods to the facts of the case.

Note that a "scientific" basis is no longer necessary. Other kinds of "specialized" knowledge can suffice. "Reliable principles and methods" may sound similar to a "generally accept[ed]" scientific basis, at least for scientific testimony, but hold on: instead of "general" acceptance, a consensus in the field, we have the judge deciding what's "reliable." F.R.E. 702 and the *Daubert* standard may have been intended to expand what would be considered expert testimony, but some say the opposite has occurred, with counsel managing to persuade judges either that the principles and methods involved aren't reliable, or that they aren't being properly applied.

Most courts presume that expert testimony is admissible unless the other side makes a motion to exclude it, but some judges consider themselves authorized to raise *Daubert* issues "sua sponte" (on their own, with no request prompting them). The more expert testimony is expected in a case, the more likely the court will require any *Daubert* challenges to be raised before trial, via a motion in limine (25.G.).

In the federal courts and some state courts, the "proponent" of expert testimony, the party who wants it admitted, has the burden of proving that it passes the applicable test. Relevant factors will include whether the underlying principles have been published in peer-reviewed publications and how often and thoroughly they've been tested.

SF-minded authors could have fun with attorneys trying to qualify experts in fields like xenobiology or ESP.

What about the expert who waffles, refusing to be pinned down about whether some fact (often the cause of an injury) is anything close to certain? If all the expert says, or what they retreats to saying when cross-examined, is "it's possible," is that such worthless testimony that the other side can get it stricken (see 22.M.)?

Probably not. This sort of halfhearted assertion may not be enough to support a judgment all by itself; but if there's any other evidence pointing the same way, the testimony is probably admissible. The wishy-washy nature of the testimony "goes to the weight of the evidence." In other words, the jury, or the trial judge in a bench trial, can decide what that evidence is worth, if anything.

Who pays for expert testimony in a criminal trial where the defendant is indigent (see 3.E.) and is represented by a public defender?

The U.S. Supreme Court, in 1985, supplied a few rules, which different states have interpreted somewhat differently, about when the government (usually the county) has to pick up the tab. The basics:

- The defendant must show there's a plausible defense for which expert testimony is needed.
- The expert hired needn't be the priciest top-tier expert around.
- For psychiatrists and the like, the defendant isn't entitled to pick their own (which doesn't mean a judge will never allow it).

There may also be a right to hire experts to investigate complicated facts, rather than to testify. Check the law of the jurisdiction in question.

12. Vouching and Testifying to Ultimate Conclusions

The trier of fact, especially a jury, may believe that when a lawyer calls a witness (other than a hostile witness), the lawyer implies by so doing that they believe what the witness is saying. Judges tend to be more realistic about the limited choices lawyers have in choosing who will testify. In any event, going beyond any such implicit suggestion and putting the same idea in words, even in hints, is called "vouching" for the witness, and it's generally considered improper.

Prosecutors may be particularly tempted to vouch for the truthfulness of child witnesses, so as to assuage any concern that the child doesn't realize the importance of telling the truth. They are, however, supposed to resist that temptation.

A child on the witness stand is potentially a sad spectacle in any event. A child struggling to please a loved one by testifying as that loved one has urged, and a lawyer's carefully calibrated exposure of that coaching, could make for quite a compelling scene. States differ on what, if anything, an expert witness is allowed to say about whether a child has been coached to give certain testimony. It's often permitted for the expert to describe the signs a coached witness will display. Some jurisdictions go further and allow the expert to say whether the child in fact displayed those signs, and/or whether the expert believes the child had been coached. A compromise position allows the expert to give their opinion that the child hasn't been coached if the defendant "opens the door" by implying or arguing the opposite.

If the witness is testifying in return for some sort of plea bargain (see 9.A.) that requires the witness to testify truthfully on pain of losing the deal, may the attorney ask questions to elicit that fact, or would that constitute vouching? There is a split among the courts, even among federal courts, as to whether this is permitted. Some allow it only after the opposition has attacked the witness' credibility, while others either allow it more generally or prohibit it entirely.

A related rule (mentioned in 22.H.7.a.) prohibits the prosecution from implying that if only the jurors knew what the prosecutor knew, they would have no qualms about believing the witness.

Under the common law (see 2.L.3.), expert witnesses were precluded from testifying as to the "ultimate issues" in the case. Ultimate issues are legal conclusions the party calling the witness wants the trier of fact to decide in that party's favor. In those courts that still apply this rule, not even an experienced tort attorney, for example, is allowed to testify that the defendant's conduct constituted negligence. This sort of testimony is viewed as improperly invading the province of the trier of fact. (Refresher: the trier of fact is either the jury or, in a bench trial, the judge. See 19.B.)

Where a court will draw the line in applying the ultimate issue rule is not always predictable. At least in some courts, for example, a doctor called as an expert witness in a medical malpractice case may testify as to what constitutes the reasonable standard of care in a particular field, even though (a) other evidence establishes that the defendant didn't meet that standard and (b) not meeting the standard constitutes medical malpractice. An expert in the fallibility of eyewitness testimony will in some courts be allowed to list all the defects in the police lineup procedure, even if they are not allowed to take the final step of saying, "In my expert opinion, this witness' recollection is unreliable."

In 1975, the federal courts adopted evidentiary rules, thereafter imitated in many states, which allowed expert witnesses to testify about ultimate issues if such testimony would be "helpful" to the judge or jury. Jurisdictions that adopted this rule, or courts within those jurisdictions, do not always interpret what is "helpful" in the same way.

John Hinckley Jr., accused of attempting to assassinate President Reagan, may have taken advantage of this rule (depending on how broadly one interprets it) in his insanity defense, calling an expert who testified that Hinckley was emotionally unable to appreciate the wrongfulness of his actions (see 13.E.3.). Public outrage at Hinckley's acquittal led to a 1984 revision of the Federal Rules of Evidence, specifying that an expert in a criminal case "must not state an opinion about whether the defendant did or did not have a mental state or condition that constitutes an element of the crime charged or of a defense." Some states adopted this exception in their turn. However, courts have not always found its language fully self-explanatory.

I. Privileges that Can Prevent Testimony

I've already discussed attorney-client privilege (4.D.). There are several other privileges that can keep otherwise relevant evidence from being admitted.

One limitation on all these privileges: if there's someone who can hear what the person said, and that listener is outside the privileged relationship, the communication isn't privileged.

1. Doctor-Patient Privilege

Doctor-patient confidentiality, like attorney-client confidentiality, is more than just an evidentiary privilege: where it exists, it prohibits disclosure in any but a very few contexts, not only in judicial proceedings.

An initial caveat: this privilege does not derive from the common law (see 2.L.3.), and is not universally recognized. The federal courts do not honor doctor-patient privilege. Nor do the Uniform Rules of Evidence include it. The rest of this discussion deals with the large majority of states that nevertheless recognize it to a greater or lesser degree. If a plot point in your story turns on this privilege, you'll need to check the law of the state in question.

To be confidential in the context of court proceedings, a communication from patient to doctor has to have something to do, directly or indirectly, with the patient's purpose in seeing the doctor (diagnosis or treatment). A comment such as "How about them Packers!", even if somehow relevant to the litigation (perhaps a prosecution for illegal gambling?), would not normally be subject to the privilege, although one could give it a try if the patient sought treatment because of an injury suffered at a Packers game. . . .

The privilege covers not only the patient's statements but their medical records, as well as the doctor's medical opinions and conclusions. It also includes communications between the patient and the doctor's professional staff. Less clear: communications with non-medical staff such as receptionists on non-medical matters. For example, the statement "I can't make an appointment this week because I'll be in Albuquerque" might possibly be admissible as inconsistent with the patient's alibi of being in Detroit.

The privilege survives the end of the doctor-patient relationship. (That's why the judge in the book *Presumed Innocent* was so ticked at a prosecutor who claimed that the privilege didn't apply because the doctor was no longer treating the patient. Any prosecutor would know better.)

If the patient sues the doctor for malpractice, the privilege disappears.

In criminal cases where the defense claims insanity or diminished capacity (see 13.E.3.), or in civil cases where a party's medical condition is at issue, a party may need to consent to examination by the state's or other party's medical expert. In such cases, the privilege won't apply to any statements made during the examination, or to the expert's records and opinions.

There's one well-established exception to doctor-patient privilege: if the patient's statement indicates that the patient is about to go out and hurt someone, the doctor is allowed to notify the authorities, or the intended victim if they have been identified. This is most likely to arise when the doctor is a psychiatrist. Almost every state has a "duty to warn" or "duty to protect" statute covering this situation, but not all of them actually require the doctor to take action: some only go as far as allowing the doctor to do so in spite of doctor-patient privilege.

If the doctor keeps quiet, then in states that make a warning mandatory, the eventual victim could sue the doctor, and the doctor could also have to answer to those in charge of discipline in the medical profession. Some states, such as California, make it a misdemeanor to violate certain professional codes, so failure to give warning might be criminal conduct. (Compare this to how California, until recently, handled attorney-client privilege, refusing until 2004 to allow a lawyer to give warning of an intended murder (see 4.D.1.).)

There's another exception to this privilege in most, though not all, states if the communication concerns child abuse (and sometimes child neglect). This exception may either be explicit in rule or statute, or implicit in broad reporting requirements. The same exception applies to therapist privilege (where there is such a privilege) and to clergy privilege, both discussed in 22.I.2. below. (Note that attorney-client privilege isn't limited in this way. See a pattern here?)

Psychiatrists are medical doctors, so aside from the exceptions just noted, there's no problem asserting psychiatrist-patient privilege. What about other psychotherapists and the like? Read on.

2. Those Other Counselors: Clerics and Therapists

As just noted (22.I.1.), most state courts recognize doctor-patient privilege. Psychotherapist-patient privilege is even more broadly accepted, existing to some extent in all state and federal courts. There's much more variation, however, where those in related fields, such as "social workers," are concerned, even though the sort of confidences made to them, and the purpose of those confidences, are often similar to what you'd find in a psychotherapist's office. A state may differentiate between "psychologists," as to which a privilege exists, and "counselors," as to which it does not. As with doctor-patient privilege, you'll need to check the law at the place and time involved in your story.

If your character wants to tell someone their troubles without any fear of seeing the confidant on the witness stand, they are fairly safe choosing a member of the clergy. The clergy privilege, also called (in misleadingly specific language) the priest/penitent privilege, protects communications between a religious adviser and the one advised. While it'll be an easier sell if the adviser is functioning within an established religion, any arguably religious title may suffice if one can convince the judge that one was seeking religious advice/assistance from that person in that conversation. Context matters: what one says to a religious official in a secular conversation, where one wasn't seeking religious counsel, will *not* be protected.

Note that I'm talking about the present day. At least in some states, the rules used to be more particular: e.g., it might have been required that adviser and advisee be members of the same religion.

As for who "holds" the privilege (that is, who has the right to assert it), the states are about evenly divided between those who say it's up to the clergyperson, those who give the power to the one seeking religious counsel, and those who say that both must consent to any waiver of the privilege.

The requirement to report possible child abuse conflicts with the religious obligations of some counselors such as Catholic priests — who might conceivably end up going to jail for contempt to protect the sanctity of the confessional. In states that don't have a child abuse exception to the clergy privilege, things could get complicated if the clergyperson is also a therapist of a sort that *is* required to report suspected child abuse. It's then up to the trier of fact to decide what hat this person was wearing when they received the communication: religious or therapeutic.

3. It's Good to be Married: Spousal Privileges

There are two separate evidentiary privileges available to spouses, or in one case former spouses; and it'd be easy to confuse the details of the two.

The "marital confidences" privilege, also called the "marital communications" privilege, involves statements by one spouse to another during the marriage. In its broader form, this privilege prevents either spouse from testifying to such communications, whether they want to or not, and even after the marriage is over. The idea is that protecting marital confidences protects the institution of marriage as such. It outlasts the marriage itself because at the time of the communication, the two were married, and shouldn't have to watch their words out of concern that the marriage might fall apart later.

Summing up the basics of the marital confidence or marital communications privilege:

- It outlasts the marriage.
- It applies only to statements, not to events or observations.
- It applies only to statements made by one spouse to the other during the marriage.
- In its broader form, neither spouse may waive the privilege: the testimony is prohibited, period.
- It's gotten a lot narrower in many places in recent decades.
- It applies in both criminal and civil proceedings (with exceptions noted below).

One could use this privilege and attorney-client privilege in the same story. An attorney blabs to their spouse about a client's confidential information; the client has reason to suspect as much, wants to get the attorney in professional trouble, and manages to recruit the spouse, but (in a state where both spouses hold the marital confidences privilege) the spouse can't testify.

The second marriage-related privilege is commonly called the "spousal testimonial" privilege, or sometimes the "spousal incompetence" privilege (because the one spouse is not a "competent" witness (see 22.H.2.) against the other) or the "spousal immunity" privilege. While a few states apply this privilege in civil cases, it's more often confined to the criminal context — though even there, it's recognized by fewer states than in the past. This privilege prevents the state (or, if applicable in civil cases, either party) from forcing one spouse to testify against the other. It protects an existing marriage against the intolerable strain of one spouse's being made to injure the other. But if the marriage is over, or if the spouse is happy to wreak such an injury, the privilege doesn't apply.

Recap:

- The spousal testimonial privilege applies to testimony about any communication or observation or event, before or during the marriage.
- When the marriage ends, the privilege evaporates.
- If a spouse *wants* to testify against the other, they may. The privilege protects witnesses, not parties.

- It most often applies only to criminal proceedings, if it applies at all.

Historical note: until the late 1800s, both these privileges were so broadly applied in the U.S. that there wasn't much of a distinction between them.

Spousal privileges apply to common-law marriages recognized by the state, but at least so far, they don't apply to other informal cohabitation. A few states have explicitly made these privileges applicable in state-recognized civil unions or domestic partnerships, but in others the question isn't yet settled.

Typically, these privileges can't be invoked when the spouses or ex-spouses are actually suing each other, or where one is the complainant in a criminal case where the other is the defendant. That would most likely be a domestic violence case or a child abuse case, where the parent who isn't accused would be viewed as the child's advocate.

Some states deny the privileges to spouses charged jointly with a crime, and/or where a marital communication was made as part of a criminal or fraudulent scheme — a pretty severe pruning of the basic rule. Even more severe: allowing the use of marital communications against the other spouse in a divorce or a lawsuit for nonpayment of child support.

In Massachusetts, the Supreme Judicial Court (the state's highest court) held in 2006 that the wording of the state's statutes left a substantial hole in the privilege: spouses could be compelled to testify against each other in grand jury proceedings. Whether any other state's statutes have similar gaps, I couldn't say. It's also possible that in some states, either or both of the spousal privileges might not apply in one or more types of administrative hearings.

J. "Bad Acts"

If a man is on trial for assaulting his neighbor, may the prosecution show that he beats his wife? Generally not. Proving the defendant's prior "bad acts" is considered likely to prejudice the trier of fact (especially a jury) against the defendant, without actually showing that the defendant is more likely to have committed the particular crime with which they are charged.

Well, how about proving that the defendant assaulted a stranger in a bar last year? What if he was convicted of that assault? No, one is still not allowed to use that conviction to show that he's more likely to have assaulted the neighbor this year. Major caveat: in sex offense cases only, the federal courts and many states now allow proof of prior similar offenses for the purpose of showing a defendant's "propensity" (inclination, tendency) to commit this kind of crime. (See 13.F.)

If the defendant was convicted of something obviously unrelated, like writing bad checks, one can't get that information in either (unless one is impeaching the defendant as likely to be a dishonest witness, per 22.H.7.).

The prosecution may be able to introduce evidence of a prior conviction, or of the underlying act, if they're trying to prove something more specific than "once a thief, always a thief." For example, if the details of that previous theft are distinctive and match the details of the theft with which a defendant is now charged, then the prosecution can get the previous theft in as evidence of pattern. One may also introduce evidence of other crimes or wrongdoing in order to prove things like motive or preparation.

A related issue: if a defendant is charged with several similar crimes, can the trial cover all of them at once? If so, there's a danger that evidence about one could taint the jury's views about the other(s). A defendant can ask the trial court to "sever" or separate the case into multiple trials. Whether this motion will be granted may depend on whether there are common threads, such as (again) a pattern of conduct, or an ongoing plan.

Whether a second crime is tried with the first or merely mentioned at the first trial, here's a tactic one lawyer used that you could consider borrowing. A man was charged with blowing up a building. During voir dire (19.D.1.), the day's haul of potential jurors told the judge they could consider the evidence impartially. Then the defense attorney told them the man was also charged with trying to hire a hit man to kill a witness. Juror after juror then expressed doubt that they could be impartial after all. Finally the judge sent them all home and summoned another group the next day, ordering the defense attorney not to make another such revelation.

The point? The defense had been trying to persuade the judge that admitting evidence of the "hit man" charge would be too prejudicial. The voir dire stunt demonstrated just how prejudicial it could be. (Nevertheless, the judge allowed the evidence in.)

K. "Well, He Said to Me...":

Hearsay and Its Exceptions

With certain exceptions, Person A won't be allowed to testify that Person B said something. For example, unless one of the exceptions applied, a police officer could not testify: "Mrs. Myopic told me the mugger was a short fat guy with curly red hair." Normally, there would be no reason for such testimony unless one was trying to prove that the attacker *was* a short fat guy with curly red hair. If that's what one is trying to prove, one usually needs the person who saw the mugging to come and testify, rather than bringing in that testimony secondhand through the police officer. The reason: the other side needs to be able to cross-examine the person whose honesty, memory, and/or eyesight is at issue. (There's also a constitutional issue, discussed in 34.F.)

However, if the mugger is conceded by all to have been a thin bald fellow, and if the witness to the mugging also witnessed some other crucial event, then the point of the police officer's testimony could be that the witness is unreliable — and *that* would make the officer's testimony admissible. Similarly, Person A is allowed to testify about what Person B said if the point to be proved is Person B's state of mind. For example, if one needs to prove that John is delusional, one may call Mary to testify that John declared himself to be the god Apollo, because one is not trying to prove John's divine status, but rather, his mental condition. The applicable legalese: one isn't trying to get John's statement admitted "for the truth of the matter asserted."

Not all prior (past) statements are barred by the rule against hearsay, even when the statement *is* offered to prove the truth of the statement's content.

For example, someone may testify that the defendant made a damaging admission. That's either an exception to the rule against hearsay, or excluded from the definition of hearsay: the rule varies. The rationale (aside, perhaps, from some basic sense that it's fair to hoist the defendant on their own petard): the defendant is right there and can present their own explanation of the statement.

A somewhat similar exception (always, as far as I know, treated as an exception, rather than being excluded from the definition of hearsay) is a "statement against interest." When a witness testifies about someone else's out-of-court statement, and that statement casts the speaker in such an unfavorable light that they could have been charged with a crime or sued (or, possibly, fired) based on its contents, that statement may be introduced via the testimony of whoever heard it, and used to prove that the speaker spoke truly. The idea is that the speaker wouldn't have said something that would get them in that much trouble unless it were true. (Likely legalese to find in a discussion of this exception: "against pecuniary interest" if the statement could have gotten someone sued (or, possibly, fired); "against proprietary interest" more generally.) The rule doesn't take into account the possibility that someone will want to brag, and lie in the bragging, in order to look tough. **Your lawyer could try to keep out a damaging "statement against interest" by arguing that for the speaker in question, looking tough is safer to life and limb than looking wussy.**

This "statement against interest" exception *only* comes into play if the original speaker can't be brought into court to testify to whatever facts the statement covered. (Legalese for this: the speaker is "unavailable.") Not being able to remember the content of a statement, and testifying to that lack of memory, counts as being unavailable.

Another type of prior statement that either falls within an exception to the hearsay rule or doesn't count as hearsay: prior statements inconsistent with what the same witness previously said under oath. Obviously the speaker, the witness, is available, so the issue of availability doesn't arise. The witness must be given a chance to explain the prior statement. (See 22.H.7.)

Also permitted in some jurisdictions: prior statements that *are* consistent with the same witness' recent testimony, when the opposition claims the witness has "fabricated" (made up) that recent testimony. One may only use a prior consistent statement if it was made before the witness had, or the other side claims they had, a motive to fabricate. (Again, see 22.H.7.)

In most states, prior inconsistent or consistent statements aren't admitted for the truth of what they assert, but only to show inconsistency or consistency. (One more time: see 22.H.7.) But few attorneys expect juries to apply that distinction.

Here are some other common exceptions to the hearsay rule:

"Excited utterances": "My God, that's my Aunt Ruth carrying the flamethrower!" It is presumed that someone blurting out a statement in great excitement or under great stress will be telling the truth. This kind of statement may be admitted via someone else's testimony even if the original speaker could have been called to testify, since the speaker is no longer in the condition that made the statement supposedly reliable — or at least (an important caveat), more reliable than most hearsay.

"Present sense impression": similar to an excited utterance, this means the speaker had just observed the fact or event when they made the statement, before their memory had a chance to fade or change, and before they had time to come up with a lie (or a reason to lie). As with excited utterance, this exception applies even if the speaker could be called to testify, since the rationale for admitting the statement no longer applies.

Statements made "under belief of impending death," also called "dying declarations": most jurisdictions assume that people don't want to lie with their close-to-last breath. Again, this exception doesn't require that the speaker have actually died or otherwise become unavailable. **Your lawyer could try to argue that this particular speaker was an atheist and wouldn't have cared two hoots about entering an afterlife with a lie echoing in the air.**

A recent Indiana case raised an interesting question: what if a paramedic assured the dying speaker that they wouldn't die? As another Indiana case stated the rule, "the trial court may consider the general statements, conduct, manner, symptoms, and condition of the declarant." In this particular case, the trial court applied the exception in spite of the paramedic's inaccurate prediction, and the appellate court decided that facts including the declarant's symptoms, plus his repeatedly asking whether he was dying, passed the test. (The fact that he actually died may have influenced the court as well.)

Statements made in order to obtain medical diagnosis or treatment: the legal system assumes that most people tell the truth to the doctor, nurse, etc., from whom they're trying to get treatment from illness or injury. I suspect that a poll among medical professionals might undercut the validity of this assumption. **You could find story material in that discrepancy.** (Presumably, though I haven't seen this overlap discussed, these statements would only be admissible if the law of the jurisdiction doesn't render them privileged or if the patient waived the privilege. See 22.I.1.)

I recently read a police procedural where a detective was allowed to consult his notes and answer numerous detailed questions based on the notes' contents, without any discussion of whether this was appropriate. Unless there is, in a particular county or courtroom, an understood and accepted practice of ignoring such technicalities, a competent defense attorney would object to this use of notes. Recorded recollection, also called "past recollection recorded," is allowed if and only if the witness used to remember something relevant to the lawsuit, and wrote it down or made some other record at the time, but has since forgotten. This exception is probably a pragmatic accommodation to the limitations of human memory. Opposing counsel may cross-examine the witness about their state of mind at the time the record was made, trying to show that the record could be inaccurate. In most jurisdictions, the record itself won't be admitted as an exhibit: a writing will be read into evidence, or a recording played for the jury, to try to reproduce as closely as possible what the jury would experience if the witness still remembered the factual material. However, if opposing counsel thinks the notes sloppy or contradictory enough that it's worth letting them in, they could decline to object to the other attorney offering them as evidence, or even offer them themselves.

If, as is usually the case, the record that's substituting for a witness' memory doesn't become an exhibit, the jurors won't get to take the record with them when they deliberate, since the record is a substitute for verbal testimony and having the record handy might give it more weight than the testimony the jurors have to remember.

Hearsay is frequently an issue with documents. Many written reports are partially or entirely inadmissible, because they are essentially secondhand accounts of someone's assertions about facts. Here are some exceptions and other issues dealing with documents. Most of these exceptions require that the person who wrote the assertion down be unavailable to testify.

Business records: if a business routinely makes a record of certain information as part of doing business, then the business has a financial motive to do it accurately. That's usually good enough to get such records past the hearsay rule. Conversely, if the business would normally have made a record of a transaction or event, the fact that there is *no* such record may be shown as evidence that the transaction or event never happened. A similar rule applies to records typically kept by religious organizations (e.g., births, deaths, marriages, baptisms).

Governmental records: in a touching display of wishful thinking, the legal system assumes that governmental entities are just as careful in conducting their affairs as businesses whose continued existence depends on reliable and accurate record-keeping. However, realism does take hold at some point: if a governmental record was generated during a process that could be viewed as preparation for litigation, it generally can't be introduced to prove the truth of its contents in that same litigation.

Expert's reports: in some jurisdictions, these will at least sometimes fall into another "not actually hearsay" category. The rationale: scientific and technical experts are opinion witnesses, not witnesses testifying to facts. For example: "In my expert opinion, this blood spatter resulted from a downward blow by a right-handed assailant." The expert witness did not see the blow they're describing. Therefore, in jurisdictions accepting this analysis, the expert's report, as well as their testimony, may be admitted into evidence. Based on my admittedly limited research, however, federal courts are unlikely to admit expert reports as evidence, instead treating them as hearsay. In general, admission is less likely if the expert doesn't actually testify.

By the way, jurisdictions differ as to whether preliminary drafts of expert reports must be turned over if included in a discovery request (see 10.A.). In late 2010, the federal courts switched from "yes, discoverable" to "no, protected from discovery."

If your story turns on evidence that may be hearsay, check the law of the jurisdiction in question for other possibly applicable exceptions. The underlying principle for any exception will be the same: some circumstances exist which make the out-of-court statement likely enough to be reliable, so the system is willing to dispense with the safeguard of cross-examining whoever made the statement.

L. Judicial Notice

There are some facts so well established that it would waste the time of everyone involved to require that they be proved. The mechanism for bringing such facts into the record is called "judicial notice."

A jurisdiction's rules on how a court may take judicial notice will be found in that jurisdiction's rules of evidence.

The federal courts, and most or all state courts, allow judicial notice of any fact "that is not subject to reasonable dispute because it: (1) is generally known within the trial court's territorial jurisdiction; or (2) can be accurately and readily determined from sources whose accuracy cannot reasonably be questioned."

Courts must take judicial notice of a fact when a party requests it and supplies information showing that the fact meets these requirements. The opposing party must, however, be given a chance to argue that those requirements haven't been met after all. A court may also, if it chooses, take judicial notice of some fact sua sponte (on its own initiative). However the judicial notice comes about, if the trial is a civil jury trial, the court should instruct the jury to treat the judicially noticed fact as conclusively established (proved, plain and simple). In a criminal jury trial, however, the correct instruction informs the jurors that they may accept the fact as proved but have the option not to do so.

Courts may take judicial notice of the existence of statutes, local ordinances, and published rules and regulations, as well as official government records, within the United States or its territories. Depending on logistical details, it may or may not be feasible for a court to take judicial notice of the laws or records of foreign jurisdictions. (See also 32.J.)

Some frequently "noticed" facts include geographic locations and boundaries, from state borders to streets and buildings; chronological facts like the time the sun rose or set on a particular date; and the dates of historical events. **You might try to come up with situations where a lawsuit or prosecution would require the date of a historical event to be established.**

In some or all states, a court may take judicial notice at any stage of a proceeding. This may be more controversial if an appellate court explicitly takes judicial notice of a fact of which the trial court didn't take judicial notice first. It's fairly common, however, at least in some appellate courts, for the court to accept briefs full of citations to articles in professional journals, even though those articles contain multiple assertions of facts that haven't been established either by judicial notice or by properly admitted evidence. These briefs are commonly called "Brandeis briefs," after the lawyer (and later U.S. Supreme Court Justice) who introduced them. (See also 32.M.)

1. The Problem of the Curious Judge

I've already mentioned (at 19.E.) the difficulty of keeping jurors from looking up facts on the Internet. Judges acting as triers of fact in bench trials (19.B.) are subject to the same temptation if some evidentiary issue isn't getting the attention the judge thinks it should, or if the judge has doubts about the accuracy or completeness of what some expert had to say. The traditional view would be that such investigation is improper, and that the only facts the judge can reach out for are those subject to judicial notice. That view is coming under some pressure these days.

Appellate judges are also doing more Web-browsing these days, and not only on the subjects typically covered in Brandeis briefs (see 22.L., just above, and 32.M.), but on various other factual issues. This, too, is controversial, as not only stepping outside the judicial role but outside the trial court record as well. In one recent Seventh Circuit case, an inmate sued prison officials for ignoring his need for appropriate treatment for a serious digestive disorder. The eminent Judge Posner wrote a majority opinion reversing summary judgment (see 25.I.) for the defendants, and based that reversal in part on Posner's online research about the medical issues. That research included the National Institute of Health website, WebMD, the Mayo Clinic website, and even Wikipedia. Posner's opinion defended his use of facts gleaned outside the summary judgment record, contrasting it with "mak[ing] a fetish of adversary procedure" and noting the inmate's practical difficulties in doing his own factual research. Judge Hamilton wrote a strongly worded partial dissent (an opinion "concurring in part and dissenting [disagreeing] in part"), calling this reliance on judicial online research "unprecedented," "contrary to long-established law," and likely to raise "a host of practical problems."

M. Objections

First, some terminology: objections aren't "denied," like motions. They're "overruled." Same difference. Similarly, objections are not granted or approved: they're "sustained."

Objections must be specific. The objecting attorney must state (briefly) what rule is violated by the question being asked or the exhibit being offered. A word or two can be enough. "Objection — hearsay." And the attorney had better pick the right ground for objection. A party may not object on one basis and then argue later, on appeal, that a completely different objection applied. Failing to make a possible objection constitutes a "waiver" of that objection, and in most cases, that means the party may not assert it on appeal or even in a post-trial motion (see 32.B. and 32.J.3.).

One rare situation when an objection may survive, even though the attorney (or a pro se party) failed to make it at trial, is where circumstances show that the objection would have been futile. If the judge has just overruled a series of similar objections, getting more irate every time, the attorney may not be required to make things worse for their client by making yet another. But the general presumption that judges do things right will make this a tough point on which to prevail.

If an attorney just calls out "Objection!" without stating a ground, and the judge asks why, it's not that unusual (though possibly embarrassing) for the attorney to withdraw the objection. On the other hand, I recently heard about a federal judge well known for his knowledge of and intense interest in the details of evidence law. Lawyers who frequently appeared in front of this judge became aware that if they missed making some objection that the judge thought appropriate, he would glare at them. Some of those lawyers made it a habit to yelp "Objection!" any time they were on the receiving end of such a glare — and the judge would often sustain the objection immediately, even though the attorney who made the objection had no idea what they had done right.

Naturally, judges sometimes make errors in deciding whether to sustain an objection, but if a judge overrules a whole series of clearly valid objections, that could be a sign that something fishy is going on. The same could be true if an attorney who isn't asleep or incompetent misses making many valid objections. On the other hand, judges sometimes overrule valid objections made by the side that seems to be winning already, in order not to hand the probable loser an issue to raise on appeal.

Attorneys arguing about an objection are supposed to, and usually do, face and speak to the judge rather than each other. If you want to show that your lawyer character is particularly upset, you could have them start talking directly to opposing counsel instead. That could well get them reprimanded by the judge.

If there's a jury listening, any prolonged back-and-forth about the objection, tying it to evidence that has or may be introduced, could be improper, and some judges will cut it short, summoning the attorneys to a "sidebar" (muttered conference at the bench) or dismissing the jury for a few minutes.

Technically speaking, if the witness has already answered an objectionable question, the attorney should "move to strike" the answer rather than objecting. (I don't know how often this rule is ignored.) Also, if the attorney wants to be able to argue later (on appeal, say) that the improper answer to the question really hurt the client's case, they have to do what they can to reduce the damage — or rather, to do something that would reduce the damage if human nature were somewhat different. The lawyer is supposed to ask the judge, in these circumstances, to instruct the jury to disregard what it's just heard (or, sometimes, to consider it only for some particular limited purpose). This judicial instruction is also called an "admonition." Problem is: people generally can't disregard what they've just heard, especially something juicy. As mentioned earlier (9.D.), lawyers (including Jimmy Stewart's character in the movie *Anatomy of a Murder*) often describe this effect by saying that one can't "unring the bell." Admonitions can even have the counterproductive effect of highlighting the objectionable evidence. One judge recently told attorneys at a seminar about a juror who, hearing an attorney's long and emphatic request for an admonition, elbowed another juror and asked excitedly, "What'd I miss?"

If you want your judge to be particularly sensitive to this problem, they might instead instruct the jury, at the beginning of the trial and/or before the jury goes off to deliberate, to ignore any question as to which an objection was sustained, and any testimony that was stricken. Of course, the jurors may have trouble remembering what evidence that affects; but maybe one of them will.

If a lawyer in a jury trial is too obvious about "ringing the bell" with references to objectionable material, the result could be a mistrial (see 9.D.) and/or a later disciplinary proceeding (4.A.).

If an attorney is offering evidence (whether testimony or an exhibit), and the judge refuses to admit that evidence into the record, a good attorney will make an "offer of proof" spelling out just what they were trying to get admitted. Otherwise, the appellate court won't be able to properly assess whether the trial court should have admitted the evidence. If the trial court has refused to allow testimony of some kind, the attorney may ask that the jury (if there is one) be excused while the attorney questions the witness, to show how the witness would have testified if allowed to do so. Failure to make some sort of offer of proof will usually prevent a party from arguing on appeal that the judge should have let the evidence in.

This is a rule that can lead appellate attorneys to tear out their hair, assuming they have any. Many trial lawyers don't like to make offers of proof: they believe such offers will annoy the judge by slowing down the trial and by emphasizing the fact that the lawyer is thinking of appealing the trial court's decision. Trial lawyers put a very high priority on keeping the judge happy, since that may increase the chances of winning in the first place, which (for reasons explained in 32.J.) is much better than bringing even the most meritorious appeal. Appellate attorneys often plead in vain for some attention to the possibility that the judge will rule against the client, in which case preservation of issues for appeal may prove crucial.

There used to be an additional hoop to jump through in order to preserve an objection for appeal: the "exception." If the judge overruled an objection, the attorney had to utter the single word "exception," or give up the right to challenge the ruling on appeal. At the end of the trial, the attorney might be required to submit a list of all the exceptions on which he (usually he, in those days) intended to appeal. This list was called a "bill of exceptions." The judge would make the bill of exceptions part of the official record by signing and sealing it.

The federal courts abandoned the use of exceptions in 1938. I can't say for sure whether attorneys are still required to interject "exception" after overruled objections in any state's courts, but I doubt it. **You could show that an elderly attorney, coming out of retirement to aid a friend, relative or cause, was out of touch with the latest procedure by having him pipe up with an "exception." But given how long ago most courts stopped requiring exceptions, you might need to set this scene some years in the past.**

Texas retains the idea of exceptions, or of a bill of exceptions, as a way to preserve error for appeal if something occurred at trial that the court reporter did not record at the time. At least some other states have other procedures to accomplish the same thing. **Issues possibly worth exploring include what happens if one party disagrees with another party or with the judge about what actually took place.**

1. Fundamental Error

In criminal trials, there's an escape hatch for the waiver of an objection: "fundamental error." While definitions may differ slightly, the essence of fundamental error (in the words of one Indiana case) is "an error so prejudicial to the rights of a defendant that a fair trial is rendered impossible. . . . To be considered fundamental, an error must constitute a blatant violation of basic principles, the harm or potential for harm must be substantial, and the resulting error must deny the defendant fundamental due process." As you might imagine, this is a very high hurdle.

Some or all of the federal appellate courts use the term "plain error" instead of "fundamental error." According to the Ninth Circuit Court of Appeals' guidelines, "[p]lain error is invoked to prevent a miscarriage of justice or to preserve the integrity and the reputation of the judicial process." Federal "plain error" may not be quite as difficult to prove as state court "fundamental error," at least in criminal cases. The Ninth Circuit guidelines for civil proceedings describe plain error as "proper only for a 'manifest miscarriage of justice,' . . . or if "there is an absolute absence of evidence to support the jury's verdict'"; but its guidelines for criminal cases use this language:

> Under the plain error standard, relief is not warranted unless there has been: (1) error, (2) that was plain, (3) that affected substantial rights, and (4) that seriously affected the fairness, integrity, or public reputation of the judicial proceedings.

One common basis for a claim of fundamental error is prosecutorial misconduct (see Ch. 23), either during the presentation of evidence or during opening or closing argument. **Here's an exercise: make your prosecutor misbehave so egregiously that an appellate court is likely to find the "fundamental error" standard has been met.**

CHAPTER 23

Prosecutorial Misconduct

W hat would you call it if the prosecutor in a criminal trial tells the jury about evidence that the trial court has already decided to exclude? Or withholds exculpatory evidence (evidence that could help the defense) from defense counsel? Or even destroys such evidence (22.G.)? Or knowingly offers perjured testimony (4.F.)? Or calls defense counsel scurrilous names in front of the jury? Or makes disparaging remarks about a defendant exercising their constitutional right to remain silent (34.D.)?

Well, aside from various other available labels, you'd call it prosecutorial misconduct. And it can lead to a reversed conviction and a new trial.

If the misconduct is obvious during trial, defense counsel had better object, and request either an "admonishment" (the trial court telling the jury that the prosecution misbehaved, and instructing them to ignore what happened) or a mistrial (9.D.). Otherwise, the misconduct has to be so egregious as to amount to "fundamental error" (22.M.1.) for the defendant to have any recourse.

If the dirty deed doesn't come to light until afterward, it could be the basis for a motion for new trial (see 32.B.), or a petition for post-conviction relief (32.C.).

In rare cases, a misbehaving prosecutor may be disciplined by the appropriate authorities (4.A.).

Why is there a special category for prosecutorial misconduct, with no matching specific tag for defense misconduct? Well, the roles of the prosecution and defense are different in a very important way. The defense attorney, like attorneys in civil cases, is supposed to devote their efforts to getting the best possible result for the client. The prosecutor, on the other hand, is not supposed to win at any cost, but rather, to ensure that the guilty and only the guilty are convicted of crimes. While either defense counsel or the prosecutor might conceivably make improper arguments or suppress evidence, society has a special stake in keeping prosecutors honest.

Of course, as discussed in 9.D., an attorney in a civil trial may also misbehave so badly as to cause a mistrial; but the more stringent constitutional safeguards for criminal defendants increase the opportunities for a prosecutor's misconduct to have this effect.

CHAPTER 24

Lost in Translation:
Foreign Language Interpreters

Trying to understand legalese, court procedure, et cetera is bad enough for a party or witness who speaks the local language. What happens to those who seek justice, or who have no choice but to come into court, if they don't speak or aren't fluent in English? Note that this possibility includes deaf people who communicate in sign language. (It may be especially hard to find an interpreter for deaf people who depend on lip-reading, but there are fewer of these than many people imagine. Lip-reading is *hard*, folks.)

It appears to be well established that criminal defendants who can't understand the proceedings, or can't make themselves understood, have a constitutional right to an interpreter. This can be crucial not only in any courtroom proceedings, but in plea bargain negotiations: what if the defendant doesn't properly understand the plea agreement?

However, this doesn't mean that in practice, there will always be a qualified interpreter available. If the price of an interpreter is a wait long enough that it'd ordinarily violate the right to a speedy trial (8.B.), well, so much for speed. More fundamentally, it's up to the judge to decide whether someone needs an interpreter or not. That decision may sometimes be made in a casual or cursory manner.

There's also the issue of waiver. Theoretically, a defendant would have to make a "knowing, intelligent, and voluntary" waiver of the right to an interpreter. In practice, the court may not investigate too thoroughly, especially if defense counsel asserts that the defendant has waived the right. **You could explore the situation where a defendant didn't adequately understand the explanation of what they were about to give up.**

What about parties to civil (tort, contract, family law, etc.) proceedings? That depends on whom you ask. The U.S. Department of Justice, Civil Rights Division, takes the position that these parties have the right to an interpreter at public expense. They've been periodically reminding state court administrators of that fact. Not all state courts act like they're convinced. If this is an issue in your story, you'll need to check the law and practice of your state. (Last I saw, Georgia did provide interpreters in civil court and California didn't. Check for yourself, even there.) If interpreters are provided in civil cases, they may be required in court-ordered mediation as well, and perhaps in publicly funded voluntary mediation, where such exists. (As I write, there's a plaintiff in federal court arguing the latter.)

What if it's a witness, rather than a defendant or other party, who can't speak English well enough to make themselves understood or to understand the questions of counsel? If it's a defense witness in a criminal trial, the right to a fair trial should embrace the right to examine that witness in a language both the witness and the trier of fact can comprehend. In a civil trial, some authorities suggest that interpreters are at least as likely to be provided for the witness as for a party. In criminal trials, at least some authorities indicate a need for *two* interpreters if a witness interpreter is needed, so that one can handle attorney-client communications during the testimony and translate procedural details while the other translates the questions to and answers from the witness.

Where the language ability of a party or witness is borderline, tactical considerations will become more important. Using an interpreter can reduce the impact of testimony, as it separates the verbal from the nonverbal elements (expression, body language). It also makes the proceedings take longer, which could annoy the judge (always an important consideration) and will make things more expensive for a litigant who's paying by the hour.

Witness interpretation is often "consecutive": the interpreter waits for the witness to finish a sentence or phrase and then translates it. Interpreters for defendants ideally translate "simultaneously" (really a beat or two after the original utterance).

Witness interpreters should swear or affirm to translate faithfully, accurately, and impartially. Jurisdictions vary as to whether party interpreters must do the same. An attorney should do everything possible to prevent the interpreter from tweaking the testimony, e.g. by adding polite touches (like "sir") that the witness did not, or using phrasing more or less decisive than that of the witness.

The glaring weak spot in all this protection: is the interpreter any good at their job? Rules for how the trial court assesses the qualifications of interpreters vary greatly, where they exist at all. Since the court reporter only takes down the English translation, not the foreign language statements, the only way for an appellate or post-conviction court to deal with interpreter shortcomings is to examine any audio or audiovisual recording, or for someone who was present to testify or file an affidavit describing the interpreter's errors.

What if the judge is, or claims to be, bilingual? It's still better to have an interpreter, for the sake of everyone else involved, and for the sake of a more complete record. (Even an all-English record of the complete proceedings is better than a record with huge gaps where the judge listened to a foreign language and supposedly understood it.)

In a notable application of common sense to legal proceedings, the involvement of an interpreter does not vitiate the attorney-client privilege (see 4.D.).

CHAPTER 25

Motions

A motion is a request. An attorney (or unrepresented party) "moves" the court to do something. Motions can be verbal or in writing, usually the latter. (Some must be in writing.) Motions can be filed before, during, or after a trial.

Sources differ on whether, in general, a "petition" is the same thing as a motion. Petitions are usually in writing. There may also be different requirements, per statute or rule, for a motion and a petition that essentially seek the same kind of relief. One of the oldest and most venerable petitions is the petition for habeas corpus (see 32.E.).

Here are some of the most common motions.

A. Motion to Dismiss

In federal practice, some motions to dismiss are called 12(b)(6) motions, after the federal rule governing one popular kind of motion to dismiss. That's a motion based on the assertion that the complaint doesn't manage to set forth a claim on which relief can legally be granted, even if everything alleged in the complaint is assumed to be true. But there can be other grounds for a motion to dismiss. For example, a motion to dismiss can be used to challenge the court's jurisdiction, or to assert that a party waited too long to take some required action.

Depending upon the reason for a dismissal, it may either be "with" or "without" prejudice. If there's something that can still be done, within the time before the statute of limitations or any statute of repose (Ch. 11) runs out, to fix the complaint, a dismissal without prejudice gives the plaintiff the chance to make that fix. If the complaint is incurably deficient, it'll be dismissed with prejudice. (Same vocabulary, different situation: if a case is dismissed as a penalty for major misconduct, such as egregious spoliation of evidence (22.G.), it'll be dismissed with prejudice.)

B. Motion for Judgment on the Pleadings

This is very similar to a motion to dismiss, except that it may be filed by either side. It asserts that based on everything alleged in the complaint (7.A.1.), everything admitted and denied in the answer, and any affirmative defenses asserted in the answer (7.A.2.), the side making the motion must prevail as a matter of law, with no need for a trial on the facts.

The odds are that a motion to dismiss or a motion for judgment on the pleadings will lose. Attorneys sometimes file such motions for the same reason doctors sometimes order probably-unnecessary tests: to avoid any risk of a malpractice lawsuit down the road.

C. Motion for Change of Venue

This dry legalese covers situations with many dramatic possibilities. A motion for change of venue asserts that the case should be moved to a different county or assigned to a different judge. (NOTE: improper venue may also be asserted in the answer to a complaint. See 7.A.2.)

Maybe a rape or murder so grieved and shocked the community that no jury made up of locals is likely to be impartial. The defendant can move for a change of venue to a county where people are less involved. Maybe the plaintiff in a civil case jilted the judge when they were both in high school. That plaintiff can move to have a different judge hear the case.

Frequently, each party has a right to get one change of venue (either type) shortly after the case gets going. After that, the party would have to persuade the judge (who may be the problem the party is asserting), and if that attempt fails, try to take the matter up right away in an interlocutory appeal (see 32.A.).

For a related but different basis for changing where a lawsuit will proceed, see forum non conveniens, 6.B.

D. Motion to Compel

When a party (or in some situations, a nonparty) is supposed to do something — for example, respond to a discovery request (see 10.A.), or turn over property after a divorce decree, or pay child support — and doesn't do it, the aggrieved party can tattle to the court and ask the court to put some pressure on, by filing a Motion to Compel.

These motions are filed most often in discovery disputes, and often filed when they could have been avoided with a little negotiation. Judges hate having to deal with discovery disputes, and they spend a great deal of time doing it. If an attorney files a motion to compel without a sincere attempt to work things out with opposing counsel, that attorney will probably annoy the judge. That's never a good idea. State or local rules may actually require an attempt to resolve the dispute before filing a motion to compel discovery.

If you're writing about a brand-new attorney, unnecessary and/or unnecessarily combative motions to compel might be a good way to show how much your attorney has to learn. The judge could provide the lesson in a pithy and/or scorching manner.

E. Motion for a Continuance

I'm only guessing, but this might win the prize for the motion most often filed (with motions to compel probably running second).

Cases may be delayed for many months as first one and then the other party asks the court to "continue" (postpone) a hearing or trial. The motion could be based on any of a number of grounds, such as the attorney's schedule, a key witness' schedule, the amount of material dumped on the attorney in response to a discovery request, a change of attorneys . . . .

The trial court has a great deal of discretion on whether to grant a continuance. Due to the nature of the beast, any claim that the trial court "abused" that discretion (made a ruling too outrageous for the appellate court to stomach) will probably have to do with the decision to deny a continuance. Why? Because if the court grants the continuance, that ruling comes a long time before the case is over. Even if the rules offer a way for the unhappy party to appeal that decision, an appeal might well take longer than the delay caused by the continuance itself. If a court denies a continuance, the next step may be a final judgment, and if the loser is the party who opposed the continuance, that party can challenge the denial of the continuance as part of an appeal.

F. Motion for Separation of Witnesses

To reduce the chance that one witness' testimony will consciously or unconsciously influence another witness, an attorney may move for "separation of witnesses." If the motion is granted, none of the witnesses may be in the courtroom before they give their own testimony.

Of course, this doesn't prevent witnesses from getting together and synchronizing their stories ahead of time — but when it comes to testifying in court, people don't always say just what they planned to say, or what they told others to expect. And a court may actually order witnesses to refrain from seeing each other or communicating with each other outside the courtroom, although I believe this is much less common.

Since parties have a right to be present during their own litigation (unless they forfeit it by disrupting the proceedings), this motion may not be used to exclude the parties. A party might also argue that a nonparty witness' presence in the courtroom, prior to the witness' testimony, is essential for some reason (for example, if the party requires constant skilled nursing care and the nurse will be a witness). Local, state, or federal rules may provide other exceptions.

If your story features a particularly frightened or emotionally vulnerable witness, separation of witnesses could deprive that witness of the person on whom they depend for courage or stability, putting the witness under dramatically useful stress.

G. Motion in Limine

A motion in limine asks the judge to decide before trial that certain evidence should or (more often) should not be admitted. This may be particularly important in jury trials, as any mention of the evidence could do damage that no judicial admonition (see 9.D.) can undo.

The peculiar thing about a motion in limine, at least in some jurisdictions, is that even after it's granted, if opposing counsel ignores (or conveniently forgets) that the motion was granted and starts to offer the evidence at trial, the party whose motion succeeded still has to object to the evidence, or else possibly lose the right to challenge its admission on appeal. Similarly, if the motion in limine was denied before trial, the party who wanted the evidence excluded may lose the right to challenge it on appeal unless they object to the same evidence at trial. (See also: motions to suppress, coming up next in 25.H.)

II. Motion to Suppress

This motion is usually filed in a criminal case, asking the court not to consider, or not to let the jury consider, some piece of evidence. It is often based on the claim that the evidence was discovered in an unconstitutional fashion. Interesting side note: if a case is dismissed for insufficient evidence because all the good stuff was suppressed, that's one of the very few situations in which the state may appeal in a criminal case (see 32.A., 32.H.).

In some jurisdictions, if a pretrial motion to suppress (aka a motion in limine, just discussed in 25.G.) is denied, the defendant must still raise the issue during the trial in order to preserve it for appellate review.

I. Motion for Summary Judgment

Sometimes, in a civil case, the parties don't disagree about any facts that could make a difference to the outcome. A party may then file a motion for summary judgment, asking the trial judge to hold that there is no genuine issue as to any material (significant) fact, and that the party filing the motion should win on the law.

In a motion for summary judgment, the moving party is asserting that the key facts are established, so the moving party must offer some proof. There are pretty particular rules about when and how one provides that proof, but parties generally use sworn written statements called affidavits, or sworn testimony taken before trial in a deposition (part of the discovery process, described in 10.A.).

The other side can try to show that there are, too, important facts on which the evidence conflicts, so that the truth needs to be determined by a judge or jury. Similar rules will cover when and how the party opposing summary judgment must present proof of those facts. Alternatively, the other party could file their own motion for summary judgment, claiming that the undisputed facts actually support a ruling in their favor.

Sometimes a party will seek, or a judge will grant, partial summary judgment: a judgment on one or more aspects of the case, leaving the others to be fought out in an evidentiary hearing.

J. Post-Trial Motions (Tune in Later)

After the trial judge has issued a final judgment, the losing party may make a motion for a new trial, based on any of many claimed errors in the first trial. Another approach, more efficient where it's allowed: a motion to "correct errors" or a "motion to alter/amend the judgment." I'll talk about these motions when I talk about appeals (32.B.).

K. Motion to Reconsider

Any time a party doesn't like the trial judge's ruling on a motion, they can try filing a motion to reconsider (unless state or local rules say otherwise). However, this motion may not have the effect of tolling any applicable deadline, such as a deadline for filing an appeal. If the motion adds no new arguments, it's very unlikely to succeed, but if it does break new ground and is made too late, the moving party may be deemed to have waived (given up) the new argument by failing to make it earlier.

If a party files a motion after an adverse final judgment and calls it a motion to reconsider, they may be able to argue later that it was really some other post-trial motion (see 32.B.) in substance, and therefore did toll the appeal deadline.

L. Motion to Stay

Lay folk (non-lawyers) often assume that if they appeal a judgment, the judgment can't be enforced during the appeal. That's rarely the case, at least not once some short period (e.g. 10 or 30 days) has passed. Usually, something extra is required beyond simply filing the appeal if the appellant (the party filing the appeal) wants to preserve the status quo while the appeal grinds on. This would be a motion to stay the judgment, discussed further in the chapter on appeals (at 32.I.). (Massachusetts is currently an exception: appeals generally act to stay the judgment being appealed. There may be other jurisdictions that follow this approach as well.)

Some courts will automatically stay a judgment that would, under state law, operate as a lien (see 14.D.1.) on the loser's property.

M. Motion to Withdraw Representation

Whether an attorney who wants out must ask the court's permission depends on the applicable rules. In federal court, the starting place is Federal Rule of Civil Procedure 74. Per that rule, an attorney may simply give notice to the court, the client, and all other parties of their plan to withdraw unless a motion or trial is currently pending. The opposing party is then supposed to make sure the bereft client knows that they are no longer represented. This is done by serving a notice telling the party either to appear personally or to hire another lawyer. The proceeding is then on hold for three weeks unless the unrepresented party waives (gives up) that delay or the court changes it in some way. The same procedure is followed if an attorney dies or gets disbarred or suspended from the practice of law (see 4.A.), or if the court kicks the attorney off the case for something like a conflict of interest (see 4.C.).

What if a motion is pending, or even worse, the trial is coming up soon? Then the attorney must file a motion seeking the court's permission to withdraw. While F.R.C.P. 74 doesn't get into details about what the attorney must prove to be released, federal district courts may include these and other specifics in their own local rules. For example, the local rules of one Minnesota federal court require the attorney to file a motion to withdraw unless they file a notice showing that only one of several attorneys representing the attorney is withdrawing, or that the client has already obtained substitute counsel. This local rule also requires a motion for attorneys seeking to withdraw within 90 days of a civil trial or 30 days of a criminal trial. (One might expect the opposite in terms of lead time, given the life-or-liberty interests at stake in a criminal trial. This rule might be based on the likely complexity of civil cases that actually go to trial rather than being settled (see 9.B.), as opposed to criminal cases in which a defendant decides they have little to lose by going to trial.)

State court rules will vary as to how many hurdles they place in front of attorneys seeking to withdraw and what grounds are likely to suffice. Here are some of the reasons attorneys might move to withdraw, where such motions are required.

(a) They aren't getting paid. This is probably one of the most common reasons attorneys try to withdraw. Whether it's a good enough reason, from the court's point of view, will depend on the timing and the client's alternatives, as well, perhaps, as how much more unpaid work the attorney would have to perform if they stayed in. The attorney might, at some point, be able to argue that having to continue work for a nonpaying client constitutes involuntary servitude and violates the Thirteenth Amendment to the U.S. Constitution.

As mentioned in 3.G., attorneys often possess a lien on any client property in their possession, including the case file, until they get paid. However, where state rules prevent an attorney from withdrawing if that withdrawal will harm the client in any substantial way, some courts might decide that this rule trumps the attorney's right to assert a lien. After all, if the attorney withdraws, any attorney taking over the case would need the case file to properly represent the client. If the attorney isn't allowed to withdraw, any battle over the file is postponed until after the case concludes.

(b) The attorney-client relationship is in shambles. This is often how things end up if an attorney ignores the warning signs of a troublesome client (see 4.I.) This ground for seeking to withdraw has several subsets, all of them offering potential for drama and suspense:

- The attorney can't find and/or can't reach the client. Attorney-client communication can be crucial on such matters as upcoming court dates, settlement or plea offers to be accepted or rejected, or the decision whether the client should testify.
- The client continually rejects the attorney's advice about trial tactics and achievable goals.
- The client loses their temper in the courtroom, incurring the judge's wrath, and the attorney has been unable to restrain the client.
- The client has filed a complaint about the attorney with the disciplinary commission.
- The client has threatened to harm the attorney or their family.

(c) The attorney is having some medical or emotional crisis that will prevent them from continuing to offer adequate representation.

(d) The client insists on offering false evidence (see 4.F.). Court rules may vary about whether a motion to withdraw is an adequate response to such a plan, and about how explicit the attorney must be about why they are filing the motion. See more on the latter issue below.

(e) The attorney finds out that they are likely to be called as a witness at trial, a role incompatible with continuing as an attorney in the case. **It's not unknown for lawyers to list opposing counsel as witnesses in order to precipitate such a crisis.** Courts are likely to scrutinize any such listing quite closely.

(f) The attorney discovers a conflict of interest (4.C.) that was somehow not evident, or that the attorney's carelessness kept them from realizing, when the attorney was first retained.

Court rules are likely to require that an attorney seeking to withdraw notify the client, in writing and possibly by certified mail or the like, of that intention some set number of days before actually filing the motion. The notice might have to include details of any upcoming court proceedings. If such a notice is required, it will probably have to be attached to the filed motion, and the motion will have to include a sworn statement from the attorney giving what the attorney believes to be the client's contact information. However, it's not terribly likely that anyone on the court's staff will check that information. **If the notice goes to a phony or obsolete address, the client might not find out that they're without an attorney until crucial court dates have come and gone. This could occur because the attorney was afraid the client would react violently to being dumped, or because some underworld figure has coerced the attorney into letting the client down.**

One often thorny problem is how an attorney can maintain attorney-client confidentiality (4.D.) while explaining the need to withdraw. Some, but not all, courts will accept a general statement, e.g., that the attorney must withdraw in order to avoid violating rules of professional ethics, or that the client has not fully complied with all aspects of the retainer agreement. If the court demands more detail, the attorney must try to reveal as little as possible while still getting the job done. Possible approaches include citing the relevant professional rule(s) by number, without elaboration.

More problems could arise if the court requires the attorney, as a condition for granting the motion, to help the client obtain substitute counsel. **This could be a nasty trick to play on a fellow lawyer if one is withdrawing because the client is impossible to work with, or dangerous, or intent on presenting false evidence. One might have to look for attorneys whose standards for potential clients are notoriously lax.**

N. None of the Above

If none of the usual motions suits a lawyer's needs, it's possible to make one up. Lawyers do this from time to time. They just find a reasonably concise descriptive title for it, starting with "Motion To" or "Motion For."

O. Petitions

As already mentioned, the word "petition" is sometimes synonymous with "motion," as in a petition for the trial court find someone in contempt of court (though in some places, this is called a motion instead, a motion asking the court for "an Order to Show Cause"). Other times, a "petition" is the equivalent of a "complaint," the opening salvo in a legal proceeding. Divorce cases start with "petitions" for "dissolution." Attempts to get the U.S. Supreme Court to involve itself in a case start with "petitions" for certiorari. Habeas corpus proceedings start with "petitions," as do requests for some other "writs" (commandments from a court that some official body do or stop doing something).

CHAPTER 26

The Original,
Whatever that Means

The "best evidence" rule is both less sweeping and more precise than it sounds. It is not a value judgment or hierarchy about types of evidence in general. It's actually about how to prove the contents of a document, photograph, audio recording, or video. (I'll just say "document" for the rest of this discussion, to keep my sentences simpler.) Basically, per the more stringent version of this rule, if the "original" document exists and is available, that's what a party must offer in evidence. And if the original no longer exists or is unavailable for some other compelling reason, then one may only use a copy if someone can testify that its contents are the same as the original. This could be the person who wrote the document, or someone who saw it and is persuasive about remembering it with enough precision to give the necessary assurance.

Cue some young person, born after personal computers became ubiquitous: "What's an original?" Well, children, back before word processors and computers, documents had to be written by hand or typed on a typewriter, unless multiple copies were being made and a printing press was used — which wouldn't happen for contracts, wills, deeds to real property, single photographs, etc. That handwritten or typed document was the original. If someone wrote it out a second time, or took a picture of it, or used a mimeograph machine (or later, a photocopier) to make a copy, that copy wasn't an original.

The Federal Rules of Evidence and many state rules have relaxed this requirement somewhat. In federal court and in states that have followed its lead, a duplicate is just as admissible as an original "unless a genuine question is raised about the original's authenticity or the circumstances make it unfair to admit the duplicate." Circumstances may, but won't always, have this effect if the document is the center of the case, as in a dispute about the authenticity of a will.

If the party against whom the document would be used had control of the original and knew it would be needed at trial, and that original has since disappeared, the party seeking to admit the document will be able to prove its contents by other means, whether with a duplicate or with testimony.

If a document started life as electronic bits, then any printout will suffice as long as whoever is offering it as evidence lays the proper foundation. That means showing that the printout comes directly from the source document, how the document came to exist, and other such background. The details of how thoroughly one must show the origin, the method of data storage, etc. may vary from state to state and from judge to judge.

What about claims that the digitally created document has been digitally altered? This is significantly easier to accomplish than altering a paper original. Still, if the required foundation has been laid, the burden of showing any such alteration will be on the party opposing admission of the document.

Those entering into contracts, or otherwise trying to make sure an electronic document is recognized as authentic, sometimes use digital signatures, essentially a type of secure computer code. However, this level of proof is not required for most electronically generated documents.

By the way, if a recording requires translation into English, that would require expertise of the sort that falls under rules re expert witnesses (22.H.11.).

A related point: it being easier to hack computers than to break into offices or homes and steal paper, it is more likely that whoever opposes admission of digitally created evidence will claim the evidence was illegally obtained. In a criminal trial where the government wants the evidence admitted, proof that the government, or someone working with the government, obtained the evidence in some unauthorized manner would probably keep the evidence out. Otherwise, it's likely to come in, though some courts will exclude an illegally obtained document in a subsequent civil proceeding, or in a proceeding that's "quasi-criminal" in nature. Quasi-criminal proceedings could include civil contempt of court (see 30.D.), a claim for punitive damages (30.B.3.), or (in some jurisdictions) a civil forfeiture proceeding (34.G.2.).

CHAPTER 27

Instructions, Verdicts, and Judgments

A. Defaults and Default Judgments

I've already talked about motions to dismiss and motions for judgment on the pleadings (25.A. and B.), which, if granted, will end a lawsuit before any judgment as such can be issued. There's another way a lawsuit can end prematurely, compared to the usual procedure: default and default judgment.

If the defendant was properly informed about the lawsuit (via "service" of a "summons", discussed in 7.A.1.) and doesn't file any responsive pleadings (see 7.A.2.), or if the defendant fails to show up at the trial after having been properly notified of the time and place, the trial court may enter a default. If the defendant wakes up and realizes what's happening, they can try explaining to the court why the responsive pleading wasn't filed, and the trial court might allow a belated filing, though it might also require the defendant to reimburse the plaintiff for the costs of seeking a default.

A default by itself doesn't accomplish much, but once there's a default, if the defendant doesn't act quickly enough to seek relief or if the trial court doesn't grant relief, the plaintiff may ask for a default judgment that gives the plaintiff whatever the lawsuit was seeking. The plaintiff would usually have to attempt to notify the defendant a few days beforehand about the impending request.

If the complaint seeks payment of a set sum of money, or the relief is otherwise clearly stated in the complaint, the court might not require any actual evidence to be submitted. Otherwise, there may be a one-sided evidentiary hearing.

Some states limit the kind of relief one can get in a default judgment. (For example, last time I checked, one couldn't get quiet title relief (14.D.5.) in a default judgment in California.) There may be defendants against whom one can't get a default judgment, including (per a federal statute that also binds state courts) people in active military service. There may also be special rules if the defendant is currently incompetent, for example because of age or mental illness, or if the defendant is a governmental entity. Re that last, West Virginia, for example, decrees by statute that no default judgment is available unless it's clear that the government didn't intend to respond to the complaint.

Not all foreign jurisdictions will enforce default judgments. A party shouldn't bother to get one if the judgment would be useless without the assistance of one of those jurisdictions.

A defendant can try to get a default judgment set aside or (same thing) vacated by showing "good cause." This isn't as hard as you might think, because courts are supposed to prefer trying cases on the merits, looking at the law and facts, rather than declaring "game over" without a trial. The defendant could claim that they didn't receive the summons or required other notice(s). (Dirty tricks involving service of the summons or other notices, amounting to fraud by the plaintiff, at some point picked up the piquant label "sewer service.") "Excusable neglect," which to some extent means whatever the trial court wants it to mean, can also provide the required good cause for vacating a default judgment. Some judges will view an attorney's screwup as excusable; others won't.

The court is likely to consider whether the defendant, now that they have shown up, has something worth saying, i.e. "a meritorious defense," or whether the plaintiff's case is such a slam-dunk that there's no point undoing the default judgment. This isn't about previewing or weighing the actual evidence: it's enough if the defendant alleges (asserts) facts that, if true, would constitute a proper legal defense to the plaintiff's claims. In that way, it's similar to what happens when someone files a motion for judgment on the pleadings (25.B.).

The court will usually consider, as well, how much the actual defendant (as opposed to the defendant's attorney) was responsible for the default; whether there's some less drastic way to punish the defendant for breaking the rules; and whether the time the plaintiff had to waste waiting for the defendant's response, getting a default, and then getting a default judgment will make it significantly harder for the plaintiff to present a winning case. That last factor is called "prejudice" to the plaintiff.

B. Let's All Pretend They Understand:
Jury Instructions

A jury has to decide what facts have been proved, and then figure out who should win and lose based on those facts. Who should win and who should lose, given the facts, depends on the law. How do juries know what the law is? Supposedly, the judge explains it to them by giving them jury instructions.

The problem is that until recently, and to this day in many places, jury instructions are made up of often-impenetrable legalese. Until fairly recently, jurors never even received these instructions in writing. Instead, they were somehow expected to hear them in one or two extended sittings: at the beginning of a trial (sometimes) and at the end (always). It was then, supposedly, the jurors' task to remember the contents of these instructions throughout hours or days of deliberations — not to mention applying the instructions to evidence they'd heard without the framework provided by the final set of instructions.

Now, it's more common, though not by any means universal, for the jurors to receive binders at the end of the trial with printouts of the instructions, on the only slightly less unlikely assumption that they will consult the instructions at the right times, concerning the right points, and understand what they read.

Judges and attorneys have typically joined in pretending that the jurors understood the instructions and would apply the law correctly as a result. **One could address how particular jurors or a set of jurors try to deal with a pile of verbiage they can't understand, given the weighty responsibility they've been given.**

More and more jurisdictions are replacing traditional jury instructions with "plain English" jury instructions. The latter may not always be crystal clear, but they increase the chance that a jury will actually follow the applicable legal rules.

Here are a couple of "before" (traditional) and "after" (plain English) jury instructions.

Traditional version: Circumstantial evidence is evidence that, if found to be true, proves a fact from which an inference of the existence of another fact may be drawn. A factual inference is a deduction that may logically and reasonably be drawn from one or more facts established by the evidence.

Plain English version: Some evidence proves a fact directly, such as testimony of a witness who saw a jet plane flying across the sky. Some evidence proves a fact indirectly, such as testimony of a witness who saw only the white trail that jet planes often leave. This indirect evidence is sometimes referred to as "circumstantial evidence." In either instance, the witness's testimony is evidence that a jet plane flew across the sky.

(Source:
http://www.plainlanguage.gov/examples/before_after/jury.cfm)

Traditional Version: *Causation – Strict Products Liability* If you decide that the product was defective or unreasonably dangerous, you must consider whether the product caused or enhanced Plaintiff's injuries. To meet this burden, Plaintiff must only show that the greater likelihood or probability that [sic] the harm complained of was due to the defective nature of the product. Conduct of the Defendant is irrelevant to this inquiry. The only focus is on the product itself. The product must be a legal cause of Plaintiff's injury. If the harm would have occurred anyway, then the Defendant is not liable. It does not matter whether other concurrent causes contributed to Plaintiff's injuries, so long as you find the product contributed to the harmful result in a material or important way. That this contribution was not slight, insignificant or tangential to causing the harm.

Plain English Version: If you find the lawnmower was defective, you must decide whether it caused or worsened Mr. A's injuries. Mr. A must prove that it is more likely than not that the defective nature of the lawnmower, and not something else, caused his injuries. If you find that Mr. A would have been injured even if the lawnmower was not defective, ABC Manufacturing, Inc. is not responsible for Mr. A's injuries.

(Source: http://dritoday.org/post/Plain-English-Jury-Instructions.aspx)

C. Did I Win or Lose?: Verdicts

When there's a jury trial, the jury is sent into deliberations with a verdict form to fill out once it has reached its decision(s). This form can be so simple that only the most hopeless foreperson would get it wrong — or so complicated that the verdict ends up showing a result seriously different from what the jury intended. It depends on how the form is laid out and on how many choices and decisions the jury has to make.

The simplest verdict form, appropriate in some criminal cases, will have space only for two ultimate results: Guilty and Not Guilty. However, many criminal cases involve multiple "counts," accusations of different crimes arising from the alleged facts, and will require a Guilty/Not Guilty finding for each count. If the crime is defined in legalese, this is a chance for confusion to enter in.

A civil case appropriate for jury trial will involve money. The simplest possible verdict in such a case is a finding for the defendant, with no one getting any money (unless that jurisdiction lets the jury decide whether the winner gets court costs reimbursed). Everything else will be more complicated.

Sometimes the jury will be given a series of questions to answer, either instead of or along with the thumbs-up or thumbs-down decision. If there are only specific questions, that's a "special verdict" (as opposed to a "general verdict") form. If a verdict form has both specific questions and an ultimate finding (for example, a finding for the plaintiff plus details that will guide the judge in calculating damages), that's a hybrid verdict, also called a general verdict with interrogatories. Depending on the judge and trial lawyers involved, the jury may get a list of questions separately addressing almost every factual issue involved in deciding who should prevail at trial.

Special verdicts reduce the chance of the jury tossing out the legal rules, to the extent they understand them, and going with their collective gut ("jury nullification," discussed in 19.G.). It'd be much more work, and feel more dishonest, to answer detailed questions in a way that adds up to the result that feels fair to the jury. Some courts have actually held special verdicts unconstitutional in criminal cases, due to the way they constrain jury independence. What may actually happen is the opposite: the jury may intend a different winner and loser than they actually produce, given their incomplete knowledge or complete misunderstanding of either the questions or the questions' legal import. **This could make for compelling frustration on the part of would-be activist jurors, who might then resort to some more extreme way of attempting to see justice done.**

In some situations, special verdicts are mandatory. For example, the federal crime of treason is defined by the U.S. Constitution as requiring "the Testimony of two Witnesses to the same overt Act, or on Confession in open Court." Jury forms for treason therefore require the jury to specify which overt act they've agreed took place, unless the defendant confessed during the trial. Far more common are special verdicts involving facts that determine the appropriate sentence. For example, cases where the prosecution seeks the death penalty, among others, require the weighing of "aggravating" circumstances (those that make either the crime or the criminal seem worse) and "mitigating" circumstances (the opposite), and many states require the jury to list such circumstances. Typical aggravating circumstances include torture, lying in wait, and multiple killings. Typical mitigating circumstances include diminished capacity, childhood abuse, a previously clean record, and remorse.

Another example of a mandatory special verdict: some states require that if the use of a firearm during a crime leads to a more severe sentence, the jury must specifically find that a firearm was so used.

It is possible for the jury, rather than picking a single winner and loser, to split the difference. In a criminal trial with multiple charges, this is easy: find the defendant guilty on some and not others. If there is only one charge, then *if* the jury instructions gave the jury a sufficient hint, the jury may find the defendant guilty of one or more "lesser included offenses." These are crimes for which conviction requires proof of only some of the elements of the crime the prosecution decided to charge. For example, if the jury isn't convinced beyond a reasonable doubt that the fellow who pushed open a door and entered a house intended to steal something, it may find the defendant not guilty of burglary (13.G.) but guilty of criminal trespass (13.M.). Or if the jury considers a killing partly excusable but not legally justified, it may find the defendant not guilty of murder but guilty of manslaughter (13.E.).

"Lesser included offense" isn't the same as "a different version of the situation." Thus, if a defendant was charged with being an accomplice (see 13.Q.) to a shooting, the jury (or the judge in a bench trial) may not find the defendant guilty of planning to beat up the victim. Such a conviction would violate the defendant's due process right (see 34.G.) to fair notice of the charges against them.

In a civil case, a partial victory for the plaintiff could be a victory on one of several claimed torts or contract violations; or it could be an award of less money or other relief than the plaintiff asked for. Occasionally, when the jurors feel that the plaintiff was correct on the law but really should have let the matter go, the damages will be "nominal" — next to nothing — or actually zero.

If the same overall fact pattern is used to charge the defendant with multiple related crimes, and the jury comes up with a verdict of "guilty" on only one, there's potential for an inconsistent verdict. For example, let's say the defendant is charged with cooking meth and possessing meth. The only meth they're charged with possessing is the stuff they cooked. There's no evidence that they got meth from someone or somewhere else. The jury finds them guilty of possessing meth, but not guilty of cooking meth. Huh? . . .

Or in a civil suit alleging negligence, let's say the jury is given a special verdict form to fill out, with a list of questions to answer. The questions include whether the defendant's conduct "proximately caused" the plaintiff's injury. (See 14.G. for what "proximate cause" means.) The jury finds that no, the defendant didn't cause the injury in any way that counts. And yet, in response to a later question, the jury finds the defendant 35% responsible for the plaintiff's damages. What? . . .

English common law required a new trial in a criminal case with inconsistent verdicts. What's developed in the U.S., however, is, well, inconsistency.

The federal courts will uphold a guilty verdict inconsistent with a simultaneously issued not guilty verdict on a different charge. Aside from various "explanations" that don't explain much (e.g., it'd be OK if two different juries reached inconsistent verdicts based on the same evidence, so it's OK if the same jury does it . . . why, exactly?), there's one explanation that does make sense. As discussed in 19.G., juries are allowed to be more lenient than the law appears to require. Where there's an inconsistent verdict, the federal courts assume that the jury meant to give the defendant a break they didn't legally deserve, and that the guilty verdict is the accurate part of the apparent confusion.

The courts of some states, however, will throw out a conviction in at least some instances of inconsistent verdicts. In California, if the "essential elements," the statutory requirements, of two crimes overlap, *and* the defendant is charged with both, *and* the prosecution can't lawfully obtain a conviction for Crime B without proving the elements of Crime A, *and* the jury acquits the defendant of Crime A and convicts them on Crime B, then the conviction won't stand. For example, as discussed in 13.Q., to convict someone of "conspiracy," the prosecution must prove at least one overt act in furtherance of the conspiracy. If the jury convicts the defendant of conspiracy, but acquits them of every crime charged that could serve as an overt act in furtherance of the conspiracy, and the state didn't prove some other overt act, then California would throw out the conspiracy conviction. And the State probably can't retry the defendant because of the rule against "double jeopardy" (see 34.I.), as well as the more general versions of that rule (see Ch. 28 re "res judicata" and "collateral estoppel").

Alaska goes further, pretty much scoffing at the federal courts' assumption that jury inconsistency equals excessive jury leniency. Rather than assume or otherwise try to decide whether the jury is being charitable as opposed to hopelessly confused, Alaska allows for retrial in the case of obviously inconsistent verdicts.

In 2010, the Iowa Supreme Court held that "a jury verdict involving compound inconsistency [multiple inconsistencies] insults the basic due process requirement that guilt must be proved beyond a reasonable doubt." The court also prohibited any retrial on double jeopardy grounds. Whether that'd happen in the other states I've discussed is complicated enough that I'm going to punt and tell you to ask an attorney who practices in that state (or set your tale in Iowa). Similarly, if you want your story set in a state I haven't discussed, you're on your own.

In civil cases, where the rationale of leniency doesn't apply, both state and federal courts are willing to toss out inconsistent verdicts. If the verdicts are genuinely inconsistent and the evidence would support either of the inconsistent approaches, the usual remedy is a new trial.

1. Polling the Jury

A single juror, the foreperson, announces the verdict. But if the losing attorney has the slightest suspicion that any juror still has doubts, or even if that attorney just likes to leave no stone unturned, there's a way to put every juror to the test. And it could make a terrific scene in your story. I'm talking about "polling the jury."

The jury may be polled in a criminal or civil case, upon request of either party or on the judge's own initiative. The judge asks each juror to state aloud, in the courtroom ("in open court"), whether the verdict announced by the foreperson is that juror's verdict. If there is more than one charge (in a criminal case) or cause of action (in a civil case), a sensible judge will do a separate poll for each.

And what if at least one juror breaks ranks and says that no, that verdict isn't their verdict after all? If even one juror does this, the polling must stop. At this point, the judge may either order the jury to go back and de-liberate so more, or else declare a mistrial (9.D.).

There are ways a judge can behave in connection with polling the jury that would be reversible error (32.J.1.), not to mention potentially dra-matic. These could include refusing a request to poll the jury; coercing a juror to adhere to the announced verdict or to disclaim it; or implicitly coercing one or more jurors by polling the jury over and over on the same charge or cause of action.

It would be a particularly good idea for an attorney to have the jury polled if the jurors had previously told the judge they were deadlocked (unable to come to an agreement), and only reached a verdict after being sent back to try again; or if the verdict form shows possibly inconsistent verdicts or other jury confusion.

Here's a tale you could tell. A prejudiced or corrupt judge, financially or emotionally invested in the victory of one party or the defeat of anoth-er, rejoices over the announced verdict, or is improperly responsible for it. When an attorney requests that the jury be polled, the judge bristles and tries to intimidate the attorney into withdrawing the request. Failing at that, the judge orders all spectators to clear the courtroom, thus violating the "open court" aspect of the procedure. When a juror, with trembling knees and voice, reveals that they don't support the verdict, the judge browbeats the juror into stating support for the verdict after all. The court reporter's transcription of these events mysteriously disappears, and the attorney must convince one or more of the jurors to help see justice done....

D. What Jury? Directed Verdict and Judgment Notwithstanding the Verdict

Once the jury acquits someone of criminal charges, that's that. It doesn't matter how poorly the jurors may have understood the law, nor how thoroughly they may have ignored it. But in other situations, the judge is not so helpless.

If, after all the evidence has been presented, the judge decides that reasonable jurors could only make one decision, the trial court may "direct" a verdict for the party the judge believes must win, cutting the case short without the jury ever getting to deliberate. The judge may not, however, direct a verdict for the prosecution in a criminal trial.

A directed verdict demonstrates the judge's belief that the party with the burden of proof — the prosecution in a criminal trial, the plaintiff in a civil trial — hasn't proved what's necessary to prevail. A directed verdict means that (a) the judge believes that no reasonable jurors could bring in a contrary verdict, and (b) the judge doesn't feel like waiting to see whether the jury agrees. Many judges in this position prefer to give the jury the chance to make the right decision, and will rarely or never enter a directed verdict.

If the judge lets the case go to the jury, and the jury's verdict is one that (in the judge's view) no reasonable jury could have reached, the judge may issue a "judgment notwithstanding the verdict." The abbreviation for a judgment notwithstanding the verdict is JNOV, not JNTV, because it's based on a Latin phrase no one uses any more. Again, as stated already, a JNOV may not be used to set aside the acquittal of a criminal defendant.

A directed verdict or JNOV is just as binding as the jury's verdict would have been, with one big exception: while the prosecution may not appeal a jury's acquittal of a criminal defendant (see 32.A.), the prosecution may usually appeal a directed verdict or JNOV acquitting a criminal defendant.

Courts generally take the role of the jury very seriously, and as a result are quite reluctant to grant either of these motions.

Many jurisdictions, including the federal courts, require the party seeking a JNOV to file a motion asking for it, and won't allow the court to issue a JNOV sua sponte (on its own initiative). Some jurisdictions (not including the federal courts) require a motion before the judge may issue a directed verdict. Some (including the federal courts) also require a motion for a directed verdict as a prerequisite for filing a motion for JNOV after the verdict comes in. A motion for either a directed verdict or a JNOV may have to, and in any case had better, be quite specific about why the judge should grant it.

In federal court, even though (as just mentioned) the two types of motions are treated differently, they no longer have different names: both are now called "motions for judgment as a matter of law." Some states may have their own labels or abbreviations.

It's likely that state court rules will require a trial judge who enters a directed verdict or a JNOV to include specific factual findings about what was wrong with the jury's verdict. That way, the appellate court can decide if there was a good enough reason to preempt or override the jury's decision.

Some states allow a party to make two alternative motions at the same time, a motion for directed verdict/JNOV and a motion for a new trial. If either is granted, the other is deemed denied. The exception: the trial court may explicitly grant both, in a conditional sort of way. The idea is that if the appellate court overturns the directed verdict or JNOV, the grant of a new trial would still stand.

E. What Jury, Part Two: Remittitur and Additur

Many people have heard about the woman who won a jury verdict of almost three million dollars from a fast food chain in a lawsuit about scalding hot coffee. Not so many people know that the judge drastically reduced that award. The judge did so in response to a motion for remittitur.

Remittitur is the trial court's reduction of the amount of damages a jury has just awarded in a civil case. Remittitur may, as in the hot coffee case, follow a motion by the defendant, or the court may issue the order sua sponte (on its own motion). The usual grounds for remittitur, which could overlap, are:

- The jury has awarded substantially more than the plaintiff asked for, and/or substantially more than any of the plaintiff's evidence would support.
- The award, in the court's view, is unconscionably (shockingly) high.

The disappointed plaintiff has the choice of accepting the lowered verdict or starting over with a new trial. It may, however, be possible for the plaintiff to settle the case for something more than the revised verdict, given that the defendant would otherwise face the expense and trauma of another trial. In fact, the hot coffee case was settled in just this way.

Remittitur is not without its critics. At least one commentator has argued that as practiced in the federal courts, remittitur is an unconstitutional denial of the right to trial by jury because the "new trial" option is more illusory than real: the same judge would generally preside over any second trial and would impose the same limit on damages. In 1998, the New Mexico Supreme Court held that remittitur as it had been practiced in that state violated the state constitutional right to trial by jury because New Mexico procedure seriously limited the plaintiff's ability to appeal the alteration of the jury's verdict.

Appellate courts may also reduce damage awards, though the term "remittitur" is less likely to be used in that context. Since there is no right to jury involvement in an appeal, the same constitutional concerns do not apply.

What if the plaintiff or the court thinks the jury verdict was unreasonably small? May the court, per a plaintiff's motion or sua sponte, increase the amount of the verdict?

Such an increase is called additur; and it's a good deal less likely to be available.

In 1935, the U.S. Supreme Court decreed that the use of additur in federal courts violated the defendant's Seventh Amendment right to trial by jury. Its rationale: the Seventh Amendment, ratified in 1791, refers specifically to the common law, and therefore protects the right to trial by jury as the common law defined that right at that time. In 1791, judges were generally authorized to grant remittitur, because the remaining portion of the award was still an award the jury had granted; but additur created a portion of the award with no jury origin, and therefore violated the defendant's rights.

This ruling did not affect state courts: as already discussed, the U.S. Constitution doesn't require the states to provide trial by jury in civil, as opposed to criminal, cases. (See 19.B., as well as Ch. 34's discussion of the Fourteenth Amendment's partial "incorporation" of the Bill of Rights.) But many or most states have limited the situations in which additur is permitted. Some allow it only for punitive damages (see 30.B.3.). As with remittitur, the party affected, in this case the defendant, has the choice of accepting the altered judgment or choosing a new trial.

It is not entirely clear whether the federal ban on additur applies in a federal diversity case (see 6.A.1.), as opposed to a federal case involving federal law. Of those few federal appellate opinions that have dealt with the question, most either state or assume that additur is unavailable in such cases. A recent Tenth Circuit opinion, however, suggests that since the outcome of a diversity case will usually depend on the law of one of the states from which the parties come, additur might be permitted if that state permits it.

F. Judgments in Bench Trials

A verdict answers questions posed by the judge to the jury. In a bench trial, where the judge is the trier of fact, there's no need for such a format. Instead, the judge writes up a more or less detailed account of the case and its result.

In federal bench trials, the trial court must "find the facts specially and state its conclusions of law separately." It may recite or read these findings and conclusions on the record at the end of the trial or write them up separately. State rules will vary: for example, in Indiana, specific findings and conclusions are only required in bench trials if a statute so indicates or a party makes a written request for them, but judges are free to throw them in even if not requested. (See also 32.J. re how reviewing courts may treat required and optional findings and conclusions differently.)

G. Conditional Judgments

There are some situations in which a judge may enter a conditional judgment, a judgment that will only take effect if specified conditions occur. I gave one example in the discussion of directed verdicts and JNOV's (27.D.). Here are two more fairly common examples.

Vocabulary note: I use "order" rather than "judgment" in some of the following because that's how these judgments are most often described. In many cases, including these, "final order" and "judgment" are synonymous.

One sometimes sees conditional judgments when money from a third party, such as an employer, is being garnished (see Ch. 33) to pay a past-due or ongoing debt. If the garnishee (the employer, or whoever else is supposed to pay a portion of some cash flow to the creditor) ignores the garnishment order, a judge may issue an order that if the garnishee doesn't shape up within some set period of time, the garnishee becomes directly responsible for the debt.

Second: some custody awards come with conditions. If there's an issue of whether a parent is planning to move away from the region where the other parent lives, the trial court may issue a custody order with the condition that if such a move takes place, the court will consider modifying custody in favor of the parent staying put. However, if the order says that the move will *automatically* result in a change of custody, that's likely to be reversed if the relocating parent appeals, since possible custody modifications are supposed to be weighed in light of current circumstances.

CHAPTER 28

You Had Your Chance!:
Res Judicata and Collateral Estoppel

One of the principles underlying our judicial system is that (in a commonly used phrase) one doesn't get very many "bites of the apple." Among the applications of that principle: if a party files a lawsuit and could have raised some issue in that litigation, the party probably can't come back years later and drag the other party into court again over the omitted issue. If a party actually did raise the issue and lost, then that party is really out of luck. The first of those related doctrines is called "res judicata"; the second, "collateral estoppel."

Let's say someone did a lousy job repairing a roof, and the roof ended up leaking. The homeowner sues and seeks damages for the furniture that got ruined. But the carpet was ruined, too, and the plaintiff didn't mention it.

The plaintiff gets a judgment against the defendant, and the case is over. Then, six months later, the plaintiff files suit for the damage to the carpet. Does the defendant have to put their life on hold, pony up for more legal fees, and head back to court? No, because the plaintiff could have raised the issue of the carpet the first time around and didn't. The carpet damage is "res judicata." That's Latin, or something close to Latin, for "the thing adjudged" — but as you can see, it includes "the thing that would have been adjudged if you'd been thorough the first time around."

Res judicata, in this context, may also be called "claim preclusion," because it precludes (prevents) making the previously omitted claim.

For claim preclusion to operate, any second lawsuit has to involve the same parties as the first, or at least a party who's "in privity" with one of the original parties. Examples of being in privity include a successor corporation to the corporation initially involved, or the purchaser of one original party's claim against the other (see "choses in action" in 14.N.).

"Res judicata" is a broad term. "Collateral estoppel," a narrower one, falls under the "res judicata" umbrella, but it's helpful to use the more precise term when it's appropriate. Collateral estoppel, or "issue preclusion," prevents the parties to the earlier lawsuit from re-arguing the same issue in a second suit. If our homeowner had lost the first suit because the trier of fact decided the leak wasn't the roofer's fault, the homeowner can't go back to court with any theory that depends on the roofer's negligence and try again, because it's already been determined that the roofer wasn't at fault.

What happens when the subsequent lawsuit involves somebody new? To return to our leaky-roof example (the version where the homeowner wins something the first time around): let's say the plaintiff claimed that one of the ruined pieces of furniture was a valuable antique. The defendant successfully argued that no, it was a contemporary reproduction, and any damages should be far less than the plaintiff was claiming. Now the homeowner makes a claim on their homeowner's insurance, asserting (once again) that the piece is an antique. The insurance company balks at paying that much, and the matter ends up in court. Is the homeowner "estopped" from claiming the greater value, even though the insurance company wasn't part of the earlier litigation?

The answer used to be: no, the insurance company in this example wouldn't be able to use collateral estoppel as a defense, because it wasn't a party to the first lawsuit. These days, at least in many jurisdictions, the answer is yes. (If your setting is not contemporary, you'll need to find out when the rule changed, if it did change, in that particular jurisdiction.) The new party (the insurance company in our example) is asserting the previous ruling defensively, as a metaphorical "shield," against someone who *was* a party to that previous lawsuit, someone who had a full and fair opportunity to fight about that issue in court. Therefore, in many states, the newcomer may invoke "non-mutual defensive collateral estoppel" (phew!), and keep the homeowner from getting the proverbial second bite of the proof-of-value apple.

What if the original ruling went the other way, and the judge in the first case found that the armoire really did come from some 17th century Continental palace? May the homeowner use that prior ruling against the insurance company? No, because the insurance company never had the chance to put on its own proof to the contrary.

What if the roofer was found to be negligent, and a different tenant (under the same roof) wants to bring a new lawsuit? May that other party use the factual findings made in the first lawsuit? That's called non-mutual "offensive" (as opposed to defensive) collateral estoppel, or more colorfully, using collateral estoppel as a "sword" rather than a "shield." Like the non-mutual defensive version, it didn't used to be allowed. Now, in some states and some circumstances, it is. Relevant factors include:

- Whether the party who would end up on the losing end in the new suit had a "full and fair" opportunity to battle it out in the former suit.
- Whether the amount at stake the first time around was worth fighting over. If the former lawsuit involved a relatively small claim, such that a reasonable litigant might decide to limit the resources spent in court, it's less likely the unfavorable finding may be used offensively in later litigation.

So if a second tenant brings a new action against the roofer, saying the issue of the roofer's shoddy workmanship has been settled by the first lawsuit, the result will depend on where the lawsuit is happening and on factual details. The roofer may not have fought that hard in the first lawsuit because there was only one plaintiff, and that plaintiff wasn't claiming a huge amount in damages. If the first tenant had been claiming destruction of a world-famous art collection, the roofer might have hired a top-notch lawyer, even if it meant mortgaging the home office. . . . It wouldn't be fair, the reasoning goes, to expand the consequences of that first lawsuit beyond what the original defendant would reasonably have expected. Some courts would also view such a result as unfair because if the contractor had won the first lawsuit against the first tenant, that wouldn't do the contractor any good against a brand new plaintiff.

CHAPTER 29

Criminal Penalties

N otwithstanding the "jeopardy of life or limb" language in the Fifth Amendment, we don't punish people in this country by chopping off hands. Acknowledged physical punishments — as opposed to sending people to prisons where various forms of physical abuse are tacitly expected — have gone out of fashion. In historical fiction, however, you can revisit our more openly bloodthirsty past.

It's beyond the scope of this book to investigate exactly which physical punishments were available at what stages of our national history; but our Founders were not necessarily opposed to all forms of corporal chastisement. Thomas Jefferson, in 1778, drafted "A Bill for Proportioning Crimes and Punishments" including the following penalties for rape, polygamy, or "sodomy with man or woman" (which probably included homosexual acts as well as various heterosexual activities): "if a man, by castration, if a woman, by cutting thro' the cartilage of her nose a hole of one half inch diameter at the least." Deliberate disfigurement of a victim was to be punished by infliction of that same disfigurement, along with forfeiture of half the criminal's lands and goods to the victim. Mr. Jefferson also makes a canny argument against (from his perspective) overly severe penalties: that prosecutors may be reluctant to prosecute, and juries reluctant to convict, where the penalty is disproportionate. (See jury nullification, discussed in 19.G.)

The Eighth Amendment to the U.S. Constitution, which at least on this point restricts the states via the Fourteenth Amendment (see the introduction to Ch. 34), prohibits the infliction of "cruel and unusual punishment." Whether a punishment violates the Eighth Amendment is determined according to a somewhat fuzzy standard: does the punishment violate "evolving standards of decency"? That, in turn, is supposed to be based on particular facts showing that community standards have changed.

So what punishments does our legal system currently have at its disposal?

A. Categories of Offenses and their Penalties

Let's start with a few categories of offenses, since the category often determines the range of penalties that may be imposed.

1. Infractions

Violation of local ordinances are called "infractions." The typical penalty is a fine, probably no more than one or two hundred dollars. In places where the cost of everything else is high, the fines for infractions might be also.

2. Misdemeanors

Next up the ladder is the "misdemeanor," a crime defined by its penalty. A crime is a misdemeanor if it is punished by no more than a year in a county jail, or no more than some set amount in fines. That amount is likely to be a good deal higher, possibly as much as ten or more times higher, than the maximum fine for an infraction.

Typical misdemeanors include vandalism, prostitution, disorderly conduct, public intoxication, and the lesser versions of theft ("petty theft" as opposed to "grand theft") and assault ("simple" as opposed to "aggravated").

The lightest consequence that can come from a misdemeanor charge, assuming it isn't dismissed as unfounded, is a process called either deferred adjudication or pretrial diversion. The difference between the two is likely to be that deferred adjudication happens after a guilty or no contest plea (9.A.1.), while pretrial diversion kicks in earlier. Such programs may also be called deferred prosecution, pretrial intervention, or other names. Most states have some version.

The essence of these programs is that if the defendant satisfies certain conditions, they won't end up with a criminal record for that offense. These programs are most likely to be available to first offenders, and/or for drug-related crimes or (perhaps less defensibly) domestic assaults. A state statute may say who's eligible, but the prosecutor usually has substantial discretion as to who gets this relatively favorable treatment. Either the prosecutor or the judge will have the final say. In some states, the alleged victim has a veto. If the defendant has been in pretrial diversion before, they probably won't get that chance again.

Conditions may include some period of probation (see 29.F.), counseling, and/or community service. The defendant will probably also have to give up (waive) some procedural rights, such as the right to a speedy trial (8.B.) or the protection of the applicable statute of limitations (Ch. 11).

The most serious consequence of certain misdemeanor convictions may be the loss of the right to possess or own a firearm. State law may impose this consequence, but that hardly matters when the federal government has stepped in. The federal statute discussed in 29.A.3., below, disarms anyone convicted of a domestic violence misdemeanor. This prohibition continues unless and until the state restores the convicted individual's civil rights (see 32.G.). **If both the parties to a dysfunctional intimate relationship accuse the other of domestic violence, and the more manipulative and persuasive of the two prevails to the extent of obtaining the other's misdemeanor conviction, the actual victim could be deprived of any effective defense against future attacks from their former partner.**

A federal misdemeanor conviction for any crime under the "alcohol, tobacco, firearms and explosives" umbrella also triggers this federal prohibition. One may apply to the U.S. Attorney General's office or to the Bureau of Alcohol, Tobacco and Firearms (BATF) to have one's right to bear arms restored, but the BATF in particular is widely believed to ignore these applications. One could also seek federal executive clemency (see 32.G.).

3. Felonies

Then we get to felonies, for which someone can be locked up in state prison for anywhere from just over a year to the rest of their life. (As for the more extreme possibility, the death penalty, see 29.J.)

There was a time when it was common for crimes to have indeterminate sentences, e.g., "from 10 to 30 years," or "from 20 years to life." This alternative, one facet (along with the idea of parole or conditional release, discussed below) of an overall shift toward rehabilitation as the goal of imprisonment, arose in the latter part of the 19th Century. (For more details, see 29.B.)

One common element of punishment for felonies is deprivation of the right to vote and/or hold office. In most states, these rights are restored once the felon leaves prison, and in a couple (Vermont and Maine, as of this writing), felons may vote from prison by absentee ballot. In a few states, however (currently including Florida, Kentucky, and Iowa), these rights are lost for life, or unless and until the governor and/or a clemency board decides to restore them. Some states (e.g. Florida) have actually gotten tougher in this respect in recent years or decades.

You could have someone running for elective office in a state where voting and office-holding rights aren't automatically restored, and an opponent's research team finding out about a long-ago felony conviction. You could then have the former felon file a belated petition for restoration of their rights, or challenge the restriction on some constitutional grounds (e.g. substantive due process, discussed in 34.G.).

Another consequence of a felony conviction is losing one's right to possess a firearm. Every state has such a rule; and the federal government has gotten into the act as well, based on yet another expansive interpretation of the Commerce Clause (see 34.L.). The federal prohibition applies to state as well as federal felony convictions, though the federal statute does not actually include the term "felon" or "felony," referring instead to crimes punishable by imprisonment for more than one year. There's a fairly broad exception that could be called the "white collar crime" exception, covering "antitrust violations, unfair trade practices, restraints of trade, or other similar offenses relating to the regulation of business practices." There is also an exception to the one-year rule for state misdemeanor convictions in states where a misdemeanor may be punished by imprisonment of two years or less. In those states, a sentence exceeding two years becomes the threshold.

Even where a particular state doesn't consider someone a felon for purposes of its own firearms prohibition, the federal government may.

The federal statute prohibits the convicted felon from owning or possessing a firearm unless and until the state restores that felon's civil rights through its own procedures. (While the term "civil rights" often refers to discrimination,in this context it means what are often called "civil liberties,", e.g. the right to vote, to serve on a jury, and to hold political office.) State laws on which felons' civil rights may be restored vary a good deal, with the nature of the crime often a key factor. In addition to the predictable concern for arming those convicted of violent crimes, some states are particularly wary of restoring firearm access to those convicted of drug offenses or crimes of dishonesty. If the restoration of rights expressly excludes the ownership or handling of firearms, the federal prohibition will remain. A pardon (see 32.G.) may or may not restore the felon's firearm ownership rights, depending on its details.

For federal felony convictions, absent a pardon or some more specifically applicable order, the prohibition is permanent.

Since the U.S. Supreme Court's recent acknowledgment of individuals' Second Amendment right to keep and bear arms, some lower courts are considering whether it violates that right to forbid firearm ownership by those convicted of nonviolent felonies. The U.S. Court of Appeals for the Third Circuit has discussed the sort of showing that might lead to such a ruling, and at least one federal trial court in the Third Circuit has followed its suggestion. In September 2014, the U.S. District Court for the Eastern District of Pennsylvania found the federal prohibition unconstitutional as applied to a man convicted almost 17 years earlier for a consensual, though illegal, sexual relationship with a 17-year-old boy. (The felony in question was "corruption of a minor," not statutory rape.)

As noted above, a few misdemeanor convictions also come with this consequence, as do some court orders outside the realm of criminal law. See 34.A.2.

B. Sentencing - Who Decides and How

There are two quite different possible approaches to criminal sentencing, particularly for felonies; and the American justice system has to some extent swung back and forth between them, with the current status quo somewhere in the middle.

"Determinate" sentencing is conceptually quite simple: for each specific crime, one specific sentence. Armed robbery: x years. Kidnapping: y years. First degree murder: z years, or death, or life in prison. With the more extreme sort of determinate sentencing, the trial court has little in the way of discretion: unless it throws out the jury's verdict on a particular charge (see 27.D.), the court will have to impose a mandatory sentence required by statute. In other forms, the judge may sentence the offender to some alternative other than prison (e.g. home detention or community service), but has no discretion to impose a shorter prison term.

An alternative approach, "indeterminate" sentencing, arose in the 19th century as a reform, intended to allow for recognition of a prisoner's rehabilitation. An indeterminate sentencing might be "10 to 30 years," or "20 years to life."

It was not intended to be a form of cruel and unusual punishment.

**But take a man with a daughter two years old, lock him away, and leave him to wonder: will he, might he, get out in time to attend her confirmation or bat mitzvah? Will he, might he, be there to see her awkwardly introduce her date for the prom? And might he, could he, be out before her wedding, and walk her down the aisle?

Then let him watch one milestone, and then the next, pass beyond recall.**

We might call this cruel indeed; and call it, also, yet another example of the Law of Unintended Consequences.

Indeterminate sentencing gives great power to parole boards, who decide when a prisoner was sufficiently reformed to be released. Such power might be applied capriciously, or in accordance with the biases and prejudices of the board's members. The actual sentences served by two prisoners convicted of the same kind might end up drastically different.

There are, however, some potential benefits to indeterminate sentencing. The trial court, if allowed to fine-tune the range, has more discretion to fit the sentence to the perceived character of the defendant. The prisoner has incentives to follow prison rules and avail themselves of any job-training and educational opportunities available.

State and federal governments began moving back toward determinate sentences around the 1970s. A common compromise these days is a nominally fixed sentence that may in fact be reduced. For example, in some states, any prisoner who avoids violations of prison rules will end up serving only half, or three-quarters, or eighty or eighty-five percent, of the imposed sentence. This reduction is commonly called "good behavior" or "good time" credit, or a reduction or time off for good behavior.

But mandatory minimum sentences, either for particular offenses or for a series of offenses, still remain. One variety that can lead to appalling injustice: "three strikes, you're out." Such laws require a very long sentence, possibly life in prison, upon conviction of a third serious or violent offense, or sometimes a third felony. In the latter case, a third conviction for nonviolent theft or drug possession might send the offender to prison for longer than a single conviction for premeditated murder.

In some jurisdictions, prosecutors may be able to ask for a waiver of a determinate or mandatory sentence where the offender cooperates with police and/or testifies against other defendants.

In 1984, Congress passed a Sentencing Reform Act meant to reduce the wide disparities in federal sentencing. A federal sentencing commission came up with federal sentencing guidelines. Not simply spelling out sentences for different crimes, the guidelines required judges to make findings concerning various factors that weighed toward a longer or shorter sentence, such as prior criminal history or the defendant's role in the crime. This meant that even in cases tried to a jury, the trial judge was required to make crucial findings of fact that directly affected the criminal's punishment.

In a series of cases between 2000 and 2005, culminating in *U.S. v. Booker*, the U.S. Supreme Court held that sentences could only be based on facts either admitted by the defendant or proved beyond a reasonable doubt (with the exception of prior convictions, whose existence is pretty much irrefutable) — and that if the defendant had exercised the right to trial by jury, those facts (again, unless admitted by the defendant) must be found by the jury, not the judge. In *Booker,* the Court also held that federal sentencing guidelines could not be binding requirements and must be advisory only. In practice, many federal judges still follow them closely. There have, however, been claims that since *Booker,* there is once again a higher correlation between the defendant's race and the length of the sentence.

One key decision to be made, in any criminal case where the defendant is convicted of more than one crime, is whether the sentences for the separate crimes will be served concurrently (at the same time) or consecutively (one after another). This is also an issue where a defendant already serving prison time is convicted of a new offense. The choice of concurrent or consecutive sentencing can have a major impact on when, or even whether, the offender will be released.

The federal sentencing guidelines have special provisions dealing with concurrent versus consecutive sentencing, and I'm not going to attempt to summarize them. In general, however, the default is concurrent sentencing, with consecutive sentences needing some kind of explanation (based on particular factors or an applicable statute specifying consecutive sentencing).

Whenever the court has some discretion as to what sentence to impose, there is usually a pause of several weeks between conviction and sentencing. During that time, probation officers prepare what's called a presentencing report for the judge's use.

The probation officer, and/or some social worker or psychologist who works for that office, will interview the defendant; check the defendant's criminal record; and talk to the victim(s). A competent defense lawyer will feed information to whoever's preparing the report about any mitigating factors in the defendant's past, and about anything the defendant is currently doing, such as addiction treatment, that puts the defendant in a better light. Some defense attorneys will go so far as to have a private presentencing report prepared, so the judge will have more than the official version to consult. These are usually written by folks who used to be probation officers, so they know the drill. But they aren't cheap.

In a small county, and/or a locale where the defendant is very well known to the judge, the judge may not bother with a pre-sentence report.

C. House Arrest

Probation or parole may include "house arrest," namely the requirement that the offender stay within the confines of their home (including the immediately surrounding private property) either full time or outside of work hours. Those on house arrest typically must wear some electronic gadget that alerts the authorities if they leave wherever they're supposed to be. That's especially likely if they're allowed to leave their homes to go to work. The device should be programmed to account for the offender's usual route to and from work. **Road work forcing an unexpected detour could lead to serious complications.**

The offender may well have to pay a fee to cover the costs of the electronic monitoring. However, if the offender has been found to be indigent (see 3.E.), that fee should be waived.

D. Fines

Fines, as a criminal penalty, may be imposed by themselves or in conjunction with probation, jail time, or time in prison. Fines are paid to the government, not the victim(s).

Fines are subject to constitutional limits, specifically the Eighth Amendment's prohibition on imposing "excessive" fines. A fine could be deemed excessive if it's seriously out of step with the fine other states impose for the same offense; if the process by which it was imposed was "arbitrary and capricious," and/or lacking in procedural due process (34.G.); or if it strikes the appellate court as outrageously high.

Theoretically, per a 1983 U.S. Supreme Court decision, a criminal sentenced to pay a fine can't be jailed for inability to pay that fine. But if the convict could pay the fine and doesn't, or if they don't try hard enough to earn or borrow the money to pay it, then into the lockup they could go. Such imprisonment would be a form of civil contempt (30.D.), meant to coerce the convict into paying, though practically speaking, imprisonment would probably make such payment more difficult. Some states add the cost of jail room and board to the amount of the fine itself.

E. Restitution

Restitution is much like a fine, but is paid to the victim rather than to the state, and is meant to make the victim whole, as much as possible, for the harm the crime caused. It's similar to the restitution that may be ordered in delinquency proceedings (13.W.) or as part of some civil damages (see 30.B.1.). It has evolved from a requirement that a thief disgorge illegal gains to something potentially much broader in scope, sometimes mirroring civil awards for economic or emotional injury.

Restitution is usually ordered along with some other sentence, like probation or imprisonment.

Even though the impact of restitution on the defendant may be identical to that of a fine (29.D.), many courts have refused to treat restitution as subject to the Eighth Amendment's "excessive fines" clause. However, a 2014 U.S. Supreme Court decision suggested that the Eighth Amendment does limit restitution orders, although the decision did not rest entirely on that holding.

F. Probation and Parole

It's common for someone convicted of a misdemeanor to be put on "probation" — a period of supervision, with rules to be followed based on the particular offense — rather than sent to jail.

Probation is more likely to be an option for first-time offenders, and for crimes against property rather than crimes involving physical violence or the threat of same. Caution: if you're writing historical fiction and plan to include probation, make sure it was already a sentencing option.

While on probation, the probationer must fulfill various conditions, which are likely to include remaining (or attempting to become) employed; maintaining a particular residence and/or notifying authorities of any change in residence; consenting in advance to searches of oneself and one's residence; taking regular drug tests; checking in regularly with a probation officer; avoiding possession of firearms; and/or following a curfew. Abstention from alcohol may also be included.

Those convicted of felonies may also be lucky enough to get probation instead of prison time. As to felons, probation is generally reserved for first-time offenders or those who, for whatever reason, the court (maybe a judge who's known the offender all their life) considers unlikely to re-offend.

Parole (sometimes, especially in older sources, called conditional release) is a lot like probation, except that it follows a jail or prison sentence. Someone convicted of a felony is more likely to end up on parole, after some time served, than on probation.

In addition to the state's or county's standard conditions applicable to everyone on probation or parole, particular convictions may give rise to other, more tailored conditions. If the offender violates any of these conditions, they can be sent to jail (or prison) for whatever sentence or portion of a sentence was hanging over them. (See below for the procedures used in that situation.)

A probationer or parolee will probably be deemed to have consented to a search of their dwelling by authorities checking on their compliance with the conditions imposed.

The term for either probation or parole is most often between one and three years, but can be longer. Where sex offenses are involved, it can be a lot longer, due to the doubt many judges have about whether sex offenders can be rehabilitated.

As already mentioned, the offender must come to the probation or parole officer's office at regular intervals and check in. If that doesn't happen, or if there's some other reason to think the offender has violated a condition of probation or parole, there'll be a court hearing. There are fewer procedural safeguards in such hearings than in the original trial. There's no right to a jury. The state doesn't have to prove beyond a reasonable doubt that the offender violated the terms of their probation or parole: the standard is the much less rigorous "preponderance of the evidence" (more likely than not). The offender has the right to a neutral trier of fact; this person may be a parole or probation officer, but not the one who initiated the proceeding. The offender has the right to written notice of the claimed violation, along with the right to be heard and otherwise to present evidence; but the tribunal may admit evidence like hearsay (22.K.) that would normally be excluded. (Caveat: at least in some states, hearsay alone isn't enough to sustain revocation.) The offender also must receive a decision in writing setting forth the facts on which the decision is based.

There's still some inconsistency out there about whether the offender is entitled to a court-ordered, county-paid lawyer in a probation or parole revocation hearing.

Where a felony involves child abuse of any kind, the offender may be prohibited by parole conditions from being within some specified distance of children and/or any location where children congregate. **But what if the offender is a parent?** Different courts or other relevant officials may respond differently to this situation, depending on local policies, the crime in question, the offender's prior record, or their own predilections.

Similarly, **a sex offender may be relying on their religious faith to help them reform, with the help of the pastor of a particular church. But what if the church is located near a school? Even though there are no students at the school on Sundays, their parole conditions might conflict with their church attendance. If the state has some statute similar to the federal Religious Freedom Restoration Act (see 34.A.1.), the parolee could assert that the parole condition violated their rights under that statute.**

Sex offenders, especially those whose offenses involved the use of computers or the Internet, may find themselves with probation or parole conditions that bar them from using these modern essentials, or even from living or working in places that contain them. Such a condition will greatly increase the offender's already considerable difficulties in finding employment. If the offender is a teenager who slept with a younger teenager and was convicted of child molesting (see 13.F.2.), a prohibition against using the Internet would be socially as well as academically and professionally devastating.

1. Parole Hearings

There will usually be a hearing when a prisoner becomes eligible for parole. Some jurisdictions automatically notify victims ahead of time; others do so only if the victim has requested notification. (There may be some states that don't have any notification setup, but I'm not aware of them.)

Concerned individuals may testify at parole hearings. It's fairly common for victims or their families to testify against releasing the prisoner on parole. It's a good deal less common for a victim to testify in *favor* of the prisoner's release — but it does happen.

A recent study suggests that in many states, parole boards routinely fail to release prisoners whose original sentences were imposed on the assumption that they would in fact be paroled. There may be few if any restrictions on what sort of input or factors the parole board may consider. There may be equally few requirements for becoming a member of the state's parole board. In most states, the governor appoints these board members; and while the job might not sound like an appealing prize, the salaries can make it so, with the result that political cronies can end up deciding the fates of countless state prisoners.

Does a prisoner have any constitutional rights in connection with the grant or denial of parole? Not many. The theoretical possibility of parole does not create a constitutional "liberty" interest (see 34.G.) in that possibility, unless the statute's language restricts the board's authority enough that a prisoner could develop realistic expectations of release based on meeting prescribed requirements. The precedents are murky as to what, if any, degree of procedural due process (again, see 34.G.) may be required in parole hearings; but clearly it is far less than most judicial or administrative hearings must satisfy. At most, a parole board may be required to give the inmate an opportunity to be heard, and to provide some explanation if parole is denied.

G. Solitary Confinement

In a June 2015 concurring opinion, Justice Kennedy of the U.S. Supreme Court painted the following vivid picture of the psychological damage done by solitary confinement:

> The human toll wrought by extended terms of isolation long has been understood, and questioned, by writers and commentators.

Eighteenth-century British prison reformer John Howard wrote "that criminals who had affected an air of boldness during their trial, and appeared quite unconcerned at the pronouncing sentence upon them, were struck with horror, and shed tears when brought to these darksome solitary abodes." The State of the Prisons in England and Wales 152 (1777). In literature, Charles Dickens recounted the toil of Dr. Manette, whose 18 years of isolation in One Hundred and Five, North Tower, caused him, even years after his release, to lapse in and out of a mindless state with almost no awareness or appreciation for time or his surroundings. *A Tale of Two Cities* (1859). And even Manette, while imprisoned, had a work bench and tools to make shoes, a type of diversion no doubt denied many of today's inmates. One hundred and twenty-five years ago, this Court recognized that, even for prisoners sentenced to death, solitary confinement bears "a further terror and peculiar mark of infamy." . . . [R]esearch still confirms what this Court suggested over a century ago: Years on end of near-total isolation exacts [sic] a terrible price.

Justice Kennedy estimated that 25,000 prisoners in the United States are serving all or a substantial part of their prison sentences in solitary confinement.

Despite all this scholarly consensus as to the effects of solitary confinement, the punishment in itself is not treated as "cruel and unusual" punishment for Eighth Amendment purposes. **However, it may violate the Eighth Amendment to put a prisoner in solitary whose pre-existing mental condition makes them particularly vulnerable to mental illness.**

H. Pregnancy in Prison

If you want a gut-wrenching collision between the sympathetic and the grim, try a woman in prison, pregnant and about to give birth. Among the many constitutional rights that prisoners lose is the right to raise their children, at least while they're incarcerated.

By some estimates, around four percent of female inmates are pregnant when they enter state prisons. The estimate is slightly lower for federal prisons. Of those in state prison, more than half may, if the authorities so choose, end up giving birth in shackles. (They could be cuffed by the wrist or by the ankle.)

Federal regs establish some medical prenatal services (screening, nutritional help, counseling), but the actual care pregnant inmates receive varies greatly. States also differ as to whether a prisoner gets access to abortion services or counseling.

Unlike the usual practice in some other countries (e.g. the UK), it's a very rare female inmate who gets to keep her newborn baby with her. If no relative steps forward (and is deemed an acceptable guardian), the infant will go straight into foster care.

I. Life in Prison

"Life in prison" can be a very different sentence depending on the qualifier, "with" or "without possibility of parole." It's the difference between "you might spend the rest of your life in prison, or you might get out" and "You're going to die behind bars." In some jurisdictions (Indiana, for example), appeals where the prisoner has been sentenced either to death or to life in prison without possibility of parole go directly to the state supreme court, bypassing the intermediate appellate court.

Which brings us to the "ultimate" penalty: death, aka "capital punishment."

J. Death

(By the way, this section only briefly addresses the death penalty available in military courts-martial. For more on that subject, see 31.D.)

As the wording of the Fifth Amendment suggests, the death penalty is part of our American tradition. All the pre-Revolution colonies provided for it. With the exception of four years in the 1970s, it has remained available, though in a decreasing number of states, ever since.

What happened during those four years? Well, in 1972, the U.S. Supreme Court ruled that the death penalty was being imposed in a manner that violated the Eighth Amendment. That decision, *Furman v. Georgia*, did not make the grounds for this ruling entirely clear, as the various Justices in the majority did not agree on much of anything except the result. Factors in one or more of the opinions included racial discrimination in the penalty's application; inconsistent application of the penalty; and the prejudicial effects of having the same jury determine guilt and penalty.

Justices Thurgood Marshall and William J. Brennan, Jr. considered the death penalty unconstitutional under any circumstances.

Thirty-seven states responded by tweaking their statutes in an attempt to get over the various hurdles mentioned in one of the *Furman* opinions. Some of them attempted to eliminate arbitrary or inconsistent application of the death penalty by going to the other extreme, making death the only available sentence for certain crimes. Sound a buzzer here: no, the Court stated in 1976 and 1977, that wasn't the solution. However, also in 1976, the Court did approve a procedure bifurcating (dividing in two) the guilt and sentencing phase of trials where the death penalty was a possible sentence, with the jury in the second phase considering various "aggravating" and "mitigating" factors: that is, facts making the crime appear more or less heinous, or the criminal appear either less culpable or beyond redemption (see 27.C.). I say more on this procedure a little later on.

As of this writing, neither the mentally retarded nor those who were under 18 years of age at the time of the crime may be executed.

"A life for a life" is the current general rule: since 1977, when the U.S. Supreme Court prohibited using the death penalty for rape, that penalty is usually reserved for murder. Before that time, various states at various times had the death penalty for, among other things, rape, train robbing, sodomy, wrecking a train, stealing a horse, arson, armed robbery, slave revolt, counterfeiting, forcing a woman to marry, or desecrating a grave. **If one of these suggests a story idea, check for the details.**

There are exceptions to this rule. The federal government authorizes the death penalty for treason (one of three federal crimes explicitly provided for in the U.S. Constitution), espionage, and certain crimes under military jurisdiction (see 31.D.), as well as for kidnapping if the victim dies in the kidnapper's custody. The latter is a form of felony murder (see 13.E.1.). By the way, murder is not usually a matter for the federal system, but when it hitchhikes on an interstate kidnapping charge, it can be. The same might be true of a murder in a national park. **One could have a turf battle between a federal prosecutor and the authorities of the state where a park was located.**

Oh, if you're curious, the other two federal crimes mentioned in the U.S. Constitution are (1) counterfeiting federal coins and (2) piracy and other felonies committed on the high seas (see 15.D.).

Theoretically, a certain federal statute concerning "drug kingpins" allows for the death penalty, even where there is no dead victim in the picture, but no one has been sentenced to death under this provision. Should such a sentence be imposed, one could be sure of a major legal battle — unless the defendant had inadequate counsel *and* none of the many groups involved in either drug policy or sentencing issues stepped in to assist.

One currently active legal battleground is the acceptable means of killing the convicted.

In our gorier past, colonies and states have employed methods of execution including burning, crushing, hanging in chains, firing squad, and even breaking on the wheel, although hanging soon became the most common method and remained so until around the end of the 19th century.

The first electric chair (a method later nicknamed "Old Sparky"), meant to be kinder than hanging, was built in 1888 and first used in 1890. Execution by lethal gas was introduced in 1921 and first used around 1924. The first attempt didn't involve the "gas chamber" used later, but was an unsuccessful effort to kill a prisoner by pumping gas into their cell. The cell leaked.

The present controversy concerns death by lethal injection, first authorized in 1977 and first used in 1982. Not content with the sort of euthanasia long used on ailing cats and dogs, those in charge of executions have come up with several methods involving sequences of drugs. This has become more challenging as drug companies become less willing to sell their drugs for use in executions. Various court challenges have contended that particular drugs administered in particular sequences are so inhumane as to be "cruel and unusual." For example, if the first or second drug paralyzes the prisoner, they could be unable to signal any failure in the drug(s) meant to provide anesthesia.

Federal executions are supposed to use the method of the state where the conviction took place. **One could imagine a ghoulish version of forum-shopping in which a serial killer, having dispatched victims in multiple states, sought to be tried in the state with what they considered the least objectionable form of execution.**

Certain rituals are almost ubiquitous in approaching the fateful moment. Texas may be the only state in which the condemned prisoner does not receive some sort of special meal. (Condemned prisoner Lawrence Russell Brewer reportedly ruined it for later Texans by requesting a huge final meal and then refusing to eat any of it.) While called a "last meal," it could occur a day or two beforehand. Different states have different rules as to its contents, cost, etc.; but whether because of Puritanical views or practical considerations, alcohol is generally prohibited. Nor may the prisoner, though almost certainly beyond any danger of lung cancer, enjoy a final smoke.

The United States is almost alone among industrialized democracies in continuing to inflict the death penalty. Our principal comrades in this fraternity are underdeveloped and/or totalitarian countries.

As of 2000, less than half the states had requirements beyond mere bar membership for attorneys representing defendants in potential death penalty cases. Things have improved since then, with some such requirements in around three-quarters of the states. In Indiana, for example, the Rules of Criminal Procedure include the following requirements for lead counsel and co-counsel in capital cases:

> (1) Lead Counsel; Qualifications. One (1) of the attorneys appointed by the court shall be designated as lead counsel. To be eligible to serve as lead counsel, an attorney shall:
>
> (a) be an experienced and active trial practitioner with at least five (5) years of criminal litigation experience;
>
> (b) have prior experience as lead or co-counsel in no fewer than five (5) felony jury trials which were tried to completion;

(c) have prior experience as lead or co-counsel in at least one (1) case in which the death penalty was sought; and

(d) have completed within two (2) years prior to appointment at least twelve (12) hours of training in the defense of capital cases in a course approved by the Indiana Public Defender Commission.

(2) Co-Counsel, Qualifications. The remaining attorney shall be designated as co-counsel. To be eligible to serve as co-counsel, an attorney shall:

(a) be an experienced and active trial practitioner with at least three (3) years of criminal litigation experience;

(b) have prior experience as lead or co-counsel in no fewer than three (3) felony jury trials which were tried to completion; and

(c) have completed within two (2) years prior to appointment at least twelve (12) hours of training in the defense of capital cases in a course approved by the Indiana Public Defender Commission.

So how does a trial proceed when a guilty verdict could result in death?

First of all, if the defendant has chosen trial by jury, the guilty verdict wouldn't immediately result in anything. The trial will be divided into a guilt phase and a sentencing phase, though the jurors will generally be the same. (See 19.D.1. on the role a potential juror's views on the death penalty may play in jury selection.) While the jurors won't hear any instructions about the death penalty until that second phase, at least one study suggests that about half of them make at least a tentative decision about that penalty before the penalty phase even begins. So much for keeping the jurors ignorant of sentencing options during the guilt phase.

There are also studies bringing the disheartening, if unsurprising, news that many jurors don't understand their duties in the sentencing phase. For example, they might not realize that they are allowed to consider mitigating factors (see 27.C.); or they might believe that the jury must all agree on a particular "mitigating" factor.

The U.S. Supreme Court held in 1994 that if the only alternative to death is life imprisonment without parole, the jury must be told as much, so that the possibility of "future dangerousness" doesn't affect their decision. However, jurors still tend to assume that if they don't choose death, the defendant will eventually be paroled, whether or not this is true. (See 27.B. on the problem of incomprehensible jury instructions in general.)

If the presence of some "aggravating" factor must be found for a death sentence to be imposed, then as of a 2002 U.S. Supreme Court decision, the jury (if there is one) must find that the aggravating factor exists.

By the time a jury is considering sentencing, it often has only two choices: death, or life in prison without possibility of parole. Depending on the jurisdiction and the crime, the judge may or may not be able to override a jury's recommendation of a death sentence. In a federal case where RICO (see 15.C.) is the vehicle for a murder charge, the judge may have no such option, according to *The Hanging Judge*, a recent novel written by a judge who has been in this position. In Alabama, though possibly nowhere else, the judge may actually override the jury's decision *not* to impose the death penalty. Apparently, when overriding the jury's decision, Alabama judges chose death over life far more often than the reverse.

Studies indicate that the death penalty is imposed inconsistently. The racial makeup of the jury tends to make a difference. For example, white jurors are a little more likely to vote for death, at least on the jury's first ballot, than black jurors.

Serving as a juror in a death penalty case can take a heavy emotional toll. The jurors may suffer a sort of post-traumatic stress for years afterward, and the actual execution (usually delayed for years, as I'm about to discuss) can make things worse.

The various appeals and other post-judgment attacks on a sentence of death are typically so prolonged that the condemned prisoner has a reasonable chance of dying in prison. Almost certainly, they will serve many years before the execution finally takes place. Some prisoners have insisted on ending the suspense and the appeal process, even while their attorneys want to keep fighting until the last. **The dramatic possibilities of such a situation are legion. For example, how would the prisoner's loved ones react? How might they try to change the prisoner's mind? And what if that happens at the last possible moment?**

A typical sequence of appeals, etc., might go as follows:

- The defendant files a direct appeal (see 32.A.) from the conviction and/or sentence. This might go directly to the state supreme court, or to an intermediate appellate court and then to the supreme court.

- If the conviction and sentence are upheld on appeal, the defendant may seek some sort of "collateral review." (See 32.C.) This would involve grounds that for some procedural reason couldn't be raised on direct appeal. The most common is "ineffective assistance of counsel," the claim that the defendant's trial attorney performed below the locally prevailing professional norm, and that this deficient performance probably contributed to the conviction and/or sentence. (See 32.C.1.) The collateral review application starts at the state trial court level, and can then work its own way up the appellate ladder.

- If state collateral review leaves the sentence intact, the defendant can seek federal or state "habeas corpus" relief. This is a complicated and much-tinkered-with process, and if you plan to write about it, you'll need to go beyond the confines of this book (but see 32.E.). The basic idea is to ensure that the state court judicial process functioned in a fundamentally fair manner, not trampling too egregiously on the defendant's constitutional rights. Under some circumstances, more limited than you might expect, the defendant may bring up new evidence of actual innocence.

These various, increasingly desperate attempts can continue up to the very last minute — hence the possibility, however remote, of a last-minute reprieve.

The crowds who used to throng to the spectacle of a public execution until well into the 20th century might be amazed that executions are no longer a display for the edification of the masses. These days, executions are by invitation only, with precautions to prevent public viewing. Relatives of the defendant, the victim(s), or both, will sometimes be present, as may the defendant's attorney(s). (In Texas, last I heard, Associated Press reporters had a standing invitation.)

CHAPTER 30

Civil Remedies

A. Introduction: Categories of Relief in Civil Cases

What can one get by suing somebody?

One can get money, known as "damages."

A judge can also order a defendant to do something or stop doing something. That's called "injunctive relief," or "obtaining an injunction."

An order to affirmatively do something is a "writ of mandamus" or "writ of mandate." One "petitions" for writs as opposed to "filing" motions (25.O.). When a government official, including someone working for a court, isn't doing what they're required to do, one can seek a writ of mandate from a higher court to kick them into gear.

An order to stop doing something is sometimes called a "writ of prohibition." When someone infringes an artist's copyright and the artist wants them to stop selling the copycat artwork, the artist would want a writ of prohibition. Sometimes one wants both kinds of writ: for example, injunctions to stop selling a book and also to turn over the plates used to print it.

Injunctive relief is also sometimes called "specific" relief. One type of specific relief is "specific performance," discussed below.

Injunctions are to be granted only when a judgment just giving the plaintiff money won't really solve the problem or "make the plaintiff whole." Put another way, an injunction, including a preliminary injunc-

490

tion, is supposed to be issued to prevent "irreparable harm." That means harm that money alone can't prevent or cure.

If the plaintiff has only asked that some fact or principle be made clear in a binding manner for future reference, the plaintiff has asked for "declaratory relief" or a "declaratory judgment." It's not always clear whether a dispute is "ripe" for a court to entertain such an action, especially in federal court, where the U.S. Constitution's requirement of a "case or controversy" prohibits "advisory" opinions. But if someone's threatening some other kind of lawsuit, the one threatened might act first by seeking a declaratory judgment. Actions for quiet title (14.D.5.) are one specialized way of requesting declaratory relief.

Sometimes, when something has gone wrong in a contractual relationship, the parties may seek, or the court may decide to steer things toward, a "reformation," meaning a revision, of the contract, instead of just presiding over its funeral and ordering damages.

The various types of relief a court can order that aren't "pay this much money" are, as a category, called "equitable relief." (See 19.B. for more about "equity.")

Some types of litigation come with their own particular kinds of relief. If someone owns property with someone and doesn't want to have to deal with them any more, the disgruntled co-owner can get a court to partition the property: either to divide it up, or to order it sold and the proceeds divided. That's similar to what happens to marital property in a divorce, but the order in a divorce will typically include other relief as well. (For details, and for what "marital property" is, see 14.H.2.) If the partners in a partnership want to dissolve it, and for some reason they haven't included binding dissolution procedures in the original partnership agreement, they can go to court for a dissolution proceeding not unlike the one used for divorces.

B. Contract and Tort Damages

Back to money.

Different kinds of civil litigation result in different kinds of money damages. And in a minority of breach of contract cases, the plaintiff can get something more.

A reminder: for how the type of harm suffered determines whether the plaintiff collects contract or tort damages, see 14.F.'s discussion of the "economic loss" rule.

1. Remedies for Breach of Contract

In contract disputes, damages are typically aimed at putting the plaintiff in the same financial position as if the contract had been fully performed ("expectation" damages). Other approaches, rarely used in the contract context, include "reliance" damages and/or "restitution" damages: whatever money, or the value of whatever resources, the plaintiff spent in reasonable reliance on the contract being performed, and/or actually gave to the defendant. However the damages are calculated, they have to be based on "reasonably certain" figures, not fuzzy speculation.

If money can't put the plaintiff in essentially the same position as performance of the contract would have done, then the judgment may go beyond money damages. For example, real property is considered unique, so if the contract called for the transfer of real property, the judge can order that transfer to take place. Such relief is called "specific performance."

Specific performance is generally not available where a contract for personal services is concerned, since courts view compelling such services as "involuntary servitude" prohibited by the Thirteenth Amendment to the U.S. Constitution. Some courts have also commented on the likelihood that trying to force personal services would not, given human nature, end well for any of those involved.

Some contracts include an agreement on what reasonable damages would be in the event of a breach. Such estimated damages are called "liquidated damages." Liquidated damages can't be disproportionately large, or they become unenforceable penalties.

Contracts that fall under the Uniform Commercial Code (see 14.B.1.) have their own methods for calculating damages, though those methods are intended to fulfill the same goals.

"Consequential" damages, also called "special" damages, may be available for breach of contract, but only if the plaintiff proves the defendant knew about special circumstances that would lead to such damages if the defendant failed to perform as promised. This is an exception to the usual rules for contract damages.

a. Interest on the Judgment

Sometimes, when it's been clear right along how much money was involved, the plaintiff can get prejudgment interest on the damage award. That's interest, usually at some rate prescribed by statute, that starts accruing before the judgment is even entered.

When does prejudgment interest start accruing? In a contract case, it'll start when the payment or some other easily valued performance was due. In tort cases, it's less likely the necessary clarity existed for prejudgment interest to be available in the first place — but if it is available, the date it starts accruing will depend on the particular facts.

Anyone who recovers money damages can also collect post-judgment interest on those damages (again, at some rate fixed by statute), generally starting when the judgment comes down. However, when the award of damages includes attorney fees, there's disagreement among the different federal appellate courts, and probably among state courts as well, about when the clock starts for post-judgment interest on those fees. Is it when the court says attorney fees should be awarded, or when the court decides on the quantity of that fee award?

A related question: who gets to keep the post-judgment interest on attorney fees, the successful plaintiff or the attorney? A 2001 Ohio decision implies that the plaintiff does, which makes sense if the plaintiff actually paid the fees and has been deprived of the use of that money. In California, however, per a 2014 decision, the attorney gets that interest. Elsewhere, I don't know.

2. Tort Damages

In tort actions, damages are supposedly aimed at "making the plaintiff whole." If someone's personal property, like a car, is banged up, the damages could be whatever it costs to repair it, unless it'd be cheaper to replace it. In that case, the damages would be the fair market value of the car (before the damage). The same rules apply to real property.

Tort damages tend to look further into the future than contract damages. What would be unavailable consequential damages in a contract case are routinely available as "compensatory damages" in tort cases, with the limit being what future injuries were reasonably foreseeable.

The damages in a tort case can go well beyond tangible losses. The trier of fact may well end up trying to quantify such deprivations as loss of future earnings, loss of reputation, loss of "consortium" (the companionship and/or intimate favors of a spouse), or the inability to engage in a favorite hobby. And in any tort case that involves physical or emotional harm, it's common to award damages for "pain and suffering." "Making [whoever] whole" is a somewhat inappropriate label for such damages (and where the plaintiff has lost a limb, particularly so). How can a court use money to "make someone whole" for the physical pain of an injury or the emotional pain of seeing their husband hit by a car? What the plaintiff gets is whatever amount the plaintiff's attorney can convince a judge or jury is somehow appropriate, possibly constrained by what's typically awarded in that jurisdiction for comparable injuries.

Theoretically, the amount shouldn't (so to speak) amount to a punishment imposed on the defendant. But in tort cases, if the plaintiff carries some additional burden (which varies from state to state), the trier of fact *is* allowed to punish the defendant by awarding the aptly named "punitive damages," discussed in 30.B.3. below.

Whenever the award of money is meant to compensate for some ongoing or future injury, the trier of fact must take into account two factors that point in opposite directions: (1) the expectation that the dollar will keep decreasing in value over time, but also (2) the fact that money received now can be invested to earn more money in the future. These calculations, done together, provide the "present value" of the future amount necessary to compensate the plaintiff, and will be used to come up with the total damage figure.

Many states have damage "caps" that limit certain kinds of tort awards. Where compensatory damages are at issue, the most common cap, present in more than half the states, covers awards for medical malpractice. The cap may apply to the entire award, or only to the "non-economic" portion of it (see 14.F.) covering such damages as pain and suffering or loss of consortium. State legislatures have capped the maximum medical malpractice award for a very practical reason: to reduce the number of doctors being driven either out of business or out of state by soaring malpractice insurance premiums.

Somewhat fewer states cap damages for all non-economic damages. Where such caps exist, they have exceptions, either removal of the cap or a higher ceiling, for cases involving either death or serious permanent injury.

Damage caps on compensatory damages may be fixed dollar ceilings, or they may limit damages to the greater of a dollar amount or a figure reached through some calculation, using such factors as the plaintiff's life expectancy.

Caps on punitive damages, discussed in 30.B.3. below, are also common.

Where a damage cap exists, it is likely that the jury won't know about it, and might issue a verdict that the judge will later cut down to size.

3. Punitive and Multiple Damages

For many torts, a successful plaintiff may be awarded not only the "compensatory" damages meant to make them whole, but damages specifically intended to punish the defendant and deter future tortious conduct. Not surprisingly, these are known as punitive damages.

In deciding on whether to award punitive damages, the trier of fact focuses not on the plaintiff's injury but on the defendant's conduct, especially the defendant's state of mind and intentions. State statutes or cases are likely to use such words as "willful," "malicious," "wanton," and "deliberate." The more knowingly and callously the defendant acted in injuring the plaintiff, the more likely an award of punitive damages. In most states, the plaintiff must prove the facts justifying punitive damages by clear and convincing evidence rather than merely a preponderance of the evidence (see 20.A. and 20.B.).

Once the trier of fact decides to award punitive damages, how large will the award be? Factors contributing to the amount of punitive damages include how profitable the wrongdoing was to the defendant and how much money the defendant has. An individual living near the poverty line who egregiously slandered the plaintiff and gained no particular financial benefit by doing so would be punished quite severely by an award of $50,000. On the other hand, the officers and directors of a multinational corporation that stole a trade secret might not even notice punitive damages under $50,000,000. The goal is to remove the incentive for future similar wrongdoing, and to hit the defendant hard enough to hurt, without destroying the defendant altogether.

Because punitive damages are by definition a form of punishment, the proceeding in which they're imposed must satisfy constitutional concerns of due process (see 34.G.).

But why should the plaintiff, rather than society as a whole, benefit from this punishment of the defendant? Some states address the "windfall" factor with statutes diverting portions of any punitive damage award to (no surprise) the state, or to some specific and appropriate state program.

Many states have imposed damage caps on punitive damage awards. This is probably due to these states' desire to attract and keep businesses, for whom the process of unlimited punitive damages in some future litigation could be a serious deterrent to locating there. These caps may be fixed dollar ceilings, ranging from a low of $250,000 to a high of $10,000,000, or maximum multipliers, so that punitive damages may not exceed some multiple of the compensatory damage award.

A few states used to have, and at least one may still have, a peculiar hybrid cause of action called "tortious breach of contract." If the defendant breached the contract in a particularly egregious way, the plaintiff could collect punitive damages. To the extent this made sense, it made sense in situations where a big company entered into multiple identical contracts. If the company's standard operating procedure was to breach those contracts in some manner profitable to the company, having to pay contract damages from time to time might not be enough of a deterrent to put an end to that practice. Being hit with a big ol' punitive damages award, however, might get the shareholders' attention.

Indiana, for example, used to recognize tortious breach of contract. However, in 1993, the Indiana Supreme Court decided that punitive damages would henceforth be available in Indiana only when an actual tort had been established.

Some other states that used to allow actions for tortious breach of contract, including at least Hawaii, Idaho, Michigan, Ohio, South Carolina and Wisconsin, have either disdained or abandoned the idea; but last I checked, it survived in Connecticut, and might still exist elsewhere.

In a state that still has this cause of action, you could have some intrepid attorney digging it up as a way to deal with a company that makes a habit of cheating its customers or vendors. But if you want to avoid looking sloppy, you'd better make clear that it's unavailable in most states.

Some statutes allow a plaintiff to receive "treble [triple] damages": an award of compensatory damages will be three times as great as it would be otherwise. (The plaintiff doesn't get the compensatory damages *plus* three times as much.) A few statutes may exist providing for other multipliers.

Essentially a variety of (and hence an alternative to) "punitive" damages, treble damages may, but don't always, require a similarly high burden of proof. There may be greater variation on the question of what level of willful or malicious conduct the plaintiff must prove to obtain these damages. Since some statutes use the possibility of treble damages as a way to encourage private enforcement of socially useful rules, there may be less focus on the nastiness of the defendant's conduct or intent.

Foreign governments that won't help collect punitive damages probably won't help collect treble damages either, at least not the two-thirds in excess of the compensatory damages.

Types of cases in which a plaintiff may have a chance at treble damages include patents, trade secrets, medical malpractice, and some personal injury cases in some states. In suits under the Clayton Antitrust Act (see 15.A.) or RICO (see 15.C.), treble damages are mandatory. In states where treble damages are available for medical malpractice, any state cap on the total amount of malpractice awards may still apply.

At least when treble damages are optional rather than mandatory, the plaintiff may need to demand them in the initial complaint.

---

4. Who Pays What: Joint and Several Liability

When a plaintiff obtains a judgment against more than one defendant, who pays what?

Some states use a rule called "joint and several liability," in which all the defendants are equally responsible for the entire judgment, no matter their degree of fault. The plaintiff may choose whether to collect the entire sum from one defendant, presumably the one with adequate resources to pay it, or from more than one. Any defendant who ends up paying more than a pro rata share may then sue the others for partial reimbursement; but if one or more of the other defendants can't pony up, the defendant originally chosen has no further recourse.

Joint and several liability, when applied to this extent, greatly reduces the chance that the plaintiff will end up unable to satisfy the judgment. It also ignores the likely differences in culpability between the defendants, and can thus lead to obviously unfair results. A variety of hybrid approaches have therefore arisen.

Some states use joint and several liability only for defendants whose share of fault exceeds some set percentage. Others use it only for "solvent," as opposed to bankrupt or about-to-be-bankrupt, defendants, whose share of the damages is distributed among the solvent defendants. If the plaintiff was partly at fault and is insolvent, the plaintiff's share may be part of what's so distributed.

Some states use joint and several liability only for economic loss (see 14.F.), with each defendant paying the noneconomic damages for which that defendant is responsible. Others use joint and several liability only in tort cases, not in contract cases; or only in cases involving intentional torts (14.F.) and/or torts where the defendants conspired (14.F.9.).

What if one or more of the defendants settle with the plaintiff before a judgment is issued? How does the court take that settlement into account in awarding damages against the defendants who didn't settle? States generally use either a "pro rata" or a "pro tanto" rule. The pro rata approach looks at the settling defendant's (or defendants') percentage of fault, as determined by the trier of fact, and gives the non-settling defendant(s) a credit for that percentage of the award. Thus, if a defendant 60% at fault settles with the plaintiff, the remaining defendants are left with 40% of the award to pay, shared or divided under whatever rule the state applies. The pro tanto rule looks instead at the amount of the settlement, giving the non-settling defendant(s) a dollar-for-dollar credit in that amount.

C. Rescission

Under some circumstances, one party to a contract can go to court to get the contract "rescinded" (unmade). If the parties had seriously different understandings of what the contract terms meant, or were mistaken about some key fact, *and* if nobody has already done what the contract required of them, rescission is appropriate.

For example, let's say a homeowner enters into a contract with a local fellow to paint a house. The homeowner assumes that the painter has their own ladder; the painter assumes the homeowner will supply the ladder. When this confusion comes to light, if the painter hasn't made any major investment in paint or turned down another job, it'll probably be less hassle for all concerned to rescind the contract.

Here's another example: a man obtains medical insurance for himself and his family. The application has questions about health risks, including cancer, in the immediate family. The man doesn't realize these questions apply to his wife and children as well, and therefore doesn't mention that his wife's sisters and mother had breast cancer. If the insurance company figures this out (maybe by cross-referencing files), it could (unless prevented by some statute) rescind the contract. In fact, a controversy arose a few years ago when it was discovered that one insurance company was making a special point of investigating the backgrounds of women with breast cancer. **If your story is set at a time when insurers could decline to cover pre-existing conditions, and if the company doesn't rescind the contract until the wife's found a malignant lump, rescission could put the family in a terrible bind.**

If some third party has already been involved in the contract in some way, benefiting from it or giving up something in reliance on it, rescission is probably a non-starter.

Rescission may or may not be available if only one party was seriously confused about the underlying facts. It's more likely to be granted if the savvier party would be "unjustly enriched" otherwise. Say, for example, the contract called for a payment of $500.00 if Joe-Bob goes to "Georgia" to pick up merchandise and brings it back to MegaCorp in Chicago, IL. Joe-Bob thought "Georgia" meant the southern U.S. state — but somewhere in the fine print was the clue that it meant the country, on the shores of the Black Sea between Russia and Turkey. MegaCorp would normally have to pay $5,000.00 for this service, and would be unjustly enriched if it got away with paying $500.00.

When a contract is rescinded, everyone gives back anything they received as part of the deal, with certain exceptions. If the Joe-Bob/MegaCorp contract is rescinded, Joe-Bob will have to return the $100.00 partial payment he received — unless he's already spent it on gasoline and renting a truck. Since the goal is an equitable (fair) resolution, Joe-Bob probably won't have to pay back the $100.00 he spent in good faith; though this might depend on the judge's sense of what's fair, which may include an assessment of whether Joe-Bob should have known better.

Rescission can't be delayed for long once the party seeking it knows about the facts that justify it. For some sorts of contracts, federal or state statutes give the buyer the right to rescind within some short period of time (e.g., 24 hours, or three days). These contracts might include contracts someone makes with a door-to-door salesperson, or other purchases made from home (more and more common these days), or some types of contracts for services. The latter sometimes include contracts for such self-improvement programs as gym memberships and diet management, the sort of contracts one might make under the short-term influence of a New Year's resolution.

If one party to a contract was defrauded (see 14.F.6.), that party has the choice of suing for tort damages or seeking rescission of the contract.

If one party was mentally incapacitated when the contract was made, the contract can be rescinded even if the other party didn't realize that fact. Unless the incapacitation was being too drunk to see straight. Unless, on the other hand, one party got the other party drunk in order to get the contract signed.

A party can seek to rescind a contract if the other party fails to perform in some way that makes the contract essentially useless to the innocent party. For example, if the contract was for catering a wedding, and the caterer shows up a week late . . . . In such a case, however, it would probably be more lucrative for the plaintiff to sue for damages.

D. Civil Contempt

There's another type of remedy that's nominally civil rather than criminal: civil contempt. Civil contempt is meant to be coercive rather than punitive. It's used to pressure a recalcitrant party. A fine can be imposed, or someone can even be imprisoned, until the person "purges" the contempt by following the court's order.

Civil contempt is "direct" if it arises from some conduct during the proceeding itself, and "indirect" if someone files a petition claiming that someone else has failed to follow a court order.

One real-life example of a judge using civil contempt involves a lawyer as lawbreaker. This lawyer embezzled money (see 13.H.1.) and got caught. Planning for that possibility, he had invested the stolen money in overseas real estate. The lawyer knew that a court in the U.S. couldn't issue any order that would effectively compel someone overseas to sell the property. Presumably he hoped that when he got out of prison, his ill-gotten gains would be there waiting for him. The judge, however, ordered him held in jail for civil contempt for as long as it took to get him to set the sale of that property in motion and bring the money back home, where the victim of the embezzlement could get at it.

Civil contempt can be quite dramatic in operation, whether in art or in life. **For example, parents can be jailed for refusing to deliver their children to noncustodial parents, or to relatives such as grandparents, whom the parent considers dangerous to the child.** In one such case, the court had ordered the mother to give her child into the temporary custody of a relative who had threatened to "take [the girl] where no one will ever be able to separate us," or words to that effect. The mother spent weeknights in jail for several weeks before some sort of compromise was reached. You can imagine, and help your readers imagine, the terrible pressures and choices such a parent would face.

Civil contempt is improper if the subject of the order didn't intend to disobey the court order at issue, or has no power to do whatever the court is trying to coerce them to do. Courts are not always realistic about what someone has the power to do: for example, they often assume that a parent can compel a teenager to go on court-ordered visitation.

(Direct criminal contempt, by the way, is behavior during a trial or other proceeding that disrespects the court or disrupts the proceeding. See 13.X. for more details.)

CHAPTER 31

Military Justice

Courtroom drama set in a military context derives additional dramatic tension from the nature of the military itself. The accused is abruptly yanked from a position defending their country, and defending themselves from the enemy, to a very different defensive posture. It could be called the judicial equivalent of "friendly fire."

The Uniform Code of Military Justice (UCMJ) covers officers and enlisted personnel in the U.S. military. It applies whether these personnel are accused of offenses that would also be crimes in the civilian world, or such offenses as insubordination or being absent without leave (AWOL), which violate only the military's rules. There will be "charges" and "specifications": the former list the Article of the UCMJ allegedly violated, and the "specifications" (logically enough) specify how.

There are several types of military justice proceedings, but I believe the accused has the following rights, at least theoretically, in all three:

- The right to a free defense attorney supplied by the military, a "Judge Advocate" (or JAG officer) from the Judge Advocate General's Corps for the military branch in question.
- The right to instead hire a private attorney at their expense.
- The right to wait for that attorney before answering questions.
- The right to a showing of probable cause before any search or seizure.

- The right to a fair trial, though not one conducted in an identical manner as a civilian trial, as you'll see below.

A. Article 15 Proceedings

For less serious charges, there's a proceeding commonly called an Article 15 proceeding, but also called a summary court-martial or "non-judicial punishment." The latter label may suggest the likely outcome of whatever fact-finding takes place. These proceedings may also be called "captain's mast" in the Navy and Coast Guard, or the incongruously low-key "office hours" in the Marines.

The accused is entitled to refuse the Article 15 proceeding altogether, at the risk of a full court-martial (see 31.C. below). Since Article 15 has fewer procedural protections, but lower maximum penalties, than any full court-martial, a service member guilty of the offense in question would be taking a serious gamble by declining an Article 15.

In an Article 15 proceeding, a single military officer, the commander, investigates the facts, interviewing accuser and accused, and possibly asking a JAG officer to answer legal questions. For the type of Article 15 proceeding with the most severe possible penalties (see below), the commander must be a major or higher rank in the Army, or equivalent ranks in the other services.

The standard of proof varies from "clear and convincing" (20.B.) in the Navy and Marines to "beyond a reasonable doubt" (20.C.) in the Army and Air Force. At least one source expresses doubt that all commanders in charge of Article 15's are aware that these standards must be met.

The accused may not have a JAG officer at the summary court-martial, though they may ask some non-lawyer to act as a spokesperson. The accused might not be allowed to have privately hired counsel present either, though in that case, they could ask for out-of-court JAG assistance.

Before the court-martial, often at a preliminary hearing, the accused has the right to see the charges and to know who's making them, and to be told the names of witnesses and what sort of documents (if any) will be used to bolster the accusation.

At the proceeding itself, the accused is entitled to plead guilty or not guilty; to present witnesses, sworn statements, or other evidence; to testify or not, with silence not to be construed against the accused; and to be informed of the maximum potential sentence. The officer in charge has the job of getting hold of defense witnesses. The Military Rules of Evidence, similar in most respects to the rules of evidence used in federal criminal trials, apply. If found guilty, the accused has the option of making a statement or presenting evidence intended to persuade the officer in charge to reduce the punishment. A written record is prepared, a copy of which the accused is entitled to receive.

A finding of guilt in an Article 15 isn't treated as a federal criminal conviction. Some Article 15 records are expunged (see 32.G.) after two years, but not all. If the accused was arrested as part of the lead-up to the proceeding, that arrest might be reported to the FBI.

There are three levels of Article 15 proceedings, listed here in increasing order of severity: Summarized, Company Grade, and Field Grade. Aside from the rank of the commander (see above), the difference lies in the maximum possible penalties.

The maximum for the lowest grade (at present and per my sources) is 14 days extra duty and/or 14 days "restriction." Restriction limits the places the offender is allowed to go. The permitted locations include work areas, barracks, mess hall, place of worship, and medical facilities.

One level up, and the commander may also impose any or all of the following: "correctional custody" (for certain lower levels of enlisted personnel only) for up to seven days; forfeiture of seven days' base pay; a verbal and/or written admonition or reprimand (my sources differ as to whether written reprimands are an option); reduction in rank by one grade, under some circumstances; and, if aboard a vessel, the time-honored confinement with rations of only bread and water (for up to three days).

The most senior commanders may impose up to 60 days "restriction," or up to 45 days extra duties or extra duties plus restriction; up to 30 days of correctional custody for certain lower ranks; two months' forfeiture of one-half base pay; reduction in rank under some circumstances; an oral admonition or reprimand; and/or (on board ship) those three days of bread and water again. The rules about which of these more serious penal-

506 • MILITARY JUSTICE

ties may or may not be combined, and how they could or couldn't add up, are confusing enough that I'm going to leave the details for you to explore.

In most cases, the subject of the proceeding may appeal to the commander's next higher officer, who may deny the appeal, set aside the finding (the equivalent of ordering a not guilty verdict), or reduce the punishment, but may not increase the punishment. However, if the armed services member is in the Navy or Marines, and is on board ship or assigned to a vessel, they may seek a reduced punishment on appeal, but may not challenge any other aspect of the decision.

Appeal or no, the sentence usually takes effect immediately, but the commander may delay it due to circumstances such as upcoming leave, field exercises, or illness. (**If the planned leave is supposed to include a wedding, it could put quite a damper on the festivities.**)

B. Letters of Reprimand

There are written reprimands that can go into a service member's file with a minimum of procedural protections, and they can bring the member's military career to a screeching halt. A LOR (letter of reprimand) can come from the member's immediate commanding officer or anyone higher in that chain. A General Officer Memorandum of Reprimand (GO-MOR) may be issued by any officer of "general" rank. In the Army, Air Force, and Marines, that's an officer above the rank of colonel, i.e. Brigadier General and up. In the Navy: above Captain, starting with the quaintly labeled "Rear Admiral, Lower Half."

Letters of reprimand are supposed to follow an "objective decision by competent authority," but there's little oversight to ensure it. Critics of these procedures claim they're used when the evidence wouldn't support an Article 15. Once an officer decides to file a letter of reprimand, the service member may appeal it; but the burden of proof is on the member — by clear and convincing evidence, yet! (see 20.B.) — that the letter's allegations are untrue or unjust. **If your main character is the subject of a vendetta from higher up, this might well be the weapon of choice.**

C. Special and General Courts-Martial

Not counting Article 15's, there are two levels of courts-martial (that's the plural): "special" and "general." Special courts-martial are used for offenses comparable to misdemeanors, general courts-martial for the equivalent of felonies.

Once the case is "preferred" (initiated), there must be some degree of investigation before it is or isn't "referred" for an actual court-martial. The investigation may be informal for a special court-martial, but where a general court-martial is sought, an "Article 32" or probable cause hearing must take place before an Article 32 hearing officer (also called an investigating officer). How is this officer chosen, you may ask? Well, the commander who preferred the case in the first place gets to choose them, unless that commander is the actual "accuser" who set everything in motion (or ordered someone else to do so), or has more than an official interest in what goes down. In that event, the buck passes to an officer higher in the chain of command.

At least the commander no longer gets to choose the JAG officer appointed to the defense.

The hearing officer presides over the Article 32 hearing. Per a December 2013 order of the Secretary of Defense, effective December 2014, the hearing officer should be part of JAG wherever this is "practicable" (feasible). This change will increase the likelihood that the hearing officer is expert in military law; but it could lead to logistical complications and delays if the hearing must take place in a remote location. For severe enough delays, or where the nature of the charges make it preferable that the hearing officer have some specialized knowledge, the "not practicable" exception could kick in.

Other rule changes made at the same time include providing a special "victim's counsel" to provide support and advice. This could include keeping the victim in the loop as to upcoming proceedings, as well as ensuring that victim protections such as the military's version of the rape shield rule (see 13.F.) are applied. Also per the new rules, alleged victims are no longer required to attend the hearing or to testify at it. How this will play out remains to be seen: the absence of the alleged victim could reduce either the likelihood of a "referral" for prosecution (see below), or possibly, on the other hand, the showing required for such a referral.

Unlike a judge in a civilian probable cause hearing, the Article 32 hearing officer doesn't ultimately decide whether the case goes to trial, though they do make a recommendation. Who does decide? Our old friend the preferring commander, though with the same important caveat that if the commander is the accuser or has a personal interest, the task gets kicked upward. If necessary for any bureaucratic reasons, the preferring commander may have to pass the matter up or down the hierarchical ladder to another officer. Whichever officer ends up holding the ball becomes the "convening authority."

The prosecutor must give the accused any exculpatory evidence (evidence favorable to the defense) they possess. If the accused chooses to participate in this hearing, they may have either military or privately retained counsel, who may cross-examine witnesses, challenge the admissibility of evidence, and present defense witnesses.

If the case is "referred," the judge, a JAG officer, is supposed to hail from a unit independent of that from which the accused and their commander come. If the accused chooses a trial by jury, the commander gets to pick the jurors, called the "members panel." As discouraging as that sounds, the odds of a conviction, always high, are even higher when the case is tried to a judge alone rather than to a jury.

In capital cases, a member panel is required.

There must be at least three members for a special court-martial, and at least five for a general court-martial (12 for a death penalty case). The members must be at or above the rank of the accused (above, for enlisted personnel). If the accused is an enlisted man/woman, they may request that at least one-third of the members be enlisted personnel as well. Except for death penalty cases, the accused may choose to be tried by a military judge instead (like waiving the right to jury trial in civilian court).

The prosecutor will be a JAG officer unless the military situation makes that impractical.

The applicable code specifically prohibits "unlawful command influence" by a commander or other convening authority: any attempt to intimidate, pressure, or order those involved in the proceeding in a particular direction. **Of course, the exercise of such influence could make for good story material.**

The accused will not necessarily be allowed to go about their business pending trial. A commanding officer with authority over the accused may order anything from "conditions on liberty" (particular activities which the accused must engage in or from which the accused must refrain) all the way up to actual confinement. All these fall under the heading of "restraint." Restraint is not always required, and is not supposed to be any more rigorous than what's necessary to make sure the accused stays put pending trial or to prevent "foreseeable serious criminal misconduct."

Where there is a jury, a two-thirds vote is required for a guilty verdict (except for death penalty cases, as explained in 31.D. below). The members vote from junior to senior rank, to ensure that the more junior won't feel any pressure to vote the same way as those more senior to them.

If the accused is convicted, the sentencing phase ("extenuation and mitigation") begins immediately. Plea bargaining is possible at or before this phase. Based on such negotiations or on their own initiative, the convening authority has the discretion to set aside the panel's findings altogether or to reduce the sentence. However, as part of the same package of rule changes already mentioned, the convening authority may no longer decide on their own to reject a finding of guilt for any felony offense for which the accused has been sentenced to a discharge and/or more than six months' imprisonment. Nor may they make any changes to any findings involving any kind of sex crime.

Other rule changes prevent the convening authority from considering "the military character of the accused" in deciding how to dispose of a felony case, and require that if the convening authority disagrees with the decision to proceed with a general court-martial, the Secretary of that branch of the Armed Forces will decide whether to go forward. There are other procedural complexities for sexual assault cases, which I won't attempt to summarize.

In case you were wondering, the catalyst for this set of changes involved a convening authority setting aside a finding that a former inspector general had committed aggravated sexual assault.

For most offenses, there's no minimum sentence in a special or general court-martial, but for a few, e.g. "non-capital" premeditated murder, there are. In the case of non-capital murder, that minimum is life in prison with the possibility of parole.

The maximum sentences for special and general courts-martial are as follows:

- Special: twelve months confinement, twelve months forfeiture of two-thirds pay, three months hard labor, and a bad-conduct discharge. (Before 2002, those "twelve"s were "six"es.)
- General: dishonorable discharge, life imprisonment, or . . . death.

D. The Military Death Penalty

The death penalty is available for a range of military offenses, including some quite far from what are considered capital crimes in the civilian sphere. A sentence of death may be imposed for any of the following (in order of the "Articles" listing the offenses in the relevant statute):

- Desertion in time of war.
- Assaulting a superior officer in time of war.
- Disobeying a lawful order in time of war.
- Mutiny (various actions intended to "usurp or override" lawful military authority).
- Sedition (various actions intended to overthrow or destroy lawful civil authority).
- Failure to do one's utmost to prevent or suppress mutiny or sedition, or failure to use all reasonable methods to inform superiors about attempted or actual mutiny or sedition.
- "Misbehavior before the enemy," such as running away, surrendering under the wrong circumstances, failing to do one's "utmost" to capture or destroy enemy troops or objectives, leaving one's duty post to "plunder or pillage," or failing to provide all "practicable relief and assistance" to troops, vessels, or aircraft engaged in battle.
- Surrendering or attempting to force a surrender without proper authority.

- In time of war, revealing a "parole or countersign" (essentially types of passwords, though not necessarily words) to someone one doesn't believe was authorized to receive it.
- "Forcing a safeguard" (an action meant to overcome protection put in place by our forces around enemy or neutral places, people, or property).
- Aiding or attempting to aid the enemy with arms, ammo, supplies, money, other tangible things, or information.
- Knowingly communicating with the enemy without proper authorization.
- In time of war, spying on any place under armed forces control or performing work that aids the war effort.
- Espionage (including attempted espionage) involving nuclear weaponry, military spacecraft or satellites, early warning systems, or other "means of defense or retaliation against large scale attack," if:
    o the members of the court martial unanimously find one or more of a list of aggravating circumstances (for some of which you'd have to go beyond the statute and look at the regulations), and
    o the members also agree that aggravating circumstances outweigh mitigating circumstances.
- "Willfully and wrongfully" putting a seagoing "vessel" (ship or submarine) in danger of loss or of injury to its crew, or allowing someone else to do so.
- In time of war, sleeping or getting drunk while on sentinel/lookout duty, or leaving that post before being relieved in the required way.
- Premeditated murder or murder while committing or attempting to commit burglary, "sodomy" (defined as "unnatural" copulation with any degree of penetration, under a since-repealed separate Article making sodomy a punishable offense), rape, robbery, or aggravated arson.
- Rape committed before October 1, 2007. (The statute that revised the military's sexual assault provisions, effective after October 1, 2007 doesn't mention the death penalty and probably doesn't authorize it.)

512 • MILITARY JUSTICE

Whether you find any of these possibilities alarming may depend on how cynical or pessimistic you are about abuses of authority in general. If your imagination tends toward the dystopian, there's considerable near-future story potential in some of these offenses. For example, there's that "in time of war" category. **What happens if a soldier has endured a long series of insulting or harassing comments and undeserved punishments from a superior officer, and finally loses their temper and hits that officer, only to learn too late that war was declared a few minutes before?** **The same situation could turn sneaking off lookout duty a few minutes early, or a prank that involves revealing a countersign, into a potentially deadly error.**

It may seem unlikely that the powers that be would actually seek the death penalty in such situations, and there's little or no reason to believe the U.S. military has abused this authority in the past; but what if **there's some personal animosity involved, carried over from peacetime civilian events?** Or what if **the war is so unpopular, and morale so low, that some martinet wants to set an example by imposing the harshest possible discipline?** This last may have historical precedent. I have heard that in the British military during World War I, some soldiers who cracked under the pressure of months of shelling, or officers who refused suicidal orders, were executed for such offenses as failure to obey orders after trials grossly deficient in due process.

Unrealistic and/or politically motivated expectations in the higher ranks about what constituted "doing one's utmost" to achieve some military objective, or what constituted "practicable relief" to troops under fire, could lead to capital charges against some convenient scapegoat.

And then there's knowing and unauthorized communication with the enemy. **It wouldn't be hard to construct a Romeo-and-Juliet scenario involving violation of this Article.**

Here's one last scenario I'll toss out: **A soldier is related to, or a life-long friend of, someone who's involved in radical political activities. A political adversary of that radical decides that the soldier should have told their superior officers about the friend's/relative's activities as attempted "sedition."**

Keep in mind, as you consider potential story lines, that the U.S. hasn't actually "declared war" since December 11, 1941. Given the context, "time of war" would probably be narrowly construed, and therefore wouldn't apply to any of the armed conflicts in which we've engaged since World War II. So if you want to use any of the "time of war" offenses, you'll either have to do the research involved in historical fiction or else speculate your way a few years into the future.

E. Military Appeals

If the sentence includes a "punitive discharge" ("dismissal" for officers, dishonorable or bad-conduct discharge for enlisted personnel) or at least a year of confinement, there's an automatic review by the Court of Criminal Reviews for that branch of the service, unless the service member waives it (possible for all but death sentences). Even then, a JAG officer will review the case for legal errors. Unlike the regular appellate courts in many states, the Courts of Criminal Reviews may reweigh the evidence, though these courts are likely to keep in mind the difficulty of judging credibility, etc., from a "cold record" as opposed to live testimony.

As already mentioned, death penalty cases require 12 panel members, and may not be tried to a judge alone. The panel must vote unanimously on four points:

- The conviction itself (guilt).
- Proof beyond a reasonable doubt of a specific aggravating circumstance. Most such circumstances are similar to those involved in civilian prosecutions (for example, victim under 15 years of age, intentional infliction of prolonged pain on the victim, murder to effect an escape from custody); but some depend on the military context, such as committing the offense in time of war or to avoid hazardous duty, or knowingly endangering a mission, or killing an officer who was performing their officer duties. And there's one aggravating circumstance that may or may not be part of any state criminal codes: murder of the President of the United States.
- That the agreed-upon aggravating circumstances substantially outweigh all mitigating circumstances.

- That death is the appropriate sentence to choose.

The verdict must then be reviewed by the Court of Criminal Appeals for the particular branch of service (Army, Navy-Marine Corps, Air Force, or Coast Guard); and if affirmed there, by the U.S. Court of Appeals for the Armed Forces (called, until 1994, the Court of Military Appeals); and if affirmed there, potentially by the U.S. Supreme Court (but only if that Court grants cert (see 32.F.)). And after all that, the Commander in Chief, aka the President of the United States, must approve the sentence. Even *then*, the condemned individual may seek habeas corpus relief (see 32.E.) from a non-military federal court.

At present, all military executions are conducted by lethal injection — but with growing opposition to and litigation concerning this method, that may change, and we may see the return of firing squads (logistically easy to arrange, if psychologically problematic) or some other approach.

F. "Just Following Orders"

What if a superior (as in senior) officer orders a member of the armed forces to perform some act that constitutes a crime under military law?

Despite the usual emphasis, to put it mildly, on the necessity of following orders, "I was just following orders," known more formally as the superior orders defense, is very unlikely to succeed. Whether it has any chance of success depends on how obviously the order was unlawful. The Court of Military Appeals, in one case involving the killing of a Vietnamese civilian, put it this way: "[T]he justification for acts done pursuant to orders does not exist if the order was of such a nature that a man of ordinary sense and understanding would know it to be illegal." This rule is often called the "manifest illegality" standard. Put another way, members of the armed forces are to presume that orders are lawful, but must remain alert to the possibility that they are not.

The U.S. military followed this approach early on, but it has not consistently done so.

An 1804 U.S. Supreme Court opinion held that naval commanders obeying the President, aka the Commander in Chief, who issued an unlawful order "acted at their peril" and could be held criminally responsible.

An 1813 opinion from a lower federal court agreed, holding that following orders is no justification if the defendant "knows, or ought to know" that the order is illegal. An 1851 U.S. Supreme Court opinion suggested that having followed orders could mitigate punishment, but not negate guilt. Following the Civil War, the commandant of the Confederacy's Andersonville POW camp was tried, convicted, and executed, despite his claim to be following the orders of his superiors.

In 1914, however, the U.S. followed international authorities in changing course and treating obedience to orders as an absolute defense. Only the officer who gave the unlawful order would be treated as guilty. The transition back to the current rule occurred during and after the post-World War II Nuremberg trials, in which various Nazi officers were tried for crimes against humanity.

Some controversy has arisen recently about the U.S. Attorney General's announcement that the AG would not prosecute CIA employees who interrogated detainees in ways that may have constituted torture and violated federal law, when these employees relied in good faith on written assurances of legality by the Office of Legal Counsel. While the CIA is not part of the U.S. military, this "good faith" defense might be used in the military context to argue that a defendant of "ordinary sense and understanding" might rely on an opinion issued by some military legal office.

CHAPTER 32

Are We There Yet?, Part Two:
Appeals and Other Post-Judgment Relief

H aving one's day in court doesn't necessarily mean that justice is
done.

Judges get things wrong. Judges fail to absorb evidence or legal
points. Lawyers fail to present evidence or make legal arguments. The
judge believes the dishonest instead of the righteous.

So if the judge gets it wrong, what can the losing party do?

Well, they can appeal, if they can afford it. What good it will do: well,
that depends.

A. What and When: Appealable Orders

When can a party appeal what the trial court has done?

Most of the time, someone appeals a "final" order or judgment. All
judgments are orders, but most orders aren't judgments. A final order may
also be called a judgment; so may an order of "summary judgment" or "partial summary judgment," described in 25.I., but as explained in a moment,
the latter may not be a *final* judgment.

Sometimes, it's simple to figure out whether a trial court's order is final. There are only two parties; they're fighting over a small set of issues;
and the order decides all these issues, with nothing left for the court to do

later (unless the winner asks the court to enforce the judgment — see Ch. 33). But it can be much more complicated than that.

What if there are multiple parties, or multiple claims? An order isn't final unless every claim, concerning every party, has been resolved. Any order issued before that time (including an order granting a partial summary judgment) is an "interlocutory" order. The general rule is that one may not immediately appeal an interlocutory order, even if one's claim has already been dealt with, unless (a) the trial court authorizes an interlocutory appeal (and at least in some states, the appellate court must agree as well), or (b) the order is one of the few (see below) that may be appealed right away without such authorization. Instead, one must wait until the case wraps up, and then add criticism of the interlocutory order to any other grounds one may have for appealing.

What about family court, where nothing ever seems to end? If the order mentions another hearing to come, or some unresolved issue (the sale of the marital home, an award of attorney fees), then it's probably not ripe for appeal. (That's oversimplifying the quite confusing issue of what sorts of future hearings keep an order from being final.)

In any given jurisdiction, there may well be a few interlocutory orders for which there's an automatic right to appeal before the case is over. While this is an area where different states may have quite different rules, these immediately appealable orders will most often be orders that can't easily be undone later on, such as orders to pay money, execute a document, or transfer real property. The refusal to transfer a case to another county or another judge would also meet this test and could well be appealable right away, before the trial takes place. A party has the right to appeal the grant, and possibly the denial, of a preliminary injunction (see 7.A.4.). Similarly, one may be able to immediately appeal the appointment or refusal to appoint a receiver (see 7.A.4. again).

Absent these exceptions, the only way to appeal a case that isn't over is to seek permission from the trial court. In Indiana, for example, if the trial court says no, that's it: the would-be appellant must wait until a final judgment is issued before appealing anything that happened on the way. If the trial court does approve an interlocutory appeal, the party must still ask the Court of Appeals if it feels like taking the appeal.

The federal courts and those of some states have a sort of hybrid procedure: the trial court, on its own or upon a party's motion, may declare that even though its order isn't final, it should be immediately appealable. Per Indiana's version of this rule (Trial Rule 54(B), matching the number of the federal rule), even when not all claims have been resolved as to all parties, the court may "direct the entry of a final judgment" anyway — so long as that judgment expressly states that it is in fact a "judgment" and "that there is no just reason for delay." In Indiana, at least, the court has to use this precise language: believe it or not, the case law concerning this rule describes the required language as "the magic words." If the magic is properly invoked, then the Court of Appeals will generally take the appeal, unless the order in question is so obviously not ripe for appeal that even magic cannot perfect it.

If a party does have the right to file an interlocutory appeal, but waits too long to file it, that party may or may not be able to raise the issue after entry of final judgment.

Even though it can be tricky to figure out whether one is entitled to appeal, one had better do so quickly, because there is often a pretty small window of time in which to get an appeal started.

This window may not be the same size in all cases. For example, under the federal rules, it's 30 days for most civil appeals, but 60 days when various federal officers or agencies are parties. Federal criminal appeals must be started within 14 days of the entry of judgment, unless the case is one of those where the government may appeal (see below) and the government does so. In those cases, the government has 30 days to appeal, after which the defendant, if they also want to appeal, gets 14 days from whenever the government filed its notice of appeal.

In some states, the time for filing the necessary initial paperwork is a true, absolute, drop-dead deadline in civil appeals. One day late is too late, period, no matter what or how much is at stake. **If you want to subject your lawyer-protagonist to appalled, heart-pounding terror (on a professional level, rather than via personal danger), then have them discover, or think they have discovered, that they miscalculated the due date for a high-stakes appeal and missed the deadline.** Better make it a civil appeal:

in at least some states, there are procedures for seeking leave to file a "be-lated" (overdue) criminal appeal.

If you want to rescue your lawyer after they've panicked for a while, put them in a state like Missouri or Illinois or Michigan. Missouri (if nothing's changed since I did my research) has a very short 10-day win-dow for filing the notice of appeal, but compensates by allowing a party to at least try for leave to file a belated civil appeal within six months after the judgment becomes final. Illinois (same caveat) has a 30-day window, but one may seek leave to file within the following 30 days with a showing of "reasonable excuse." Michigan has a 21-day window for civil appeals, with the ability to beg for mercy for up to six months from the date of the trial court order. On the other hand, if you want your lawyer to be sued for malpractice, they can miss the deadline in California, where the length of the window varies from 60 to 180 days based on all sorts of factors, and there's no escape hatch if one calculates it incorrectly. California also has various tricky rules about who must file what kind of appeal after the grant of a judgment notwithstanding the verdict (27.D.).

If there's a post-judgment motion filed in the trial court (see 32.B.), then the clock doesn't start ticking for the appeal until after that motion is granted, denied, or deemed denied. "Deemed denied" is what happens in at least some jurisdictions if the trial court takes an unduly long time to rule on the motion. The rules eventually treat the motion as effectively denied.

As long as the timing is correct, then anyone can appeal a final judg-ment, right? Wrong. In criminal cases, if the defendant is acquitted, that's the end of it. It doesn't matter how obviously and outrageously the trial court may have blundered, nor how flagrantly the jury ignored the evi-dence or the judge's instructions: the prosecution may not appeal the ac-quittal, at least not in any way that affects the result. (One possible exception: when the trial court directs a verdict in the defendant's favor or overrides the jury's guilty verdict. See 27.D.) In some jurisdictions, in a few situations, the state may be able to appeal in an attempt to clarify how things should have been done, for the sake of the future; but the defendant still goes free.

On the other hand, if a criminal case is dismissed because the state's key evidence is excluded, either because a search is held to have been illegal or for some other reason, then the prosecution may usually appeal that ruling (see 32.H.).

B. Not an Appeal: Post-Trial Motions

There's a step the losing party may take before appealing. Or rather, there's at least one such option.

In the federal system and in most or all states, one may respond to an unsatisfying judgment with a motion for a new trial. The rules don't specify what the grounds may be, except to refer to the grounds available at common law. Permissible bases for seeking a new trial include:

- The verdict goes against the weight of the evidence. This is sometimes called the "13th juror doctrine," as it involves the judge deciding that the jurors got the case so wrong that a reboot is necessary.
- The damages awarded are either excessive or inadequate. In practice, they'd better be "grossly" out of line with the evidence, and/or with how the law is supposed to be applied to the evidence.
- The judge gave one or more significantly erroneous jury instructions, or failed to give one or more important instructions.
- The judge made one or more significant errors in admitting or excluding evidence.
- The verdict was based on false testimony.
- An attorney's misconduct had a serious effect on the trial.
- Something about the way things went at trial constituted "unfair surprise." That could mean that the judge allowed evidence that should have been excluded because of the failure of the party offering it to disclose it ahead of time.
- One or more jurors were guilty of misconduct. (This is a difficult argument to make: see 19.G.)
- A party has discovered new and crucial evidence. This only works if the party had no reasonable way to find this evidence before the final judgment. If it isn't likely to change the outcome, it isn't crucial enough. The evidence can't be simply cumulative of what's already come in, and it can't be relevant only as impeaching a witness' credibility (22.H.7.).

The federal rules also allow for a "motion to alter or amend the judgment." This would let the court change the judgment rather than restarting the whole trial process. Such a motion may be filed to take advantage of a change in the law since the judgment was issued; to deal with new evidence, with the caveats already mentioned; to give the court the chance to correct a legal error; or to prevent a "miscarriage of justice." These motions are more common following bench trials (see 19.B.) or summary judgment orders (see 25.I.).

As you may have noticed, many of the possible grounds for post-trial motions amount to an attempt to persuade the trial court that it goofed. "Trial courts" being, in fact, trial judges of the human variety, a motion based on that premise is a tough sell. But a successful motion to alter or amend the judgment, in particular, would be much quicker and much cheaper than an appeal. Success is slightly more likely when the judge got confused in an easily tracked manner, or overlooked clearly applicable law of which they were informed before making the ruling.

Federal Rule of Civil Procedure 59, governing post-trial motions, only allows these motions to be filed for 28 days after the judgment is issued. States that basically follow the federal rule may have their own cutoff dates. Indiana, for example, allows 30 days.

Indiana calls its equivalent of F.R.C.P. 59 a "motion to correct error." (I've seen examples of federal motions with this name, though the federal rules don't use that terminology.) You could check other jurisdictions for any reference to a "motion to correct" or a "motion for review," which might be essentially the same critter. But take care not to confuse this motion with the much more limited motion to correct clerical errors, available in California and possibly elsewhere.

Until at least the late 1970s, Indiana's motion to correct error was a mandatory first step for any appeal. Given how rarely these motions get granted, that requirement amounted to a waste of everyone's time and resources. Nowadays, the only time a motion to correct errors is required before an appeal is when it's based on either (a) newly discovered evidence or (b) excessive or inadequate damages.

Generally, one may not raise an issue via a post-trial motion if one didn't raise it before the judgment, unless the judgment itself raised the issue for the first time (for example, if the judgment included factual findings entirely unrelated to the evidence).

Applicable rules may or may not divide what must be filed into a shorter motion and a longer brief or memo (sometimes called a "memorandum of points and authorities").

The deadline for starting an appeal will probably be "tolled" (i.e., the clock is stopped) until the judge rules on the post-trial motion — although as noted in 32.A., if the trial court is too slow to act, a time may come when the applicable rules determine that the motion shall be treated as denied, and the clock starts up again. Attorneys may file a post-trial motion even if they very much doubt it will succeed, as a way to buy time for their client to decide about (or raise money for) an appeal. If there are multiple parties on the losing side, however, one party's motion may or may not act to toll the other parties' appellate deadlines.

Trial lawyers who don't do much writing may be intimidated by the prospect of drafting this kind of motion; but they'll be a lot more familiar with what happened at trial than an appellate attorney would be. It may be a good idea for the two to collaborate.

C. Not an Appeal: Post-Conviction Relief

In criminal cases only, there's something called post-conviction relief that can happen either before, after, or instead of an appeal, and may involve quite a different procedure. While appeals, as you'll see below, concern only the record already developed in the trial court, a post-conviction petition generally claims that facts not already in the record make the conviction illegal, unconstitutional, or unjust. This sort of petition is called a "collateral" attack on the judgment, as opposed to an appeal's "direct" assault. (Caveat: this isn't the only use of the word "collateral.")

Post-conviction relief is not supposed to be a substitute for an appeal, particularly since it is often brought after the time for an appeal has expired. The hurdles tend to be even higher than those presented to appellants.

1. Not Really Better than Nothing:

Ineffective Assistance of Counsel

One of the most common bases for a post-conviction relief petition is "ineffective assistance of counsel": that the lawyer did such a poor job as to deny the accused their Sixth Amendment right to legal representation (see 2.M.).

There are usually two prongs to this argument: the lawyer's performance was so deficient that it doesn't count as "assistance," *and* the poor performance actually prejudiced (hurt) the defendant's case. If no sentient juror or judge could possibly have failed to find the defendant guilty, it won't matter how bad the lawyer was.

Often, this would be a difficult or impossible claim to assert based solely on the trial court record. In a post-conviction relief hearing, the defendant may call legal experts, experts on issues neglected at trial (e.g. psychiatric or medical conditions), and/or the original trial lawyer as witnesses. The trial lawyer's participation is likely to be pursuant to a subpoena (a summons to testify), rather than a gesture of selfless benevolence. **Fictional treatments of such testimony could include the lawyer's struggle with the temptation to lie, or at least waffle, under oath.** Of course, the state may call trial counsel and give them the more congenial task of defending their conduct of the case.

There's a strong presumption that the lawyer wasn't *that* bad. Post-conviction courts have held, and appellate courts have affirmed, that defense lawyers who slept through part of the trial or were high on narcotics weren't deficient enough to establish ineffective assistance. On the other hand, if the defense lawyer suggested that the defendant would have lied under oath if they'd testified, or if the lawyer failed to challenge any potential jurors, that might do the trick. In the latter example, the defendant probably wouldn't prevail unless many of the jurors actually ended up problematic, e.g. friends and relatives of the police.

One could test the boundaries of the pro-attorney presumption and generate suspense doing so.

There are some circumstances in which, once the defendant establishes deficient representation, the necessary prejudice is presumed. If the state interfered with the lawyer's representation of the client, or (to a lesser extent) the attorney had an actual conflict of interest in representing the client, the likelihood of prejudice is great enough that requiring proof of prejudice may be unnecessary.

A convicted defendant may also claim that an appellate attorney's representation during an appeal as of right (2.L.) was ineffective. This is a very hard argument to sell: an appellate attorney's tactical choices about which arguments to make get a great deal of deference. One probable reason: no one in the appellate court system wants to see appellate attorneys pressured to assert weak arguments, of which there could be quite a few in any appeal.

One drawback to asserting ineffective assistance of counsel in a postconviction relief petition is . . . the need for the assistance of counsel to do the job properly. While criminal defendants are still entitled to counsel on appeal — and can, as just mentioned, assert ineffective assistance of appellate counsel as well as of trial counsel — that right doesn't extend to postconviction relief proceedings.

D. Not an Appeal: Motions to Set Aside the Judgment

In the federal courts and in many states, there's a way to seek relief from a judgment even after the time to file an appeal has long since expired. Many states follow the federal system in numbering the applicable rule 60(b) (or (B)). The details are likely to vary from state to state, but here's the gist of it.

Within some fixed period, probably a year, of the date the judgment was entered, a party may file a motion to set that judgment aside on any of the following bases:

- Mistake, surprise, or excusable neglect.
- Newly discovered evidence that couldn't have been discovered in time for a post-trial motion (see 32.B., above) by the exercise of due diligence.
- Fraud, misrepresentation, or other misconduct of the adverse party.

Just what do those terms mean: "mistake," "surprise," "excusable neglect"? Nothing very well defined; and the terms overlap to some extent, as so many strings of legal terms do. "Excusable neglect" is especially tauto-logical (logically circular): neglect is "excusable" if the courts usually decide to excuse it.

Sloppiness on the part of a lawyer or a lawyer's staff isn't necessarily excusable, but sometimes it will be, if the judge sympathizes with the circumstances. If the lawyer was suddenly taken ill and not in a position to make sure something got filed, some courts would accept that as excusable. It might also be excusable to rely on an oral promise from opposing counsel to overlook some technicality. If the party is asking the court to set aside a default judgment (27.A.), and the party was for physical or logistical reasons unaware of the lawsuit or unable to respond to it (**comatose, traveling for an extended period in some remote location, lost in the wilderness, abducted by aliens**), that might also suffice for "surprise" and/or "excusable neglect."

Some states will allow a motion to set aside a judgment based on late-discovered facts that aren't strictly evidence, facts that could have formed the basis for a post-trial motion — again with the proviso that the moving party couldn't have dug up those facts before the time for a post-trial motion expired.

Once a year has passed, it gets a lot tougher. Still, within whatever the court deems a "reasonable" time under the circumstances, a party may move to set aside a judgment by claiming that:

- it's already been satisfied (by payment or agreement) or discharged (as in bankruptcy).
- it's based on an earlier judgment that's been reversed or vacated.
- it's void. This means there was some fundamental element missing. For example, if the court that issued the judgment had no jurisdiction over that type of case under state law, the judgment is void and may be challenged at any time.

Then there are two rather squishy categories.

One is related to the claim, just mentioned, that the earlier judgment has been reversed or vacated. What if the earlier judgment is still valid, but somehow the circumstances make it inequitable (unfair) to enforce it in the future? Theoretically, at least some jurisdictions, including the federal courts, will grant relief in this situation, although they're very reluctant to find that such circumstances exist. Here's an example where they might, based loosely on a hypothetical in a Florida case. Let's say a court issues an order establishing a guardianship for a terminally ill patient. Based on the available evidence, the court determines that the patient would want to be kept alive as long as possible by any means necessary, and the guardian is ordered to act on that assumption. Then, a year later, someone stumbles on the patient's health care directive, stating that the patient does not want any life-sustaining measures. A court might find it inequitable to continue to enforce the original terms of the guardianship.

Finally, there's often an open-ended catch-all provision along the lines of "any other reason that justifies relief" (that's the federal wording). Courts are generally quite leery of granting relief under this catch-all clause.

One claim still available more than one year after the judgment (under the catch-all subsection, if the rules don't list it separately) is "extrinsic" fraud or "fraud on the court." This doesn't mean that one party lied to another, even if the lie induced the latter to take some action to their detriment. Nor does it mean concealing unfavorable evidence. Those count as "intrinsic" fraud, in this context, which usually has to be alleged within a year of the judgment. Even perjury isn't enough to get around that one-year limitation. The fraud has to be both egregious (extreme, outrageous) and somehow aimed at the judicial system itself: for example, a party bribes a judge or juror, or an attorney (who's automatically considered an "officer of the court") fabricates evidence. To pass this test, the fraud must involve intentional misconduct and/or intentional intent to deceive the court.

E. Not an Appeal: Habeas Corpus Petitions

The U.S. Constitution states: "The Privileges of the Writ of Habeas Corpus shall not be suspended unless when in Cases of Rebellion or Invasion the public Safety may require it." It doesn't define the writ or describe these "privileges." Many years of case law, and several statutes, have provided the details lacking in this clause.

A habeas corpus petition says, in essence: "I'm being illegally held in government custody, and the court should order my release." With important limitations discussed below, habeas corpus petitions may be filed by those being held in federal or state government detention, whether as a result of a criminal conviction; pretrial detention; immigration/deportation cases; or military justice proceedings (courts-martial, detention by military authorities, or proceedings before military commissions). Technically, it's a civil petition filed against the government agent, e.g. a warden, who's holding a prisoner (or a "detainee") in custody; but in substance, it's a collateral attack, an attack from a different angle, directed at some stage of the criminal justice process.

A habeas corpus petition may be used to challenge pretrial detention, based on the denial of bail or alleged excessive bail (see 12.A.); a refusal to find double jeopardy (see 34.I.); the failure to provide a speedy trial (see 8.B.); or a somehow improper plan to extradite the detained person to another country. It's also one of two ways to get a federal constitutional claim into federal court after a criminal conviction in state court. The other, seeking a writ of certiorari to the U.S. Supreme Court, has long odds against getting past the first procedural obstacle. (See 32.F., next.)

For a federal habeas corpus petition, the detainee must have tried every non-federal avenue available, up to and including asking the highest state appellate court to review the case. The petition must be in a signed writing, and either the detainee or someone acting for the detainee must verify the petition's allegations (that is, affirm under penalty of perjury that the allegations are accurate to the best of that person's knowledge).

A prisoner may also file a petition for habeas corpus in state court, but this seems to be less common than filing in federal court.

A successful petition leads to a writ ordering the prisoner's release.

Congress narrowed the scope of federal habeas relief several times in the last few years of the 20th century. In 1996, Congress imposed a one-year statute of limitations; limited federal habeas relief for state prisoners to cases where the state court's determination clearly ran counter to federal law established by the U.S. Supreme Court; and required federal appellate approval of a second or later petition. A second petition by the same detainee will be dismissed out of hand unless there are new grounds the second time around. At least so far, these limitations have not been deemed a "suspension" of the writ.

Some states have similar limits in their own habeas rules.

When does the one year in the federal one-year statute of limitations start to run? That depends. The clock starts ticking at the latest of four times: (1) when the state appellate review process is complete; (2) when any illegal practical obstacle imposed by the government was removed; (3) when facts supporting the claim could be discovered, using "due diligence" (a reasonable amount of effort); or (4) when the U.S. Supreme Court declares some new right that would help the detainee and also declares that this new right applies retroactively (to past cases).

In 2005 and 2006, Congress decreed that detainees at the military base in Guantanamo Bay, Cuba, could not use the habeas procedure, being limited instead to military commissions and then appeals of commission rulings to the D.C. Circuit. However, the U.S. Supreme Court threw out that limitation in 2008.

Per case law, the executive branch (the President and those under the President's authority) can't decide it's time to suspend the writ of habeas corpus (make it unavailable) without Congress saying so first. That order of events hasn't always been followed: Abraham Lincoln suspended the writ during the Civil War without prior approval from Congress. At that time, the writ was deemed to apply only to federal prisoners; but after the Civil War, most of the Bill of Rights was gradually interpreted to bind state governments via the Fourteenth Amendment (see the intro to Ch. 34), and habeas corpus came to apply to state detainees as well.

F. Sort of an Appeal: Seeking Transfer or Cert

Whichever party loses on appeal may want to go one more rung up the ladder to the state supreme court. That's assuming the appeal wasn't one of the rare ones that are heard in the state supreme court in the first place. In some states, sentences of death, or of life imprisonment without possibility of parole, are appealed directly to the state supreme court, skipping the mid-level appellate court. If the state has a special tax court, appeals from that court may also go straight to the state supreme court. And appeals from federal courts in the Virgin Islands now go straight to the U.S. Supreme Court, bypassing the Third Circuit Court of Appeals. So if the case in your story is out of the ordinary and the appeal venue matters, double-check.

A party with a claim based on the U.S. Constitution may, after going through all available appeals on the state level, ask the U.S. Supreme Court to get involved.

Most of the time, once a party has appealed a case and lost, whether that party may go on to a state supreme court — or in the federal system, the U.S. Supreme Court — is up to that higher court. The process of asking such a court to take a case may be called petitioning for a writ of certiorari (cert for short), as in the federal system, or moving for or petitioning for transfer, or possibly something else.

Most such motions and petitions are denied. Success is more likely when the lower appellate courts in that jurisdiction don't agree on some question of law; or the lower appellate court seems to have ignored prior Supreme Court precedent; or the issue is of substantial public importance; or the case law everyone's been applying has come to seem seriously out of date.

One practical obstacle: if a criminal defendant has a state-provided attorney, the state may not be obligated to pay for such an attempt, nor for any resulting briefs and oral arguments.

One not infrequently sees headlines declaring that a state supreme court or the U.S. Supreme Court has "ruled" thus-and-so, when a closer look would show that the court did no such thing. Refusing to accept transfer or to grant cert is not a "ruling." It is a decision not to decide, and it has no value as precedent (i.e., it may not be cited in any future litigation). That decision may or may not offer a clue as to any particular judge's (or, to use a term common for supreme court judges, "justice's") views on the issue involved. Members of a supreme court may decline to take a case because it doesn't, in their view, present the issue in the clearest terms, or because there has not yet been disagreement among the lower appellate tribunals. For example, the U.S. Supreme Court's delay in taking a same-sex marriage case was probably due to how long it took for one federal appeals court to disagree with the others. **One could delve into the behind-the-scenes discussions and analyses in a controversial case, possibly a case involving a clearly presented legal issue but also a less-than-sympathetic party seeking transfer or cert.**

G. Not an Appeal:

Executive Clemency and Expungement

A pardon is official forgiveness for a crime. A pardon doesn't wipe out the record of a criminal conviction, but it puts an end to all direct penalties for that conviction. If a prisoner is pardoned, they will be released. If a criminal is out on parole, they will no longer have to meet the various conditions of that parole (see 29.F.).

It's actually possible, though quite unusual, for someone to be pardoned before they've been convicted or even tried. President Ford issued such a pardon to former President Nixon, to the dismay of many American citizens, after Nixon resigned to avoid impeachment. (See 5.C., explaining impeachment in the context of getting rid of federal judges.)

A pardon is one kind of "executive clemency." Others include the commutation (shortening) of a sentence; the remission (canceling) of a fine or an order requiring restitution; and a "reprieve," putting the criminal process on hold while some review or decision is made.

Anyone who's been convicted of a crime may ask the chief executive of the jurisdiction for executive clemency. For a federal conviction, that means the President; for a state conviction, that state's governor.

In practice, however, there may be some agency set up to handle such applications. For example, requests for federal executive clemency go to the Office of the Pardon Attorney, which is part of the U.S. Department of Justice. The Office of the Pardon Attorney investigates the underlying facts and makes a recommendation that gets signed by the Deputy Attorney General. In the rare cases where executive clemency is granted, the President signs the "warrant" granting that clemency. The application, the decision about it, and any warrant are all public records that people can get to see using the Freedom of Information Act.

In some states, the governor may not act alone to grant executive clemency: a state board of pardons either must agree, or may act independently.

Being pardoned isn't the same as having the record of the crime expunged (see below). The criminal conviction still officially happened and may continue to have consequences. However, the pardon may eliminate some of those consequences. It may serve to restore civil rights such as the right to vote, to serve on a jury, or to hold public office. Under some circumstances, it will prevent the person from being deported (evicted from the U.S.). A federal and/or state pardon may allow the convicted person to regain the right to own a firearm. The details vary from state to state, and may be mind-bogglingly convoluted. (See also 34.A.2.)

Different jurisdictions will have different rules about when one may request executive clemency. For example, a request for a federal pardon won't even be considered until at least five years after the individual's release from their most recent confinement, even if that's for a different conviction than the one for which they are seeking the pardon. That rule doesn't apply to a request for commutation of a federal sentence, or there'd be no way such a request could ever be granted.

Executive clemency is rarely granted, and pardons even less often, although the beliefs and personality of a particular executive, as well as state tradition, could make a difference. When a pardon is granted, it may be based on a criminal's repentance and reformation; or it may, even more rarely, be a recognition that the person should never have been convicted in the first place. **A newly elected governor or president could stir a great deal of controversy by making substantial use of their executive clemency powers, particularly if they focused on pardoning those convicted under laws they opposed.**

When a criminal has been sentenced to death (29.J.), requests for a reprieve, followed by a request for commutation of the sentence to life in prison (29.I.), are part of the usual prolonged process by which defense counsel tries to save their client's life. At least one state governor has commuted multiple death sentences on their way out the gubernatorial door.

Expungement, unlike executive clemency, rewrites history. It almost entirely erases a criminal conviction or an arrest from one's records. Depending on state statutes, it may be handled by a different agency than the one in charge of executive clemency, or by the courts. Some states refer to expungement with confusing terminology like "expungement pardons."

Some states only allow expungement for first-time offenders, or for juvenile offenders, or for nonviolent crimes. Some allow arrest records to be expunged if and only if there's no conviction resulting from the arrest. Some will expunge a first felony conviction, but no subsequent ones. Some will only expunge the conviction if doubt later appears as to whether the conviction was justified. Some distinguish between expungement and the more limited relief of "sealing" records from public view; others treat expungement and "sealing" as synonymous.

States may have different waiting periods for expungement of different sorts of arrests or convictions. States may also list certain convictions as too informative or too heinous to expunge. These excluded offenses may be obviously serious crimes like rape or murder, or more surprising choices, such as driving under the influence (several states) or hunting law violations (South Carolina).

A state may also limit the effect of expungement for certain crimes. For example, in California, an expunged conviction for a crime including gun violence still prevents the offender from receiving a firearm carry permit or becoming a police officer.

Once a conviction or an arrest has been expunged, the subject is no longer obligated to reveal the conviction on job applications, leases, etc. However, if they get in trouble again, the court in charge of any future criminal proceeding will probably be able to see the record of the expunged conviction and take it into account. An expunged conviction may also be relevant in future deportation proceedings.

H. Appeals by the Prosecution

Most of the time, the prosecution in a criminal case doesn't get to appeal when the defendant wins (see 32.A.). But there are a few exceptions, including these:

- The trial court grants a motion to suppress crucial evidence (see 25.H.) and the case falls apart, or is very much weakened.
- A court order puts an end to the criminal case in some other way, such as holding that it's barred by double jeopardy (34.I.) or by the

prosecution's failure to move fast enough to satisfy speedy-trial requirements (8.B.).

- The prosecution claims the judge made a mistake in sentencing the defendant.

I. Meanwhile: Stays of Appealed Orders

Like just about everything in the legal system, appeals take a long time. From start to finish, it's a rare appeal that lasts less than six months. The typical appeal lasts at least as long as a human pregnancy, and often longer than a donkey's. (The latter takes one year. This is probably not the origin of Mr. Bumble's famous dictum, "The law is an ass.") While some states require court reporters to put together the transcript of the trial or hearings in as little as 30 days, those states may grant extensions more liberally than those who allow a longer initial period (e.g. 90 days).

If the loser is stuck with the results of the trial court's decision during that time, the appeal could end up worthless. Say the defendant was ordered to pay $50,000. The plaintiff wouldn't have to try very hard to spend the whole award before the appellate court speaks up and says the defendant shouldn't have had to pay after all. If the defendant had to turn over real property, it might have a different house on it before the defendant (if successful on appeal) could get it back again. And if the judgment concerns child custody, the effects could be far more profound.

Just filing an appeal doesn't necessarily, by itself, prevent the judgment from taking effect. However, there are ways for a party who plans to appeal a judgment to seek a "stay" of the trial court's order, postponing its implementation. The process begins by filing a "Motion to Stay Pending Appeal," or something of the sort.

Where there's a money judgment, the appellant seeking a stay will generally have to ensure that enough money to pay the judgment, and more (see below), will still be available when the appeal is over. To get a stay, the appellant typically must file some sort of "security," such as an "appeal bond" or an "irrevocable letter of credit," with the court or with any entity the court designates for that purpose. The amount covered by this security will typically be the amount of the judgment, plus post-judgment interest

(30.B.1.a.) for the expected length of the appeal, plus at least some of the costs the appellee (the party who didn't start the appeal) will incur because of the appeal. And unlike bail bonds (see 12.A.), appeal bonds aren't usually available for a small fraction of the amount at stake.

In practical terms, this means that if a party is ordered to pay money damages, that party won't be able to appeal unless they could afford to put even more than the amount of the judgment on ice for several months to a year. Otherwise, the appeal can go forward, but in the meantime, the winner may still collect the judgment (see Ch. 33). Thus, those with the most compelling need to appeal may gain the least by doing so. **One could come up with various Kafkaesque scenarios illustrating this point.**

If the judgment can be paid off gradually, it may be more practical to go ahead and start paying it, hoping to get the money back if one wins on appeal. **You could chronicle the payment of installments of a money judgment while the appeal is pending, and how the party who won at trial squanders that money.**

When the fight is over something other than money, getting a stay of the judgment is likely to be a matter of persuading rather than paying, and the odds are not terrific of being sufficiently persuasive. Such non-monetary judgments could include, for example, a judgment to dissolve a partnership, or to transfer real or personal property, or to modify custody of a child, or to modify the amount or type of parenting time a noncustodial parent gets. If the appellant can get either the trial court, which just ruled against the appellant, or the court in charge of appeals, which doesn't know much about the appeal yet, to decide that things should stay the way they are until the appeal is over, then the appellant can get a stay. **The denial of a stay in such circumstances has plenty of dramatic possibilities, as the harm threatened by the trial court judgment draws closer or begins, while the appeal drags on.**

If property with a known value is at stake, an appeal bond or similar security may well be required, just as with a judgment for money damages.

If the judgment actually preserved the status quo ante (the state of affairs before the judgment was issued), and the appellant's hoping to change things, a stay is unlikely. In that situation, getting a motion for a stay granted is a sign of a crackerjack lawyer and/or a very strong appeal.

J. Apples and Appeals: What the Appellate Court Will and Won't Consider

The idea that one only gets "one bite at the apple" (see Ch. 28) applies to appeals as well. Most often, an appeal is not a factual do-over. The appellate court reviews the existing trial court record. Only under very limited circumstances may a party offer any new evidence on appeal. (One of those circumstances: when the trial court has denied a post-trial motion (32.B.) for a new trial based on recently discovered evidence.) The court will, however, review a trial court's decision to exclude evidence, at least if the appellant's attorney made an offer of proof at trial (see 22.M.).

Appellate courts recognize that the trial judge, who sees and hears the witnesses, is in a much better position to assess the witnesses' testimony than an appellate judge reviewing a "cold" record. That's why, in some states, the appellate court will accept the trial court's call on a disputed factual issue, as long as there is *any* evidence that supports that call. Other states use a slightly more demanding "substantial evidence" standard. Similarly, appellate courts will usually uphold a jury verdict supported by substantial evidence (in some states) or any evidence (in others), as long as it's consistent with the applicable law.

In reviewing a jury's guilty verdict, the standard will be whether the evidence was sufficient to allow rational jurors to find the defendant guilty beyond a reasonable doubt (see 20.C.). Any conflict in the evidence will be resolved in favor of the conviction.

Besides the fact that the trial judge or the jury sees and hears the witnesses, complete with facial expressions and body language, there's also an institutional preference for finality. The judicial system tends to limit the reasons for any kind of trial court reboot.

In some states, however, at least in certain kinds of cases, the appellate court will look at the evidence presented at trial with a fresh eye, judging the weight of the evidence each way, while still deferring somewhat to the trial judge's assessment. This is called de novo review (law Latin for "anew"). Last time I researched the matter, the states with de novo appellate review for at least some appeals included Iowa (for all equity cases (see

19.B.)); Nebraska (for equity cases where the appellant seeks review of factual findings, instead of just making a legal argument); and Oregon (only in appeals of termination of parental rights (14.H.13.)). Missouri doesn't *say* it allows de novo review, but its appellate courts may reverse judgments in equity cases if those judgments are deemed contrary to the weight of the evidence.

In the federal appellate courts, a trial court's findings of fact in a civil bench trial are reviewed for "clear error," a fairly difficult standard to meet (though it's not quite as deferential to the trial court as the "any supporting evidence and it's upheld" standard mentioned above). Conclusions of law, on the other hand, are reviewed de novo. In this context, de novo review doesn't mean reweighing facts, but rather, assessing the legal issue without deference to how the trial court analyzed it. A federal jury's verdict will be upheld on appeal if it is supported by "substantial evidence" and isn't based on any legal errors.

In criminal cases up on federal appeal, the appellate courts still apply the "clear error" standard to factual questions, and the de novo standard to legal conclusions; but it won't rely on an alternate justification for the ruling if the judge's reasoning was wrong.

In a state with a distinction between required and optional specific findings (see 27.F.), the appellate court may approach the latter differently. In Indiana, for example, when a party has requested findings and conclusions, at least some evidence must support the findings, and the findings must legally support the conclusions, or the appellate court must reverse the trial court's decision. When the trial court doesn't have to make findings and doesn't bother to do so, the judgment may be affirmed based on any evidence in the record and any legal theory that fits that evidence. This is called a "general judgment" standard of review. If a trial court makes findings sua sponte (on its own initiative), the stricter standard of review applies to any facts or legal points the findings and conclusions address, but if those optional findings and/or conclusions fail to address any issue, the general judgment standard takes over as to that issue. For example, if a defendant in a civil case raised the affirmative defense of estoppel (see 7.A.2. and Ch. 17), and the trial court ruled in the defendant's favor without mentioning estoppel, the appellate court could still uphold that judgment if the evidence supported an estoppel defense, as long as neither party asked for specific findings and conclusions.

It may not be obvious to the parties, and isn't always obvious to lawyers, what is a question of fact, on which the appellate court will defer at least somewhat to the trier of fact, and what is a question of law, as to which the appellate court does its own analysis. This distinction is also key in resolving motions for summary judgment (25.I.), which may be granted only when no real controversy exists on any significant question of fact.

Questions of law include, for example, what burden of proof (see Ch. 20) applies to a particular set of facts; what a statute or part of a statute means; whether a statute of limitations (see Ch. 11) has expired; whether a written contract is ambiguous (14.C.7.); and whether allowing a child of some particular age to play unsupervised or to stay home alone constitutes neglect.

In one 1995 Alabama case, a couple advertised a house as "new" even though they were living in it. The buyers knew that, and also signed a contract saying they were buying the house "as is." The house had defects the buyers hadn't known about, and the buyers sued the sellers and the real estate broker for fraud. The trial court granted summary judgment for defendants. The Alabama Supreme Court reversed, on the ground that if the house were new, there would be an implied warranty of habitability (i.e., that it meets certain minimum requirements in such areas as heat, water, plumbing, and freedom from vermin — see also 14.D.9.). That raised a question of fact as to whether the house was actually "new" as defined by law. (However, in 2010 Alabama changed its judicial mind on the legal issue involved, holding that an "as is" real estate contract precludes any action for fraud.)

Where an issue concerns the law of some foreign jurisdiction, if there is no straightforward way for the court to take judicial notice of that law (see 22.L.), the party who wants to rely on it will have to prove it as a question of fact.

"Mixed" questions of law and fact require delicate handling on appeal. Courts are not fully consistent as to how to handle these. Some try to disentangle the factual and legal threads, applying the usual standards of review to the separate legal and factual issues. Others use a "sliding scale," giving more or less deference to the trial court according to how important the factual and legal components appear. Still others pick either the more deferential or less deferential standard and apply it to the whole messy problem.

The following issues, for example, might be seen as presenting mixed questions of law and fact:

- Whether someone sued for negligence had a duty of care, if the facts of the defendant's relationship to the plaintiff are in dispute.
- Whether an enforceable contract exists, which would depend on what happened between the parties as well as on contract law.
- Whether a defendant voluntarily waived the right to remain silent (34.D.) or the right to counsel (see 2.M.), which involves reconstructing what took place and then applying constitutional law to those events.
- Whether a victim's identification of the defendant in a lineup or show-up satisfies due process concerns (see 22.H.10. and 34.G.), which depends both on what took place and on the constitutional requirements for such procedures.

Finally, an important though seldom acknowledged tactical point: even where there's no de novo review, and the appellate court is supposed to view the facts in a light favorable to the judgment, the applicable law often provides some degree of wiggle room. If appellate counsel finds a way, within the procedural limitations (or dancing along the edge of them), to describe the facts in a way that makes the appellate court *want* to provide some relief, the court can frequently find a way to do it.

1. "Harmless" as Opposed to Reversible Error

Try hard enough, pore over the transcript long enough, and one can find some sort of error in many or most trials. But not every error is considered "reversible error," error important enough to justify a complete or partial do-over.

Error that's not serious enough to justify relief on appeal is called "harmless error." What constitutes harmless error may vary from one jurisdiction to another. Sometimes the court will say that a particular error does not affect any "substantial right" of the party concerned. Sometimes the formulation will be that there must be a substantial probability that the verdict would have been different if not for the error. In criminal trials, where the defendant claims some piece of evidence should not have been admitted, and where the court finds "overwhelming" evidence of guilt even without that evidence, any error in admitting the challenged evidence will be considered harmless error.

But what if the defendant is appealing the exclusion of evidence, rather than admission of evidence? If the evidence was "highly relevant and necessary," or was a key piece in building the structure of defendant's case, its exclusion is reversible error. Even where evidence could be called "cumulative," repeating some point made by other evidence, excluding it may be reversible error if that point would have been more impressive with additional corroboration. A finding of reversible error is particularly likely if the excluded evidence would have corroborated the defendant's version of what took place.

If the claimed error in a criminal trial was the denial of some constitutional right, the reviewing court must decide whether the error was harmless beyond a reasonable doubt.

If the error consisted of denying a criminal defendant's right to cross-examine an adverse witness for impeachment purposes, the court must assume "that the damaging potential of the cross-examination [would have been] fully realized." The factors to be weighed include, per a 1986 U.S. Supreme Court case, "the importance of the witness' testimony in the prosecution's case, whether the testimony was cumulative, the presence or absence of evidence corroborating or contradicting the testimony of the witness on material points, the extent of cross-examination otherwise permitted, and, of course, the overall strength of the prosecution's case."

Certain types of error that affect the fundamental fairness of the trial itself may never be deemed harmless. For example, complete denial of the right to legal counsel is per se (automatically) harmful, because it is the attorney's job to protect all the other rights the defendant has. Denial of the right to a jury trial is another, given the great latitude juries have to focus on justice and fairness rather than legal technicalities (see 19.G.).

2. Invited Error

Another kind of error that gets an appellant nowhere: "invited error." If, at trial, a party asked the court to do something, or clearly accepted the court's doing something, then that party can't turn around and holler "reversible error!" about it.

This could be called an equitable principle in action; or, for Yiddish speakers, a "limitation of chutzpah" rule.

3. Waived Error versus Fundamental Error

Normally, if a party doesn't object to something at trial, when the trial judge could still do something about it, the party has waived (given up) any claim to assert that error on appeal. But some errors are so important that they can't be waived, though courts won't always agree in detail as to what they are. The general category is called "fundamental error," and it's discussed in more detail back in 22.M.1.

4. Holes in the Record

As I've already mentioned, appellate courts base their decisions on the record of what took place at trial. But what if that record has holes in it?

Records can be incomplete for various reasons. A judge may habitually decline to have the court reporter record "bench conferences," where the judge and attorneys huddle together briefly to discuss some procedural issue. A court reporter might have enough trouble keeping up with a fast-talking witness, or hearing a mumbling witness, or understanding a witness not fluent in English, that bits of testimony go unrecorded or are recorded inaccurately. The court reporter's recording could be lost or damaged or destroyed, due to anything from floods to tornadoes to electrical surges.

The trial or appellate rules will generally include some procedure for reconstructing missing transcripts or missing portions of transcripts. Pro se litigants (see 2.K.) are often unaware that such procedures exist, and therefore more likely to go into an appeal with some crucial portion of the record missing. Trial lawyers who seldom handle appeals may share such ignorance.

These procedures may be quite challenging, involving not just piecing together what occurred, but getting opposing parties and/or the judge to agree on what happened and/or on who said what. If these folks can't agree, the rules may require that the competing narratives be placed in the official record for the appellate court to wrestle with.

K. Appellate Briefs (Which Aren't) and Cross-Appeals

Appellate courts typically look at a typed transcript of the trial court proceedings (prepared by the court reporter once an appeal gets started) and at the exhibits admitted at trial, plus whatever motions and such the attorneys filed with the trial court.

Some jurisdictions have looked into using videos of the trial instead of typed transcripts. This has some serious logistical disadvantages. Transcripts these days typically exist in electronic as well as typed form, which makes them easily searchable. Finding a particular word or phrase in a video? Not so easy. And in writing their briefs, instead of citing an easily consulted numbered page, the attorneys would have to cite the exact moment of the tape, designated by a counter of some kind; and the appellate judge or clerk reading the brief would have to scoot around in the tape to find the cited testimony or argument. A pilot project to use videos on appeal just died in Indiana, and I wasn't a bit surprised.

But the appellate judges don't just sit down and go through the record to decide what they think of it. They depend on the lawyers for the appellant (the one bringing the appeal) and the appellee (the one happy with the judgment) to guide them through. To do that, the attorneys write "briefs," usually not-so-brief presentations of why the trial court did or didn't make the right decision(s). The specific format will vary from state to state, but can be found in the state court rules. Typically, the appellant files an opening brief; the appellee files a response; and the appellant gets the last word.

Briefs may seem long now to the weary appellate judge, but they used to be longer. For example, until 1980, the U.S. Supreme Court put no limits on the lengths of briefs, and in consequence regularly received monsters several hundred pages long. Finally fed up, the Court limited briefs to a maximum of 50 pages unless a party received permission to run on longer. More recently, in 2007, the Court switched to word limits (15,000 words for the main briefs and 7,500 for reply briefs).

What if the trial court didn't make anybody altogether happy? If both sides want to appeal, that'll alter the process somewhat. In all the jurisdictions I know about (which does *not* necessarily mean all U.S. jurisdictions), if the appellee also wants to appeal some aspect of the judgment, the appellee doesn't have to say so until after the appellant has filed a notice of appeal. At that time, the appellee can decide to "cross-appeal." How much time the appellee has to start a cross-appeal, how that's done, and what happens next will all depend on that jurisdiction's court rules.

In Indiana, for example, the appellee's brief may also be a "cross-appellant's" brief, and that can be the first clue anyone has that a cross-appeal is happening. The appellant would then file a combination of a "reply brief," the appellant's usual last word, and a brief responding to the cross-appeal. In this scenario, the original appellee, as a cross-appellant, files the final reply brief. In Alaska, on the other hand, a cross-appeal must start with a notice of appeal, just like the initial appeal.

Whether there's an advantage to being the initial appellant or the cross-appellant may depend on the rules of that particular jurisdiction, as well as on what the particular attorney considers an advantage. For example, some lawyers would prefer to file the first brief, while others prefer to have the last word. Where, as in the federal court system, the initial appellant may file a longer brief, some attorneys will relish that opportunity, while others pay more attention to the pleas of many appellate judges to be concise.

By the way, the Federal Rules of Appellate Procedure didn't provide much guidance about cross-appeals until 2005.

Attorneys who aren't used to handling appeals can get themselves in trouble writing appellate briefs. Some state appellate courts are very sticky about getting the format right and won't accept a brief that isn't 100% in compliance, though the attorney may get a few days to fix what's wrong. As for substance: if, as is true in many states, the appellate court always takes the trial court's side in any factual dispute (see 32.J.), then the appellate attorney has to argue that even assuming the trial court believed the right witnesses and exhibits, it *still* made reversible legal errors. In these jurisdictions, one may not re-argue the facts, and doing so will just annoy the tribunal, which is never a good idea.

It makes matters worse if an attorney indulges in snarky language, or makes veiled or explicit accusations of incompetence, corruption, or fraud on the part of opposing counsel. Most attorneys, experienced or no, have more sense than to do this — but it does happen. One sees such behavior more often when appellants go pro se (2.K.). This sort of improper attitude can get an appeal dismissed, sometimes with the party and/or attorney ordered to pay the other party's attorney fees. **It could be a particularly bad idea to badmouth the trial court judge, who may have previously been a colleague or even a mentor of one of the appellate judges.**

L. Thinking on Your Feet: Appellate Oral Argument

Some appellate courts routinely hold oral argument, where each attorney has some period of time (typically 20 or 30 minutes) to highlight important points and answer the judges' questions. In other appellate courts, oral argument is rare, with the court deciding the case based only on the written materials. In those courts, the appellant may request oral argument, but that request isn't necessarily granted. Courts where oral argument is the exception may order it where the briefs leave some aspects of the issues unexplored, or where the panel is undecided and wants a chance to explore the matter as fully as possible. Some appellate courts also have what attorneys irreverently refer to as "road shows," holding oral arguments outside their usual chambers in venues such as law schools, other schools, and retirement homes. These appeals are often chosen more for their relevance to the community than for their difficulty or importance.

If the appellate judges go into the argument well informed about the case, the judging panel is informally referred to as a "hot bench." Such judges will have little patience with a lawyer who wastes their time repeating the basics of the case. With a "cold bench," however, one had better start by getting the judges up to speed. Appellate attorneys should know enough about the appellate court in question to be able to predict which type of panel they'll be facing. **If you want to show a new attorney's embarrassing mistakes, those mistakes could include a presentation aimed at the wrong type of judging panel.**

It's a good idea for attorneys approaching their first oral argument in a particular appellate court to pull up videos, if available, of the court's previous oral arguments. If the court discloses ahead of time which judges will be on the panel, the attorney can study the questioning style of those judges. If the court keeps that information secret until the day of the argument, as some do, the attorney can simply look at a series of arguments to be sure of seeing all the judges in action. More generally, many attorneys' preparation for oral argument includes "moot," or mock, oral arguments with other attorneys playing the part of judges and asking the toughest questions they can dream up.

Oral arguments are not, not, NOT evidentiary hearings. No one is sworn, no one testifies, and no new evidence may be introduced — although the issue may concern whether new evidence should be brought before the trial court, in which case the nature of that evidence will be discussed.

The attorneys take turns, with the appellant going first. Usually, the appellant has the choice of saving a portion of the allotted time for a final word.

Attorneys usually prepare a statement to recite or read to the panel, but they often don't get to use much of it. Sometimes the attorney will barely get through a sentence or two before being peppered with questions. These questions may or may not provide hints as to which way the judge is leaning. Some judges tend to play "Devil's advocate" regardless of whether they're inclined to agree with the attorney's position.

If for any reason an attorney brings the client along, the attorney had better prepare the client for the customary questioning, **or the client, particularly a nervous or suspicious client, could lose confidence in the attorney's competence.**

What if the attorney is answering one judge's question when another judge interrupts with a new question? At least in some courts, it's proper protocol to answer the second question while hoping for an opportunity to finish the answer to the first question afterward. Some chief judges or chief justices, including Chief Justice Roberts of the U.S. Supreme Court, will act as traffic cops to assist attorneys in this situation.

Judges may use their questions to the attorney as a way of talking to other judges on the panel, addressing points the judges have already raised in preliminary discussions and seeking answers that will bolster the position taken by the questioning judge.

It occasionally happens that one of the judges confuses two somewhat similar cases and starts asking questions based on the wrong case. **You could challenge your lawyer character to straighten out this confusion diplomatically.**

One common error attorneys make in oral argument — and this really, really annoys the judges — is to evade the question. Who do they think they're fooling? If the attorney doesn't know the answer, they should say so, give a tentative answer if possible, and offer to submit a supplementary brief (unless the court rules explicitly prohibit such briefs). If the answer will be unfavorable, the attorney needs to squirm as little as possible, give the bad news briefly, and then find ways to say why the unfavorable aspect is unimportant or doesn't really apply. **You could show a young lawyer learning this lesson the hard way from an exasperated judge.**

And speaking of newbie mistakes: one may address the judge by name (Judge Black, Justice White, Mr. Chief Justice Gray) or simply as "your Honor," but if you go with the name, you'd better get the judge's name right. . . .

Another major blunder, one that some male lawyers still make (no doubt without realizing it), is to talk over questions asked by female judges, while giving proper deference to male judges. Believe me, the female judges will notice.

M. Amicus Curiae, aka Kibbitzing on Appeal

Sometimes an appeal — especially, though not always, an appeal that's reached a state supreme court or the U.S. Supreme Court — involves a legal or public policy issue in which many people besides the parties are interested. In such cases, there's a mechanism whereby outsiders can get a word in. A nonparty who files a brief (or, less often, participates in oral argument) is called an amicus curiae (amicus for short), or "friend of the court." ("Kibbitzing," for those unfamiliar with that Yiddish term, means looking over someone's shoulder and giving advice.)

The mechanisms for permitting an amicus to take part vary from court to court. Sometimes the parties have the ability to smooth the way or to leave procedural hurdles in place.

An amicus often focuses on the big picture rather than on how the law applies to the particular facts before the court. It's a good idea for an amicus who supports one side to coordinate with the attorney(s) representing that side, to avoid repeating arguments the party will already make. (Since the parties' briefs have higher priority, an amicus must take special care to write concisely and avoid wasting the time of judges and staff, who could easily just quit reading.)

It's quite common for an amicus brief to rely heavily on sources other than case law, such as scientific and/or sociological research. Briefs, whether submitted by parties or by amici curiae (yeah, a Latin plural), that cite many of such sources are called "Brandeis briefs," after Louis Brandeis. Before Brandeis got to the U.S. Supreme Court, he pioneered the use of briefs like this. Not everyone in the legal community is a fan of Brandeis briefs. Opponents focus on the niggling little detail that few or none of the cited studies, which are essentially sets of factual assertions, have been admitted in evidence in the case in question. (See the related discussion in 22.L.)

If an amicus does take part in oral argument, the amicus' attorney will have to share the time allocated to the party the amicus is supporting. This probably explains why amicus briefs are more common than amicus appearances at oral argument.

N. Appellate Opinions

There's quite a bit of variety in the decisions, aka opinions, that appellate courts write. They can be dry and technical, or sprinkled with vivid images and footnoted references to popular culture (e.g. *Star Trek*). **You could come up with an appellate judge whose analogies and metaphors reflected their hobbies, be they skiing or video games.** **You could also feature a judge with gradually escalating mental illness, and their increasingly cryptic or even violent written imagery.**

Appellate opinions can be based on the facts of a particular case, or broader in scope. For example, *Bush v. Gore*, the U.S. Supreme Court decision that resolved the November 2000 presidential election, at least claimed that its holding was confined to the unique facts of that case.

Many jurisdictions distinguish between "published" cases and "unpublished" cases, or between "opinions" and "memorandum decisions," or some such categories. These days, both types of case may be published online and available to researchers. The difference: the first category is supposed to be "precedent" controlling the decisions of the decisions of lower courts (and in some states, courts at the same level), while it's either discouraged or outright prohibited to cite the second category in a brief or argument. **This can be incredibly frustrating for a lawyer who finds the perfect case and can't cite it, and/or a trap for the careless or inexperienced lawyer who doesn't know the difference.** Some appellate lawyers deal with this limitation by borrowing, verbatim, portions of the case they can't cite.

One interesting aspect of appellate decisions is the occasional use of "dicta." "Dicta" (Latin plural for "word" or "saying," though generally treated as a singular noun) is a statement in an opinion that isn't actually essential for the resolution of the case. Some judges are such good writers that their dicta is often quoted and later becomes the rule. (Of course, it helps if that later case comes to the same court while the judge is still there.) The more powerful the court, the more impact dicta will have. **If your judge character is particularly eloquent and/or eccentric, dicta would be a good place for those qualities to show up.**

"Concurring" opinions agree generally, but not entirely, with the majority opinion. Their points, too, often become the law later on.

O. Round Two: When Appellate Courts Remand the Case

An appellate court may "reverse" a trial court judgment, saying it should come out the other way. Frequently, however, the court will "remand" the case without reversing. A remand might send the case back to the trial court for a new trial on one or more issues; or the remand may require some other trial court action, such as a more complete explanation of why the trial court decided as it did.

Depending on the state or local rules, when a case is remanded to the trial court, and especially if any new (or previously excluded) evidence is to be considered, the appellant may have a short window in which to ask that a new trial judge be appointed. This is often a good idea, as judges who believed themselves to have made the right call in the first place will often find a way to reach the same conclusion in spite of the new evidence being forced down their metaphorical throats. **However, in counties where there are few judges available, the personalities and abilities of the particular judges could make this a complicated or difficult choice.**

Whether with a new judge or the original one, a remand that involves the presentation of new evidence is going to be an expensive victory, with legal fees for trial preparation (including preparation of any witnesses) and the trial or hearing itself.

CHAPTER 33

Collecting the Spoils:
Enforcement of Judgments

Most romance novels and movies end shortly before, during, or shortly after the wedding. Similarly, many courtroom dramas involving civil cases end with the jury awarding some huge sum while the victors rejoice. Anyone who's been married knows that the wedding is just the beginning of the drama. The same holds true with collecting a judgment.

If the defendant appealed and had to post an appeal bond or similar security before appealing (see 32.I.), then at least the money is there to be got at. But most judgments aren't appealed.

In auto accident cases and other actions where the defendant has applicable insurance, it will probably be relatively straightforward to collect the judgment from the insurer. Insurance companies are used to paying out after settlements or (more rarely) verdicts, and can be expected to be pretty businesslike about it. Corporate defendants will also generally accept the need to pay up at this point, rather than to expend corporate resources on ultimately fruitless evasive maneuvers. But in many civil cases, there's no insurer or corporation from which to collect.

One generally can't start collecting a judgment until it's clear whether the loser is filing an appeal and seeking a stay (32.I. again). If there's an appeal plus a stay, the tentative winner can't collect until the appeal is officially over. One consolation for the delay: one generally gets something extra out of it. As discussed in 30.B.1.a., states set a rate of "post-judgment interest" to be added to all money judgments, usually starting from the date the judgment was entered, in order to compensate the winner for any delay in cashing in. If the lawsuit involved a contract that had a different rate, the latter will apply.

Of course, collecting that interest is just part of the overall task of collecting the judgment.

How does that work? Well, depending on the temperament and the financial situation of the loser (the "judgment debtor"), the winner (the "judgment creditor") may have to go back to court. So much for any momentary illusion of having finally escaped that purgatory!

The proceedings for collecting a judgment are known as "proceedings supplemental" or "proceedings supplementary" ("pro supp" for short). In this round of hearings, the judgment creditor's attorney and/or the court will try to dredge up all the details about the judgment debtor's income and assets. The court can order the judgment debtor's wages, salary, or accounts receivable to be "garnished", meaning partially withheld by the payor (that's whoever would normally be paying the judgment debtor). That portion will instead be paid to the judgment creditor or to the court. State or federal law may limit what percentage of the judgment debtor's income may be garnished.

There's another device similar to garnishment, used frequently in divorces, to ensure payment of installments of a property settlement or child support, and also in Chapter 13 bankruptcies (see 14.R.): an "Income Withholding Order," often called an IWO for short. Proceeds from such an order normally go to a court or to some state agency in charge of processing such payments. The limits on what percentage of income may be scooped up by an income withholding order may differ from the limits for garnishment.

If the judgment debtor's cash resources and cash flow are insufficient to pay the judgment, the judgment creditor can try going after non-liquid assets like real estate, vehicles, or miscellaneous personal property. This is typically more expensive and time-consuming than garnishment.

The animosity between the parties, however intense it may be after months or years of litigation and possibly of appeals, can reach new heights (or depths) when the impact of the judicial result becomes so tangible and potentially life-altering for the loser.

CHAPTER 34

The Constitution in the Courtroom

he U.S. Constitution sets some limits on what the government
may do in the courtroom. These rights surface mainly, but not
entirely, in the context of criminal trials.

These protections are found in the Bill of Rights, namely the first ten
Amendments to the Constitution, and in the Fourteenth Amendment.
The Fourteenth Amendment was passed soon after the end of the Civil
War, and has gradually been interpreted to "incorporate" some of the Bill
of Rights. That means that while the Bill of Rights only limits what the
federal government is allowed to do, the Fourteenth Amendment extended certain protections so that they restrict the power of state governments.
To date, the First, Second, and Fourth Amendments have been fully "incorporated," as have most of the Fifth Amendment (all except the portion
dealing with grand juries) and the Sixth Amendment (all except the restrictions on where jurors should reside), and that portion of the Eight
Amendment dealing with cruel and unusual punishment (but not the portion dealing with excessive fines, while the legal picture is confused as to
excessive bail). The U.S. Supreme Court hasn't dealt with whether the
Third Amendment has been incorporated, but the Second Circuit Court of
Appeals has held that it is.

If your story is set anywhere between 1873 and the early or middle
1920's, the Bill of Rights should be viewed as limiting only federal power.

The Fourteenth Amendment has also been held to protect some rights
that aren't spelled out either there or in the Bill of Rights. How this came

about is quite a tale, but not one I'll try to shoehorn into this book. We'll get to the result in a bit.

A. First, Some Constitutional Rights Not Directly Courtroom-Related

We've already touched on some constitutionally protected rights that make a difference in the courtroom: the rights to a speedy trial (8.B.), to trial by jury (19.B.), to the "beyond a reasonable doubt" standard for criminal trials (20.C.), and to assistance of counsel in criminal and a few other trials (2.M.). Before we get to other rights of this kind (see 34.B. through 34.K. in particular), let's discuss some constitutional rights that don't directly deal with the judicial system, but do restrict what someone may be sued for and what the state may criminalize. These rights include the rights set forth in the First and Second Amendments. I've mentioned the First Amendment in discussing invasion of privacy (14.F.7.), but read on for a more comprehensive overview.

I'll also be talking about a Fifth Amendment right unrelated to "taking the Fifth": a property owner's right to receive payment when the government decides it wants that property.

---

1. The First Amendment

The First Amendment plus the Fourteenth (see the intro to this chapter) prevent the federal, state, and local governments and their agents from:

- "establish[ing]" any religion;
- "prohibiting the free exercise" of any religion;
- "abridging" the "freedom of speech," the "freedom of the press," "the right of the people peaceably to assemble," and the right of the people "to petition the government for a redress of grievances."

None of these restrictions on government power are straightforwardly defined, and the definitions keep changing. What government actions constitute an "establishment of religion" is a particularly tangled thicket, with frequent litigation about whether a town hall may open with a prayer (currently, yes, if the prayers are theoretically open to all religions) and whether religious symbols such as Nativity scenes may be erected with public funds or on government property (currently, no, unless there actually are a variety of comparable secular displays in the same location as well).

As for what constitutes an unconstitutional restriction on the free exercise of religion: the current general rule is that a government may prohibit behavior in a general way, even if that prohibition happens to cover someone's religiously inspired behavior such as drug use or animal sacrifice. However, the federal government's ability to do this has been restricted by federal statute, and the same is true in some states, with varying caveats. The usual label: "Religious Freedom Restoration Act," or RFRA. The controversial U.S. Supreme Court case commonly called "the Hobby Lobby case," holding that Congress couldn't require a privately held corporation to fund activities that violated its owners' religious beliefs, involved the federal RFRA, not a claim under the Free Exercise clause of the First Amendment.

Freedom of speech covers only *government* restrictions on speech. If, for example, a magazine refuses to publish certain points of view, that's not "censorship" in the sense of a violation of the First Amendment: the magazine, as a private entity, has every right to decide what speech it will tolerate.

The definition of "free speech" has been stretched over the years to include a good deal of nonverbal-but-expressive conduct, such as nude dancing (if the context is arguably artistic). It can also include loudly airing one's displeasure at what a police officer is doing, though at some point such conduct could shade over into "disorderly conduct," "disturbing the peace," or interfering with the officer's performance of their duties" (see 13.O.). When someone yells obscenities or insults at a police officer, states may differ as to whether police officers should be treated as having a higher threshold of endurance than the general public. More generally, there is often a two-stage analysis:

1. Did the state restrict expressive activity?

2. Did the defendant "abuse" their free speech rights to the point that they're no longer protected?

The court may combine several balancing tests, looking at how much the state interfered with the speech, and at how much of a nuisance or injury the defendant's conduct imposed on bystanders, nearby property owners, etc. If the speech had political content, even if liberally larded with obscene emphasis, the state will have to show more in the way of damage done.

Free speech definitely includes expressing unpopular and "offensive" opinions and trying to persuade people to come around to those opinions. That's why rules that try to "protect" students at public universities from being offended or upset run afoul of First Amendment concerns.

What about "fighting words"? The idea that some insults provide so much provocation as to put them outside First Amendment protection comes from the 1942 *Chaplinsky* case, in which the U.S. Supreme Court held that calling a city official a "damn racketeer" and a "damn Fascist" fell into an unprotected "fighting words" category. The Court defined "fighting words" as words "which, by their very utterance, inflict injury or tend to incite an immediate breach of the peace." It elaborated the latter as "epithets likely to provoke the average person to retaliation, and thereby cause a breach of the peace."

During the latter part of the 20th century, the Supreme Court retreated somewhat from that earlier position, emphasizing that provocative speech likely to lead to disputes and anger was still generally protected. To the extent the "fighting words" doctrine survives, it now refers only to personal insults directed at specific people, and does not allow even those insults to be punished under statutes that could also be used to punish a broader variety of offensive statements.

State and lower federal courts have often disagreed as to just what insults may still be treated as crimes. As already mentioned, there may be a tendency to treat insults directed at police officers as constitutionally protected comments on governmental activity, where the same insults aimed at a private citizen would have no such protection.

Some state college administrators, whose colleges come within the rules for governmental institutions, fall back on the fact that the Supreme

Court never explicitly overruled *Chaplinsky* as allowing them to prohibit "offensive" speech. This argument has not fared well in the courts.

Another much-misunderstood notion is "clear and present danger," for which the best-known example is shouting "Fire!" in a crowded theater. This example was used in a 1919 U.S. Supreme Court case that actually involved a very different sort of speech, namely encouraging young men to resist the draft during World War I. (This period was not exactly a high water mark for U.S. civil liberties.) If speech posed a "clear and present danger" of leading to consequences the government could legitimately seek to prevent, it could be prohibited and punished.

The Supreme Court overturned this ruling around fifty years later. Abandoning the "clear and present danger" standard, the Court held that speech could not be made illegal unless it incited "imminent lawless action." "All of you go out right now and burn down the theater!" would presumably qualify.

What about falsely hollering about a fire for the fun of watching people stampede out of the theater? Recall that no such event was actually involved in the U.S. Supreme Court case that introduced this image. I'm not aware that anyone has ever been charged with a crime, let alone been sued, for such conduct. Despite the overruling of that 1919 case's actual holding, which didn't involve this scenario, there's a decent argument that one could charge such a mischief-maker with the crime of disturbing the peace (13.O.), or that one of the victims could sue them for intentional infliction of emotional distress (14.F.8.). Not every use of language constitutes protected speech: blackmail (13.K.) and intimidation (13.L.) are examples of crimes perpetrated by the use of words. The key could be whether the court viewed the false exclamation as fundamentally expressive, or as conduct that happened to involve a verbal utterance. **Feel free to explore the matter further and tell the story.**

Governments may regulate the "time, place, and manner" of speech. These regulations may protect such interests as keeping public grounds undamaged and maintaining the flow of traffic. However, such rules must be content-neutral, or else pass the very restrictive "strict scrutiny" test (see 34.G.), which they're unlikely to do. For example, as the U.S. Supreme Court clarified in June 2015, a town may not have separate rules for size, total display time, etc. for signs, depending on whether the signs are "ideological," "political," or "temporary directional." These distinctions flunk the "strict scrutiny" test for content-based restrictions on speech, since they don't further a compelling governmental interest and aren't "narrowly tailored" to serve such an interest.

For some reason, discussions of how public demonstrations may be regulated rarely analyze the question in terms of "freedom of assembly" or the freedom to petition . . . for a redress of grievances," the neglected metaphorical stepchildren of the First Amendment. However, all these rights together have been held to provide "freedom of association": the right to gather, physically or otherwise, for political, religious, or cultural reasons. This concept arose in the 1950s and 1960s.

Freedom of the press was a simpler concept back when everyone knew what and who a journalist was. With the advent of the Internet, blogging, etc., the boundaries of this protection have expanded, but just how far is not yet clearly established. (See also 14.F.3.)

Freedom of the press includes some degree of access to information about governmental operations and activities, with many and varying limitations. These limitations flow from, e.g., the need to preserve the privacy of individuals mentioned in such records, the desirability of allowing frank debate in legislative bodies, and on the federal level at least, national security.

"Shield laws" in almost every state provide protection for reporters who consider it necessary to keep their sources confidential. (The first such law was passed in 1898, the second not until 33 years later, but by 1973 half the states had passed shield laws of their own.) There is no shield law at the federal level, but as of 1972, journalists have a "qualified" privilege to refuse to disclose their sources. To overcome that privilege, the government must "convincingly show a substantial relation between the information sought and a subject of overriding and compelling state interest."

"Prior restraint" of speech by government is rarely permitted. Whether the government outright prohibits speech that hasn't been spoken, e.g. by getting an injunction (30.A.) against it, or makes the speaker get a permit before speaking, that's almost always an unconstitutional prior restraint. Requiring a permit as to the "time, place, and manner," however, is allowed.

The boundaries of the prior restraint rule are somewhat fuzzy. The U.S. Supreme Court has ruled against prior restraint of the publication of classified documents, but a majority of the Justices suggested that national security concerns would sometimes allow such a prior restraint. There's also something less than clarity about whether and when a court may issue a gag order preventing the press, as opposed to participants, from publicly discussing a court proceeding.

One area where the courts have recently been active concerns symbolic speech as to which the government issues some sort of permission, such as customized automobile license plates and federal trademarks.

Many states allow drivers to pay something extra so that their license plate will bear a message of some kind. Given the space constraints, these will not always be intelligible to the general public, but states generally prohibit at least the more obvious sorts of obscenities and racial or ethnic slurs. Some states also provide specialized visual designs at the behest of some organization, again for an additional fee. In June 2015, the U.S. Supreme Court held (in a 5-4 decision) that the state may prohibit what it considers an offensive symbol, in this case the Confederate battle flag. The rationale: even though the drivers may view these plates as a form of self-expression, they are actually government speech which the government is free to restrict.

Wasting no time, a federal district court applied the same rationale to registered federal trademarks in a July 2015 decision (discussed at 14.M.2.).

a. Obscenity, or I Know It When I See It

"Indecent" speech and expressive conduct have First Amendment protection. "Obscene" speech and expressive conduct don't. Good luck telling the difference.

I should add that the federal government does claim the right to prohibit the broadcast of "indecent" or "profane" speech during certain hours on certain media, and the courts have upheld that claim. "Profane" language includes the words that comedian George Carlin publicized, to his cost, as "the seven words you can never say on TV." If you're unsure which seven, it's easy to find the list online. I have my doubts as to whether #7, "tits," is still considered dangerous to public morals, but I haven't investigated the matter.

So what speech, etc., is "obscene"? The legal standard has changed over time, not always in the direction of allowing more naughtiness.

In the late 19th century and the first half of the 20th, the U.S. used a rather unilluminating British test: "whether the tendency of the matter charged . . . is to deprave and corrupt those whose minds are open to such immoral influences, and into whose hands a publication of this sort may fall." This test took no account of any artistic value the "matter charged" might have.

In 1957, the Supreme Court stated that obscene material was "utterly without redeeming social importance," but that language was apparently descriptive, rather than describing any test for whether material was or wasn't obscene. The test adopted at the same time: "whether to the average person, applying contemporary community standards, the dominant theme of the material taken as a whole appeals to a prurient interest." "Prurient" meant "lewd or lustful." This test, while not clearing matters up enormously, did add the element of "community standards," making the likely success of an obscenity charge dependent on the geographical location.

In 1964, in a widely quoted concurring opinion, Supreme Court Justice Potter Stewart stated that a particular French film was not "hard-core pornography," and that while he couldn't provide a coherent definition of such pornography, "I know it when I see it."

In 1966, the Court made obscenity prosecutions more difficult, by using "utterly without redeeming social value" as part of the test to be applied. Another case that year, however, held that if someone used the U.S. mail to send advertisements meant to appeal to the recipient's "prurient interests," that still counted as obscenity the feds could prosecute.

In 1969, the Court shifted its focus from the distributor to the consumer, holding that the First and Fourteenth Amendments protected those who possessed even "obscene" material from being prosecuted for that possession.

Then, in 1973, the Court stepped back from its earlier "utterly without redeeming social value" language, substituting this three-part test:

(a) whether the "average person, applying contemporary community standards" would find that the work, taken as a whole, appeals to the prurient interest ..., (b) whether the work depicts or describes, in a patently offensive way, sexual conduct specifically defined by the applicable state law, and (c) whether the work, taken as a whole, lacks serious literary, artistic, political, or scientific value.

The majority opinion also provided some helpful specifics. Obscenity included "'hard core' sexual conduct," and *that* included "patently offensive representations or descriptions of ultimate sexual acts, normal or perverted, actual or simulated ... masturbation, excretory functions, and lewd exhibitions of genitals."

The Court modified (but hardly clarified) the "contemporary community standards" test in 1987, stating that courts should ask not "whether an ordinary member of any given community would find serious literary, artistic, political, and scientific value in allegedly obscene material," but rather, "whether a reasonable person would find such value in the material, taken as a whole."

That's essentially where things stand today. As for applications of these rules: laws criminalizing such telephonic conveniences as "Dial-a-Porn" have been struck down, but only when such laws cover "indecent" speech as well as obscenity. Various attempts to restrict obscenity on the Internet have fallen afoul of one or another aspect of the constitutional standards. On the other hand, while nude dancing may be protected "expressive" conduct, it's all right for local governments to use zoning to restrict where nude dancing may be offered as entertainment.

One situation not yet resolved at the Supreme Court level is whether a parent who takes pictures of their own child naked may be prosecuted for obscenity. **Given how often parents take "cute" bathtub snapshots, there's potential for a "legal nightmare" story line here.** **Or you could have a different sort of narrative tension by at least suggesting that your photographer really was intending to satisfy consumers of child porn.**

Another sort of story could follow the trials, literal and metaphorical, of a playwright seeking to challenge their audience with sexually charged subject matter; or, on the other hand, **the attempts of a brothel owner to avoid prosecution for preliminary entertainment provided to customers before they picked their partners.**

---

2. The Second Amendment

It would have been rather more convenient if the Framers of the Constitution had had the advice of a few good time-travelers. Without that assistance, they often failed to foresee how societal changes would render the wording of constitutional provisions somewhat unclear to their descendants. The Second Amendment is a case in point:

> A well regulated Militia, being necessary to the security of a free State, the right of the people to keep and bear Arms, shall not be infringed.

The first few words, known as the "militia clause," have inspired many a heated debate. Does this subordinate clause limit the reach of the primary clause, and if so, how?

Nowadays, we're so used to our large federal military establishment that we forget how very suspicious Americans were of the idea of a "standing army." The citizenry at the time the Constitution was written and ratified expected the primary military force of the nation to remain the citizens themselves, armed with their own weapons and organized into militias supervised by the various states. Given that assumption and the importance of an armed citizenry, the Framers emphasized the need for an armed militia in the wording of the Second Amendment.

Various writings that remain to us from that era show other concerns that may have contributed to the passage and ratification of that amendment. These included what has now become quite controversial, the need to preserve the people's ability to rebel against any future government tyranny, as the new nation had recently rebelled against the British crown.

A linguistic shift since the late 18th century may have further muddled things. According to some authorities, "well regulated," at that time, meant something like "well-disciplined," rather than "subject to sufficient government regulations."

For many years, the federal judiciary interpreted the Second Amendment into unimportance, treating it as dealing only with formal militias and the like (e.g. the National Guard) established by the state and/or federal governments. Then, beginning in the 1980s, a rising tide of legal and historical scholarship ultimately led the U.S. Supreme Court to hold that the Second plus the Fourteenth Amendments do, to some extent, protect the right of individual Americans to possess and carry at least some weapons. The limits of that right are still being defined.

A historical note: when the Fourteenth Amendment was proposed and debated, one explicitly discussed rationale was the need to protect the rights of newly freed slaves and other black Americans to possess defensive weapons, given the threat of attack from hostile white locals.

As discussed in 29.A.2. and 3. above, federal law prohibits most felons and various others from owning or possessing firearms unless certain procedural obstacles have been successfully negotiated. The applicable statute covers not only all but an exempt group of felons, and not only those convicted of domestic violence misdemeanors and misdemeanor BATF violations, but the following as well:

- Fugitives from justice.
- Those using or addicted to illegal drugs (with various federal regulations about from what facts one may infer either status).
- Those subject to restraining orders having to do with domestic harassment or stalking.
- Those adjudicated as "mental defectives" (which includes, among other categories, those found either insane or incompetent to stand trial in a criminal case, and those found to lack the mental capacity to conduct their own affairs), or who have been involuntarily committed to a mental institution.
- Noncitizens unlawfully present in the U.S., as well as some of those admitted on nonimmigrant visas.
- Those dishonorably discharged from the U.S. military.
- Those who have renounced their U.S. citizenship.

Many of these prohibitions suggest ideas for compelling fiction. For example, **someone with intractable mental illness, in and out of psychiatric wards, may feel that they have utterly lost control of their life. They could find that, somewhat paradoxically, the only way they can make it from day to day is by recalling that they retain the freedom to end their life with a single gunshot. Then they are confronted with the fact that even that option is legally denied to them. Might they react with violence toward someone other than themselves?** **What if a cancer patient has been using medical marijuana in a state that has not yet legalized that usage, or during a period when the federal government has been ignoring state laws allowing it? They may live in a neighborhood where owning and/or carrying a pistol is exceedingly prudent, and giving up that defensive weapon could have grievous consequences.** Or **take the case of a gay man dishonorably discharged from some branch of the military for homosexuality before the fairly recent change in that policy. What if he has been making a living by teaching marksmanship and safe firearm handling? (To avoid complexities about whether the federal statute applies to discharges that would no longer take place under current rules, you might want to set this story before the policy change.)**

3. Power but with Payment: the Takings Clause

What if the state, in its not-so-infinite wisdom, decides that a family farm is the perfect place to put a new highway off-ramp? Do the farmers have any rights?

The good news is, they do. The bad news is, they lose the farm anyway. The other good news is, they get paid for it.

The Fifth Amendment, binding on the states via the Fourteenth, guarantees that "private property [shall not] be taken for public use without just compensation." This language is known as the Takings Clause. The taking itself is called "eminent domain." The government, most often a state or local government, is usually supposed to pay the owner the fair market value of the property the government is taking. If the owner doesn't think the government's offer constitutes fair market value, the owner may bring an "inverse condemnation" action to force a higher payment — if it's worth the attorney fees to do so. Some states offer partial compensation for such fees. I'm told that Florida lets the owner recover all attorney fees and appraisal expenses, but check before you rely on that.

What if the state takes other property, with the effect that someone's property becomes totally useless? For example, let's say there's no longer a way to get to some piece of land. If the owner can no longer use the property at all, that counts as a taking. But if "all" the owner loses is the use they have been making of the property, or the most profitable use for the land, they are probably out of luck.

What if someone doesn't own the property, but merely leases it? If the lease gave the tenant a particularly good deal, the tenant might be entitled to compensation. That doesn't mean it'll be worth suing to get it.

What if the state takes part of someone's property, and by doing so makes the rest of their property *more* valuable? For example, maybe the remaining property becomes more accessible, or is now near a good school or some other attraction. Then the increase in value of the remaining property is offset against the amount the owner would otherwise get for the lost portion of the property.

Here's a use of eminent domain that really raises hackles. What if the county wants to take someone's land, not for a road or school or other public function, but to give or sell to some other private party? Incredibly enough, they may be able to do so, if the private party will supposedly serve some public purpose with it. If the targeted property is "blighted," meaning it's part of a slum or otherwise a notorious eyesore that does nothing for the community, then the government can take it, pay the owner (probably not much) for it, and give it to someone who says they'll build something that will boost the local economy, such as a shopping mall or business park. They may be able to do the same thing if the property is perfectly inoffensive, such as a house in good repair, so long as the planned development will supposedly put more money in municipal coffers. The U.S. Supreme Court affirmed this latter power in 2005, in a fiercely criticized decision called *Kelo v. City of New London*.

It's not uncommon for the private projects for which land is thus confiscated to end up tanking. The private development for which New London took Susette Kelo's house was never built, and the land now sits empty.

Kelo caused sufficient public outrage that some states subsequently passed statutes limiting takings of private property for private projects.

However, these statutes often had enough exceptions and other complexities that they were less than fully effective.

Is there any reason the Fifth's "private property" language should be confined to real property? There have been folks who thought so; but in June 2015, the U.S. Supreme Court held that the Takings Clause does indeed cover personal property. While it was at it, the Court held that if a federal agency requires farmers to hand over some percentage of a crop, so the agency can use artificially limited supply to increase demand for that crop, that requirement is a taking for which the farmers must receive just compensation. And the higher prices that are supposed to result don't count as the required compensation.

B. Limits on Search and Seizure and on Arrests

The right of the people to be secure in their persons, houses, papers, and effects, against unreasonable searches and seizures, shall not be violated, and no Warrants shall issue, but upon probable cause, supported by Oath or affirmation, and particularly describing the place to be searched, and the persons or things to be seized.

Once upon a time, the King's agents could search anyone, any time, for anything. Their authorization: "writs of assistance," also known as "general warrants," good for the lifetime of the king whose government issued them. The American response: the Fourth Amendment to the U.S. Constitution, quoted above. Gone were the all-purpose, all-encompassing general warrants. Instead, warrants had to specify what the searchers were hoping to find and where they could look for it. And there had to be a good reason, "probable cause," for thinking that evidence of a crime was there to be found.

To be a little more specific, "probable cause" means something like: the known facts and circumstances would make a reasonable person conclude that a crime has been, or is about to be, committed.

Whoever's seeking the warrant provides information under oath to a neutral judge or similar official, often a magistrate (5.A.), sort of a junior judge, with qualifications that vary from "lawyer" to "literate." That official then decides if there really is probable cause, and should also make sure the warrant isn't overbroad in any respect.

Whether or not the police need a search warrant depends in part on whether the place they want to search is one for which the object of the search has a "reasonable expectation of privacy." New technologies constantly test the boundaries of this notion. For example, in 2001 the U.S. Supreme Court decided (though by a 5-4 margin) that homeowners' reasonable expectation of privacy in their homes meant that thermal imaging of the home constituted a search requiring a search warrant, in the absence of any of the usual exceptions (see 34.B.1. below). That opinion drew a so-called "bright line" at the "entrance" to the home. This probably would not mean a gate into the yard, but rather the main door to the dwelling. The surrounding yard is part of the "curtilage," as to which a somewhat lesser standard applies: unless there's a "No Trespassing" sign, the police may walk through the curtilage, and may then take note of whatever's in "plain view" there (again, see 34.B.1.).

A recent Indiana case decided that people have a reasonable expectation that the contents of a GPS will remain private, so that a search warrant is needed (once again, absent the recognized exceptions discussed in 34.B.1.) before those contents may be searched. The losing argument in that case: that a GPS is a "container" within an automobile, and subject to the "automobile" exception. State courts have been split as to whether a cell phone carried in a car comes within that exception, but the U.S. Supreme Court came out with a decision in 2014 that seems to settle that question in defendants' favor. That ruling, however, depended not so much on the defendant's reasonable expectation of privacy as on the substantial degree to which searching a cell phone actually invades the owner's privacy.

Hearsay that couldn't be admitted in an actual trial (see 22.K.) may be used in an application for a search warrant as long as it meets some tests (which vary by jurisdiction) for reliability. One example of such a test, from Indiana:

(1) the witness has given correct information in the past, (2) independent police investigation corroborates the informant's statements, (3) the basis for the witness's knowledge is demonstrated, or (4) the informant predicts conduct or activity by the suspect that is not ordinarily easily predicted.

Note the "or."

Humans are excellent at sniffing out loopholes. Here's one: where in the Fourth Amendment does it actually say that all searches or arrests have to be conducted after getting a warrant?

What has developed, then, is a series of exceptions to the warrant requirement.

1. Exceptions to Requirement for a Search Warrant

Concerning search warrants, here are the usual exceptions.

- When someone's being arrested, and the arrest is legal, the police may search the person's "person" (their body) and surroundings to make sure there's nothing dangerous to be grabbed, and also to prevent the destruction of evidence. This is called a search "incident to arrest." If what the police find is not at all dangerous, but highly useful in a criminal prosecution, it may be so used. The courts actually use the poetic term "wingspan" for the distance within which it's reasonable to search.

  What if the arrest turns out to be unlawful? Well, that depends on what makes it unlawful. If the arrest wasn't based on probable cause (see the Fourth Amendment's language about "seizures" and probable cause), then the "exclusionary rule" (34.E.) applies, and the state may not use whatever it found. But if the police violated only a state law, rather than a federal constitutional limitation, that doesn't trigger the exclusionary rule, which is federal. However, if the state has a separate constitutional limit on search and seizure, and an exclusionary rule to go along with it, then the defendant can keep the evidence out.

- If the police have a legitimate reason to be somewhere, and they can see evidence of illegal activity "in plain view" from that vantage point, they may seize that evidence without a warrant.

- If the police are responding to an emergency (also known as "exigent circumstances"), and/or are in "hot pursuit" of a fleeing perpetrator, so that waiting for a warrant might endanger the police or the public, they may overlook what would otherwise be legally impassable thresholds. Then they may make note of and/or seize any evidence of illegal activity that they happen to notice. However, if the police caused the emergency in the first place, that excuse won't wash.

- Since moving vehicles are likely to move out of reach while police are obtaining a warrant, the police don't have to wait, so long as they have probable cause to think the vehicle contains evidence of a crime, the "fruits" of a crime, stuff used to commit a crime ("instrumentalities" of the crime), or stuff it's illegal simply to possess ("contraband"). But what part of the vehicle or its contents they may search depends on what they have probable cause to think is going on. If the police think there's a dead body there somewhere, that doesn't allow them to search the glove compartment (unless it's the stolen body of a research mouse).

- The "stop" element in the limited type of search known as "stop and frisk" (see 34.B.2., below) doesn't require full-out probable cause, let alone a warrant: it only requires "reasonable suspicion" that evil (oh, okay, that crime) is afoot. For the "frisk" part to be permitted, the police must have reason to believe the person they've stopped is "armed and dangerous" (i.e., armed). If this "stop" goes on too long, however, it turns into a seizure, requiring probable cause.

- Finally, there's an exception that's obvious once one thinks of it: consent. If the person whose body or space is being searched without a warrant says that's perfectly okay, then it is. Complications arise when more than one person has some claim to the place being searched, and only one of them has consented to the search. Generally, that consent is good enough for a search of any part of the space that the person who consented actually uses.

One interesting point: while minors, in generally, can't give binding consent in the area of contracts (see 14.C.4.), minors may be considered competent to consent to a search, depending on the judge's assessment of such factors as maturity and intellectual capacity.

2. Exceptions to Requirement for an Arrest Warrant

We've talked about searches incident to arrest, but what about the arrest itself?

As mentioned earlier (see Ch. 12), the requirement for an arrest warrant has even broader exceptions than the requirement for a search warrant. If a police officer personally sees the crime occur, they may make an arrest. And when that hasn't happened, if the police convince a judge later that they had "probable cause" to think the person had committed or was about to commit a crime, then the arrest is deemed legal.

Someone arrested without a warrant is generally supposed to get a hearing within 48 hours about whether the arrest was lawful.

Of course, the Fourth Amendment doesn't refer to "arrests," but to "seizures" — language which includes arrests but goes somewhat beyond it. If a reasonable person would not, under the circumstances, feel free to walk off whistling Dixie, they have probably been "seized." Typical supporting circumstances include (a) a show of authority on the part of the police, such as waving handcuffs around, using intimidating language, or actual physical contact, and (b) that the person in fact stays put rather than leaving.

"Seizures" that don't amount to arrests are allowed with no warrant if they're "reasonable under the circumstances." When the police reasonably believe that some criminal activity is going down in a particular place, they're allowed to stop people they suspect, ask them questions, and pat them down to check for weapons that could be pulled before the conversation is over. This sort of encounter is called a "Terry stop" (named after a case), a "Terry frisk" (same case), or a "stop and frisk." The police may ask for the subject's ID, but the subject doesn't have to produce it. If they don't, however, that plus some other events may sometimes add up to probable cause for a warrantless arrest.

The U.S. Supreme Court, in its wisdom (whatever the degree of that wisdom), has also held that general dragnets used to briefly stop and question random drivers, in the hope of catching unlawful immigrants or those driving under the influence, are constitutional seizures as well.

C. Excessive Bail versus No Bail

The Eighth Amendment provides that "[e]xcessive bail shall not be required." But what about cases where bail is denied?

At first blush, it might seem as if this language in the Eighth Amendment contains an accidental loophole, such as I've suggested (see 34.B.) might exist in the Fourth. Didn't the Founders intend for bail to be available in all cases?

Probably not. The distinction between bailable and non-bailable offenses has been around for centuries. While neither the Eighth Amendment nor its predecessor, the 1689 English Bill of Rights, spelled out the difference, common sense suggests that when the death penalty looms, financial interest, whether one's own or one's family's, may be insufficient to induce someone to stand trial and risk execution. (See also 12.A.)

As noted above, the case law is somewhat murky as to whether the states are bound by the federal constitutional prohibition against excessive bail.

D. The Right to Remain Silent

"[N]or shall any person . . . be compelled in any criminal case to be a witness against themselves . . . ."

The right to remain silent, protected by the Fifth (quoted above) and Fourteenth Amendments, means that I don't have to help the state convict me of a crime. As long as I speak up and say, in some reasonably explicit way, that I'm asserting my constitutional right to shut up, I don't have to answer any questions.

You've almost certainly heard some fictional (or actual) police officer rattle off some verbiage beginning, "You have the right to remain silent."

If you include these warnings in your story, make sure it's set no earlier than 1966, when the U.S. Supreme Court's *Miranda* decision established that those being interrogated needed to be told about their rights in so many words. The full Miranda warning must use these words or something close to them:

> You have the right to remain silent. Anything you say can and will be used against you in a court of law. You have the right to speak to an attorney, and to have an attorney present during any questioning. If you cannot afford a lawyer, one will be provided for you at government expense.

But what about before 1966? Did the courts pay any attention to whether the cops beat a confession out of someone, or interrogated them into an exhausted daze? Yes. The defense could assert that a confession/incriminating statement wasn't "voluntary." The defense still can.

When the defense asserts that the defendant's statement was involuntary, the prosecution theoretically must prove the opposite. However, the standard of proof in some jurisdictions is only "preponderance of the evidence" (20.A.), and courts and jurors often tend to believe the police version of any disputed facts. Recordings of interrogations were less common in pre-*Miranda* days, and are still far from routine in many states.

Massachusetts has a rule that other states might do well to copy. If a police interrogation isn't recorded and results in a confession, the defendant is entitled to a jury instruction that more or less encourages the jurors to question whether the confession was voluntary, and points out that (per the Massachusetts standard of proof on this point) the prosecution must prove the confession voluntary beyond a reasonable doubt.

Once someone has asserted the right to remain silent, is that the end of the matter? Not necessarily. The police may try again to get the person to talk, if they have been out of custody for at least two weeks in the meantime. (See 2.M. for a similar rule involving invocations of the right to counsel.) The details of this rule are likely to keep evolving, so if it's important to your story, check for recent developments.

As for the familiar *Miranda* litany, that's only required once someone is being subjected to "custodial interrogation." What constitutes custodial interrogation, or being in custody, can be a complicated question. In general, if the circumstances would give a reasonable person the impression that they aren't free to go about their business, that's being in custody. One doesn't have to be in jail or prison, or in a police car. However, even if no one who's been subjected to a traffic stop really believes they can just drive away in the middle of it, the courts have held that a traffic stop, by itself, doesn't constitute custodial interrogation.

The right to remain silent extends beyond criminal investigations. One may also remain silent in any other proceeding — a civil suit, or testimony before Congress, or whatever — to avoid giving the government ammunition in any future prosecution.

What if someone has an urgent reason to say something incriminating in a civil proceeding? This sometimes comes up when the authorities in charge of child welfare (see 14.H.13.) have decided that a child has been abused. The parent may be ordered to participate in some therapeutic program that requires admission of guilt; and refusal to make that admission may, at least in some states, be treated as failure to succeed in therapy, with no Fifth Amendment excuses allowed. That in turn can make it easier for the government to permanently sever the parent-child relationship (again, see 14.H.13.). **There's obviously gut-wrenching story material here.**

If a defendant in a criminal trial asserts their Fifth Amendment rights and refuses to testify, may the prosecutor suggest that an innocent defendant would be eager to get up and tell their story, and that the defendant's silence betokens guilt? No.

Will the jury jump to that conclusion anyway? Probably.

The judge in Scott Turow's novel *Presumed Innocent* tries to deal with this likelihood by rhapsodizing about the right to remain silent, and explaining that the defendant can't really get the full benefit of that right if the jury is thinking the defendant ought to explain what happened. But even this defendant's dream of a judge probably wouldn't fully succeed in overcoming the human tendency to expect the innocent to declare their innocence. Defense attorneys who don't want their clients to testify, for any of a number of reasons, will probably try to impanel a jury intelligent and dispassionate enough to understand the "beyond a reasonable doubt" standard; or else, they'll try the case to a judge rather than a jury, and concentrate on poking holes in the prosecution's case.

What if the defendant who invoked their Fifth Amendment rights is later sued for conduct related to the previous criminal case? In many jurisdictions, the plaintiff in this later civil action would be allowed to offer the defendant's earlier silence as implying liability. The U.S. Supreme Court held in 1976, citing "the prevailing rule," that "the Fifth Amendment does not forbid adverse inferences against parties to civil actions when they refuse to testify in response to probative evidence offered against them."

What if a witness starts to answer questions and then realize they shouldn't have? May they stop? That's not easily determined, but the answer will often be "Sorry, no." There's a similar issue when someone first takes the Fifth and then answers a few questions: those answers may be viewed as a waiver of the just-asserted right to remain silent. Case in point: when a certain employee of the Internal Revenue Service appeared before a Congressional committee and "took the Fifth," then presented a rambling series of self-justifications, many people expected that she'd be found to have waived the Fifth's protections. After some suspense, however, the U.S. attorney decided otherwise, declining to prosecute her for contempt of Congress.

1. Immunity: Compelling Speech the Government Can't Use Against the Speaker

Government agents may, after all, compel a person to make potentially incriminating statements, if they first enter into a binding agreement never to use those statements in any future prosecution. This is called a grant of "immunity." Calling it an agreement is a mite misleading: once the government offers immunity, it is, to borrow a well-known phrase, an offer the person can't refuse. Anyone who refuses to testify after being given immunity can be held in contempt and jailed until they talk (see 30.D.).

There are two kinds of immunity: "use immunity" and "transactional immunity." Use immunity is the more limited. If the government can dig up some other evidence of the same fact revealed in the witness' immunized testimony, the prosecutor can get the fact into evidence, as long as they don't use the immunized testimony to do it. It doesn't matter that the prosecution might never have known enough to start digging if the witness hadn't been compelled to testify.

Transactional immunity, also called "blanket" or total immunity, plugs this loophole: the fact the witness revealed may not be used, period. Naturally, transactional immunity is a lot harder to get. Only if the potential witness is likely to hang tough, even if locked up for contempt, and/or if the information they could provide is particularly valuable will the prosecution reluctantly grant transactional immunity. The federal government no longer gives transactional immunity at all. New York, on the other hand (unless something has changed recently), gives transactional immunity to all witnesses called before grand juries, unless the witness is so careless as to mention a crime they committed that's completely irrelevant to the grand jury proceedings.

Once a witness receives use immunity from a state and testifies as required, may the federal government use that compelled statement as the basis for its own prosecution? No. Once one jurisdiction gives a witness immunity, that immunity protects the witness to the same extent in other jurisdictions.

E. The Exclusionary Rule

So we have all these limits on what the police may do. What if the police don't play by the rules?

Well, an aggrieved defendant, already embroiled in criminal proceedings, could try suing the police officer and/or department. Such a party would have the labyrinth of sovereign immunity (see Ch. 16) to deal with, and besides, it's gets harder to handle litigation if one is locked up (though not impossible — see 2.K.1.). Nor is it necessarily an easy task to convince a trier of fact that the police violated one's constitutional rights. Such suits are possible (see 34.M.), and sometimes they eventually succeed in costing the government money. But that doesn't help the criminal defendant much in the meantime.

Or the system could protect defendants' rights by making violating the Constitution less productive.

From early in our history, the Fifth Amendment has been read to mean that any testimony a defendant was forced to give must be excluded, its truth or falsity notwithstanding. It took until 1914 for the same principle to be applied to unconstitutional searches.

Excluding improperly discovered evidence has always been more controversial than excluding coerced confessions. Confessions made under duress may well be unreliable, but objects found in an illegal search have just as much probative value as those found in accordance with the rules. Applying the "exclusionary rule," as it's called, to such evidence is quite likely to result in letting the guilty go free. This result becomes more likely when one applies a corollary rule: if illegally gained evidence leads the police to other evidence, the latter is "the fruit of the poisonous tree," and will generally be excluded as well. Only if this other evidence would (according to a somewhat psychic determination) have "inevitably" been discovered through some less problematic route, or if the connection to the illegal evidence is a pretty long chain with some weak links, may this "fruit" be, so to speak, consumed.

One real and gruesome example of "inevitable discovery" involves a man arrested on suspicion of murder. Police misconduct led to his disclosing the location of the victim's body, in which DNA matching that of the defendant was found. The trial court held that within another couple of weeks, the body would have started to stink, and that since a nearby grassy area was mowed and cleared of trash regularly, the body would have been discovered by its odor before maggots would have destroyed the portion of the body containing DNA evidence. An appellate court upheld this ruling.

1. The "Good Faith" Exception

The state and its citizens pay the heavy price of excluding relevant evidence of guilt in criminal trials in order to punish and deter unlawful police conduct. That reasoning has led to an ever-widening escape hatch known as the "good faith exception." If the police believed in good faith that they were following the law, then the fact that they were wrong doesn't prevent the evidence from coming in. For example, if the police or the magistrate relied on obsolete case law, and the current law makes the search unlawful, the resulting evidence may still be admitted. If a magistrate doesn't properly scrutinize the warrant application and shouldn't have issued the warrant, the evidence discovered by a police officer who knew nothing of that sloppiness would still be admissible. Critics of this latter application argue, so far in vain, that it increases the likelihood of magistrates rubber-stamping warrant applications.

Given the tendency of judges to believe the sworn testimony of police officers as to what they did and what they believed, the "good faith exception" threatens to swallow the exclusionary rule.

2. "New Crimes"

In many state and federal courts, there's another exception to the exclusionary rule called the "new crime" exception. Or you could call it a failure to extend the rule.

If the police engage in an illegal search or seizure, and the defendant's response includes committing another, separate crime, the defendant may be charged with the new crime. The new crime wouldn't have occurred if not for the illegal police conduct, but the courts in some jurisdictions have decided that they don't really care.

As the Indiana Court of Appeals recently put it: "Because the purpose of the exclusionary rule — to deter police misconduct — is not advanced by suppressing evidence of a new crime committed by a defendant after an illegal search or seizure, we apply the new-crime exception to the Fourth Amendment's exclusionary rule."

Is it so crystal clear that excluding evidence of the new crime wouldn't deter police misconduct? For that matter, could police officers be tempted to push the envelope on illegal searches or seizures if they know that by doing so, they might provoke the defendant into some rash reaction that could give them a "collar" (an arrest) and a prosecution?

Feel free to agree or disagree with the Indiana court's assessment.

F. The Right to Confront Witnesses

The Sixth and Fourteenth Amendments give a criminal defendant the right "to be confronted with the witnesses against them." This is generally treated as including something more active: namely, the right to do some confronting, including cross-examination. This right overlaps with, but may go further than, the hearsay rule (22.K.), which arises from the belief that if a statement isn't coming from the mouth of a witness who can be cross-examined, there had better be some very good reason to consider it reliable.

When does the Confrontation Clause, as it's called, require exclusion of evidence that could otherwise come in under an exception to, or a limitation of, the hearsay rule? That gets quite complicated, and the U.S. Supreme Court tinkers with the issue fairly frequently.

For example, the Court held in June 2015 that a statement by a three-year-old boy to a teacher about who caused the marks on his body wasn't covered by the Confrontation Clause. The reasoning: (a) the "primary purpose" of the teacher's inquiry wasn't to create a substitute for trial testimony, but rather, to deal with an immediate threat to the child's welfare; (b) the child showed no sign that he intended his statement to be used to punish the defendant; (c) at the time the Constitution was written and ratified, statements like this were generally considered admissible; and (d) the teacher wasn't part of any law enforcement team or process, despite a legal obligation to report suspected child abuse.

G. Due Process, Procedural and "Substantive"

The Fifth Amendment to the U.S. Constitution provides that no "person," citizen or not, may be "deprived of life, liberty, or property, without due process of law . . . ." That restriction originally applied only to attempts by the federal government to inflict such a deprivation, but the Fourteenth Amendment added similar language applicable to the states.

What is "due process of law"?

At first blush, the phrase seems to concern procedure: rules of evidence, indictments, how trials are conducted, and the like. And it certainly includes such matters. Unsurprisingly if redundantly, that sort of due process is known as "procedural due process." The essentials of procedural due process include notice of the threatened deprivation, notice of the charges on which it'd be based, and an opportunity to be heard on the subject before an impartial decision-maker. This hearing must involve evidence, not just allegations, and an opportunity to respond. Except in emergencies, the hearing must take place prior to the deprivation. (For the way government authorities get around all these niceties in "civil forfeiture," see 34.G.2., below.)

Beyond these basics, procedural due process isn't a fixed set of required procedures. The courts will look at three factors in deciding whether the procedures used in a given situation were good enough to satisfy the Due Process clause. Here are those factors as stated in a 1976 U.S. Supreme Court case (*Mathews v. Eldridge*) and repeated many times since:

> [F]irst, the private interest that will be affected by the official action; second, the risk of an erroneous deprivation of such interest through the procedures used, and the probable value, if any, of additional or substitute procedural safeguards; and, finally, the Government's interest, including the function involved and the fiscal and administrative burdens that the additional or substitute procedural requirement would entail.

Consideration of these factors will, in different cases, lead to different burdens of proof, or to more fundamental differences like whether a court needs to hear evidence before taking action. For example, the way the U.S. Supreme Court has assessed things, one is entitled to an evidentiary hearing on whether one should receive welfare benefits, but not on whether one should get Social Security disability benefits. Another example: given how many people must drive to work, having a driver's license is treated as an important enough "property" interest that if some statute or regulation may cause your license to be suspended, you have a right to a hearing.

Being deprived of "life" is a pretty obvious condition, and actually means the same thing in law as in everyday parlance. But what counts as "liberty" or "property" for purposes of procedural due process?

"Liberty," in this context, means more than whether or not one is incarcerated. It also includes deprivation of some freedom guaranteed by the U.S. Constitution, a state constitution, or a statute.

What if someone is already locked up, and the prison authorities impose some further punishment like solitary confinement? Unless it's much harsher than what's usual in that prison, or the prisoner is punished for doing something they had a right to do, like blowing the whistle on corrupt prison officials, they probably can't challenge how the punishment was imposed. It's different, however, if the punishment would extend how long someone is imprisoned: for example, losing "good time" credits that reduce a prisoner's sentence if they stay out of trouble (see 29.B.). Then the prisoner has at least some rights to notice, hearing, etc. As for how long a stretch in solitary (see 29.G.) would be harsh enough to give a prisoner some recourse, that varies from court to court, but if it's close to a year, chances are good that the prisoner may challenge the procedures used.

"Property" includes not only real property and tangible personal property, but intangible entitlements like the driver's license I just mentioned. If it was the government that owed someone something in the first place, or if it acted intentionally or recklessly in a way that caused a loss, the person so deprived may have some recourse.

Over time, and possibly because of questionably narrow interpretations of other constitutional provisions, "due process" has been stretched beyond its obvious procedural meaning to include what some have called an oxymoron: "substantive due process."

"Substantive due process" is a label for various non-procedural rights, some of which aren't explicitly protected elsewhere in the constitution. The right to privacy, the right to marry, and the right to raise one's children as one sees fit have been accorded U.S. constitutional protection via this rubric, with some assistance from other related amendments. The Third and Fourth Amendments, along with the Due Process amendments, are said to exude a "penumbra" implying the right to privacy and its more specific progeny.

The right to privacy has various subsidiary rights included in it, such as the right to use contraception, the still-controversial right to have an abortion, and (since 2003) the right to engage in homosexual sex, discussed further in a moment.

Some rights, such as the right to marry, are sometimes described as aspects of the right to privacy and sometimes treated as "liberty" interests. Some commentators believe that the latter formulation is becoming more important. Supporting that view, in the recent U.S. Supreme Court decision finding a constitutional right to same-sex marriage, the term "liberty" appeared far more often than the term "privacy."

Do people have a right to die as they see fit? Many states used to treat suicide, or practically speaking, attempted suicide, as a crime. None of them still do; but that's not the same as having a recognized right to kill oneself. If people jump through enough hoops, they may be able to dictate in advance the circumstances under which they shouldn't be subjected to medical procedures to prolong life. **If someone missed a hoop, or if conflicting evidence turns up, things could get ugly.** And so far, there's no established "substantive due process" right to help a loved one commit suicide, no matter the quality of their life. But the Supreme Court last addressed that question in 1997 (in *Washington v. Glucksberg*). **Maybe it's time for someone to find out if they've changed their minds on that as well.**

With the exception of abortion, which occupies a fuzzy realm of its own (discussed further below), the rights I've been discussing are deemed "fundamental" rights. So what's a "fundamental" right? If someone is sitting on land that I own and won't get off it, don't I have a "fundamental" right to that property? Well, no. The U.S. Supreme Court has defined "fundamental rights," in this context, as "rights and liberties which are 'deeply rooted in this Nation's history and tradition' and 'implicit in the concept of ordered liberty'."

All clear?

Some fundamental rights are well recognized and protected in the Bill of Rights, like freedom of speech, freedom to exercise one's religion, and the right to keep and bear arms (see 34.A.1. and 2.). However, where we're dealing with "fundamental rights" that need substantive due process for their protection, one decade's impertinent assertion can become the next decade's fundamental right. Courts dealing with the issue of what's a fundamental right tend to play definitional games. If the majority of the judges want to find that a right doesn't exist, they'll find the narrowest or most specific plausible phrasing for the claimed right, and then claim that there's an inadequate historical basis for recognizing it. If they're more inclined to recognize the right, they'll find a general and expansive way to categorize it. Compare, for example, the 1986 opinion in *Bowers v. Hardwick*, declining to find a fundamental right "[for] homosexuals to engage in sodomy," with the 2002 opinion in *Lawrence v. Texas*. *Lawrence* overruled *Bowers* on the basis of fundamental rights described variously, in the majority opinion, as the right to "[make] personal decisions relating to . . . family relationships," "a realm of personal liberty which the government may not enter," and "the right to define one's own concept of existence, of meaning, of the universe, and of the mystery of human life." (**One could write an interesting family saga that included the span from *Bowers* to *Lawrence*.**)

When the government infringes on fundamental rights, that infringement will be found to violate the "substantive" aspect of the Due Process clause unless it's necessary to achieve some "compelling" governmental purpose. Even then, unless the infringement is "narrowly tailored" to achieve that purpose, making it the most "narrowly drawn" means toward that end, it's still unconstitutional. These rules, taken together, constitute the "strict scrutiny" standard. You'll see this standard again in equal protection law (34.H.).

When we get outside the realm of fundamental rights (and, once again, leaving abortion out of it), "substantive due process" doesn't make a whole lot of difference. If someone challenges government action as violating substantive due process, and the court decides that the asserted right isn't fundamental, then all the government has to show is that the statute or other government action is "rationally related to a legitimate government purpose." This test, also called the "rational basis" test, usually sets a very low bar. Indeed, courts have held that the so-called "rational basis" for a statute doesn't actually have to be rational in the usual sense. A statute based on junk science and lousy logic may still pass muster. Every once in a while, however, a court gets feisty and requires that such a statute actually make sense and be likely to serve its intended purpose.

So how does the right to an abortion fit in?

Initially, the U.S. Supreme Court's 1973 *Roe v. Wade* decision treated the right to control one's procreation, including the right to an abortion, as an aspect of the right to privacy, although it treated the government interest as progressively stronger as an embryo or fetus got closer to full term. In the first trimester (first three months) of pregnancy, the state could only impose regulations protecting a mother's health, in much the same way that it could do in other medical contexts. In the second trimester, still prior to the date (at that time) when a fetus would be "viable" (would probably survive if born), the state could interfere only to protect the mother's health. After viability, the state could prohibit abortion unless the abortion was necessary to protect the mother's health.

However, the Court's 1992 decision in *Planned Parenthood of Southeastern Pennsylvania v. Casey* backtracked somewhat from *Roe's* rationale and framework. *Casey* held that states could regulate abortion prior to viability as long as those regulations didn't impose an "undue burden" on the mother's rights, which meant erecting a "substantial obstacle" to abortions of nonviable fetuses. Given advances in medical technology, the threshold for viability was tentatively estimated at 20 weeks. We don't find this "undue burden" or "substantial obstacle" language in substantive due process analysis either for fundamental or for non-fundamental rights.

What these dividing lines mean in practice is continually in flux. If your story involves restrictions on abortion, you'll need to check the latest cases in your locale.

---

1. Controversies at the Borders of Parental Rights

You may have seen stories recently, in newspapers or online, about cases where child welfare authorities or the police have confronted parents who allow their children to play unsupervised in public parks or to stay home alone, sometimes at ages (such as 9 or 10) where such activities used to be commonplace. There has also been blowback against the ways some schools have enforced federal guidelines about the content of school lunches, particularly where a parent has made a point of packing what they consider a nutritious meal.

Such disputes, in the view of some parents and commentators, demonstrate excessive government interference with the fundamental parental right, discussed just above in 34.G., to raise one's child as one sees fit.

This same right may be implicated in cases where child welfare authorities order a parent already involved in CHINS or similar proceedings (see 14.H.13.) to refrain from all corporal punishment, even forms that the state does not consider child abuse. The ultimate resolution of such controversies may or may not turn out to be the expansion of what society considers criminal child abuse. For now, **this issue may be a flash point where authorities from one ethnic background confront parents from a quite different cultural milieu.**

Those who take the view that such governmental actions usurp parental rights might be interested in exploring near-future dystopian extremes of these trends.

2. Property on Trial: Civil Forfeiture

Let's get back to actual procedural rights for a minute. The Fifth and Fourteenth Amendments prohibit the state and federal governments from depriving any "person" of "property" without "due process of law." What's the minimum in procedural protection required before the government may take someone's property away?

Don't be too quick to think you have the answer. Yes, I just told you about notice and a prior hearing before an impartial arbiter. But government officials at various levels have found a way around all that. It's called "civil forfeiture" or "civil asset forfeiture," and it begins with the legal fiction that not the person but their property is on trial.

Civil forfeiture involves "in rem" jurisdiction (see 6.A.2.). In civil forfeiture cases, in rem jurisdiction often results in strange case captions: e.g., State v. One Thousand Gold Doubloons.

Civil forfeiture started out in this country as a way to deal with smuggled cargo. The owner of a ship might not be within reach, but the cargo was right there and could be confiscated to pay the customs duties. Civil forfeiture started to become much more common in the early 1980s, as the

"War on Drugs" heated up. As currently practiced, it lets law enforcement organizations in at least forty states and in the federal government take and keep forfeited property for their own use.

In civil forfeiture, the property's owner doesn't have to get prior notice. In fact, it could be months before the owner finds out what's going on, if circumstances don't make it apparent sooner. As for the burden of proof, that's where that legal fiction comes in handy (for the government). To prevail and permanently keep the property, the government must prove that the property was involved in criminal activity — but only by a preponderance of the evidence (20.A.), a far weaker standard than would apply if the government was trying to convict and fine the owner. And the government may use evidence collected after it took the property in the first place.

Once the government has met this lax standard, the *property owner* is the one with the burden of proving, again by a preponderance of the evidence, the "innocent owner defense": namely, that they weren't aware of or involved in that criminal activity, or that once they found out, they did their best to stop it. And it's not unknown for the authorities to threaten property owners with criminal charges if they continue to contest the forfeiture.

There are rules about what happens if someone purchases the property after the criminal activity took place, and other such details, but that's civil forfeiture in a nutshell.

Here's how this might work, though the procedural details will vary from place to place.

The police make a traffic stop because a car had no lights on at night. They find a bag of cocaine on the front seat. The driver is a young woman; the car belongs to her uncle, who lives in an adjacent county and had lent the car to his brother, the young woman's father.

A few days afterward, the uncle contacts the police in his county of residence and reports the car stolen. The uncle and his brother, the girl's father, have quarreled since the loan of the car, and no one in the family tells the uncle about the arrest.

Eight weeks later, the uncle is served with a summons: there's going to be a hearing about whether his car is forfeit. He talks to a lawyer, who quotes him a retainer greater than the value of the car.

The police have no trouble proving that there was cocaine in the car. Now it's up to the uncle to prove that he didn't know about his niece's drug trafficking, or even let her use the car. It's his word against — well, against no one's, but the judge doesn't have to believe him. The girl has been told to keep her mouth shut if she doesn't want more serious charges filed against her. The police department gets to keep the car. They sell it and use the proceeds, along with proceeds from other forfeited property, to buy an armored van for late-night no-knock raids.

Not every state lets police departments and the like keep the proceeds of forfeited assets; but when they don't, the department can, or could until recently, use something called "equitable sharing" to turn the proceeds over to the federal government, which would eventually give 80 percent of the asset's value back to the state agency. This practice was somewhat restricted in mid-January 2015, but reports vary greatly as to the impact of that change. Some describe it as applying to most equitable sharing, while others estimate it will affect less than twenty percent of equitable sharing arrangements.

In late March 2015, the outgoing U.S. Attorney General (a status that may or may not be coincidental) announced new restrictions on federal forfeitures of bank accounts, specifically forfeitures based on "structuring." Structuring is depositing cash in the bank in quantities under $10,000. Never mind how many restaurants and such have occasion to do this: making such deposits is supposedly a sign of unlawful activity. The exact nature of the new restrictions isn't clear to those of us not in the inner circle: some critics say they still leave federal officials with too much discretion (e.g., too much ability to pick and choose whom to target).

Many states don't even require any sort of reporting of assets forfeited or the uses made of the proceeds.

What if the property is the owner's primary residence, or is crucial to the running of the owner's business? In the federal system, under these circumstances there's some limited availability of something analogous to bail, giving the owner back possession of the property pending completion of the forfeiture proceedings. The owner is also entitled to a Legal Services Corporation attorney if they can't afford to hire counsel. (For the details, look up 18 U.S.C. §983, paragraphs (f)(3) and (f)(8).) There's one key exception: the business owner can't get temporary return of money, no matter how much it's needed to keep the business going, unless the *whole* business has been seized and the money is a business asset. In one recent case, a business had substantial operating funds seized because the owner had found it convenient to make periodic deposits of less than $10,000 ("structuring" again), and that triggered official suspicion of black market activity. Despite repeated attempts, the business didn't get its money unfrozen until unrelated events made the situation politically ticklish.

Did I say one case? As I was writing this section, I came upon a report that between 2005 and 2012, the IRS seized *hundreds of millions of dollars* from thousands of bank accounts based on the same technicality. Four-fifths of these seizures were under civil forfeiture procedures, which took an average of one year to resolve. Over half of the money was in fact forfeited.

So if you want your Kafkaesque situation to involve deprivation of property rather than imprisonment, civil forfeiture makes for ideal subject matter.

The Eighth Amendment to the Constitution prohibits imposition of "excessive fines." The Eighth Amendment is one of those applied against the states via the Fourteenth Amendment (see the intro to Ch. 34). However, this clause only applies to civil forfeitures in very limited circumstances. In a 5-to-4 1998 decision, the U.S. Supreme Court held that where someone took more than $300,000 out of the country without reporting the fact, and a federal statute required such a report for sums over $10,000, forfeiting the entire amount of more than three hundred grand constituted a criminal penalty and an unreasonable fine. However, one key factor was that the applicable federal statute only allowed this forfeiture as an additional punishment for someone convicted of the underlying crime.

An update: as I write this, there's apparently a bill in Congress that would raise the government's burden of proof (when the government has the burden) in civil forfeiture cases from "preponderance of the evidence" to "clear and convincing," and would also require that indigent property owners (see 3.E.) have appointed counsel. Of course, that doesn't do much for a property owner who ends up indigent because of the forfeiture.

Also, New Mexico recently passed a law pretty much banning civil asset forfeiture as it's generally used. The state may now take property only after its owner is convicted of a crime in which the property was used; and the proceeds go into the general fund rather than to the police. A future edition of this book may be able to report that other states have followed this lead.

H. Equal Protection

Unlike the right to due process (34.G.), which existed as a restraint on the federal government before the Fourteenth Amendment, the right to "equal protection of the laws" only became an explicit part of the U.S. Constitution with that amendment.

The full wording of the Equal Protection Clause goes like this: "nor shall any State . . . deny to any person within its jurisdiction the equal protection of the laws." Does that mean Congress, the legislature of not-a-state-but-the-federal-government, may deny such protection? The U.S. Supreme Court rescued us, at least partially, from that potential incongruity in 1954, holding that the federal right to due process includes at least some aspects of equal protection. But the Court could always change its mind. . . .

One crucial point on which many people get confused: equal protection is *only* about government action. Discrimination is perfectly legal unless the government gets involved somehow, or unless some federal or state statute prohibits that private discrimination. A federal statute, for example, prohibits discrimination based on "discrimination or segregation on the ground of race, color, religion, or national origin" in any "public accommodation." Public accommodations include restaurants, bars, hotels and motels, gas stations, theaters, race tracks, etc. — places that provide some good or service to the public at large. (By the way, small bed-and-breakfast places, those with five or fewer rooms for guests, are exempt, at least from the federal statute.)

A host of federal statutes deal with discrimination in employment. Some may serve as the basis for a lawsuit under 42 U.S.C. §1983 (34.M.), while the others provide their own enforcement mechanisms. Here's a list, which I am not promising is complete.

- 42 U.S.C. §1981, which covers hiring and other workplace practices that have an unjustified "disparate impact" on employees because of race. This statute is usually enforced by the Equal Employment Opportunity Commission (EEOC). However, per a 2008 U.S. Supreme Court case interpreting the statute, §1981 also lets employees sue on their own, rather than needing the EEOC to do it for them, if an employer retaliates in some way against an employee who's previously filed a complaint about racial discrimination.

- Title VII of the Civil Rights Act of 1964 prohibits discrimination based on "race, color, religion, sex or national origin" in "hiring, discharging, compensating, or providing the terms, conditions, and privileges of employment." "Sex," in this context, includes pregnancy, childbirth, and medical conditions arising from either, as well — per the EEOC — as sexual orientation or transgender status. Title VII also covers labor unions' membership requirements and any classifications unions make about types of employment. This statute applies to employers, labor unions, and employment agencies engaged in "interstate commerce" (whose very loose definition you can read about in 34.L.) and that have more than 15 employees.

- The Age Discrimination in Employment Act (ADEA), similar to Title VII, but covering employees over age 40. In 2008 (a busy year for discrimination law, apparently), the U.S. Supreme Court held that it wasn't enough to show that some employer action affected folks over 40 differently: the EEOC had to show that the employer intended to discriminate against older employees.

  A potential plaintiff could struggle with the notion that at the not-so-ancient age of, say, 43, they were covered by an "age discrimination" statute, and would have to admit being "older" in order to take advantage of it.

- The Equal Pay Act, which amended a federal labor law in 1963, prohibits employers and unions from paying (or, in the case of unions, demanding) different wages for "equal" work based on gender. Two jobs are "equal" if they require "equal skill, effort, and responsibility" and are "performed under similar working conditions."

- The Americans with Disabilities Act, a very broad statute passed in 1990. It covers businesses engaged in interstate commerce, as well as state governments. It prohibits discrimination based on disability in a number of areas, including employment, transportation, public accommodations, and communications. That last means that people providing land lines, cell phones, pagers, or the services of phone operators — remember those? — must do what's reasonably possible to make sure that people with disabilities can use them. This statute is enforced by multiple federal government agencies.

- The Uniform Services Employment and Reemployment Rights Act (USERRA) protects employees of public or private employers from discrimination based on past or present military service. That means, among other things, that if the employee was deployed overseas for years, they are supposed to have the same seniority and seniority-related perks when they return as if they'd never left. They must be employed in the same position they had before, or a better one, unless they can't do the work despite reasonable efforts by the employer to make adjustments. An employee may ask the Secretary of Labor to act on their behalf, or may file their own lawsuit. The employer may defend against such a lawsuit by claiming that the employee's changed circumstances make reemployment impossible or unreasonable, or would impose an undue hardship on the employer, or would require the employer to create a useless job. **You could write a gripping story, with rights and wrongs as clear or unclear as you liked, about an employer afraid that a returning employee's PTSD would cause problems in the workplace.**

- The Black Lung Act prohibits mine operators from firing or otherwise discriminating against miners suffering from "black lung disease" (pneumoconiosis). This statute doesn't cover totally disabled miners, who could probably give the Americans with Disabilities act a try.

- The Nineteenth Century Civil Rights Act, amended in 1993 and perhaps at other times, fills in gaps in some other statutes about what damages may be awarded and suchlike.

All of these statutes pull in their wake a monumental quantity of federal regulations.

Congress claims the constitutional authority to make such laws in two ways: via the Commerce Clause, already mentioned (see 34.L.), and based on any "State action" that "supports" whatever the private party is doing. Back when there were state and local laws enforcing racial segregation, there was clearly "state action" "supporting" such segregation. The Civil Rights Act also says discrimination is supported by state action if it's "carried on under color of any custom or usage . . . [e]nforced" by state or local officials.

Given many of these statutes' reliance on the Commerce Clause, and the broad reach of the Commerce Clause under its current federal interpretation, there haven't been that many tests of just what constitutes "state action" supporting private discrimination. The factors that would probably be relevant include:

- any circumstances suggesting that the state approves of the discrimination or is lending it some symbolic support;
- a close, symbiotic relationship between the government and the private business.

As with substantive due process (34.G.), the rigor of equal protection depends on whether strict scrutiny is applied. Until that test appeared, the toothless "rational basis" test governed equal protection analysis. Strict scrutiny was first hinted at, though not applied, in a footnote to a 1938 case. Its first actual use was not exactly promising: the U.S. Supreme Court claimed to be applying strict scrutiny when it upheld the roundup of Japanese nationals and Japanese-American citizens during World War II. But eventually strict scrutiny became very strict indeed. Applying strict scrutiny usually, though not quite always, means striking down the governmental action at issue.

Distinctions made on the basis of a "suspect classification" always trigger strict scrutiny. These include race, national origin, and ethnicity. Gender, however, doesn't make the cut. Distinctions based on gender get "intermediate scrutiny," discussed below.

Distinctions that affect fundamental rights (again, see 34.G.) also trigger strict scrutiny. This makes the description of the distinction very important, and (as noted in 34.G.) courts can play definitional games in order to reach the result they prefer. At one time, laws limiting marriage to one man and one woman weren't treated as impinging on the right to marry, because marriage itself was defined as involving different genders. In June of 2015, however, the U.S. Supreme Court (or at least, five Justices thereof) embraced the idea that the right to marry had no such limitation. The majority opinion cited equal protection as well as substantive due process. While that opinion coyly avoided saying outright that it was applying strict scrutiny, it did link its equal protection ruling to the fundamental right to marry.

Prior to that decision, some proponents of same-sex marriage made a different equal protection argument, one based on gender. They asserted that letting a woman marry a man, but denying a man the right to do the same, constituted gender-based discrimination. That argument has a certain clarity lacking from the recent Supreme Court analysis; but it came with the drawback of requiring only "intermediate" scrutiny. Intermediate scrutiny, which first appeared in 1988, is used for distinctions based on "quasi-suspect" classifications. Such a distinction, to pass constitutional muster, must be "substantially related to an important governmental objective." The most common "quasi-suspect" classifications involve gender, but distinctions based on legitimacy (birth within a marriage) also qualify.

I. Double Jeopardy

[N]or shall any person be subject for the same offense to be twice put in jeopardy of life or limb . . . .

Aside from its reference to amputation as a criminal penalty, this passage from the Fifth Amendment is noteworthy for its limitation on what's commonly known as "double jeopardy."

Double jeopardy prevents the government from being a certain type of sore loser in criminal prosecutions. Once a defendant is acquitted of a particular crime, or their trial has ended in certain kinds of mistrials (I'll get to that in a second), they can't be tried again for that same crime. Even if previously unknown evidence crops up, even if the former defendant sells a tell-all confession to the tabloids, even if the jurors completely misunderstood the facts or the law, once acquitted is forever acquitted.

And if the government does succeed in convicting someone, and the conviction survives any appeals and such, they can't just pile on and keep trying and convicting them over and over again, hoping for a more severe sentence.

Now it gets complicated.

The Fourteenth Amendment as (eventually) interpreted by the U.S. Supreme Court makes this limitation applicable to state courts as well as federal courts. That's good for criminal defendants, since most of them are tried in state courts for crimes defined by states; but this broader coverage adds importance to a question lurking in the constitutional language. What counts as "the same offense"?

As happened in some other constitutional contexts, the wording of this phrase was based on assumptions that no longer apply. At common law, what a layperson would regard as a single crime resulted in a single prosecution. Now, however, we have all sorts of detailed and inventive ways to characterize the different aspects and interludes that may make up a criminal episode. (Prosecutors often use these variations to inflate the number of charges facing a defendant, so as to have easy concessions to make during plea bargaining. See 9.A.) The question becomes: for how many of those crimes may the government, or more than one government, charge and try the same defendant?

In 1932, the U.S. Supreme Court (in *Blockburger v. United States*) held that a government can't impose a separate punishment for two offenses unless each offense, by definition, requires proof of some factual element that the other offense doesn't. (See the definition of "element" in 2.J.) You can scale this up as many times as you like. However many offenses you're looking at, each must have some unique element.

For some reason, this test, used nationwide to decide whether a defendant has been subjected to multiple punishments, isn't always the one used to determine whether a defendant already acquitted, or already convicted, of one crime may later be charged with another. At least, the prosecution could be allowed to proceed under the *Blockburger* test, but still be barred from bringing a second prosecution under one of the other tests floating around.

Some state courts, but no federal courts, use a "same transaction" test to resolve this question. According to that test, if two or more offenses are committed during one uninterrupted episode with common facts (whatever that means) and with a single goal or intent, the state may not try the defendant for any more of them if the defendant has already been acquitted or convicted of one.

Both state and federal courts have sometimes used the "actual evidence" test to resolve this same issue. The *Blockburger* rule focuses on what facts, in *general* terms — what elements — must be proved for particular crimes. The "actual evidence" test looks at the details of the particular case. What evidence did the prosecution introduce the first time around? The key question: is it likely that the trier of fact in the second case would base a conviction on the same facts with which the prosecution tried to prove the first case? If so, the second prosecution is barred by double jeopardy.

For a few years, the federal courts used a "same conduct" test, which some states still use. This is a more straightforward, less technical approach than the others. If the prosecutor in Trial #1 proved, or tried to prove, the same conduct that would be at issue in Trial #2, forget about Trial #2. End of discussion.

All this is constitutional law applicable to criminal prosecutions only. (Two related doctrines that apply in both the criminal and civil contexts, "res judicata" and "collateral estoppel," are discussed in Ch. 28.)

What about trials in two different states for some crime that crossed state lines, like auto theft or fleeing from police? There's no constitutional rule against both states' prosecuting someone in that situation, but some states have their own statutes preventing it. And the prosecutor might consider it a waste of taxpayer money, if the other state was doing an adequate job of nailing the perp.

Ready to analyze a bizarre and unlikely situation and decide whether double jeopardy applies? Well, let's consider the movie called (aptly) *Double Jeopardy*. **SPOILER ALERT** — though if you read anything about the movie, you'll find this out:

A woman wrongly convicted of killing her husband finds out, years later, that he's still alive. She figures that since she's already been convicted of killing him, she can go ahead and do the deed, and they can't prosecute her again. Her parole officer, a former law professor, backs her interpretation.

Are the woman and her parole officer correct?

Sorry, but no. For one thing, she was convicted of killing her husband in one state, and by the time she tracks him down, he's in another. Also, the time and place of the supposed murder are usually considered elements of the crime, and they'd be different. As for the actual evidence, that'd just about *all* be different.

So what could this woman have done? She could have used the extraordinary circumstances as a basis for a motion to set aside the verdict (32.D.) or a request for executive clemency (32.G.).

Back to mistrials. (As to what those are in general, see 9.D.) If a trial proceeds to conviction or acquittal, the defendant has clearly been "put in jeopardy." But what about cases that end in a mistrial? When, to use the usual if archaic term, does jeopardy "attach," and will it prevent the prosecution from starting over?

To answer the first question, jeopardy attaches as soon as the jury is sworn, if there's a jury, or as soon as the first evidence is heard, for a bench trial (19.B.). But when is a second prosecution permitted?

A lot depends on the defendant's role, if any, in the mistrial. If the defendant requested or consented to the mistrial, they can probably be tried again, unless they requested it because either the judge or the prosecution seriously misbehaved. (See 9.D. for examples of prosecutorial or judicial misconduct.)

If the jury is deadlocked, resulting in a "hung jury" (which is not a reference to vigilante justice by outraged attorneys), the case can be retried, if the prosecution fancies its chances on a second go-round.

What if the jury finds the defendant guilty of a "lesser included offense" (see 27.C.), but deadlocks as to the more serious crime? If the judge enters judgment based on that verdict, double jeopardy kicks in as to the more serious offense. But in at least one state (Indiana), if the jury finds the defendant guilty of a lesser included offense, and the judge issues a JNOV (27.D.) ordering the defendant retried on all the charges instead of entering a judgment on the lesser included offense, then the new trial can proceed on all the charges. (Don't expect your readers to know that, or even to believe it, without some explanation.)

If some catastrophe, such as the courthouse roof collapsing or being carried off by a tornado, prevents continuation of the trial within a reasonable time, the prosecution can start over when conditions allow.

Our Founders probably expected the number of federal crimes to stay small, just as they probably expected the federal government itself to stay small. It didn't occur to them to address what should happen when a federal prosecutor wants to try someone for a federal crime based on the same facts that gave rise to a previous state prosecution. So, as some of you will have guessed, the federal courts have decided double jeopardy doesn't apply in this context. That means, for example, that if a defendant is charged with murder in state court and acquitted, a federal district attorney can decide to charge the defendant with the federal crime of violating the civil rights of the deceased, based on the same events.

J. More Time Travel: Ex Post Facto Laws

What if someone is convicted of a crime, and while that person is in prison, state legislators decide that it's an even worse crime than they thought? What if they change the law and double the minimum sentence to be served? Will that change apply to the prisoner?

No. That'd be, as to the prisoner, an ex post facto law, and it'd violate the U.S. Constitution.

There are actually two provisions in the U.S. Constitution prohibiting ex post facto laws, both in Article I. Art. I, §9, paragraph 3 states that "[n]o . . . ex post facto Law shall be passed." In context, that means Congress can't pass one; but then, §10, paragraph 1 states that "[n]o State shall . . . pass any . . . ex post facto Law." The same rule might have ended up applying to the states as an aspect of due process (see 34.G.), but §10 makes that unnecessary.

What counts as an "ex post facto" law?

- A law that reaches back in time and makes conduct that's already happened into a crime.

- A law that, as in our starting example, retroactively increases the punishment, the criminal penalty, for a crime that's already been committed.
- A law that, by changing the elements of a crime, the defenses to that crime, or the standard of proof to be used in the trial, makes it easier to convict someone of a crime that took place before the law was passed.
- Extension of a criminal statute of limitations, if used to revive the possibility of prosecuting someone for whom the previous limitations period has already expired.

Applying these principles can get tricky. For example, what's a criminal penalty? Courts claim to look at the essence rather than the label, but as far as federal constitutional law goes, none of the following count as ex post facto laws, even if passed and applied years after the triggering criminal (or other) activity:

- Civil forfeiture (see 34.G.2.).
- Changes in the scheduling of parole hearings (see 29.F.1.) that may have the effect of delaying a prisoner's parole.
- Deportation (requiring someone who isn't a U.S. citizen to leave the U.S.).
- "Three strikes" laws that increase penalties for a current conviction based on the existence of previous convictions. In other words, it doesn't matter that there was no such thing as a "strike" of this kind when the earlier crime was committed.
- At least in some jurisdictions, changes in the rules of evidence that make a conviction easier to get.
- Extension of a criminal statute of limitations, if the extension happens after the crime but before the statute of limitations would have expired in its original form.
- Laws requiring offenders to pay "extradition" costs (the costs of sending them to another state for trial).
- Civil commitment of a sex offender whose sentence has been completed, based on the offender's remaining "sexually dangerous."

One area where many state and federal courts disagree, and where details of the statutory scheme may be crucial: sex offender registration requirements that arise or are extended years after the underlying conviction or delinquency finding.

Generally, factors the courts might consider in distinguishing between a "criminal" penalty and a civil one, for ex post facto purposes, include whether there's some plausible purpose other than punishment, such as streamlining administrative procedures or protecting the public; whether the penalty is excessive as a way to serve that alternate purpose; and whether it's triggered by a finding of "scienter" (some sort of intention). These last two factors would point toward treating the penalty as criminal, subject to the ex post facto prohibition.

A few states have their own separate state constitutional provisions about ex post facto laws. Given the U.S. Constitution's Article 1, §10, these additional rules only make a difference if they provide more protection than the U.S. Constitution does. Several states, including Missouri and Colorado, extend ex post facto principles to legislative changes in contract obligations, privileges, and immunities. New Hampshire goes further, applying the ex post facto prohibition to civil cases in general.

K. Judgments that Follow People Around the Country: Full Faith and Credit

If a party loses in court, can that party just move to another state and pretend it never happened? No. As part of setting up a nation with states more closely bound together than in the original Articles of Confederation, the U.S. Constitution (in Article IV) has what's called the Full Faith and Credit Clause. §1 of this clause reads:

> Full faith and credit shall be given in each state to the public acts, records, and judicial proceedings of every other state. And the Congress may by general laws prescribe the manner in which such acts, records, and proceedings shall be proved, and the effect thereof.

(Historical footnote: the original text, still lying there waiting to startle the modern reader, also went on (in §2) to say: "No person held to service or labor in one state, under the laws thereof, escaping into another, shall, in consequence of any law or regulation therein, be discharged from such service or labor, but shall be delivered up on claim of the party to whom such service or labor may be due." That's coy constitution-ese for: if a slave escapes and makes it to a state without slavery, the slaveowner can still come and get the slave. The Thirteenth Amendment, which outlawed slavery, made this text a dead letter.)

The Full Faith and Credit Clause is usually applied to make a civil court judgment from one state just as binding in another state, although the winner will have to go to the courts in the second state and get the judgment "recognized" or some such term.

There have been situations where this didn't happen. Until the 1970s, states didn't all recognize custody or visitation orders from other states, and many parents distressed by such orders fled their states with their children in tow. The Uniform Child Custody Jurisdiction Act was drafted to deal with this situation, and by the mid-1980s, every state had adopted some version of it. A later tweak of the uniform law, the Uniform Child Custody Jurisdiction and Enforcement Act, achieved almost as wide acceptance. Then Congress weighed in, in 1980, with the Federal Kidnapping Prevention Act, saying that valid custody decrees were entitled to full faith and credit. That still didn't always settle the matter. For example, in one or more Florida counties, courts have refused to recognize grandparent visitation orders from other states, because those orders would have flunked the constitutional tests applied by higher courts in Florida. (The inconsistency in how different states' courts deal with grandparent visitation petitions is the result of the U.S. Supreme Court's failing to rule on some crucial aspects of these petitions. See 14.H.10.)

A similar uniform act, the Uniform Interstate Family Support Act (UIFSA), covers child support orders (14.H.5.). Using the familiar threat of withholding federal highway funds, the federal government has induced all the states to adopt either the 1996 or a later version of the UIFSA — at least where child support orders are concerned. The UIFSA also has provisions covering spousal support, sometimes known as alimony (see 14.H.6.), but they differ substantially from the statute's treatment of child support. For example, while a child support order may be modified by the court of another state if all the parties have left the original state, only the state whose court issued the original spousal support order may modify it. Not all states have adopted the spousal support portions of the uniform statute.

Until late in the 20th century, states routinely recognized marriages performed in other states, even if those marriages would have been illegal under their own laws: for example, due to a family relationship between the spouses that was closer than the second state's laws would allow. Then, when a few states started allowing same-sex marriages, other states that didn't want any truck with such marriages started passing laws, or amending their state constitutions, to say that no same-sex marriages would be recognized. The federal government jumped in with the "Defense of Marriage Act" (DOMA), which not only defined marriage as between one man and one woman for federal purposes, but also provided that states could refuse to recognize same-sex marriages performed in other states. In 2013, the U.S. Supreme Court struck down the part of DOMA dealing with federal law; and in 2015, it held that states could not refuse to recognize other states' same-sex marriages.

L. The Elastic Commerce Clause

I've mentioned several times that the Commerce Clause, contained in Article 1, §8 of the U.S. Constitution, has been used to justify all manner of federal legislation, a great deal of which could land someone in court. So what is this clause?

The Commerce Clause authorizes Congress to "regulate Commerce with foreign Nations, and among the several States, and with the Indian tribes." It was inspired by such pre-Constitution problems as states imposing taxes or other burdens on goods coming from other states. There is some debate about whether the term "commerce" originally referred only to the trade in or exchange of goods, or whether it had some broader meaning that included, for example, manufacturing and/or agriculture. Many of those involved in the process of drafting the Constitution, and in defending it in the debates over whether it should be ratified, clearly intended the narrower meaning, but that intention was not necessarily universal. (It is clearer that some of those involved *wanted* Congress to have broader powers than that they thought the ultimately chosen language *provided* those powers.)

Over the many years since then, as federal power in general has expanded both explicitly (the post-Civil-War amendments), by judicial interpretation, and by successful Congressional assertions of authority, "commerce" has come to have a very broad meaning indeed. Under the current interpretation of the Commerce Clause, "commerce" means any activity that could directly or indirectly affect any aspect of any economic transaction taking place in the interstate marketplace. Any such activity may therefore be regulated by Congress, or by some agency to which Congress has delegated authority.

We recently came within one Supreme Court Justice's vote of allowing Congress to use the Commerce Clause as a basis for regulating *in*activity, namely the failure to buy health insurance, which failure could arguably affect the nationwide market for health care. By five votes to four, the Court held that Congress could, to some extent, *tax* such inactivity, and upheld the Affordable Care Act on that basis — but not as a proper exercise of the Commerce Clause.

Here are two striking examples of the broad interpretation in action.

Wickard v. Filburn: This case grew out of Depression era wage and price controls. Farmer Roscoe Filburn grew wheat for use on his own farm. He grew more wheat than the federal regulations allowed, so he was ordered to destroy his perfectly good wheat crop and to pay a fine.

Roscoe Filburn wasn't selling wheat across state lines. He wasn't selling it at all. He was growing it to feed his farm animals. Where, he asked, did Congress get the authority to tell him how much wheat he could grow for his own use?

Well, the Court explained, because Filburn grew so much wheat, he didn't have to buy any. And because he didn't have to buy wheat to feed his animals, that reduced the demand for animal feed. And when he and other farmers met their own needs with their own wheat and thereby reduced demand, that affected the price of wheat. And people sell wheat across state lines. So . . . burn that wheat, Farmer Filburn!

Gonzales v. Raich: This 2005 decision was a surprise only because of the *Lopez* decision ten years earlier (see below). *Raich*, as it's usually known, held that the Commerce Clause let the federal government prohibit the use of marijuana for medical purposes, even if the defendants had grown their own weed for their own use. It's essentially *Wickard* revisited, but with an illegal market substituted for the price-controlled wheat market of the Depression.

Aside from the Affordable Care Act ruling mentioned above, the only U.S. Supreme Court decision in modern times to suggest that the Commerce Clause has its limits was 1995's *U.S. v. Lopez*. *Lopez* held that the Commerce Clause didn't authorize Congress to designate schools as "gun free zones." The Court held that possessing a firearm in a local school zone just wasn't any kind of economic activity. One could, applying the *Wickard* reasoning, argue otherwise: mightn't a prohibition on carrying guns at schools depress the market for pistols, which are frequently sold across state lines?

M. Section 1983: Civil Suits for
Violations of Civil Rights

Anyone in the United States, whether or not a citizen, may sue a state government official, or anyone working in concert with a government official, for violating their federal constitutional rights. The defendant must have been acting "under color of" state law: that is, acting under the authority provided by a state statute or regulation, or as directed by a state official enforcing a statute or regulation.

Such lawsuits spring from a federal statute, 42 U.S.C. §1983, often referred to simply as "section 1983." Section 1983 has been around a long time, passed as part of the Civil Rights Acts of 1871 in the post-Civil War period. But it became much more useful after a 1961 U.S. Supreme Court decision that held one could sue a police officer under section 1983 even if the officer's conduct actually violated state law. The Court's reasoning: since the officer was in a position to violate the plaintiff's rights only because of the authority the state had given them, the officer was still acting under color of state law.

Section 1983 also allows lawsuits based on rights that derive from certain federal statutes rather than from the U.S. Constitution. For example, many suits for violations of federal anti-discrimination laws (see 34.H.) are brought under section 1983. However, if such a statute has its own enforcement mechanism, section 1983 can't be used instead.

The plaintiff may sue in either state or federal court. Wherever the suit, the state's statute of limitations for personal injury lawsuits is usually applied. But when the section 1983 claim accrued, which starts the statute of limitation's clock, is a question of federal law. In general, the date that counts is when the plaintiff knew or had reason to know that their rights were being violated. But in employment discrimination suits under section 1983, the key date is when the challenged conduct occurred, even if that isn't when the discrimination had its most severe effect.

Section 1983 uses the term "person" both for potential plaintiffs and potential defendants. The definition of "person" for the latter purpose is quite complicated. A state official or employee may be sued for damages only in their "personal" capacity, meaning that their government employer can't be made to pay those damages under a respondeat superior theory (see 14.Q.). However, a state employee or official may be sued in their "official" capacity if the plaintiff is seeking future-oriented relief, e.g. declaratory or injunctive relief (see 30.A.).

Municipalities, namely cities and towns and counties, may be sued as "persons" under section 1983, though only where the deprivation of constitutional rights may be attributed to the local government's policies rather than simply the actions of some employee or official. Whether the actor's conduct may be attributed to municipal policy will depend on each state's laws about such issues as how much autonomy municipalities have.

What if a municipality, acting as a creator of government policy, does something that indirectly leads to the violation of someone's rights? For example, say a city hires a racist police chief, who then makes a point of arresting people for "driving while black." Let's further posit that under that state's law, the city has enough authority that its employment guidelines constitute a government policy. May one of those arrested sue the city? Not unless the city was "deliberately indifferent" to the possibility that it would end up hiring a racist vigilante. That's only true if the deprivation of civil rights was a "plainly obvious consequence" of the city's decision to adopt certain employment policies.

One way in which local governments and actual flesh-and-blood people are treated differently is on the very important subject of "qualified immunity." An individual sued under section 1983 will not be held liable if a reasonable person in their position would not have known that their conduct violated a "clearly established federal right." However, at least where compensatory damages (see 30.B.2.) are concerned, a municipal entity may not assert qualified immunity. Another difference, but this time benefiting the municipality, concerns punitive damages (30.B.3.). These may be awarded only against individuals, not municipalities.

Exactly what a plaintiff must establish for a section 1983 suit based on deprivations of various different federal rights is beyond the scope of this summary.

N. Obscure Constitutional Oddities

Some constitutional provisions haven't gotten much attention in the last couple of centuries, but one never knows when circumstances will draw attention to them.

1. Third Amendment

For example, you don't hear much talk about the Third Amendment.

No Soldier shall, in time of peace be quartered in any house, without the consent of the Owner, nor in time of war, but in a manner to be prescribed by law.

Think it's just a quaint anachronism? One major U.S. Supreme Court privacy case invoked this amendment, among several others, as having a "penumbra" (like a shadow, but even less distinct) protecting against government intrusions; and that argument may resurface in future discussions of such issues as governmental collection of private data. But leaving aside penumbras and such, we might want to look at the literal meaning of the Third Amendment.

What with our ongoing "war on terror," which clause currently applies? Is this a "time of peace" or "time of war"? If, as some now fear, the military starts conducting drone operations within the U.S., and if a future Commander in Chief decides it's cost-effective to post drone operators in private residences, the interpretation of this amendment may become more than academic.

A recent case claimed that municipal police violated the Third Amendment by taking over a home in order to get a tactical advantage over suspected criminals next door. The federal district court didn't buy it; but a commentator noted that professional, armed-to-the-teeth police forces didn't exist when the Amendment was passed and ratified, and wondered what the Amendment's contemporaries would think about its proper scope now that we have such police.

Going back to the military itself, here's another interesting possibility: even in time of "peace," can the feds get around the Third Amendment by using eminent domain?? **"Oh, of course, sir, we can't turn your home into a drone operations base without your consent. Too bad it isn't your home any more. Have a nice day."** In reality, it'd no doubt take considerably longer than that — but could it happen?

2. Congressional Power to Limit Supreme Court Jurisdiction

Article III, the constitutional provision that establishes the U.S. Supreme Court and gives Congress the power to set up lower federal courts, also says that the Supreme Court has appellate jurisdiction "with such Exceptions, and under such Regulations as the Congress shall make." When the Supreme Court takes a case that has worked its way up through lower courts, that's the exercise of its appellate jurisdiction. No amendment to the Constitution has monkeyed with this language.

That means that if Congress passes a statute that claims to change any of the constitutional rules we know and love (or know and loathe), Congress may also have the power to say, at the same time, that the Supreme Court can't do anything about it.

3. What Else?

Why don't you sit back with a copy of the Constitution and see what other obscure provisions you can find? They might be worth a story.

4. State Nullification?

This section isn't so much about little-known language in the Constitution as about little-known approaches to defending the Constitution.

If you've heard of the concept of "state nullification," it may have been in the context of the antebellum South, where some future Confederates spoke of nullification and secession in the same breath. However, the idea of nullification, a state's refusal to follow what its leaders consider unconstitutional federal laws, has a longer and less sullied history.

In 1798, only seven years after the Bill of Rights was ratified, Congress passed the Alien and Sedition Acts at the urging of President John Adams. The Alien Acts made it easier to deport foreigners and harder for immigrants to become citizens, while the Sedition Act allowed the feds to fine or imprison people for "false, scandalous and malicious" writings critical of the government. A number of newspaper editors were locked up for violating the Sedition Act, sometimes for statements that we would nowadays classify as protected statements of opinion. One example: calling out President Adams for his "unbounded thirst for ridiculous pomp, foolish adulation, and self avarice."

At that time, the Supreme Court had not yet asserted its power to strike down federal statutes as unconstitutional. (The arguments for that power are primarily structural: the language of the Constitution doesn't explicitly include it.)

Founding Fathers Thomas Jefferson and James Madison responded by drafting resolutions for the states of Kentucky and Virginia respectively, declaring that the states would have nothing to do with enforcing or otherwise abiding by this unconstitutional legislation. These resolutions asserted that it would never do for the federal government to be the sole arbiter of whether it was violating the Constitution. Whether this argument has become less persuasive, now that we have the Supreme Court's power to overturn legislation as part of the federal mix, is open to debate.

The Kentucky and Virginia resolutions didn't mention some constitutional text that could be claimed to support nullification. In Article VI, paragraph 3, the Constitution requires that all state officials, whether executive, legislative, or judicial, swear or affirm to support the Constitution. It does not say: "to support the federal government's interpretation of the Constitution." The question is whether this is a meaningful distinction, allowing or even requiring state officials to resist what they view as unconstitutional federal initiatives, or whether the long-established practice of treating the Supreme Court as a final arbiter of constitutionality renders this linguistic point insignificant.

The Supreme Court's 1958 *Cooper v. Aaron* decision firmly rejected the idea that states could rely on their own assessments of what was or wasn't constitutional. That has not prevented the idea of state nullification from reviving in recent years, even becoming a hot topic in some state legislatures. Those currently active in promoting the idea tend to be moved by intense views on a few topics, including illegal immigration, the Affordable Care Act, and/or environmental regulations that impose economic burdens on certain industries. **Efforts in a state legislature to force a confrontation with the federal government could provide the basis for a political thriller.**

CHAPTER 35

Tricks and Tactics: A Small Sampler

I am not, and have never really been, a trial lawyer, though I did serve as "second chair," a sort of legal gofer, in a trial or two. I'm therefore not much of an authority on trial lawyers' various ways of manipulating judges and (especially) jurors, driving opposing counsel insane, etc. But here are just a few of the many tactics your trial lawyers could use.

- Before trial, prepare like hell!
  - ○ For example, some trial lawyers summarize every page of every deposition, noting the deponent (the person deposed) and the page number on each summary.
  - ○ A litigator shouldn't rely on some underling's summary of the case law, let alone the facts, without at least double-checking. If expert testimony is critical, they should spend as much time as they can spare with that expert, learning as much as possible about the expert's area of expertise.
  - ○ It's also a good idea to keep up on the local news, the better to predict the judge's or jurors' frame of mind.
  - ○ Proper prep for an appellate attorney includes knowing just what's in the trial record and how to find anything important in a hurry.
- If opposing counsel is unfamiliar with one's capabilities, one could disguise those capabilities for as long as possible during the early

phases of the litigation, in order to later catch the opposition un-prepared. For example, some lawyers will make a point of appear-ing disorganized and absent-minded during pretrial depositions (see 10.A.) But any such games must not make their way into the courtroom where they could make a bad impression on the judge.

- While lawyers will disagree on the ideal order of witnesses, most would agree on both starting and ending the day with a strong wit-ness giving riveting (or at least, not soporific) testimony.
- The lawyer should ask the jury early in the proceedings whether they can hear what the lawyer is saying.
- It's a good idea to distract the jury during potentially damaging tes-timony. If the lawyer knows the witness taking the stand is going to hurt the lawyer's case, they could start making a paper clip chain, or turn paper from a legal pad into origami. There's a limit to what sort of facial expressions and body language one may use before drawing an objection and/or alienating the judge (if not the jury), but alternating between puzzlement, sorrow, and restrained indig-nation might help. Related tactic: stay calm and unconcerned if one's own witness says something that hurts one's case.
- The lawyer can emphasize aspects of their personality so as to fit the audience or to claim underdog status. (For one or both, see Jimmy Stewart's character in the movie *Anatomy of a Murder*, de-scribing themselves as a simple country lawyer up against the fella from the big city.) However, it would be easy to take this too far. Juries are generally good at sniffing out insincerity.
- Treat the client like a treasured friend, someone who completely deserves the lawyer's and the jury's protection. Rest a hand on their shoulder briefly when passing by the counsel table. Show care and concern in one's body language while engaging in brief inaudible colloquies.

How theatrical should a litigator get?

Sometimes a physical demonstration of some point is more effective than a verbal description. (It also helps keep jurors awake.) For example, in the movie *Suspect*, Cher plays the defense attorney in a murder case. The victim's throat was cut. At one point, Cher is examining an expert of some kind. Rather than asking him about how a right-handed versus a left-handed killer would cut someone's throat, she asks the witness (after, I believe, getting the court's permission) to stand. Then she positions herself as a killer might, first for right-handed and then for left-handed cutting, illustrating the witness' answers about the direction in which such a killer would cut.

Cher then calls to her client to "catch!" and tosses him her keys. He catches them left-handed — and the judge barks out a reprimand. This stunt, in the court's view, crossed a line. Why? Well, the attorney didn't ask permission; the client wasn't on the stand; and the client might well be able to catch the keys with either hand, particularly if he'd practiced.

Two somewhat similar demonstrations go over better in the novel *To Kill a Mockingbird.* **SPOILER ALERT:**

> Tom Robinson is on trial for raping and beating a girl. Defense attorney Atticus Finch has already established that given the girl's injuries, her attacker was probably left-handed. Cross-examining the girl's no-good father, he asks whether the man can read and write, and then asks him to demonstrate. The demonstration reveals that the father is left-handed. Later, when the girl testifies, Atticus asks her to point to the man who attacked her. She points to Tom. Atticus asks Tom to stand up. When Tom stands, he reveals his short left arm and shriveled left hand, injured long ago in a cotton gin accident.

In both these examples, the bit of theater fit within the examination of a witness, though indirectly in the second instance; and the circumstances of neither would lend themselves to fakery.

Closing arguments can be a good stage for effective drama. The following example may err on some detail, but it's close to what happened.

A legendary trial lawyer in Indiana, seeking a very large punitive damages award, brought a large supply of pennies to the counsel table. Before starting his closing argument, he carefully stacked the pennies in multiple piles, one by one. Then he explained that each penny represented one million dollars of the defendant's net worth. The jury awarded record-breaking punitive damages . . . which the Indiana Supreme Court swept out of existence by changing the law about when such damages could be awarded. (See 30.B.3. for the story.) Life sometimes provides its own ironic twists.

Theatrical elements like this, which some lawyers and judges refer to as "parlor tricks," can backfire. Juries may be put off by such stuff, especially if something about the setup feels artificial or suggests that the lawyer doesn't think much of the jurors' intelligence. Here's one example a judge I know mentioned to a group of lawyers. A defendant's attorney arranged for someone strongly resembling the defendant to sit at the defense table where a defendant usually sits. Then the lawyer asked a witness to identify the person who committed the crime; and the witness pointed to the lookalike. Some of the jurors told the judge, after the trial, that this trick offended them and didn't really prove much about the strength of the witness' identification.

There are some trial tactics that violate local rules or are just so obvious that they can get the perpetrator slapped with sanctions. Discovery (see 10.A.) is an area where such tactics abound. For example, many a party has responded to a request for production of documents with the equivalent of: "You want documents? We'll give you documents! Warehouses full of 'em!" To some extent, such a response is common, as mentioned in 10.A., but there's a point past which the recipient is likely to invoke the court's intervention, though just when that point is reached will depend on the size and complexity of the case.

Beyond tricks and tactics, the job of a trial or appellate attorney comes down to one fundamental task.

There's a well-known legal adage that goes something like this: "If you've got the facts, pound the facts. If you don't have the facts, pound the law. If you don't have the law or the facts, pound the table."

"Pounding the table," engaging in highly passionate displays, is not actually that good an idea. It's questionable etiquette at best, hence risky at trial and even more so on appeal. That said, the saying's priority list makes sense — because, whether presenting a case to a jury or to a judge, a lawyer is addressing human beings. And human beings love to hear stories.

Stories move us and stay with us where recitations of abstract fact make little impression. Stories help us concentrate and help us learn.

Whatever their personal style, whatever the constraints imposed by the evidence and the applicable law, the lawyer needs to find a story to tell: a story in which the client may be the hero or the victim, but a story that shows the trier of fact, judge or jury, why the result the lawyer is seeking provides the best possible ending.

CHAPTER 36

Technology on the March

T he Internet has changed even the hidebound world of legal procedure. Courts are not only using email, but are beginning to accept
electronic filing of pleadings, briefs, etc., and to make case files
and/or appellate opinions available online.

These technological advances come with possible glitches that you
could use in your stories. For example, what happens if a case file is
hacked? **Your hacker could alter exhibits, or replace a technically adequate brief with one that violates court rules, or change the record of
when something was filed to make it appear untimely (in violation of time
limits).** Less nefarious but more likely: the possibility of system crashes
that lose or corrupt one or more court files. **If this occurs a little ways in
the future, at a time when paper backups have become positively rare, it
could wreak substantial havoc.**

Some courts already allow parties or attorneys to participate in hearings by telephone. Skype, Facetime, and other audiovisual real-time setups
are likely to be used more and more when personal attendance is difficult
or impossible.

Technological advances will also bring new legal problems to be
solved. For example, what rules will govern collisions between spacecraft,
or space habitats, and space junk? Will negligence (14.G.), strict liability
(14.G.4.), or some other framework govern such disputes? Where the junk

used to be a satellite launched by a government, will that government be liable or immune (see Ch. 16)?

When some of us live in inhabited space stations and planetary colonies, what laws or treaties will govern ownership and boundary disputes between Earth-based governments, and/or between companies with some role in establishing these habitats? There's already some precedent on that question: there are treaties in place dealing with the settlements established in Antarctica, a region almost as sterile and forbidding as many a distant planet may be.

Water will be an enormously valuable commodity in space. Will interplanetary water laws resemble those of the eastern U.S., or the more water-deprived West (see 14.E.)?

CHAPTER 37

Last Words

You may think I've gone well beyond what you want or need to know about lawyers, judges, courtrooms, etc.; but there's plenty more to learn. Here are a few ways to learn more.

Find a glossary of legal terms. Just reading through it will not only prepare you to get the language right, but give you a capsule legal education.

When you're trying to find your way through some legal maze, get a guide. Ask a lawyer to explain things to you. If you know any lawyers, they're probably sick of being expected to answer their friends' legal questions for free, but sharing their expertise with a novelist might well be a refreshing change. If you're approaching a stranger, you may have to pay for a short consultation — or you might get away with simply thanking the lawyer in your Acknowledgments section. (Find out ahead of time whether the lawyer expects to be paid for answering your questions.)

Read other books that help non-lawyers understand the law. I'll mention a couple, but I'm sure there are many.

My first tentative title for this book included the phrase "order in the court," commonly used by bailiffs at the start of courtroom proceedings. While writing the book, I researched that potential title and discovered attorney David S. Mullally's book *Order in the Court: A Writer's Guide to the Legal System*, published in 1999 and currently out of print. While I have not actually read Mullally's book, I have read its description and Amazon reviews, and have glanced at the book itself. I recommend it to those who would like a more exhaustive and encyclopedic (and less flippant) approach to the subject than what I have provided, from an attorney with far more courtroom experience than I can claim.

For those especially interested in courtroom drama, here's another book, one I've only glanced at but look forward to reading. *Reel Justice: The Courtroom Goes to The Movies*, by Paul Bergman and Michael Asimov (both law professors), summarizes more than 150 law-related movies, analyzes them for legal accuracy, critiques the lawyers' trial tactics, and discusses public policy issues the films raise. The book groups the films according to such categories as "Courtroom Heroes," "Courtroom Comedies," and "Prejudice on Trial," as well as substantive topics like "Family Law" and "The Death Penalty."

I'll repeat one very important caveat I mentioned at the beginning: while I've worked hard to make this book as accurate as possible, please don't rely on anything I've said as legal advice. If you need such advice, hire a lawyer to provide it!

Finally, a note on updates: I expect to update the ebook version of this guide fairly often, and the paperback less often but eventually. I'll post the same updates, and possibly others, on the book's website at http://cttf.karenawyle.net. You can also find a few other online extras there, such as deleted material (generally rants I decided would be distracting or impolitic to include).

Acknowledgments

My beta readers for this book were especially and exceptionally hardworking, helpful, and generous with their time. I most humbly and heartily thank (in alphabetical order): Ronald L. Chapman, Maggie Scheck Greene, Steven Karel, Robert Mann, J. Alex Tanford, Wendy Teller, Rich Weyand, and Linda Williams. None of them, of course, should be held accountable in the slightest for the errors I am certain to have made.

My thanks also to my husband Paul Hager and daughters Livali Wyle and Alissa Wyle for patiently providing requested input on everything from the cover to various subject matter and word choices. I did not always follow their advice, and you should assume that any regrettable choices were my doing rather than theirs.

Index

(order, continued)

    distinguished from judgment: 516

    military, following: 514-515

ownership, forms of: see property

pain and suffering: 220, 222, 273, 494, 495

paralegal: 18, 20, 46, 113, 241

pardon: 473, 530-531

parental rights (see also constitutional rights): 45, 82, 92, 167, 173, 226, 234, 235, 236, 237, 238, 239-241, 243-245, 248-249, 253, 394, 480, 572, 582-583

    termination: 45, 234, 239-241, 243, 244, 248-249, 373, 536

parenting time: see visitation

parole: 31, 103, 472, 474, 477, 479-481, 510, 530

    hearing: 480-481, 596

    life in prison without: 159, 483, 487, 488, 528

    revocation: 44, 103, 479-480

partner, law: 16, 19, 46, 51, 52, 65, 328

partnership (see also limited liability partnership): 229, 322, 327

    dissolution of: 27, 491, 534

patent: 7, 12, 13, 288, 291, 298-301, 305, 334, 387, 497

penalties, criminal (see also criminal law): 123-124, 469-489

pension: 227, 228, 268, 273, 274, 323-325

    ERISA: 324-325

per capita: 264

per stirpes: 264

perjury: 24, 31, 34, 63, 93, 138, 140, 231, 262, 358, 364, 387, 395, 397, 398, 432, 520, 526, 527

    suborning: 63, 138, 432

personal jurisdiction: see jurisdiction

petition: 38, 48, 57, 106, 237, 238-239, 243-244, 249, 250, 253-254, 275, 321, 432, 437, 447, 472, 501, 522-524, 526-528, 529

petit jury: 356

plea: 93, 120, 505

    Alford: 102-103

    bargain: 14, 17, 44, 45, 93, 99-101, 103, 109, 147, 341, 412, 434, 445, 509, 592

    no contest (aka nolo contendere): 30, 102

pleading: 26, 31, 86-90, 438, 451, 611

post-conviction relief: 44, 45, 48, 432, 436, 522-524

post-judgment interest: see judgment

postnuptial agreement: 167, 229-230

precedent: 25, 31, 43, 342, 343, 481, 529, 547

preemption: 75, 83-85

ABOUT THE AUTHOR

Karen A. Wyle is an award-winning appellate attorney with more than thirty years' experience. A *cum laude* graduate of Harvard Law School, she worked for law firms and the California Court of Appeal before establishing her solo practice in Bloomington, Indiana.

Wyle has filed amicus briefs in the U.S. Supreme Court and seven state supreme courts. She has also written and published five novels. One-quarter of her novel *Division* is set in a near-future courtroom.

For online extras including updates and deleted passages, as well as contact information and links to Wyle's professional and fiction websites, please visit this book's website at cttf.karenawyle.net.